THE RECOVERY PROBLEM
IN THE UNITED STATES

A Da Capo Press Reprint Series

FRANKLIN D. ROOSEVELT
AND THE ERA OF THE NEW DEAL

GENERAL EDITOR: FRANK FREIDEL

Harvard University

THE
RECOVERY PROBLEM
IN THE
UNITED STATES

By Harold G. Moulton
and Others

Da Capo Press • New York • 1972

Library of Congress Cataloging in Publication Data
Main entry under title:

The Recovery problem in the United States.
   (Franklin D. Roosevelt and the era of the New Deal)
   Original ed. issued as Publication no. 72 of the
Institute of Economics of the Brookings Institution.
   1. U. S.—Economic conditions—1918-1945.
   2. U. S.—Economic policy—1933-1945.
   I. Moulton, Harold Glenn, 1883-1965. II. Series.
   III. Series: Brookings Institution. Institute of
Economics. Publication no. 72.
HC106.3.R44   1972   330.973'0917   73-176337
ISBN O-306-70421-8

This Da Capo Press edition of *The Recovery Problem
in the United States* is an unabridged republication
of the first edition published in Washington, D.C.,
in 1936 as Publication No. 72 of the Institute of
Economics of the Brookings Institution.

Published by Da Capo Press, Inc.
A Subsidiary of Plenum Publishing Corporation
227 West 17th Street, New York, New York 10011

THE RECOVERY PROBLEM IN THE
UNITED STATES

THE RECOVERY PROBLEM
IN
THE UNITED STATES

WASHINGTON, D.C.
THE BROOKINGS INSTITUTION
1936

Printed in the United States of America

George Banta Publishing Company

Menasha, Wisconsin

PREFACE

This volume is not designed as a presentation of any general theory of cyclical movements. It does not even pretend to assess the causes of the particular depression which began in 1929 nor to suggest means for preventing the recurrence of depressions in the future. Such contribution to cyclical theory as it may contain is merely an incidental by-product of a general analysis focussed strictly upon the problems of recovery in the United States at the present juncture.

To provide adequate background and foundation, it has been deemed essential to review the great economic changes which have occurred in recent years. In Part I, entitled "The Sweep of World Events," an attempt is made to make clear the international setting of the dislocation which has occurred in the United States. The second division of the analysis, "Readjustments in the United States," is a more detailed study of the course of depression and recovery to date as related to major aspects of American economic life. In the final section, "Readjustments Required for Recovery," an effort is made to integrate the analysis as a whole and to indicate the primary requirements for stimulating and safeguarding further progress.

Because of its comprehensive character, the carrying out of the project has necessarily required the collaboration of numerous specialists. Harold G. Moulton planned and co-ordinated the analysis as a whole and collaborated in the writing of Chapters VIII, XI, and XII. He is primarily responsible for Parts I and III, except for Chapter XIX. Maurice Leven is responsible for Chapters VI, VII, IX, and X. Leo Pasvolsky collaborated on Chapters I, II, and V and contributed Chapters XV, XVI, and XIX. Charles O. Hardy is the author of Chapters XIII and XIV. Malcolm Merriam assembled the data and collaborated in the writing of Chapters XII and XVIII. George Terborgh is responsible for the bulk of the material in Chapter VIII, but, as a result of a new commitment, was unable to participate fully in the final writing of the chapter. Hugo Bezdek, Jr. acted as general assistant and collaborated in Chapters II, III, IV, V, and XI. Kathryn R. Wright collaborated in the preparation of Mr. Leven's chapters. Sheldon B. Akers assisted in the statistical work, and Louise H. Bebb in the preparation of the charts. Dr. Nonny Wright, of Geneva, Switzerland, rendered valuable assistance in the assembling of the foreign material, especially that presented in Appendix B.

The comprehensive factual foundation of this inquiry was greatly facilitated by the availability of a wide range of economic data currently gathered by the agencies of the federal government. The international comparisons presented in this volume were largely made possible by the exhaustive statistical and analytical studies issued by the Financial and Economic Sections of the League of Nations Secretariat.

The study has been conducted under a special grant of funds from the Maurice and Laura Falk Foundation of Pittsburgh.

Edwin G. Nourse
Director

Institute of Economics
December 1936

CONTENTS

PART I

THE SWEEP OF WORLD EVENTS

CHAPTER I

THE BACKGROUND OF THE DEPRESSION

Although it is beyond the scope of this investigation to attempt any systematic or detailed analysis of the causes of the world depression which began in 1929, it is essential that the reader have in mind a general picture of the world economic situation out of which the depression emerged. Thus without trying to indicate the relative importance of the numerous factors which combined to produce a depression of unparalleled severity we may in this introductory chapter note the range and complexity of the forces and factors involved. Some of these were essentially international in character, while others grew primarily out of domestic conditions.

Certain phases of the profound maladjustments which have characterized the depression period are rooted in the economic consequences which flowed from the World War. In attempting to appraise the cost of a war one naturally thinks first in terms of the destruction of life and property; and the consequences are ordinarily assumed to be measured chiefly by the reduction of labor power and the loss of capital which the conflict entailed. Less apparent but of much greater ultimate importance are the indirect results which a great war may produce through disrupting the mechanism by which the economic activities of the world are carried on.

The economic system may be likened to a complex and delicately adjusted machine. When each part of the mechanism is properly balanced with reference to other parts, and when all parts are geared or meshed with one another, the machine as a whole functions smoothly and yields maximum results. But if the mechanism gets out of balance or adjustment at any point, the efficiency of operation is immediately impaired. Moreover, the economic system, like the physical machine, may at a given time be out of balance in several places. The war, in fact, resulted in a series of maladjustments which seriously impeded the functioning of the economic system. It was this impairment of the economic mechanism rather than the loss of life and property that proved to be of continuing significance throughout the post-war period.

I. MALADJUSTMENTS ARISING OUT OF THE WAR

The World War produced three types of economic maladjustment: First, it upset the equilibrium or normal balance in international financial and economic relations both within Europe and between Europe and the rest of the world, especially the United States. Second, it destroyed fiscal and financial stability in many countries. Third, it led to territorial realignments and modifications of national policies of far-reaching consequence. The significance of each of these types of maladjustment may be briefly indicated.

1. Trade and financial changes. The war thoroughly disrupted the former balance in international trade and financial relations. The changes which occurred were in part the direct result of the diversions of trade movements which accompanied the division of Europe into two belligerent camps. They were even more largely attributable, however, to the fact that in order to finance the war most European countries had not only to sacrifice much of their present wealth but also to mortgage their future. The steps in this process were fairly clearly defined.

In the first place, early in the war there was an extensive movement of gold from belligerent to neutral countries for the purchase of war supplies. The result was an undermining of currency foundations in some countries and in others the accumulation of excessive reserves. While the flow of gold was checked in due course by resort to government loans, the extensive shifts that occurred served to complicate the problem of restoring financial equilibrium at the end of the war. Moreover, for several years after the war the process of shipping gold from deficiency to surplus areas continued.

In order to finance the war, foreign investments were also liquidated. For example, British and French investors were asked by their governments to sell American railroad and other bonds purchased in preceding years in order that the proceeds might be available for buying munitions and other war supplies. Many private loans were negotiated through American banks for the same purpose. After April 1917 the governments themselves borrowed tremendous sums from the United States government. Thus the United States was converted from a debtor to a creditor country, whereas the European nations were transformed wholly or in part from lenders to borrowers. To these financial changes were added the complications resulting from the assessment of stupendous reparation obligations against the defeated powers.

The industrial and agricultural changes which occurred during the war were quite as important as were these financial shifts. While European economic activities—except in war production lines—were curtailed, there was great expansion in countries outside the war zone. The expansion of both agricultural and industrial output in the United States was particularly stimulated in consequence of shipping exigencies.

When the war ended, the European countries found themselves with greatly decreased productive power, but also with greatly increased foreign obligations which could be met only with the fruits of production. On the other hand, the United States and certain other countries possessed greatly expanded productive facilities, but found reduced market opportunities abroad. For a brief interval indeed—in 1919-20—American exporters made large foreign sales, chiefly on short-term credits, for the purpose of enabling European countries to replenish empty larders; but thereafter, until about 1924, sales abroad were restricted because of the lack of adequate purchasing power in Europe and the general economic and currency instability which made the extension of foreign credit precarious.

2. *Financial disorganization.* The financial requirements of the war seriously undermined fiscal and monetary stability. While methods of financing the war differed materially in the various countries, in every case there was a huge growth of public indebtedness, and all of the European belligerents suspended the gold standard. The degree of financial deterioration of course varied widely in the several countries, being, with the exception of Russia, least among the Allied countries and greatest among the Central Powers. The difference was to some extent attributable to the varying methods employed in financing the war, but more largely to the greater accumulated reserves of the Allied nations, together with their ability to borrow abroad. Through the repercussions of the war upon the economic life of the world as a whole, financial stability was impaired also in neutral countries.

The depreciation of the foreign exchanges was a result of the combined influences of internal fiscal and monetary disorganization and external trade and financial readjustments. During the course of the war the depreciation was checked by control devices, which need not here be discussed, and the full extent of the disorganization which had occurred was thus not fully revealed until the war was over. The relative extent of the depreciation of the exchanges in the various countries reflected in a rough way the relative degree of economic and financial disintegration which they had sustained.

This general disorganization of national finances seriously complicated the problem of recovery. The accumulation of indebtedness, both domestic and foreign, greatly increased the burdens of taxation; and the instability of currency enhanced the risks of business and fostered speculative activity. Thus the basic foundations for the conduct of private business operations were substantially undermined.

3. Territorial readjustments. The process of world recovery was impeded by the shifts in national boundaries which resulted from the war. The dismemberment of the Russian, German, and Austro-Hungarian empires resulted not only in enlarging the territory of some of the victorious countries, but also in creating a substantial number of new independent states. The efforts of the new states to achieve a large measure of economic independence naturally led to extensive readjustments in commercial and financial relations. Similarly, both the enlarged and the dismembered countries found it necessary to reorganize their economic activities in the light of changes in their frontiers. Both of these developments served temporarily to retard the re-establishment of a smoothly functioning economic system.

Whatever the political importance of the realignment of territories which followed the peace, whatever the cultural and spiritual values involved in the establishment of new national entities, and whatever the ultimate economic results may prove to be, there is not the slightest question that the territorial changes which occurred greatly increased the difficulties of restoring normal economic activity. Long established commercial and financial relationships were disrupted, and an extensive international organization was very seriously impaired. The resulting confinement of commerce and finance within narrower boundaries, and the effort on the part of each nation to be economically self-sufficient, seriously interfered with the economic life of a large part of continental Europe.

The situation was further complicated by the fact that the treaties of peace imposed a condition of economic inequality upon the Central Powers. This was especially true in the field of commercial policy. Under the terms of the treaties, the defeated countries were virtually deprived—for varying periods of time—of their freedom of action as regards tariff policies and were placed under an obligation to grant the Allies unilateral most-favored-nation treatment. It was not until 1925, when this condition of inequality finally disappeared, that European trade in general was freed from the disturbing influence of these artificial restrictions.

The combined effect of these maladjustments was to produce in the early post-war years more or less continuous financial instability and economic uncertainty. Taking the world as a whole there was, it is true, an extensive expansion of production. But in Europe recovery was spotted and halting, and much of it was inflationary in character. Not until a series of disastrous financial breakdowns occurred in Central and Eastern Europe was a serious effort made under international auspices to re-construct the shattered financial and economic system.

II. CONFLICTING RECONSTRUCTION POLICIES

The reconstruction policies inaugurated after the war were intended, on the one hand, to mitigate burdens and solve immediate difficulties, and, on the other hand, to provide a basis for the recovery and expansion of economic activity. The re-establishment of the gold standard and stable international exchanges was conceived to be the essential foundation for economic rehabilitation. A succession of financial stabilization plans, beginning with that for Austria in 1922, were formulated and put into operation by international agreement. Each involved, on the one hand, reductions in the schedule of reparation payments and, on the other hand, the extension by a group of interested creditor governments of large reconstruction loans to the afflicted countries. Thus were funds provided with which to re-establish the gold standard, and at the same time to ease the immediate strain upon the foreign exchanges.

Beginning in 1923 a series of settlements were negotiated with respect to the inter-Allied debts, which had been in suspense since the end of the war. These "settlements" pertained not only to the debts to the United States, but also to the intra-European governmental debts.

These various international reparation and debt adjustments also laid the basis for new private credit operations on an extensive scale. The European countries which had suffered financial collapse following a period of disastrous inflation found themselves denuded not only of the raw materials and supplies required by industry, but also of the liquid funds, or "working capital," essential to the operation of a pecuniary system. Funds with which to finance the rehabilitation and expansion of plant and equipment were also in many cases imperatively required. In consequence, these countries were willing to assume large new foreign obligations bearing high rates of interest. This circumstance provided what appeared to be highly profitable outlets for the abundant investment funds of the creditor countries, particularly the United States.

Accordingly, following the negotiation of the various debt agreements, new private loans—both long- and short-term in character—were extended in amounts which usually greatly exceeded the current interest instalments on the inter-governmental debts. These credits were advanced not merely by the United States but also by Great Britain, France, Sweden, and other creditor countries. It is to be noted too that loans were being extended on an extensive scale not only for the reconstruction of impoverished Europe, but also for expansion in other parts of the world, especially in South America and Australia.

For a few brief years this financial reconstruction process was acclaimed by most observers as a genuine solution of the financial and trade difficulties which had resulted from the war. The pressure of international debt payments on the foreign exchanges was completely eliminated. At the same time the rapid acceleration of business enterprise materially eased the internal budget problems of the borrowing countries.

To the superficial observer it seemed that a means had also been found whereby the United States could play the role of a creditor country without receiving any excess of imports over exports, and whereby the European nations could meet their indebtedness while yet continuing to have large excesses of imports over exports. To be sure, it was commonly recognized that ultimately, as the new interest obligations mounted, there would have to be readjustments in trade relations, but it was urged that this would come about by such gradual stages as to have imperceptible effects. That is to say, although the new foreign loans involved costs usually amounting to from 8 to 10 per cent, it was nevertheless blithely assumed that the productive enterprise thus fostered would not only permit the payment of interest, but would also make it possible to liquidate the huge accumulation of war indebtedness as well.

This reconstruction effort did not, however, eliminate the basic financial maladjustments which originated in the war days. Instead of liquidating foreign indebtedness, the new loans of course served to increase the external obligations of most European countries. Had these loans been confined to essential requirements the net result might have been altogether beneficial; but under the happy philosophy which prevailed the volume of new credit expansions bore little relation to economic possibilities. Thus difficulties were accumulating for the future.

Meanwhile commercial policies continued to impede economic recovery. The war had destroyed the network of commercial treaties which had governed trade relations among the nations of Europe and had substituted direct government control over the physical volume of trade for the traditional device of customs tariffs as a means of regulating trade movements. It was deemed necessary to continue these measures of quantitative control in the early post-war years, especially since the disruption of currencies tended to nullify the effectiveness of tariffs as a defense against the dumping of goods and other methods of unfair trade competition. International commerce in Europe was for a time conducted on the basis of what amounted to inter-governmental barter.

It was not until 1921 that general conditions became sufficiently stabilized for the nations of Europe to begin re-employing customs tariffs as the principal method of regulating trade. A return to the type of commercial agreement that had served before the war to stabilize trade relations among nations was obstructed by the condition of economic inequality to which the defeated nations of Central Europe had been subjected by the treaties of peace. The desire to achieve economic self-sufficiency as well as to provide employment led many countries into a rapid increase of protectionism. The movement in this direction became intensified when Germany and the other defeated nations regained their freedom of action in tariff matters in 1925.

This rapid rise of trade barriers, proceeding side by side with a widespread reintroduction of the gold standard and an increase of international loans, soon began to cause apprehension in some responsible circles. The League of Nations Assembly, meeting in September 1925, discussed the problem and decided to convoke an international economic conference to consider the situation. The World Economic Conference met in May 1927 and unanimously recommended the need of arresting the protectionist movement and of liberalizing commercial policy in general if the laboriously re-established monetary stability were to be maintained, and a system of international credit relations were to function effectively. The Conference, in fact, made a categorical statement that "the time has come to put a stop to the growth of customs tariffs and to reverse the direction of the movement." It was suggested that this might be accomplished in three ways: (1) by the individual action of particular states in reducing tariffs; (2) by joint agreement between two nations; and (3) by multilateral agreements among several countries.

For a few months, some progress was made in the sense that numerous contemplated increases in tariffs were not put into effect, and a number of trade arrangements designed to improve trade relations were concluded. But, in late 1928 and 1929, a movement for higher protection again gained momentum, being precipitated mainly by the increasing depression in agriculture in various countries. This European movement was stimulated by the alarm and resentment felt in many countries over the increased duties of the Smoot-Hawley Tariff Act in the United States, which after a year of discussion was finally passed in June 1930.

Thus not only were the recommendations of the World Economic Conference never carried out, but the barriers to international trade were markedly increased at a time when the need of expanding international commerce appeared most necessary. In particular, the increasing restrictions on imports by some creditor countries continued to work at direct cross purposes with the trade necessities involved in the servicing and liquidation of the mounting international indebtedness.

III. THE RAPID RECOVERY OF WORLD PRODUCTION

One of the most striking features of the post-war era was the remarkable rapidity with which the volume of economic activity reached and exceeded pre-war levels. Gauged by productive output alone, recovery from the war appeared truly phenomenal.

The recovery of agricultural production began in Europe almost immediately after the war. Since farming

is a relatively simple type of enterprise, production began to expand just as soon as demobilization relieved the
shortage of farm labor. Agricultural recovery was also
stimulated by government aid, especially in the restoration of devastated areas. Moreover, agricultural development came to be fostered by many European countries as an important part of the policy of promoting
national economic self-sufficiency. By 1925 agricultural
output in most European countries was back virtually to
pre-war levels.

While European industrial recovery, as already noted,
was retarded for many years by financial instability, after
1924 the growth of productive capacity was very rapid.
Not only was there restoration and expansion of industrial production in the old industrial countries, but there
was also substantial growth of industry in regions hitherto primarily agricultural. By means of tariffs, subsidies,
and other aids governments were everywhere fostering
industrial development, not only as a means of achieving
greater economic independence, but also with a view
to providing employment.

As early as the year 1925, the production of foodstuffs
and raw materials in the world as a whole exceeded pre-
war levels. Output—on a per capita basis—was 10 per
cent greater than in 1913. Even the European continent
had attained a level of production in these lines equal to
that of the last year before the war. The volume of world
trade was, however, still slightly below the pre-war
level; and European trade was 9 per cent below, with
exports lagging as much as 14 per cent.

Between 1925 and 1929 industrial activity and international trade tended to catch up with the previous increase in agricultural output. World population increased about 4 per cent, the production of foodstuffs 5

per cent, raw materials 20 per cent, and world trade 19 per cent. Available data indicate that the production of finished manufactures increased more rapidly than the output of raw materials. For example, the world production of pig iron rose 28 per cent and steel 33 per cent.

The second distinguishing feature of the period 1925-29 was the relative increase in European production. Whereas up to 1925 expansion had been considerably greater in other countries than in Europe, after 1925 the expansion was more rapid in Europe than in other parts of the world. Concretely, Europe with an increase in population of 5 per cent showed an expansion in trade of 22 per cent; while the rest of the world, with an increase of 3 per cent in population, showed only a 12 per cent expansion in volume of trade. This remarkable growth in European production and trade was of course greatly facilitated by the enormous international credits which were extended during those years.[1]

Thus it appeared—on the surface of things—that within a very few years the productive power of the world, and even of war-stricken Europe, had been fully re-established. From a curve indicating the trend of world production in 1900, 1913, and 1929, it would be difficult to observe that the war had had any lasting effect upon the wealth producing capacity of the world.

IV. CONTINUING INTERNATIONAL MALADJUSTMENTS

The costs of the war had, however, in no sense been liquidated. Profound maladjustments in agriculture and industry and in trade and financial relations which had been produced by the war were not only still existent but had in some respects been gravely complicated by the

[1] For detailed data, see League of Nations, *World Economic Survey*, *1931-32*.

reconstruction process. We may consider first the situation with respect to agriculture.

The restriction of agricultural production in Europe during the war had enormously stimulated agriculture in other parts of the world, especially in North America, the prevailing high prices making it profitable to open up extensive new areas to cultivation. The recovery of European agriculture after the war was not, however, accompanied by any corresponding readjustment in agricultural production in other countries. As a result, the great increase in agricultural production in the post-war period was accompanied by a persistent decline in farm prices. After the precipitate collapse of 1920-21, the price of wheat recovered materially; but from 1925 on the decline was almost continuous. Cotton, wool, silk, sugar, and coffee showed similar trends; while the prices of a number of other farm products, notably rice, tea, cocoa, jute, hemp, and flax, began to fall in 1926-27.

This expansion of world agricultural output, moreover, led to a progressive accumulation of unsold stocks of farm commodities. Instead of each year's production being completely disposed of, for whatever the crop would bring, prices were often sustained by temporarily withholding supplies from the market, and by "valorization" schemes supported by government credit. The outcome was a persistent piling up of unsold stocks of the principal agricultural commodities. With such supplies hanging over the markets, and with production constantly increasing, the world agricultural situation was highly unstable.[2]

There were maladjustments of a similar sort in the

[2] For a detailed study of the movement of agricultural prices and stocks, see Vladimir P. Timoshenko, *World Agriculture and the Depression*.

field of industry. The reconstruction and "rationalization" of industrial plant and equipment in the old industrial countries of Europe, and the expansion of industry in nations hitherto primarily agricultural had not been accompanied by any corresponding readjustment in the productive capacity of the United States. On the contrary, the large foreign markets, made possible in part through credit policies, contributed toward further expansion of productive capacity in the United States in nearly all lines of production. By the end of the period competition in international markets was becoming more intense; and it was this in part which accounted for the development of new tariff restrictions, to which reference has already been made. At the same time, the greatly expanded volume of international indebtedness had increased the necessity for ultimate modifications in the currents of international trade.

In short, the stimulation of business activity through the granting of huge international credits and the internal subsidization of agriculture and industry led to a great concurrent expansion in the volume of production. But the process did not restore the pre-war state of economic equilibrium. On the contrary, it served to increase some of the existing maladjustments and thus to magnify, as we shall see in the following chapter, the extent of the economic dislocation of the ensuing years.

Mention should also be made of the divergent movements of prices in different countries. The stabilization of currencies that began about 1923 was far from uniform in character, being effected in the different countries at widely different levels. As a result, the relations between price levels in different countries were disturbed for varying periods of time. It is possible that even by 1929 the readjustment of costs and prices to the changed monetary units had not been completed. Maladjustment in the international price system, however, was probably not an important factor in the situation.

V. INTERNAL MALADJUSTMENTS

Economic stability is dependent not only upon external trade and financial relations, but also, and in no small degree, upon domestic policies and conditions. Accordingly, this survey of the economic background of the depression of 1929 would not be complete without some consideration of the purely domestic factors in the situation. Again, we shall not attempt any detailed statistical study designed to·show the relative importance of various factors or the time sequence in the movement of events. While our primary interest is in studying the problem of recovery as it presents itself in the United States, it is necessary to mention certain factors of maladjustments existing in other countries.

In foreign countries. In the first place, many countries were confronted with difficult fiscal situations. Both as a legacy from the war and as a result of extensive post-war public loans for reconstruction and relief, the budgets of central governments were in many cases seriously unbalanced. These fiscal difficulties were not only increasing the burdens of taxation, but were also complicating the problem of maintaining monetary and exchange stability.

It should be pointed out, also, that in many countries domestic credit was being employed for purposes of expansion on an extremely large scale. Extensive loans were being made by banking institutions for the development of private business activity, and at the same time large public and quasi-public loans were being floated for purposes regarded as socially important. In the case of countries borrowing in the international markets, these internal loans were in fact made possible by the inflow of foreign funds. The mounting burden of indebtedness —both public and private—was to prove a factor of great difficulty once the depression had begun.

While the situation varied materially in different countries, there were numerous cases in which business activity had for years been greatly stimulated by reconstruction activities, by a boom in housing, and by the upbuilding of domestic agriculture and industry as a part of the process of territorial and economic readjustment. With the tapering off of such activities, economic difficulties were here and there beginning to manifest themselves. In some countries, moreover, notably in Great Britain, the whole process of post-war economic and financial reorientation had produced continuing economic difficulties.

In the United States. In considering the factors of maladjustment within the United States, it will be helpful first to recall the general trend of business in the post-war years. From early 1919 to the spring of 1920 there was a commercial boom, accompanied by rapidly rising commodity prices, which was directly related to the replacement—both in the United States and in Europe—of depleted stocks of commodities required for ordinary consumption. The so-called "buyers' strike" of May 1920 was followed by an acute depression involving a precipitate decline of prices and a drastic liquidation of commercial credit. Recovery began late in 1921 and continued with slight interruption until the spring of 1924. Then came a sharp curtailment of industrial production which lasted, however, only until the autumn of that year. Another moderate recession extended over the greater part of the year 1927. On the whole, how-

ever, the period from 1922 to 1929 is not inaccurately
described as one of great and well-sustained prosperity;
and in any event we are not here concerned with the
minor fluctuations which occurred.

A number of factors, apart from large foreign sales,
combined to produce the great business activity of the
twenties. Of greatest significance were the enormous expansion in the field of construction, made necessary by
the shortages produced by the war, and the phenomenal
growth of the automobile industry. These two developments require a few words of explanation.

During the course of the war, except in fields directly
related to the war program, building operations were
largely suspended. This was, of course, particularly true
of the housing field. Moreover, during the brief prosperity period of 1919-20, there was but a moderate increase in building activity. With population, particularly
in urban centers, steadily increasing, five or six years of
suspended construction inevitably served to create a great
shortage of housing accommodations. The recovery of
1921 was undoubtedly stimulated by the increase of construction which began early in the year and steadily
gained momentum. As prosperity returned, there was,
moreover, a cumulative increase in all forms of construction, including industrial plant and equipment, railroad
and public utility replacements and improvements, public works—federal, state, and local—and a number of
new industries as well.[3]

The phenomenal growth of the automobile industry
was closely related to developments in housing. The
higher levels of income made it possible for vastly in-

---

[3] For further data on trends in the construction industry, see **Chap.
VIII and Appendix D.**

creased numbers of people to own automobiles; and, in turn, the ownership of automobiles greatly stimulated the housing industry by shifting population from urban to suburban regions. Similarly, also, the growth of the automobile necessitated a vast program of highway construction. Thus widespread business activity was cumulatively accelerated.

In view of the rapid expansion, particularly in the fields of construction and automobile production, the question whether the pace could be maintained was frequently raised. In the case of houses, it was pointed out that the rate of increase had been faster than the rate of increase in population; and it was frequently observed that the saturation point would sooner or later be reached with respect to automobiles. Without endeavoring to analyze the issue thus raised, it is clear that just as the existing shortage of housing facilities in 1920 and 1921 had created a situation helpful to recovery, so also might the surplus of housing in the late twenties lead to general depression. The data show a gradual decline in housing construction from 1925 on; but this was more than offset by expansion in other construction.

Economic expansion was also facilitated by the liberal use of credit. In addition to the extensive international loans to which reference has been made, credit also played a large role in the domestic field. On the consumption side, sales on the instalment plan made possible a substantial increase in purchases of automobiles and a wide range of household commodities. Similarly, houses could be bought on time payment plans involving but small initial investment. State and local governments also employed their credit in floating securities for the purpose of financing highway construction and other public enterprises.⁴ Commercial bank credit was, more-over, extended on a large scale for both short- and long-term financing.

The distribution of national income was manifesting increasing inequality. During the post-war period there was a rapid increase in the total national income. The per capita income from current production activities (in-flationary gains excluded) increased between 1919 and 1929 by as much as 23 per cent. This increase was not, however, participated in equally by all portions of the population. For example, as a result of the persistent de-cline in agricultural prices, the income of the farm popu-lation as a whole did not expand. Wages which, as al-ready noted, were relatively high after the price declines of 1920-21, continued to increase. But wages did not increase in proportion to the increase in productive effi-ciency or to the national income as a whole. The most rapid rate of increase occurred in the high income groups, including salaried officials and receivers of profits from business enterprises.

In consequence of the increasing concentration of in-comes in the higher brackets a larger percentage of the national income tended, as the years passed, to be saved for investment. That is to say, the proportion of the total income that was directed into consumption channels did not grow as fast as the amount that was directed into savings channels. The results were manifested in two ways.

On the one hand, producers of consumer goods, con-stantly confronted with markets inadequate to permit the

⁴ For chart showing growth of state and local government debt, see p. 310; for detailed data and discussion of the growth of debt in general, see Chap. XII.

full utilization of their productive resources, sought to expand sales by means of liberal credits both at home and abroad. Intensive efforts by means of advertising and enlarged selling organizations were made to overcome what was called "sales resistance," but which was in reality inadequate purchasing power among the masses, whose income is directed chiefly to the purchase of consumption goods. There was, however, no piling up of inventories, the volume of actual production being in most lines adjusted to sales.

On the other hand, the flow of funds into investment channels was greatly in excess of the current needs of business enterprisers for the development of additional capital in the form of plant and equipment. This situation, together with the abundance of commercial bank credit available, promoted developments such as the Florida real estate boom, the flotations in American markets of a great variety of European and South American securities, many of them highly speculative in character, and the issuance of investment trust and holding company securities, not for the purpose of financing new capital construction, but of acquiring control of existing corporations. It was this superabundance of investment money, still further enhanced by commercial credit loans for stock speculation, that was chiefly responsible for the phenomenal rise in the prices of stocks.[5] Short-term interest rates were high, as a result of Federal Reserve policy; but rates and yields on bonds were not, while yields on stocks were unprecedentedly low (see page 369.) Mention should also be made of the large flow of foreign funds to the United States in 1928-29—

[5] For a fuller discussion of this problem, see H. G. Moulton, *The Formation of Capital*, Chap. X.

attracted by high rates of interest on short-term funds as well as by the possibilities of speculative gains in the security markets.

In short, the flow of funds through consumption or trade channels was inadequate to call forth the full utilization of our productive capacity; while, on the other hand, the flow of funds into investment channels was greater than business men would use under the existing conditions in building additional plant and equipment. A maladjustment of a fundamental character had thus arisen out of the distribution of the national income.

VI. SUMMARY OF ECONOMIC SITUATION IN 1929

The decade of the twenties was an era of exceptional economic activity, built upon insecure foundations. While the direct losses resulting from the war appeared to have been overcome in an incredibly short period of time, and although the volume of world production and trade materially exceeded that of pre-war days, the situation was nevertheless fundamentally unstable. The economic machine was seriously out of adjustment in several important respects; or perhaps one might better say it was vulnerable in a number of places. Without endeavoring to assess their relative importance in producing the intense depression which was soon to begin, we may nevertheless conclude this discussion of the economic background by enumerating in summary form the major sources of maladjustment then existing:

International trade and financial relations were fundamentally unbalanced, being supported for the time being by a continuous stream of funds from creditor to debtor nations.

The stabilized international exchanges were in many instances dependent solely upon the continuance of credits, particularly those of short duration.

The reconstruction of plant and equipment in the old industrial countries of Europe and the fostering of manufacturing development in the new nations established at the end of the war were intensifying international competition and further stimulating the growth of trade barriers.

The recovery and expansion of world agricultural production had depressed the prices of basic farm products everywhere, and at the same time unsold stocks were steadily accumulating.

The governments of many countries were burdened with domestic indebtedness, and in few cases were budgets safely in balance.

The expansion of private credit, for both productive and consumptive purposes, had proceeded at a pace which could not be indefinitely maintained and which was storing up troubles for the future in meeting interest obligations.

In the United States the prolonged boom in the construction industry had served to replace deficiencies by surpluses, while the output of automobiles had reached a level difficult to maintain.

The distribution of income in the United States was becoming increasingly concentrated, and the flow of funds into consumptive channels was persistently inadequate to purchase at prevailing prices the full potential output of our productive establishments.

The flow of savings and of bank credit into invest-

ment channels was excessive, producing an inflation of security prices and consequent financial instability.

Such, in brief, was the general economic situation on
the eve of the depression, the course of which we shall
trace in the ensuing chapter.

CHAPTER II
THE COURSE OF THE DEPRESSION

In the analysis of the trend of economic events prior to 1929, no effort was made to assess the relative weight or significance of the several types of maladjustment which were found to exist on the eve of the depression. Moreover, we shall not undertake to make such an appraisal in the present chapter. Our major purpose is rather to trace the course of events during the depression and to reveal the interacting and cumulative consequences of the various maladjustments which existed.

We are not interested in attempting to determine *the cause* of the depression—for the analysis of the first chapter indicates that the depression was the outgrowth, not of some one single disturbing element but of a number of factors. Inasmuch as the world economic system was vulnerable in several important respects, it was only a question of time until a break would occur somewhere —the precise moment and place being perhaps more or less a matter of accidental circumstance. Moreover, once a serious break occurred at any place in the complex mechanism the effects would spread throughout the entire system.

It may be useful, however, in helping to show the complexity and the geographic spread of the forces involved to note here that economic changes were manifesting themselves in various ways and in various places before the acute break which came in the New York stock market in October 1929. In Australia and the Dutch East Indies the depression clearly began in the last quarter of 1927. The year 1928 showed business recession in Germany beginning early in the year and in Finland and Brazil in the third quarter. In 1929 Poland showed a decline in the first quarter, Canada and Argentine in the second, and Italy, Belgium, Egypt, and the United States in the third.[1] The extent of the recession was, however, in most cases not pronounced and, as revealed in the preceding chapter, world production was in the aggregate continuing to expand. It was not until after the break in the American stock market that the stage of severe depression may be said to have begun.

The recession involved two distinct phases. The first extended until the spring of 1931, and the second from then until 1932-33—the date of the upturn, as we shall see in the following chapter, showing considerable variation from country to country. The first phase was comparatively moderate in character, resembling in many respects an ordinary business recession. While the extent of the business decline was extremely severe, there was no acute breakdown of the economic structure, and it seemed to many observers that the processes of normal recovery would shortly manifest themselves. The second, and acute, stage of the recession was marked by a collapse of international credit and monetary systems, and by a profound disruption of the internal banking and financial structure of many countries.

The spread of the depression throughout the principal countries of the world and the intensification of the economic dislocation are indicated in the accompanying diagram. The quarterly movements from 1929 to 1933 shown in this diagram are based on a composite series of statistical indexes which have been compiled by the

[1] See accompanying chart; also League of Nations, *World Economic Survey, 1931-32*, p. 65.

League of Nations Secretariat, for the purpose of reflecting changes in national income.[2]

In studying these diagrams the reader should bear in mind that the data do not pretend to measure the extent of the reduction in the volume of business activity, but only the direction of movement from one quarter to the next. It will be observed that in general the recession developed slightly earlier in Oceania, the Americas, and Asia than it did in Europe, that it spread rapidly in late 1929 and early 1930, and that by 1931 it was practically universal and steadily growing in intensity.

In the first major division of this chapter we shall indicate the extent and character of the early phase of the depression. In the second section we shall show the bearing of the international debt situation on the acute financial crisis which came in the spring of 1931. In the third and fourth divisions we shall analyze the profound effects of this crisis upon the financial and economic structure of the world with particular reference to the United States.

I. SEVERE BUSINESS RECESSION, 1929-31

The most striking and significant developments during the first phase of the recession—from late 1929 to the spring of 1931—were as follows: (1) a sharp decline in the prices of stocks; (2) a drastic fall in the prices of foodstuffs and raw materials; (3) a substantial curtailment of industrial production; (4) a marked de-

[2] The original charts from which the accompanying diagram has been adapted will be found in League of Nations, *World Economic Survey, 1931-32*, p. 64; and same for 1933-34, p. 320. The explanatory notes accompanying the original charts state that they summarize changes in economic conditions as recorded in the publications of governments, central banks, and business cycle institutes in the various countries; and that in certain cases the national summaries available have been supplemented by using the statistics of production, employment, and trade in the countries concerned.

The Trend of World Economic Conditions, 1929–33[a]

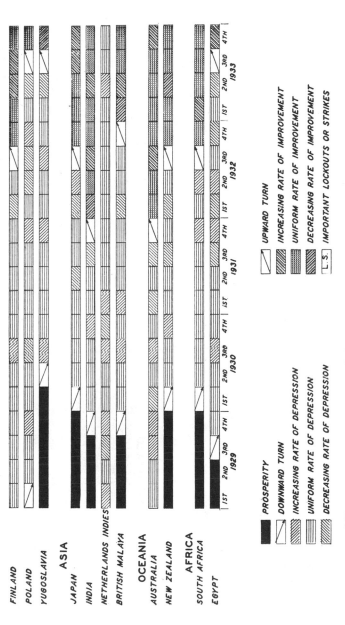

FINLAND
POLAND
YUGOSLAVIA

ASIA
JAPAN
INDIA
NETHERLANDS INDIES
BRITISH MALAYA

OCEANIA
AUSTRALIA
NEW ZEALAND

AFRICA
SOUTH AFRICA
EGYPT

| 1ST | 2ND | 3RD | 4TH | 1ST | 2ND | 3RD | 4TH | 1ST | 2ND | 3RD | 4TH | 1ST | 2ND | 3RD | 4TH | 1ST | 2ND | 3RD | 4TH |
1929   1930   1931   1932   1933

PROSPERITY
DOWNWARD TURN
INCREASING RATE OF DEPRESSION
UNIFORM RATE OF DEPRESSION
DECREASING RATE OF DEPRESSION

UPWARD TURN
INCREASING RATE OF IMPROVEMENT
UNIFORM RATE OF IMPROVEMENT
DECREASING RATE OF IMPROVEMENT
L.S. IMPORTANT LOCKOUTS OR STRIKES

ᵃ For source, see note 2, p. 29.

crease in world trade; and (5) a rapid reduction in the
flow of new international loans. The course of each of
these developments may be briefly summarized.

 1. The break in stock prices. While, as we have seen,
a slight business recession was occurring here and there
before the autumn of 1929, the first striking evidence
that the boom period was over was afforded by the sudden collapse of stock prices in the New York market.
The movement of stock prices in leading international
markets from September 1929 to June 1931 is revealed
by the following indexes, which are based on September
1929 as 100.

		New York	London	Paris	Berlin
1929,	September	100	100	100	100
	December	68	84	89	86
1930,	March	75	81	92	89
	June	66	78	85	87
	September	64	76	81	74
	December	47	69	66	62
1931,	March	52	67	68	66
	June	40	57	62	54

The collapse of the security market boom in the
United States was quickly reflected in general business
activity. The transformation of speculative profits to
losses checked certain types of consumptive expenditures, particularly of the luxury variety, and at the same
time the shock to confidence led to the curtailment of
new business commitments. In the early spring of 1930
there was a substantial rise in security values. Further
drastic liquidation took place in the second half of 1930,
followed by a slight recovery in the first quarter of 1931.
The coming of the acute stage of the depression in the
second quarter of 1931 precipitated a new downward

movement. The trend in European financial centers was similar, though a little less pronounced in character.

2. *Decline of foodstuff and raw material prices.* Supplies of many of the basic foodstuffs and some of the important raw materials had been accumulating and prices had been declining for some time before 1929. With the coming of the depression, a catastrophic fall occurred in the prices of both foodstuffs and raw materials. Efforts to arrest the decline by means of valorization schemes and cartel agreements were of no permanent avail.

The following table shows the extent of the decline in the world market prices of a selected group of foodstuffs and raw materials. The first column reveals the percentage decline from the average of the year 1928 to the average for the month of June 1930; the second indicates the magnitude of the cumulative drop from the same 1928 base to June 1931.

Foodstuffs	June 1930	June 1931	Raw Materials	June 1930	June 1931
Wheat	28	61	Wool	38	68
Rye	48	64	Cotton	28	55
Corn	25	60	Silk	29	54
Rice	13	51	Hides	37	65
Coffee	44	50	Tin	40	54
Sugar	32	48	Copper	15	42
Bacon	12	50	Petroleum	31	43
Butter	27	36	Rubber	43	72

It will be observed that in some cases prices held up comparatively well in the first nine months of the depression, but that drastic declines everywhere ensued in the second year.

The prices of manufactured commodities fell much less than those of foodstuffs and raw materials. In the United States, for example, price indexes show a decline between June 1929 and June 1931 of about 20 per cent in finished manufactured products, 33 per cent in industrial raw materials, and 37 per cent in foodstuffs and agricultural raw materials.

This smaller relative decline in the prices of manufactured products is attributable to several factors. There had been no great accumulation of unsold stocks of goods in manufacturing lines, the flow of production having been adjusted rather closely to current demands. It was also possible for industry in some measure to adjust production schedules to changed conditions, whereas agricultural output proceeded unabated. However, the attempt on the part of debtor countries producing agricultural products and raw materials to meet debt obligations by forcing exports exerted a downward pressure on the prices of these primary commodities.

3. Curtailment of industrial production. The first phase of the recession showed a substantial decline in the volume of industrial production in all manufacturing nations. The reader will find on pages 56-67 the annual changes in the volume of production in manufacturing, crude foodstuffs, and raw materials for the whole period 1925-35. The decline of industrial production in the United States by quarterly intervals from September 1929 to June 1931 is shown by the following table. These monthly index numbers are based on the average for the year 1929 as 100.[3]

1929,	September	103
	December	85
1930,	March	87
	June	82
	September	76
	December	71
1931,	March	73
	June	70

[3] For monthly data to June 1936 see Appendix A, Table 10.

4. Reduction of world trade. The decline in the total value and "quantum"[4] of world trade from the third quarter of 1929 through the second quarter of 1931 is indicated below. The figures are based upon the average for the year 1929 as 100.[5]

Quarter	"Quantum"	Value
1929, July-September	98.3	98.3
October-December	105.9	102.2
1930, January-March	94.8	89.1
April-June	92.6	82.4
July-September	88.0	75.7
October-December	95.7	76.1
1931, January-March	84.5	62.5
April-June	84.4	59.9

It will be seen that the volume of international trade held up reasonably well throughout this period, but the value declined sharply after the middle of 1930 and continued to fall through the first half of 1931. This sharp decline in the total value of world trade, occasioned mainly by the collapse of the prices of many basic commodities entering into international trade, helped, through its repercussions upon the international credit structure, to weaken the economic position of many countries, particularly those exporting raw materials.

5. Contraction of new international loans. The flow of international loans began tapering off well before October 1929. Foreign loans from the United States were declining. At the same time French funds which had in

---

[4] These so-called quantum figures are not, strictly speaking, physical units. They are derived from the value figures corrected for price changes; and they therefore reflect the volume of trade in a rough way. This measure is used here because physical quantity data are not available for all countries.

[5] The figures have been compiled by the League of Nations Secretariat. See *Monthly Bulletin of Statistics*, December 1934, p. 531.

preceding years been invested abroad were returning to France. On the debtor side the borrowings by such countries as Germany, Poland, and Hungary were declining.

Perhaps the best means of indicating what was occurring in the field of international financial relations during these years is to show the net movement of funds, whether arising out of new loans, repayments, or withdrawals of investments. The accompanying table shows the net outflow of funds from principal creditor countries and the net inflow to principal debtor countries from 1927 to 1931 inclusive.

NET INTERNATIONAL MOVEMENT OF FUNDS, 1927-31[a]
(In millions of dollars)

Country	1927	1928	1929	1930	1931
United States	+ 518	+1,113	+225	+295	0
United Kingdom	+ 385	+ 570	+574	+112	−313
France	+ 504	+ 237	− 20	−258	−787
Germany	−1,058	− 974	−508	−120	+506
Poland	− 82	− 124	− 67	− 1	+ 5
Hungary	− 89	− 91	− 38	− 24	− 39
Australia	− 188	− 188	−214	− 15	+ 56
India	− 121	− 67	− 37	− 92	+ 86
Argentine	+ 127	− 184	− 4	−243	+ 27

[a] League of Nations, *Balance of Payments*, 1931 and 1932, p. 21. These figures have been derived not from recorded data but from analyses of the annual balances of payments of the respective countries. The plus sign means net outflow; the minus sign, net inflow.

It will be seen that the outward flow of foreign credits from the lending countries was enormously reduced by 1930 and disappeared in 1931; indeed there was a substantial inflow to France in 1930 and 1931, and also to Great Britain in the latter year. The net outflow from Germany, Australia, Argentine, and India which began in 1931 reflects, of course, not the extension of new credits but rather the repayment of existing debts, and—

in the case of Germany—a flight from the mark during the period of panic.

During the first stage of the depression there were recurring waves of optimism as to the possibilities of recovery. Many observers sought to explain the developing situation in terms of previous downswings of the business cycle and were inclined to regard the events of 1930 as representing the normal operation of the forces of readjustment. The slight improvement manifested in the early spring of 1930 led many to conclude that the depression was over, and there was widespread confidence that recovery would not be long delayed. An important British economic journal, in analyzing developments in the United States in 1930, described them as constituting "continuous but orderly deflation in security prices, commodity prices, credit outstanding, and in the manufacture, distribution and sale of goods."[6] With the new slight improvement which manifested itself in various countries at the beginning of 1931, the remarkable resiliency of the economic system became the subject of widespread comment.

The apparent stability in the international economic situation contributed greatly to sustaining the prevailing spirit of hopefulness. The international monetary system which had been laboriously restored in nearly all countries between 1924 and 1930 remained, in general, firmly anchored to the gold standard; and the structure of international indebtedness, public and private, which had come into existence as a result of the war and post-war developments, showed no sign of imminent breaking. The only important countries to depart from the gold

[6] "Commercial History and Review of 1930," *The Economist*, Feb. 14, 1931.

standard during this period were Australia and Argentine, which suspended gold payments as early as December 1929. The currencies of Bolivia, Brazil, Panama, Uruguay, and Venezuela declined from their gold parities, but there was no official abandonment of the gold standard. On the other hand, in two countries, Japan and Yugoslavia, the gold standard was for the first time since the war re-established during the year 1930. By and large, international debt payments, both public and private, continued to be met on schedule, notwithstanding the substantial curtailment in the volume of new international credits.

It is true that some uneasiness was occasioned by the inability of Australia and Argentine to meet their international obligations without abandoning the gold standard; but in general there was inclination to regard the difficulties of these countries as special in character, because of their dependence upon the exportation of foodstuffs and raw materials, chiefly wheat and wool, which had suffered unusual price declines. While it was not regarded as impossible that some debt concession might become necessary in the case of other countries, if they were to avoid monetary breakdown, it was not believed that such readjustments would need to be of substantial character. In September 1930 the Young Plan was put into effect in the belief that the payments required, which represented only a moderate reduction from the Dawes Plan schedules, were well within the economic power of Germany to fulfill.

II. INTERNATIONAL DEBTS AND THE CRISIS OF 1931

The factor directly responsible for the disastrous breakdown which occurred in the second quarter of 1931 was the huge volume of international indebtedness. It would be idle to speculate on the question whether, in the absence of the extraordinary international debt situation, the severe business depression might shortly have been arrested by the normal processes of adjustment. It is possible that serious difficulties might in any case have developed because of the numerous other forms of maladjustment which existed. However this may be, it is certain that the financial collapse of 1931 was made incvitable by the international debt situation. Hence, as a preliminary to an analysis of the second phase of the depression, it is essential to indicate the character of the international debt problem at this juncture.

The volume of international indebtedness had assumed proportions which dwarfed that of pre-war days. While precise data as to the extent of international debts —both long- and short-term, and public and private— are not available, they may be conservatively estimated as aggregating at the end of 1930 at least 60 billions of dollars. The interest and amortization charges on this vast sum required payments across national frontiers approximating 3 billion dollars annually.[7]

As we have already seen, the instalments on both public and private indebtedness continued to be paid through 1930 without apparent difficulty. However, the process by which the debtor countries succeeded in making these payments and at the same time in preserving monetary stability was directly contributing to subsequent difficulties. Unable to borrow as much as before, and at the same time faced with a reduction of income per unit of exports

---

[7] The reparation and inter-Allied indebtedness as funded aggregated at the end of 1930 a principal sum of approximately 20 billion dollars. The League of Nations Secretariat estimates that the volume of private fixed interest indebtedness was 35 billion dollars at the end of 1932; no estimate has been made for direct investments in business enterprises and securities.

as a result of the sharp decline in the prices of basic export commodities, they found it necessary to make drastic efforts to obtain means with which to meet foreign debt payments. They strove simultaneously to reduce imports and to expand the physical volume of exports as a means of offsetting the reduction in the value per unit. Most of them succeeded in varying degrees. Imports were curtailed, in part as a result of conscious policy and in part as a natural consequence of the depression, while the physical volume of exports was stimulated mainly by means of price concessions.

In the table below we show the changes in the physical volume of trade and resulting effects upon the monetary balance of eight debtor countries; also the reverse effects upon the trade of the principal creditor countries.

TRADE CHANGES IN SELECTED COUNTRIES, 1928-30[a]

Country	Exports (In thousands of metric tons)			Imports (In thousands of metric tons)			Balance of Trade (In millions of old U. S. gold dollars)		
	1928	1929	1930	1928	1929	1930	1928	1929	1930
DEBTORS:									
Germany...	45,013	54,770	57,103	66,005	66,778	56,953	− 298	+ 9	+ 592
Hungary....	2,173	2,873	2,462	6,628	6,710	4,885	− 67	− 4	+ 11
Rumania...	5,886	7,065	9,215	953	1,102	805	− 32	− 3	+ 33
Bulgaria....	368	313	543	360	508	317	− 2	+ 14	+ 9
Poland.....	20,424	21,038	18,922	5,165	5,088	3,571	− 98	− 33	+ 10
Brazil......	2,075	2,189	2,274	5,838	6,108	4,881	+ 33	+ 40	+ 57
Australia...	4,686	5,289	6,646	5,889	6,067	4,598	− 23	− 117	− 41
Argentine...	17,029	16,703	11,027	12,538	13,040	12,364	+ 210	+ 88	− 102
CREDITORS:									
United States	57,035	57,475	49,731	45,642	50,985	47,563	+ 738	+ 382	+ 386
United Kingdom......	...	...	...	...	...	...	−1,718	−1,854	−1,878
France.....	41,128	39,906	36,681	49,340	59,462	60,921	− 129	− 435	− 506
Switzerland.	977	1,045	919	8,020	8,711	8,553	− 104	− 115	− 151
Netherlands.	15,725	16,302	16,606	29,851	30,989	31,395	− 281	− 306	− 281

[a] The plus sign means excess exports; the minus sign, excess imports.

The process indicated by the table had repercussions of far-reaching importance. The stimulation of the physical volume of exports, consisting mainly—except in the case of Germany—of foodstuffs and raw materials, tended to drive down still more the already depressed prices of these commodities, and thus to render increasingly difficult the maintenance of international income by the debtor countries. The resulting intensification of competition led to demands on the part of producers in creditor countries for protective measures against this flood of low-priced imports. The contraction by the debtor countries of imports, consisting largely of manufactured goods, reduced the exports of industrial countries and tended to depress the prices of manufactured goods and to curtail industrial activity generally. The optimism engendered by the stability of the gold standard and the structure of international indebtedness was thus built on shifting sands.

A particularly dangerous feature of the international debt situation was the large accumulation of short-term obligations. By the end of 1930 obligations of this type constituted from 12 to 14 billions of dollars. Of this total 7 or 8 billions was in the form of *commercial credits* arising out of trade transactions. The remainder represented the *investment of funds*, and included the foreign exchange holdings of central banks, amounting to approximately 2.5 billions of dollars.[8]

The abnormal amount of international short-term investments was attributable in part to the fiscal and monetary disorders of the post-war years, which created a

---

[8] These estimates of short-term indebtedness are based on the foreign exchange debts and claims of the three principal countries—the United States, Great Britain, and Germany—and on less complete data for several other countries. The distribution by types is arrived at in the following manner: the figure for central bank holdings is obtained from official reports of the banks, while the volume of commercial credit is assumed to be from 12 to 15 per cent of the total value of world trade. The estimate is of necessity a very rough approximation, but is in close correspondence with an estimate of 14 billion dollars made by the Bank for International Settlements at the end of 1930 (see its *Fourth Annual Report*, p. 27).

widespread feeling that short-term loans were safer than long-term investments. Second, there were large shiftings of funds from one country to another to take advantage of the possibilities of speculative profits. Third, central bank policies contributed to the creation of such indebtedness in a twofold way. The re-establishment of an international monetary system based on gold had involved the wide adoption of what is known as the gold exchange standard, under which central banks were permitted to include in their reserves not only metallic gold but also foreign exchange instruments representing claims to gold in other countries. In addition to the gold exchange banks, many other central banks adopted the policy of holding large amounts of foreign exchange among their assets as a convenient and presumably liquid form of short-term investment. In fact, the volume of foreign exchange holdings by these banks was much larger than that of the banks operating under the gold exchange system. The Bank of France was of overwhelming importance in this situation, its foreign exchange holdings alone exceeding at the end of 1930 those of the ten principal central banks operating under the gold exchange system. All these holdings of foreign exchange represented international short-term indebtedness and the funds involved were subject to removal from one country to another at a moment's notice.[9]

The world's greatest debtors on short-term account were the United States, Great Britain, and Germany. The large volume of short-term debts owed by the United States and Great Britain were the result of two factors: the predominant role which these countries played in the financing of international trade; and the

[9] For detailed data relating to foreign exchange holdings of the world's principal central banks, see Appendix H, Table 9.

fact that they were the repositories of short-term funds from other countries which were seeking safety or investment opportunity. Germany's short-term indebtedness represented in part credits granted by foreign financial centers, chiefly New York, London, and Paris, and in part direct commercial obligations arising out of trade relations with various countries. We present in the following table the short-term debts and claims of the United States, Great Britain, and Germany respectively as of the end of 1930.[10] The figures are in billions of dollars.

Country	Debts	Claims	Net Debts
United States	2.7	1.8	0.9
Great Britain	2.0	0.8	1.8
Germany	2.5	1.2	1.3

The intricate inter-relationship of short-term debts and claims and the constant movement of liquid funds across national frontiers, operating as a sort of endless chain, presented no difficulty so long as confidence prevailed. But the moment a break in the chain occurred at any place, accompanied by withdrawals on a large scale, panic was certain to ensue. The total volume of short-term obligations abroad was in the case of many countries, including Germany and Great Britain, much greater than the total monetary reserves of the central banks; hence large withdrawals would precipitate an exchange panic and force the suspension of gold payments. The situation was identical with that of an individual bank which holds demand deposits greatly in excess of cash reserves. So long as there are no unusual

[10] The data for the United States are from Department of Commerce, *The Balance of International Payments of the United States in 1930;* for Great Britain from the *Report of the Macmillan Committee;* for Germany from the *Report of the Wiggin Committee.*

demands for payment the credit structure is safe; but once a run on the bank begins the suspension of payments becomes inevitable.

III. FINANCIAL AND MONETARY COLLAPSE

Although surface indications seemed reassuring at the beginning of 1931, the foundations of the international financial and economic structure were steadily being undermined and the inevitable collapse was near at hand. The forces immediately responsible for the financial crisis which occurred in the second quarter were in part economic and in part political.

On the economic side, the continued decline of productive activity was imposing an increasing strain on the internal finances of practically every country. At the same time, the sharp shrinkage in the value of world trade which began in the first quarter of 1931 as a result of the cumulative effects of the trade adjustment policies that had been pursued gravely complicated the ability of the debtor countries to continue meeting international debt payments. (Refer again to trade data on page 33.)

Political factors in the situation were also serving to weaken the financial situation, especially in Central Europe. The growing strength of the Nazi movement in Germany, disclosed by the elections held in October 1930, served to frighten foreign creditors, especially the French, into substantial withdrawals of short-term funds. Similarly, the autumn elections served to induce many Germans to transfer their funds abroad in the hope of obtaining greater security. This outflow of funds, slow at first but increasing in magnitude as the months passed, was reflected in a gradual diminution of the gold and foreign exchange holdings of the Reichsbank, which decreased between December 1930 and March 1931 by more than 100 million dollars.

The financial collapse of Central Europe in May 1931 was precipitated by political developments. On March 11 Germany and Austria announced the conclusion of a customs agreement—a move which was construed as a violation of the treaties of peace. This action led immediately to large withdrawals of foreign funds, particularly by France. Within a few months this drain, together with internal difficulties, brought the Austrian financial system to the stage of collapse, the first outward appearance of which was the failure of the country's largest bank, the Kreditanstalt. This event produced a panic among the short-term creditors of all Central European countries. The ensuing withdrawals quickly forced the abandonment of the gold standard and the suspension of a substantial part of the international debt payments, both public and private.

No financial catastrophe of the past had ever compared with this one in the magnitude of the economic shock produced and in its terrifying implications. Apprehension transcending human experience prevailed in every political and financial center in the world. In an effort to stem the tide of financial dissolution drastic steps were soon taken both in the countries directly concerned and by governments and financial institutions in all the nations involved. The Hoover moratorium of June suspended reparation and war-debt payments for a period of one year. The foreign short-term creditors of Germany and Austria agreed to "stand still" agreements with their debtors under which withdrawals of foreign funds were either suspended or reduced to a minimum. Large new short-term loans were extended to Germany, Austria, and Hungary by the principal central banks, as well as by the Bank for International Settlements. In addition, various means for controlling capital movements were introduced by some of the Central European countries themselves.

While these measures served to retard the process of financial disintegration in Central Europe, new strains soon developed elsewhere. The freezing of a huge volume of short-term funds in Central Europe inevitably led to apprehension over the safety of short-term funds in other quarters, and a mad scramble began for the repatriation of liquid funds while there was yet time. The most immediate, and by far the most serious, effect was the strain placed upon Great Britain, the second weak link in the short-term credit structure.

Great Britain was on the whole in a very strong creditor position. But, as we have seen, her short-term obligations abroad exceeded her short-term claims against other countries. Her long-term investments could not quickly be converted into cash, and at the same time a large part of her short-term claims had become unrealizable because of the situation in Central Europe. Meanwhile, however, Britain's short-term obligations to foreigners were payable on demand.

Within a short time the run on the relatively slender gold reserves of the Bank of England precipitated a foreign exchange and monetary crisis. In an attempt to meet the strain and prevent a collapse of the financial and monetary structure, the Bank and the British Treasury contracted loans in the United States and France during the late summer of 1931 to the amount of 650 million dollars. But even these resources were insufficient to meet the double drain occasioned by the simultaneous withdrawal of foreign funds and the flight of British capital which followed the revelation of an acute budget situation. On September 21 the British government took the momentous step of abandoning the gold standard.

In October the strain was transferred to the United States. As in the case of Great Britain, the long-term debts due the United States were of no immediate use and the short-term claims were largely frozen. As a result of large withdrawals of short-term claims held by foreigners, American gold soon began to flow abroad; in the month of October as much as 338 million dollars of gold was exported. But thanks to the enormous accumulation of gold in the United States resulting from war and post-war trade and financial relations, this country was able to withstand the strain. While there was grave concern for a time over the increase of internal hoarding and the flight of capital, the outflow of gold soon ceased. Great Britain lost the gold standard; the United States lost only gold.

Great Britain's abandonment of the gold standard resulted in a wholesale breakdown of the international monetary system. The British act of September 1931 was a signal for similar action on the part of a large number of other countries. As soon as the gold standard system began to crumble, governmental control of foreign exchange transactions also began to be widely introduced. Some countries used exchange control in conjunction with the abandonment of gold for the purpose of regulating fluctuations in foreign exchange rates; others employed it to prevent depreciation of their currencies, thus insuring a nominal maintenance of the gold standard. In either case, these artificial measures represented essentially an abandonment of the gold standard.

The rapidity with which the international gold standard system disintegrated is shown graphically in the table on the following page.

DISINTEGRATION OF THE GOLD STANDARD SYSTEM

I. Countries Which Abandoned the Gold Standard

Prior to 1931	Jan.–Aug. 1931	Sept.–Dec. 1931	Jan.–June 1932	July–Dec. 1932	Year 1933
Argentine Australia	Mexico	Bolivia Canada Colombia Denmark Egypt Finland India Ireland Japan Malaya Norway Palestine Portugal Salvador Sweden United Kingdom	Chile Ecuador Greece Peru Siam	South Africa	Austria Estonia United States

II. Countries Which Introduced Exchange Control

Brazil Chile Germany Hungary Spain	Argentine Austria Bolivia Bulgaria Colombia Czechoslovakia Denmark Estonia Greece Latvia Nicaragua Uruguay Yugoslavia	Costa Rica Ecuador Rumania	Japan Paraguay	United States

The disintegration of the gold standard in its turn exerted a profound influence upon trade and tariff policies. The struggle to maintain financial solvency, the collapse of international credit, and the sudden alteration in the terms of commercial competition resulting from the new depreciation of currencies with respect to gold led to utter turmoil and confusion in the field of commercial policy. As already noted, numerous debtor countries had, in 1930, resorted to restrictive trade policies with a view to maintaining financial equilibrium. While the United States in June of that year had passed the Smoot-Hawley Tariff Act, it was not until after the financial crisis of 1931 that commercial policies everywhere turned sharply in the direction of violently restrictive action.

The following enumeration of some of the methods adopted during this period gives a graphic picture of the trade war that followed the breakdown of the gold standard.

In the sixteen months after September 1, 1931, general tariff increases had been imposed in twenty-three countries, in three of them twice during the period—with only one case of a general tariff reduction. Customs duties had been increased on individual items or groups of commodities by fifty countries, in most cases by a succession of enactments which, in several countries, numbered over twenty tariff changes in the sixteen months. Import quotas, prohibitions, licensing systems and similar quantitative restrictions, with even more frequent changes in several important cases, had been imposed by thirty-two countries. Import monopolies, for the most part of grains, were in existence in twelve countries; milling or mixing regulations in sixteen others. Export premiums were being paid in nine, while export duties or prohibitions had been imposed in seventeen.

This bare list is utterly inadequate to portray the harassing complexity of the emergency restrictions that were superimposed upon an already fettered world trade after the period of exchange instability was inaugurated by the abandonment of the gold standard by the United Kingdom in September 1931. By the middle of 1932, it was obvious that the international trading mechanism was in real danger of being smashed as completely as the international monetary system had been.[11]

In due course many countries, especially those of South America, defaulted outright on international in-

[11] League of Nations, *World Economic Survey, 1932-33*, pp. 16-17.

debtedness, while others adopted novel devices for relieving the strain of foreign payments. Various countries declared "transfer moratoria" under the terms of which annual payments to foreign creditors would be made in domestic currency to a designated institution within the country, but would not be subject to conversion into foreign currencies except under certain prescribed conditions. In many cases, even current payments on account of commercial transactions were "blocked" or suspended, and a considerable part of international trade thus came to represent merely forced loans by exporters in one country to importers in another.

Finally, out of all these difficulties grew the system of clearing arrangements, under the operation of which a substantial portion of international trade was reduced to barter terms. Since a clearing arrangement could be operated successfully only between two countries, the use of such arrangements naturally tended to bring about a direct trade balance between each pair of countries. The growth of this bilateral balancing process greatly reduced the scope of roundabout trading operations, diverted commerce from its accustomed channels of economic advantage, robbed the trade process of much of its necessary flexibility, and served to intensify the vicious interaction between trade shrinkage and financial and monetary disintegration.

The constriction of world trade and the continued reduction in prices which accompanied the breakdown of the international financial system is revealed by the table on the opposite page, which shows the "quantum" and value of international trade, quarterly, from the middle of 1931 to the middle of 1933.[12]

---

[12] The figures are based on the average for the year 1929 as 100. For preceding quarterly data, and source, see p. 33.

Quarter		"Quantum"	Value
1931,	April-June	84.4	59.9
	July-September	82.1	55.8
	October-December	90.3	52.4
1932,	January-March	76.2	41.9
	April-June	73.0	39.8
	July-September	67.9	35.3
	October-December	78.4	39.2
1933,	January-March	72.7	34.9
	April-June	71.8	34.1

The ultimate consequence of this series of national measures—the suspension of gold payments, exchange controls, increased tariffs, import quotas, monopolies, licensing systems, each of which was introduced with a view to maintaining the stability of a particular country —was to produce profound instability in the international economic system as a whole. However unavoidable or inescapable some of these policies may have been, once the breakdown of the international monetary system had begun, the net result was greatly to reduce production, increase unemployment, and impoverish the people of the world.

IV. REPERCUSSIONS UPON THE UNITED STATES

The collapse of the international system served not only to contract the volume of international trade but also to intensify the internal depression in every country. The resulting curtailment in the volume of industrial production for the world as a whole, as well as in selected countries, may be seen by studying the diagrams on pages 65 and 68. There were, moreover, further drastic declines in the prices of commodities and in security values. Since the focal point of our interest in this study is the United States, we shall confine our analysis of the effects of the breakdown of the international system to its repercussions upon the American economic situation.

The American export trade was very sharply reduced. In 1929 the value of American exports was well above 400 million dollars monthly. In 1930 it had shrunk to an average of 320 millions monthly, and in 1931 to 202 millions. By July 1932 it was down to 107 millions, with the monthly average for the year 134 millions. Imports showed a corresponding decline.

Notwithstanding the previous severe decline in the prices of foodstuffs and raw materials, there was further collapse. From an average of 70.6 in March 1931 the price index of American foodstuffs declined to a low of 42.8 in March 1933. Raw material prices fell during the same period from 69.4 to 49.4. The price of wheat dropped from 76 cents a bushel in May 1931 to a low of 46 cents in December 1932, while cotton fell from 10.9 cents per pound in March 1931 to 5.3 cents in June 1932.

The depression of American industry was also greatly intensified by the international collapse. The effect manifested itself both directly and indirectly. At the same time that exports of manufactured goods were sharply curtailed, the deepening of the agricultural depression led to a great shrinkage in the demand for manufactured goods from the agricultural areas of the country. The index number of industrial production, which stood at 70.6 in January 1931, fell to 62.2 in December 1931, and to a low of 48.7 in July 1932. Data showing the monthly changes in industrial output are given in Appendix A, Table 10.

The shrinkage of industrial output and of corporate earnings, together with increasing pessimism as to the ability of the economic system to withstand the strain to which it was being subjected, led to renewed drastic declines in the prices of securities. Although the index of stock prices in New York had already shown a decline of 50 per cent from the peak in 1929, between March 1931 and July 1932 two-thirds of the remaining values were wiped out. The monthly indexes from July 1931 to July 1932 are shown in the table below.

The prices of bonds also declined heavily during this period. Up to the middle of the year 1931 they had remained practically stationary; indeed, as is common in periods of depression, they rose several points during the first year of the recession. But after June 1931 the collapse in the prices of low-grade bonds was comparable to that of stocks; and even high-grade issues suffered a heavy depreciation. The monthly price indexes of representative groups of stocks and bonds were as follows (September 1929 is equal to 100):[13]

Quarter	Stocks	Bonds
1931, July	42	105
August	41	104
September	35	101
October	30	94
November	31	94
December	25	86
1932, January	25	85
February	25	85
March	25	85
April	19	84
May	18	79
June	16	76
July	17	78

The wholesale shrinkage in values produced a grave debt crisis. Even before the depression began, the persistent decline in agricultural prices had created a diffi-

[13] Stock price indexes are from *Standard Statistics*; bond price indexes from the *Federal Reserve Bulletin*.

cult farm-debt problem. Mortgage obligations incurred
on the basis of war-time prices of farm lands could not
readily be met even on the basis of prices obtaining in
1928-29. With the drastic decline in agricultural prices
which came during the first stage of the depression, the
farm-debt problem was rendered acute; with the further
drastic decline in 1931-32 the meeting of farm-debt obligations became virtually impossible.

Meanwhile the debt situation was also becoming increasingly serious elsewhere. State, city, and local government units, which had for years been borrowing for
various and sundry purposes, were finding it increasingly
difficult to meet interest obligations. In the field of urban
mortgages, large numbers of individuals whose incomes
were steadily shrinking were unable to continue meeting
interest and mortgage instalments. Urban real estate
mortgage companies and their bond issues, which were
inadequately secured even on the basis of pre-depression
values, were falling into default. The railroads seemed
threatened with wholesale bankruptcy, while many public utility and industrial corporations were also in serious condition. The stability of insurance companies and
other financial institutions, of trust and endowment
funds, was directly dependent upon the continuance of
the flow of interest and mortgage payments. Involved in
the whole network of relationships was the safety of the
deposits and investments of all classes of people.

The final stage in the process of financial disintegration was the collapse of the American banking system.
Small-town and country banking was, of course, dependent upon the prosperity of agriculture.[14] During the first

[14] For some years before the depression, rural banks had been failing
by the hundreds annually, partly because of agricultural depression but
more largely on account of the decline in importance of small towns
occasioned by automobile transportation.

stage of the depression the mortality rate was greatly increased, and in the second stage the whole rural credit structure was undermined.

The country banks were in turn closely articulated with "correspondent" banks in the larger cities. For years city institutions had been helping to carry their country bank clients along in the hope of gradual improvement. The situation which developed in 1931 made it apparent that it could be only a question of time until this aid would have to be withdrawn. Many city banks were, moreover, heavily involved in urban real estate financing, and when this situation broke wholesale bank failures became inevitable.

Meanwhile, also, the decline in the value of securities was adding to banking difficulties; and a race for liquidity began. As margins on collateral loans became inadequate, payment was demanded and often the collateral had to be taken over by the bank and sold at a loss. The shrinkage in the value and the income of bonds directly owned by banks also presented a serious problem. Fearful of still further shrinkage in value, and often in need of cash, the banks attempted to sell their holdings of second-grade bonds. The combined result of the liquidation of the collateral of distressed borrowers and of their own investments was to demoralize still further the security markets. The greater the efforts of the banks to save themselves by the liquidation of securities, the greater became the demoralization of security values.

In due course the situation led to a renewed flight of funds to other countries and also to extensive hoarding within the United States. The flow of gold abroad was resumed on a large scale; in the six months January-June 1932 the net ouflow was 620 million dollars. The situation was relieved somewhat by the moderate recovery which occurred both in business activity and security prices in the second half of 1932.[15] But in the winter of 1933 the business situation again became worse, and the collapse of the banking structure ensued.

Whether the situation might have been tided over by governmental action at an appropriate time is a matter of speculation into which we do not care to enter. Our object here is merely to reveal the chain of events, world-wide in scope, which led us in four short years from the heights of 1929 to the depths of 1932-33.

[15] See diagram, pp. 78-79.

CHAPTER III

THE WORLD IMPACT OF THE DEPRESSION

Thus far in the analysis we have been concerned merely with outlining the successive stages of the business recession which began in 1929 and with revealing its international ramifications and repercussions. We shall next consider the general magnitude of the depression and the force of its impact on the economic life of the world. How severely were production, trade, and employment reduced? What were the relative effects upon the different divisions of economic activity? Were all countries more or less equally or quite differently affected? To what extent has recovery occurred in the various countries? In what ways have governments attempted to influence the recovery process? Several chapters will be required to answer these questions. The primary objective of the present chapter is to reveal the effects of the depression on the economic activities of the world conceived as an aggregate entity, and also to show the relative severity of the depression in the principal countries.

In order to reveal the impact of the depression upon the economic activities of the world as a whole—our first task—we present a series of diagrams covering world trends in production and trade. As a means of indicating the varying intensity of the depression in different sections of the world, we are also showing, in the cases where data are available, the trends by continental areas. The data are given, where possible, for the years 1925-35 inclusive, thereby revealing more adequately the contrast between economic activities in a period of prosperity and in a period of depression.

I. WORLD FLUCTUATIONS

In studying the diagrams presented in the following pages, the reader should bear in mind that no adjustment has been made for the growth in population, which amounted to approximately 10 per cent over the ten-year period.[1] All of the production diagrams are based on index numbers, with the average volume of production for the five-year period 1925-29 as a base of 100 per cent.

1. Production of foodstuffs. The chart on page 57 shows the trend in the production of crude foodstuffs for the world as a whole and also for continental divisions. Inasmuch as agricultural production is ordinarily not centrally controlled to any appreciable extent, one would naturally expect fluctuations in the production of foodstuffs during a period of depression to be relatively small in magnitude as compared with changes in industrial output.

The upper diagram on the opposite page shows that the fluctuations in aggregate world production of foodstuffs have been indeed slight. The range between 1928 and 1934 was only two points. The slight decline in 1935 is clearly attributable to the decrease in production in North America—as a consequence largely of the drought and in lesser degree the agricultural adjustment program of the United States government.

The data for the continental areas reveal some interesting variations in trend. Europe (including Asiatic

[1] Nor is allowance made for any increase in productive efficiency since 1929. In discussions of production trends in the United States during the depression period, in Chap. VII, allowance is made both for population increase and changes in productivity.

WORLD PRODUCTION OF CRUDE FOODSTUFFS, 1925-35[a]
(1925-29 average = 100)

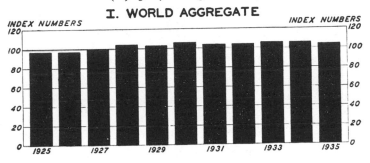

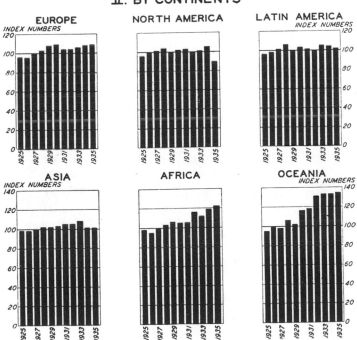

[a] For data, see Appendix A, Table 1.

Russia) shows an appreciable increase during the period of the recession. Separate figures for Europe, with the Soviet Republic excluded, reveal a similar upward trend. The most marked increases in agricultural output, not only during the recession but over the whole period, occurred in Africa and Oceania (which includes Australia and New Zealand).

On the whole, it appears that the depression did not appreciably affect world production of foodstuffs. As we have seen, however, there was a drastic decline in agricultural prices, which profoundly affected the income of agricultural producers. (See pages 31 and 32.)

2. *Production of industrial raw materials.* This general classification includes such agricultural raw materials as textiles, tobacco, vegetable oils, wood pulp, and rubber; and such non-agricultural raw materials as fuels, metals, non-metallic minerals, and chemicals. The chart on page 59 shows the production of all raw materials for the world as a whole and by continents; the double chart on page 61 reveals the fluctuations in agricultural and non-agricultural raw materials respectively; while the diagrams on page 63 show the fluctuations of output in a selected group of raw materials.

There was a steady increase in aggregate world production from 1925 to 1929. The decrease between 1929 and 1932 amounted to 29 per cent. In the next three years over two-thirds of the lost ground was recovered. North America shows much the greatest decline, amounting to 42 per cent. The decrease in Latin America was about 32 per cent and in Europe (including Asiatic Russia), about 23 per cent. But Europe, exclusive of the Soviet Republic, showed a decline of as much as 30 per cent. In Soviet Russia the production of raw materials increased throughout the period, except in the

WORLD PRODUCTION OF RAW MATERIALS, 1925-35[a]

(1925-29 average = 100)

I. WORLD AGGREGATE

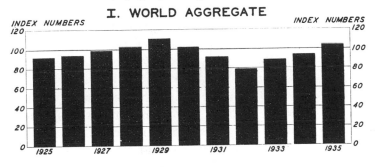

II. BY CONTINENTS

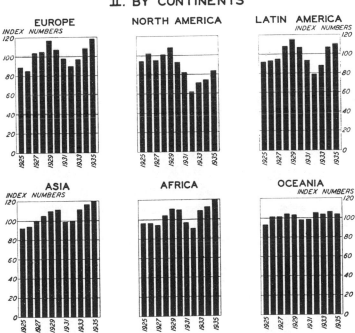

[a] For data, see Appendix A, Table 2.

single year 1932. The index number stood at 75 in
1925, at 126 in 1929, and at 232 in 1935. The decline
in Africa amounted to 20 per cent.

In Asia and Oceania the declines were not only much
less, but the bottom was reached at an earlier date—in
Asia in 1931, and in Oceania in 1930. In Asia (excluding Asiatic Russia) the peak of raw material production
was reached in 1930 and the decline amounted to only
12 per cent. In Oceania, 1928 was the year of greatest
production and the decline was only about 6 per cent. In
these three continents, the output in 1935 was above the
levels attained in the preceding prosperity period.

When we turn to the fluctuations in agricultural and
non-agricultural raw materials respectively, as shown
in the diagrams on page 61, we find some interesting
contrasts. Comparing first the world figures, it will be
seen that the decline in the output of agricultural raw
materials was very much less than in the non-agricultural raw materials, amounting between 1929 and 1932
to 10 per cent in the former class and 34 per cent in the
latter.

It is of interest to note that the production of agricultural raw materials in North America was substantially lower in 1934 and 1935 than in 1932—owing no
doubt to the drought and the agricultural curtailment
program in the United States. Europe, including or excluding Russia, is the only continent which shows a
steady yearly gain in the production of agricultural raw
materials since the bottom was reached in 1932.

The decline in the production of non-agricultural
raw materials was very much greater in North America
and Latin America than elsewhere. The percentage decrease in North America was 47 per cent and in Latin
America 43 per cent. In Europe, including Russia, the

WORLD PRODUCTION OF AGRICULTURAL AND NON-
AGRICULTURAL RAW MATERIALS, 1925-35[a]

(1925-29 average = 100)

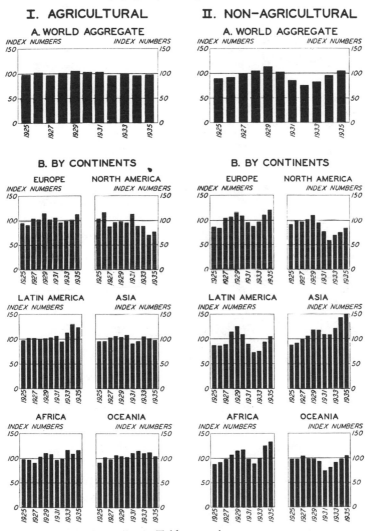

I. AGRICULTURAL

A. WORLD AGGREGATE

B. BY CONTINENTS

EUROPE   NORTH AMERICA

LATIN AMERICA   ASIA

AFRICA   OCEANIA

II. NON-AGRICULTURAL

A. WORLD AGGREGATE

B. BY CONTINENTS

EUROPE   NORTH AMERICA

LATIN AMERICA   ASIA

AFRICA   OCEANIA

[a] For data, see Appendix A, Tables 3 and 4.

decrease was only 25 per cent; with Russia excluded, it was 30 per cent. Russia showed a steady increase from 137 in 1929 to 323 in 1935.

Africa and Oceania showed an extreme decline of 25 per cent, and Asia a maximum of 8 per cent. In Africa the decline did not manifest itself until 1931, while in Oceania the low point was reached in that year.

The relative effects of the depression upon a selected list of raw materials is revealed in the diagram on page 63. Sharp differences in the degree of recession are here in evidence. In some cases, it will be observed, the maximum decline was comparatively small—with the output in 1935 equal to or in excess of that of 1929; in other cases the reductions were of catastrophic proportions.

The greatest declines were in pig iron (59 per cent), copper (52 per cent), potash (45 per cent), and sulphur (37 per cent). The smallest declines were in wool, cotton, and petroleum, amounting to 4, 9, and 13 per cent respectively. Cotton was lower in 1934 than in any preceding year of the depression.

3. Manufacturing activity. The term "manufacturing activity" is somewhat less inclusive than the term "industrial production." The latter classification includes both manufacturing and mining. Since mining has already been included in the discussion of raw materials, we shall here present only the index of manufacturing activity. In any event, because of the close relationship of manufacturing to raw material production the indexes vary but slightly. In the diagram at the top of page 65 we give the aggregate index of manufacturing activity from 1925 to 1935 inclusive, and also indexes for North America and Europe exclusive of Russia. Separate data are not available for all the continental areas.

It will be seen from the chart that the aggregate

World Production of Selected Raw Materials, 1925-35
(1925-29 average = 100)

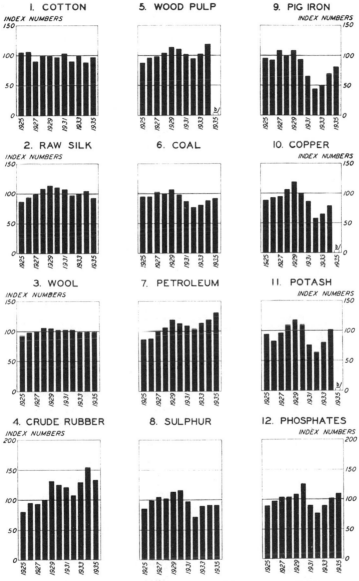

[a] For data, see Appendix A, Table 5.   [b] Data not available.

63

index of manufacturing activity declined precipitately from 1929 to 1932, the amount of the reduction equalling 31 per cent. The decline in North America was appreciably greater than that in Europe, even with Russia excluded. The extreme decline from 1929 to 1932 was 46 per cent in North America and 30 per cent in Europe.

4. *The volume of world trade.* In the second diagram on page 65 the effects of the depression on the aggregate movement of goods between countries is revealed for the period 1929-35. At the bottom of the diagram the fluctuations in the international movements of foodstuffs, raw materials, and manufactured articles are given separately. The aggregate decline amounted to 25 per cent. Trade in foodstuffs declined, at the maximum in 1934, by 16 per cent. Trade in raw materials and manufactured articles, which reached bottom in 1932, declined by 18 per cent and 42 per cent respectively. The recovery to the end of 1935 had been slight. This aspect of the general problem of world recovery will be enlarged upon in Chapter XIX.

5. *Unemployment.* All of the data thus far presented merely record the impact of the depression in physical terms. The ultimate effects of the changes thus recorded are manifest in the reduction of individual incomes throughout the world. The decrease in productive activity has affected practically all forms of income, whether derived from direct services or from investment in properties. World data with respect to national incomes are not available; hence we shall attempt here merely to indicate the effects upon the volume of unemployment.

Data with respect to unemployment everywhere leave much to be desired, and the reliability of the figures varies widely in different countries. Nevertheless, the

World Manufacturing Activity, 1925-35[a]
(1925-29 average = 100)

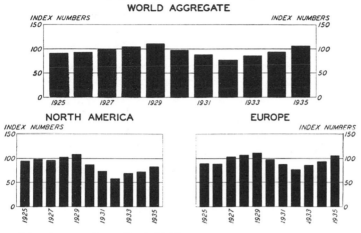

WORLD AGGREGATE

NORTH AMERICA   EUROPE

[a] For data, see Appendix A, Table 6.

Volume of World Trade, 1929-35[a]
(1929 = 100)

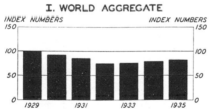

I. WORLD AGGREGATE

II. BY GROUPS OF COMMODITIES

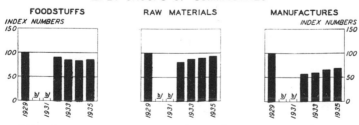

FOODSTUFFS   RAW MATERIALS   MANUFACTURES

[a] For data, see Appendix A, Table 7.   [b] Data not available.

65

general trend from 1929 to 1935 is revealed by an international index of unemployment computed by the International Labor Office. Owing to the increased emphasis that has been placed upon the collection of unemployment data during the course of the depression, it is probable that the data for 1935 are more inclusive than those for 1929; therefore the upward movement may be slightly overstated. We present the figures, however, as the best available evidence as to unemployment tendencies in the world as a whole. With the volume of unemployment in 1929 taken as 100, the figures for the period 1929-35 are as follows:[2]

1929	100	1933	274
1930	164	1934	221
1931	235	1935	193
1932	291		

It will be observed that, as in the case of the series dealing with production and trade, the peak of unemployment was reached in 1932. The subsequent improvement has, however, been of moderate proportions only.

It is not possible, by way of concluding this survey, to present any precise quantitative measurement of the effects of the depression upon world economic activity as a whole. One can, however, make a number of rough generalizations, as follows: industrial and manufacturing activity decreased by approximately one-third; the output of agricultural raw materials fell only about 10 per cent; while the production of foodstuffs showed no appreciable decline. The depression was most acute in the industrial areas of North America and Europe, with

[2] League of Nations, *Statistical Yearbook*, 1935-36, p. 75. Data compiled by the International Labor Office are given for 18 selected countries in our Appendix A, Table 9.

the closely articulated raw material producing areas of Latin America following.

II. FLUCTUATIONS IN SELECTED COUNTRIES

We may now indicate in brief summary fashion the effects of the depression upon the economic life of 23 selected countries. For this purpose we shall use general indexes showing the physical volume of industrial production, and shall not attempt to break the discussion down into the effects upon different divisions of economic activity. In considering these data it should again be borne in mind that the production figures are not on a per capita basis, and hence do not take account of the growth of population, which has varied materially in different countries.

The production indexes which are presented are those published by the League of Nations. In each case the year 1929 is taken as a base of 100 per cent. The reader should bear in mind that the method of compiling and computing indexes is far from uniform in the different countries. The number of groups or series of products, as well as the number of individual commodities included, varies widely. Accordingly, these indexes do not permit any close or precise measurements of the relative effects of the depression upon the different countries. They do, however, afford a fair general idea of tendencies within each country, and also a rough gauge of the relative severity of the decline in the various countries. The detailed figures and an indication of their general character and reliability will be found in Appendix A, Table 8.

In the diagram on pages 68 and 69 we show the course of production from 1929 to 1935, for 23 countries. The countries selected include both highly developed indus-

INDUSTRIAL PRODUCTION IN

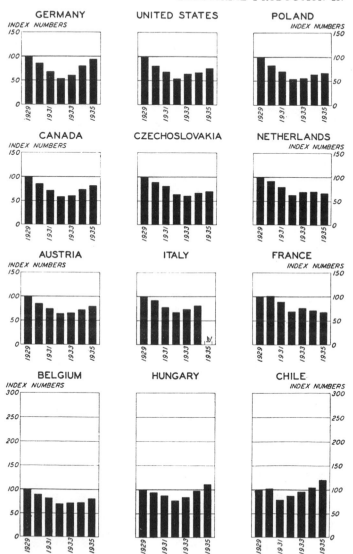

ᵃ For data, see Appendix A, Table 8.
ᵇ Data not available.

SELECTED COUNTRIES, 1929-35[a]

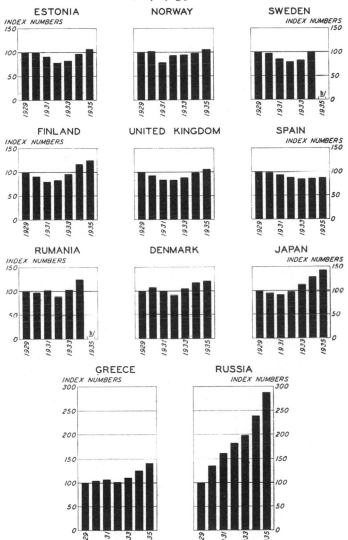

trial nations and agricultural and raw material producing countries, and they show a wide geographic distribution. Australia and New Zealand are omitted because
of lack of data. The countries are arranged in the order
of the degree of decline from 1929 to the low point of
the depression, as shown by the production index.

The group showing the greatest degree of depression
includes Germany, the United States, and Poland. Production declined in Germany by 46.6 per cent, in the
United States by 46.2 per cent, and in Poland by 46.1
per cent. In each case the year 1932 marked the low
point of the depression.

The second group comprises Canada, with a 41.9
per cent decline, Czechoslovakia with 39.8, and the
Netherlands with 37.7. In Czechoslovakia the low year
was 1933; in the others it was 1932.

Included in the next group are Austria, Italy, France,
and Belgium with declines respectively of 35.7, 33.1,
32.6, and 30.9 per cent. Austria, Italy, and Belgium
show 1932 as the low year; but in France 1935 appears
as the low year. In should be noted also that the level
of production in France in 1930 was slightly above that
of 1929.

In the fourth group are six countries with reductions
as follows: Hungary, 23.1 per cent; Chile, 22.1 per
cent; Estonia, 21.9 per cent; Norway, 21.7 per cent;
Sweden, 20.9 per cent; and Finland, 20.0 per cent. In
three of these countries—Finland, Norway, and Chile—
1931 appears to be the bottom of the depression, with
1932 marking the low point in Sweden, Hungary, and
Estonia. Norway and Chile show no recession for the
year 1930.

In the next group are the United Kingdom and Spain.
The former shows a decline of 16.5 per cent to a low

in 1932, while the latter shows a reduction of 15.6 to a low in 1933.

Rumania, Denmark, and Japan show reductions of 11.5, 9.0, and 8.4 per cent respectively. In Japan the low year was 1931, and in the other countries it was 1932. It is of interest that production in Denmark was substantially higher in 1930 than in 1929.

Greece showed a continued expansion of production in 1930 and 1931, and the decline of 1932 still left the volume of output slightly above the level of 1929. The production index of Russia shows a sustained expansion throughout the period under review, which coincides closely with the period of planned industrial development in that country.

In general the nations and the continental areas which are prevailingly agricultural show a smaller degree of depression than the highly developed industrial regions. It should be borne in mind, however, that the degree of decline shown reflects both differences in the composition of the index numbers themselves and—since they are all figured from a 1929 base—differences in the degree of prosperity in the base years. For example, the year 1929 was one of only moderate activity in the United Kingdom, whereas in the United States and many of the continental countries activity was exceptionally high.

The course of production in the various countries finds general support in the available data with reference to unemployment. While unemployment figures are not available for all of the countries which we have covered above, in those countries for which we have them as a rule they show tendencies similar to those of the production data—this despite the widely varying completeness and accuracy of unemployment data.

CHAPTER IV

THE EXTENT AND CHARACTER OF THE RECOVERY

In Chapter II we traced the downward course of the depression through its two stages, covering the period from the autumn of 1929 to the spring of 1933. We noted in this survey that, in many countries, the bottom of the depression seemed to have been reached in the middle of 1932, but that elsewhere it continued with little interruption until the second quarter of 1933. In the present chapter we shall focus attention upon the revival, endeavoring to locate the upturn in time and place, to show the extent and character of the revival in the leading countries of the world, and to reveal the significant characteristics of the recovery movement.

Unfortunately there is no completely satisfactory means of following the course of economic conditions as a whole. The best method would obviously be to show changes in aggregate income; but reasonably satisfactory figures are available for only a few countries, and even for these the figures are on an annual basis. The most significant single index is that showing fluctuations in industrial production; but this does not, of course, reflect changes in the agricultural situation, which is of dominant importance in certain countries. Nor does it disclose the degree to which expansion may be attributable to military outlays, emergency public works, and other subsidies, as distinguished from a recovery of normal private enterprise. Industrial data are, however, very useful in giving a rough indication of the course of economic conditions in general.

72

I. WHEN AND WHERE RECOVERY BEGAN

In seeking to determine the time at which recovery began in the various countries, we are able to present two types of evidence. In addition to industrial indexes showing *monthly* changes in the volume of production there are quarterly measurements, which reflect in a rough way changes in national income. These quarterly movements have already been presented in the diagram following page 28, which shows fluctuations from 1929 to 1933 inclusive. The reader should bear in mind that this chart does not reflect quantity changes, but indicates only the direction of movement.

It will be seen from the diagram that in the last quarter of 1931 a change was evident in a few countries, namely, the United Kingdom, Brazil, India, and Australia—with Argentine showing a change in the first quarter of 1932. In the United Kingdom, Brazil, and Argentine the improvement did not last, but in India and Australia no new recession is indicated.

In the third quarter of 1932 an upward movement is indicated in Germany, France, Finland, the United States, Japan, South Africa, and New Zealand, with the United Kingdom, British Malaya, Belgium, and the Netherlands showing improvement in the fourth quarter. However, the United States showed renewed recession in the first quarter of the year 1933.

Italy began to show improvement in the first quarter of 1933, while in the second quarter the upward trend is evident in all countries but Austria, Norway, Poland, Switzerland, Czechoslovakia, the Irish Free State, Yugoslavia, Egypt, Argentine, Brazil, and the Dutch East Indies. It may be said that by the end of 1933 the recovery movement was practically universal, except that a number of countries, mainly those which remained on the gold standard, suffered a slight recession in the last quarter of the year.

The evidence afforded by monthly indexes of industrial production reveals much the same story as do the general indexes of business activity. Data are not available for some of the important countries included in the other series, such as Australia and New Zealand, Argentine and Brazil, India and British Malaya; but nearly all of the leading industrial nations of the world are covered.

The date of the lowest point of the depression in a group of twelve selected countries is shown in the table below. The final column shows the lowest level to which production declined as measured from a base of 100 per cent in 1929.

Country	Date of Low Point	Production Index at Low Point
Japan	March 1931	85.1
Hungary	4th quarter 1931	62.7
Chile	January 1932	65.0
Belgium	July 1932	48.5
United States	July 1932	48.7
Sweden	July 1932	67.3
Germany	August 1932	50.3
France	August 1932	66.4
United Kingdom	3d quarter 1932	77.7
Czechoslovakia	December 1932	54.0
Canada	February 1933	48.0
Poland	March 1933	46.0

In some of these countries, however, subsequent recessions occurred, and a noteworthy improvement is not revealed until several months later. This is especially the case with the United States, Germany, and Hungary.

In the chart on pages 78 and 79 we show the monthly fluctuation of industrial production in twelve countries from January 1931 to June 1936. The indexes are based on 1929 as 100 per cent. It will be observed that the recovery dates shown by these industrial indexes correspond fairly closely with those for general business recovery presented in the chart following page 28.

A sustained forward movement in industrial production began in Japan and Chile in February 1932; in Belgium, Sweden, and Hungary in the late summer and early fall of 1932; in the United Kingdom in the last quarter of 1932; while in Germany, the United States, Poland, Czechoslovakia, and Canada a sustained upward movement is not revealed until the early spring months of 1933.[1]

In concluding this discussion of the turning points of the depression, it should be emphasized that while in many countries an increase in industrial production was evident in the second half of 1932 the recovery movement remained somewhat sporadic in character and moderate in proportions until the spring of 1933. Perhaps the safest statement would be that in general the bottom of the depression was clearly reached in the summer of 1932, but that a strong and broad forward movement did not begin until nine months later.

We shall make no attempt here to answer the moot question: What forces were responsible for arresting the depression and bringing about a new advance in business activity? To settle this issue would require a detailed analysis of the movements of statistical series in all countries; and even then the answer would be inconclusive—on account of imperfect and inadequate statistical data and because of imponderable elements in the situa-

---

[1] Evidence that improvement was under way in the late summer of 1932 is also afforded by the moderate rise in the prices of some basic raw materials.

tion, such as the state of business psychology and the influence of governmental policies.[2] Whether, for example, the new hopes for enduring peace and a co-operative solution of economic difficulties which were raised by the Lausanne Conference of July 1932 played an important role, as many believe, in restoring business confidence, no one can definitely establish.

In any case, it is a fact of striking interest that the recovery began within so short a time after the depression entered its acute stage. It was little more than a year after the financial collapse in Central Europe in the second quarter of 1931 that the bottom of the depression was reached and the slow, if halting, process of recovery was under way.

II. THE COURSE AND EXTENT OF THE RECOVERY

We turn now to the more interesting question, namely, the degree to which the recovery movement has proceeded. Did the improvement once under way continue at a steady pace? Was it more or less uniform in different countries, or are marked variations in evidence? How near have we approached the levels of 1929?

The extent of the recovery for the world as a whole through the year 1935 has already been indicated in the world trade and production data given in the diagrams in the preceding chapter. In considering these data, it should be remembered that since 1929 world population had increased by about 5 or 6 per cent. World production of foodstuffs in 1935 was one per cent above the 1929 level; production of industrial raw materials stood at 92 per cent of the 1929 total; while manufacturing activity had risen to 96 per cent of the 1929 level. Since in time of depression the *output* of agricultural

[2] See Chap. II.

products does not show wide variations, accounts must be taken of the trend of agricultural *prices* when the degree of recovery is being considered. Relevant data for a series of countries cannot conveniently be presented here; but the fact is that, in general, farm prices have risen considerably more than industrial prices, thereby expanding farm purchasing power.[3]

The recovery movement in the various countries has developed irregularly and has followed a very uneven course. It will be seen from the monthly figures of industrial production shown in the diagrams on pages 78 and 79 that the expansion of industrial production when once under way was more or less continuous in Japan, Sweden, the United Kingdom, Hungary, and Chile, but that the rate of expansion varied considerably. In Poland and Czechoslovakia there were mild recessions in the second quarter and in the last half of 1934 respectively.

In the United States the upward movement shows a very irregular trend. After the sharp rise in production in the spring and early summer of 1933 there was a substantial recession in the autumn. Through 1934 and the first half of 1935 there were periodic advances followed by more or less corresponding declines. It was not until the middle of 1935 that a strong and persistent advance occurred. The movements in Canada correspond in general to those in the United States but have been less pronounced.

In Belgium, following the upturn in 1932, production remained practically stationary until the end of 1934. In France, after one year of expansion in 1932-

---

[3] The degree to which pre-depression price relations between farm and industrial products has been restored in the United States is shown in Chap. XI. The data for several countries will be found in League of Nations, *World Production and Prices, 1934-35*, pp. 109-11.

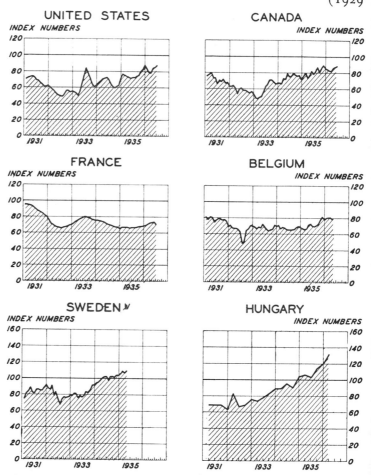

PRODUCTION, 1931-36[a]
= 100)

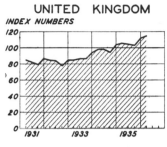

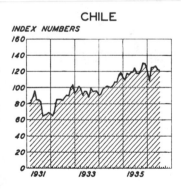

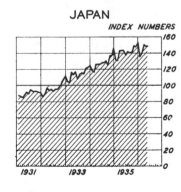

33, production declined throughout 1934 and showed little recovery thereafter.

The degree of recovery in a group of important countries is indicated in the following diagram, which shows the volume of industrial production in June 1936 as compared with the level obtaining in 1929. It should be

INDUSTRIAL PRODUCTION, JUNE 1936, COMPARED
WITH 1929[a]
(1929 = 100)

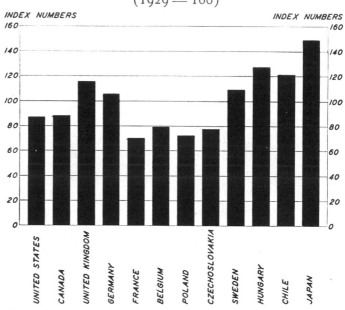

INDEX NUMBERS

UNITED STATES • CANADA • UNITED KINGDOM • GERMANY • FRANCE • BELGIUM • POLAND • CZECHOSLOVAKIA • SWEDEN • HUNGARY • CHILE • JAPAN

[a] For data, see Appendix A, Table 10.

borne in mind when studying the diagram that the figures are not altogether satisfactory for the purpose of comparing the trends in different countries. In the first place, the degree of prosperity in 1929, the base year, varied considerably in the several countries; and, in the second place, the figures of industrial production do not make allowance for a growth in population which has been rapid in some countries and practically stationary in others. The data do, nevertheless, afford a fair general picture of the degree to which pre-depression levels in industrial production have been restored.

It will be observed that in Japan, Chile, Hungary, Sweden, Germany, and the United Kingdom industrial production in 1936 actually exceeded the level in 1929. France and Poland show the smallest degree of recovery.

III. SOME CHARACTERISTICS OF THE RECOVERY

Some interesting features of the world business recovery have already been revealed. For example, the revival has proceeded much further in Asia and Oceania than it has in the more highly industrialized continents of North America and Europe. And, as we have just seen, the rate and degree of improvement have been far from uniform in the various countries. Attention will now be directed to other significant features of the recovery movement.

First, the current recovery movement has been unusually slow and halting. According to such records as are available for previous periods of expansion, no recovery of the past has been interrupted by as many minor reversals as has been the case in the present instance; and the general pace of recovery, except perhaps in one or two countries, has heretofore never been so restrained. As a rule, full recovery has occurred in less than half the time that has elapsed since the beginning of the present advance.[4]

In this connection it is of great interest to note that the current expansion has not only been at a slow pace,

---

[4] Based on Leonard Ayres' index, "American Business Activity since 1790," published in current numbers of the *Cleveland Trust Company Business Bulletin*.

but has already continued for a much longer time than is usually the case before a new recession occurs. As measured from the low levels of 1932, more than four years have elapsed since the upturn began, and, figuring from April 1933 when the forward movement definitely began in the United States, 42 months have passed. The average length of 20 expansion movements since 1855, according to the studies of the National Bureau of Economic Research, has been 25 months, and, if the Civil and World War periods are omitted, the average is 23 months. The longest advance was 36 months. Whether the greater duration of the upswing is attributable to its restrained and hesitant character, or to other factors, we shall not attempt to determine.

Second, the recovery of international trade has lagged behind the expansion of world production. Although the degree to which international trade has recovered varies materially in different classes of goods, we find that in manufactures and foodstuffs foreign trade has recovered much less than world production. In the case of raw materials, however, production and trade show similar growth. The table below indicates the quantity increase in production and in international trade in these categories of commodities from 1932 through 1935.

INCREASE IN WORLD PRODUCTION AND TRADE, 1932-35[a]

(1929 = 100)

Commodity Class	Production				Trade			
	1932	1933	1934	1935	1932	1933	1934	1935
Manufactures.........	63	71	77	84	58	60	66	69
Raw materials........	71	79	85	92	82	88	90	94
Foodstuffs............	101	101	100	100	91	85	84	86

[a] League of Nations, *World Production and Prices, 1934–35*, p. 94.

The very substantial lag in the recovery of international trade in manufactured goods reflects not only the disorganizing effects of currency instability but also the growth of commercial regulations designed to protect and stimulate domestic industry. It will be seen that the recovery of trade in raw materials kept pace with the revival of world production in 1933 but lagged in subsequent years. In the first year of the recovery the increase is largely attributable to the necessity of replenishing depleted stocks; in 1934 and 1935 the lag reflects the interference with the free movement of international commerce which resulted from the bilateral trade agreements arising out of the system of exchange control. While world production of foodstuffs has shown little variation from the 1929 level, the volume of international trade in this class of commodities declined materially during the depression and has remained well below former levels.

A third interesting aspect of the present recovery is the continuance of an unstable situation in the sphere of international monetary relations. In former depressions there were sporadic instances of suspension of specie payments, but such financial breakdowns usually did not last long and did not result in substantial alterations in the foreign exchange rates of the currency units involved. During the current depression the breakdown of the gold standard has been almost universal and changes in the foreign exchange rates have been of very great magnitude.

Prior to the present depression, the abandonment of the gold standard and the depreciation of national currency units as registered in the foreign exchanges were generally regarded as unfortunate and unavoidable consequences of profound economic dislocations. This was true in some countries during the recent collapse of the gold standard; but in a number of important cases the abandonment of gold and the depreciation of the currency unit were the result of deliberate policy, designed either to relieve the strain of falling gold prices or to improve the nation's competitive position in international trade.

Adherence on the part of statesmen to the various theories of monetary management, which were for the first time put to the test of practical application during the current depression, has been in large measure responsible for the failure of the nations of the world to return to a system of stable foreign exchanges. It should be noted, however, that since the middle of 1935 a de facto stability of the principal currencies has been maintained although the exchange rates of these currencies have not been definitively linked together.

A fourth feature of the present recovery has been the failure of commodity prices to rise appreciably since the first stage of the revival. Notwithstanding the extraordinary decline that had occurred, the upward movement since the low points of 1932-33 has been very moderate. The chart on pages 86 and 87 shows the movements of wholesale commodity prices in a group of countries from 1929 to 1936. It will be seen that since the first year of recovery there has been little advance in the general level. Regardless of the fact that foodstuff and raw material prices have risen appreciably, it is evident that the industrial expansion has been accompanied by little if any rise in the prices of manufactured goods.

This comparative stability of prices is especially interesting in view of the existence of powerful forces which it is believed were bound to produce rising prices. In addition to the stimulus to price advances which expanding business demands ordinarily provide, governmental policies have in many countries been designed to promote "reflation." Among these the most important, of course, have been the depreciation of currency values and the extensive employment of government credit in expanding purchasing power. In addition there has been in many countries an abundance of loanable funds available at low rates of interest.

The stability of prices in the United States is particularly remarkable in view of the powerful and many-sided "reflation" program that was undertaken by the government. Nearly all of the rise in prices that has taken place occurred in the first few months of the recovery period. Since the autumn of 1933 the prices of industrial products in the United States have remained practically stationary, standing at 85.3 in October 1933, and at 86.0 in June 1936.

A fifth characteristic of the recovery movement is the lag in the recovery of the durable goods industries. In a period of depression the decline in the production of capital equipment, housing facilities, and other durable products which involve substantial outlays, is naturally much greater than the decrease in the output of goods required for current consumption. The explanation of this phenomenon is given in Chapter VIII, which is devoted to a discussion of the situation of the durable goods industries in the United States. During the present depression, the output of goods required for current consumption declined in general by 20-30 per cent, whereas the output of durable capital and consumer goods decreased by 40-60 per cent—even more in particular instances.

Since 1933 the output of goods destined for current consumption has approached much nearer to normal

Movements of Wholesale Prices

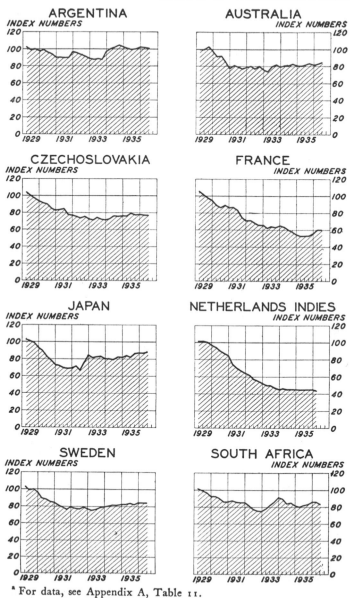

ARGENTINA
INDEX NUMBERS

AUSTRALIA
INDEX NUMBERS

CZECHOSLOVAKIA
INDEX NUMBERS

FRANCE
INDEX NUMBERS

JAPAN
INDEX NUMBERS

NETHERLANDS INDIES
INDEX NUMBERS

SWEDEN
INDEX NUMBERS

SOUTH AFRICA
INDEX NUMBERS

* For data, see Appendix A, Table 11.

IN SELECTED COUNTRIES, 1929-36*

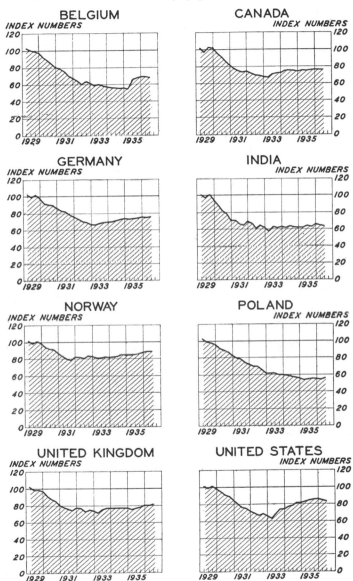

than has the production of capital equipment; and in many countries housing facilities and other durable products also show a substantial lag. The methods of compiling data with reference to so-called producer and consumer goods vary materially in different countries; hence close direct comparisons should not be attempted. But figures for various countries show conclusively that the volume of output of productive capital goods in the form of plant and equipment is nearly everywhere still lagging behind the output of current consumption goods. It is of interest to note, however, that in some countries, notably in the United Kingdom, Sweden, and the Netherlands, building construction has more than kept pace with the expansion of output of goods destined for current consumption. In the United States the lag is very great both in capital goods proper and in housing.[5]

Many observers have pointed to the persistence of an extraordinary volume of unemployment as perhaps the most outstanding characteristic of the present recovery movement. It is contended that this reflects continued technological improvement as well as the growth of population. Data with respect to both employment and unemployment are not sufficiently accurate to permit reliable statistical measurements. However, unemployment data as compiled by the International Labor Office for a group of selected countries are given in Appendix A, Table 9; and an appraisal of the unemployment situation in the United States will be found in Chapters VI and IX.

A final noteworthy feature of this recovery to which

[5] For data showing the degree of recovery in the production of producers' investment goods, current consumption goods, and durable consumptive commodities in various countries, see Appendix A, Table 12. For detailed discussion of durable goods in the United States, see Chap. VIII.

attention should be called is the accompanying extraordinary increase in public indebtedness. In former periods of depression the people did not commonly depend upon the government to carry a substantial part of the financial losses and burdens incident to the depression itself, or look to the government to use its powers and financial resources to stimulate recovery. Such deficits as occurred were largely due simply to a decline in revenues. The present reliance upon government aid is in part an inevitable outgrowth of the greater complexities of modern life; but it is also in part attributable to the evolution of a theory that increased governmental expenditures may be made to counteract the effects of the curtailment of private expenditures and thus serve both as a balance-

GROWTH OF PUBLIC DEBTS, 1932-36[a]
(In millions of the standard monetary units of the respective countries)

Country	1932	1933	1934	1935	1936
United States......	19,487	22,539	27,053	28,701	33,779[b]
Japan.............	4,939	5,984	7,268	8,210[c]	...
Germany.........	8,918	9,290	10,347	10,720[d]	12,473[e]
France...........	276,058	303,537	322,380[f]	337,874[g]	352,500[h]
Italy............	95,572	97,215	102,622	105,710[i]	107,078[j]
Belgium..........	28,956	30,178	30,428	33,279[k]	...
Hungary.........	259	327	357	432[l]	456[m]
Poland..........	449	759	1,346	1,475[n]	...
United Kingdom...	6,557	6,799	6,994	6,866[o]	6,987[p]
Australia.........	586	607	629	650[q]	...
Sweden..........	2,155	2,359	2,349	2,487[r]	2,380[s]
Norway..........	783	827	810	837[t]	...

[a] Data from League of Nations, *Statistical Yearbook, 1935-36*, pp. 294-303.
[b] June 30. [c] March 31. [d] March 31.
[e] Dec. 31, 1935. These data do not include the "unrecorded" future short-term obligations of the Reich arising from advance tax certificate transact'ons, interest subsidy transactions, short-term financing of the employment creation program, national highway construction, rearmament. The total of "recorded" and "unrecorded" debts amounted to 25,500 million reichsmarks in March 1933 and 33,000 millions in March 1936.
[f] December. [g] December (unofficial). [h] March 27 (unofficial). [i] June 30.
[j] Sept. 30, 1935. [k] December 31. [l] June 30. [m] March 31. [n] December.
[o] March 31. [p] Dec. 31, 1935. [q] June 30. [r] June 30. [s] February 1936. [t] June.

wheel and a stimulus to revival. It is assumed, of course, that once the revival is well under way government expenditures can again be reduced and fiscal stability restored. Moreover, in many countries military programs have played an important part in piling up government debts.

The table on page 89 shows the changes in the internal public debt of a group of important countries, as officially reported. The figures represent millions in terms of the national currencies of the respective countries. Owing to the prevailing tendency among governments to conceal, or at least to delay showing, the full extent of the growth of the public debt, these figures in many cases materially understate the existing situation. Thus recovery has been accompanied by developments which may have serious repercussions in the future. The trend of federal, state, and local indebtedness in the United States, and its significance from the standpoint of recovery, will be fully discussed in later chapters.

It is apparent from this analysis of the extent and character of the recovery movement that, great and widespread as the improvement has been, the economic condition of the world is still far from stable. The problem of unemployment with its social and political implications remains everywhere grave. The position of agricultural populations has been somewhat improved as a result of more favorable price ratios, but farm incomes still remain well below the levels of 1929. The problem of maintaining fiscal and monetary stability has been seriously complicated by the universal expansion of public indebtedness; and heavier tax burdens are in store for the future. World trade and financial relations are still profoundly abnormal, and, although the surge of economic nationalism appears definitely on the wane, extraordinary barriers to international commerce remain. We are still endeavoring in substantial measure to operate an international economic system on principles of national independence.

Moreover, a new development—arising largely from disturbances incident to the depression itself—has come to menace the resumption of international trade, the stability of public finance, and the whole process of economic recovery. Vast military programs threaten the peace of the world. While currently contributing to the expansion of industrial activity and employment, military outlays make no permanent contribution to recovery. They do, however, imperil the foundations of the economic system.

CHAPTER V

GOVERNMENT POLICIES IN RELATION
TO RECOVERY

For the first time in industrial history the powers of government have been extensively invoked to stem the tide of depression and to stimulate recovery. Hence any account of the world recovery movement, however general and tentative in character, must give some attention to the role played by government policies. In the nature of the case, it is impossible in a general analysis of this kind to make a conclusive appraisal of the results of governmental actions in each of the leading countries. It may well be doubted, indeed, whether it would be possible in any case to disentangle the complex and repercussive effects of various policies, both public and private, in such a way as to indicate beyond question whether the results of governmental intervention have on the whole been helpful or detrimental. Moreover, the final evidence is not as yet available, for the experiment is far from finished.

A brief summary of the recovery measures adopted should, however, serve to correct prevailing erroneous impressions as to the general character of the programs of different countries and at the same time afford interesting comparisons. In this chapter we shall accordingly present, in bird's-eye proportion, a picture revealing the variety and character of the recovery policies which have been employed in leading countries. Many of these have been developed by individual governments as purely national programs while others have involved extensive international co-operation. We shall first re-

view the efforts that have been made to promote world
revival through international action and then give a
brief account of the policies adopted in the principal
countries to stimulate domestic recovery. Consideration
of the American recovery program will be deferred to
Chapter XVII.

I. ATTEMPTS AT INTERNATIONAL ACTION

Efforts to promote world recovery through concerted
international action have been of varied types. Some have
had for their objective the adoption, by all the nations
of the world, of common policies in dealing with certain
outstanding international economic problems. Some have
been more limited in scope, both as regards the problems
involved and the number of nations participating. Some
of them have centered upon questions of commercial
policy; while others have been chiefly concerned with
international financial and monetary relations.

The first large-scale attempt at international action,
made soon after the depression began, was concerned
primarily with the problem of commercial policy. It
grew out of the World Economic Conference of 1927,
to which reference has elsewhere been made. That conference, in addition to recommending to governments the
need of liberalizing their commercial policies, suggested
the creation, by the League of Nations, of an Economic
Consultative Committee, to meet periodically for the
purpose of taking stock of current developments and of
making further recommendations to governments. The
Committee met only twice, in 1928 and 1929. On the
occasion of its last meeting, which coincided with the
second anniversary of the Conference, the Committee
came to the conclusion that the governments did not appear disposed to act upon the recommendations which

had been embodied in the resolutions of the Conference and reiterated in the Committee's own reports. This conclusion was made the subject of discussion at the Tenth Assembly of the League of Nations, meeting in September 1929, and, as a result, the League decided to attempt a new approach to the whole problem.

Whereas the Conference of 1927 and the Economic Consultative Committee were merely advisory in character, the new approach was to be through the medium of a diplomatic conference of official government representatives, authorized to negotiate the necessary conventions. The principal task assigned to the Conference was the conclusion of a tariff truce as the first step in the process of demobilizing trade barriers.

The new parley, at first officially known as the Customs Truce Conference, took place at Geneva in February and March 1930. It was predominantly European in character, consisting of representatives of all the countries of Europe, with the exception of the Soviet Union, and of only three other nations—Japan, Peru, and Colombia. It was marked by a strenuous but fruitless effort to carry out the task of negotiating a tariff truce. Finally, in order to mask its failure, it renamed itself officially a Preliminary Conference for Concerted Economic Action and contented itself with negotiating a Commercial Convention, under the terms of which the signatories undertook, for one year, not to denounce their existing commercial treaties, except under certain prescribed conditions, and with signing a protocol embodying a program of future negotiations in the sphere of economic relations.

This first attempt was not conceived in terms of any policy of recovery, but rather as a part of a continuing effort to place international commercial relations upon a sounder basis. At the second Conference for Concerted Economic Action, convened in November 1930, the discussion of commercial policy was, however, dominated mainly by considerations of economic recovery. The Conference was entirely European in character and was devoted to an effort to direct the trade policies of the European nations away from the channels of increased protectionism into which the developments of the depression period had been pushing them. Although by that time the relation of the growth of trade barriers to the continuation and intensification of the depression was beginning to gain wide recognition, the nations represented at the Conference utterly failed to find a basis for agreement. After a wholly inconclusive session, the Conference was adjourned until March 1931; at which time the participating governments agreed that there was no possibility of putting into effect even the relatively innocuous Commercial Convention negotiated a year earlier, and the whole attempt was abandoned. The increase of protectionism in the United States, manifested by the enactment of the Smoot-Hawley Tariff Act in June 1930, contributed in some measure to the failure of the European attempt at tariff reduction.

In the meantime, another movement on a European scale had been inaugurated at Geneva. In September 1929 Premier Briand of France proposed the creation of a European Union for the purpose of improving the political and economic relations among the nations of Europe. After a year of preliminary studies, a Commission of Inquiry for European Union was created under the auspices of the League of Nations. The Commission set up a number of committees for the examination of specific problems, mainly in the field of economic relations, in an effort to bring about at least partial improvement in this sphere.

During this period, also, three attempts were made, on an even more narrowly regional scale, to improve international trade relations. Representatives of the agricultural countries of Eastern Europe met several times in the summer and autumn of 1930, and finally succeeded in working out a program of action which called for coordinated national control of exports and a system of tariff preference to be granted to the agricultural countries by the industrial nations of Western Europe. This program was submitted to the Second Conference for Concerted Economic Action, but failed of endorsement and could not, therefore, become operative, at least with respect to the system of preference. In December 1930 representatives of Holland, Belgium, and the three Scandinavian countries signed the Oslo Convention, which was designed to stabilize their mutual tariff relations; the Convention failed of ratification and was never put into effect. In March 1931 Germany and Austria concluded a Customs Union, but subsequently gave up the project under pressure from former Allies.

By the middle of 1931, the rapid unfolding of the financial crisis pushed into the background the problem of commercial policy. Attempts at international economic action shifted to the field of debt relations. The Hoover moratorium of June 1931 led to a series of conferences in which some or all of the countries concerned with the reparation and war-debt payments took part. The principal purpose of these conversations and negotiations was to find some sort of solution for the German debt problem which, by that time, had come to be almost universally recognized as an important disruptive factor in the economic life of the world.

A meeting of the official representatives of the seven principal nations concerned with the war-debt problem, held in London in July, was immediately followed by meetings of specially constituted committees of financial experts and central bank representatives. These conferences resulted in implementing the Hoover moratorium and in devising other international measures of financial relief. A meeting of Germany's short-term creditors, which took place in Berlin about the same time, negotiated the first "standstill" agreement with that country. Similar agreements were negotiated by the short-term creditors of Austria and Hungary. In December 1931 the Bank for International Settlements convoked a meeting of its Special Advisory Committee for the purpose of canvassing the whole German situation and making recommendations with regard to permanent measures. All these were steps in the process of international action designed to salvage the financially prostrate countries of Central Europe.

The process culminated with the convocation of the Lausanne Conference, which was held in June-July 1932. At that momentous parley, the slate was virtually wiped clean as regards the vexatious reparations problem which since the end of the war had plagued the economic life of the world. The statesmen gathered at Lausanne realized, however, that reparations constituted a segment of a very complicated problem of international indebtedness. Moreover, by that time the international gold standard was in almost complete collapse, the international credit structure had broken down, international commerce was being throttled by unprecedented barriers to trade, and unrelieved depression was almost everywhere deepening. They decided, therefore, to inaugurate an attempt to deal, by means of international action, with the entire complex of economic factors which were making for a prolongation and intensification of the depression.

The new attempt was to be in the form of an official monetary and economic conference, in which all the nations of the world would be asked to participate. The Lausanne Resolution dealing with the convocation of the new conference emphasized in particular "the necessity of restoring currencies to a healthy basis and of thereby making it possible to abolish measures of foreign exchange control and to remove transfer difficulties," and urged "the vital need of facilitating the revival of international trade." In order to achieve these objectives, it was thought necessary to submit the following questions to a thorough examination: monetary and credit policy; exchange difficulties; the level of prices; the movement of capital; tariff policy; prohibitions and restrictions of importation and exportation, quotas, and other barriers to trade; and producers' agreements.

In the opinion of the Lausanne conferees, the procedure was to involve two distinct steps. First, a preparatory committee of experts was to explore these and other related problems and to suggest the measures which would be needed to deal with them. Second, a conference was to be called to examine the recommendations of the experts and to negotiate the necessary agreements and conventions requiring concerted action on the part of the governments concerned. The League of Nations was to be entrusted with the preparation and convocation of the new parley.

The committee of experts met in October-November

1932, and again in January 1933. It produced for submission to the governments an Annotated Agenda, in which the basic economic problems of the world were subjected to a systematic analysis. The committee refrained from recommending specific measures, leaving their determination to the forthcoming conference. But it reiterated emphatically the fundamental ideas which really constituted the motive force behind the Lausanne Resolution. They were strikingly expressed in the following passage:

It will not be possible to make substantial progress by piecemeal measures. A policy of "nibbling" will not solve this crisis. We believe that the governments of the world must make up their minds to achieve a broad solution along the whole front. Action in the field of economic relations depends largely upon monetary and financial action and vice versa. Concerted measures in both fields are essential if progress is to be made in either.

When the World Economic Conference convened in London in June 1933 it was soon evident that the principal nations of the world were still unprepared to proceed along these lines. The Conference foundered on the rock of discordant monetary policies. The United States refused to accept any commitment with respect to the stabilization of foreign exchanges, although it was willing to discuss trade problems; while France and the other countries which remained on the gold standard announced their conviction that any discussion of economic problems was entirely useless while the principal nations remained unwilling to achieve a solution of the monetary problem.

The failure of the London Conference left unchecked the drift toward concentration of attention by individual nations upon purely domestic policies of recovery, which the whole effort begun at the Lausanne Conference was intended to arrest. Since the adjournment of the London Conference in July 1933 no more efforts have been made, on a large scale, to attempt "a broad solution" of the depression problem by means of international action.

Attempts to attain more limited objectives along the lines of international recovery policies were made, both shortly before and since the London parley. Just after the Lausanne Conference adjourned, the Netherlands, Belgium, and Luxembourg signed an agreement at Ouchy, under the terms of which they undertook a gradual mutual reduction of tariffs which would be extended to other nations willing to enter upon a similar undertaking. Like the Oslo Convention, the Ouchy Agreement was never made operative.

A system of regional economic agreements was created in August 1932 at Ottawa by Great Britain and the other self-governing members of the British Commonwealth of Nations. This system was based upon the principle of exclusive imperial preference. While it provided a basis for improved trade relations within the British Empire, it constituted a backward step from the point of view of general commercial policy. The Ottawa agreements were based upon a general increase of protectionism on the part of the nations concerned as against the rest of the world. They led to substantial diversions of trade and in actual application have not proved to be fully satisfactory even to the British nations themselves. They were originally negotiated for a period of five years, and are now in the process of revision.

In September 1932 a conference at Stresa attempted to find a solution for the acute economic difficulties experienced by the smaller countries of Central and Eastern Europe. This conference grew out of another decision of the Lausanne Conference, in accordance with which a special body was to be set up for the purpose of examining these difficulties and reporting its findings to the Commission of Inquiry for European Union. The Stresa Conference worked out two series of proposals. The first dealt with trade problems and called for the granting, by the industrial countries of Western and Central Europe, of special trade and financial concessions to the economically weaker nations of the continent, especially those of a predominantly agricultural character. The second envisaged a reconsideration of the short- and long-term debts of the heavily indebted countries and the creation of an international Currency Normalization Fund to assist in a regularization of monetary conditions in the countries of Eastern and Central Europe. The proposals of the Stresa Conference were reviewed by the Commission of Inquiry for European Union and were referred by the latter to the Monetary and Economic Conference. They disappeared from the scene with the demise of that ill-fated parley.

One of the principal objectives sought by the Stresa Conference—an improvement in the position of the agricultural countries of Eastern Europe—bid fair for a time to be achieved in another way. An outgrowth of the London Conference was an attempt to deal, on a world scale, with the acute problem presented by the disastrous fall in the price of wheat. After much preliminary consultation and negotiation, a Wheat Conference assembled in London in August 1933, and an agreement was signed between the wheat-exporting and wheat-importing countries. The object of the agreement, as stated in its preamble, was "to adjust the supply of wheat to effective world demand and eliminate the abnormal surpluses which have been depressing the wheat market, and to bring about a rise and stabilization of prices at a level remunerative to the farmers and fair to the consumers of breadstuffs." The exporting countries undertook to reduce their output and to limit their exports in accordance with an agreed schedule. The importing countries undertook to cease all efforts for the encouragement of wheat production within their frontiers and, after the world price of wheat had reached an agreed level, to begin a reduction of their customs duties on wheat. The agreement was never fully put into effect because of the recalcitrance of some of the exporting countries, and the machinery set up under it is now in the process of liquidation.

The last formal attempt so far made to improve international economic relations by international action was the adoption of the Seventh International Conference of American States, held at Montevideo in December 1933, of an agreement, proposed by the United States, which related to the application of the most-favored-nation principle in the case of multilateral economic conventions. In order to encourage the conclusion by groups of nations of arrangements designed to promote economic relations among them, the signatories of the agreement undertook to refrain from invoking their rights under the most-favored-nation principle unless they chose to become parties to the multilateral arrangements and to assume all the obligations thereof. The agreement stipulated that it applied only to conventions "which are of general applicability, which include a trade area of substantial size, which have as their objective the liberalization and promotion of international trade or other international economic intercourse, and which are open to adoption by all countries." The agreement has been ratified by the United States and a number of other American nations. So far, however, no multilateral convention of the type contemplated has been negotiated.

II. NATIONAL RECOVERY MEASURES

In every important country in the world the current depression has been marked by vigorous efforts on the part of the government to influence or control the course of business. In part because of a growing belief that the government may be used as a sort of balance wheel in the economic system but more, perhaps, because of sheer desperation, the powers of government have recently been utilized in ways which are wholly incompatible with the economic and political philosophy of the nineteenth century.

The measures that have been adopted by individual governments during the course of the depression and recovery have been of widely divergent types and have had varying objectives. Many of the earlier acts were primarily of a defensive nature, intended to check the downward spiral of deflation or to bring relief to economic groups in acute distress. Other measures were essentially offensive in character, designed to start a stalled economic engine and promote a new forward movement. In some cases primary reliance was placed upon monetary and fiscal policies; in others the main emphasis was upon stimulating industrial and agricultural revival. Some of the measures employed have been deflationary in character, that is, directed toward reducing costs and prices as a means of establishing a sound basis for revival; others have conceived the way out to be through a "reflation" of prices, accomplished either by monetary policies or by the artificial expansion of purchasing power. Some countries show considerable specialization in the matter of recovery policy, while others have employed a wide variety of measures, sometimes inconsistent with one another.

Because of the complex and varied character of recovery legislation it is in most cases impossible to discover any clearly defined, coherent program which might be made the subject of a clean-cut, simple appraisal. Accordingly, we shall have to be content for present purposes with indicating the principal types of measures that have been adopted in the leading countries. A summary statement of the depression and recovery legislation of fourteen representative countries—Great Britain, France, Belgium, Germany, Sweden, Norway, Finland, Poland, Denmark, Italy, Austria, New Zealand, Australia, and Japan—will be found in Appendix B. Only by glancing over such a digest as is there given can one obtain any real conception of the extent to which government aid in the solution of our problems has been sought, and only by studying the summary with some care can one appreciate the range and far-reaching implications of the policies that have been adopted. The recovery measures of the United States government are not included in this summary.

The measures passed in the various countries may as a rule be grouped as affecting: (1) money and credit; (2) the budget; (3) labor and unemployment; (4) agriculture; (5) industry; and (6) foreign trade—though, to be sure, the effects in many cases are interacting in character. This classification has been followed, in most cases, in the appendix digest. For purposes of general comparison a brief, but necessarily over-simplified, characterization of the depression and recovery legislation is given at this place. Its principle value is in indicating the relative emphasis upon various types of measures in the various countries.

In Great Britain, the gold standard was abandoned; fiscal stability was maintained; agriculture and industry were protected and encouraged by new commercial legislation; and employment was stimulated through the granting of subsidies, particularly for the construction of houses.

France maintained (until 1936) the value of the currency; vainly tried to maintain a balanced budget; and sought to reduce costs and prices in industry. But with this deflationary policy was coupled an extensive program of agricultural aid through subsidies and the control of production and prices, and extensive appropriations for public works as a means of relieving unemployment.

Belgium followed in the main a deflationary policy until the spring of 1935; but it then devalued the currency, reorganized its financial system, and embarked upon a systematic policy of stimulating recovery, especially by means of expenditures for public works.

In Germany two distinct stages are in evidence—before and after the emergence of the National Socialist Party. In the former period major emphasis was placed upon monetary and credit stability, the balancing of the budget, and the reduction of costs and prices with a view to stimulating exports. In the second period the government exercised strict control over production, prices, and trade, and largely eliminated unemployment through a simultaneous reduction in the number of "available" workers and an increase in the number of jobs through extensive programs of public works and by vast outlays for military purposes. Gold parity has been maintained, though with extensive exchange control; while the budget has been seriously unbalanced.

The Swedish government, contrary to prevailing assumptions, did not adopt an extensive recovery program. The currency was linked to the pound sterling; the budget was only moderately unbalanced; aid was extended to agriculture; and provision was made for the relief of unemployment.

In Norway we find a wider range of legislative measures. As in Sweden, primary emphasis was placed upon monetary and fiscal policies. The currency was adjusted to the pound, and vigorous efforts were made to maintain a balanced budget.

Finland remained on the gold standard, and attempted to maintain a balanced budget through rigid economies and increased taxation. On the other hand, extensive aid was extended to agriculture, and appropriations were made for public works as a means of relieving unemployment.

The government of Denmark carried through a very extensive program, involving not only the alleviation of distress but the regulation of production, trade, and prices.

Poland maintained the gold standard; endeavored by rigorous methods to maintain a balanced budget; reduced "inflexible prices" by negotiation or decree; and "stabilized" industry by means of syndicates or cartels. A moratorium was proclaimed on agricultural debts, and financially distressed industries were relieved by a compulsory general bankruptcy law.

The Italian program extended to practically every phase of economic activity, great emphasis being placed upon the control of production, prices, and wages. Gold parity was maintained until the autumn of 1936, and systematic but unsuccessful efforts were made to keep the budget in balance.

The Austrian government, during the acute stage of the depression, devoted its energies chiefly to the re-establishment of financial stability, with the co-operation of the League of Nations. The gold standard was definitely abandoned in 1933. Relief aid, particularly to agriculture, was extended throughout the whole period.

The government of New Zealand concentrated attention upon monetary, credit, and fiscal policies. The gold standard was abandoned and fiscal stability maintained. Extensive aid was given to agriculture, and a public works program was instituted.

The Australian recovery program is distinctive for the systematic effort made to lower costs of government and the level of commodity prices by means of reductions in wages and interest rates. At the same time relief was extended to distressed debtors and to the unemployed.

In Japan we find perhaps the most extreme case of inflationary action. Not only was the gold standard abandoned, but public credit was extensively employed for the promotion of industry, the development of foreign trade, and the carrying out of a military program. No effort was made to maintain a balanced budget, and most of the government's loans were placed directly with the central bank.

In the light of this summary sketch of the efforts made in various countries to modify or control economic trends, what conclusions if any may be reached as to the results attained? One thing is altogether obvious—that under modern conditions governments cannot possibly escape the adoption of *defensive* measures designed to check the collapse of economic institutions and to afford relief to distressed individuals, whatever their effects upon business conditions may prove to be. The issue of primary importance is whether positive *offensive* government measures may be made to stimulate an earlier and more extensive recovery than would occur were business allowed to run its "natural course." On the basis of the record can one say what types of recovery program have the greatest merit? Does the degree of recovery attained in the various countries show any positive correlation with particular recovery policies? While it is not possible to answer such questions with the conclusiveness which one naturally desires, certain observations may be made which should be helpful in clarifying some popular misconceptions.

(*1*) *It is not possible to prove from the available evidence whether recovery has been impeded rather than promoted by governmental activity.* In no country did the government entirely refrain from interference with private economic activity; hence it is impossible to compare the results in countries which invoked the powers of government with the outcome in countries following a policy of strict laissez faire. If one is to establish a presumption for or against government intervention it must still be by means of theoretical reasoning. The most that might be said on the basis of the data is that in some countries recovery was apparently under way before extensive governmental recovery programs were launched.

(*2*) *It is not possible to measure with any precision the relative merits of specific types of recovery effort.* This is because nowhere do we find any clear-cut adherence to a single method of promoting business revival and expansion. As a rule several methods have been employed simultaneously, and at best there have been varying degrees of emphasis upon different types of recovery policy. It is accordingly impossible to disentangle the interacting and in many cases conflicting results of recovery programs.

(3) Countries which remained on the gold standard show as a rule a considerably smaller degree of recovery than do those which abandoned or modified that standard. It does not follow from this fact, however, that the abandonment of the gold standard promoted world recovery—for it disorganized international economic relations and profoundly affected the volume of world trade. All that is indicated by the fact that the "gold bloc" countries remained relatively depressed is that they suffered from the consequences of the policies of other nations. It is to be noted that in some countries recovery began before the gold standard was abandoned, and, also, that in some cases the degree of recovery in countries which did not depreciate the currency compares favorably with that in countries which did. Finally, it should be pointed out that in some cases the abandonment of the gold standard has been accompanied by deflationary fiscal and business policies, while in others it has been combined with inflationary measures. Similarly, some of the countries which refrained from depreciating the currency have endeavored to maintain a balanced budget, while others have not.

(4) The degree of recovery does not correlate closely with the extent to which government funds have been employed for the purpose of promoting expansion. Among the important countries showing the greatest degree of recovery are Japan, Great Britain, Australia, Sweden, and Germany. While Japan and Germany have made prodigal use of public funds, in the other three there has been but a moderate increase in the public debt,

and in consequence the present fiscal situation is comparatively stable. On the other hand, it should be observed that in some countries with decidedly lagging recoveries the public debt has rapidly increased, as in France, Belgium, and Poland; in these cases the recurring deficits are of course in substantial part attributable to the continuance of severe depression of business.[1]

Perhaps the inference that may most definitely be drawn from a comparison of government recovery measures with the degree of recovery attained is that no significant positive correlation is apparent. By and large the extent of recovery appears to be more or less independent of the particular program adopted. Certainly it is impossible to discover from this summary outline any sure formula by means of which the processes of recovery may be controlled. One other conclusion may with certainty also be drawn—that statesmen are scarcely to be envied the responsibilities they assume.

[1] For data on the debt increase in various countries, see p. 89.

PART II

READJUSTMENTS IN THE UNITED STATES
1929-36

INTRODUCTION

The primary purpose of Part I was to place the American depression in its world setting. That is, we sought to reveal the interacting and ramifying forces at work in the world economy as a whole, with particular reference to their impingement upon the economic life of the United States. We did not, however, give detailed attention to the ways in which the depression affected the different divisions of the American economic system or to the extent and character of the recovery movement in this country. This will be the task of the second division of the analysis.

We shall review in turn the effects of the depression upon employment and production, upon wages and prices, upon government and private finance, and upon international trade and financial relations. In each of the eleven chapters which comprise this section we shall be primarily concerned with revealing the facts with reference to the changes which have occurred in connection with important phases or divisions of economic activity. The data thus assembled will be found to throw light upon numerous theoretical issues pertaining to cyclical movements, as well as upon various practical questions of current importance. They provide also the essential groundwork for the interpretative analysis and recommendations which make up the third division of the study.

CHAPTER VI

EMPLOYMENT AND UNEMPLOYMENT

Production and employment are basic and ultimate points of reference in modern industrial life. Depression, like prosperity, is a phenomenon which is significant primarily in these terms, and no understanding of the factors of recovery may be gained without a thorough consideration of these two elements of economic activity. Production refers to the volume of commodities and services which is made available for consumption; and employment gauges the degree of utilization of available human energy in the productive process. Employment, moreover, serves as a means of distributing the national product, for it is through employment that the majority of the people acquire claims to the goods and services which are being produced. Employment, therefore, is itself a determinant of production.

In this and in the following three chapters we shall attempt to set down the basic facts on employment and production with a view to indicating the magnitude of the problem of re-employment and what is involved in its solution. We shall address ourselves first to a consideration of the available labor force—its composition, growth, and employment immediately before and during the depression. Subsequently we shall examine the changes which have taken place in the volume and character of production. Special consideration will be given to the durable goods industries, which are usually so important in accentuating both prosperity and depression. The material to be presented in these chapters is basic in character and should serve as a background for all proposals seeking to lead the country towards full recovery.

I. THE LABOR FORCE

On April 1, 1930 there were 48.8 million persons reported by the Census of Occupations as "gainful workers." This means persons who, whether or not actually employed at the time, had gainful occupations and constituted the working force of the nation. This group, including business and professional people as well as farmers, factory workers, and laborers, comprised almost 40 per cent of the total population. On the basis of the proportion of gainful workers in the population of working age in 1930, the most recent year for which we have adequate data, we estimate that the "gross labor force" of the nation at the end of 1936 will number about 53 million individuals.[1]

The over-all figure of the labor force does not, however, convey an accurate impression of the volume of effective human energy available for production. In order to gain a clearer picture of the full magnitude of this force, it is necessary to examine its composition. For lack of more recent data we must again consider figures recorded for the beginning of 1930. The results will then be applied, in summary, to the situation as it is today.

1. A bird's-eye view of the labor force in 1930. A detailed analysis of the distribution of the working population at the beginning of the depression will be found in Tables 1 and 2 of Appendix C. For convenience of presentation the salient facts are depicted in a series of simple graphs on page 117. Agriculture is treated separately because of its peculiar position with regard to

---

[1] See Appendix C, Table 3.

employment and production. The non-agricultural labor force, which comprised nearly 80 per cent of the aggregate, was divided roughly as follows: manufacturing (which was the largest single group), 24 per cent; wholesale and retail trade, 15 per cent; domestic and personal services, 10 per cent; transportation and communication, 9 per cent; professional services, 6 per cent; and building construction, 5 per cent. The remaining 9 per cent was attached to numerous smaller industries.

From Figure 1 it will be seen that although farm workers comprised little more than 20 per cent of all workers, agriculture contained the major portion of the self-employed. Outside of agriculture there were only 3.6 million persons who were earning their living as independent enterprisers. On the other hand, agriculture included only 2.8 millions of the 37.5 million employees. Because of the high proportion of enterprisers in agriculture, the labor force in that industry is more stable and less subject to the problems of unemployment, in the usual sense, than the non-agricultural group which consists for the most part of employees.

Figure 2 shows the age composition of the working population. In 1930 over 2 millions of the 48.8 million gainful workers were under 18 years of age, and a slightly larger number were 65 years and over. Thus, those of active working age numbered only about 44.5 millions, or 91 per cent of the total reported. Female workers, who constituted about 22 per cent of the total, comprised a larger proportion of minors and a smaller proportion of elderly people than did the male contingent of the gainfully employed. As will be shown later, a high percentage of the young workers were on farms and were to a large extent "unpaid family workers."

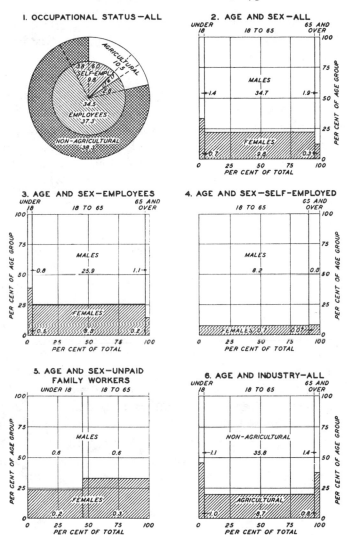

I. OCCUPATIONAL STATUS—ALL

2. AGE AND SEX—ALL

3. AGE AND SEX—EMPLOYEES

4. AGE AND SEX—SELF-EMPLOYED

5. AGE AND SEX—UNPAID FAMILY WORKERS

6. AGE AND INDUSTRY—ALL

[a] Numbers within the diagrams represent millions of gainful workers. For data, see Appendix C, Table 1. A correction in the table which shifted about 200,000 non-agricultural workers from the self-employed to the employee group has not been incorporated in this chart. Figures 1, 3, and 4 are affected.

The sex and the age composition of the employee group alone are shown in Figure 3. Females constituted only 25 per cent of the total number of employees within the 18-64 age group and nearly 40 per cent of those under 18. But the proportion of females in the ages 65 and over was only about 15 per cent. Almost half of these elderly women were in occupations connected with domestic and personal services. The male employees 65 years of age and over were well distributed through the various industries, the majority being urban wage earners.

Figure 4 shows that the self-employed group contained a considerable proportion of individuals above 65 years of age. While among employees only about 3.5 per cent were reported in the older groups, more than 9 per cent of the self-employed were 65 years of age and over. Only a small proportion of the entire group were females.

As may be seen from Figure 5, nearly one-half of the unpaid family workers were under 18, and 29 per cent of the total were females. Unpaid workers are more or less an anomaly. They are neither employees nor self-employed, and their contribution to production in the narrow sense of the word is not ascertainable. Moreover, although there is a counterpart of this group in urban pursuits—in retail trade, for instance, and in some "sweat-shop" hand trades where the whole family assists in the business—the Census records only the number in agriculture. We shall have occasion later to discuss the relationship of unpaid family workers on farms to the problem of employment and unemployment.

The age composition of gainful workers in non-agricultural and agricultural pursuits is shown in Figure 6. About 20 per cent of the active adult labor force were in agriculture. But it is significant to note that the minors working on farms constituted approximately 45 per cent of all workers under 18 years of age, and the agricultural workers 65 years of age and over about 38 per cent of the total number of gainful workers in this age group.

In the foregoing paragraphs special attention has been given to the age composition of the working population. While the age limits used are arbitrary, the classification is helpful in the analysis of the problem. Children and aged workers, though still important in our industrial organization as a source of productive energy, present problems of employment and unemployment which are sufficiently different from those encountered in connection with the main current of the nation's labor force to warrant separate consideration. The inclusion of minors and superannuated workers in the count of the gainfully employed somewhat distorts the picture of the labor force and its potential productive capacity. Moreover, it confuses the problem of re-employment since their peculiar position in society may well indicate solutions which are not applicable to others—as, for example, the raising of educational age requirements and the establishment of an adequate system of old-age pensions.

2. *The increase in the number of gainful workers.* The labor force is a function of population. Although the ratio of one to the other is modified in the long run by various social and economic trends, the change is usually slow enough to make it possible to estimate the number of available workers in intercensal years from estimates of population on the basis of a ratio obtained from the data for the preceding Census. The effect of the social and economic changes is partially eliminated if

the gainful workers are correlated with a pertinent section of the population (a specific age group, for instance) rather than with the entire population. The differences existing in current estimates are due largely to the use of different population bases.

The estimates of the number of gainful workers since the last decennial Census shown in the chart on page 121 have been made on the basis of the population of the ages 15-64 inclusive. This choice of base has been considered advisable in view of the fact that restriction of immigration,[2] decrease in birth rates, and prolongation of life have introduced progressive changes into the age distribution of the population. Because of these tendencies the rate of increase in the older groups has been and will no doubt for some time continue to be considerably different from that of the population as a whole.[3]

Exclusive of unpaid family workers, the ratio of persons in gainful occupations to the population 15 to 64 years of age has remained stable at about 59 per cent in the last three Census enumerations. This ratio applied

[2] The restriction of immigration has had two opposing influences on the age distribution of the population and hence the number of gainful workers: in the first place, because the birth rate is usually higher for the immigrant than the native population, it has reduced the proportion of young persons in the population; and, in the second place, it has cut off a supply of adult labor.

[3] The restriction of the population base has been made possible by recent estimates of future population by broad age groups prepared by Warren Thompson and P. K. Whelpton of the Scripps Foundation for Research in Population Problems. See *Estimates of Future Population by States,* National Resources Board, December 1934.

In further explanation of the difference between the estimates here presented and those used in other studies it should be stated that the ratio calculations have been made after excluding the "unpaid family workers on farms." It is believed that the number of these workers varies not with the growth in general population but with the economic position of farmers. However, in order to obtain rough estimates of the aggregate number of gainful workers within the Census definition, the number of unpaid family workers as reported for April 1930 has been added as a constant to the other estimates.

to population yields an estimate of about 51 million workers for July 1936. The addition of the unpaid family workers raises this estimate to 52.7 millions. Thus, between January 1, 1930 and July 1, 1936 the labor force was increased by 4 millions.

THE INCREASE OF GAINFUL WORKERS, 1930-36[a]

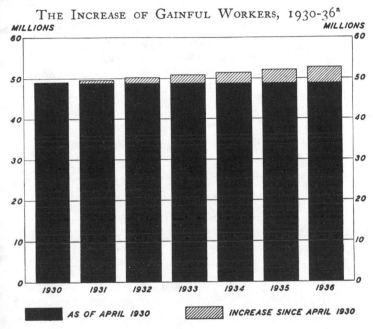

MILLIONS   *MILLIONS*

[a] For data, see Appendix C, Table 3.

The estimates indicate that the number of workers available for gainful occupations in the past six or seven years has increased at a higher rate than has the total population. Estimates on the basis of total population would show, in fact, that in July 1936 the total number of available gainful workers, including unpaid family workers, was 51 millions, or only 2.3 millions higher than at the beginning of 1930, as compared with our estimate of 4 millions.

The difference is clarified by the comparison of the age composition of the population in 1930 with that in 1935, which is recorded in Appendix C, Table 4. The table shows that while the total population increased only about 4.6 millions in the five years, the number in the age groups 15 years and over was increased by more than 6 millions, the difference being made up by a loss of 1.5 millions in the age groups under 15. In other words, the gain in population was confined to the ages from which most of the gainful workers are drawn. As a matter of fact, the increase in the number of persons of working age surpassed by some 15 per cent the net increase in the entire population.

Seen in this light, the problem of employment with which we are now faced assumes more than cyclical significance. It would appear that the present depression is complicated by the operation of a deep-rooted secular change in the population of the United States. Both the decrease in birth rates and the increase in longevity tend to increase the supply of workers relative to the total population. The first, in addition to increasing the ratio of adults to the total population, tends to release women from the home for gainful employment, and the second increases the labor force by lengthening the average period of active employment.

While in the long run this phenomenon is favorable to greater prosperity, immediately it intensifies the problems of readjustment. It puts a greater premium on the available jobs, the number of which has been restricted by the purely cyclical factors of the depression, and it also undoubtedly creates basic disturbances in demand. In an advanced industrial society, where food constitutes a comparatively small fraction of the budget and items generally called "sundries" such a large proportion, needs change with age. The requirements of adults are different from those of children, and it is reasonable to believe that the shift in the age composition of the population has introduced significant changes in the character of goods entering into consumption. Although the tendencies toward an "older" population were in evidence even before the depression, it appears that the movement is now in a phase of acceleration.[4] Indeed it may itself be accentuated by the depression. Certainly the normal decrease in birth rates has been intensified by the cyclical decrease in the marriage rate resulting from the depression. Be that as it may, the problem is not one of re-employment alone but of added employment as well. Even beyond the measure of the statistics, the reduction of family incomes has produced a larger number of would-be gainful workers than the number required to re-establish the 1929 level of per capita production. It should be noted, however, that not all of the individuals seeking employment under present conditions would be available under prosperity. Many would undoubtedly prefer leisure and non-pecuniary activities if family incomes were re-established on a more or less secure basis.

It is necessary to draw attention to an additional feature concerning the excess of persons desiring jobs over the number employed. In so far as greater longevity and better health add to the labor supply, it is possible to have a volume of employment commensurate with pre-depression levels and still have unemployment. In

[4] The proportions of the total population represented by those 15 years of age and over, as shown by the last four enumerations of the Census of Population, are as follows: 1900, 66 per cent; 1910, 68 per cent; 1920, 68 per cent; and 1930, 70 per cent. Thompson and Whelpton have estimated that in 1935 this group formed 73 per cent of the total and that by 1940 it will have increased to 75 per cent. See *Estimates of Future Population by States*, p. 3.

other words, production and employment in proportion to population might be as high and even higher than in 1929 and yet leave unemployed workers. Presumably if the distribution of the products of industry were dependent on some principle other than employment, the population would be no worse off; but, in our economy, having a job is for the bulk of the people the only means of getting a share in the national product. Aside from the fact that the people could use more goods and services and that unemployment represents a waste of social energy, the nation cannot be satisfied with bringing employment back to the best pre-depression standards, if that means that some persons who are able and willing to work will be unemployed or under-employed.

3. *Deterioration of the average efficiency of the labor force.* The labor force of the United States, like the population itself, is constantly undergoing changes in composition through losses from illness, death, and retirement, and through replacements and additions. Skill, knowledge, and efficiency, which have long distinguished American labor, must, therefore, be carried and transmitted through the flowing stream of new workers. Should the instruction and training of the young be halted for one reason or another, the most important element in the productive capacity of the nation would become lost with the disappearance of the older workers.

Such a degeneration has in fact gone on throughout the depression. Many of those who have entered the ranks of would-be workers during the past six years have still to find their first real work, and hence have yet to acquire the skill and efficiency that come only through experience at the job.

It is impossible to determine with any precision the extent of deterioration of the working force of the nation which has taken place during the depression. Some idea of the situation may, however, be gained from the fact that in the six and one-half years following January 1930 some 10 million experienced workers dropped from the effective working personnel of the country and that a large proportion of those who came in have as yet had no opportunity to obtain work and acquire occupational skill. The new workers who came in during the period indicated, together with the addition to the working personnel resulting from the growth in population, numbered about 14 million persons at the middle of 1936 and constituted about 27 per cent of the entire labor force.[5] Normally replacements occur so gradually that at any given time the number of inexperienced workers is comparatively small.

The composition, by sex and probable location in industry, of the group which reached the bread-winning stage during the depression is as follows (in millions):

Agriculture:
Males	1.62
Females	0.20
	1.82

All other activities:
Males	8.30
Females	4.15
	12.45

It may be assumed that in so far as agricultural labor is concerned working efficiency has not suffered on account of unemployment. Unemployment in agriculture is never a significant factor since most of the work is done by the farm operators themselves. Also, during the de-

[5] See Appendix C, Section I for description of the method of arriving at these estimates, and Table 5 for the data.

pression a larger number of workers have remained on the home farms than in pre-depression years when the farm population was supplying labor for other industries; and remaining on the farm is for the most part tantamount˙ to engaging in the business. The young workers who are destined to take over the farm work of the country have therefore not been without training in this occupation during the depression. Only those who will leave the farm for industrial pursuits when economic conditions improve will enter their occupations as inexperienced recruits.

The lack of training and skill among those who look to non-agricultural industries for employment presents a far more serious problem. This is because the numbers involved are much larger, and because, unlike unpaid family workers on farms, they have little opportunity to learn how to work without a bona fide job. The estimates given above show that more than 87 per cent of the total, or about 12.5 million new workers, would be needed in non-agricultural industries to maintain the labor force of 1930 and to allow for population growth. In this group there would be about 4.2 million females and 8.3 million males.

The loss of efficiency attributable to the fact that new female workers have been unsuccessful in obtaining jobs is somewhat mitigated by two interacting factors. The first is the temporary character of most women's participation in industry. The second is that, in general, women enter occupations requiring comparatively little skill. The estimated annual replacement rate[6] for all female workers outside of agriculture exceeds 5 per cent as compared with less than 3 per cent for males. The turnover

[6] The rate of replacement is used here to describe entrance into and exit from the category of "gainful workers"; it does not take into consideration changes from one job to another.

among females is particularly great in the occupations requiring no extended preparation and training. For instance, among telephone operators it is about 8.5 per cent, among clerks 7.8 per cent, and among stenographers and typists between 11 and 12 per cent. On the other hand, in some of the professions (medicine, for example) the replacement rate among females is not much higher than among males.

In this connection it is of interest to see in which occupations the majority of the female gainful workers outside of agriculture are to be found. The following distribution is based on the 1930 Census:

Occupational Group	Percentage Distribution[7]
Self-employed, professional	0.6
Self-employed, others	3.7
School teachers[8]	8.8
Trained nurses	2.9
Professional and executive employees exclusive of school teachers and trained nurses	2.8
Foremen and lower managerial employees	2.9
Clerical and other lower salaried employees	31.2
Skilled wage earners	0.4
Semi-skilled wage earners	21.6
Unskilled wage earners	25.1
Total	100.0

The foregoing tabulation fails to give an accurate picture of the allocation of the 4.2 million new female

[7] Based on Table 2, Appendix C. The classification is of necessity very rough.

[8] Not including college teachers; they are grouped with "professional and executive employees." A very large proportion of the school teachers who are in rural and elementary schools cannot properly be considered professional workers. They enter teaching with little training and for the most part remain only a short time. The replacement rate among school teachers as a group (the data do not permit of a more detailed analysis) appears to be about 7.3 per cent per year.

128   *THE RECOVERY PROBLEM*

workers who entered the labor force since the beginning of the depression. Because of the differences in the rates of replacement the proportions of new workers in the non-skilled occupations would be larger and in the skilled occupations smaller than shown in this tabulation.

More serious has been the effect of the depression upon the efficiency of the male contingent of industrial and other non-agricultural workers. In 1930 this group included 28.5 million individuals or more than 58 per cent of the total number of gainful workers, distributed as follows:

Occupational Group	Percentage Distribution[9]
Self-employed, professional	1.6
Self-employed, others	9.7
School teachers and trained nurses[10]	0.7
Professional and executive employees exclusive of school teachers and trained nurses	5.6
Foremen and lower managerial employees	2.8
Clerical and other lower salaried employees	16.6
Skilled wage earners	18.9
Semi-skilled wage earners	18.9
Unskilled wage earners	25.2
Total	100.0

In addition to being the most important group numerically, it contained by far the highest proportion of

[9] Based on Table 2, Appendix C. An attempt was made to make this comparable with the tabulation for females; teachers and trained nurses are therefore listed separately. The classification is not precise. It is obvious that the class descriptions cannot have exactly the same meaning for males and females.

[10] Not including college teachers; they are grouped with "professional and executive employees." The proportion of trained nurses is less than 0.1 per cent. See note 9 above.

skilled workers. While experience and training are important factors in all occupations, they are especially significant in skilled trades, in the professions, and in executive and managerial occupations. From the accompanying tabulation it may be seen that these selected groups comprised at least 30 per cent of the total number of males in non-agricultural activities. It is significant that the replacement rate among these workers is higher than among the semi-skilled and unskilled.[11] A rough estimate indicates that of 9 million male workers in 1930 whose productivity depended upon skill or prolonged training and experience,[12] little more than 7 millions are now available for active employment—a loss of nearly 2 million men. If with revival of business activity we should need the same proportion of this type of worker as before the depression, the total required at the end of 1936 would be roughly 10 millions, which means an aggregate of about 3 million new workers since 1930.

For male workers as a group the personnel enumerated by the 1930 Census has been reduced through natural causes at the rate of 2.8 per cent per year. In the

[11] In this respect males differ from females. Among females—because of their temporary stay in industry—it is in the occupations requiring little skill that we find the highest replacement rates.

It is found that while for the entire group of male non-agricultural workers the rate was 2.8 per cent, the rate for skilled wage earners was 3.1 per cent, for foremen and lower managerial workers 3.3 per cent, and for officials and executives in manufacturing 3.5 per cent. (For method of estimating these rates, see Appendix C, Section I.)

The National Industrial Conference Board has estimated that the "obsolescence and mortality rate" among skilled artisans in normal years was 5 per cent per year and that "the percentage has probably been higher during the depression." (National Industrial Conference Board, *Wanted: Skilled Labor*, June 1935, p. 4.)

[12] Included in this category are skilled wage earners, professional men, executives, and foremen and lower managerial employees, as well as a portion of the entrepreneurs.

meantime the stream of available workers has not only been kept numerically intact through replacements but has been increased as a result of growth of population. It is estimated that at the middle of 1936 the number of males available for gainful employment, exclusive of agriculture, was about 31.6 millions, and that it included 8.3 million individuals, or 26 per cent, who came in after January 1930. How many of the 8.3 million new male workers have had an opportunity to acquire the necessary training during the depression is, of course, not known.[13]

In so far as formal education and training are concerned, the labor force probably has not suffered during the depression. Colleges and universities granted more degrees in the academic years 1931-32 and 1933-34 than in any previous years.[14] However, many of the graduates have not been able to establish themselves in their chosen work and have drifted to other activities. This, by the way, has happened among the older professional men as

[13] One approach, which would tend toward the conclusion that the new workers have been at a competitive disadvantage in applying for the available jobs and have, therefore, not been able to get much experience, is an examination of statistics of unemployment by age groups. The available data are limited to the federal Census of Unemployment made in 1930 and a study made in Massachusetts in 1934. (See Appendix C, Tables 6 and 7.) Both show that the percentage of unemployment was higher among males under 25 years of age than in the other age groups. In 1930 about 15 per cent of the urban male employees 15 to 19 years old were unemployed and 12 per cent of those 20 to 24 years, as compared with approximately 9 per cent for the groups 25 to 45 years. The contrast is more marked in the Massachusetts survey in January 1934. About half of the male "employables" under 25 were unemployed while for those from 25 to 55 years the ratio was less than 25 per cent. These are over-all figures which make no distinction as to skill.

[14] U. S. Department of the Interior, *Biennial Survey of Education, 1931-32*, Chap. III, p. 26 for 1931-32; 1933-34 figure from unpublished data.

well. How many will have returned when full recovery has been achieved and to what extent they will be able to regain their former efficiency is of course unknown. It is certain, however, that the loss of potential productive efficiency through occupational and geographical dislocations is considerable.

The deterioration of skills during the depression is somewhat offset by a relative decrease in demand for skilled workers which has been brought about by changes in technology. The NRA report on the automobile industry indicates not only a displacement of labor by new machinery but also a substitution of non-skilled or semi-skilled for skilled workers.[15]

The extent to which recovery will be impeded because of the deterioration of the labor force cannot be measured quantitatively from the available data. But expressions in the press and results of industrial surveys indicate that a shortage is already being felt in some lines.

II. CURRENT ESTIMATES OF EMPLOYMENT AND UNEMPLOYMENT

Several series of estimates measuring employment and unemployment have had currency during the depression, the most commonly quoted being those of the American Federation of Labor, the National Industrial Conference Board, and the President's Committee on Economic Security. The methods of deriving these estimates differ only in detail, and, since the same basic data are used in all, the results are very similar.

The methodology consists in (1) establishing the em-

[15] Research and Planning Division, NRA, *Preliminary Report on the Study of Regularization of Employment and Improvement of Labor Conditions in the Automobile Industry*, Appendix B, Exhibit 16, Jan. 23, 1935.

ployment situation as it existed in April 1930 when the first federal Census of Unemployment was taken; (2) projecting estimates of employment in the several branches of industry on the basis of indexes of the United States Bureau of Labor Statistics, the Interstate Commerce Commission, and miscellaneous employment surveys; (3) projecting estimates of total gainful workers reported in the Census of Occupations in 1930 in accordance with a population factor; and (4) subtracting the number employed from the total number of gainful workers—the residual representing the number of gainful workers unemployed.[16]

1. Total employment and unemployment. The course of unemployment during the depression as depicted by the three series of data is shown in the accompanying chart. It will be observed that although at the beginning of the depression the estimates of unemployment almost coincide, in 1936 there is a difference of more than 2 millions between the lowest and the highest. The American Federation of Labor estimates (line *A*) indicate that in August 1936 we had approximately 11 million unemployed persons. as compared with an average of about 2 millions in 1929. All three series show that the highest unemployment in absolute terms was reached in the first half of 1933. In March of that year the American Federation of Labor estimated total unemployment at 15.7 millions; the President's Committee on Economic Security at 15.1 millions; and the National Industrial Conference Board at 13.5 millions.[17]

[16] For further discussion, see Appendix C, Section II.

[17] The present and subsequent references to the estimates of the N.I.C.B. pertain to the series made available prior to the Board's revision of Nov. 13, 1936. The new estimates follow very closely those of the A. F. of L. and the President's Committee on Economic Security. (See "New Estimates of Employment, Unemployment and the Size of the Labor Force," *Conference Board Bulletin*, Nov. 13, 1936.)

There is closer agreement among the different esti-
mators as to the number of persons employed than to the
number unemployed. Thus in 1930 the three series show
the total number employed as 44.0 millions, 44.0 millions, and 43.9 millions respectively. In 1935 the averages still run close together. The lowest of the three is
39.1 millions, as estimated by the President's Committee on Economic Security, and the highest is 40.3 millions, as estimated by the National Industrial Conference Board. The estimate of the American Federation
of Labor stands practically in the middle, 39.6 millions.
The reason why the three estimates of the number

ESTIMATES OF UNEMPLOYMENT IN THE UNITED STATES
BY REPRESENTATIVE AGENCIES, 1929-36[a]

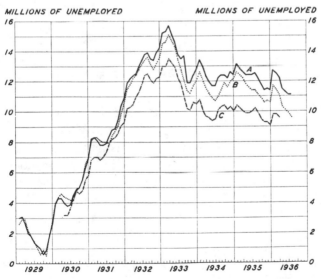

A. AMERICAN FEDERATION OF LABOR
B. PRESIDENT'S COMMITTEE ON ECONOMIC SECURITY
C. NATIONAL INDUSTRIAL CONFERENCE BOARD

[a] For data, see Appendix C, Table 8. See also note 17, p. 132.

employed could be so close together while the estimates of the unemployed were at considerable variance is that the three series were based on quite different estimates of the aggregate number of available workers. Consequently we prepared the new set of estimates of the total number of gainful workers shown in the table on page 135, which are based on population within the ages 15-64 inclusive. By subtracting the number of employed used in each of the three series under discussion from our estimates of gainful workers, we obtained revised unemployment figures which are shown in the last three columns of the table. It will be seen that the revised estimates of unemployment are invariably higher than the original ones but are in closer agreement among themselves. The published figures of the American Federation of Labor come nearest to our adjusted estimates —the Federation's figure for 1935 being 12.3, as compared with our 12.5 millions.[18] For 1929 the estimates are 1.9 millions and 2.2 millions respectively. (The difference of about 200,000 is carried through the entire period. See Appendix C, note 3.)

From these figures it appears that the average number unemployed in 1929 was in the neighborhood of 2 million persons. The reader should bear in mind that this figure included some 600,000 persons classified by the 1930 Census as voluntarily idle or out of work because of illness.[19] Considering the fact that under any circumstances a substantial number of people are in the process

---

[18] By using our estimates of gainful workers in combination with the employment estimates of the President's Committee on Economic Security the average number unemployed in 1935 is 13.0 millions instead of 11.4 millions. Similarly, the National Industrial Conference Board estimate would appear as 11.8 millions instead of 9.8 millions.

[19] By the interpretation of the American Federation of Labor, "many

UNITED STATES, 1929–36
(In millions)

Year	Total Number of Gainful Workers as of July 1[a]	Number of Employed[b]			Number of Unemployed[c] (Our revision)		
		American Federation of Labor[d]	President's Committee on Economic Security[d]	National Industrial Conference Board	American Federation of Labor	President's Committee on Economic Security	National Industrial Conference Board
1929	48.4	46.2	46.8	....	2.2	1.6	....
1930	49.0	44.0	44.0	43.9[e]	5.0	5.0	5.1
1931	49.6	40.7	40.6	40.9	8.9	9.0	8.7
1932	50.2	36.9	36.8	37.5	13.3	13.4	12.7
1933	50.8	37.0	36.7	37.5	13.8	14.1	13.3
1934	51.4	38.9	38.6	39.7	12.5	12.8	11.7
1935	52.1	39.6	39.1	40.3	12.5	13.0	11.8
1936	52.7	41.1[f]	40.8[f]	[g]	11.6	11.9	[g]

[a] See Appendix C, Table 3. [b] See Appendix C, Table 8.

[c] Obtained by subtracting respective series of the number employed from the total number of gainful workers shown in the first column. The results are therefore not exactly as reported by the respective agencies.

[d] It should be noted that the figures in these series, for 1934 and 1935, at least, understate the actual employment within the definitions used on account of an under-estimate of the number of gainful workers in agriculture. Each series presumes that a "gainful worker" on the farm is an employed person. The under-estimates are disclosed by the Census of Agriculture for 1935, the results of which were not available at the time the estimates were prepared. From the Census it appears that at the beginning of 1935 there were about 2 million more workers on farms than are included in these estimates. Not all of this difference, however, should be considered a correction of the estimates. Part of it is due to the inclusion in the 1935 Census of a larger number of part-time farmers than in the 1930 Census. See p. 146.

The National Industrial Conference Board made no attempt to estimate changes in agricultural employment but assumed that the number working on farms remained constant. (This does not apply to the Board's revision of Nov. 13, 1936.)

[e] Average for last nine months of year.

[f] Estimated by applying ratio of employment in first eight months in 1936 to same period in 1935 to the average employment for the year 1935.

[g] Series has not been continued beyond March 1936.

of shifting from one job to another, it would seem that the amount of outright unemployment in 1929 indicated by these estimates was perhaps less than a million.[20] Within the limitations of the assumptions underlying the estimates, it appears that in 1935 the gross[21] number of unemployed was something like 12.5 millions.[22]

2. *The course of employment by industries.* The total number of workers who are unemployed gives us a general idea of the magnitude of the volume of re-employment necessary for recovery. In order to make a more concrete approach to the problem, however, we must know in which industries employment has been most seriously curtailed. The existing statistical measures of unemployment by industrial divisions are less reliable than those of total unemployment. It has already been explained that the number who are unemployed can be estimated only indirectly by subtracting the number em-

---

of these 600,000 persons, perhaps even two-thirds of them, were actually unemployed . . ." (quoted from a letter from the Federation). See also Appendix C, Section II.

[20] This figure is undoubtedly too low. In reviewing this paragraph Mr. Robert R. Nathan, who compiled the estimates for the President's Committee on Economic Security, made the following statement: "Personally, I believe the 1929 estimates are understatements. When we consider the marked seasonal variations in such industries as manufacturing, mining, construction, agriculture, and trade, and also the lack of mobility of employment as among these industries, I doubt very much whether the average unemployment could possibly be less than a million in any recent year. . . . My own thought is that there were anywhere from 1.5 to 2.0 million persons actually unemployed in 1929. I appreciate the fact that the estimates do not indicate this total, after adjusting for certain factors, but this deficiency can be traced to the 1930 Census, which perhaps was not adjusted sufficiently."

[21] This figure should be compared with the 2 millions for 1929. It, too, includes unemployables and the minimum number of those who are unemployed because of shifting from job to job. Included in the 1935 estimate of unemployed are also more than 3 million persons on work relief and, as will be shown later, a considerable number who have temporarily "returned" to agriculture.

[22] For reference to a recent survey of employment in industry and trade by the *New York Sun*, see Appendix C, Section II.

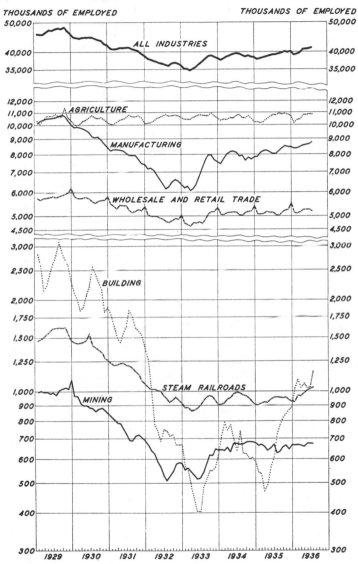

THOUSANDS OF EMPLOYED

ALL INDUSTRIES

AGRICULTURE

MANUFACTURING

WHOLESALE AND RETAIL TRADE

BUILDING

STEAM RAILROADS

MINING

[a] For source, see note 23, p. 138.

ployed from the estimated number of gainful workers. But so many changes have taken place in the industrial line-up during the past five or six years that assumptions as to the allocation of available personnel among individual industries would very probably yield misleading results. The best that can be done on an industrial basis is to examine the course of employment. The changes which have taken place in six basic industrial divisions as indicated by estimates originally prepared by Robert R. Nathan for the President's Committee on Economic Security, are shown in the chart on page 137.

The first thing on the chart that catches attention is the relatively steady employment shown for agriculture. This is explained primarily by the assumptions underlying the definition of agricultural employment in this series. In preparing the estimates it was postulated that all the gainful workers who moved from the city to the farm during the depression found employment in agriculture as farm operators or supplementary workers. Agricultural unemployment was taken account of only in the small contingent represented by agricultural wage earners.[23] As a matter of fact, data made available by the recent Census of Agriculture (which were not in existence at the time the estimates were prepared)[24] indicate that the number "employed" in agriculture increased considerably between 1930 and 1935. Accordingly, the estimates of agricultural employment, in-

[23] For detailed description of these estimates see Robert R. Nathan, "Estimates of Unemployment in the United States, 1929-1935," *International Labour Review*, Vol. XXXIII, No. 1, January 1936, pp. 57, 65, and 72.

[24] Mr. Nathan based his computations of city-to-farm and farm-to-city movements of gainful workers on the preliminary estimates of the Department of Agriculture of total population movements. It now ap-

stead of showing a horizontal trend, should indicate a considerable upward movement during the period. The Census shows that in January 1935 there were 12.4 million persons "employed" on farms, including family labor and hired help,[25] whereas the series plotted in our chart shows only 10.2 million persons employed as of that date. The difference of 2.2 millions is highly significant, for if we accept the basic assumption that all those who went to the farm were employed, the estimates of aggregate employment would be increased by about 2 millions,[26] while the estimates of unemployment would be decreased by this substantial amount. The

pears from the Census of Agriculture that the shifts in workers from city to country have not been proportional to population. The increase in the number of workers between April 1930 and January 1935 was in fact greater than the increase in farm population. The number of workers in January 1935 was reported to be 12,407,000 as compared with about 10,693,000 in 1930 (the number of farm operators, as reported in the Census of Agriculture, plus the unpaid family workers, wage earners, and other workers except managers, as reported by the Census of Occupations). Thus between 1930 and 1935 there was an increase of 1,714,000 workers on farms; the farm population increased only 1,356,000 in the same period.

The discrepancy between increase of workers and increase in population may be explained mainly by the fact that unemployed agricultural laborers have moved off the farm and that tenant farmers with large families have been replaced by adults without families—sons and daughters who have returned to the home farm from the city. The latter also explains in part why the Census shows that those who came from nonfarm residences exceeded the net increase in farm population during the period. A fact also in point is that while the number of white persons living on farms has increased, the number of colored has decreased. Part of the difference may, of course, be due to differences in definition from Census to Census. As indicated in Appendix C, the 1935 Census included a larger number of part-time farmers.

[25] "Farm Labor," *United States Census of Agriculture: 1935* (rotoprint release), p. 2.

[26] Some of the individuals reported by the 1935 Census as working on farms were undoubtedly engaged part time in other occupations. It is impossible even to approximate the duplication contained in the workers represented by the 2.2 million difference.

validity of the assumption will be discussed later (see page 146).

In absolute numbers the greatest decline in employment from 1929 to 1933 appears to have been in manufacturing industries, but in relative terms the greatest drop was in building construction. In the latter industry the loss in employment from the highest month in 1929 to the lowest in 1933 was more than 85 per cent. The decrease of 5 millions in manufacturing represented only 45 per cent. Mining and steam railroads paralleled manufacturing in the downward movement, while the decline in trade was less pronounced than in any of the other industries except agriculture.

In the recovery period the several industries show more or less the same order as in the decline. The greatest degree of recovery in percentage terms has been made by building construction, where employment nearly doubled in the first eight months following the middle of 1933. In this case, however, recovery of 100 per cent from the low mark represented only 400,000 workers. The gain, moreover, was not maintained very long—in 1935 employment in building construction reverted almost to its 1933 low. Even in the middle of 1936 employment in this industry was still less than half of the 1929 level.

Recovery in manufacturing has been more substantial. Since the low of 1933 the industry has absorbed some 2.5 million workers. The spectacular rise in the summer of 1933 somewhat exaggerates the degree of actual recovery during that period. As will be pointed out in connection with the discussion of equivalent full-time employment, the increase in the number on payrolls was in a large measure due to work-spreading. The rise also reflected the speculative boom which preceded the inauguration of the NRA codes—a boom which soon spent itself. The retarded rate of increase in employment since the initial spurt is due in some degree to the fact that during this period expansion has in part been made by reinstatement of more normal hours for those already on payrolls.

Most of the foregoing discussion applies to the other industries as well as manufacturing. In practically every case illustrated in the chart most of the recovery registered so far appears to have been accomplished during 1933, the progress since then being very moderate.

The difference between the number employed in the several industries in July 1929 and July 1936 as disclosed by the estimates under discussion is as follows (in millions):

Industry	Employed in July 1929	Employed in July 1936	Difference between 1936 and 1929
Agriculture	10.8	10.8[27]	0.0[27]
Manufacturing	10.5	8.8	−1.7
Wholesale and retail trade	5.8	5.2	−0.6
Building	2.8	1.2	−1.6
Steam railways	1.6	1.0	−0.6
Mining	1.0	0.7	−0.3
All other industries	15.0	13.5	−1.5
All industries	47.5	41.2	−6.3

In viewing the employment curves in the chart and the summary just preceding, it is necessary to bear in mind that changes in employment with respect to 1929

[27] If it is assumed that the discrepancy between the Census figure of the total workers on farms for January 1935 and the estimate incorporated in this series for the same date has been carried as a constant in the estimates for the subsequent months, the 1936 employment in agriculture would be close to 13 millions and the difference between 1929 and 1936 would become about plus 2 millions instead of zero. See note d to table on p. 135.

fail to tell the full story of the unemployment problem as it is today. It should be recalled that the number seeking employment has since been augmented by at least 4 millions; moreover, even for July 1929 the estimates show unemployment to the extent of about one million workers.[28]

III. EQUIVALENT FULL-TIME EMPLOYMENT

General figures of employment dealing with the number of persons on payrolls fall short of measuring the changes in the amount of time actually devoted by the population to production. At the height of economic activity there is usually a considerable amount of overtime work which a mere count of workers does not disclose, and in a period of slackening activity there is not only a decline in the number of employed but also a decrease in the average time worked by those retained on payrolls.

During this depression the discrepancy between the number employed and the time worked was particularly important because the tendency to spread work was fortified by government pressure. Hence the employment series which have been discussed in the foregoing section tend to overstate the volume of employment in the past few years and to understate the volume of unemployment.

To overcome this deficiency, an attempt has been made to represent the movement of employment in terms of full-time equivalents. It is self-evident that the concept and measurement of full-time employment are different for wage earners, salaried workers, and self-employed. For wage earners, full-time employment may be represented by an accepted number of hours per week

[28] This estimate, which includes those unemployed because of illness and voluntary leave and those who were in the process of changing jobs or seeking employment for the first time, is probably too low. See note 20, p. 136, and note 4, Appendix C.

or year, and the estimate may be made by converting payrolls into man-years. Salaried workers are not paid by the hour and therefore hours of work cannot be used as a criterion of full-time employment; but it is possible to arrive at fair approximations of the number of salaried workers by converting payrolls into man-years on the basis of full-time annual rates of pay. A definition of full-time employment is more difficult when we consider the self-employed, for in their case the relationship between earnings and time given to work is obscured by other factors. Hence correction for partial employment on the part of entrepreneurs can be made only in a very rough manner, and that only for a limited group. But even though the composite estimates of full-time equivalents obtained by such methods do not possess a high degree of precision, they are believed to give a more accurate picture of the course of depression and recovery than do the more general employment data.[29]

1. Wage earners and salaried workers. In viewing the decline in the number of employees during the depression it is well to recall that even in 1929 there was considerable slack. In that year there were about 37 million wage earners and salaried workers in the country, but the aggregate volume of employment, computed on a full-time basis, was equivalent to the employment of 34.3 million workers.[30] Thus even in 1929 the margin between available personnel and the actual full-time employment amounted to about 2.7 million persons.[31]

[29] For a description of the method by which equivalent full-time employment was estimated see Appendix C, Section III.

[30] This estimate is practically the same as that obtained by the Department of Commerce. See Appendix C, Table 9.

[31] It should be stated that approximately 600,000 of the 37 million employees in 1929 were not working because of illness or voluntary leave. But this is offset by the fact that the estimate of equivalent full-time employment included the time given to work for pay by those classified as self-employed.

By 1932 the full-time equivalent of employees had declined to 23.9 millions, a drop from 1929 of over 10 millions, or almost 31 per cent. In the meantime, however, the total number available as employees had increased to at least 39.3 millions. Hence the unused human energy represented by unemployment among wage earners and salaried workers in 1932 was equivalent to about 15.4 million "man-years," or 39 per cent of the total. When put on a full-time basis, employment in 1933 was not any higher—and perhaps slightly lower—than in 1932. Since then there has been some recovery, in terms of full-time employment, but not so much as was shown by the general estimates of employment and unemployment. The explanation is that a great deal of the apparent increase in employment, during the life of the NRA at least, was accomplished through the increase in the amount of part-time employment; that is, the decrease in the average number of hours. If the final figures for 1936 were available, it is not unlikely that they would show that the situation has been reversed; the increase in equivalent full-time, or total number of hours, would be greater than the increase in the number on payrolls.[32]

[32] The American Federation of Labor has called attention to this fact in a report submitted to President Roosevelt which decries the lengthening of hours since the abolition of the NRA. The Federation estimated that "at least 4,576,501 workers were affected by the breakdown of labor standards between June 1935 and March 1936 as a result of the invalidation of the NRA. . . . 4,073,901 workers alone have suffered from the lengthening of hours. . . . As a direct result of this lengthening of the hours of work, 839,123 wage-earners have been deprived of possible re-employment in the current recovery." (The *A. F. of L. Weekly News Service*, July 11, 1936.)

For manufacturing alone the increase in average hours of work between the first eight months of 1935 and the same period for 1936 was nearly 7 per cent as compared with an increase in the number on payrolls of 5 per cent. Thus the rise in employment due to expansion of hours was apparently greater than that due to added workers.

2. *The self-employed.* At the beginning of 1930 there were about 9.6 million "gainful workers" in the United States who were self-employed. This figure, however, is not informative with respect to the productive human energy actually represented by the so-called entrepreneurial group. The group is composed of a variety of types whose position in the economic structure of the nation is not easy to define. The shoestring peddler who is part merchant and part mendicant is technically an entrepreneur and self-employed; likewise the self-sufficient mountain farmer who in a primitive fashion ministers to his own needs in practically the entire range of social and economic activity and whose contact with the main current of economic life is negligible is also an entrepreneur. Contrasted with these are the operators of large enterprises and professional practitioners, such as doctors, lawyers, consulting engineers, and the like. The difference in the position of the two broad classes of self-employed in our economic system is obvious, and it is significant that during the depression the number in the first group has increased, while that in the second—especially if active employment is considered—has decreased.

The self-employed include agricultural enterprisers and individuals in numerous trades and professions. In both classes there are some who are not operating on a commercial basis; that is, they are not producing goods for sale or exchange in the market. Most of these are found in agriculture[33] though many of our artists, painters, and sculptors work for themselves in the true sense of the word and only in a minor degree with a view to selling their wares. Available data are insuffi-

[33] As many as 498,000 farmers were reported as "self-sufficing" by the Census in 1930.

cient to warrant an estimate of the number outside of agriculture thus employed; but the group is in any case comparatively small.

During the depression self-employment in agricultural and in non-agricultural pursuits moved in opposite directions. Because of the limited business opportunities, the volume of self-employment in industry, trade, and the professions has materially decreased, for in these fields self-employment still means "working for others." Agriculture, on the other hand, although it now furnishes less employment to wage earners, has attracted an additional number of workers on a self-employed basis. Between April 1, 1930 and January 1, 1935 the number of farms was increased by 523,700.[34] Since obviously it was not an expansion of market demand for agricultural products that attracted city workers to the country, we may safely assign all the new farmers recorded in the 1935 Census to the non-commercial farm group.[35]

It would be unsafe to assume that these new farmers constitute a permanent addition to agriculture. For the most part they have come to the farm to weather the depression and will undoubtedly return to the city as soon as urban employment is re-established. Although technically they are employed, they may still be regarded as part of the non-agricultural labor force and

---

[34] "Reports for States with Statistics for Counties and a Summary for the United States," *United States Census of Agriculture: 1935*, Vol. I, p. xvi.

[35] The Bureau of the Census in commenting on the increase during the depression in the number of persons living on farms states that the increase "occurred around industrial centers, mining sections, and in areas often designated as 'subsistence farming.' Areas showing large increases in farm population include the southern Appalachians, eastern Ohio, and western Pennsylvania, the Ozarks, eastern Oklahoma, the Birmingham industrial area, New England, northern Minnesota and Wisconsin, and the Puget Sound and Willamette Valleys." "Farm Population," *United States Census of Agriculture: 1935* (rotoprint release).

from this standpoint they are part of the unemployed. Unless we assume that the depression has ushered in permanent changes in our social and economic life which involve a lower degree of inter-dependence and greater individual self-sufficiency—that is, a return to a lower material standard of living with perhaps greater independence and security—we must look for a reversal of the city-to-farm migration and a re-establishment of the pre-depression trend.[36]

In estimating the full-time equivalent of the self-employed in agriculture, the farm operators have been divided into two groups—those operating on a commercial basis and those who are self-sufficing. We have assumed that all additions to the number of farmers recorded by the Census between 1930 and 1935 fall in the self-sufficing group—for the reason that there has been no increase in production of or demand for farm products. In addition to farm operators, allowance has been made for unpaid family workers devoting full time to farming.[37]

No plausible method for estimating the extent of employment and unemployment among entrepreneurs outside of agriculture can be developed. The Department of Commerce has made rough allowances for fluctuations during the depression which we are accepting for the purposes of our estimates.

3. All workers. The results of the several adjustments which we have made in order to show a full-time equivalent of employment are combined in Tables 12 and 13, Appendix C. The estimates referring to commercial activities only are perhaps more significant than those

[36] The renewal of the farm-to-city migration is already apparent in the population estimates of the U. S. Department of Agriculture.

[37] For method employed and discussion of the estimates derived, see Appendix C, Section III.

which include self-sufficing farmers. These estimates, as well as the approximations of total unemployment based thereon, are shown in the chart below.

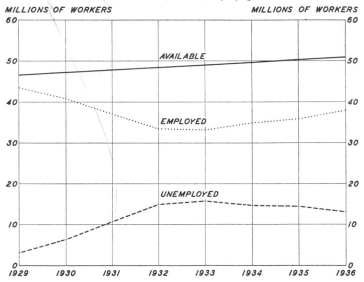

FULL-TIME EQUIVALENT EMPLOYMENT AND
UNEMPLOYMENT, 1929-36[a]

[a] Exclusive of non-commercial activities. Estimates for 1936 are preliminary. For data, see Appendix C, Table 13.

The gravity of the depression and the task of recovery is indicated by the fact that in 1933 the full-time equivalent of 15.8 million workers were unemployed. In 1935 the number was still about 14 millions out of a total of 50 millions. While data in terms of full-time equivalents are not available by months for the year 1936, other data on unemployment indicate that some 23 per cent of the nation's labor force remains unutilized in the fall of 1936.

The reader should bear in mind that in computing

this full-time equivalent, we made no allowance for any shortening of hours since 1929 for industrial wage earners; that the unemployed include some non-effectives;[38] and that the data take no account of those added to farming or those on work relief.

In conclusion, it would be of interest to compare the approximations of full-time equivalent employment and unemployment with the general estimates of unemployment treated in a previous section. Unfortunately the two methods of approach are quite different and no consistent comparison can be made on the basis of over-all figures. All that may be said is that the full-time equivalent figures show that there has been a greater waste of human energy during the depression than is shown by the general figures of unemployment.

4. Workers in manufacturing industries. For manufacturing, better data are available for comparing full-time employment with the more usual measures of employment. But even here the concept of full-time employment can be applied more concretely to wage earners than to salaried workers or entrepreneurs.[39] The comparison of the average number of wage earners on payrolls and the full-time equivalent in manufacturing is shown in the chart on page 150. Both are expressed in terms of 1929 as 100.

In 1929 the difference between the average and the equivalent full-time expression was insignificant. By both calculations the number of wage earners was about 8.8 millions. In subsequent years, however, the divergence is considerable. By the index based on the average number on payrolls, manufacturing employment in 1932

[38] For adjusted figure of unemployment, see Chap. IX, p. 234, and Appendix C, Table 16.
[39] A summary for all workers in the industry is shown in Appendix C, Table 14.

stood at about 61 per cent of 1929; but, in terms of man-hours, employment in 1932 went down to almost 50 per cent of 1929. Likewise, recovery from the 1932 low has progressed less in terms of total man-hours (that is, full-time equivalents) than in the number of workers on payrolls.[40] In 1935 the average number of wage earners

EMPLOYMENT OF WAGE EARNERS IN MANUFACTURING
INDUSTRIES, 1929-35[a]
(1929 = 100)

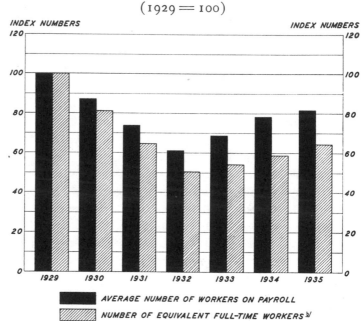

[a] For data, see Appendix C, Table 15.
[b] Computed at constant average hours per year.

[40] As stated elsewhere, two stages in re-employment may be distinguished. During the NRA period additions to payrolls represented to a large extent reduction of hours. Later, after recovery got under way, some expansion of employment was made by reinstating more normal hours for those already employed as well as by taking on additional workers.

employed in manufacturing was nearly 82 per cent of the average in 1929. The total number of man-hours, however, was less than 65 per cent of the 1929 level. In other words, in 1935 wage earners in manufacturing worked on the average only about four-fifths as many hours as in 1929. Part of this decrease was in accordance with the normal trend for reduced hours of work which was established prior to the depression and does not represent deterioration in income; but a large part represents involuntary restriction of working time and earnings due to the depression. The pre-depression trend in the standard hours of work shows an annual rate of decrease of about one-half of one per cent. If this is assumed to be still applicable, hours worked in 1935 would be about 97 per cent of those in 1929.

The question of what the full-time working hours in manufacturing *should* be today as compared with 1929 is a matter of opinion. Some argue that 30 hours a week, or about 1,500 hours a year, are at present socially desirable and possible. Since the average for manufacturing in 1929 was about 2,400 hours, the reduction to 1,500 hours would mean a decrease of about 37.5 per cent. At the rate of 1,500 hours per wage earner, the aggregate man-hours worked in 1935 would represent an equivalent number of workers surpassing the actual number employed in 1929. If 40 or some other number of hours were regarded as desirable, a very different result would be obtained. It is essentially by this sort of manipulation that advocates of the shorter working week hope to eliminate unemployment.[41]

If we may assume that, in the absence of the disturbances produced by the depression, working hours would have been reduced approximately in accordance with

[41] Possible effects upon production are not here in question.

pre-depression trends, the working week in 1935 would have been about 97 per cent of what it was in 1929 (see above). Corrected by this percentage, the equivalent full-time manufacturing employment in 1935 stood at approximately 66.5 per cent as compared with 100 in 1929. On this basis manufacturing employment in 1935 was still one-third below the 1929 level, which is the same as saying that an increase of 50 per cent in manufacturing employment in 1935 would be necessary before the 1929 volume would be reached.

The employment situation in manufacturing during the depression may be further clarified by comparing the equivalent full-time employment with the number of persons attached to the industry. Such a comparison can, of course, be made only in the broadest terms for, in the first place, the number attached to manufacturing ean be no more than a hypothetical approximation,[42] and, in the second place, there is a difference in quality between the employed portion of the workers and the total which cannot be equalized. Theoretically, at least, the average efficiency of the employed is higher than that of the entire group, which includes those who are unemployed on account of inefficiency. None the less, it is useful to relate employment even to the rough estimates of the number attached to manufacturing in order to obtain an approximate expression of the volume of unemployment.

In the chart on page 153 full-time employment of wage earners in manufacturing since 1919 is expressed as percentages of the number attached to the industry. In 1932 less than 50 per cent of the labor force assigned to

[42] For a description of the method by which the number of wage earners attached to manufacturing was estimated, see note *d* of Appendix C, Table 15.

manufacturing industries was used as compared with about 93 per cent in 1929 and 66 per cent in 1921. Recovery since 1932 has been slow. In 1935 full-time employment was still little more than 60 per cent of the

FULL-TIME EMPLOYMENT AND UNEMPLOYMENT OF
WAGE EARNERS IN MANUFACTURING INDUSTRIES,
1919-36[a]

[a] In percentages of the total number of wage earners attached to manufacturing; full time is taken as 2,400 hours per year. Estimates for 1936 are preliminary. Based on data in Appendix C, Table 15.

number attached to manufacturing. In 1936, if we may judge from partial data, it is still running at only about 70 per cent of 1929.

Before we leave the discussion of the employment situation in manufacturing it is significant to note that since the World War there has been a marked tendency toward contraction in the volume of employment furnished by manufacturing. Despite the increase in population, the number of wage earners in 1929 was lower than in 1919. The decrease cannot be explained by cyclical differences in economic activity between the two years for in 1929 manufacturing production was the highest ever attained and was, in fact, almost 50 per cent higher than in 1919.

An opposite tendency from that observed in the case of wage earners is found for salaried workers (see Appendix C, Table 14). The number of the latter has tended to increase. But even when wage earners, salaried workers, and entrepreneurs are combined, the evidence forces the conclusion that in absolute numbers manufacturing is barely holding its own in furnishing direct employment and, like agriculture, it is becoming relatively less important.

This point, although most important in its bearing upon the question of economic progress in general, is of great significance in the consideration of the problem of re-employment. The decrease in the relative importance of agriculture may to a large extent be ascribed to physical and extraneous causes. For the most part the products of agriculture are subject to an inelastic demand, and even moderate advances in agricultural efficiency are sufficient to keep up the requirements of an increasing population without the need for expansion in agricultural employment. (This is not to imply that the American people have reached the saturation point in the consumption of agricultural products.) Moreover, American agriculture had to a considerable degree been developed on the basis of an export market which is being contracted. Loss of foreign markets for agricultural products may in itself be (though it has not been during this depression) a mark of better economic opportunities in non-agricultural fields which tend to drain the farm population into other occupations.

An entirely different situation is encountered in manufacturing. Manufactured products, by their very nature and variety, are not subject to the same limitations of demand as the products of agriculture. Even when we disregard the new products which are being developed daily, we can see that the requirements of the nation for manufactured commodities have no limits short of those set by the labor supply. The failure on the part of manufacturing to absorb an increasing labor force is therefore conditioned not by physical but by economic factors which are subject to modification.

In brief, the United States is emerging from the depression with an enlarged but weakened labor force. Although there are now over 4 million more workers than in 1929, efficiency has been lost through deterioration in skill and through occupational and geographical displacements. Such degeneration in the labor force as has taken place, however, is temporary and is being overcome by the process of recovery.

Unemployment has decreased considerably since the bottom of the depression. None the less, the number unemployed in 1936 may still be placed between 9 and 10 millions—some 7 to 8 millions more than in 1929. Under-employment on account of short hours would raise these estimates.

On a full-time basis such as prevailed in 1929, more than 20 per cent of the nation's labor force remains unutilized in 1936. This percentage, however, somewhat exaggerates the re-employment problem, since it is subject to a downward adjustment on account of the shortening of work hours for industrial workers incidental to the normal course of economic progress. Also, it disregards work relief and other temporary depression pursuits.

CHAPTER VII

PRODUCTION AND PRODUCTIVITY

The inter-dependence of employment and production in relation to depression and recovery was emphasized at the beginning of the preceding chapter, which dealt with the employment aspect of the problem. If it were not for changes in productivity the estimates of full-time equivalent employment, in so far as they are themselves reliable, should fully reflect the course of production. Productivity has, however, been changing both with respect to the operation of long-run factors and because of shorter-run cyclical influences. It has responded not only to technological changes but also to shifts in the composition of industrial activity and in the composition of personnel within plants.

For example, the curtailment of production in capital goods industries and the relative maintenance of output of consumers' goods, particularly perishable goods, have given an entirely different value to the productivity factor of industry in the aggregate, since productivity in capital goods industries is in general different from that in other industries. Likewise, curtailment or expansion within a plant is likely to change the average productivity for the plant, even without any change in the technology, merely because personnel and equipment of lower or higher degrees of efficiency than the original average were either withdrawn or reinstated.

The study of production must therefore supplement that of employment in the analysis of the factors of depression and recovery. The condition of existing statistics makes it possible, moreover, to view the situation through production from angles which are inaccessible through the medium of figures on unemployment. The question of productivity also has a place in a discussion of recovery. To those who approach the problem of re-employment primarily from its distribution aspect—that is, as a means of distributing purchasing power—increasing productivity appears as an obstacle to recovery. Hence, in the present chapter, after examining the data on production, a brief statement is made with respect to changes in productivity before and during the depression.

I. THE COURSE OF PRODUCTION

In analyzing the changes which have occurred in production we shall consider changes in aggregate output as well as fluctuations in selected industries.

1. Volume of output. In the chart on page 158 the course of physical volume of production between 1919 and 1935 is traced by means of three annual indexes. The index for manufacturing and the composite index for eight major industries, including manufacturing, are based chiefly on direct measures of physical output,[1] while that for all industries and services is a rough measure based on estimates of all income from productive activities and an index of prices of commodities and services produced.[2]

The three indexes give a composite picture of what happened to output before and during the depression and suggest the degree of recovery which has been made since 1932. From each of the three indexes it appears that physical volume of production in 1932 approxi-

---

[1] Compiled by the National Bureau of Economic Research.

[2] Neither the income estimates nor the price index is of a high order of precision. The price index, particularly, is a rough instrument of known as well as unknown shortcomings. In fact no really satisfactory index of the general price level can be constructed. None the less it is helpful in portraying the general movements in total product, though it is not to be relied upon for fixing minor changes.

mated that of the low point reached in the depression of
1920-21. However, since in the meantime the population
had increased more than 15 per cent and productive effi-

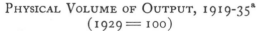

PHYSICAL VOLUME OF OUTPUT, 1919-35[a]
(1929 = 100)

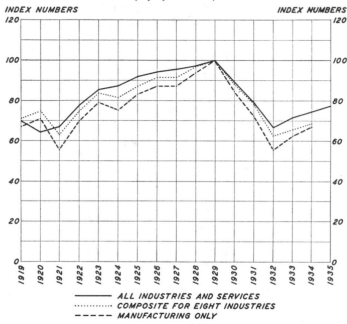

———— ALL INDUSTRIES AND SERVICES
·············· COMPOSITE FOR EIGHT INDUSTRIES
– – – – MANUFACTURING ONLY

[a] For data, see Appendix C, Tables 17 and 18.

ciency had increased also, relatively speaking the volume
of production was reduced much more drastically in the
depression of the thirties than in 1920-21. Preliminary
estimates indicate that, in terms of the indexes plotted in
this chart, the physical volume of output at the middle
of 1936 was at the rate of about 88 per cent of that in
1929.

Recovery is a relative term; it implies comparison
with a standard of "normalcy." The selection of the

standard of comparison is therefore important. The most acceptable standard is not a point in the past nor an average for a past period, but a trend tracing the probable performance which would currently obtain if the temporary factors responsible for economic disturbances were eliminated. Thus, for instance, it would not be fair to judge recovery in production by reference to any single year or the average for any series of years in the pre-depression period. Both the growth in population and in technological progress should justify a much higher level of production in 1936 than in any previous year. Though the trend is the most appropriate standard of comparison, its use for the purpose of measuring the degree of recovery from the low point reached in 1932 is fraught with difficulties; the extraordinary duration of the depression makes it necessary to extrapolate for more than six years beyond the point for which usable data are available. It is therefore important to keep in mind that such results as we obtain in connection with the trends computed on pre-depression data are tentative and rough approximations only.

An examination of the existing production data indicates that prior to 1930 output in manufacturing was increasing at the rate of about 4 per cent per annum and that total product in all industries and services was increasing at the annual rate of about 2.5 per cent.[3] From the projection of these trends it would seem that manufacturing production should have been about 26 per cent higher in 1935, and 31 per cent higher in 1936 than in 1929. Likewise, the total national product in 1935 should have risen to about 116 per cent of 1929 and in 1936 to 119 per cent.

[3] Per capita production in all industries and services appears to have grown at the rate of about one per cent per annum. For data, see Appendix C, Table 18.

COMPARISON OF ACTUAL PRODUCTION SINCE 1929 WITH PRODUCTION TRENDS ESTABLISHED PRIOR TO THE DEPRESSION[a]

(1929 = 100)

I. Actual Production Compared to Pre-Depression Trends

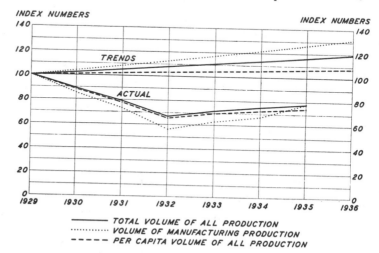

TOTAL VOLUME OF ALL PRODUCTION
VOLUME OF MANUFACTURING PRODUCTION
PER CAPITA VOLUME OF ALL PRODUCTION

II. Production Adjusted for Pre-Depression Trends

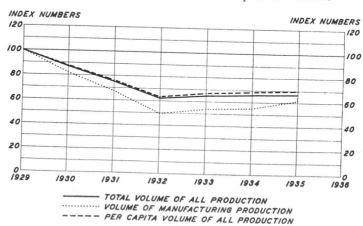

TOTAL VOLUME OF ALL PRODUCTION
VOLUME OF MANUFACTURING PRODUCTION
PER CAPITA VOLUME OF ALL PRODUCTION

[a] For data, see Appendix C, Table 18.

In the upper chart on page 160 the estimated output in all industries and in manufacturing alone since 1929 is compared with pre-depression trends. The gravity of the depression is here emphasized by the opposite movement of actual production and production trends. In 1932 manufacturing output was 44 per cent below that of 1929, while, hypothetically, it should have been about 12 per cent above. The degree of recovery since 1932 is minimized by the fact that in the meantime the *expected* output, as measured by trend, has increased. By 1935, although a very considerable expansion in output had taken place, the deficiency in product—that is, the difference between actual output and "normal"—was still not much smaller than in 1932.

The course of production since 1929 is further shown in the lower chart on page 160. Here the indexes of output are expressed as percentages of their pre-depression trends and therefore show actual production as proportions of what might have been expected had normal trends continued. As in the previous chart production in 1929 is taken as 100.[4]

From this chart it appears that manufacturing production (adjusted for trend) descended in 1932 to about 50 per cent of the 1929 level. It increased to about 54 per cent in 1933 and to 61 per cent in 1935. In the middle of 1936 it reached about 70 per cent. Similarly, the total output of all industries reached a low in 1932 of about 62 per cent of the 1929 level and recovered to about 67

---

[4] The fact that 1929 is taken as 100 implies the acceptance of the production in that year as "normal." This is not strictly in accord with the statistical concept of normal, since in reality the output of 1929 was above the trend. For our purposes, however, it is reasonable to take 1929 as a point of departure. The slack in employment and in physical capacity which existed in that year indicates that 1929 was not an abnormal year with respect to what was reasonably possible.

per cent by 1935[5]. Official figures of national income, which served as a basis for estimating the total annual product, are not available for 1936, but a rough estimate indicates that the total output as of the middle of this year (corrected for trend) was approximately 74 per cent of 1929. In other words, it appears that by the middle of 1936 we were still 25-30 per cent below the adjusted 1929 level in both manufacturing production and total output of goods and services. It is emphasized again that the figures should be taken only as approximations and that the hypothetical normal which has been projected perhaps sets too high a standard from which to gauge recovery.

2. *Output in selected industries.* The indexes for the eight industries for which the composite is given in the chart on page 158 are plotted in the chart on page 163. The indexes are expressed in terms of 1929 as 100, without any correction for trend. Construction volume fluctuated most violently during the period. From a 1928 peak of 108 the index for this industry dropped to 28 in 1933, a decline of almost 75 per cent. Agricultural production fluctuated the least: the lowest point reached by the index during the period under observation was not during the present depression but in 1921. The highest was in 1931, when it stood 11 per cent higher than the average for the entire period. Figures for output in manufacturing, mining, and transportation show approximately the same characteristics. Electric light and telephones reflect the strong upward secular trends of expanding industries, while the curve for street railways is modified by the fact that the industry is declining. In all cases, however, except agriculture, the decline from

---

[5] On a per capita basis the recovery was slightly greater. The difference is due to the change in the rate of population growth.

INDEXES OF PHYSICAL VOLUME OF OUTPUT IN
EIGHT INDUSTRIES, 1919-34[a]
(1929 = 100)

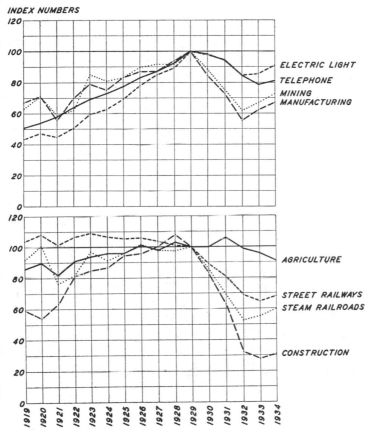

INDEX NUMBERS

ELECTRIC LIGHT

TELEPHONE

MINING
MANUFACTURING

AGRICULTURE

STREET RAILWAYS
STEAM RAILROADS

CONSTRUCTION

[a] For data, see Appendix C, Table 17.

1928-29 was halted about 1932. The turning point from depression, as shown by the monthly index of manufacturing output, has already been shown in Chapter IV.

II. CHANGES IN PRODUCTIVITY

Existing data are not sufficiently accurate to yield a precise measure of productivity. A rough index of productivity in manufacturing industries may, however, be obtained by combining our estimates of the number of equivalent full-time workers with an index of physical volume of production in manufactures which has been constructed by the National Bureau of Economic Research.

1. Productivity in manufacturing industries. It will be observed from the chart on page 165 that the index of productivity has, except for a few abnormal years, increased at a constant rate throughout the period from 1919 to 1935. The fitted trend shows that productivity per equivalent full-time wage earner in manufacturing increased at the rate of 4 per cent per annum.

This rate of increase, which is based on figures covering wage earners alone, somewhat exaggerates the actual increase in efficiency. The decline in the number of wage earners which accompanied the increase in efficiency has been offset to some extent by the increase in the proportion of salaried workers. Moreover, there is reason to believe—although no accurate measurements are available—that some of the functions formerly performed by the personnel of manufacturing firms—advertising, for instance—are now transferred to specialized agencies and services. Both the increase of office personnel and the transfer of functions, if incorporated into the index of productivity, would show a lower rate of increase than is obtained when productivity is computed on the basis of wage earners alone. A full correction is impossible, but when the salaried workers and proprietors and firm members are included, the rate of increase for the period is 3.5 per cent a year instead of 4.0 per cent.

MAN-HOUR PRODUCTIVITY IN MANUFACTURING, 1919-35[a]

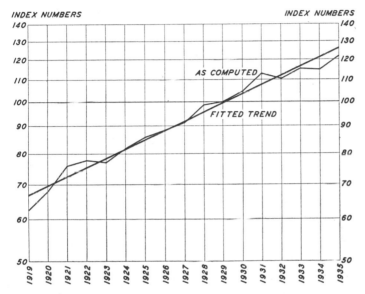

[a] Wage earners only. For data, see Appendix C, Table 21.

The annual deviations from the trend of productivity in manufacturing industries are traced in the chart on page 166. The period covered is not long enough to permit definite conclusions with respect to the course of productivity during prosperity and depression in general, but tentative observations may be useful.

It is generally accepted that productivity rises during depression and falls during prosperity. The logical explanation for this tendency is that during depression the less efficient workers are eliminated and those who remain, fearing loss of employment, apply themselves to their jobs with more than normal diligence and efficiency; at the height of prosperity, on the other hand, not only does efficiency suffer from the fact that marginal workers are drawn into industry, but the personnel in general becomes lax on account of the increased opportunities for finding other employment. This generaliza-

ANNUAL DEVIATIONS FROM TREND OF MAN-HOUR
PRODUCTIVITY IN MANUFACTURING, 1919-35[a]

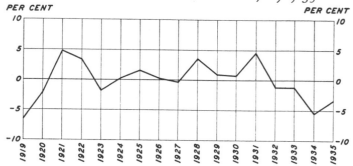

ᵃ Wage earners only. For data, see Appendix C, Table 21.

tion is completely supported by our data in so far as the depression of 1921 is concerned. Man-hour productivity, which had fallen below normal during the post-war boom, increased in 1921 and, while remaining considerably above the trend in 1922, declined to a low point with the expansion of industrial activity in 1923. Since then tendencies appear mixed. In spite of increasing prosperity, the index of productivity rose above the trend in 1928 and 1929 and contrary to expectations fell considerably below normal in the later years of the depression. The situation in 1928 and 1929 may of course be explained by the fact that the forces making for greater efficiency were so powerful in the late twenties that they overcame the tendencies toward lowered efficiency engendered by prosperity.[6] As a matter of fact, the productivity index was lower relative to the trend in 1929 than it was in 1928, which is in accord with the general theory.

During the first two years of the depression productivity ran according to expected behavior. The index rose in 1930 and again in 1931, reaching in the latter year a height above normal commensurate with that reached in 1921. However, instead of continuing to rise as the depression progressed, productivity fell sharply in 1932 and then again in 1934. This downward movement in the productivity index is not contradictory to the experience in previous depressions. It simply indicates that the factors favorable to increased productivity per manhour cannot be depended upon to operate when the depression lasts for a long time, for then the adverse forces become strong enough to offset the gains. In 1934 the operation of the NRA was undoubtedly an important factor in lowering man-hour productivity. The indiscriminate lowering of the working hours of those fully employed and the introduction of new workers were bound to lower the average efficiency, whatever compensating benefits may have resulted therefrom. Also, deterioration of equipment no doubt became an adverse factor during the later years.

2. *Productivity and technological unemployment.* Much confusion of thought has arisen during the depression with regard to increased productivity and tech-

[6] In part it may reflect only the inaccuracies of the data and the effect of including 1934 and not including 1935 in the calculations. (The index for 1935 has been excluded because only a preliminary estimate is available.) Without 1934, or with 1935, the trend would be lifted somewhat.

nological unemployment. The rapid rise in productive efficiency, which prior to the depression was regarded as a beneficial force leading to higher standards of living for the people, has since come to be feared as an increasing source of permanent unemployment. Drastic reductions of working hours have been advocated in order to spread the allegedly decreasing volume of work among the available workers. Aside from the obvious fact that the age of plenty is not yet here and that the majority of the people still have many unsatisfied wants, the actual increase in productivity has been grossly exaggerated.

Undue emphasis has been given to the problem of technological unemployment by reference to isolated cases of technological advances which have displaced labor. Some startling examples of what has taken place in the automobile industry in the short period since 1929 noted in a report of the NRA[7] have been unduly "universalized" and have intensified the fear of technological improvement. We do not mean to imply that technological unemployment resulting from sudden changes in technique is unimportant, but it is necessary to face the problem calmly and apply remedies which will overcome the strain without destroying the advantages. While the problem of technological change and its effect upon employment should not be under-estimated, it should also be kept in mind that the advances in the automobile industry can be duplicated only in limited areas of production.

While it is true that rapid progress in output per manhour has been made in certain industries, notably in manufacturing (see page 164), the net result for the entire range of economic activity as measured by per

[7] *Preliminary Report on the Study of Regularization of Employment and Improvement of Labor Conditions in the Automobile Industry*, Appendix B.

capita real income has not been so phenomenal. In *America's Capacity to Consume* it was roughly estimated that between 1900 and 1929 the per capita product from all economic activities, with price changes eliminated, in-

TREND OF PRODUCTIVITY IN MANUFACTURING[a] AND OF
OUTPUT PER GAINFUL WORKER IN ALL
ECONOMIC ACTIVITIES[b]
(1929=100)

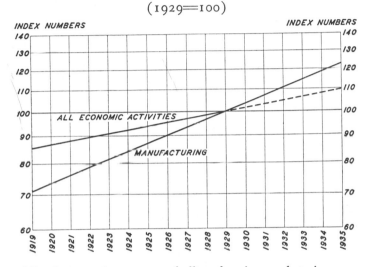

[a] Based on man-hour output of all workers in manufacturing, 1919-34. For data, see Appendix C, Table 20.
[b] Based on income produced adjusted roughly for price changes, 1909-29, with abnormal war and post-war periods eliminated. For data, see Appendix C, Table 18.

creased about 38 per cent. From the extension of a trend fitted to the estimates for the period 1909-29, with the years disturbed by the war eliminated, it appears that, were it not for the depression, the index, which in 1929 stood at 137.7, would in 1936 be about 147.5.[8] That is, following the normal rate of growth of general productivity, and under normal employment conditions, the in-

[8] The index is that shown on p. 150 of *America's Capacity to Consume* and refers to 1900 as 100.

crease in total per capita product in the seven years from
1929 to 1936 would be little more than 7 per cent,
despite the fact that productivity in manufacturing industries alone (as measured by trend) increased about
27 per cent in the same period. The trends of productivity for manufacturing alone and for all economic activities are compared in the chart on page 169. The difference in slope of the two lines shown indicates clearly
that the progress of productivity in economic activities
as a whole was much slower than it was in the limited
field represented by manufacturing.[9]

The reason why individual instances of phenomenal
technological advances are so misleading becomes clear
when we examine the figures concerning the occupational
and industrial distribution of the working population.
The area from which most of the examples of technological displacement of labor are generally drawn appears to be quite restricted. Manufacturing, where the
application of power machinery is most feasible and
where increased productivity has been most noticeable,
had less than 25 per cent of the country's workers in
1929 (11.8 millions out of 48.8). Even this number
included a considerable proportion of owners and salaried employees, who are not as susceptible to techno-

[9] The concepts of productivity represented by the two lines differ
somewhat. The line for manufacturing represents total manufacturing
output divided by an approximation of aggregate hours of actual work,
while the trend for all economic activities refers to total national product
divided by the total number of gainful workers corrected for changes in
the standard hours of work. The latter reflects the effect of non-techno-
logical as well as technological factors, whereas the former does not. A
further difference, necessitated by the nature of the data, is that while the
trend of manufacturing productivity is computed on the basis of all
years for which adequate data are available, normal as well as abnormal,
the trend of "over-all" productivity is computed on the basis of normal
years alone, the depression period being omitted. See Appendix C, Tables
18 and 20.

logical displacement as are factory operatives. Only about 9.3 million wage earners were attached to manufacturing industries at the height of production in 1929. Even if we assume that great technological progress, corresponding to that in manufacturing, is still possible in mining and in some of the industries—principally steam railroads—reported by the Census under transportation and communication, the aggregate number of wage earners in all the industries subject to such progress would appear not to have exceeded 12 millions in 1929, which is less than 25 per cent of the enumerated gainful workers.

The other 75 per cent of the working population found employment in the direct-service occupations and the industries where hand labor is still the general rule. Here changes in productivity are slow, and serious displacement of workers by machines or other technological advances not of immediate likelihood. Trade, public service, the professions, domestic and personal services, clerical occupations, and miscellaneous services comprised some 22 million workers, or about 45 per cent of the working force, while agriculture, the building industry, and miscellaneous transportation activities included the rest of the 48.8 million workers reported by the 1930 Census of Occupations.

Potentially a very great amount of human energy may be released from the activities which have lagged in technological development. In the building industry prefabrication holds out hope for a substantial increase in output per worker. Likewise there are prospects that merchandising and distribution in general will in time be placed on a more efficient basis so that the required services will be rendered with a relatively smaller number of workers. In agriculture, too, technological changes are in sight which may release—particularly in the southern Cotton Belt—a portion of the agricultural workers for other pursuits. But on the whole a much smaller rate of increase in productivity may be expected in the activities which, with agriculture, comprise 75 per cent of the workers, than in the mass production operations. A large part of the goods and services entering into consumption will always remain of the "handmade" or "made-to-order" types which do not lend themselves to significant technological changes.

The professional and personal services, for example, cannot be subjected to mass production, and such improvements as will take place there will be through a better utilization of working time. In this connection it may safely be affirmed that such improvement as may occur in the efficiency of supplying these services will not result in a relative decrease of their personnel but in an expansion of the quality and volume of service rendered. We may be sure, for instance, that an increased productivity of personnel engaged in rendering medical services, which may result from a reorganization of medicine, would not mean a reduction of the number of physicians and surgeons per 1,000 population but in more and better service. The same applies to the building industry. The unsatisfied wants in housing are so great that it may reasonably be expected that lowering of costs of construction resulting from increased productivity will for a considerable period be followed by an expansion of the volume of construction rather than by a decrease in the demand for labor in the building industry.

Without minimizing the problem of technological unemployment—for there can be no doubt that changes in the processes of production through the introduction of labor-saving machinery work hardship upon the displaced workers by outmoding skills acquired through years of experience and by necessitating a readjustment to new conditions and loss of time and wages in the search for new employment—it is none the less clear that in general increased productivity can mean only increased prosperity. A rise in productivity in one industry in itself means increased demand for its own products or for the products of other industries, so that by and large it generates employment at the same time that it curtails it.

Increased productivity signifies that a given volume of product may be produced with a smaller number of workers than formerly and that the cost of production in terms of human effort has been decreased. In the simplest though not the usual case the entire saving in cost goes to those who remain as producers in the industry. When this is true the smaller number of participants, if they maintain full production, obtain an added product which is equivalent to the former production of the individuals who have been released. This extra product will presumably be placed on the market in exchange for new goods, the production of which will employ the released workers.

Presumably the increased demand for new production will materialize whether the added product per working hour resulting from the change in productivity is distributed in the form of higher wages to labor, lower prices to consumers, or higher profits or dividends to the entrepreneur or investor.[10] In other words, irrespective of how it is distributed, it has the potentiality of yielding more product for the population as a whole with no

[10] To be sure, the process may be interfered with by maladjustments arising from a disproportion between spending and saving. For full discussion, see H. G. Moulton, *The Formation of Capital*, especially Chap. X.

diminished employment (except temporary unemployment during the period of readjustment following any dislocation), rather than the same volume of production with a smaller number of persons employed. The increased prosperity resulting from the increase in productivity may of course be taken in the form of shorter hours. It is conceivable that in balancing additional goods and services against added leisure, the people would choose the latter. As a matter of fact, as the general productivity of the nation has grown, its benefits have been passed on partly in the form of more product and partly in shorter hours of work.

The idea of forcing lower hours (irrespective of whether or not we prefer added leisure to more goods and services) as a means of preventing technological unemployment is nothing but a revival of the blind machine-smashing days of the early stages of the industrial revolution. The idea acquires plausibility only in the darkness of despair. It is not based on mature analysis of the causes of unemployment and of the maladjustments underlying the depression in general; nor does it appear to be the result of an analysis which takes into consideration the long-run progress of the nation. While provision must be made for the victims of technological advances the process of rising productive efficiency must not be interfered with. It still remains to be proved either by logic or fact that restriction of hours of work for the purpose of spreading the "available jobs" at a time when we need an expansion of the supply of goods and services will solve even the immediate economic problems with which the nation is faced.

Those who see in shorter working hours a solution of unemployment are handicapped in their thinking by the fallacy that the nation is divided into two fixed groups—

those who have work to offer and those who seek employment—and that the amount of work to be done and the amount of funds available for wages are also fixed. Reasoning from this premise leads to the conclusion that a forced reduction of the hours of work would spread employment and wages to include everybody who is willing to work.

But, as a matter of fact, employers and employees (in the broad sense) are in essence not two separate and rigidly fixed groups. Under modern conditions we all work for one another and the employers and employees are fundamentally the same people. The manufacturer and the merchant offer employment only in so far as the people—composed chiefly of employees—are in a position to use goods and services. Employment and production are complementary concepts: one generates the other—one is not independent of the other. Maintaining or expanding the purchasing power of those employed, lowering prices to consumers, and making ample provision for those temporarily dislocated by technological changes would therefore seem to offer a more pertinent approach to the problem of technological unemployment than work spreading.

The production and productivity situation may be briefly summarized. Considerable recovery has been achieved in the output of goods and services in the United States in the past three years. By the middle of 1936 the output was only about 13 per cent below that of 1929, as compared with about 35 per cent in 1932. This statement, however, does not tell the whole story. When growth of population and normal progress are taken into account, output in 1936 appears to be 25-30 per cent below that indicated by the 1929 level.

Except for the possible setbacks incident to the deterioration of the labor force and capital equipment, and other temporary factors, there is no reason to believe that the trend in productivity has been retarded during the depression. On the other hand, there is no evidence that it has been accelerated. During 1930 and 1931 man-hour productivity was somewhat above normal, but since then—in manufacturing at least—various factors have kept it below the trend line. It is not unlikely that, with the re-establishment of more normal conditions, productivity will turn upward and the pre-depression rate of growth may be resumed.

In general it appears that increased productivity and the dire consequences sometimes attributed to it have been greatly exaggerated. Examples of startling technological change have necessarily been drawn from limited fields of economic activity. The majority of the people are normally engaged in work which is only moderately subject to the application of labor-saving devices. As a result, even though man-hour productivity in manufacturing has been increasing at the rate of about 3.5 to 4.0 per cent per year, for the economic system as a whole it has proceeded at the rate of only about one per cent per year.

CHAPTER VIII

ACCUMULATED NEEDS IN DURABLE GOODS

Much has been heard in recent years of the role of the so-called "durable goods" in the depression. Indeed the extraordinary decline of these industries from 1929 to 1933 and the tardy recovery of some of the most important of them since recovery began have been thoroughly publicized. We have been told variously that the revival of durable goods production is an indispensable condition of recovery, that genuine prosperity is impossible without full activity in the construction industry, that the "heavy industries" must be stimulated by public works' outlays, and so forth. The importance of the issues thus raised is evidently such as to warrant special consideration of the situation in these industries.

The durable goods industries are, moreover, regarded as of fundamental importance from the standpoint of providing work. It is contended that if existing unemployment is to be eliminated a large portion of the unemployed must be absorbed in the production of durable goods, where the greatest slack and the greatest production deficiency exist. In the present chapter we shall accordingly study the situation in the major divisions of the so-called durable goods industries with a view to indicating, as accurately as the available data will permit, the extent of the latent requirements or needs there existing. Then, in the ensuing chapter these production requirements will be translated into terms of employment possibilities.

As a preliminary to this discussion, it seems desirable to get a bird's-eye view of the nature and extent of the durable goods industries and to note their distinguishing economic characteristic.

First, what is meant by durable goods? For the present purpose they may be somewhat arbitrarily defined as goods having a normal useful life in excess of three years. They include buildings of all kinds, producers' plant and equipment, public works, and consumers' goods such as automobiles, refrigerators, vacuum cleaners, washing machines, furniture, and the like. The term is thus distinctly broader than capital goods or producers' goods, the function of which is to facilitate the processes of production. It includes a substantial proportion of the total supply of consumers' goods, the most important groups being private housing, household equipment, and automobiles. The reason for grouping producer goods and consumer goods having a long life under the single classification of durable goods is that they possess certain characteristics which make for similarity of behavior during periods of expansion and depression. Their primary common characteristic is the postponability of the demand for them.

Three principal factors account for the relative postponability of the production of durable commodities. The first is that current consumption of all such commodities need not be eliminated when new production ceases. A suspension of the production and distribution of food would result in almost immediate distress, while a cessation of house building would occasion no acute shortage of facilities for several years. As long as a community has an unconsumed stock of durable goods, it can continue to enjoy their use even though current output is entirely suspended.

The second factor relates to the relative urgency of the need for durable as compared with non-durable commodities. In the first place a great many durable commodities fall in the class of luxuries, and hence are more readily dispensable than are necessities. Postponement of the production of capital goods involves another consideration, namely, that in a period of recession the supply of existing capital goods greatly exceeds current demands for the products which can be turned out. Thence considerations of profit serve to postpone new construction until a more favorable time. Moreover, the curtailment of output in consumer goods industries results in a postponement of replacements of plant and equipment and thus in the demands upon capital goods industries for such equipment. In general, however, the decrease in the production of replacement equipment and repair materials is very much less than the decline in the output of new plant and equipment.

The third factor affecting the demand for durable goods is the availability of credit. Since durable goods commonly involve relatively large commitments, the buyers thereof usually find it necessary to supplement their own funds with borrowed money. This is especially the case with houses and with capital goods, both private and public. Under these circumstances, even when individuals are willing to assume the risks involved, the lenders of funds may be unwilling to make the necessary advances. The supply of credit available for the purchase of durable goods is itself subject to psychological swings. In certain types of loans, for example real estate mortgages, there are times when money is almost unobtainable on any terms. In consequence, the fluctuations in the demand for durable goods may be amplified by fluctuations in the availability of credit.

The construction and repair of durable goods ordinarily absorb a substantial portion of the productive energies of the nation. In the chart on page 181 we show the value of the annual output during 1919-33 of finished durable commodities, as compared with non-durable goods and with total production of commodities; also the relative importance of the principal types of durable commodities.

The durable portion of the total commodity production generally ranges between 30 and 50 per cent, the average for the entire period covered by the chart being about 42 per cent. It should be borne in mind that these figures relate to commodity production only, services being excluded; hence they overstate somewhat the relative importance of durable goods in the aggregate productive activity of the nation.[1] When allowance is made for services (for which no comprehensive and continuous statistics are available), it appears that on the average about one-third of the total productive effort goes into durable goods, the range of variation being roughly from 25 to 40 per cent.[2]

As the chart indicates, the decrease in the output of durable goods during the depression was vastly greater than that of non-durable commodities. Between 1929 and 1933 the value of durable goods produced decreased from 32 billion dollars to about 12.5 billions, while the output of non-durable commodities declined only from 36.8 billions to 31.2 billions. Statistical compila-

[1] The estimates of production of durable goods are *gross* and hence include goods currently consumed.

[2] The National Bureau of Economic Research has estimated that in 1929 the volume of services "not directly related to the production, transportation, and distribution of commodities" was about 17.5 billions (*Bulletin 52*, p. 5). This indicates that in that year the production of physical goods absorbed about 80 per cent of the entire economic activity of the country. Durable goods alone absorbed 39 per cent.

RELATIVE IMPORTANCE OF DURABLE GOODS
PRODUCTION, 1919-33[a]

I. ALL COMMODITIES

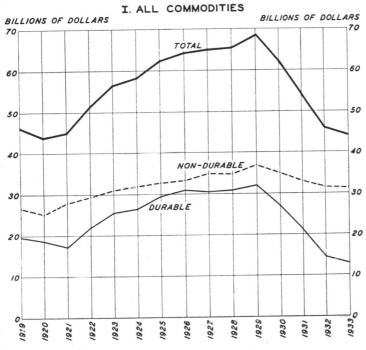

II. DURABLE COMMODITIES

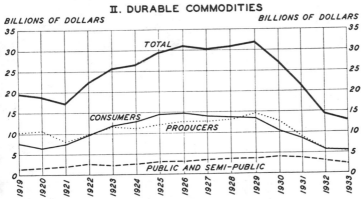

[a] The data have been computed throughout in terms of 1929 prices in order to eliminate, so far as possible, variations due to changing price levels. The figures for durable goods include repair parts and some, but not all, of other expenditures for upkeep and maintenance. For statistical sources and methods, see Appendix D, Section I.

tions are not yet available showing the degree of the recovery in the durable and non-durable lines since 1933, but in general it is true that the output of non-durable commodities is much closer to pre-depression levels than is the case with durable goods. The chart also indicates that the decline in producers' durable and consumers' durable goods was roughly in the same proportion. The decline in public and semi-public construction was somewhat less than that in the output of private durable goods.

The relative importance of the principal classes of durable goods production, including repairs, for the five-year period 1925-29 is shown in the accompanying table. Since the data are not precise they are given in round figures, within the probable range.

PRODUCTION OF PRINCIPAL TYPES OF DURABLE GOODS, 1925-29

Class	Five-Year Average Value (In millions of dollars)
Consumers' durable:	
Residential construction	4,500– 5,000
Passenger automobiles	3,750– 4,000
Other	5,000– 5,500
Total consumers' durable	13,250–14,750
Producers' durable:	
Steam railroads	2,600– 2,700
Public utilities	2,100– 2,200
Industrial enterprises	7,000– 7,500
Agricultural enterprise	900– 1,100
Total producers' durable	12,600–13,500
Public and semi-public construction	3,500– 3,700

There is very little difference in the aggregate volume of production of consumers' durable and producers' durable goods. Industrial enterprises, housing, and automobiles constitute the three most important groups. In the following pages each of these divisions of the durable goods industries will be given separate consideration.

I. RESIDENTIAL CONSTRUCTION

Because of the long life of houses and other residential buildings, readjustments in the fundamental factors of supply and demand require a long time to work themselves out. There is indeed some evidence of the existence of a typical building cycle of from 15 to 20 years' duration.[3] Consequently it is essential that the present housing situation be viewed in a considerable time perspective.

The chart on page 185 reveals the basic trends in residential construction from 1919 to 1936. Since the statistical data with reference to housing construction, demolitions, vacancies, and so forth, are far from precise, the chart must be regarded as representing merely a reasonable picture of changes in the supply and use of housing, based upon a careful appraisal of the evidence available. It should also be noted that the figures relate only to the non-farm housing of the country.

It will be seen that the peak in residential construction was reached in 1925. Thereafter the continued increase in vacancies and the decline in rents and values of existing properties resulted in a steady reduction in the volume of construction. By 1929 the output was only about one-half that of the peak year 1925. The extraordinary range of activity in the construction industry is indicated by the fact that in 1925 as many as 900,000 housing units (residences and apartments) were

[3] See chart by J. R. Riggleman in the *Journal of the American Statistical Association*, June 1933, p. 175. See also recent issues of the *Real Estate Analyst*, and the study by Homer Hoyt entitled *One Hundred Years of Land Values in Chicago*.

erected, whereas in the low year of the depression, 1934, only 60,000 units were built.

The enormous fluctuation in the number of houses constructed reflects their exceptional durability. The average life expectancy of new housing units is somewhere between 50 and 100 years. Since probably 90 per cent of the residential structures now standing in American cities are under 50 years of age, the volume of old-age demolitions is of insignificant proportions.[4] Even if we include demolitions from all causes, the total is relatively small; hence new construction needed to replace old dwellings destroyed is ordinarily but a small part of the total. In the decade of the twenties new building was roughly ten times the volume of demolitions, the latter averaging about 70,000 a year.[5] This means that the predominant factor in the demand for new housing is not replacement but expansion in the total number of units occupied. This expansion is governed primarily by the growth in the number of families.[6]

The line on the diagram marked "potential occupancy" indicates the occupancy that would have been expected under prosperity conditions. The difference between actual occupancy and potential occupancy reflects three factors: (1) doubling up of families, (2) post-

---

[4] The *Real Property Inventory*, covering 64 cities at the end of 1933, found 91.7 per cent of such buildings under 50 years of age. F. J. Hallauer's computations based on this inventory lead him to believe that the average life expectancy of new dwellings exceeds 100 years ("Population and Building Construction," *Journal of Land and Public Utility Economics*, February 1936). Roy Wenzlick has found in a study of St. Louis that 72 per cent of residential structures are standing on their 50th anniversary (*Real Estate Analyst*, May 1934).

[5] See Appendix D, Section III.

[6] Individuals maintaining separate living quarters are considered as families.

poned marriages, and (3) a shift of urban population to farms. The first two of these factors are clearly of a temporary character; and in view of the fact that the farm population of the country remained practically sta-

TRENDS IN THE HOUSING INDUSTRY, 1919-36[a]

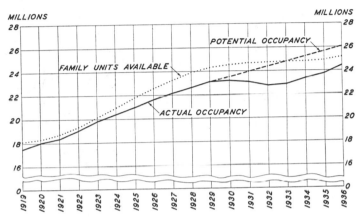

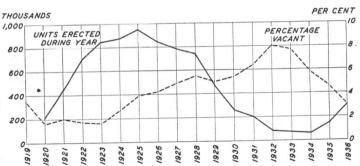

[a] For sources and methods, see Appendix D, Section II. All data except those for dwellings built each year relate to December 31.

tionary throughout the twenties it is reasonable to assume that, with the return of prosperous conditions, there will be a return flow from farm to city; in fact the movement has already begun. In any event, that line on the chart represents the potential occupancy on the basis of the assumptions here made.

In the light of this brief survey we may now ask: What are the construction needs in the near future, resulting from the restricted building of the last seven years, demolitions, and the normal growth of population? The amount of new building needed cannot, of course, be indicated with *precision* for it depends to a considerable extent upon indeterminate factors. It is nevertheless possible to gauge the probable requirements in a crude way on the basis of certain assumed trends. If we assume that the rural population in the future will be no larger than it was in the decade of the twenties,[7] that population growth and marriage will proceed at the rate currently indicated, and that the demolition of houses will continue at a somewhat increased rate, we can indicate the approximate number of housing units that will need to be constructed in the near future if the population is to be housed on the same plane as before the depression.

For the purposes in hand we shall project these requirements over a period of five years, from 1937 to 1941 inclusive. They depend upon: (1) the present accumulated deficiency or arrearage resulting from population growth and restricted construction during the last seven years; (2) the increase in the number of families requiring housing accommodations in the next five years; and (3) the rate of demolition of existing houses. On a conservative basis the estimated requirements work out as follows:

[7] The farm population was practically stationary in the twenties and it seems not improbable that the return movement to the farms during the depression will prove a temporary phenomenon and that, with the return of full prosperity, the farm population will be no larger than it was in 1929.

Accumulated deficiency, 1930-36 .... 2,000,000 units
Increase in urban families, 1937-41 .... 2,000,000 units
Demolished housing replaced, 1937-41 ..... 500,000 units

If spread equally over the five-year period the total number of units required would be approximately 900,000 annually, representing a value at current prices of over 4 billion dollars a year. Repairs on the housing inventory as a whole would increase this total to about 5 billions annually. It will be recalled that this computation relates to non-farm residential construction only.

In this computation we have not assumed any new shifts in the location of urban population such as occurred in the twenties. Nor has allowance been made for any possible wholesale destruction of old houses, either as part of social slum-clearance programs or because of new developments in housing construction which would provide better accommodations at much lower costs.

This annual average requirement of approximately 900,000 units during the next five years may be compared with an actual average of 750,000 during the five years 1925-29, and an average of only 160,000 during the last seven years. To give this country by 1941 housing facilities equal, on a per capita basis, to those of 1929 would require an average annual construction about 20 per cent greater than that during 1925-29, over five times as great as the average during the last seven years, and three times as great as that in 1936.

Again it must be emphasized that we are not here indulging in prophecy as to the actual volume of construction which will be undertaken in the next five years. Developments will depend in part on the general trend of business and in part upon factors peculiar to this industry itself, particularly the level of costs in relation to rents and values. We are for the present concerned

only with indicating in a rough general way the potentialities in the field of residential construction. What
these potentialities mean in terms of employment will
be considered in the following chapter.

It should be noted, in passing, that the great bulk of
the present construction is under private auspices. Notwithstanding the strenuous efforts of the Public Works,
Relief, and Resettlement Administrations in the erection
of urban housing, only about 50,000 units will have been
constructed in a period of three years. Even this paltry
volume promises to be greatly reduced with the completion of existing projects; and it remains to be seen
what efforts may be made along this line in the future. In any case, public construction will doubtless play
a relatively minor role in the next few years.

II. PASSENGER AUTOMOBILES

The purchase and repair of passenger automobiles is
of a magnitude comparable to that of residential construction, amounting between 1925 and 1929 to roughly
4 billion dollars annually. Significant changes in this
field of activity are shown in the chart on page 189.

The use of passenger automobiles, as indicated by
their total gasoline consumption, showed remarkable
stability during the depression, the low year (1932) being about the same as in 1929 and the average for the
period 1930-35 being materially higher. Despite this
high level of consumption, however, the sale of new
cars suffered a drastic decline. In the low year the number marketed domestically was only one-third of the
1925-29 average, while for the years 1930-35 the average was but 60 per cent of the pre-depression level.

This curtailment of new car output and distribution
served to halt for a time the growth in the number of
cars in use, but it was insufficient to effect any great

PRODUCTION, CONSUMPTION, AND SUPPLY OF
PASSENGER AUTOMOBILES, 1925-35[a]

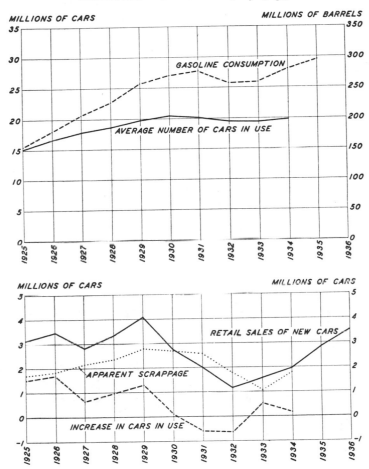

[a] For sources of data and methods, see Appendix D, Section IV.

reduction from levels previously attained, the maximum
shrinkage being something like 6 per cent. The smallness
of this contraction was in part due to a reduction in
scrappage rates during the depression as a result of the

use of cars beyond their normal age and condition for retirement; but an even more important contributory factor was the low average age of the pre-depression automobile inventory.

Because of the rapid expansion of that inventory (the number of cars in use rose 43 per cent in the five years prior to 1930) it was relatively overweighted with young units, and it contained, therefore, an exceptionally large volume of unconsumed mileage. This is estimated to have been two-thirds of the mileage contained by an equal number of absolutely new units at the end of 1929.[8] Thus there was a large reservoir from which withdrawals could be made during the depression. That these withdrawals far exceeded replacements is strikingly evidenced by the estimate that the unconsumed mileage in the car inventory fell from 1,067 billions of miles at the end of 1929 to 671 billions at the end of 1934.[9] By the end of 1936 little progress will have been made in the refilling of this reservoir, despite the fact that the number of cars now in use is probably at least as high as before the depression. Indeed, it appears that 1936 was the first year since 1929 during which there was any expansion of the unconsumed mileage in the inventory.[10]

[8] J. W. Scoville estimates the average mileage expectancy of a new car at 77,500 miles, and the average unused mileage of cars in use at the end of 1929 at nearly 54,000. *Behavior of the Automobile Industry in Depression*, p. 19.

[9] The same, p. 19.

[10] If we assume that the average car runs 10,000-11,000 miles a year, and that the potential mileage of the average new car is 75,000-80,000 (see Scoville, *Behavior of the Automobile Industry in Depression*), we conclude that 1936 saw a mileage consumption of 200-220 billions, as against additions to the inventory of 260-280 billions. On this basis it would appear that the unconsumed mileage inventory at the end of 1936 would be approximately 720 billions.

Since the extraordinary volume of unconsumed mileage in 1929 was the result of an age distribution of the car supply to be found after a period of rapid growth, it must not be assumed that it represents a norm to be regained irrespective of the future rate of growth.

The present passenger car inventory is relatively over-weighted with units that are approaching superannuation and retirement, and underweighted with units of recent vintage. Although, as we have just observed, the inventory as a whole is as large as it was at the end of 1929, the number of cars under three years of age is smaller by nearly 2 millions (8.2 millions as against 10.1), while those under four years of age fall short by nearly 4 millions (9.7 millions as compared with 13.6). Some millions of people are driving cars older than they are accustomed in good times to "trade in" for new ones, while other millions whose circumstances are such that they ordinarily turn in one used car for another are likewise driving vehicles older than they would continue to use in prosperity.[11] This qualitative deficiency of the present inventory in relation to the prosperity standards of the car-using public is certain to take the form of released demand with improvement in economic conditions. It should be added in this connection that the large number of old cars in the present stock indicates exceptionally heavy scrappage in the near future, a factor that will convert a qualitative deficiency into a quantitative one.

Even the present supply of cars appears deficient quantitatively in relation to potential prosperity demands. The number of cars in use has not increased since 1929 in proportion to the growth in population. The number of families in the United States is now about 10 per cent greater than it then was. This would indicate a

[11] The state of the inventory in the hands of those who ordinarily buy their cars new is of course more directly related to the prospective demand for new output than is the condition of the inventory in the hands of those who trade one used car for another. The latter is significant indirectly, however, through its effect on the used car market and on the relationship between new and used car prices. This relationship has much to do with the demand for new units.

considerably further expansion in the number of cars even if the ratio of cars to family population remained unchanged. That ratio was, however, rapidly expanding before the depression, and there appears no convincing reason to doubt that a return to prosperity and reasonably full employment would see considerably higher ratios than then prevailed. The potential deficiency of cars attributable to these factors is evidently large.

While much progress has been made since the bottom of the depression in freshening up the passenger car inventory of the country and while there has been a moderate expansion in its size, it is nevertheless clear that the process has considerably further to go before the potential deficiency resulting from the curtailment of production during the depression has been eliminated.

The requirements for passenger car construction over the next five years may—on the basis of certain assumptions—be indicated in a rough general way. These assumptions are: (1) that a normal situation with respect to the age of cars would be one in which on the average their life was nearly half spent—a little over 50 per cent of their mileage unconsumed; and (2) that the number of automobiles in proportion to population would be at least as great in 1941 as it was in 1929.

As has been pointed out, because of the preponderance of old cars, the unconsumed mileage, on the average, was below "normal" at the end of 1936. We estimate that to obtain a normal inventory situation would require nearly a million new cars. The per capita ownership of automobiles has also declined; and we estimate this deficiency at the end of 1936 at approximately 2 million cars. The total backlog is thus about 3 million cars.

To provide for the growth of population in the next

five years would require well over a million cars. In addition, there is the normal replacement of worn-out cars. If we assume an average life of seven or eight years, the replacement requirements in the next five years would amount to more than 3 million cars a year. The total requirement, thus computed, is roughly 20 million cars in the next five years—or an average annually of about 4 million cars. This may be compared with domestic sales between 1925 and 1929 of about 3.4 million cars. On the basis of the present average price per car, this would represent an expenditure of about 3 billion dollars annually.

Whether such a volume of automobile demand will actually develop will of course depend upon the state of business activity as a whole, about which we are here making no prediction. The estimate merely affords a rough indication of minimum requirements if the per capita consumption of automobiles is to be on a plane equal to that of the years just before depression. If we may judge by the experience of the past the actual production might, under favorable business conditions, be even higher than these estimates.

III. OTHER CONSUMERS' DURABLE GOODS

Apart from housing and automobiles, durable consumers' goods constitute a miscellany of items such as household furniture, refrigerators, vacuum cleaners, washing machines, ironers, radios, and mechanical equipment generally. In the late twenties consumer expenditures for this group of commodities averaged in excess of 5 billion dollars yearly.

The durability of most of these articles is not very great—a matter of a few years—and their initial cost as compared with houses and automobiles is small. Both of these characteristics help to account for the fact that despite wide variations in the behavior of different items the group as a whole displayed a greater degree of resistance to decline during the depression than did houses or automobiles.[12] A further factor in this relatively good resistance is the existence of a number of component items the sale of which prior to 1930 was increasing rapidly. This condition obtained in the case of articles recently introduced or recently brought within reach of the mass market. Examples are especially numerous in the field of electrical equipment, such as refrigerators, radios, ironing machines, ranges, clocks, dishwashers, heating pads, percolators, toasters, and waffle irons. The effect of the depression on items for which the sale during prosperity had been rapidly expanding was in general a much smaller decline from 1929 levels than would have occurred had the market been already saturated. In extreme instances it merely slowed up without stopping the growth in unit sales, while in some other cases unit sales remained at about the 1929 figure.[13] Such items helped to make the decline in the "all other" consumers' durable goods category as a whole less than that shown by established goods with relatively saturated markets such as household furniture, physical sales of which declined about 60 per cent from 1929 to 1932.[14]

Notwithstanding a considerable number of new and rapidly spreading items like radios and mechanical refrigerators, the fact remains that the bulk of the demand

[12] If adjustment is made for price changes, the maximum decline from prosperity high to depression low (in annual terms) was over 90 per cent for new housing, and over 70 per cent for new automobiles, as compared with a little over 50 per cent for the "all other" category.

[13] See *Electrical Merchandising*, January 1936, p. 3.

[14] Estimated from trend of furniture store sales, with adjustment for price changes.

in the "all other" category is of a replacement character. The number of households in the country seldom expands at a rate exceeding 2 or 3 per cent annually. It is obvious, in view of the limited durability of most articles in this category, that for those already in general use the normal replacement market is many times as great as that arising from the increasing number of consumers. This applies especially to such things as furniture and standard house furnishings which are employed in some form by every household. Even for a commodity so recently introduced as the radio, however, it has been estimated that 73 per cent of the current output goes for replacement and only 27 per cent for extending the number of users.[15]

The rate at which the existing inventory of these goods was consumed or worn out probably did not change very materially during the depression. Their owners continued to use them as long as they could be made to serve regardless of whether they could be replaced when discarded. Whether, or to what extent, the inventories actually declined in terms of number of units it is impossible in most cases to say. It is certain, however, that in many cases they failed to keep pace with the growth of population, and thus some deficiency undoubtedly exists in 1936.

As to the accumulation of a qualitative deficiency in the existing inventories there can be even less doubt. The age distribution of the inventories shifted unfavorably and came to have an abnormally large proportion of old and obsolete units. For many of the articles in this

---

[15] *Radio Retailing*, January 1936, p. 14. The calculation excludes automobile receiving sets. The early appearance of replacement demand in this and many other cases is due more to rapid obsolescence than to actual wear. Many articles of recent introduction are improved so fast that they become obsolete in short order.

field, obsolescence from style changes and mechanical improvements is very rapid, and any aging of the inventories due to a suspension of purchasing during the depression builds up a strong potential demand to be released by more favorable conditions.

Comprehensive data for the output of this class of goods since 1933 are not available; but it is evident from fragmentary evidence that we have already had a recovery that has placed the sale of many items in new high territory and has lifted the class as a whole most of the way back to former levels. It seems certain, however, that the bulk of the deficiency accumulated during the depression remains to be repaired.

Because of the wide range of commodities included in this classification and the unsatisfactory character of much of the data, it is particularly hazardous to present estimates of requirements over the next five years. However, that a deficiency of considerable magnitude will exist at the end of 1936 is not open to doubt. Moreover, if new residences are constructed during the next five years at the rate indicated in a preceding section, it is evident that there will be accompanying needs for new household furnishings and equipment. Taking account of the deficiency in existing household furnishings and equipment, the increase in the number of households, the normal replacement, and figuring on the basis of present prices, we would estimate that the minimum requirements over the next five years would represent a level of production at least 10 per cent above that of the 1925-29 period. This would be at the rate of approximately 6 billion dollars a year.

IV. STEAM RAILROADS

Railroad expenditures for capital and maintenance purposes averaged from 1925 to 1929 over 2.5 billion dollars annually. The average for the period 1930-36 inclusive has been only half this total. In the low year of the depression these expenditures shrank to only 825 millions; in 1936 the outlays have increased to nearly 1.5 billions.[16] As a basis for the discussion which follows, we present on page 199 a graphic picture of some of the major factors and trends in the railway situation.

A glance at the top section of the chart shows the drastic curtailment in the construction of both equipment and new roads which occurred after 1930. For five years the output of new rolling stock was almost negligible, falling so far short of the current scrappage of old units that the total stock of equipment owned by the railroads shrank continuously (see second section of the chart). Notwithstanding a considerable increase in the production of equipment in 1936,[17] it did not suffice to prevent a further decline in the existing inventory during that year.

In the case of roadbed and structures the effect of the curtailment of new capital outlays was not to reduce inventories but rather to check the modernization of facilities already under way. The scrappage of railway lines has been comparatively negligible, abandonments amounting between 1929 and 1936 to only 2 or 3 per cent of the total mileage in operation, but the roads have fallen far behind their original program for improving their trackage and structures to meet the requirements of modern operating standards. The *Railway Age* observes that the railroads "have never gone through a period of five years when they bought so little new equipment, and in which so many changes in the equip-

[16] Maintenance expenditures are computed exclusive of charges for depreciation and retirements.

[17] No satisfactory figure for the year as a whole is available at the time of writing.

ment offered them were made, as in the last five years. The prolonged lack of buying, the changes in transportation competitive conditions, and the development of new kinds of equipment and materials have made a vastly larger part of railway facilities obsolete than ever was the case before."[18]

Because of the complicated character of the problem it is exceptionally difficult to estimate the construction and maintenance requirements of the railroad industry. Unlike other durable goods industries, no increase in basic plant (miles of railway line) is necessary, but extensive rebuilding and re-equipping is essential if the railroads are to be placed in condition to handle satisfactorily an increased tonnage. At the same time, however, there have been marked improvements in the character of equipment and in operating efficiency which tend to lessen the amount of investment required for a given volume of business. Nevertheless, it is possible to arrive at a rough estimate of requirements—on the assumption that traffic increases not only to pre-depression levels but expands in proportion to the increase in population. It is necessary to consider the situation separately with respect to roadway and structures and equipment.

1. Way and structures. During the depression there was a drastic curtailment of improvements in the form of heavier rails, additional ballast, new signal systems, grade reductions, straightened track, and so forth, outlays for such purposes in 1933 being less than 20 per cent of those in 1929. The under-maintenance of road-

---

[18] *Railway Age,* Jan. 4, 1936, p. 4. See also the following reports by the Federal Co-ordinator of Transportation: *Technical Improvements in Railroad Equipment, Roadway and Structures,* Jan. 27, 1935; *Inspection of Freight Cars and Locomotives,* Jan. 4, 1934; *Freight Car Equipment,* Nov. 25, 1933; and *Steam Locomotives,* Apr. 24 and June 9, 1934.

RAILROAD PLANT AND EQUIPMENT, 1921-36[a]

I. ROAD AND EQUIPMENT BUILT
(1929=100)

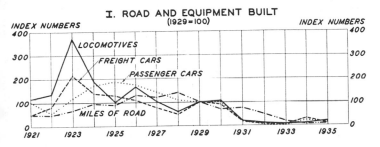

II. AMOUNT OF EQUIPMENT OWNED, DEC. 31
(1929=100)

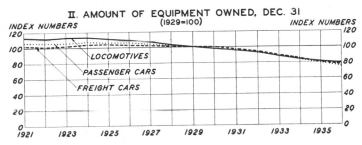

III. MAINTENANCE OF ROAD AND EQUIPMENT

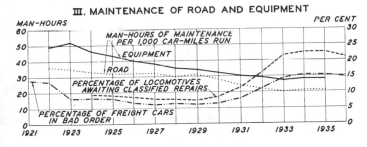

IV. MAXIMUM PERCENTAGE OF EQUIPMENT ACTIVE

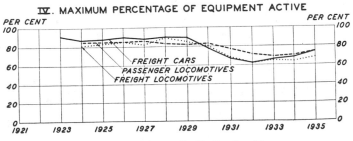

[a] For data and sources, see Appendix D, Section V.

bed is indicated on the chart on page 199 by the reduction in man-hours of road maintenance per 1,000 "car-
miles run" from 31 in 1929 to 20 in 1933 and 21 in
1934-35. The under-maintenance of roadbed is further
evidenced by the fact that in the five years 1930-34 the
tonnage of rails laid in replacement averaged only about
half as much in relation to car mileage as in the preceding five years, while the corresponding comparisons for
the number of crossties laid shows about 80 per cent.[19]

In 1933 the *Railway Age* published an estimate of
700 million dollars for necessary outlays on roadway
and track, if a general "physical rehabilitation" of the
railways was to be made. In January 1936 the same
journal stated that "a statistical study in which an effort
was made to take all . . . factors into account indicates
that the expenditures for maintenance of way and structures during each of the . . . years 1932-35 inclusive, has
amounted to not more than 70 per cent of the outlay
that would have been required to maintain the condition
of properties." This, according to the Railway Business Association, would mean an accumulated deficiency
of approximately 650 million dollars.

Other students arrive at much smaller estimates. It
is pointed out that the number of tons of rails laid in
replacement during 1929 was more than normally
needed, and that the replacement problem in the next
few years would not require as large outlays, including
deferments, as was the case in the years just prior to
1929. At the same time, it is observed that railroad re-

---

[19] The test of car mileage results in a considerable understatement of
the maintenance deficiency during the depression, since the deterioration
of road and equipment from the action of weather went on irrespective
of use. It did not, therefore, contract in proportion to the decline in
car-miles run.

placement and repair work is less expensive than formerly, and that present improved methods of application tend to lengthen the life of rails. Much the same situation exists in the case of ties. With respect to ballast, it is observed that the excellent record of the railways for safe operation in recent years suggests that ballasting of the tracks has not been seriously impaired. Such considerations indicate a volume of deferred maintenance of something like 200 million dollars.

These wide differences in estimates are in part attributable to differing assumptions as to the volume of traffic which the railways may be expected to carry and as to the extent and character of the rehabilitation which railroad properties should undergo. If the computations are made upon the assumption of a substantial improvement in roadbed, structures, and so forth, to meet the needs of a volume of traffic in excess of that of 1929, one would naturally arrive at a substantially higher figure than if one is estimating merely the indispensable minimum of improvements necessary to carry a volume of traffic, say, 10 or 15 per cent above present levels. It is obvious, therefore, that any estimate can be at best but a rough approximation; but it would seem that a figure of 300 million dollars for deferred maintenance of way and structures for the railroad system as a whole would be conservative.

2. *Equipment.* The problem with respect to equipment is essentially different from that in the case of roadway and structures. Here we have to take account not only of a deterioration in the quality of equipment but also in the quantity of rolling stock. We shall consider the quantitative problem first.

At the end of 1936 there will be about 12,000 fewer

locomotives than in 1929, a decrease of 21 per cent. However, since the decrease in inventory has naturally been among the oldest, smallest, and least efficient units the loss in effective performance has been less than the decline in mere numbers would suggest. Average tractive power per unit in fact increased from 44,801 to 48,367 pounds. Taking account of this increase in average efficiency of the existing inventory and the greater tractive power of the newest type of locomotives, and allowing for the fact that there was some excess of stock in 1929, it would appear that something like 6,000 or 7,000 new locomotives would be necessary to give us a tractive power the equivalent of that of 1929. To handle an increase in traffic proportionate to the growth in population between 1929 and 1936 would require nearly 2,000 additional engines. A deficiency of, say, 8,000 locomotives represents a cost of about 800 million dollars at present prices.

The number of freight cars at the end of 1936 was approximately 500,000 (20 per cent) less than in 1929, while passenger cars showed a proportional decline, to the number of 12,000. Allowing on the one hand for a surplus of cars in 1929 and increased efficiency in the use of rolling stock, and on the other for a growth of traffic proportionate to the increase in population, the deficiency would be some 400,000 freight cars and about 6,000 passenger cars. This accumulated deficiency would represent a cost of approximately a billion dollars.[20]

A second point to be considered in connection with equipment is that the existing facilities, both locomotives

---

[20] In 1935 the average cost per unit of the rolling stock constructed was: locomotives $103,450; passenger cars $31,145; and freight cars $2,133 (based on unpublished data furnished by the Interstate Commerce Commission).

and cars, are in a state of unusual disrepair. A glance at the third section of the chart on page 199 discloses an extremely high percentage of bad order equipment even in 1936.[21] The proportion of unserviceable freight cars increased from 6 per cent in 1929 to 14 per cent in 1935. This tangible evidence of under-maintenance is corroborated by the indicator (see chart) showing the change in the number of man-hours of labor put into the upkeep of equipment for every 1,000 car miles run, which declined from 34 in 1929 to 28 in 1935.

While the figures thus point to a very considerable under-maintenance of equipment during the depression years, there is no method of estimating its exact extent. An estimate of 100 million dollars for locomotives and cars appears highly conservative.

Thus we arrive at a total deficiency for way and structures and rolling stock combined of approximately 2,200 million dollars as of the end of 1936.

In estimating the additional requirements over the next five years several factors need to be taken into account. Because of the high average age and obsolete character of a substantial percentage of the locomotives

---

[21] These data probably understate the growth in unserviceability, for two reasons: (1) a significant part of the idle equipment accumulated during the depression and reported as serviceable was, in fact, in disrepair; (2) many of the units reported merely as unserviceable were in exceptionally bad condition. A special investigation of the condition of freight locomotives reported in 1933 as "stored serviceable" showed only 78.7 per cent of these actually ready for use. The same examination applied to freight cars disclosed 4.4 per cent unfit for any service and only 56 per cent fit for the service for which they were designed. (Statement by the Federal Co-ordinator of Transportation, Jan. 4, 1934.)

In a statement dated Dec. 15, 1935 President H. A. Wheeler of the Railway Business Association observed that "a large proportion of the 'bad-order' car total is composed of freight cars bought during the World War or shortly after it. Repairs frequently become so expensive that it is a waste to rebuild as an alternative to acquiring more modern rolling stock."

and cars, the replacement of rolling stock should proceed at an unusually rapid rate, and allowance has to be made for a continued growth of population and traffic. On the other hand, the volume of maintenance and upkeep, both equipment and roadway—once the present deferments have been made good—should be substantially lower than it was in the late twenties; and at the same time the present level of costs is appreciably below that of the pre-depression years. On balance it would appear that the normal requirements of the next five years would be considerably less than in the late twenties when total expenditures aggregated over 2.5 billion dollars a year. An estimate of about 2 billion dollars annually for normal maintenance, replacements, and increases would appear highly conservative.

If, in addition, we are to make good in the next five years the 2.2 billion dollars of accumulated deficiency at the end of 1936, we would have a level of railway expenditures about equal to that of the years 1925-29.

To keep the railways abreast of current technical developments and to provide transportation on an increasingly economical basis would necessitate much heavier replacements of existing rolling stock and a more extensive physical rehabilitation of roadways and structures than have been contemplated in the analysis above. But leaving such improvements out of the reckoning and considering only the accumulated deficiency and ordinary maintenance and replacement requirements we would still need to make in the next five years annual outlays about equal to those of the pre-depression period.[22]

Some students of the railway problem, however,

[22] It is of interest to note that in the first eight months of 1936 orders for freight cars, locomotives, and passenger cars were 478, 638, and 256

point to an important possible offset to these requirements. They expect to see the railways playing a role of declining relative importance in the transportation of the future, in consequence of the assumed greater efficiency of other types of transportation, and also because of industrial shifts which may tend to lessen the total movement of goods in proportion to the total volume of national production.

If it is granted that the former assumption has validity, it remains none the less evident that the railroads are going to make vigorous efforts to retain traffic, both passenger and freight, and that the effort will itself involve the installation of new railway equipment. Moreover, it should also be noted that a transfer of traffic from railways to other forms of transportation would in any event require something like a corresponding increase of facilities in other lines of transportation. Thus the net effect of such a trend upon the transportation equipment problem is not likely to be great. The effects of the shifting of industry and population work themselves out only gradually; and it may well be doubted whether we are entering upon a stage in which railway transportation is of declining importance.

V. PUBLIC UTILITIES

Another broad category of durable producers' goods includes electric power, gas, electric railways, telephones, and telegraphs.[23] Combined capital and maintenance expenditures of these utilities during the pre-

---

per cent respectively of the orders of a like period of 1935, while rail orders in the first seven months of 1936 exceeded those for the entire year 1935. (Data are those of the *Railway Age.*)

[23] Waterworks systems are classed under public works and are therefore considered under that heading.

depression years 1925-29 averaged a little less than those of steam railways in the same period, namely 2.25 billions a year as compared with over 2.50 billions for the railways. Their relative importance and their trends over a period of years are shown in the diagram on the opposite page.

1. Electric power. The electric power industry, as the term is used here, covers central stations, public and private, which produce electricity for sale rather than for their own use. It thus excludes generating plants of manufacturing establishments, street railways, irrigation projects, and the like, even though in some cases there is an incidental sale of power to the public. The municipal plants account for less than 6 per cent of the total capacity and output. While they are included in the statistics which follow, the discussion of factors affecting capital expenditures refers primarily to the privately owned establishments. A still smaller fraction of the industry—in this case not included in our figures—consists of hydro-electric developments owned by the federal government. Most of these are still under construction, but even when completed their initial capacity will be only a little over 2 per cent of the present total for the industry.[24]

The electric power industry underwent a very rapid expansion during the twenties, its capacity and output growing at the astonishing average rate of about 10 per cent annually. Outlays for new plant and equipment ranged between 1925 and 1929 from 700 to 900 million dollars annually. As a result of this rapid expansion

---

[24] *National Power Survey*, Series No. 1, p. 31. This statement relates to projects now authorized, Boulder Dam being included. Their "ultimate" capacity is estimated at about four times the "initial."

CAPITAL AND MAINTENANCE EXPENDITURES IN
PUBLIC UTILITIES, 1919-36[a]

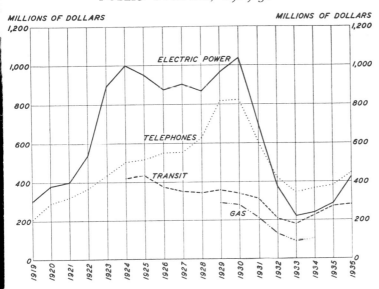

MILLIONS OF DOLLARS

MILLIONS OF DOLLARS

[a] For sources and methods, see Appendix D, Section VI.

the industry entered the depression with a heavy preponderance of recently constructed units. At the end of
1930 about two-thirds of the total capacity was under
ten years of age, while approximately 90 per cent of it
was under twenty years.[25] This had the double effect
of holding repair and maintenance expenditures to relatively low levels and of reducing the volume of new
facilities required to replace scrapped units.

The total generating capacity continued to expand,
though at a diminishing rate, until 1933. Since it takes
two years to plan and build a large steam generating

[25] Estimated from data in *National Power Survey*, Series No. 1, pp.
22, 23.

station, and from two to seven years for a large hydro plant, it is evident that an abrupt curtailment of outlays for such purposes is not easy. In any event, capacity reached its highest level about the time that demand for electric power was at its lowest ebb. Thus for the time being there was an exceptional surplus of unused capacity.

The eventual curtailment of new capital outlays, though belated, was drastic. In 1933 and 1934 such outlays amounted to but 20 per cent of the pre-depression peak. Combined with maintenance expenditures, which declined only moderately, they reached a depression low of less than 30 per cent of the corresponding figure for 1929. Beginning with 1935 there has been a gradual recovery both in new capital outlays and in maintenance, this development being largely in response to a growth in power consumption which commenced in 1933.

So rapid has been this expansion in the demand for power that at the present time (the autumn of 1936) the output is currently running from 15 to 20 per cent above pre-depression highs for the same period of the year, and appears to be expanding at a rate even in excess of that prevailing prior to 1930.[26] Not only is the number of customers about 7 per cent higher than in 1929, indicating an increased size of distribution facilities, but the current rate of utilization of generating capacity is back approximately to the former level. This suggests a fairly complete absorption of the additional facilities installed during the depression.

A lively controversy has been carried on as to the imminence of a "power shortage" and the immediacy of

[26] The output for the first eight months of 1936 was 13.5 per cent over that of the similar 1935 period.

the need for additional generating capacity to meet the rapid growth in demand to which we have just referred.[27] We need not enter into the details of this dispute, many of which are of a highly technical character, nor even into its essential merits. Not only is much of this discussion predicated on conditions of two or three years ago, but the differences of view, once allowances are made for mutual misunderstandings, are not sufficient to concern us here. Granted that an exact estimate of the maximum output obtainable from the present facilities is impossible, and granted, therefore, that it is impossible to say precisely when their capacity will be overtaxed by the growing demand for power, there will be little dissent from the proposition that if output continues to expand at anything like the present rate of revival large-scale expenditures for new facilities cannot be much further delayed. There are marked differences among the various regions of the country with respect to the imminence of power shortages, and the revival of the construction of new generating capacity would therefore tend to be for a time rather spotty and uneven.[28]

A return to pre-depression ratios of output to generating capacity for the country as a whole supports this presumption. It is true that there was a liberal amount

[27] Compare, for example, the findings in *National Power Survey*, Series No. 1, with the criticism of certain utility executives, *Electrical World*, Apr. 13, 1935, p. 35, and the comments of the editor of that journal, Apr. 27, 1935, p. 23.

[28] *National Power Survey*, Series 1, p. 27. The completion of federal hydro-electric projects now under construction will produce a power surplus in certain adjacent areas and will of course postpone the need for new private generating capacity therein. The construction of transmission and distributing facilities, usually a major fraction of all capital outlays in this industry, will of course go on irrespective of the source of the power.

of reserve and stand-by capacity in 1929, and that a good deal of slack could have been taken up had the peak load been suddenly increased. This was in part due to the perfectly legitimate practice of "building ahead of demand." The amount of this reserve capacity in 1929 is held by competent authority not to have been significantly in excess of the requirements of good operating policy nor in excess of previous practice in the industry.[29] In the absence of unforeseen improvements in load factors (through increased inter-connection of generating stations or otherwise) it appears that the industry will soon find itself underbuilt by the pre-depression standard. In view of the liberal reserve capacity provided by that standard the underbuilding may continue for a time without producing severe power shortages under peak loads, but such a makeshift policy would have a very limited duration. The restoration of normal reserves of capacity thereafter would, of course, require a compensatory over-expansion of capital expenditures in the process.

We would conclude from this survey that, while perhaps no significant deficiency has accumulated as a result of the depression, the construction requirements for the next five years are well above those of the late twenties. With output and sales already from 15 to 20 per cent above pre-depression levels, and with markets constantly broadening, it is evident that a considerable expansion of capital is required in the near future. The average outlays for the period 1925-29 were about 900 million dollars. Allowing for somewhat lower prices in the next five years a similar figure would seem to be a

[29] For a discussion of this subject, see F. G. Tryon in *America's Capacity to Produce*, Chap. XV.

conservative estimate of requirements.

2. *Telephones.* The telephone industry ranks second among public utilities from the standpoint of capital and maintenance expenditures, averaging from 1925 to 1929 a little over 600 million dollars a year. Like electric power, it has a history of very rapid and continuous growth up to the recent depression, with the double result of a predominantly youthful equipment inventory and a relatively high prosperity ratio of new capital outlays to maintenance expenditures. The new capital expenditures during the period 1925-29 averaged about 450 million dollars annually, while maintenance outlays ran a little more than a third as high.

The industry presents two very distinct features. The first is the necessity for its plant and equipment to expand more rapidly than its output, as measured by the number of telephones in use. The reason for this is simply that since the telephone system must provide the means of connecting every subscriber with every other, the number of potential connections increases in geometric ratio to the growth in the number of users.

The second peculiar feature of the industry is its extraordinary concentration of ownership. The companies controlled by the American Telephone and Telegraph Company own about 80 per cent of the country's telephones and roughly 90 per cent of its wire mileage and plant investment. By virtue of this monopolistic position both capital and maintenance expenditures may be controlled to an unusual degree by long-range planning.

There was very little decrease in construction outlays during the first two years of the depression. Outlays in 1930 were as high as in 1929, while those in 1931 were larger than in any year prior to 1928.[30] With the number of telephone users declining between 1929 and 1933 by 17 per cent, the result was an unprecedented surplus of facilities in relation to current utilization. It was not until 1932 that new additions to capital proved less than retirements.

The expansion in telephones installed, which began in 1934, has thus far regained only about half of the ground lost during the depression. Although the total number of installations has been increasing recently at the rate of more than 800,000 a year, it will be over two years even at that rate before the 1930 level is attained. In view of the extensive additions to the telephone plant that have been made since the former peak was reached, it does not appear that there will be any acute general shortage of facilities for some time. Indeed, it has been estimated that the Bell System alone can add 2 million telephones to those now in use with only minor expenditures for equipment.[31]

While the large reserve capacity of the basic telephone plant argues against any very heavy capital outlays in the immediate future, it should not be inferred that these outlays will remain at their depression level. They have already risen from 170 million dollars in 1933 to 250 millions in 1936, in addition to which there has been a moderate expansion in maintenance expenditures.[32]

The general adequacy of the present plant does not

[30] The amounts were 610 millions in 1930; 405 millions in 1931; 250 millions in 1932; and 170 millions in 1933.
[31] Standard Statistics Company, *Standard Corporation Records*, A37, Mar. 13, 1936, p. 4. The estimate is actually 3 millions, but applies to conditions at the end of 1935.
[32] Estimates by the American Telephone and Telegraph Company. The 1936 figure is preliminary.

prevent the development of shortages in specific local situations. Much water has flowed under the bridge since 1930 and 1931. Because of the shifting of population during the depression and the development of new residential areas with the revival of housing construction, the demand for new telephone connections is certain to fit only imperfectly the reserve facilities created several years ago, and some outlay for basic plant such as cable lines and central office equipment will be needed despite existing unused reserves in many localities. Moreover, there is an elastic field of expenditure in the replacement or improvement of old facilities which fall short of the best current standards. The entire telephone plant has aged during the depression, and there is an increased scope for renovation.[33] The growth in capital expenditures, therefore, need not wholly await a normal utilization of the plant reserves created in earlier years, but can proceed prior to their general absorption.

There is undoubtedly a considerable deficiency in capacity resulting from the various factors outlined, but it is impossible to express it in terms of figures. A considerable portion of the millions of families still on public or private relief will need and install telephone service when their incomes are restored. This demand, added to that arising from the normal extension of telephone service to meet the needs of an expanding population, will require heavy capital programs. The requirements during the next five years would seem to approximate those of 1925-29.

3. The transit industry. This industry, as defined by

[33] Scrappage was fairly heavy during the first three years of the depression, but has since fallen short of the level that appears to be indicated by past trends.

the Census, includes electric railways of all kinds and motor-bus lines operated by electric railways and by their affiliated subsidiary or successor companies. The definition is sometimes broadened to include city bus lines operated by independent companies. The electric railways are in any case of dominant importance, carrying in 1935 about 85 per cent of the urban traffic.[34]

While the importance of this industry from the standpoint of durable goods activity is not sufficient to warrant any extended discussion here (capital outlays and maintenance expenditures averaged about 350-375 million dollars a year in the late twenties) it is interesting as an example of a mature industry in a declining phase of its career. Owing to the growing use of private automobiles the total number of passengers carried by electric railways and city bus lines failed to grow materially after 1920, and after 1926 it entered a gradual decline. The depression accelerated the downward movement, and by 1933 the traffic was only 65 per cent of the 1926 level. A modest recovery in 1934 and 1935 raised the percentage to 72.[35]

The result of this shrinkage in the total volume of traffic was evident even before the depression in a relatively low level of capital outlays for the transit industry, averaging for the period 1925-29 about 125 million dollars annually, despite an investment in plant and equipment exceeding 4 billions and an annual expenditure for maintenance averaging 250 millions. During the depression the contraction of the facilities of the industry was greatly accelerated, the number of electric cars on surface lines declining one-third between 1929

[34] *Transit Journal,* January 1936, p. 6.
[35] The same, p. 6.

and 1935, a shrinkage only partially offset by an increase in the number of motor buses and rapid transit cars in city use.[36] The mileage of surface tracks in operation declined 30 per cent during this period, here again with only a partial offset in the expansion of urban bus routes and rapid transit lines.[37]

This shrinkage in total facilities during the depression suggests that a recovery of traffic to prosperity levels, even though it stops considerably short of pre-depression volume, will necessitate substantial expenditures to enlarge the carrying capacity of the industry, not to mention those needed to offset current scrappage on continuing operations.[38] Although many of the routes abandoned in recent years will not be re-established, the growth and movement of population and the development of fresh residential areas will give rise to many new ones, while increasing traffic on existing routes will call for additional facilities there.

The volume of capital expenditures, moreover, will be conditioned not only by the volume and distribution of the existing facilities but also by their character. The industry is in the throes of a technological revolution. In small and medium-size cities, and for certain types of service in large cities, the motor bus is steadily superseding the conventional street car. Thus from 1922 to 1930 total street-car trackage declined from 42,200 to

[36] The same, p. 19. The number of surface cars declined 21,400, as against an increase of 7,250 buses and 1,470 rapid transit cars.

[37] The same, p. 15. Surface trackage was reduced by 11,000 miles, while bus routes increased by 2,650 miles and rapid transit lines by 175 miles.

[38] Whether during the depression there has been any considerable under-maintenance of facilities destined to be continued in service in the future it is difficult to say, but the available statistics do not seem to indicate that it has been very large.

35,500 miles while city bus routes increased from 817 to 24,750 miles. At the present time nearly one-third of all cities of over 25,000 population depend on bus service exclusively, this group including cities as large as 230,000.[39] The process of changing over from street-car to bus service, although retarded during the depression, is being resumed in force with the expansion of traffic, and will necessitate, of course, sizable outlays for new equipment.[40] Even where street-car service is continued, a vast amount of obsolete equipment will need to be replaced in the near future. Roughly 90 per cent of the cars now in existence are over 15 years old.[41] Many of these are a liability from the standpoint of attracting patronage as well as expensive to operate.

These factors have already been reflected in a volume of capital outlays for 1936 almost as high as the level of the late twenties, and nearly three times the volume of 1933. In addition, maintenance expenditures have been expanded considerably.[42] A level equal to that of the late twenties seems a reasonable estimate of needs.

4. The gas industry. This industry, which embraces the production and distribution of both natural and manufactured gas, is not of sufficient importance as a consumer of durable goods to warrant more than passing notice, its total capital and maintenance expenditures falling short of 300 million dollars even in 1929. Suffice it to say that these expenditures, after declining to a low in 1933 of about one-third of the pre-depression figure, have shown a slow recovery since then that has

[39] *Transit Journal*, January 1936, p. 15.
[40] Expenditures of the industry for the purchase of buses during 1935 were 60 per cent higher than in 1929.
[41] *Transit Journal*, January 1936, pp. 1 and 19.
[42] Estimates by the *Transit Journal*.

still left them at less than half the 1929 level. In view of the fact that there is now a larger number of gas customers than ever before, with gas sales also at new highs, and especially in view of the steady uptrend in both series since 1933, it is clear that potential capital requirements are substantially above the level of 1925-29.[43]

VI. INDUSTRIAL ENTERPRISES

The term "industrial enterprises" is merely a convenient catch-all to embrace the entire gamut of industry exclusive of railroads, public utilities, and agriculture. Its coverage is therefore both heterogeneous and vast, ranging from mining and manufacturing to merchandising and miscellaneous local services such as barbering and medicine. Although the data in this field are seriously incomplete, it appears that capital and maintenance expenditures averaged at least 7.5 billion dollars a year during the period 1925-29. This constituted about 55 per cent of the expenditures for all producers' durable goods and roughly 25 per cent of the grand total for durable goods of all kinds. It is evident, therefore, that we have here an exceedingly important group of industries from the standpoint of the present discussion.[44]

[43] It should be observed that there was a considerable building ahead of demand prior to the depression, especially in the western divisions of the natural gas industry, where enormous pipe-line developments under way when the depression began had to be completed during 1930 and 1931. (See *America's Capacity to Produce*, p. 99.)

[44] For very few indeed of the almost innumerable separate industries falling within this category do we have budgetary data on capital and maintenance expenditures comparable with those for railroads and public utilities. In lieu thereof it is necessary to rely on statistics for the erection of buildings, and for the sale of machinery and equipment of types used by industries in this field. Unfortunately, a large proportion of the individual items or classifications of buildings and machinery which are

For industrials as a whole the chart on page 219 presents the record of durable goods expenditures classified as construction and machinery and equipment. The former consists of the erection and repair of factory and commercial buildings, and does not include construction activity (if such it may be called) in the sinking of mines and oil wells. The latter covers the sale of industrial apparatus of all kinds and of repair parts.[45]

It will be noted that the outlays are preponderantly for machinery and movable equipment rather than for the construction of fixed and immobile properties. This is in sharp contrast to the situation in the fields of housing, railroad, and public utility construction, where a large percentage of the outlays are in highly durable forms of fixed capital. Partly because of this shorter life span, and in some measure also because their purchase calls for smaller blocks of expenditure than does the construction of buildings, machinery and equipment held up better during the depression than industrial construction. Sales in the low year of the depression were 40 per cent of the 1925-29 average as against a

---

statistically separable are employed in more than one industry, so that it is impracticable to compile from such data separate totals of capital expenditure by industries. The statistics are seriously deficient for another reason. Since we have no budgetary data on these expenditures and must proceed by the indirect method just described, there is no way of ascertaining the volume of spending for the wages of maintenance and repair crews. Maintenance expenditures appear in the statistics only to the extent that they are absorbed in the purchase of repair parts. For these, sales data are usually available. In the case of industrial buildings, however, a minor part of the maintenance labor is reported in the statistics of building contracts awarded.

[45] The distinction between "construction" and "machinery and equipment" is by no means clear cut, nor is usage entirely consistent from one field to another. Thus in the case of electric power plants the generating equipment is usually tabulated under "construction," while for factories only the building itself is included. This is regardless of whether the machinery installed is light or heavy, mobile or immobile.

corresponding figure of 12 per cent for construction. By 1936 the latter had risen to about one-third the former level, while fragmentary indications are that machinery and equipment were near two-thirds.

CAPITAL AND MAINTENANCE EXPENDITURES IN INDUSTRIAL LINES, 1919-36[a]

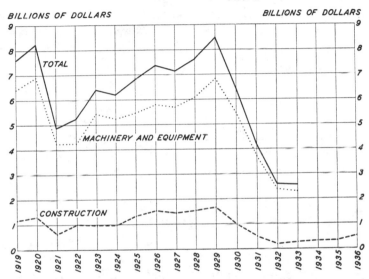

BILLIONS OF DOLLARS

BILLIONS OF DOLLARS

[a] For sources of data and methods, see Appendix D, Section VII.

Since the use of the existing inventory declined very much less during the depression than did expenditures devoted to repairing, replacing, and extending it, there is a strong probability that the period has seen a considerable accumulated deficiency in relation to prosperity needs. While it is not possible to give a precise measurement of the extent of such deficiency, something of its general magnitude may be indicated by studying the situation in some of the more important divisions of this broad field. We shall consider first the construction of buildings devoted to commercial and industrial uses.

1. Commercial and factory buildings. Expenditures for the construction of industrial, mercantile, and other commercial buildings averaged in the period 1925-29 more than 1.5 billion dollars a year.[46] They declined during the depression to almost nothing and have since shown only moderate recovery. Does this protracted interval of low building activity indicate the accumulation of a "deficiency"? If so, what is its character?

It should be pointed out, first, that there has probably been no material reduction in the number of such buildings since 1929. They are typically of long life and the number demolished was probably not much greater than the number of new structures completed. It might be inferred from this that no deficiency has accumulated during the depression except in relation to a total utilization higher than previously attained, but this is far too simple a view of the situation. Not only has there been a good deal of under-maintenance of these facilities that has not yet been corrected, but recent technological advances in design and equipment will require a sizable volume of remodeling and modernization if existing structures are to be absorbed in preference to the erection of new ones.

The importance of under-maintenance and obsolescence in commercial buildings is suggested by the results of a study of store modernization needs recently published by the Department of Commerce.[47] A few of the

[46] Factory construction averaged slightly over half a billion and commercial buildings a little over a billion. Under the latter head are included stores, warehouses, elevators, garages, filling stations, office buildings, theaters, laundries, banks, and so forth. Repair expenditures are included only in part.

[47] "Store Modernization Needs," *Marketing Research Series No. 8,*

findings of this investigation are as follows: 37 per cent of the stores need painting or repair of walls and ceilings; 21 per cent need painting or refinishing of the store front; 26 per cent need refinishing or replacement of floors; 22 per cent need replacement or installation of new fixtures; 20 per cent need repair or refinishing of fixtures. It is obvious from these and similar figures that the qualitative deficiency of existing structures is substantial.

There is, moreover, another factor to be considered. Industrial and commercial buildings are not only fixed in location but are relatively specialized in type. The period since 1929 has seen many shifts in the distribution of demand which are constantly developing shortages of particular types of building in particular locations irrespective of surpluses elsewhere. This lack of adaptability to the changing geographical and functional pattern of demand for the services of industrial buildings is a matter of considerable importance.

The depression occasioned a sharp decline in the total occupancy of most types of industrial buildings, a decline not yet completely overcome. In some cases, such as central office buildings, for example, vacancies still average much higher than in 1929. The accumulation during the past seven years of under-maintenance and obsolescence, and the shifting of demand and use which has lessened the serviceability of the existing inventory, have, however, created a multiplicity of specific shortages already reflected in a marked upturn in construction activity in this field. The fact that the aggregate space available is nearly as great as in 1929, or that total

---

August 1936. This study, covering 8,108 stores in 23 cities, was a co-operative project of the Federal Housing Administration and the Bureau of Foreign and Domestic Commerce.

occupancy is still below the former level, definitely does not contradict the fact that a sizable potential deficiency has accumulated during the depression years.

2. *Industrial machinery and equipment.* The available data in this field are too meager to enable us to say with any assurance whether the total inventory of industrial machinery is now below 1929, but with this type of durable goods the question of number of units is of comparatively minor importance. Machinery of this sort is not only relatively short lived (the average expectancy is probably between 10 and 15 years) but it is subject to very rapid technological obsolescence. Moreover, it is frequently highly specialized, with limited transferability among various users, and since it is employed in competitive industry characterized by relatively rapid shifts in the distribution of utilization, the current adaptability of the inventory to the pattern of use may be of greater consequence than its total magnitude. For these reasons considerations of age, quality, and distribution provide a better test of the accumulated depression deficiency in this field than merely quantitative changes.

That the age distribution of the machinery inventory has shifted materially since 1929 there can be no doubt. A survey by the *American Machinist* at the beginning of 1935 showed 65 per cent of the installed metalworking machinery to be over ten years of age, as against 48 and 44 per cent in 1930 and 1925 respectively. With foundry equipment, 58 per cent exceeded 10 years of age as against 36 per cent in 1930.[48] While there has been some improvement since this survey was made, it is evident that at present the proportion of new and up-to-date machinery is much lower than before the depres-

[48] *American Machinist,* Apr. 24, 1935.

sion, while the representation of old and obsolete units is greater.

The importance of accumulated obsolescence deserves special notice. Great technological advances in industrial machinery have been made during the depression, but they have been incorporated only to a limited extent into the existing inventory.[49] This has created a large accumulation of requirements if advantage is to be taken of new productive economies.

As for shifts in the distribution of demand for the services of the industrial machinery inventory during the depression, these have been extraordinarily rapid and severe. The shifting of productive activity among different establishments and geographical regions which is always going on was accelerated by the economic cataclysm. The resultant maldistribution of the supply of productive machinery was only partially alleviated by transfers of ownership and location so that an unusual proportion of the inventory was rendered ineffective. This reduction in its serviceability represents no less an

[49] The *American Machinist* observes with reference to one branch of the machinery industries: "Machine-tool builders have been prolific in the introduction of new designs, even during depression years when there was little likelihood of their cashing in on their inventiveness." Recent advances in machine tools are summarized as follows: "(1) Greater productivity—in some cases more than ten times as much material can be removed in a given time; (2) greater accuracy—machines designed and built ten years ago are incapable of working to the close limits now demanded by many customers; (3) better materials—alloy steels and irons for machine parts, greatly improved heat treatments, the application of many new kinds of cutting tools, including the hard carbides, have revolutionized design and performance; (4) incorporation of hydraulic and electric controls, ball and roller bearings, better plain bearings, automatic lubrication systems, new types of drives, and many other similar improvements have made the machine tool of 1935 an entirely different and immensely superior unit from its ancestor of 1925." (The same, Apr. 24, 1935, pp. 317 and 327.) While progress in other types of industrial machinery may have been less spectacular than in machine tools, it has been nevertheless substantial.

accumulated depression deficiency than a reduction in its size would be.

While no accurate measure of the potential machinery requirements of industry is available, there can be no doubt that with full recovery they would be enormous. An interesting indication of the attitude and expectation of machinery users on this point is to be found in the replies to a questionnaire circulated generally throughout industry by the Machinery and Allied Products Institute at the end of 1934. The respondents were asked to state the amount of machinery they would be in the market for, given "a sound government policy and restored confidence." From the returns it was estimated that the potential requirements of American industry were then 18.5 billions of dollars.[50] For a part of the returns, for which a separate tabulation was made, 53 per cent of the requirements were designated as for "replacement," as compared with 47 per cent for "additions."[51]

The replacements required would thus be about 10 billion dollars. Other methods of estimating confirm the general reasonableness of this figure. The spectacular recovery in machinery output during the last two years, moreover, confirms the view that replacement needs are of pressing importance. While no comprehensive data for this period are yet available, it is evident from the

[50] Machinery and Allied Products Institute, *Survey of Potential Machinery Requirements of American Industry*, April 1935, p. 8. The categories of machinery covered are as follows: agricultural implements; electrical machinery and apparatus; engines, turbines, tractors, and water wheels; foundry and machine shop products; machine tools; and "all other" machinery.

[51] The Institute offers the following comment: "It becomes apparent that a considerable part of the 1929 industrial plant, a part of which was nearing obsolescence in 1929, has become obsolete merely because of the passing of the five depression years. Not all of the 1929 plant was then operating at full efficiency—it is estimated that at that time about

figures for individual items or types that the shortage is already making itself acutely felt.

Again, it is possible to indicate only in the roughest way the requirements over the next five years. But a backlog of deficiency of 10 billion dollars in the field of industrial equipment represents two years' production at the levels of 1925-29. To make this good in the next five years would thus require a level of production equal to 40 per cent of the 1925-29 average. Taking into account normal replacements and population growth, and also the deficiencies indicated in commercial and industrial buildings, it is evident that requirements are in the magnitude of something like 10 to 11 billions annually instead of the 7.0 to 7.5 billions in 1925-29, or 40 per cent greater.

VII. AGRICULTURE

Capital and maintenance expenditures of agriculture prior to the depression were in the neighborhood of one billion dollars a year.[52] They declined drastically after 1929, reaching a low in 1932 of a little more than a quarter of that amount. The recovery which began in 1933 had carried them by 1935 to approximately three-quarters of the pre-depression average, and indications are that the estimates for 1936, when available, will show considerable further gains.

The high level of agricultural production throughout

---

one-fourth might have been economically replaced. Five years have since elapsed—obsolescence has been continuous, replacement almost nothing. It follows that at the end of 1934 a much larger proportion requires replacement for effective operation. Consideration of all factors involved indicates that one-half or more of the 1929 industrial plant had become obsolete by the close of 1934."

[52] Estimate derived chiefly from data published by the Department of Agriculture in *Income from Farm Productions in the United States*, 1935 and earlier issues. This figure includes estimated expenditures for the construction and repair of farm residences (unpublished data) and

the depression is sufficient evidence that the rate of consumption of farm capital did not decline appreciably. If the estimated accrual of depreciation on farm buildings and equipment is taken as a convenient indication of consumption, it is clear that for five consecutive years additions to the inventory were insufficient to maintain it.[53] In fact, it appears that the accumulated deficiency since 1929 is roughly 1.5 billion dollars. If, as now seems likely, some progress was made in repairing this deficiency in 1936, it is true nevertheless that the bulk of it remains to be eliminated in the future.

VIII. PUBLIC AND SEMI-PUBLIC CONSTRUCTION

Under this heading are included public works and a miscellany of relatively unimportant items of construction such as private schools, clubs, churches, charitable institutions, and the like. Of an average pre-depression expenditure of about 3.5 billion dollars a year for the category as a whole, public construction composed nearly 90 per cent.

Owing to the strenuous efforts made throughout the depression, first by local governments and later by the federal government, to maintain the volume of public works as a means of relieving unemployment or aiding recovery, this type of construction held up better than any other. These combined efforts nevertheless did not suffice to prevent a serious reduction of total expenditures in this field, a development reflected in the chart on the opposite page.

---

excludes expenditures on passenger automobiles and other durable consumers' goods. The latter are excluded here because expenditures by farmers have been included in the estimates for these goods already presented. Housing expenditures, on the other hand, are included because the previous discussion of housing covered only the non-farm area.

[53] The same, 1935, pp. 7 and 10.

Expenditures fell rapidly after 1930, and by 1933 had reached a total of about half the previous peak. Since then there has been a fairly continuous recovery, the

EXPENDITURES FOR PUBLIC CONSTRUCTION AND MAINTENANCE, 1923-34[a]

(In millions of dollars)

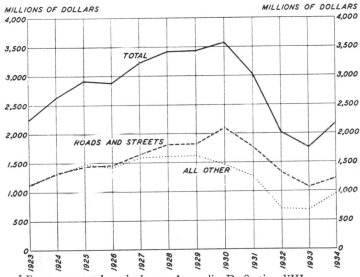

[a] For sources and methods, see Appendix D, Section VIII.

extent of which it is difficult to estimate, but which appears from preliminary indications to have reached a level in 1936 not very far below the pre-depression average.[54]

If the volume of construction and maintenance expenditures from 1930 to 1936 inclusive is adjusted for

[54] A considerable part of the difficulty of estimating for 1936 consists in determining the weight which should be given to construction expenditures by the Works Progress Administration.

changes in construction costs during the period, it appears that the average annual activity in physical terms was below the average for 1925-29 by not more than 10 per cent.[55] At first glance this does not appear to indicate much accumulated deficiency as a result of the depression. It must be remembered, however, that prior to 1929 public works construction and maintenance had been expanding rapidly, and that a mere cessation of growth may represent in effect an accruing deficiency in relation to the prosperity demands of the nation for the services of publicly owned durable goods.

In spite of the effects of the depression, the consumption of most types of public capital goods has risen above pre-depression levels. The use of highways in 1936, as measured by gasoline consumption, exceeded 1929 by 20 per cent. Total enrollment in public schools was up 7 per cent. The use of waterworks and sewers was certainly higher, though by an indeterminate amount. In so far, therefore, as construction expenditures were needed to offset the current consumption of the inventory of public capital goods, the depression justified no reduction.

A very substantial portion of the pre-depression expenditures went not for replacement or repairs but for additions to the inventory needed to accommodate the growth and movement of population and the improvement in the standards of service for which the public was willing to borrow or pay taxes. The growth of population of course went on with only a slight retardation by the depression. While its influence on the demand for public construction has been in part postponed by the virtual suspension of residential building, which

[55] See Appendix D, Table 9.

obviated the need of new streets, water lines, sewers, and schools to accommodate new communities, this construction has been no more permanently avoided than has the residential building itself. It has accumulated as a backlog for the future.[56] Another factor to be reckoned with in appraising future needs for public works expenditures is the certainty of expanding maintenance charges. When a durable goods inventory has been growing as rapidly as this one has done for many years, the volume of necessary repairs and renewals is certain to show a responsive but delayed expansion as the inventory ages. The moderate curtailment of current additions to the inventory during the depression had practically no effect on the relentless advance of these requirements. Indeed, it appears that the serious curtailment of repair expenditures for some classes of public goods resulted in a good deal of accumulated under-maintenance.[57]

It is quite impossible to make any measurement of future requirements for public works construction and maintenance, for there are many imponderable elements

[56] Technological obsolescence affects public property no less than private. Roughly half of the present surfaced mileage was constructed in the days of Model T. Much of this mileage is still narrow and tortuous, with unbanked curves and poor visability. Recent advances in highway engineering and in the technique of traffic control have made obsolete a considerable fraction even of the mileage more recently constructed, particularly trunk lines between metropolitan centers.

For an enlightening discussion of this subject see *Fortune*, August 1936, p. 85; also "Highway Progress Responsibility," an address by T. H. MacDonald, chief of the Bureau of Public Roads, before the Association of Highway Officials of the North Atlantic States, Atlantic City, Feb. 12, 1936.

[57] This was apparently worse in the case of city streets, for example, than in the case of rural highways. The available data are, however, insufficient to permit any very confident generalization as to under-maintenance, particularly since the execution of numerous Federal Relief projects for the repair of public buildings and works.

in the situation.[58] However, in the light of the accumulation of repair work, the great amount of urban street reconstruction that should be undertaken and the requirements which arise from the growth and shifting of population, it would seem that the needs over the next five years are of a magnitude at least equal to the actual construction of the late twenties.

IX. SUMMARY OF PRODUCTION REQUIREMENTS

We may now attempt to recapitulate and summarize the results of this analysis of the situation in the various divisions of the durable goods industries. It is perhaps essential first to restate the objectives of the inquiry in order that there may be no misunderstanding as to the nature and significance of the results obtained.

In brief, we have studied the changes that have occurred in the durable goods industries during the course of the depression, not with a view to predicting the assured trend of demand and production in the near future but rather for the purpose of establishing the general magnitude of the production that would be required in the next five years to equip the nation with a supply of durable goods (both producer and consumer) commensurate with that of 1929. This involved taking account of the restricted rate of production during the

---

[58] An example of these imponderables may be found in the school situation. The country has long passed the peak of grade-school enrollment, this having declined by a million from 1929 to 1935, but high school enrollment is still rising, the increase during the period being 2.5 millions. Presumably the total of both will soon begin to decline. What does this augur as to outlays for school buildings? Another example is the highway situation. The process of laying down the initial surfaced trunk-line network of the country may be regarded as approaching completion, and less new mileage of this sort will be needed in the future. Against this must be set the necessity for increased repairs and replacements on mileage previously built. What does this indicate as to total requirements?

last seven years, the extent of deferred replacement and deferred maintenance, the obsolescence factor, and the growth of population. In other words, our approach has been of an engineering character: we have endeavored to take an inventory of the existing situation in the durable goods industries and on this basis to project the production requirements over the next five years if the population in 1941 is to be as well supplied, on a per capita basis, as it was in the late twenties, no allowance being made for higher standards of living.

In most cases the data are far from precise and the estimates reached are necessarily but rough approximations. They nevertheless serve to replace mere conjectures as to the accumulated needs in durable goods industries with considered estimates based on a realistic appraisal of all the available data. A conscious effort has been made to avoid possible exaggeration by stressing *minimum* requirements. It is our view that, whatever shortcomings may exist in the estimates for the separate categories of goods, the aggregate figures may be taken as reasonable approximations.

We found that in several divisions of the durable goods industries there were in 1936 very considerable requirements growing out of deferred replacement and deferred maintenance. These were particularly large in the fields of residential construction and steam railroads. We found that current production in 1936 was still far below the levels of pre-war years. Hence, to restore by 1941 a per capita production equal to that of 1929 would involve both making good existing deficiencies and stepping up production in line with the growth of population, not only to date but over the next five years. Prices have changed materially since 1929; hence we have made our estimates on the basis of present levels of cost.

Our estimates indicate that in aggregate terms the accumulated deficiency of durable goods at the end of 1936 amounted to from 25 to 30 billion dollars. If this deficiency is to be made up in the next five years and the increasing population provided with goods equal, on a per capita basis, to those furnished in the late twenties, the level of production during the next five years would have to be something like 33 billion dollars annually. This annual average may be compared with an actual production of durable goods in 1936 of approximately 21 billion dollars.[59]

[59] For summary table on which these figures are based, see Appendix D, Table 10.

CHAPTER IX

RE-EMPLOYMENT POSSIBILITIES

In the preceding three chapters the depression and recovery have been examined from the standpoint of production and employment. We first reviewed the composition, growth, and effectiveness of the labor force over the period 1929-36. We then presented the estimates of employment and unemployment for the past seven years, and attempted to measure the unemployment volume in terms of *full-time equivalents* in order to allow for overtime as well as under-employment and outright unemployment. This analysis was followed by a brief inquiry into production and productivity as related to trends established in the years preceding the depression, with the purpose of evaluating the progress which has already been made towards recovery and the distance we still have to go before we can reasonably say that we have attained recovery. Finally, an attempt was made to indicate, within the limits of existing data, the accumulated needs of the nation for durable goods. In the present chapter we shall endeavor to recapitulate and recast in broader terms some of the conclusions reached in the foregoing analysis, toward the end of focussing upon the problem of re-employment.

I. THE MAGNITUDE OF THE PROBLEM

From the evidence available it appears that in 1936 the volume of unemployment requiring absorption is equivalent to approximately 9.5 million workers on a full-time basis. The elements involved in this total are summarized in the accompanying table (in millions):[1]

Unemployment in 1929 . . . . 3.1
Decrease in employment, 1929-36 . . . . 5.1
Increase in labor force, 1929-36 . . . . 4.3

Gross unemployment in 1936 . . . . 12.5
Allowances for voluntary and disability unemployment,
    time lost in changing jobs, and shortening of hours . 3.0
Net unemployment requiring absorption on a full-time
    basis . . . . 9.5[2]

This broad estimate of 9.5 millions refers to the net increment in the number of individuals who, though part of the labor force of the nation, are not engaged in *regular* economic activities as defined by pre-depression criteria. It includes those who may be technically employed but whose employment is incident to the depression: government work relief, for example, and transitory non-commercial activities such as subsistence farming. With this concept of "unemployment requiring absorption," it is evident that the estimates would have to be reduced if we were to assume that some modification has taken place in the system which will permanently change the economic functions of government and the behavior and attitude of individuals.

For instance, if the WPA and its activities should be made permanent, a large number of those on work relief would automatically be removed from the number

---

[1] See Appendix C, Table 16. The unemployment figures are annual averages. In the latter part of 1936, unemployment was lower than the average here shown.

[2] From some points of view the standard of full-time employment exacted by this estimate may be considered too high. It requires somewhat more complete employment (if no offset is made for the imputed reduction in working hours) than was experienced in 1929. The estimate would be reduced by something more than one million if the attainment of the 1929 employment situation were taken as the aim.

requiring employment. Likewise, if we were to assume that the gainful workers who left the city for the farm had permanently withdrawn from commercial activities, our estimate would again be reduced. In either case the number of available workers for *regular* activities would be smaller than estimated. These are corrections which the reader may make in accordance with his own conjectures. It would seem, however, that a conservative view of the re-employment problem requires the assumption that the dislocated personnel will be absorbed into regular channels of activity.[3]

II. RE-EMPLOYMENT IN RELATION TO PRODUCTION

What are the possibilities in the near future of absorbing this volume of available labor power in customary business activities? Must we maintain in permanent idleness, or make-work enterprises under government auspices, millions of people for whom there is presumably no regular work? One way to answer these questions is by referring to the needs and requirements of the nation for goods and services.

It is, of course, realized that the existence of needs does not necessarily dictate production and employment. Yet the consideration of re-employment possibilities against a background of needs—though not adequate for making a forecast—is both valid and useful. Even if the needs of the people are not sufficient in themselves to determine business activity, they should be given an important place in the determination of policies intended to cope with the unemployment problem.

Accordingly, the 9.5 millions of unabsorbed workers may be related to the requirements of the population as

[3] This is not to imply that work relief has been unproductive or that subsistence farming is less desirable than other economic activities. We are merely venturing to frame the problem in terms of long-run tendencies.

disclosed by income and production. It has been amply shown that even in 1929 the needs of the people were by no means satisfied and that the standard of living for a very large proportion of the population was far from adequate.[4] Yet the income of 1936 in terms of product appears to be not more than 87 per cent of that of 1929. In the meantime, the population has increased—about 5 per cent in total and between 9 and 10 per cent in the number of adults. Product income in 1936 *per capita* is therefore only about 82 per cent as high as it was in 1929.

It is impossible to say precisely how many workers would be required to restore the income level of 1929 with allowance for population growth, but a rough calculation indicates that under existing conditions the shortage, which amounts to between 14 and 15 billion dollars in 1929 values, represents work which would require not far from the entire unemployed force.[5] For the immediate future this presumption is conservative, although it appears exaggerated in view of the fact that the increased technological efficiency should make possible the achievement of the 1929 standard of living with a smaller number of workers relative to population. As indicated in Chapter VII, a temporarily offsetting factor to the rise in technological efficiency in some industries is the considerable deterioration in the effectiveness of the labor force which has taken place during the depression. Besides this, there has been a more than normal decrease in the accepted hours of work which may have fully

---

[4] See *America's Capacity to Consume.*

[5] In this rough computation no account is taken of the division of production between consumers' and producers' goods (nor of the questions of balance of trade and capital export). Differences in the proportioning of the same amount of productive energy may yield entirely different standards of living.

anticipated the effects of the increase in man-hour productivity.[6]

The foregoing estimate takes no account of the rise in the standard of living which might be expected in the regular course of progress. When the needs of the population of the United States are gauged by the extension of the pre-depression trend of production, they assume proportions which would considerably strain the productive capacity of the available labor force in its present condition.

The problem of re-employment would be clarified if it were possible to analyze employment possibilities industry by industry. This, however, cannot be done. As pointed out in Chapter VI, the available data do not lend themselves to measuring the volume of unemployment in individual industries. Likewise, while it is feasible to indicate the potential needs of the people in general terms, it would in most cases lead one too far afield to attempt a definition of requirements on a product or industry basis. The obstacles are particularly great in the present instance because of the lapse of such a long time since the beginning of the depression. During this period so many industrial shifts and substitutions have probably occurred that the needs constituting a seemingly unaltered standard of living might now consist of products and services quite different from those of the twenties.

By making durability of product the basis of distinction, however, economic activities can be divided into two broad categories—a division highly pertinent to the analysis of our problem. By reference to the material

[6] It is evident that the increased leisure afforded by the shortening of hours cannot take the place of the goods and services called for by the pre-depression standards of living; if anything, more leisure will result in an expansion rather than a contraction of requirements.

presented in Chapter VIII, we shall attempt to give a brief summary of employment requirements in durable goods as compared with non-durable goods and services. It has been shown that the production of durable goods is subject to greater fluctuations than that of non-durable goods and that the heaviest loss in employment during the depression has been in the durable goods industries. The full weight of this statement is indicated by the fact that durable goods, including construction, repairs, and parts, constituted about 40 per cent of the national product in 1929. In that year an equivalent of about 18 million gainful workers devoted their full time to the production and distribution of these goods, whereas at the low point of the depression only about 9 millions were afforded employment in this field.[7] A rough calculation based on preliminary data indicates that in 1936 the employment furnished by the activities connected with durable goods, as defined, is equivalent to about 14 million persons, or roughly 4 millions less than in 1929.

If the available labor force were to be assigned to durable and non-durable goods in the same proportion as obtained in 1929, the activities related to production and distribution of durable goods would have the burden of absorbing 5.5-6.0 million additional workers.[8] This would leave 3.5-4.0 of our estimated 9.5 millions to be taken up by non-durable goods and direct services.

This tentative allocation affords a rough gauge which may be applied to the conclusions reached in Chapter

[7] The estimates are rough approximations based on total value of durable goods and aggregate national product per equivalent full-time worker.

[8] The reduction of about 4 millions plus roughly 40 per cent of the increase in the number of gainful workers since 1929.

VIII. It was there indicated that the accumulated deficiency in durable goods amounts to between 25 and 30 billion dollars. At the present rate of efficiency and at current values, from 15 to 20 million additional workers would be required for one year to make up this deficiency alone. If the production necessary to restore the depleted inventories were to be spread over the next five years, the backlog would be sufficient to give employment during this period to more than 3 million persons over and above the employment necessary to satisfy the regular requirements in durable goods.

When current requirements are added to the accumulated deficiency, the needs for durable goods over the next five years indicate an average annual production at current prices of approximately 33 billion dollars whereas actual production in 1936 is running at the rate of about 21 billions. In terms of employment, the difference of 12 billion dollars represents the addition of some 8 or 9 million persons on a full-time basis. This exceeds by a considerable margin the portion of the now unabsorbed labor force allocated to durable goods.[9] Hence, to effect the indicated production program in durable goods, it would be necessary to encroach heavily upon the working personnel allocated to non-durable goods and direct services.[10]

It will be recalled that in our tentative allocation of the unemployed it was assumed that full employment would require the absorption of some 3.5-4.0 million workers into the activities related to the supply of non-

[9] This is true even when due allowance is made for the increase in the number of gainful workers over the next five years.

[10] The discussion is of necessity in very broad terms and is perhaps over-simplified. The interchange of personnel among industries, particularly between durable goods and non-durable goods and direct services, is, of course, more complicated than it is possible to indicate here.

durable goods and direct services. This constitutes an increase of about 15 per cent over the present actual employment in these fields.[11] Is such an absorption reasonably possible in the light of potential needs? Unfortunately this question cannot be settled by a precise statistical answer. But such evidence as there is would seem to establish a strong presumption that an increase in employment of 15 per cent would give the consuming public a level of consumption no higher than that of 1929. The manufacture of non-durable goods in 1936 furnishes employment to only about 92 per cent as many wage earners as it carried on payrolls in 1929. Besides, there has been a very substantial reduction in the number of hours worked by each worker.[12] When measured by man-hours, it appears that the volume of employment (for wage earners) in the manufacture of non-durable goods in 1936 is about 29 per cent lower than in 1929 despite the increase in population.[13]

No separate figures of man-hour productivity in manufacturing are available for non-durable goods. But if we assume that the increase since 1929 for all manufacturing industries applies to this section of the field— an assumption which perhaps magnifies the change—the rise in productivity would seem to fall short of com-

[11] The total full-time equivalent employment in 1936, exclusive of subsistence farming and irregular activities, is placed tentatively at 37.9-38.4 millions (see Appendix C, Table 13) and the durable goods employment at about 14 millions, leaving about 24.4 millions as employed in the supply of non-durable goods and services.

[12] Based on Bureau of Labor Statistics and National Industrial Conference Board data; 1936 estimates have been computed from incomplete data. For 1929 average hours worked per week are not given separately for non-durable goods. For all manufacturing the average was about 49 hours. The preliminary estimates for 1936 indicate an average for all manufacturing of 39.2 and for non-durable goods about 37.7.

[13] See p. 236.

pensating for the fall in volume of employment. The present rate of production and employment would have to be augmented considerably before the 1929 standard in non-durable manufactures could be re-established. What is true of manufacturing is true in varying degrees of other processes connected with the production of non-durable goods and also of direct services.[14]

All in all, it appears that the addition of 15 per cent (3.5-4.0 million workers) to the number now employed in supplying non-durable goods and service would do no more than reinstate the equivalent which entered in the pre-depression standard of living. This presumption is strengthened by the consideration that a good share of the supply in question—such as direct services—has not been much affected by new labor-saving devices.[15]

In summary, we are led to the conclusion that a production program of sufficient magnitude to replace accumulated deficiencies within the next five years and expand output to a level that would provide a consumption volume commensurate with that in 1929 would be faced by a shortage of labor. This conclusion is not to be taken as a forecast that such a situation will eventuate. Developments in production and employment depend upon a combination of many contributory factors, some of which will be discussed in the following chapters.

The foregoing conclusion refers only to the situation as it is today. The existing economic condition is marked on the one hand by a weakened productive capacity

[14] In some of the other activities reductions in hours and employment were, of course, not compensated by increase in man-hour productivity to the same degree as in manufacturing.

[15] Additional support of this presumption is furnished by the probability that the average productivity of those now unemployed would be somewhat lower than that of the personnel already at work.

with respect to plant and equipment as well as labor, and on the other hand by a more than normal need for the output of industry. Both are of course temporary factors which are being reduced in the process of recovery. But for the present—until the deteriorating effects of the depression on material inventories as well as human resources have been overcome—there does not seem to be any way of accomplishing all that appears necessary without taxing the available labor supply. The pressure may, of course, be met by expanding working hours either through lengthening the standard work week or resorting to overtime.

In this connection it should be mentioned that the existence of an accumulated deficiency in durable goods is both a boon and a danger. It will undoubtedly be instrumental in speeding recovery, but it also holds the potentialities of over-accelerated activity in certain lines and another depression. If industry undertakes to make up the accumulated deficiency at too rapid a pace, the result will be an abnormal concentration of the labor force, both industrially and geographically. The temporary nature of the activity connected with the process must eventually lead to the discharge of large numbers of workers and a consequent downward spiral of production and employment. The potential dislocation is aggravated by the tendency of both producers and consumers to extend inventories of durable goods beyond replacement needs. Our immediate problem, therefore, is not only one of recovery but also one of control looking to the prevention or at least the attenuation of another depression.

CHAPTER X

WAGE READJUSTMENTS

In Chapter VI it was shown that the great bulk of the population is dependent upon wages and salaries for a living. In fact, nearly 80 per cent of the gainful workers obtain their livelihood as employees, and between 60 and 65 per cent of the national income is disbursed in the form of wages and salaries. Wage earners alone, in so far as they can be separated from other employees, comprise more than 50 per cent of the entire labor force, and, in 1929, the wages of this group amounted to about 35 billion dollars in a total product of 81 billions. It is therefore not surprising that in discussions of depression and recovery, economists as well as politicians center much attention upon wages.

The recovery theories connected with wages may be divided into two groups: those which focus upon wages as a cost of production and those which regard them as a source of purchasing power. As a rule the two lines of approach are opposite in the contemplated immediate effect upon wage rates. The first finds that wage rates are too rigid and do not respond as quickly as other prices to deflationary tendencies, and that hence, without adjustment between costs and prices, profits disappear and production is curtailed or suspended. The remedy, therefore, is found in a reduction of wage rates to meet the reduction in commodity prices in order to make it possible for business to carry on. (Another version of the theory is that a lowering of wage rates would make possible a lowering of prices and thus result in an expansion of demand.) The purchasing power theories, on the other hand, advocate the increase of wage rates in order to place more money in the hands of workers and thus stimulate demand for goods which in turn will stimulate production. It can be seen that the two lines of reasoning have as their aim the same final result—expansion of production and employment. But while one seeks to apply the stimulus at the point of production, the other seeks to apply it at the point of consumption. The remedies flowing from the two viewpoints are sometimes classified as "deflationary" and "reflationary"—for the one attempts to adjust wages down to the lower levels reached by the flexible parts of the economic structure, while the other, although its advocates are not always aware of its implications, effects a reinstatement or even an advance of prices. The worth of either theory is, of course, to be tested not by the immediate effects but by the ultimate results in terms of the volume of production and consumption. No attempt will be made in this chapter to appraise the relative merits of these conflicting theories, but the facts here presented regarding the movement of wages in relation to income, profits, and prices have a definite bearing upon the considerations involved.

I. WAGE RATES AND WAGE INCOME

In the discussion of wages it is necessary to bear in mind the distinction between rates and totals, between earnings per hour and earnings per year. The conflict between wages as costs and wages as income is not so much in terms of totals as in terms of rates. From the standpoint of the worker, particularly that of his family, rates are not so significant as total income. Without minimizing the importance of rates of wages to labor (it is indeed out of rates that aggregates are built) it is well to realize that to be worth anything in a material sense wage rates must be associated with another important factor—duration or volume of employment. Under certain conditions volume may be more important than rates. This is particularly so when the group as a whole is concerned.

The significance of this distinction during the present depression is well illustrated by the chart on page 246, which shows the average annual earnings of wage earners engaged in manufacturing computed on three different bases: (1) to show what wages were per average person actually on the payrolls; (2) to show what earnings would have been on a full-time basis; (3) to show what earnings would have been if aggregate disbursements had been divided among all who were dependent upon (attached to) manufacturing.

It will be seen that the decline in wage rates during the depression, as indicated by full-time earnings, has been quite moderate. Those who were fortunate enough to have full employment earned, even during 1932 and 1933, an average of more than $1,100 per annum, as compared with about $1,330 in 1929.[1] The decline between 1929 and 1932 amounted to only about 17 per cent; and, as will be seen later, this loss in money wages was fully compensated by the decrease in the cost of living. By 1934 the money earnings of those who were fully employed had recovered to almost their 1929 level, and by 1935 they had surpassed it.

But not all the workers had full-time employment, and a great number had no employment at all. To those without jobs the maintenance of wage rates offered little

[1] It should be noted that the averages are affected by changes in the composition of personnel. A drop in the proportion of lower paid workers would in itself cause the average to rise or prevent it from falling even in the face of general reductions in rates.

consolation. Despite the fact that earnings per hour had been reduced only 17 per cent, the 1932 payrolls if

AVERAGE ANNUAL WAGES IN MANUFACTURING
INDUSTRIES, 1919-36[a]

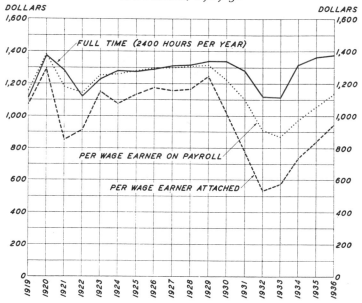

[a] For data, see Appendix C, Table 22.

distributed evenly among all the workers attached to manufacturing would have given each worker less than $550, or only about 43 per cent of the average for 1929. In 1935, though average hourly earnings for those working were higher than in 1929, the total earnings for all wage earners attached to the industry were still about 33 per cent below the 1929 level.

The difference between full-time earnings and earnings per worker attached to the industry emphasizes an important point which, though self-evident, has not been given proper consideration in the depression remedies concerned with wages. We refer to the enormous disparity between the income of the employed and the unemployed and to the fact that, once employment has been impaired, manipulation of wage rates directly affects only a part of the workers. In fact, the raising of wage rates during depression adds to the advantage of those having jobs, who are already benefiting from depression because of lower living costs, and (if a rise in prices results) to the distress of those who have suffered reduction or disappearance of income.

It appears that average hourly earnings declined considerably less during the depression than the cost of living. The result was that the real income of those who had the good fortune to remain employed increased steadily, although the workers as a group suffered great deprivation. A glance at the chart on page 248 will show that even in 1932, when the average real income of all the manufacturing wage earners was only about 53 per cent as high as in 1929, the real earnings of that portion of the wage earners who remained employed were in general about 4 per cent higher than in 1929. Conditions have improved for the group as a whole since 1932 as well as for those who had full employment; but it is significant to note that while in 1935 the average real earnings of all manufacturing wage earners were still 16 per cent below 1929, the average full-time real earnings for the same number of hours as in 1929 was about 26 per cent higher than in that year.[2]

This exemplifies a significant characteristic of depression—the tendency toward concentration of income. The concentration is, of course, different from

[2] As indicated in the preceding footnote, part of the rise in the average may be due to a change in the composition of personnel since 1929.

that which obtains in prosperity, in that it is less spectacular and less likely to attract public indignation. None the less it is far reaching in its immediate effects. In times of prosperity concentration of income is a result

AVERAGE ANNUAL "REAL" WAGES IN MANUFACTURING INDUSTRIES, 1919-36[a]

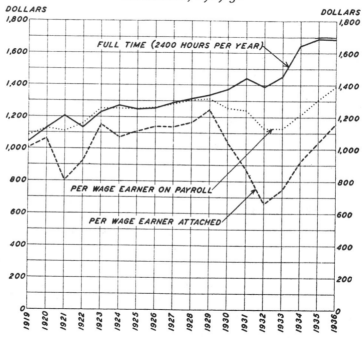

[a] For data, see Appendix C, Table 23.

of comparative plenty and takes the form of an uneven distribution of the expanded portion of the national income. But in depression the maldistribution results from a drying up of the source of income of a large portion of the population and the relative expansion of the purchasing power of those whose source of income has been left intact. The spread between the lower incomes and the higher incomes in depression may not be so wide as in prosperity, but because of the presence of such a large proportion of zero or near zero incomes, it is relatively more significant. The situation under depression is complicated by uneasiness over the future on the part of those who still have incomes.

II. WAGES AND SALARIES IN RELATION TO TOTAL INCOME

In line with the general consideration of wages, it should be of interest to note briefly the changes which have taken place during the depression in the relationship between aggregate wages and salaries and total national income. A graphic summary of these changes is given in the charts on page 250. In these charts wages and salaries are related to two totals measuring national income: that referring to the net amount of money paid out annually by business, government, and individuals to operators, employees, and investors ("income paid out") and that referring to the net income resulting from actual production during each year ("income produced"). The difference between the two totals represents the amounts retained in business as undivided profits or the deficits resulting from paying out more than is produced within the year. During the depression the differences between "income paid out" and "income produced," which are shown below the base line in the upper chart, were quite substantial, the estimate for 1932 being 8.8 billion dollars, or 22 per cent of the total produced income of 39.5 billions.

The "unproduced income" was paid out to employees as well as to other claimants, but it is to be presumed that a larger proportion of it was paid out in interest —which is a contractual and fixed charge—than in any other single class of disbursements. At any rate, interest

WAGES AND SALARIES IN RELATION TO THE NATIONAL INCOME, 1929-35[a]

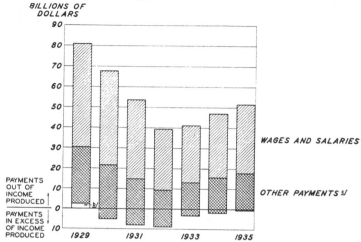

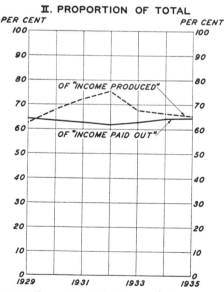

[a] For data, see Appendix C, Table 24. [b] Amount retained in business.
[c] It should be stated that some of the "payments in excess of income produced" constituted wages and salaries. In addition to the technical difficulty of showing this in the chart, there is justification for considering all payments out of surplus as applying to investors and entrepreneurs since presumably they are reflected in the decrease in the value of their property.

250

payments have remained more stable during the depression than other disbursements.

In terms of "income paid out" the percentage of total income distributed as wages and salaries declined from 1929 to 1932 and then recovered somewhat, but over the period as a whole the changes were not material. The figures underlying the chart do not include work-relief wages. If these were included the rise from 1932 to 1935 would appear larger than is indicated.

The changes in the percentages are much greater when wages and salaries together are related to the income produced. As can be seen from the chart, the proportion going to wages and salaries rose considerably during the depression, and then in the recovery period declined again toward the pre-depression ratios. The computations do not, of course, mean that wage earners became more prosperous during the depression. They merely received a larger share of a greatly reduced total.

III. WAGES AND PROFITS

In the aggregate, wages and profits are not mutually exclusive elements in our economic system. On the contrary, both are derivatives and dependents of productive activity and go almost hand in hand. When one is high the other is high, and when one is reduced the other is bound to show a reduction, too. The chart on page 252 illustrates this simple fact for manufacturing industries.

The correlation between the two, in direction at least, is quite evident. Within the period covered by the data, 1929 was unprecedented with respect to both aggregate wages and aggregate profits. Likewise, 1932 was the lowest year in both respects. There is, of course, no proportionality in the correlation between wages and profits. One reason is that while there can be no negative wages, the aggregates of profits are made up of both positive and negative amounts. Some businesses operated at a loss even in 1929. In 1931 and 1932 losses of manu-

facturing corporations exceeded gains, with the result
that aggregate profits of all corporations were negative
in these years.

An extended discussion of the relationship between

THE COURSE OF AGGREGATE WAGES AND PROFITS IN
MANUFACTURING INDUSTRIES, 1922-33[a]
(1929 = 100)

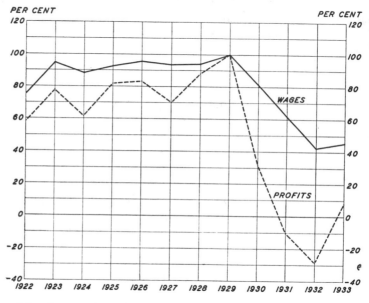

[a] For data, see Appendix C, Table 25.

wages and profits is not required here. The significant
fact is that they are co-ordinate in derivation; they both
grow out of the process of production. Ultimately it is
the consumer who pays both. Since neither is the source
of the other, one cannot be materially expanded at the
expense of the other, particularly during depression. Any
effort to raise wage payments at the expense of profits if
carried too far will trench upon capital in the case of

many enterprises and thus result in curtailment of production. Likewise, any persistent encroachment of profits upon wages will thwart expansion of consumption and will reduce opportunities for profit. The essence of the matter is that volume of production is the basis for both wages and profits.

In connection with this problem it should be borne in mind that profits are not uniformly spread over all business enterprises. Aggregates and averages are thus very treacherous to clear understanding. Policies formulated on the basis of totals may be very disruptive because of the inequality and unpredictability of their effect upon the component parts of industrial organization. For instance, the profits of all manufacturing corporations, which in 1933 amounted to 400 million dollars (before income taxes) consisted of approximately 1.6 billions in gains on the part of corporations having net income and about 1.2 billions in losses for corporations without net income. It was largely because of such factors as these that the attempt at wholesale wage increases through the NRA codes met with such difficulties. For many businesses it was utterly ruinous to meet the code requirements. The problem was not merely one of transferring profits to wages; it meant rather a draft upon capital.

The foregoing paragraphs are not intended to convey the implication that there is something sacred about profits and that they must always be safeguarded at some particular level. The facts show clearly that profits vary widely under differing conditions without destroying business enterprise. It is none the less true that in a system of private enterprise profits are a motivating force in production and have an important bearing upon employment and payrolls.

IV. WAGES AND PRICES

One of the most widely discussed features of the present depression has been the relative movement of wages and prices. Reference has already been made to the divergent theories with respect to the importance of wage and price adjustments, one group holding that inflexible wage structures have prevented recovery, and the other holding that wages must be maintained, or even increased, as a means of promoting business expansion. Without attempting at this place to settle this controversial issue, we shall present the essential facts with reference to the actual movements of wages and prices.

The chart on page 255 shows the movements of wholesale and retail prices of finished manufactured goods and hourly wage earnings in manufactures. Wholesale prices started to decline in the last quarter of 1929. Retail prices did not begin to fall until the first quarter of 1930. Wages (that is, hourly earnings) were held up to approximately their 1929 level for more than a year, and it was not until the end of 1930 that they started to fall.

Two explanations may be given of the fact that average hourly earnings held up for such a long time after the onset of the depression. In the first place, in the late twenties the philosophy that high wages were the basis of prosperity had come to be accepted by many business men. This, coupled with the belief that the drop in business activity was only temporary, apparently had a potent effect in maintaining disbursements to personnel as well as to stockholders at a higher level than later proved to have been justified. Not only were rates of wages maintained, but for a long time employees were kept on payrolls even though there was not enough work to keep them busy.

HOURLY EARNINGS IN MANUFACTURING AND WHOLESALE
AND RETAIL PRICES OF FINISHED MANUFACTURED
PRODUCTS, 1920-36[a]

(1929 = 100)

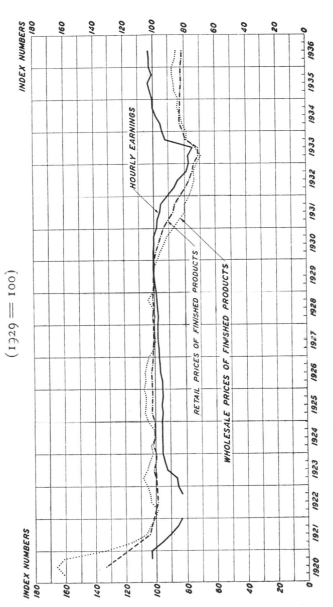

[a] For data, see Appendix C, Table 26.

255

In the second place, when reductions in personnel were finally made, the less efficient and hence the lower paid employees were dropped first. This had a tendency to raise the average earnings of those remaining on the payrolls. To the extent that the averages are influenced by the weeding out of the lower paid wage earners, our index of hourly earnings does not measure the movement of rates of wages in the abstract. The index reflects only the hourly earnings of the residual employees, that is, the earnings of those actually employed.

The lowest point in each of the three indexes plotted in the chart was reached in the first half of 1933. Prices turned up first, but they did not lead through the upward course as they did on the way down. Because of the operation of the NRA, hourly earnings recovered more rapidly than retail and wholesale prices. In the three months of the third quarter of 1933 average hourly earnings in manufacturing regained all they had lost in the eighteen months preceding. By the middle of 1934 the wage averages appear to have reached their 1929 level and have since stood above that level.[3] Neither retail nor wholesale prices experienced the same degree of recovery as wages. By the end of 1935 wholesale prices of finished goods were still about 12 per cent below their 1929 level and retail prices about 17 per cent.

V. WAGES AND PRODUCTIVITY

In current discussions productivity is related to wages in two ways. Some regard increasing productivity with apprehension and see in it the cause of labor displace-

---

[3] Attention should again be called to the fact that the average of hourly earnings is influenced by changes in composition of personnel as well as by changes in actual rates.

ment and hence of unemployment and reduced payrolls. Others accept increasing productivity with less suspicion, but are concerned with the extent to which its benefits are translated into higher wages. The phase of the subject indicated by the first point of view need not be treated here; it is covered in Chapter VII (see pages 167-75). In this section we shall examine briefly the movement of wages and productivity in recent years.

Inherently, productivity is the basis of wages, prices, and profits, and in the long run its benefits are passed on to the public in any or all of these ways. (It may also be reflected in changes of hours of work, which is another form of wage benefits.) Within short periods of time, however, the extent to which increasing productivity is balanced by any combination of lower prices, and higher wages and higher profits, is neither predictable nor precise. The factor which disturbs the equivalence is the degree of utilization of facilities. Productivity is merely a rate which to become effective must, like wage rates, be associated with duration and continuity of activity. High productivity per man-hour has no practical significance if it is accompanied by a low rate of utilization of the available man-hours. Like wages and profits, benefits through lower prices are derived from total product, and total product is the resultant of the rate of productivity and the volume of work.

In the chart on page 258 comparison is made of productivity, wage rates,[4] and prices in manufacturing industries during the period 1919-36. When prices and wages are taken separately, there is little apparent rela-

[4] Wage rates are here represented by the average hourly earnings of those employed and hence are somewhat different from rates in the abstract. But since productivity is computed on the basis of total man-hours of the same workers the comparison is consistent.

tionship between either and the growth in productivity. While the latter shows a very definite upward trend, both wages and prices—with the exception of the two

Wages, Prices, and Productivity in Manufacturing
Industries, 1919-36[a]

(1929 = 100)

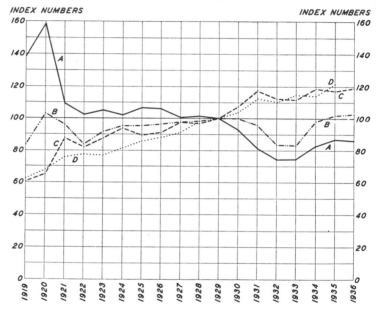

A. WHOLESALE PRICES OF FINISHED PRODUCTS
B. FULL-TIME WAGES
C. "PRODUCT" WAGES [b]
D. PRODUCTIVITY

[a] For data, see Appendix C, Table 27. Estimates for 1936 are preliminary.
[b] In terms of finished manufactured products at wholesale prices.

periods of depression—have varied within a narrow range, and the direction of their trends is only faintly perceptible. The explanation is that prices and wage rates, although they both reflect changes in productivity, are moved in opposite directions by them.

A better measure of the effect of productivity may be had by expressing wages in terms of the goods produced by the workers. The resultant index of "product wages,"[5] which reflects the effect of productivity on both wages and prices, is represented in the chart on page 258 by line C. This new line corresponds more closely with that representing productivity than either prices or wages alone.

In line with the foregoing it is found that hourly earnings in manufacturing, when expressed in terms of physical product, have increased since 1919 at the average rate of 3.6 per cent per annum. For the same period man-hour productivity (wage earners only) rose at the average annual rate of approximately 4.0 per cent, while the average rate of growth of manufacturing production per equivalent full-time person engaged, including salaried employees and entrepreneurs, was 3.5 per cent per year.[6] Thus it appears that the tendency has been for the share of labor to expand in almost the same proportion as productivity.

The wage earners, however, did not get their remuneration in the goods which they produced at wholesale prices. Their wages were paid in money which they used in buying various goods and services at retail. Hence, even though their share of their own product increased in proportion to their productivity, their "real" wages need not have grown proportionately. In trading the

[5] Average earnings adjusted by means of the index of wholesale prices of finished manufactured goods.

[6] Needless to say, the trend measurements are only approximate. It should be evident that the comparisons are in very rough terms. The price index is of necessity not wholly co-ordinate with the wage and productivity indexes.

goods he produces himself for the commodities he needs, the wage earner in manufacturing may well have been compelled to lose part of his advantage. This, in fact, is what has taken place. "Real wages," that is wages corrected for the cost of living, increased at the average rate of only 2.4 per cent per annum.

It is not possible to account precisely for this difference. A large fraction of it is due to the fact that while the factory workers use machines in the production of the goods they place on the market, they buy in a large measure goods and services produced "by hand." In other words, owing to differences in productivity it is to be expected that an increasing volume of manufactured goods should be offered for a given unit of nonmanufactures. Part of the difference is also accounted for by the fact that the cost of living includes items such as ground rent and minerals, which, because of the limited supply, are bound to increase in price with the increase in the number and income of the people. Another cause of divergence between "product" wages and "real" wages is due to the imperfections of the data. Aside from the inadequacies of the other series, the cost of living index by its very nature tends to exaggerate the prices of goods used in consumption, since it cannot incorporate changes which are constantly taking place in the pattern of consumption and cannot make proper allowances for the increasing volume of "free" goods which is made available to consumers.

A comparison of the deviations of hourly earnings and man-hour productivity from their respective trends does not reveal consistent correlation between the two during the entire period covered. In general, however, it may be said that "product" wages and productivity move together (see the chart on page 261). They went up during the first two years of the current depression, reaching a peak in 1931, and declined more or less together in the subsequent years.

The short-time fluctuations (deviations from trend) in "real" wages corresponded for the most part to the

DEVIATIONS FROM TREND OF MAN-HOUR PRODUCTIVITY
AND HOURLY WAGES IN MANUFACTURING
INDUSTRIES, 1919-35[a]

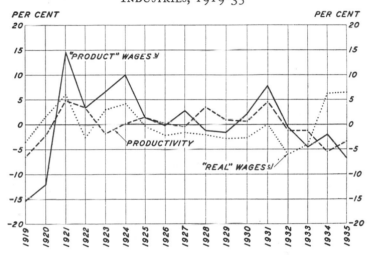

ᵃ For basic data, see Appendix C, Tables 21, 23, and 28.
ᵇ In terms of finished manufactured products at wholesale prices.
ᶜ Adjusted to cost of living.

fluctuations in "product" wages. A significant exception is found in the recovery phase of the present cycle. While "product" wages as well as productivity have continued to move down from the peak of 1931 (their low point in this movement has not yet been established by the data through 1935), "real" wages reached bottom in 1932 and then turned up, with the result that they stood considerably above "normal" in 1934 and 1935.

In other words, the cost of living had not caught up with the rise in hourly earnings in 1935 and it is apparent that if the figures were available it would be found that "real" wages are still above "normal."

The comparison of "real" wages with productivity brings us back to a point raised before but which is worthy of emphasis. The question of wage rates in terms of the cost of living has only limited significance in the general aspects of depression and recovery. The movement of "real" wages is of material interest only to those who are fully employed. An increase in average hourly earnings, whether it is expressed as real wages or money wages, is small comfort to the family which through reduced hours of work or total unemployment has lost part or all of its income. To the partly or wholly unemployed, income counts more than leisure and even more than higher rates per hour. To the population at large it is the total volume of production and the total of wages that count. Despite the increase in population, wage disbursements in the major industries in 1932, after correction for changes in cost of living, were nearly 50 per cent lower than in 1929, and the total labor income including salaries was 27 per cent lower. Even in 1935 the labor income of the country was only 86 per cent[8] of that received by a smaller number of persons in 1929.[9]

VI. WAGES AND COST OF PRODUCTION

In the introductory paragraphs of this chapter attention was called to the significance of the fact that wages are both a source of purchasing power and a cost of production. It was noted that one type of analysis em-

[8] This includes work-relief wages. Without work relief it was 82 per cent.

[9] In current dollars the three percentages last given were 59, 41, and 69 respectively.

phasizes the importance of maintaining and increasing wage rates as a means of providing purchasing power while another emphasizes the importance of reducing wages in order to obtain a satisfactory cost-price ratio.

In line with the analysis which runs in terms of wages as costs it would be of interest to examine the changes in wage rates which have occurred since 1929 in the different fields of economic activity. The existing data, however, do not permit of any conclusive analysis of the interaction of wage rates and costs during the depression. The indexes for major industries plotted in the chart on page 263 are subject to the limitations indicated in connection with the discussion of manufacturing wages (see page 246). They represent for the most part average earnings per hour for those employed and indicate only in a general way the real movement of wage rates. Even where the indexes purport to represent rates, they are of necessity based on averages for a more or less wide range of occupations and skills and so are affected by errors of sampling. On the whole, therefore, the figures reflect changes in the composition of personnel as well as actual changes in rates. Thus the averages for building construction show a decline in the first half of 1936 despite the fact that during this period the rates for both skilled and unskilled labor appear to have increased. The decline was apparently due merely to the larger proportion of unskilled labor engaged in 1936 as compared to 1935. The same factor has undoubtedly influenced the averages for other lines of activity. Moreover, changes in technology have modified in varying degrees the relative significance of wage rates in different industries.

The chart shows that there has been considerable variation during the depression in the movement of

(1929 = 100)

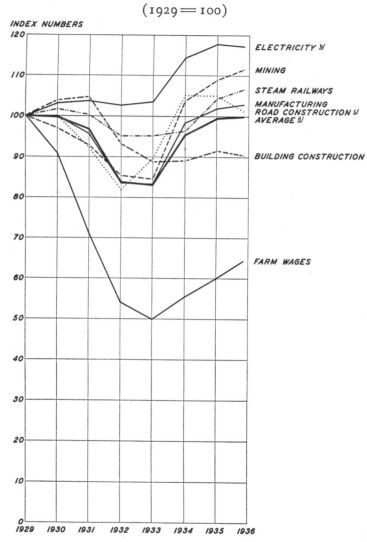

INDEX NUMBERS

ELECTRICITY [b]

MINING

STEAM RAILWAYS

MANUFACTURING
ROAD CONSTRUCTION [c]
AVERAGE [d]

BUILDING CONSTRUCTION

FARM WAGES

[a] For data, see Appendix C, Table 29. Estimates for 1936 are preliminary.

[b] Production and distribution.   [c] Common labor.

[d] Exclusive of farm wages.

average wages in the several industries. But no definite conclusion can be drawn with respect to the maladjustments created by the lack of correspondence in these fluctuations. However, the significance of this lack of correspondence is perhaps not so great as may appear. The fact that wage rates in different industries have failed to move together is not in itself an indication that the maladjustments are now greater than they were in so-called normal times.

More important than relative changes of wage rates is the consideration of labor costs as compared with wage income. The condition most conducive to prosperity and economic progress is low labor costs combined with high returns to the workers, that is, with high aggregate wages. This means technological efficiency and fully employed labor time. Unfortunately, there are important industries in which this condition does not obtain even in days of prosperity. In building construction, for instance, high wage rates combined with low output per man-hour make for high costs. Yet by and large, despite the high hourly rates, the annual incomes of the workers in the building trades are not high, for the reason that the number of hours of actual employment per year is on the average comparatively low. If the industry were so organized as to permit employment on an annual rather than daily or hourly basis and permit a fuller utilization of the workers, labor costs might be reduced without reducing earnings. Indeed, with lower costs, production might be expanded and aggregate earnings greatly increased. Building construction is not the only sphere within which improvement in the wage structure and other changes which lead to reduction of costs without infringing upon the wage income of the workers would facilitate expansion in production and employment.

CHAPTER XI

CHANGES IN THE PRICE STRUCTURE

Profound disturbances in the process of producing and distributing goods and services are nowhere more quickly or strikingly revealed than in the movements of commodity prices. Attention has already been called, in Part I, to the catastrophic decline in the world price of foodstuffs and raw materials during the course of the depression and also to the fluctuations of general wholesale prices in sixteen countries. We shall now consider in much greater detail the changes which have occurred in the structure of prices in the United States.

Some students attribute great cyclical changes in business conditions to fluctuations in the general level of prices arising out of independent variations in the available supply of money and credit. Others, particularly in recent years, have sought to explain the severity of business depressions not so much by the general decline in the level of prices as by the disruption of price relationships. The wide dispersion of prices that occurs during depression is attributed to the growth of so-called inflexible elements in the price structure resulting from monopolistic controls, governmental regulations, the power of labor organizations, and so forth. It is contended that the consequent distortion of the price structure serves not only to intensify but also to prolong depression. In line with this reasoning it is assumed that recovery cannot begin until a substantial realignment of prices has occurred; or at least that recovery will be seriously retarded so long as wide price disparities remain. In view of these varying conceptions of the significance of price changes in relation to cyclical movements, a study of price fluctuations since 1929 is evidently essential.

For the purpose in hand we shall show the fluctuations in the prices of commodities as a whole, both wholesale and retail, and then analyze the variations in the prices of raw materials and semi-finished and finished goods; major groups of commodities; selected industrial products; and the commodities bought and sold by farmers.[1]

1. Wholesale prices and the cost of living. In the chart at the top of page 268 are shown the movements of indexes of wholesale prices and the cost of living. The wholesale price index covers 784 commodities; and the cost of living index includes the retail prices of commodities, together with rents. On the downswing, it will be observed, wholesale prices led continuously and the maximum decline was some 10 per cent greater than in the case of retail prices. The turn in wholesale prices came in March 1933, and the upward movement was rapid until September. The increase in retail prices was both tardier and much less pronounced. Since the beginning of 1934 the two indexes have been close together and have remained fairly stable at a level some 15 per cent below that of 1929. It is evident that in general these over-all wholesale and retail price indexes show no striking divergences. However, when the various groups and sub-groups of commodities which comprise the general indexes are studied, much wider variations are indicated.

2. Wholesale prices of raw materials and semifinished and finished goods. In the chart at the bottom of the following page are shown the wholesale price varia-

---

[1] The relative movement of wages and prices is shown in the chart on p. 255.

INDEXES OF WHOLESALE PRICES AND COST OF LIVING, 1929 TO JUNE 1936[a]

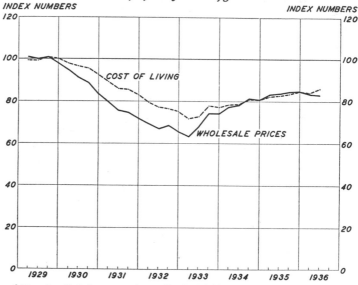

ª For detailed data, see Appendix E, Table 1.

INDEXES OF WHOLESALE PRICES OF RAW MATERIALS AND SEMI-FINISHED AND FINISHED GOODS, 1929 TO JUNE 1936[a]

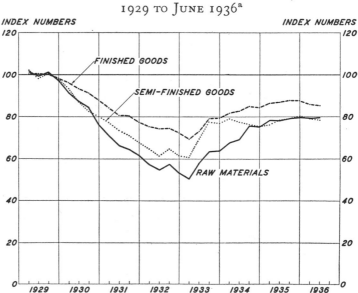

ª For detailed data, see Appendix E, Table 1.

tions of commodities classified in broad categories. Here we find considerable price dispersion. From 1929 to the first quarter of 1933 the prices of raw materials declined 50 per cent, of semi-finished goods 40 per cent, and of finished commodities only 30 per cent. The upturn began first in the case of raw materials, and by the end of 1934 the dispersion as between raw and semi-manufactured products had been eliminated. It still remains true, however, that the prices of raw materials and semi-manufactured commodities are appreciably lower, relatively to 1929, than those of finished products.

3. *Wholesale prices of major groups of commodities.* Wider variations in wholesale price movements during the course of the depression are revealed by the indexes of the ten groups of commodities which enter into the general wholesale index. The dispersion of prices is shown in the diagrams on page 270. Because of the number of groups included, it has been necessary to break the diagram into two parts.

The greatest decline occurred in the prices of farm products, which fell from 1929 to the first quarter of 1933 from 100 to 39, or 61 per cent. The smallest recession, 23.5 per cent, was in metals and metal products. The declines in the prices of house furnishings, chemicals, fuel and lighting, building materials, and the miscellaneous group were all less than 30 per cent, while the prices of foods and textile products declined more than 40 per cent.

The upturn in all cases except fuel and lighting began between February and May 1933. In the ensuing years the largest rises have been in those groups which had previously shown the most severe declines. At the present time prices of farm products are still relatively low, while those of fuel and lighting and building materials

INDEXES OF WHOLESALE PRICES OF GROUPS OF COMMODITIES, 1929 TO JUNE 1936[a]

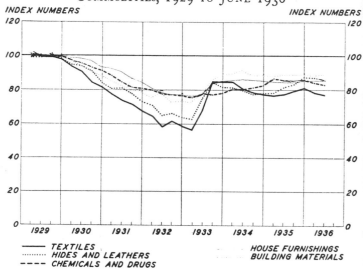

TEXTILES
HIDES AND LEATHERS
CHEMICALS AND DRUGS

HOUSE FURNISHINGS
BUILDING MATERIALS

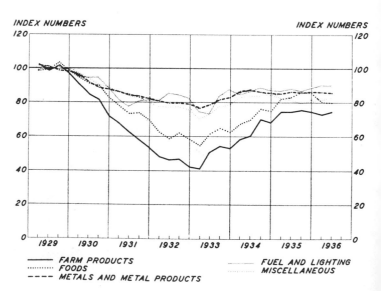

FARM PRODUCTS
FOODS
METALS AND METAL PRODUCTS

FUEL AND LIGHTING
MISCELLANEOUS

[a] For detailed data, see Appendix E, Table 2.

are relatively high. In general, however, the degree of price dispersion has been very materially reduced.

4. Wholesale prices of selected products. When we break down the major groups of commodities into types of products, still wider variations in the degree of price change are revealed. These are shown in the diagrams on page 272. Iron and steel, paper and pulp, boots and shoes, and furniture products showed a decline at the maximum of only 20 to 25 per cent. At the other extreme, non-ferrous metals (copper, lead, zinc, and so forth) declined by 57 per cent, petroleum products by 56 per cent, and cotton goods by 50 per cent. Woolens and worsteds and lumber declined by about 40 per cent and fertilizers by a little over 30 per cent.

It is of interest to compare the marked declines in the prices of non-ferrous metals and lumber with the more moderate declines in the larger groups of which they are component parts, namely, metal products and building materials respectively (see chart, page 270). Similarly, the decline in the price of the sub-group, petroleum products, was much more severe than that of the general group of fuel and lighting.

The upturn was manifested earliest in the case of lumber, fertilizer materials, non-ferrous metals, and cotton goods—in February and March 1933. At the other extreme, petroleum products and iron and steel did not begin to go up until June 1933. By June 1936 the prices of boots and shoes, woolens and worsteds, iron and steel, and paper and pulp were above 90 per cent of the 1929 level, while non-ferrous metals and fertilizers were still below 70 per cent. Thus it is apparent that there are still wide variations in prices as compared with pre-depression relationships.

INDEXES OF WHOLESALE PRICES OF SELECTED PRODUCTS,
1929 TO JUNE 1936[a]
(1929 = 100)

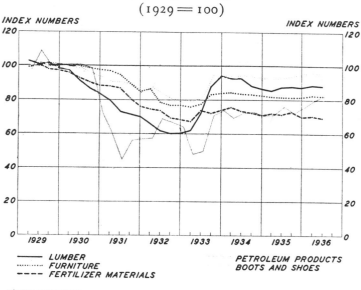

INDEX NUMBERS

——— LUMBER
·········· FURNITURE
– – – FERTILIZER MATERIALS

PETROLEUM PRODUCTS
BOOTS AND SHOES

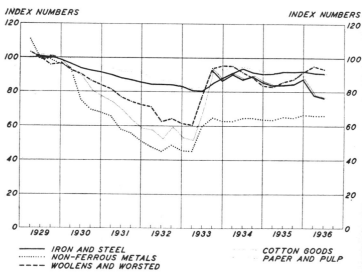

INDEX NUMBERS

——— IRON AND STEEL
·········· NON-FERROUS METALS
– – – WOOLENS AND WORSTED

············ COTTON GOODS
PAPER AND PULP

[a] For data, see Appendix E, Table 3.

5. Variations in agricultural and industrial prices.
The comparative movements of agricultural and industrial prices have occupied a central place in discussions of price relationships. Moreover, the Agricultural Adjustment program has been definitely directed toward increasing agricultural prices relatively to industrial prices, with a view to restoring what is called "price parity." From this point of view the best means of revealing the relative position of the farm population during the depression is to compare the prices which the farmer receives for the goods he produces with the prices which he pays for the commodities which he customarily purchases. For the latter purpose two indexes are employed, covering commodities used respectively for home maintenance and in farm productive operations. These indexes are shown in the diagram on page 274.

Between 1929 and the first quarter of 1933 prices paid by the farmer for articles used in home maintenance and for productive operations declined 37 and 31 per cent respectively. Meanwhile prices received for farm products declined by 62 per cent. In considering the relative position of the farm population with respect to income it is, however, necessary to bear in mind that a substantial part of the farmer's living is provided directly on the farm; and it is also to be noted that the fall in the prices paid by farmers for consumer commodities was some 10 per cent greater than the decline in the cost of living of the urban population.

Since the low point of the depression the index of prices paid by farmers for home maintenance goods has risen from 63 to 77, while that for farm production commodities has risen from 69 to 82. The rise in the prices of home maintenance goods occurred almost entirely in the first year of the recovery. Prices of goods used in farm production continued to rise until September 1934, since which time they have fallen by nearly 10 per cent.

Meanwhile the index of prices received by farmers has risen from 38 to 73. The increase in the prices of farm

INDEXES OF PRICES OF COMMODITIES BOUGHT AND SOLD BY FARMERS, MARCH 1929 TO JUNE 1936[a]

(1929 = 100)

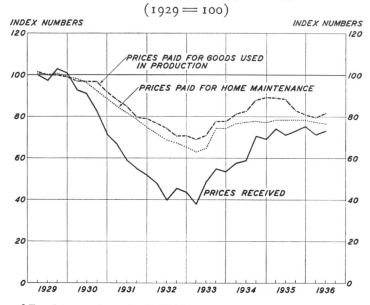

[a] For data, see Appendix E, Table 1.

products has occurred in two jumps, so to speak, the first in the spring and summer of 1933, and the second in the third quarter of 1934. Since September 1934 the general level of prices received by farmers has fluctuated within moderate limits, rising by the first half of 1936 to a point which brought prices of farm products within 10 per cent of their pre-war ratio to industrial prices. During the last few months they have risen to substantial equality with 1909-14. It should be borne in mind in this connection, however, that inasmuch as the increase in farm prices is due in substantial part to reduced production, these price changes do not necessarily reflect proportional changes in income.

We cannot at this place enter into a general discussion of the relationship between price movements and the phenomenon of depression and recovery. Two or three general observations may, however, be made. In the first place, it is apparent that recovery was not delayed until after prices had been realigned. The fact is that the recovery began at the time of greatest price dispersion; the realignments which have occurred have been an accompaniment of the process of recovery.

In the second place, there is no definite evidence in support of the view that the length of the 1929-33 depression is primarily attributable to the growth in modern times of inflexibility in the price structure.[2] The present recovery began at the end of a period during which the dispersion of prices had been occurring at the most rapid rate. During the first stage of the depression, extending to the spring of 1931, there was a considerable divergence in price movements; but the widest variations came in the stage of acute depression from the spring of 1931 to the spring of 1933—at the end of which both general business and prices began to recover.

Whether the rate and degree of recovery have been adversely affected by the relatively high prices existing in certain sectors of the economy is of course another

[2] It is of interest in this connection to note that the recent recession was of considerably shorter duration than the great depressions which occurred in the 1870's and the 1830's—before the development of monopolies, regulated utilities, and powerful labor organizations.

matter. It is our view that the extent of recovery in certain lines of activity would have been greater had costs and prices not remained substantially out of alignment with other costs and prices. Evidence—not assembled in this chapter—shows that recovery has in general proceeded furthest in lines where prices are relatively low and least where prices are relatively high.

The discussion of the present chapter is not directly related to the larger issue as to whether the depression itself is to be explained by an inadequate supply of gold or money and credit. It should be recalled here, however, that in studying the sources of maladjustment existing in 1929 we did not find that there was any shortage of gold or other forms of currency. It is our conclusion that the catastrophic fall in the general level of prices was an accompaniment of the business depression and not an antecedent cause thereof.

CHAPTER XII

THE TREND OF GOVERNMENT FINANCE

We turn in this chapter from a consideration of the readjustments which have been occurring in the realm of private enterprise to a study of the concurrent changes in the field of government finance. As has already been indicated, the situation with respect to public finance is of an unprecedented character, other depressions and recoveries having occurred without any noteworthy increase in public indebtedness. As the government assumed new burdens during the present depression, the simultaneous decline in tax revenues and increase of expenditures inevitably served greatly to increase the debt of the national government. Since the recovery began, notwithstanding a material increase in revenues the federal debt has continued to expand in consequence of the continuance of large outlays for relief purposes and the effort to stimulate revival through the medium of large disbursements from the federal Treasury. Meanwhile the debts of states, counties, and other local agencies have registered no material change. The bearing of this accumulated public indebtedness upon the stability of the fiscal and monetary system and the further progress of recovery presents an issue of paramount significance.

If we are to be in a position to gauge the importance of the issue thus raised, we must have before us a clear and accurate picture of the extent of the changes which have occurred in public finance. The central points on which light is required are: the growth of the public debt and of interest charges; the trends with respect to revenues and expenditures; and the growth of government debt burdens in relation to taxation requirements and national income.

In order to simplify the analysis as much as possible we shall divide this chapter into three major divisions. In the first we shall present the facts with reference to the trends in national finance; in the second we shall give a summary picture of the situation with respect to all governments combined—federal, state, and local; and the third section will be devoted to the relation of taxation to national income. The interpretation of the significance of the public debt situation with respect to the maintenance of financial stability and the promotion of further recovery will be reserved for Chapter XVIII.

I. THE FEDERAL GOVERNMENT

In setting forth the situation with respect to federal government finance it will be necessary to divide the analysis into five major parts, covering respectively: the growth and structure of the debt; the burden of interest charges; fluctuations in receipts and expenditures; sources of revenue; and the growth and changing character of expenditures. In order to make the presentation as graphic as possible the basic data will be presented in a series of diagrams. Explanatory comments and supporting evidence underlying the diagrams and statements made in the text are relegated to footnotes and to Appendix F.

A. The Growth and Structure of the Debt

In analyzing the situation with respect to the federal government it will be necessary to consider separately the aggregate amount of the debt; the composition of the interest bearing debt; the contingent liabilities which constitute potential additions to the existing obligations; and the assets owned by the government which may have some liquidation value. While our interest centers primarily on the increase in the federal debt in recent years, it will be helpful in giving perspective to the whole discussion if we have before us a picture of the growth of public indebtedness over a period of years. Since the great fluctuations in the federal debt begin with the entrance of the United States into the World War, we shall run our figures back as far as 1915.

1. The aggregate federal debt. The chart below shows the amount of the gross federal debt outstanding at the

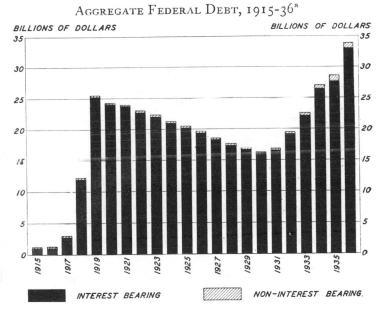

AGGREGATE FEDERAL DEBT, 1915-36[a]

[a] For data, see Appendix F, Table 4.

end of each fiscal year from June 1915 through June 1936. At the end of the Civil War the aggregate debt had exceeded 2.7 billion dollars, whereas in 1915 it was little more than a billion. The existence of this remaining debt did not reflect any inability on the part of the government to repay all its obligations. The larger portion of the interest bearing debt was used by the national banks as security for bank notes; and the bulk of the small non-interest bearing debt represented the unsecured portion of the currency in the form of United States notes or greenbacks.

As a result of the World War the gross federal debt reached an aggregate on August 31, 1919 of 26,597 million dollars. In the ensuing decade it was reduced by over 10 billion dollars, the post-war low of 16,026 millions being reached on December 31, 1930.[1] In the five and a half years since, the debt has increased by 17,753 millions; and the total on June 30, 1936 of 33,779 millions is 7,182 millions above the level reached in 1919.

Practically all of the federal debt increase since before the war has been in the form of interest bearing obligations.[2] In recent years, however, there have been significant changes in the character and proportions of the interest bearing debt to which attention must be directed.

2. *Changing character of the interest bearing debt, 1930-36.* As will be seen from the chart on page 281, there are four major types of interest bearing obligations—long-term bonds, intermediate term notes (one to five years), short-term Treasury certificates, and Treasury bills which were introduced in 1930. The maturities of bills and certificates may run up to twelve months. The difference between them is that, whereas certificates are issued to bear interest at a fixed coupon rate, the bills are sold at a discount (determined by competitive bidding), the interest being an initial deduction

---

[1] The means by which this reduction was accomplished are indicated in Appendix F, Section II.

[2] The amount of the non-interest bearing debt is given by years in Appendix F, Table 4. The increase in volume in recent years is attributable to retirements of national bank notes.

from the ultimate maturity value. They thus constitute an extremely flexible medium of financing.

INTEREST BEARING FEDERAL DEBT, CLASSIFIED, 1930-36[a]

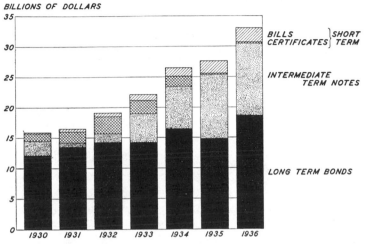

^a For data, see Appendix F, Table 5.

The striking fact revealed by the chart is the relative decrease in the proportion of long-term obligations. Although there was an increase in the total volume of bonds outstanding between 1930 and 1936 of 6.5 billion dollars, the percentage of the total obligations which was in the form of bonds declined from 76 to 56 per cent. From negligible amounts outstanding in 1931, the intermediate term notes have steadily increased to more than 11.8 billions on June 30, 1936, constituting 36 per cent of the interest bearing debt. In the short-term debt there was a preponderance of certificates until 1934, but since then the situation has been reversed.

The scheduling of maturity dates has presented a difficult problem. It would be obviously desirable during a deficit period to arrange maturities at sufficiently distant dates to preclude any possibility of their falling due while deficits were still being incurred. Various practical considerations have, however, prevented an altogether satisfactory arrangement of maturities on new borrowing. But bond maturities have been spread over a longer term of years, and spread more evenly, by the refunding of the Fourth Liberty Loan due in 1938 and the First Liberty Loan due in 1947 involving more than 8 billion dollars. The short-term debt, maturing within twelve months, has been reduced somewhat as compared with earlier years; but, on the other hand, the whole mass of short and intermediate term debt, all of which falls due before 1942, has exceeded 13.7 billions.

The maturity schedule as it appeared on June 30, 1932 and June 30, 1936 is shown in the chart on page 283. It will be observed that the bunching of maturities in 1938 and 1947 has been eliminated, and that a much more even spread has been obtained. Increasingly heavy maturities on the intermediate notes are, however, to be faced between 1936 and 1940. Discussion of what is involved in the refunding of these obligations must wait on the fuller consideration of the budget situation as a whole and the sources of borrowed funds.

Before concluding this discussion of the character of the public debt, attention must be directed to certain "special-purpose interest bearing debts." Various issues are set apart by the purposes for which they are created, the receipt of funds by the Treasury being incidental to the primary purpose of providing special types of investments. Such, for example, are the Postal and United States Savings bonds, and the special issues authorized as Social Security reserve investments. There are also special obligations for which no funds are received by the Treasury at the time of issue; in effect, these merely recognize established claims against the government pay-

able at some future date. The most conspicuous illustrations are the Adjusted Service bonds, and notes and certificates issued to the Adjusted Service Certificate Fund.

MATURITIES OF INTEREST BEARING FEDERAL DEBT[a]

I. AS OF JUNE 30, 1932

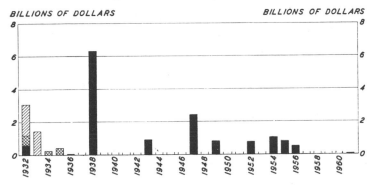

II. AS OF JUNE 30, 1936

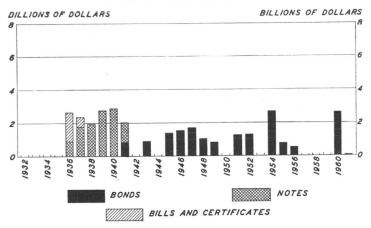

[a] For data, see Appendix F, Table 6.

At present the volume of special-purpose interest
bearing debts is not great and constitutes but a negligible
proportion of the total debt. The aggregate amount of all

such issues in 1930 was $1,458,021,350 and in 1936 it was $2,007,664,484. For a fuller statement with reference to the special-purpose government debts the reader is referred to Appendix F, Section III.

Broad questions of national policy are involved in some of these special-purpose obligations. They suggest, moreover, the possibility or necessity of a much larger permanent public debt in the future than has been the case in the past. Just as the system of bond-secured national bank note issues in former times required the maintenance of a considerable volume of federal debt, so in the future open market operations of the Federal Reserve Banks, and operations under the Social Security Act and other measures would seem to afford a permanent "repository" for a very large volume of public debt.[3]

3. Contingent liabilities of the federal government. In addition to the direct public debt of the United States government there are a number of indirect obligations which are legally recognized as contingent liabilities. In the main their origin is explained by the dependence of certain vital parts of the private economic system upon government support, regulation, or protection. As a minor exception to this, but with vast potentialities, are contingent liabilities arising out of indirect governmental borrowing. Thus in developing a specific enterprise the government may use a specially created corporation or agency which is authorized to borrow in its own name —with the assurance of ultimate support from the federal government in case of necessity.

Prior to the depression, the indirect obligations of the

[3] On the basis of tentative actuarial schedules it is believed that the Old-age Reserve Account will accumulate to about 48 billions by 1980. The Unemployment Trust Fund will be a reserve which will possibly reach proportions of from one to 2 billions. Such a prospective development of course raises very important issues, which cannot be discussed at this place.

federal government were confined largely to the maintenance of sound currency. Since 1932 a score of supplementary financial agencies, both of temporary and permanent character, have been created, particularly in the fields of home mortgage finance and agricultural credit. The extent of the contingent liabilities of the federal government, in all connections, as of May 31, 1936, is shown in the accompanying table:

CONTINGENT LIABILITIES OF THE FEDERAL GOVERNMENT,
MAY 31, 1936[a]

(In millions of dollars)

Type of Liability	Amount
OBLIGATIONS GUARANTEED BY THE GOVERNMENT.............	**4,727**
Federal Farm Mortgage Corporation bonds..............	1,428
Federal Housing Administration debentures..............	—
Home Owners' Loan Corporation bonds...................	3,046
Reconstruction Finance Corporation notes[b].	253
Tennessee Valley Authority bonds[c]......................	—
OBLIGATIONS SUPPORTED BY CREDIT OF UNITED STATES.........	**5,026**
Postal Savings system deposits (Mar. 31, 1936)[d]...........	1,244
Federal Reserve notes[e].................................	3,782
Secretary of Agriculture[f]..............................	—
GRAND TOTAL.......................................	**9,753**

[a] *Statement of the Public Debt of the United States,* May 31, 1936.

[b] These notes do not represent sales to the general public; they were issued chiefly in exchange for preferred stock and capital notes or debentures of banks in bolstering their capital structure. For its cash expenditures, the Reconstruction Finance Corporation has obtained funds by borrowing directly from the Treasury.

[c] Authorized to issue 50 million dollars of bonds. The Authority has to the present been financed from the federal Treasury.

[d] The government pledges itself to the payment of these deposits; but since about three-fourths of Postal Savings assets consist of government obligations the pledge is not of great practical importance.

[e] Technically these notes are obligations of the United States; but they are issued by the Federal Reserve Banks, on whose assets they have a prior lien. They are also protected by segregated collateral of which 40 per cent is in gold certificates.

[f] Under the Agricultural Adjustment Act the Secretary was authorized to acquire and dispose of cotton held as collateral to loans of governmental agencies; and, as an incident in the process of disposal, to borrow with government guaranty of repayment. Only a small amount was borrowed and this was promptly liquidated.

A common characteristic of these contingent liabilities is that (except for the obligations of the Secretary of Agriculture) they are the obligations of agencies set up distinct from the government proper, but functioning under financial procedures defined and restricted by federal statute. The character of these special enterprises permits a separation of collateral assets to support the indebtedness, and it is chiefly for this reason that it is proper to classify them—so long as the underlying collateral values are adequate—as only indirect obligations of the government.

Attention should also be called to the fact that as a practical matter the United States government has assumed a moral responsibility for the safety of bank deposits. While the deposits are insured by a special Federal Deposit Insurance Corporation Fund, the ultimate security rests in considerable measure on the general credit of the government.

4. Assets of the federal government. Assets owned by the federal government consist of three types: (1) public buildings and other property directly utilized in the conduct of ordinary government operations; (2) public parks, waterways, lands, and so forth constructed or acquired in pursuit of general public policy; (3) various loans and investments acquired by the Treasury in connection with fiscal operations. The first two types, with minor exceptions, do not yield any revenue and could not well be liquidated; nor are they formally capitalized. The third group represents in considerable part realizable assets which may be used for the purpose of offsetting government obligations.

The normal function of government is to provide immediate services and not to acquire and develop productive properties. But at times, and especially in periods of great emergency, the Treasury is authorized to make loans with and without collateral security, and to sponsor undertakings which bring productive assets in their wake. The variety and extent of the loans and investments held by the federal Treasury on May 31, 1936 are shown in the table on page 288.

Of the impressive total of 18 billions, we may at once place the 12 billions of foreign obligations in a state of suspended animation. This leaves a balance of approximately 6 billions, consisting largely of capital investments in subsidiary corporations and agencies, with some special loans and advances.[4] As has already been indicated, the long-term obligations of several of these subsidiary corporations appear as contingent liabilities of the United States. These guaranteed obligations, as we have seen, came into existence largely through the conversion or assumption of existing private debts.

Two purposes were in mind in the extensive use of direct investment: (1) to afford relief or protection to distressed corporations and individuals; and (2) to thaw out, rehabilitate, and stimulate the financial superstructure of the private economy in the hope of promoting recovery.[5] It is evident that in the pursuit of such objec-

[4] In the "Combined Statement of Assets and Liabilities of Governmental Corporations and Credit Agencies," which appears in the *Daily Treasury Statement*, the *proprietary* interest of the United States on May 31, 1936 is shown as $4,295,146,466, with privately owned interest amounting to $347,336,264. These private investments include 156 millions in Federal Land Banks and 160 millions in the Federal Deposit Insurance Corporation. The government's *proprietary* interest is less than the *investments* indicated in the table on p. 288, because of the elimination of certain non-recoverable Reconstruction Finance Corporation assets representing relief allocations.

[5] The first agency organized to stop deflationary liquidation was the National Credit Corporation set up in October 1931, with a revolving fund of 500 millions to be subscribed by private banks. The purpose was to make loans to distressed banks against assets ineligible for rediscount. This agency met with little success and was supplanted by the Reconstruction Finance Corporation in the early part of 1932.

SECURITIES OWNED BY THE FEDERAL GOVERNMENT,
MAY 31, 1936[a]

(In millions of dollars)

Type of Security	Amount
FOREIGN OBLIGATIONS	**$12,015**
Funded	11,156
Unfunded	205
German bonds (reichsmarks converted to dollars)	654
CAPITAL STOCK OF WAR EMERGENCY CORPORATIONS	**84**
U. S. Shipping Board Merchant Fleet Corporation	50
U. S. Housing Corporation	34
U. S. Spruce Production Corporation	b
War Finance Corporation	b
CAPITAL STOCK ETC. OF OTHER GOVERNMENTAL CORPORATIONS AND CREDIT AGENCIES	**5,310**
Panama Railroad Company	7
Inland Waterways Corporation	12
Reconstruction Finance Corporation[c]	3,849
Home Owners' Loan Corporation	100
Federal Savings and Loan Insurance Corporation	100
Regional Agricultural Credit Corporations	29
Federal Home Loan Banks	98
Federal Farm Mortgage Corporation	200
Export-Import Banks of Washington	18
Reconstruction Finance Corp. Mortgage Company	10
Production Credit Corporations	120
Commodity Credit Corporation	100
Electric Home and Farm Authority	b
Federal Deposit Insurance Corporation	150
Federal Savings and Loan Associations	49
Federal Subsistence Homesteads Corporation	b
Federal Land Banks	227
Federal Intermediate Credit Banks	100
Central Bank for Co-operatives	75
Banks for Co-operatives	64
OTHER OBLIGATIONS AND SECURITIES	**656**
Acquired by Fed. Emer. Admin. of Public Works	136
Advances from Revolving Fund of Agr. Marketing Act	110
Seed, feed, drought relief, and crop prod. loans	197
Securities received on account of sale of ships	106
Miscellaneous	107
GRAND TOTAL	**$18,065**

[a] *Statement of the Public Debt of the United States*, May 31, 1936.

[b] Under a million.

[c] A net figure. The total investment of the government in the RFC is $4,620,000,000 representing $500,000,000 in capital stock and $4,120,000,000 in notes. From this is deducted $771,037,262 representing subscriptions to capital stock and provision of loan funds for other corporations and agencies shown on this statement.

tives ordinary banking principles with reference to lending could not be closely followed. If losses should be sustained the ultimate benefits in checking depression and promoting revival might greatly outweigh the losses to the Treasury. It was hoped, however, that with recovery a considerable part of such assets might prove good. By far the most important of the subsidiary agencies is the Reconstruction Finance Corporation. It was established primarily to make loans secured by capital and other assets of private enterprises. The values were taken over at more or less of a discount, in acknowledgment of the general deflationary trend. Its assets at the end of May 1936 included loans and investments (2,443 millions); allocations to other agencies of the government for loan or investment purposes, and so forth (759 millions); and allocations for federal emergency relief (1,800 millions). Loans and investments (exclusive of allocations to other governmental agencies and for relief) made between February 2, 1932 and May 31, 1936 aggregated 6,194 millions, of which 3,751 millions or 61 per cent have been repaid. The balance may include some poor risks; but given full economic recovery tangible results will be realized even on these.

In connection with this apparently favorable recovery record, it should be noted that a considerable part of the funds received have not been used by the Reconstruction Finance Corporation to reimburse the Treasury; 1,800 millions of such funds have been allocated instead to federal emergency relief. Since such assets are not recoverable, it is obvious that the Treasury's expectations of reimbursement will have to be reduced by a like amount.

The purposes of the remaining subsidiary corporations cannot here be dealt with in detail. Most of them also owe their origin to conditions arising during the depression and the ultimate liquidation values are hence problematical.[6] If these institutions prove their worth, it is possible that in some cases their capital may be shifted to private ownership.[7]

The "other obligations and securities" listed in the table have in the main also arisen out of depression conditions; but the operations involved are not carried out by formal corporate organizations. The Public Works Administration has received various marketable securities for advances made to public and private bodies; and most of these may prove marketable under favorable conditions.[8] However, judging from other experience, the greater part of the advances to relieve agricultural distress (with the exception of mortgage loans) will not be repaid.

It is apparent from this discussion that only a portion of the 6 billions of loans and investments owned by the government can be regarded as constituting offsets to public debt.[9] In some instances they have ceased to have any value whatsoever, and the illusion that the proceeds of liquidation will be used to retire debt is being destroyed in proportion as repayments are used for relief or new ventures. While no one can predict the result with any degree of certainty, it is a safe guess that less

[6] The chief exceptions are the war emergency corporations, the Panama Railroad Company, and the Inland Waterways Corporation—a heavily subsidized enterprise.

[7] In several of the agricultural financial agencies provision is made for subscription to capital of the banks by private borrowers in proportion to the loans which they receive.

[8] On May 31, 1936 the RFC held as assets 130 millions of securities of this character purchased from the PWA. A substantial volume had previously been disposed of as market conditions favored. Of total of 406 millions purchased by the RFC, 249 millions had been sold and 27 millions collected.

[9] It should be pointed out that in practice the net debt figure given by the Treasury is derived by deducting only the net balance in the general fund from the gross public debt.

than half of the values listed will be realized by the
Treasury in the form of cash.

B. The Burden of Interest Charges

The fiscal burden of public indebtedness expresses
itself in the cost of debt charges, which must be met from
taxation. Full debt charges ordinarily include both current interest and a sinking fund for amortization of the

INTEREST CHARGES ON THE FEDERAL DEBT, 1915-36[a]

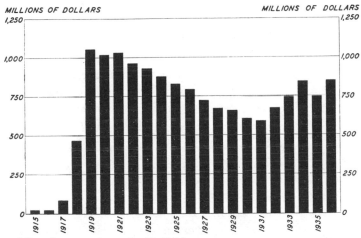

[a] For data, see Appendix F, Table 7.

principal. In the analysis which follows we shall, however, ignore the sinking fund and concentrate attention
solely upon the amount of interest charges, which represent fixed contractual agreements. The accompanying
chart shows the trend of these charges on the federal
debt from the pre-war year 1915 through the fiscal year
1936.[10]

[10] The figures used are the "computed annual interest charges." These
figures give a more accurate index for momentary comparison of interest with principal than the actual interest disbursements, which com-

The striking fact revealed by the diagram is that the growth of the debt in recent years has not been accompanied by a proportional increase in the interest burden. From 1930 through the fiscal year 1934, when the debt increased from 15.9 to 26.5 billions, the interest charge rose only 236 million dollars. Then, with an increase of over 6.5 billion dollars during the ensuing two years, the interest burden remained practically stationary. For comparison it may also be noted that the peak debt in 1919 of 25.2 billions carried an interest charge of 1,054 millions, whereas on the debt of 33 billions in 1936 the interest burden is only 845 millions.

The explanation of this phenomenon is of course to be found in the wide fluctuations in the rate of interest. The chart on page 293 shows the fluctuations from 1915 to 1936 of a computed interest rate representing a composite of the various rates of interest in the different types of government obligations making up the debt at the end of each fiscal year. For purposes of comparison the chart also shows the fluctuations in the principal of the debt.

Wide fluctuations in the interest rate are apparent. Just before the war the average rate on the outstanding debt was 2.37 per cent. It rose to a high of 4.34 per cent in 1921. Then, as the debt structure as a whole was moulded into a more permanent form and as money market conditions changed, the rate gradually declined during the twenties to a low of 3.88 in 1928, rising slightly to 3.95 in 1929.

Since the beginning of the depression the rate of interest on the public debt has steadily declined, at first

---

monly involve a lag. As may be observed from the appendix table, computed interest usually exceeds actual interest disbursements during the years of debt increase and conversely in periods of retirement.

slowly, and then rapidly as if to confound the critics of fiscal policy. From a rate of 3.95 in 1929 it fell to 3.35

FLUCTUATING INTEREST RATES ON FEDERAL DEBT, 1915-36[a]

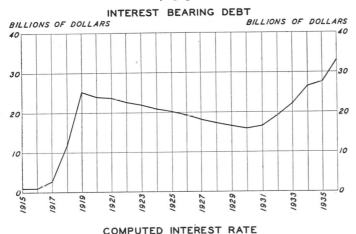

INTEREST BEARING DEBT

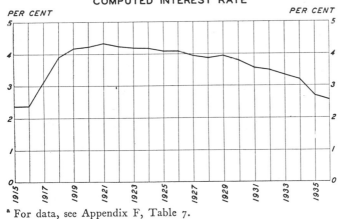

COMPUTED INTEREST RATE

[a] For data, see Appendix F, Table 7.

in 1933 and to 2.56 in 1936. On the face of things it would seem that the more the credit of the government is strained by mounting indebtedness, the stronger the government's credit becomes.

Two factors have combined to reduce the rate at which the government is able to borrow. The first is to be found in underlying conditions in the money market which have resulted in a general decline in the rate of interest. This phenomenon will be considered at a subsequent place in the analysis. The second is the great shift that has occurred from long-term to intermediate and short-term borrowing, a shift which has also been facilitated by the general money market situation.

It has already been noted that 8 billions of war loans representing about one-half of the bonded debt have been refunded, transforming obligations at an average interest rate of more than 4 per cent to roughly 2.5 per cent—yielding a saving of approximately 125 millions per year. Sinking-fund operations and other miscellaneous retirements have also aided in converting high interest bearing obligations into low ones. The maintenance of the sinking-fund system in a period of heavy deficits has thus had some practical justification.[11]

The significance of the shift in the position of the debt will be revealed by a glance at the chart already presented on page 281. The short-term and intermediate term indebtedness had by 1936 come to constitute as much as 44 per cent of the total. Since the intermediate term notes bear a rate of about 1.5 per cent and since the cost of the short-term borrowings is negligible, the increasing proportion of the total debt in these categories has served to reduce materially the interest burden on the debt as a whole—quite apart from the general decline in the interest rate.

As has already been indicated, the Treasury bills are

[11] In the fiscal years 1931-35 inclusive an annual average of 450 millions of debt has been retired by statutory provisions. For a statement showing the operation of the sinking fund, see Appendix F, Section IV.

not issued to bear a definite rate of interest. They are merely short-term obligations sold below par, the interest being the immediate deduction from the ultimate maturity value. Bills outstanding at the end of February 1936 reflected yields at time of issue as low as 0.052 (approximately 1/20 of one per cent), and as high as ¼ of one per cent on nine-month maturities.

We shall leave the discussion for the moment with this factual statement. The changes that may ultimately occur in the burden of the debt, as a result either of rising interest rates or the refunding of the huge volume of short-term floating indebtedness now outstanding, will be fully discussed in Chapter XVIII.

C. Fluctuations in Receipts and Expenditures

The growth of the public debt is of course a direct reflection of the excess of current expenditures over current revenues. A deficit may be the result either of shrinking revenues or of expanding expenditures. Accordingly if we are to have a complete picture of the trend of public finance in recent times, it is necessary to reveal the trends with respect to annual revenues and expenditures. These are shown graphically in the accompanying chart. In the fiscal year 1915 receipts and expenditures were practically in balance. The war years showed a very great increase in ordinary receipts (which exclude borrowed funds and postal revenues) accompanied by a colossal increase of expenditures.

For eleven successive years beginning with 1920 revenues were in excess of expenditures—the primary factor in the improvement being the decrease of expenditures. Revenues also showed a slightly downward tendency from 1922 to 1929. The increase in the level of expenditures between 1915 and the middle twenties is attributable primarily to expanded outlays as a consequence of the war—chiefly pensions and interest. The expenditures incurred in connection with the general and civil functions increased between 1915 and 1925 from only 273 millions to 645 millions, of which public works accounted for 100 millions.[12] This increase was not greatly out of line with the rise in wages and prices.

The low point in post-war expenditures was reached in the fiscal year 1927 at 2,974 millions. There was a moderate increase in the ensuing two years, amounting to 325 millions. Since 1929, notwithstanding a decline of about 15 per cent in the general level of wholesale prices, federal outlays have increased nearly threefold.

In an appendix table we have prepared a general budget summary showing government receipts and expenditures by major classifications for the seven-year period 1930-36.[13] Total receipts declined from 4,048 millions in 1930 to a low of 2,006 in 1932, and then rose to 4,116 millions in 1936. Expenditures (less debt retirement) increased steadily from 3,308 millions in 1930 to 8,477 millions in 1936. The resulting deficits are summarized as follows:[14]

1931..	462 million dollars	1934..3,629 million dollars	
1932..2,735 " "		1935..3,002 " "	
1933..2,601 " "		1936..4,361 " "	

Having reviewed the changing relations of revenues to expenditures and the resulting deficits and growth of public indebtedness, we turn next to an analysis of the

[12] For data showing the functional classification of expenditures in 1915, 1919, and 1925, see Appendix F, Table 3.

[13] See Appendix F, Table 9.

[14] The amount of the deficit in a particular year does not correspond precisely with debt increases, owing to changes in the amount of cash held by the Treasury between the beginning and the end of the period, and debt retirement through use of the devaluation increment.

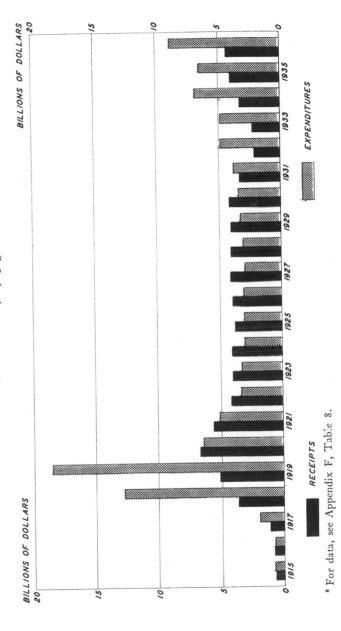

RECEIPTS AND EXPENDITURES OF THE FEDERAL
GOVERNMENT, 1915-36[a]

BILLIONS OF DOLLARS

BILLIONS OF DOLLARS

EXPENDITURES

RECEIPTS

[a] For data, see Appendix F, Table 8.

REVENUES OF THE FEDERAL GOVERNMENT, CLASSIFIED BY SOURCES, 1930-36[a]

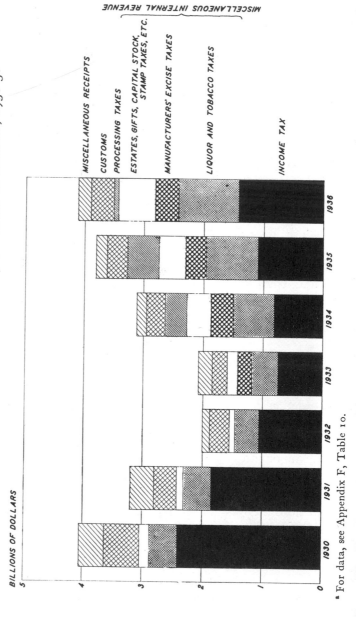

MISCELLANEOUS INTERNAL REVENUE

MISCELLANEOUS RECEIPTS
CUSTOMS
PROCESSING TAXES
ESTATES, GIFTS, CAPITAL STOCK, STAMP TAXES, ETC.
MANUFACTURERS' EXCISE TAXES
LIQUOR AND TOBACCO TAXES
INCOME TAX

BILLIONS OF DOLLARS

[a] For data, see Appendix F, Table 10.

shifting character of revenues and expenditures respectively. For this purpose the discussion will be confined to the period 1930-36.

Since the beginning of the depression there have been some noteworthy changes in the sources of federal revenue. We are referring here not to borrowing operations but to real revenues derived from taxation and other miscellaneous receipts. In the accompanying chart we present a breakdown of the revenues and other receipts there shown.

In 1930 about 62 per cent of the total revenue was derived about equally from corporate and individual income taxes, based on incomes of the calendar years 1928 and 1929. These schedules, admirably adapted to a period of prosperity and public debt retirement, were wholly unsuited to the cataclysmic conditions to follow. The tax schedules of 1928 and the temporary reduction of rates in 1929 did not anticipate the fiscal situation of 1931, in which year a substantial part of the 1929 taxes was actually paid. In the fiscal year 1933 the income tax yielded 746 millions, as compared with 2,411 millions in 1930.

Customs and miscellaneous internal revenues, the second line of support in the tax structure, shrank sharply but less violently than the receipts from the income tax.[15] Customs dropped from 587 millions in 1930 to 251 millions in 1933, and miscellaneous internal revenue from 628 millions in 1930 to a low of 504 millions in 1932—with tobacco taxes increasing in relative impor-

---

[15] Miscellaneous receipts also decreased from 422 millions in 1930 to 117 millions in 1932, chiefly as a result of the suspension of payments on war debts.

tance and constituting four-fifths of the total in the latter year.

The Revenue Act of 1932 providing for a drastic upward revision of income taxes was passed to halt the widening of the gap between receipts and expenditures. Improvement in the actual situation was, however, delayed because of the intensification of the depression and the normal lag in collections. It was not until the fiscal year 1934 that the new rates became fully effective. Even so, in consequence of the contraction of taxable income, this tax was not restored to its former relative position. From a purely revenue aspect the additional estate taxes and a variety of new or increased indirect taxes on production, transportation, communication, business transactions, and so forth were of greater significance. This does not represent a new experiment in taxation since such taxes had all been used during and after the war. They were reimposed and increased because of the relatively satisfactory way in which they had stood the test of the war period.

We cannot attempt here to catalogue the detailed changes in the tax structure since 1932 or to enumerate the specific revenue provisions of the various acts. There have been two developments of particular importance, however, to which attention must be called. These relate to emergency taxes on agricultural products and to the liquor taxes.[16]

[16] Special premium taxes authorized by the Social Security Act of Aug. 14, 1935 are a third development of far-reaching importance. Under the annuity provisions of the act, about 6 per cent of payrolls, primarily industrial, will be diverted to the government by equal employee income and employer excise taxes. The combined taxes are graduated from 2 per cent in 1937, with combined receipts of about 560 million dollars for the fiscal year 1938, to the maximum of 6 per cent in 1949 when it is estimated that they will produce slightly less than 2 billions annually. At some time between 1965 and 1970 it is believed that tax receipts and

The Agricultural Adjustment Act of May 12, 1933 authorized the Secretary of Agriculture to levy excise or processing taxes on the first domestic processing of certain basic agricultural commodities. These taxes were collected by the Bureau of Internal Revenue and placed in the general fund of the Treasury. An amount roughly equivalent to the proceeds was appropriated largely for the purpose of rental and benefit payments to farmers. Thus the specific tax receipts and particular new objects of expenditure were definitely linked in a co-ordinated plan, separable only by a tenuous technical interpretation. Collections of the processing taxes amounted to 353 millions in 1934 and to 522 millions in 1935. Invalidation of the Agricultural Adjustment Act on January 6, 1936 closed this source of revenue, but only by reason of its association with an unconstitutional purpose of expenditure.[17]

With the repeal of the Eighteenth Amendment in 1933, liquor taxes again became a very productive source of revenue. Whereas only 9 millions of miscellaneous internal revenue came from this source in 1932, as much

---

annuity payments will balance, but by then between 35 and 40 billions of surplus receipts will have been paid into a reserve fund invested in U. S. government securities. If outstanding securities are purchased in the market, these surplus receipts will not be available to cover the cost of regular government functions. If special new securities are issued to the reserve, the surplus receipts will remain in the general fund to be used for a variety of possible purposes, including a scaling down of rates of taxation or a continued expansion of expenditures. There is another 3 per cent employer excise tax levied for the purpose of unemployment insurance and a similar, but much smaller, reserve may be accumulated for this purpose. Because of the latitude of administrative policy it is impossible to predict how these special tax surpluses will be adjusted to the changing state of federal finances.

[17] In the rice millers' case decision of Jan. 13, 1936 the Supreme Court ordered the return to processors of about 200 millions of impounded processing taxes collected prior to the invalidation of the AAA. As shown by the chart, however, about 77 millions of taxes from the first half of the fiscal year 1936 were retained by the government.

as 506 millions was obtained in 1936. Thus the increase of combined revenues from liquor and tobacco, as shown on the chart, was almost entirely attributable to this re-opened field. The increase of custom duties from the same source has not been of appreciable significance.

In the receipts of the fiscal year 1936 we may observe the extension and enlargement of tendencies which had their inception in the adjustments of 1932. Total revenues of 4,116 millions were more than double the low point of 1932, and 208 millions higher than in 1930. Enlargement of the income tax base has been insufficient to offset the contraction of income, but there has been a notable improvement in that the 1936 collections of 1,427 millions are about double the 1933 amount.

The 1936 collections are, of course, based in part on the incomes of the calendar year 1934 and in part on those of 1935; and they thus tend to understate the revenue productivity of existing provisions. It remains true, however, that since 1932 the income tax has occupied a secondary position with respect to miscellaneous internal revenue, which in 1936 constituted 49 per cent of total revenues as against 35 per cent for the income tax. The tendency therefore has been to reverse the post-war trend with respect to these tax classifications, which culminated in 1930 in a preponderance of income tax receipts.

Particularly noteworthy has been the increase in miscellaneous internal revenues. Excise taxes which are based in a large degree upon essential commodities, the production of which has remained comparatively stable, have come to occupy a place of increasing importance. Taxes levied upon the windfall type of income from estates and gifts have also increased in amount. In the aggregate, miscellaneous internal revenues yielded 2,009

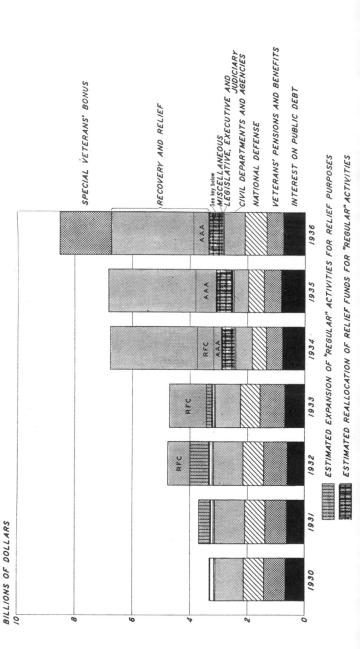

PUBLIC EXPENDITURES, 1930-36[a]

BILLIONS OF DOLLARS

SPECIAL VETERANS' BONUS

RECOVERY AND RELIEF

MISCELLANEOUS
LEGISLATIVE, EXECUTIVE AND JUDICIARY
CIVIL DEPARTMENTS AND AGENCIES
NATIONAL DEFENSE
VETERANS' PENSIONS AND BENEFITS
INTEREST ON PUBLIC DEBT

See key below

AAA
RFC

ESTIMATED EXPANSION OF "REGULAR" ACTIVITIES FOR RELIEF PURPOSES
ESTIMATED REALLOCATION OF RELIEF FUNDS FOR "REGULAR" ACTIVITIES

10 8 6 4 2 0

1930 1931 1932 1933 1934 1935 1936

millions in 1936, of which about 1,400 millions was from commodity taxes and manufactures excises. Liquor and tobacco contributed more than one billion.

E. Growth and Changing Character of Expenditures, 1930-36

It is a simple matter to show the aggregate growth of federal government expenditures since 1929; but it is difficult to reveal, with precision, the changes which have occurred in their functional character. This difficulty arises out of the fact that accounting methods have not been uniform throughout the period. Arrangements of the component parts of the total expenditures have created certain illusions as to the trend of the regular expenditures of the government—as contrasted with recovery and relief outlays. We have attempted to correct this distortion. The accompanying chart reveals the growth of expenditures classified in broad categories. (Expenditures for debt retirement are excluded from this chart.)

In reviewing these expenditures it is desirable to divide the period into two parts, corresponding roughly with the two administrations, the dividing line being June 30, 1933. The first period parallels the contraction of business into the depths of depression. To provide for the relief of individuals—the concept of *spending for recovery* not yet having emerged—the government expanded and accelerated outlays through regular departmental channels. Estimates of the amount of such expansion are indicated on the chart for the years 1931 through 1933 by the red areas crossed with black.

In the fiscal year 1931 the total of expenditures in which the primary purpose was relief was roughly 389 million dollars. This included public works (highways, public buildings, and so forth), 135 million dollars;

loans to farmers from established agencies, 85 million dollars; and increased loans and benefits to veterans, 169 million dollars. The problem of distinguishing these special categories from normal expenditures on regular activities is more difficult in the fiscal year 1932. We believe, however, that they may be conservatively estimated at 658 millions for that year.[18] This represents a continued expansion of public works, further loans to farmers (with 125 millions additional investment in the stock of the Federal Land Banks), and the continuance of liberality to veterans. In 1933, as shown by the chart, there was a sharp reduction of these accelerated expenditures to a level of about 200 millions. This was partly attributable to the non-recurrence or curtailment of previous special expenditures, but, in the main, to a shift in the method of handling relief problems which began with the establishment of the Reconstruction Finance Corporation in 1932.

The RFC introduced the recoverable loan and investment feature of recovery and relief financing and thus was an important contributing element in the subsequent development of the dual budget system, under which emergency outlays were sharply distinguished from regular expenditures.[19] The methods of the RFC indicated the assumption of a broader responsibility on the

---

[18] The method employed in arriving at this estimate is as follows: We have fairly accurate expenditure data showing that there was an increase in 1931 of 389 millions for relief purposes. Total expenditures in 1932 exceeded those of 1931 by 769 millions, of which 500 millions went for the budgeted RFC outlays. On this basis we place net increase for the regular departments for extraordinary purposes at 658 millions. This appears justifiable in view of the fact that—other than for relief—there were no new burdens or functions imposed upon the federal government in these years and a *normal* level of regular activities can be assumed. (These estimates are based on data from reports of the Secretary of the Treasury for the respective years.)

[19] A fact frequently overlooked is that the dual system of accounting was fully developed during 1932 and 1933, even though it was not

part of government for conditions of economic distress. A total of 768 million dollars was expended through this agency in the fiscal year 1932 for purposes of financial relief and of allaying the effects of deflationary panic, particularly upon banks, insurance companies, and railroad corporations. Its 1933 expenditures aggregated 1,277 millions in an expanded field of operations. Loans of 300 million dollars were made to state and local governments for relief and 118 millions allocated for farm and home relief and financial aid. Thus the apparent reduction of the exceptional expenditures under the regular departments in 1933 was largely a matter of shifting these expenditures to the RFC account.

The separation of regular from emergency expenditures which was inaugurated by the establishment of the RFC received a tremendous impetus with the advent of the new Administration. The white and black shaded areas on the chart, which indicate the costs of regular government activities, contracted moderately in 1933 and sharply in 1934. This was due in part to economy legislation passed both by the Hoover Administration and the new government, the main reduction in 1934 being in the pension item.[20] However, following 1933 a

---

acknowledged at the time and was not formalized in procedure until 1934. In the two former years a total of 2,045 million dollars was paid to the RFC, but only the stock subscription of 500 millions was shown as an expenditure and reflected in the deficit. The difference was revealed only by the increase in the public debt. The investments in the RFC were, of course, deemed recoverable. (See *Daily Treasury Statement*, June 30, 1933.) This omission has been corrected in subsequent budget statements.

[20] It is to be noted that the budget for the fiscal year 1934 was prepared and acted upon by the Hoover Administration in the early part of 1933. The incoming Administration passed economy legislation (a particular feature of which was the reduction of veterans' benefits with the view of supporting its promise of a reduction of 25 per cent in the cost of government. At the same time, however, preparation was made for extraordinary expenditures by the huge deficiency appropriation of 3,300 million dollars.

new and more elaborate distinction was made between regular government costs and those considered to be of temporary emergency origin. It is evident that some relationship was assumed between contracted revenues and regular government costs, and, on the other hand, between expanded borrowing and temporary relief expenditures. Also the new aspect of spending for recovery supplanted more conservative policies exemplified by the activities of the RFC, the net expenditures of which continued on a reduced scale into 1934.

We have prepared the table on page 305 to show the general character of special recovery and relief expenditures during the depression as a whole. We have only presented data where accounting accuracy is obtainable and have excluded various adjustments, based upon rough estimates, which are shown on the chart and interpreted in these pages.

We regard the great bulk of the expenditures in these seven classifications as falling within the government's general program of relief and reflation. In some instances, however, as in the case of expenditures for the agricultural adjustment (or soil conservation) program, broader objectives are involved and hence perhaps they may be in some measure permanent in character.

It will be seen from the table that in 1932 and 1933 segregated relief outlays were made through the RFC, whereas beginning with 1934 funds have flowed out through a multitude of specialized agencies. The emergency expenditures of primary importance are those for relief, for public works, and for aid to agriculture. While expenditures for agricultural aid and public works declined appreciably in the fiscal year 1936, relief expenditures were contracted only slightly. The latter type of outlay is primarily directed toward the relief of indi-

RECOVERY AND RELIEF EXPENDITURES, 1932-36[a]
(In millions of dollars)

Allocation	1932	1933	1934	1935	1936
AGRICULTURAL AID...............			866	885	699
Agricultural Adjustment Adminis- tration....................			289	712	532
Refunds of processing taxes....			1	31	10
Commodity Credit Corporation...			183	60[b]	130
Farm Credit Administration.....			347	154	33[b]
Federal Land Banks...........			46	48	60
RELIEF.........................			1,844	2,342	2,250
Federal Emergency Relief Adm...			707	1,814	496
Civil Works Administration......			805	11	1
Emergency conservation work....			332	436	486
Drought relief (Dept. of Agricul- ture)....................			—	81	3
Works Progress Administration...			—	—	1,264
PUBLIC WORKS..................			642	1,021	827
Administrative expenditures PWA......................			6	15	25
Boulder Canyon..............			19	24	10
Loans and grants to local govern- ments....................			79	138	172
Loans to railroads.............			71	66	128[b]
Public highways..............			268	317	215
River and harbor works........			72	148	152
Other (defense, public bldgs etc.)			127	313	381
AIDS TO HOME OWNERS			195	103	215
Home Loan system.............			192	76	37
Emergency housing............			1	6	25
Federal Housing Administration..			—	15	15
Resettlement Administration....			—	2	138
Subsistence homesteads........			2	4	—
MISCELLANEOUS..................			159	10	25
Export-Import banks..........			3	3[b]	20
Federal Deposit Insurance Corp...			150	1	—
National Industrial Recovery Adm.			6	12	5
RECONSTRUCTION FINANCE CORP....	768	1,277	566	135[b]	239[b]
TENNESSEE VALLEY AUTHORITY.....			11	36	49[o]
UNCLASSIFIED AND UNALLOCATED...			—	110	
GRAND TOTAL..................	768	1,277	4,283	4,262	3,827

[a] The 1936 figures compiled from the *President's Budget Statement* of Sept. 1, 1936. Years 1935 and 1934 based upon the *President's Budget Statement* of Sept. 29, 1935. Other years from *Annual Report of the Secretary of the Treasury.*
[b] Repayments (deduct).
[o] Includes all expenditures, general and emergency, as classified by the Treasury.

viduals; while in other cases the direct purpose is to improve the functioning of economic agencies and institutions, with individual relief an indirect but nevertheless important consideration.

In the years 1931 through 1933 we have made adjustments to bring out the expansion of regular government functions for purely relief purposes. In the succeeding years the illusion of vast relative economy in the regular government establishments is dispelled by adjustments in the relief expenditures. Particularly in the case of public works, it has been common practice to reallocate funds provided for emergency administrations back to the regular government departments where they fill in the deficiencies of their normal budgeted activities. To determine the precise extent of this reallocation is extremely difficult because of the lack of adequate data. But for the years since 1933 we have shown on the chart, in the dark areas crossed with red, the amounts which we estimate were involved. The estimates of 400 millions for 1934, 510 millions for 1935, and 437 millions in 1936, we regard as conservative minimum figures.

The heavy black line on the chart thus indicates our estimate of the division which would have been shown between regular and emergency expenditures had accounting practice been consistent throughout the period. This excludes the expanded activities of 1931 through 1933, but includes the reallocated relief funds in recent years. In the years preceding 1934 there is little evidence of change in the level of regular expenditures, which were 3,308 millions in 1930 and 3,204 millions in 1933. In 1934 they declined to 2,862 millions, but recovered to 3,015 millions in 1935 and 3,313 millions in 1936. There has been a recent tendency to restore expenditures carried in emergency categories back to their regular departmental classifications, but, in addition, certain projects of depression origin are regarded by some as permanent functions of the federal government. Thus the AAA outlays have been officially carried as regular expenditures.[21] If we were to follow this method, a glance at the chart, on which the AAA expenditures are separated, reveals that since 1934 "regular" expenditures have been far above the 1930 level, which was sufficiently high to call for economy legislation. We might further block off from the *recovery and relief* bracket the 486 millions expended on Emergency Conservation Work (CCC) in 1936 as an addition to regular costs, as they were, indeed, officially classified in that fiscal year.[22]

The readjustments which we have attempted to make in the expenditure classifications do not, of course, affect the total outlays. The hard reality of the rising total costs of government is apparent. They increased from

[21] Disregarding legalistic views of expenditure classification, there must be a considerable measure of personal judgment in the placing of this expenditure. It would appear that there was more justification for considering AAA expenditures as regular when, prior to 1936, they were met by specific revenues. On the other hand, the fact that an activity can be financed out of revenues is not the final criterion in determining government functions; more complex issues are involved.

[22] In its origins the dual budget method had certain distinct points of merit; at first in regarding special expenditures as subsequently recoverable, and later with the further assumption that expenditures which were separable as the cause of deficits, were of temporary and contractable nature. In retrospect, and with a view to the future, however, it would appear that its emergency classification has been regarded as a convenient receptacle for all expenditures which were not covered by revenues—with less emphasis upon the terminable characteristics of such expenditures as revenues continued to rise with business recovery. An excellent example of this process is afforded by the CCC expenditures which in 1934 and 1935 were considered *relief*, but appeared in the *regular* category in the budget statement of January 1936. The transition of this expenditure (which was also effected retroactively for the year 1935) was apparently with the underlying intention of showing reductions in special emergency outlays. We doubt that the move was fully justified in consideration of the origin and characteristics of the agency involved.

3,308 millions in 1930 to 4,741 millions in 1932. Although they were reduced by about 60 million dollars in the fiscal year 1933, total outlays rose from 4,681 millions in that year to 6,803 millions in 1935 and 8,477 millions in 1936—or 6,703 millions if the special bonus of 1,774 millions be omitted.[23]

For the fiscal year 1937, expenditures in excess of 7 billion dollars appear probable. The original budget estimate amounted to 6,753 millions. The President's budget statement of September 1, 1936 gives a revised estimate of 7,183 millions, excluding debt retirement of 580 millions.[24] It appears likely that further funds will be required to cover relief expenditures this year. The turning point in total expenditures has thus not yet been reached.

II. ALL GOVERNMENTS COMBINED

The United States is a country in which there is an extraordinary degree of decentralization in the administration of governmental functions. In addition to the 48 state governments there are more than 182,000 minor political units having the power to levy taxes and incur debt. Any adequate picture of the situation with respect to public finance in this country must, therefore, include these state and local government units.

[23] Total payments to the Adjusted Service Certificate Fund in the fiscal year 1936 were 1,774 millions, of which 1,673 millions was directly attributable to prepayment of the bonus in the month of June (*Daily Treasury Statement,* June 30, 1936). The latter figure, however, was not the full amount received by bonus recipients, as there is an accounting complication involving the liquidation of securities invested in the old Adjusted Certificate Fund. In the absence of precise data we use the higher figure as being a closer approximate in covering a minimum of at least 70 millions of cash from such liquidation.

[24] Expenditures for 1937 include an estimate of 560 millions to be paid to government trust funds in reimbursement for cancelled veterans' loans as a result of the bonus payment. This is a non-recurring expenditure involving a debt increase but not necessarily a cash outlay. For further details see Appendix F, Section III.

All taxes, by whatever agency imposed, must be paid by the public as a whole. Moreover, there has been a growing inter-dependence between federal, state, and local finance. The primitive concept of local economy has progressively given way to both social and economic changes which transcend traditional political boundaries. This has been especially the case as a result of the financial difficulties arising out of the economic depression. In this section of the analysis we shall therefore present in summary form the situation with respect to public finance for federal, state, and local governments combined.

A. Growth of Federal, State, and Local Debt, 1915-35

In the accompanying chart we show the growth of state and local debts, in comparison with the growth of federal

GROWTH OF ALL PUBLIC INDEBTEDNESS, 1915-35[a]

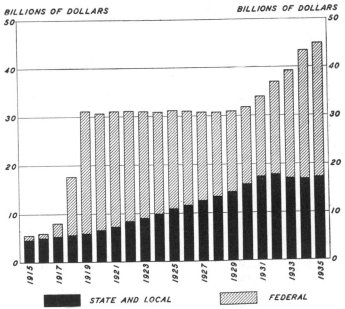

[a] For data, see Appendix F, Table 11.

debt from 1915 to 1935. In studying this chart attention should first be directed to the contrasts between the growth of federal and local indebtedness. It will be seen that, in general, the trends have been essentially different. During the World War period the state and local indebtedness showed only a very slight increase. However, during the fiscal years from 1919 to 1930, when the federal debt was being decreased by nearly 10 billion dollars, state and local indebtedness increased by practically 10 billions, or nearly threefold. In the first years of the depression state and local indebtedness increased more or less proportionally to the federal debt; but after 1932 the former declined slightly, while the federal debt showed a huge expansion.

Prior to the war the federal debt was negligible in amount. At the peak of the war-time financing it was four times as great as state and local indebtedness; but the changes in the twenties brought it to just under 16 billion dollars in 1930—virtual equality with the state and local total. By 1936 the federal debt was again nearly double that of the smaller units.[25] The change in the last few years of course reflects the assumption by the

[25] The contraction of total state and local debts between mid-year 1931 and 1935 was about 200 millions, following an increase of 300 millions from June 30, 1934. In the calendar years 1932-35 inclusive, there were 2,934 millions of new long-term issues, exclusive of refunding. (Data published in *Federal Reserve Bulletin*.) Inasmuch as defaults are included with the outstanding debt, and are deducted only when compromised, the greatest factor offsetting new financing and holding down the total was normal retirement, particularly of serial issues. The short-term debt, which is included in the totals, decreased from 1.6 billions in 1932 to 1.1 billions in 1935 (*Annual Report of the Secretary of the Treasury*, 1935, Table A, p. 425). This is explained by improvement in the tax delinquency situation, and by some funding into long-term obligations.

There are difficulties in computing the amount of municipal debts in various technical stages of default, but estimates of the percentage of government units affected are of interest. For the entire country, only 1.68 per cent of all government units have defaulted, but in seven

federal government of the responsibility not only for stimulating recovery but for aiding distressed local governments and maintaining the stability of local finance generally.

In the early stages of the depression the state and local governments attempted to deal with the relief problem; but revenues proved inadequate to the new and unequally distributed burden, and bank and investment sources of credit and capital were tightened by deflationary forces. Thus, irrespective of whether relief is logically a national or local responsibility, the burden was largely thrown upon the federal government with its extensive credit and currency powers.

The composition of the state and local government indebtedness in 1932, the latest date for which classified figures are available, is shown by the following table:[26]

State governments	2,361	million dollars
Counties	2,391	" "
Cities, towns, villages, and boroughs	8,842	" "
School districts, townships, and other civil divisions	3,983	" "
Total	17,577	" "

The origin and purpose of state and local indebtedness have been essentially different from those of the federal debt. Whereas the federal debt, until the depression period, has been attributable primarily to military outlays, that of the local governments has been created in a process of developing enterprises deemed socially

Southern states and New Jersey the percentage was highest, an average of 13.67 per cent. These states also had the highest debt-burden index, about double the United States average, and their debts were largely incurred in the twenties. (B. U. Ratchford, *The Annalist*, Nov. 22, 1935, p. 717.)

[26] Gross debt, less sinking fund assets. From *Financial Statistics of State and Local Governments*, 1932.

important, such as schools and school buildings, roads and streets, rapid transit, waterfront and harbor improvements and sewerage facilities (see page 314).

Interest charges on the state and local indebtedness are considerably larger, relatively to the principal, than is the case with the federal debt. As we have seen, the average interest charges on the federal debt have been greatly reduced in recent years, in part as a result of refunding operations, but to a greater extent by the increasing proportions of short-term borrowing at merely nominal interest rates. State and local governments have been able to benefit in the main only by refunding operations.

Because of the multitude of bond issues involved and the lack of detailed and comprehensive data, it is difficult to show the net interest charges on state and local government indebtedness as a whole. A compilation made for the year 1932, however, showed total interest payments amounting to nearly 844 millions, giving an average rate of about 4.6 per cent.[27] Since the aggregate debt has been decreased since 1932 by about 600 million dollars and the average interest rates were shaded somewhat as a result of refunding operations, the interest obligations at the present time probably amount to a little less than 800 million dollars.[28] Thus notwithstanding the fact that the state and local debt is only a little more than half the amount of the federal debt, the interest charges for 1936 would appear to be slightly in excess of the actual interest disbursements of 749 millions on the

[27] *Financial Statistics of State and Local Governments,* 1932, p. 28.

[28] The average yield on high-grade municipals was 4.29 per cent in 1929; 4.71 in 1933; and 2.72 in June 1936 (*Federal Reserve Bulletin,* August 1936). On the basis of such yields it would appear that if extensive refunding operations are carried through in the next few years the present interest burden will be materially reduced.

federal debt. If and when the federal debt is funded this comparison will, of course, change materially.

B. Growth of Expenditures

The growth of state and local expenditures in relation to federal expenditures may be briefly summarized. The expansion since 1915 is shown by the table below.

FEDERAL, STATE, AND LOCAL EXPENDITURES BETWEEN
1915 and 1934[a]
(In millions of dollars)

Year	Total	Federal	State	Local
1915............	3,379	719	490	2,170
1923............	8,918	3,117	1,208	4,593
1926............	10,196	2,853	1,499	5,844
1929............	11,709	3,046	1,943	6,720
1932............	13,417	4,712	2,257	6,448
1934............	14,449	6,784	2,044	5,621

[a] The data for 1915 were obtained from *Recent Social Trends*, Vol. II, Table 20, p. 1324 and are comparable with data for the other years, which are from National Industrial Conference Board, *Cost of Government in the United States, 1933–1935*, Table 1, p. 4. The expenditures are adjusted to exclude debt retirement and federal tax refunds. Grants-in-aid are treated as an expenditure of the first disbursing authority.

Over the period as a whole, state and local expenditures combined increased approximately threefold, while federal expenditures increased nearly tenfold. Eliminating the extraordinary federal expenditures of the last three years and making the comparison between 1915 and 1932, we find state and local expenditures increased a little over threefold, as compared with an increase of nearly sevenfold in federal expenditures. The rate of increase in state government expenditures for the period as a whole has been somewhat more rapid than that of local expenditures—though in absolute magnitude the latter show an expansion of about 3.5 billions, as compared with 1.5 billions for state expenditures. In both cases a considerable decline is evident in recent years, local expenditures having fallen by nearly 20 per cent since 1929.

The character of state and local expenditures is revealed in the following summary statement for the year 1929:[29]

Education	2,862	million dollars
Highways	1,862	" "
Welfare	568	" "
Other (administration, protection, conservation, health, etc.)	2,780	" "

Expenditures for education, highways, and welfare have shown a tendency to increase for many years. These three functions accounted in 1915 for 51.5 per cent of all state and local expenditures, while in 1929 they comprised 61 per cent of the total.

It is evident that during the depression state and local expenditures have been adjusted more closely to the level of current revenues than has been the case for the federal government. As a whole, the states and localities entered the depression with over-extended debts and, as revenues declined, there was enormous pressure to curtail expenditures. Moreover, the burden of relief was progressively shifted from local to state governments and, in turn, to the federal government. State and local governments possess no such credit expanding possibilities as are available to the federal government.

C. Growth of Taxation

In order to compare the increase in state and local taxation with the increase in federal taxation we have prepared the accompanying table, which shows the aggregate collections by the federal, state, and local governments respectively for selected years since 1913. Fed-

---

[29] Data computed from *Recent Social Trends*, Vol. II, Table 21, p. 1326.

eral taxation increased fourfold during this period, state taxation nearly sixfold, and local taxation a little over threefold.

FEDERAL, STATE, AND LOCAL TAXES BETWEEN
1913 AND 1934[a]
(In millions of dollars)

Year	Total	Federal	State	Local
1913............	2,259	662	300	1,297
1923............	7,234	3,032	917	3,285
1926............	8,605	3,207	1,264	4,134
1929............	9,759	3,328	1,612	4,819
1932............	8,147	1,789	1,642	4,716
1934............	8,767	2,892	1,732	4,143

[a] Data for 1913 from *Recent Social Trends*, Vol. II, Table 2, p. 1335; other years from National Industrial Conference Board, *Cost of Government in the United States, 1933–35*, Table 13, p. 27. Tax refunds are deducted from federal tax receipts.

The figures in the table cover tax receipts only. In addition there are various non-tax revenues (apart from borrowing). In 1932, for example, such revenues received by state and local governments amounted to 2,494 millions, as compared with 6,358 millions from tax receipts. These non-tax revenues were derived as follows:[30]

Earnings of departments and public service enterprises	942	million dollars
Special assessments	321	" "
Highway privileges, rents, and interest ..	256	" "
Subventions and grants	868	" "
Fines, donations, gifts, etc.	107	" "

While the distinction is not in all cases precise, in general the non-tax revenues represent the cost of some special privilege or benefit, whereas taxes go for the general support of government without relation to particular benefits derived by taxpayers. The subventions and

[30] Data from *Financial Statistics of State and Local Governments*, 1932. This is the only year for which complete data are available.

grants represent contributions of one division of government to another, generally for the support of some specific function, such as highway construction. These have already been included in the receipts of the governmental agencies making the subvention or grant.

III. TAXATION AND NATIONAL INCOME

To round out this summary sketch of the trend of public finance it is essential to relate the growth of taxation to the growth of national income. Has the percentage of the income of the people that is diverted through government channels been steadily increasing? How great is the proportion now required to meet government obligations? In making these comparisons we shall include both federal and state and local taxation, showing the trends for each separately, and also with respect to combined totals. The table on page 317 shows the changes from 1913 to 1936, by selected years.

It will be observed first that the national income, as expressed in dollar terms, has fluctuated widely—in part reflecting price changes and in part recurring periods of boom and depression. Thus, largely as a result of war and early post-war inflation of prices, money income more than doubled between 1913 and 1920. After the readjustments of 1921 and 1922 the income expanded at a gradual rate—with prices meanwhile showing a slight reduction. The depression since 1929 affected both the volume of business and the level of prices and resulted in a reduction in the total income from 81.9 billions in 1929 to a low of 40 billions in 1932. Since 1932 there has been an increase in the volume of business and in the general level of wholesale prices, which is reflected in a rise in national income to approximately 60 billion dollars—the preliminary estimate for the calendar year 1936.

Prior to the war federal taxes absorbed only about 2 per cent of the national income and all taxes combined about 7 per cent. In the post-war period federal taxes averaged a little over 4 per cent of the national income and all taxes about 11 or 12 per cent. Owing to the

TAX COLLECTIONS AND NATIONAL INCOME IN SELECTED YEARS, 1913-36
(Dollar items are in millions)

Year	National Income[a]	Tax Collections			Taxes as a Percentage of Income		
		All	Federal	State and Local[b]	*All*	*Federal*	*State and Local*
1913..	$31,900	$2,259	$ 662	$1,597	*7.1*	*2.1*	*5.0*
1923..	68,400	7,234	3,032	4,202	*10.6*	*4.4*	*6.2*
1926..	77,200	8,605	3,207	5,398	*11.2*	*4.2*	*7.0*
1929..	81,900	9,759	3,328	6,431	*11.9*	*4.1*	*7.8*
1932.	40,000	8,147	1,789	6,358	*20.4*	*4.5*	*15.9*
1933..	42,200	7,501	1,786	5,715	*17.8*	*4.2*	*13.6*
1934..	48,900	8,767	2,892	5,875	*17.9*	*5.9*	*12.0*
1935..	53,600	9,800[d]	3,714	...	*18.3*	*6.9*	...
1936..	60,000[c]	10,200[d]	4,062	...	*17.0*	*6.8*	...

a The income figures for the period 1913–29 are from *America's Capacity to Consume*, Table I, p. 148; the later years are a projection on the basis of estimates of the Department of Commerce (*Survey of Current Business*). The figures are for produced income rather than income paid out. We have selected the former because it more accurately portrays the real basis of taxation.

b Compiled figures are available only for the year 1932. The other figures are estimates of the National Industrial Conference Board.

c Preliminary estimate.

d For the purpose of obtaining *total* figures in 1935 and 1936 we have assumed state and local revenues to have increased to 6.1 billions.

shrinkage of income in 1932 more than 20 per cent of the national income was absorbed in taxes. In the succeeding years the percentages ranged from 17 to 18, of which the federal taxes absorbed approximately 7 per cent.

The present taxes are, however, inadequate to cover the full costs of government. While the state and local budgets, taken in the aggregate, are roughly in balance, the federal deficit in 1936 amounted to 2,587 millions—exclusive of 403 millions expended through the sinking fund and the special bonus of 1,774 millions. To balance the budget at this level of expenditure would have required federal taxes equal to 6,703 millions. A more reasonable basis on which to balance the budget would be at a level of expenditures approximating 6 billions.[31] On this basis federal taxes would absorb about 10 per cent of the present national income and all taxes a little over 20 per cent.[32]

If the tax burden is to be reduced below the levels thus indicated it will have to be as a result of a further increase in the national income. It will be of interest to indicate the magnitude of the tax burden on the assumption of a return to a level of economic activity equal to that of 1929. The income in that year was approximately 82 billions. The level of prices is now some 15 per cent below that of 1929 and a present income, in money terms, of 70 billions would be roughly the equivalent of the 1929 income. On this plane taxes aggregating 12 billion dollars would absorb about 17 per cent of the national income.

It is beyond the scope of our present inquiry to consider the distribution of the tax burden upon the various groups in society and the effects of various types of levies upon the operation of the economic system. We must here be content merely with indicating the quantitative magnitude of the problem.

[31] See discussion in Chap. XVIII.

[32] The tax burden is sometimes placed at a substantially higher percentage than that at which we have arrived. The difference is usually due to the practice of including in the state and local government revenues both the tax receipts and the non-tax revenues. Our reasons for excluding such revenues in computing the tax burden are disclosed by the analysis on pp. 315-16. Sometimes also the burden is computed as a percentage of the total expenditures of 1936, including the special bonus.

CHAPTER XIII

READJUSTMENTS OF PRIVATE DEBT

In this chapter and the following one we survey the changes which have taken place since 1929 in the amount of the debt and the ownership of the claims outstanding against various classes of institutions and individuals, in the rates of interest paid on various types of loans and investments, and in the resulting burden of interest. In this survey our primary interest is in the bearing of the debt situation on the capacity of industry to attract capital and to operate profitably, and in the ownership of the debt, as its volume and soundness affect the solvency of financial institutions and their consequent capacity to finance the expansion of business in the future. We are also interested in the changes which have taken place in the ownership of creditor claims because these are so radical in character as to evidence an important change in the financial structure of society.

I. CHANGES IN AMOUNT AND OWNERSHIP OF DEBT

The table on page 320 summarizes our estimates of the volume of debt in the United States at the end of 1929 and 1933, together with estimates for certain kinds of debt for 1934 and 1935. Because of the lack of data concerning general corporate and individual debt, no totals are shown for 1934 and 1935. These data are analyzed in detail in later sections of the chapter. It must be understood that the figures here relate to the gross debt and do not measure directly the debt burden of the country, since the debtors and creditors are to a large extent identical. The net debt for any country as a whole, apart from international debtor and creditor relationships, is, of course, zero, since there is a creditor for every debtor. The net debt of net debtors, that is, of those who owe more than others owe them, cannot be

GROSS DEBT OF GOVERNMENTAL AGENCIES, CORPORATIONS, AND INDIVIDUALS, 1929-35[a]

(In millions of dollars)

Group	1929	1933	1934	1935
Non-financial corporations.....	60,410	54,878	...	...
Financial institutions.........	104,286	85,590	...	...
Federal, state, territorial, and local governments.........	31,435	41,513	47,188	47,053
Governmental lending agencies.	1,262	1,574	5,915	6,896
Individuals.................	80,414	48,725	...	...
Total.................	277,807	232,280	...	...

[a] For sources of data, see detailed tables below.

estimated accurately, but is certainly less than half the amount of the gross debt shown in our table.[1] The governmental debt, as was shown in Chapter XII, is substantially all net, whereas nearly all the debt of financial institutions is offset by creditor claims, as is that of wholesale and retail trading corporations. Individuals as a group are creditors to a much larger extent than they are debtors, and in this respect their condition has shown a great nominal improvement during the course of the depression. However, since the entire debt of governments and governmental agencies is a contingent liability of the individuals who make up the country, the improvement in the balance sheet position of individuals is in fact offset by the increase of their ultimate liabilities as taxpayers.

[1] To use an extreme illustration: If a speculator is carrying a bond in a margin account with a broker, the corporation owes the speculator, the speculator owes the broker, the broker owes a bank, and the bank owes its depositors, but the only net debt is that which the corporation owes, in effect, to the depositors in the bank.

It will be noted that there was a net decline in the gross debt totals between 1929 and 1933 amounting to about 13.5 per cent. The reduction is greatest in connection with financial institutions and individuals. Business corporations show a decline up to 1933 of less than 6 per cent. The most striking change, however, was not the reduction in total indebtedness, but the appearance of the federal government in the role of banker-at-large to the community. The debt of the federal government increased by nearly 8 billion dollars and that of its lending agencies by 2 billions more, down to the end of 1933, and in the next two years the increase was even more rapid. As is shown below, the creditor position of the national government and the quasi-governmental lending corporations rose from 6.5 billion dollars to more than 14 billions.

What has been happening may be summarized in two statements: first, as the credit of other agencies deteriorated and that of the United States government remained unimpaired, the government substituted its credit for that of the other agencies; and second, as individual and corporate businesses contracted the scale of their operations, the government expanded its field of economic activity. Individuals who under normal conditions would have bought corporation securities or made mortgage loans have been using their savings to pay off bank loans or holding them idle in the form of bank deposits (now virtually underwritten by the government). Banks, finding little demand for sound individual and corporate loans, buy government securities. The government uses the funds to make loans which are deemed too risky by banks and other lending agencies, and also to carry on an expanded program of public works. Thus the government has become more and more the leading borrower, lender, and business manager in the country.

In the following sections we shall consider in some detail the history of the various classes of debt through the depression and recovery eras.

II. NON-FINANCIAL CORPORATIONS

The accompanying table shows the creditor position of non-financial corporations for 1929 and for 1933; later information is not available, except for railroads.

NON-FINANCIAL CORPORATIONS' DEBT, 1929 AND 1933-35[a]
(In millions of dollars)

Year	Railroads	Other Public Utilities	Corporations Other than Utilities	Total
1929:				
Long-term............	13,809	12,810	9,888	36,507
Short and demand......	1,651	5,903	16,349	23,903
1933:				
Long-term............	14,182	14,898	10,272	39,352
Short and demand......	1,568	1,919	11,739	15,226
1934:				
Long-term............	13,895	...	...	...
Short and demand......	1,784	...	...	...
1935:				
Long-term............	13,564	...	...	...
Short and demand......	2,015	...	...	...

[a] For sources of data, see Appendix G, Section I.

1. Railroads. The railroad debt was very stable during the depression, as it had been for many years before. The bulk of railway indebtedness constitutes permanent investment, and the investment in railway property cannot be recovered in any large volume even in cases where railway service is discontinued. And so long as service is maintained it is usually necessary that the investment be increased from year to year. Hence the only ways in which the debt can be reduced are by bankruptcy and write-off, and by refunding through stock issues. A significant amount of amortization out of earnings is practically impossible, even with profitable roads, because the periods when the railroads are making money are the ones in which they have the greatest need of new and improved facilities, and consequently of additions to total investment. Refunding through stock issues has, of course, been impossible during the depression. What reduction has occurred has been almost entirely the re-

HOLDINGS OF RAILWAY SECURITIES ON DECEMBER 31 OF SELECTED YEARS, 1929-35[a]

(In millions of dollars)

Creditor	1929	1933	1934	1935
Other railroads	1,449	1,547	1,264	1,224
National banks	626	530	574	582
All insured banks	—	—	981	1,026
United States Treasury	63	38	31	31
Life insurance companies	3,029	3,039	3,070	3,086
Railroad Credit Corporation	—	67	53	46
Reconstruction Finance Corporation	—	337	378	458
Public Works Administration	—	—	133	82
Other[b]	8,642	8,636	7,698	7,029

[a] For sources of data, see Appendix G, Section II.

[b] Mutual savings banks apparently hold over one billion dollars of the amount shown here as held by "others," but the amount cannot be estimated accurately because published reports do not separate railroad securities from those issued by public utility corporations.

sult of reorganization, and has been offset by the expansion of short-term debt of other railroads.

The ownership of railroad securities has changed more than has the total volume of debt, but not nearly as much as the ownership of farm and home mortgages. The accompanying table shows, as of December 31 of selected years, the holdings of railway securities reported by the more important classes of institutional holders.

It will be noted that in proportion to the total volume of railway debt outstanding, the credit extended by the emergency lending agencies of the government has been small.[2] The government thus has built up a compara-

[2] The Railroad Credit Corporation lends railroad money, and not that advanced by the federal government.

tively small equity in the railroads as compared with its stake in the financing of land ownership. The importance of the aid extended to the roads by the government, however, is greater than the figures might seem to imply, chiefly because of the extent to which railroad credit involves that of banks, life insurance companies, educational and philanthropic foundations, and the smaller taxing units.

The mileage operated by railroads in receivership or in process of reorganization under the Bankruptcy Act rose from 5,703 in 1929 to 42,168 in 1934. About three-fifths of this increase is accounted for by five roads, all but one of which were in a very weak financial situation before the depression began.[3] All the other roads which are in the hands of receivers or trustees are small, none of them operating more than 1,000 miles of line. The funded debt of the railways in the hands of receivers and trustees at the end of 1934 amounted to 1,926 million dollars, or about one-seventh of the total funded debt of the railways of the country.

In view of the number of defaults reported and the extent to which other defaults have been prevented only by the intervention of the government, the experience of the depression seems to have confirmed the popular belief that the railroads have an excessive debt burden. In this connection, however, several points are worthy of note.

First, it is to be emphasized that the distress of the railroads is not a direct consequence of the fall in the price level. Railroad rates are inelastic; they do not go down with falling prices while many railroad costs do go down. Therefore, for a given volume of business, the profit margin is higher (or the deficit margin lower)

---

[3] The five roads are the Wabash, the Seaboard Airline, the Wisconsin Central, the Missouri Pacific, and the St. Louis-San Francisco.

when prices are low than it is when they are high. It is the shrinking volume of business and not the fall of prices which causes embarrassment to railroads in time of depression. In this respect their position is similar to that of other agencies which enjoy a considerable degree of monopoly, except that they lack the freedom that an industrial monopoly has to experiment with lower and higher prices.[4]

Second, railroad debt, even if excessive, does not constitute a significant source of unemployment in the railroad service itself. Bankrupt railroads do not go out of business. They keep on hauling freight while the lawyers readjust the debt burden. Roads in financial distress do, however, commonly spend less for betterments and for equipment than they would if they had less debt.

Third, the primary importance of railroad solvency, from the standpoint of the re-establishment and maintenance of normal business activity, is in its indirect influence on the rate of investment. The solvency of the railroads has vital importance for the solvency of banks, insurance companies, and educational and philanthropic institutions. A limited amount of insolvency has no significant influence on the total volume of employment and business activity, but the coincidence of a large volume of failures in any field exerts a strong adverse influence on the willingness of holders of liquid funds to invest them. Railroad failures bring home the risks of

[4] From the standpoint of the owners of railroad securities as a group, a heavy debt is in one sense an asset because it gives them in fact—though not in legal theory—a better claim on the public for liberal treatment in the regulation of their rates. Theoretically the return which the railroads are allowed to earn depends upon the fair value of their property and not on their capital structure, but in practice there is some tendency for the Interstate Commerce Commission to give more consideration to bondholders than it gives to stockholders, even though the stock may have originated in a reorganization where bondholders were forced to exchange their securities for stock certificates. (Compare H. G. Moulton and others, *The American Transportation Problem*, pp. 294-97.)

investments directly to a very large body of potential investors, and if they are so serious as to cause failures of banks and other financial institutions, the dampening effect is enormously aggravated.

Fourth, the recent threat to the solvency of certain institutional holders of railroad securities was due not so much to the volume of railroad securities held as to the fact that the same agencies which hold the railroad securities are also large holders of urban, and especially of farm, mortgages. Moreover, those governmental units which are most heavily dependent on railroad taxes are also in many cases the ones which are most heavily dependent on taxes on farm property. The shrinkage in the ability of the railroads to pay interest and taxes during the depression coincided with the collapse of the ability of the farm population to pay interest and taxes. Consequently, the solvency of the railroads became much more vital to their most important creditors. The collapse of urban land values also hit the municipalities and made them much more dependent on railroad taxes than they would ordinarily have been. Thus the aid extended to railroads by public lending agencies, particularly the Reconstruction Finance Corporation, was essential to the solvency of institutions which under ordinary conditions would have been able to absorb the loss from a collapse of railroad prosperity. This is the real significance of the program of governmental aid to distressed railroads. Loans to railroads that were not in acute distress have also played an important part in maintaining some degree of activity in railway expenditures for construction and betterments, especially electrification, air-conditioning, and stream-lining.

2. *Other utilities.* For utilities other than railroads the change in total indebtedness is no more significant

than it is in the case of the railroads. The accompanying table shows the funded debt of certain types of public utilities for which detailed information is available.

The operating companies which furnish electric current, gas, or water have had remarkably smooth sailing through the depression, considering its severity, but the holding companies have been hit very hard. During the boom period there was a wave of consolidation of utilities

FUNDED DEBT OF CERTAIN TYPES OF PUBLIC UTILITIES,
1929 AND 1933-34[a]
(In millions of dollars)

Group	1929	1933	1934
Manufactured gas companies............	951	845	830
Switching and terminal companies.......	583	708	698
Electric light and power companies......	5,879	6,550	...
Telephone companies.................	1,214	1,079	1,048
Telegraph companies.................	77	108	127
Pipeline companies (interstate)..........	43	39	53
Electric railway companies.............	2,037	...	...
Holding companies...................	1,500	2,000	...
Express companies...................	33	32	32

[a] For sources of data, see Appendix G, Section III.

through the medium of holding companies whose chief purpose was to exploit the possibilities of "trading on the equity" by pooling the securities of operating companies and using them as collateral for bond issues, or as a credit base for the issuance of preferred stock. A few conspicuous failures in this group have brought all holding companies into disfavor with investors, and practically no securities of this sort have been issued in the last few years. Defaults which are not fully reflected in the statistics of indebtedness outstanding have brought about some reduction in the collectable indebtedness which is not yet fully reflected in statistical reports.

3. Other corporations. For the debt of corporations other than financial institutions and public utilities, our only source of information is the *Statistics of Income,* and these reports are not available for any date later than 1933. Changes from the end of 1929 to the end of 1933 were as follows:

DEBT OF INDUSTRIAL CORPORATIONS, 1929 AND 1933[a]

(In millions of dollars)

Industrial Group	1929			1933		
	Long-Term	Short and Demand	Total	Long-Term	Short and Demand	Total
Manufacturing..	5,450	7,418	12,868	5,022	5,723	10,745
Trade..........	1,252	5,730	6,982	1,127	3,624	4,751
All other.......	3,186	3,201	6,387	4,123	2,392	6,515
Total........	9,888	16,349	26,237	10,272	11,739	22,011

[a] Data from *Statistics of Income.* Compare note 1, Appendix G.

It will be noted that during these years there was a considerable reduction in the reported debt of industrial and commercial corporations. The reduction, however, was much greater in the short-term and demand debt than in the long-term debt. This reflects simply the liquidation of bank credit with the contraction of current operations. The data are affected also by the disappearance of corporations from the reporting group on account of bankruptcy or inactivity in the course of the depression. All three of the classes of corporations shown have short-term creditor assets in excess of the short-term debt shown in the table, and these creditor assets decreased between 1929 and 1933 in somewhat greater proportion than did the short-term and demand debt.[5]

[5] Long-term creditor assets for these corporations are relatively unimportant and are not reported separately from other investments.

III. FINANCIAL INSTITUTIONS

The table on page 330 brings out some of the financial repercussions of the depression. The mutual savings banks have shown at least a normal growth and the life insurance companies have also expanded, though less rapidly than they did before the crisis. Building and loan associations' mortgage loans have been reduced by more than one-third, partly through foreclosure and partly through the disappearance of associations. Other financial corporations, consisting chiefly of real estate companies and investment trusts, show comparatively little change.

There has been a very sharp liquidation of the indebtedness of investment trusts. This is accounted for to a small extent by bankruptcy, but chiefly by the fact that the managements of solvent institutions have elected to sell enough investments to pay off a large part of their bonds. Examination of the reports of the management trusts (as listed in *Keane's Investment Manual* and in *Moody's Manual*) shows that of 236 million dollars of indebtedness issued, practically all of which was outstanding in 1929, less than 7 millions was in default at the end of 1935, about 2 millions had been written off in distress reorganizations, and 104 millions had been paid off. The amount outstanding at the end of 1935 was almost exactly half that outstanding in 1929.

The increase in the assets of the Federal Reserve Banks is, of course, a reflection of the depression policy of easing the money market by large open market purchases of government securities, with a corresponding expansion of demand obligations. The increase in the accounts of the Postal Savings system is due in part to the reduction in private banking facilities, but chiefly to transfers of funds because of distrust of the banks.

CONDITION OF FINANCIAL INSTITUTIONS IN SELECTED YEARS SINCE 1928[a]

(In millions of dollars)

I. Debts

Group	1929 Long-Term	1929 Short and Demand	1933 Long-Term	1933 Short and Demand	1934 Long-Term	1934 Short and Demand	1935 Long-Term	1935 Short and Demand
National banks	—	25,008	173	18,827	482	22,563	524	24,802
State banks	—	30,324	246	15,908	484	18,531	478	20,771
Mutual savings banks	—	9,112	—	9,744	—	9,851	—	9,991
Federal Reserve Banks	—	4,318	—	6,152	—	7,652	—	10,995
Postal savings	—	173	—	1,213	—	1,229	—	1,235
Building and loan associations	—	—	—	222	—	188	—	159
Life insurance companies	15,240	856	18,436	630	21,487	1,108	22,991	1,185
Veterans' Administration	411	21	671	19	725	18	790	18
Joint Stock Land Banks	572	14	367	27	279	18	205	14
Federal Deposit Ins. Corp.	—	—	—	—	—	—	—	—
Railroad Credit Corporation	—	—	67	—	53	—	46	—
All other financial	9,912	8,325	8,247	4,641	…	…	…	…
Total	26,135	78,151	28,207	57,383	…	…	…	…

II. Creditor Assets

10,444

Group	1929 Long-Term	1929 Short and Demand	1933 Long-Term	1933 Short and Demand	1934 Long-Term	1934 Short and Demand	1935 Long-Term	1935 Short and Demand
National banks	7,472	20,292	8,717	11,756	11,085	13,469	11,919	15,207
State banks	8,958	22,902	8,281	9,949	9,246	11,363	███	12,409
Mutual savings banks	9,257	764	9,755	838	9,462	783	9,700	104
Federal Reserve Banks	281	1,505	1,494	1,475	1,927	874	1,890	924
Postal savings	26	138	292	844	615	548	853	297
Building and loan associations	7,888	631	5,541	443	4,666	374	4,259	338
Life insurance companies	15,481	697	18,103	1,088	20,083	1,348	20,886	1,442
Veterans' Administration	413	24	663	26	717	28	779	29
Joint Stock Land Banks	490	31	373	6	263	24	194	10
Federal Deposit Ins. Corp.	—	—	—	—	315	18	311	36
Railroad Credit Corporation	—	—	67	1	55	1	46	—
All other financial	2,727	9,700	2,727	5,373	…	…	…	…

By far the most important items in our table, from the standpoint of this study, are those relating to commercial banks. The long-term assets of the banks have shown a slight increase, due almost entirely to the heavy investment in government bonds. Their short-term assets have been reduced by more than 50 per cent and their demand obligations (notes and deposits) by about 25 per cent for national banks and nearly 50 per cent for state banks.[6]

The decline of bank deposit liabilities from 1929 to 1933 and the subsequent rise reflect clearly the turn from general liquidation to slow recovery, and show the radical change in the credit structure of the country which has taken place within the last seven years. There was practically no shrinkage in the volume of bank deposits before the middle of 1930. During the next three years, however, four processes were going on together which steadily reduced the volume both of bank assets and of bank liabilities.

One factor was the cancellation of deposits through voluntary payment of loans in excess of good applications for new loans. With falling prices and a falling volume of business, industrial and commercial borrowers taken as a group had less need of working capital and so reduced their loans. Second, there was much involuntary liquidation, the banks calling in loans because of impairment of borrowers' credit and because of greater caution on their own part. The lessened willingness to incur risk and the increased estimate of the degree of risk which characterized the entire depression period thus affected both the banks and their customers.

A third factor which operated to reduce bank deposits

[6] Compare Chap. XVIII.

and bank assets was the withdrawal of deposits in cash. This process, which was due to distrust of the banks, operated chiefly in the autumn of 1931, when cash in circulation increased by 664 million dollars in four months.[7] The total increase of cash in circulation from May 1930 to February 1933 was over 2 billion dollars, of which nearly one billion had been returned to the banks by the middle of 1934. Recently, however, the cash in circulation has again increased to about the peak figure.

The final factor in the decline of bank deposits was the succession of bank failures, which for the three years 1930-32 numbered 5,299. This record represents first a continuance of the post-war process of eliminating small non-profit making banks, largely in communities that were losing business to larger centers; and second, the acute distrust of banks which appeared in the fall of 1931, subsided in 1932, and reappeared in intense form in the winter of 1932-33.

The two factors mentioned first—that is, voluntary and forced liquidation of bank loans—were the most important sources of the reduction of bank deposits which went on from 1930 to 1933. Increased caution on the part of banks in making loans also tended to hold down deposit expansion during the two years immediately following the bank holiday. The ancient theory that banks should not make permanent working capital loans, which had always been honored in the breach rather than in the observance, took on new life as an explanation of the great number of bank failures, and played a significant,

[7] There were also large withdrawals in 1931-33 which took the form of transfers between banks, especially the withdrawal of funds from country and suburban banks for deposit in larger city banks. This process tended to cause bank failures but did not, of course, directly reduce the total volume of bank deposits.

though probably a minor, part in determining the lending practice of banks and the policy of bank examiners.[8] At the same time the volume of government securities was expanding rapidly. Moreover, the demand for bank loans did not revive in proportion to the recovery of business activity. The larger industrial corporations had been making a decreasing use of bank credit before the depression, preferring to obtain their working capital through the issuance of stocks, and the depression therefore found them with an abundant supply of cash. Naturally the business organizations which were in this position were more likely to survive the depression than were the smaller businesses which had not been able to finance through the security market and consequently were more heavily in debt for their working capital needs.

Since the middle of 1933 the trend of bank assets and liabilities has been very sharply upward, but the increase in assets is entirely accounted for by the rise in holdings of United States securities. Loans of all classes have decreased more than investments in private securities have increased.

Taking the period as a whole, the change in the banking situation is in most respects favorable to recovery. The distrust of banks has been relieved in two ways. In the first place, many, doubtless most, of the weakest banks have been eliminated, and many banks have been strengthened by the waiver of depositors' claims and the investment of new capital. Second, deposit insurance has in part removed the threat of another wave of deposi-

[8] Compare Charles O. Hardy and Jacob Viner, *Report on the Availability of Bank Credit in the Seventh Federal Reserve District*, pp. VI, 13-25.

tor withdrawals.[9] The asset position of the banks, viewed from the standpoint of safety, must be regarded as strong, since a large proportion of the banks' portfolios consists of government obligations. Regardless of one's opinion as to the ultimate soundness of the credit of the government, the fact that bank deposits are so largely offset by government securities is a safeguard against bank failures, since the banks' liabilities run in dollars and a collapse in government credit and consequent inflation would affect the value of the assets and of the liabilities in substantially the same way.

A large inflow of gold and a considerable expansion of Federal Reserve investments have put the banks in possession of vast excess reserves so that they are now in a position to finance an expansion far larger than that which preceded the collapse of 1929-33. Excess reserves, even after reserve requirements had been increased by 50 per cent, stood at 1,890 million dollars on August 26, 1936, sufficient to support a volume of bank deposits much greater than the country has ever had.[10]

IV. INDIVIDUALS

Direct information as to the indebtedness of individuals is fragmentary, and information concerning their creditor position is still scarcer. The table on page 335 shows the more important categories of individual debt

[9] However, so long as deposit insurance is limited to amounts of $5,000 and under, there will still be danger from this source. In the later stages of the banking crisis when the larger city banks were affected, it appears to have been the big corporate accounts rather than the small individual deposits that were the chief source of trouble.

[10] Moreover, the Treasury has free gold in the amount of nearly 400 million dollars, and the Secretary of the Treasury has unused authority to issue 3 billion dollars in greenbacks. Then there is a large potential credit expansion concealed in the silver holdings of the Treasury, and the Stabilization Fund has a reserve of sterilized gold which may be as large as 1,800 million dollars. Finally, there is in circulation a volume of currency about a billion dollars larger than the circulation at the

for 1929 and 1933, the latter year being the latest for which sufficient data are available to make such a tabulation worth while. Some of the estimates are very rough. In addition to the data shown in the table, we have more detailed information concerning certain classes of debt; these we discuss in the following sections. Because of lack of data, we offer no tabulation of the creditor position

INDIVIDUAL DEBT, 1929 AND 1933[a]
(In millions of dollars)

Type	1929	1933
Home mortgages.........................	22,000	18,740
Farm mortgages.........................	9,039	7,624
Bank loans..............................	21,825	8,533
Brokers' borrowings from non-bankers.......	3,664	391
Brokers' loans to customers...............	5,985	1,267
Debt to retailers........................	6,974	4,156
Non-corporate debt to wholesalers...........	6,866	3,003
Debt to small loan companies..............	242	222
Debt to life insurance companies...........	2,379	3,769
Debt to government life insurance..........	202	529
Miscellaneous items[b]...................	1,238	491
Total...............................	80,414	48,725

[a] For sources of data and methods of estimating, see Appendix G, Section V.

[b] Pawnbrokers, credit unions, axias, unlawful lenders, remedial loan societies, employees' loan associations, Hebrew Free Loan societies, endorsed note lenders.

of individuals as a whole, though estimates for individuals who submit income tax returns are presented in the table on page 336.[11]

peak of the post-war boom. If this currency were to be deposited in banks and redeposited by the banks in the Federal Reserve Banks, reserves would be correspondingly augmented.

[11] An attempt was made to estimate the creditor position of individuals, by deducting the known holdings of corporations and governmental agencies from data concerning the amount of securities and other obligations outstanding, but was abandoned because of the high degree of uncertainty concerning the holdings of educational and philanthropic institutions which do not file reports for income tax; and also the amounts of domestic securities which are held abroad.

1. Individuals submitting income tax returns. The items below, except for tax-exempt securities owned by individuals with incomes over $5,000, are estimated (in millions of dollars) by capitalizing figures for interest paid and received, as reported in *Statistics of Income.*

INTEREST BEARING DEBT

Group	1929	1933
Individuals with income over $5,000	15,983	3,470
Individuals with income less than $5,000	5,683	5,000
Individuals with no net income	3,000	2,250

INTEREST BEARING ASSETS

	1929	1933
Individuals with income over $5,000:		
Tax-exempt securities	5,373	4,535
Other interest bearing assets, non-fiduciary	20,960	7,045
Other interest bearing assets, fiduciary	3,686	1,677
Individuals with income of less than $5,000:		
Tax-exempt securities	. . .	. . .
Other interest bearing assets, non-fiduciary	10,921	8,985
Other interest bearing assets, fiduciary	792	861
Individuals with no net income:		
Tax-exempt securities	. . .	. . .
Other interesting bearing assets, non-fiduciary	1,920	1,795
Other interest bearing assets, fiduciary	112	182

In capitalizing interest received, it has been assumed that 55 per cent of the fiduciary income is derived from interest bearing assets. This is roughly the proportion shown in the trust portfolios of national banks.

2. Farm debt. The table on page 337 shows the changes which have taken place since 1929 in farm mortgage debt and in holdings of certain lending agencies.

It will be seen that the total amount of farm mortgages outstanding, and the amounts held by banks and life insurance companies, have decreased rapidly since 1929. Mortgage loans of the Federal Farm Loan system, on the other hand, increased slightly between the year-end dates of 1929 and 1933, and since the latter date have risen very rapidly indeed. The decrease in the total amount of farm mortgages is due only in minor degree to the liquidation of debt out of income, although because of declining land values and the enhanced desire for liquidity on the part of lenders there has been considerable pressure on borrowers to reduce their loans wherever funds were available for the purpose. To a large extent the reduction is due to the writing down of loans through compromise settlements.[12] Still more important has been the liquidation of debt through forced and quasi-voluntary sales of property to new borrowers who have taken over the property with reduced mort-

FARM MORTGAGES, 1929 AND 1933-35[a]
(In millions of dollars)

Year (Dec. 31)	Outstanding	Owned by			
		Federal Reserve Member Banks	Life Insurance Companies	Joint Stock Land Banks	Federal Farm Loan System
1929.......	9,241	388	2,100	627	1,197
1933.......	7,855	318	1,630	392	1,284
1934.......	7,770	262	1,291	256	2,458
1935.......	7,500	251	1,008	177	2,866

[a] For sources of data, see Appendix G Section VI.

gages, and to the acquisition of property by the lenders themselves.

Some indication of the extent of the latter type of loan liquidation is afforded by the statistics of life insurance company holdings of farm properties. Life insurance holdings of real estate rose from 345 million dollars in 1929 to 1,905 millions in December 1935.[13] During the same period, member banks of the Federal Reserve system increased their holdings of real estate, other than banking houses, from 184 million dollars to 551 mil-

[12] During the fiscal year 1935, 5,979 farmer cases of extension and settlement were filed under Section 75 of the Bankruptcy Act, as compared with 410 in 1934. Bankruptcies were 4,716 in 1934 and 4,311 in 1935.
[13] Estimated from reported holdings of 38 life insurance companies, having 92 per cent of total assets of all life insurance companies.

lions. However, the reduction of the mortgage loans of the commercial banks and the insurance companies has been due more to the expansion of loans on the part of the various government lending agencies than it has to voluntary or involuntary liquidation. Separate figures for farm real estate are not available, but we may infer from the change in mortgage holdings that life insurance holdings of farm property have increased through foreclosure by five or six hundred million dollars, and those of member banks by 50 millions.[14]

The short-term debt of farmers, which was roughly estimated at 3,500 million dollars in 1928, has probably been liquidated to a larger extent than has the mortgage debt. Bank loans to farmers, other than mortgage loans, were estimated on June 30, 1931 at 1,936 million dollars. This figure is known to have been greatly reduced in more recent years, but data are not available for an estimate of its present size, nor for the bulk of the remaining debt. A considerable amount of short-term debt has been refinanced on a long-term basis in connection with loans from the Farm Mortgage Corporation. Loans of production credit associations and regional credit corporations financed by the Federal Intermediate Credit Banks amounted to 137 million dollars at the end of 1935, and emergency crop and emergency drought loans, which were negligible in amount at the beginning of the depression, amounted to 173 millions in 1935. Rehabilitation loans of the Resettlement Administration amounted to 8 million dollars at the end of the latter year.

3. Urban mortgage debt. Information with regard to urban home mortgage debts is very scanty. Details are

[14] Estimate based on the fact that of the total decrease in real estate mortgages, about two-fifths in the case of insurance companies and one-seventh in the case of banks was in farm mortgages.

available with regard to the total urban mortgage loans made by banks, life insurance companies, and building and loan associations, but these data do not separate individual from corporate obligations nor home mortgage loans from those secured by liens against industrial and commercial property. The Home Owners' Loan Corporation estimates the total mortgage debt on one to four

ESTIMATED URBAN HOME MORTGAGE DEBT,
DECEMBER 31, 1934[a]
(In millions of dollars)

Agency Holding Mortgage	Amount	*Percentage Distribution*
Savings and loan associations..........	4,100	*23.1*
All banks............................	3,700	*20.9*
Life insurance companies..............	1,500	*8.5*
Home Owners' Loan Corporation........	2,200	*12.4*
Mortgage companies...................	1,090	*6.1*
Construction companies...............	80	*0.5*
Title and trust companies.............	500	*2.8*
Individuals..........................	3,800	*21.4*
All others...........................	770	*4.3*
Total...........................	17,740	*100.0*

[a] *Federal Home Loan Bank Review,* March 1936, p. 205. A home is defined as a dwelling built to accommodate one, two, three, or four families, and used primarily for residential purposes.

family urban homes at the end of 1934 to have been 17,740 million dollars and refers to an estimate of 21,000 million dollars which was made in 1931. The details of the HOLC estimate are shown in the accompanying table. The first four items are believed to be relatively accurate; the others are estimates.[15]

V. GOVERNMENTAL AND QUASI-GOVERNMENTAL AGENCIES

The table on pages 340-41 shows more clearly than does the one on page 320 the rapid expansion of the

[15] The estimated items are based on data for 61 cities collected for the *Financial Survey of Urban Housing.*

Financial Condition of Governmental and Quasi-Governmental Agencies, 1929 and 1933-35[a]
(In millions of dollars)
I. Debts

Agency	1929 Long-Term	1929 Short and Demand	1933 Long-Term	1933 Short and Demand	1934 Long-Term	1934 Short and Demand	1935 Long-Term	1935 Short and Demand
United States government	16,029	633	20,819	3,469	25,832	4,312	26,945	2,757
Federal trust funds	150	—	127	—	120	—	117	—
United States territories and possessions	—	—	—	—	—	—	—	—
State and local governments	13,423	935	16,379	1,196	16,846	947	17,844	1,025
Reconstruction Finance Corporation	—	—	180	16	249	13	252	8
Federal Land Banks	1,188	22	1,192	44	1,784	110	1,928	92
Federal Farm Mortgage Corporation	—	—	—	—	980	33	1,387	18
Federal Intermediate Credit Banks	50	2	128	3	164	5	131	2
Regional agricultural credit corporations	—	—	—	104	—	39	—	3
Commodity Credit Corporation	—	—	—	—	—	—	—	—
Banks for co-operatives	—	—	—	—	—	—	—	8
Production credit corporations	—	—	—	—	—	93	—	91
Production credit associations	—	—	—	—	—	—	—	—
Emergency crop and seed loans and crop production loans	—	—	—	—	—	—	—	—
Resettlement Administration	—	—	—	—	—	—	—	—
Agricultural Marketing Act Revolving Fund	—	—	—	—	—	—	—	—
Home Owners' Loan Corporation	—	—	103	—	2,407	26	2,914	36
Federal Home Loan Banks	—	—	—	—	—	4	—	7
Federal Savings and Loan Insurance Corporation	—	—	—	—	—	—	—	—
Federal savings and loan associations	—	—	—	—	—	10	—	19
Federal Housing Administration	—	—	—	—	—	—	—	—
Public Works Administration	—	—	—	—	—	—	—	—
Shipping Board	—	—	—	—	—	—	—	—

II. Creditor Assets[a]

Agency	1929 Long-Term	1929 Short and Demand	1933 Long-Term	1933 Short and Demand	1934 Long-Term	1934 Short and Demand	1935 Long-Term	1935 Short and Demand
United States government	68	—	44	1,218	36	1,967	36	1,575
Federal trust funds	1,049	—	535	—	593	—	628	—
United States territories and possessions	—	2,441	—	—	—	—	—	—
State and local governments	1,500	—	1,500	1,951	1,500	2,601	1,500	3,079
Reconstruction Finance Corporation	—	—	318	1,694	982	1,461	1,235	1,403
Federal Land Banks	1,239	54	1,308	85	2,040	150	2,205	129
Federal Farm Mortgage Corporation	—	—	71	—	1,196	21	2,152	67
Federal Intermediate Credit Banks	81	3	33	160	74	198	73	167
Regional agricultural credit corporations	—	—	—	153	—	93	—	49
Commodity Credit Corporation	—	—	24	—	79	37	85	278
Banks for co-operatives	—	—	—	27	113	35	128	62
Production credit corporations	—	—	—	—	—	5	—	1
Production credit associations	—	—	—	—	—	61	—	94
Emergency crop and seed loans and crop production loans	—	7	—	90	—	112	—	172
Resettlement Administration	—	—	—	—	—	—	8	—
Agricultural Marketing Act Revolving Fund	—	15	—	158	—	55	—	44
Home Owners' Loan Corporation	—	—	103	—	2,394	131	2,903	133
Federal Home Loan Banks	—	—	88	7	101	9	121	7
Federal Savings and Loan Insurance Corporation	—	—	—	—	100	2	101	2
Federal savings and loan associations	—	—	—	—	90	7	361	16
Federal Housing Administration	—	—	—	—	9	—	9	16
Public Works Administration	—	—	149	—	255	—	189	—
Shipping Board	70	—	—	—	134	—	112	6
Total	4,007	2,520	4,173	5,543	9,696	6,945	11,239	7,300

[a] For sources of data, see Appendix G, Section VII.

debtor and creditor position of the government lending agencies. We shall not discuss here the change in the debt of the United States government and of states and municipalities, since these are dealt with in another chapter of the book. The growth of government owned corporations reflects a systematic effort on the part of the federal government to relieve the depression or mitigate its effects by protecting property owners against foreclosure or other forced liquidation of their assets in order to satisfy the claims of creditors. In general the effect of this operation has not been to reduce the totals of indebtedness but rather to freeze the debt structure by substituting for a private creditor a public agency which will exercise a minimum of pressure on distressed debtors. The Reconstruction Finance Corporation has come to the rescue of the banks and the railroads; the Farm Credit Administration has protected the holders of farm lands and their creditors; and the Federal Housing Administration and the Federal Home Loan Bank system have done the same for the owners of urban homes and their creditors.

1. Loans to business. The government's program of lending money as a method of combating the depression really began with the establishment of the Reconstruction Finance Corporation early in 1932. The RFC is a hybrid agency, deriving most of its funds from direct advances from the federal Treasury, but a minor part from sales of notes in the investment market. At the end of 1935 it owed the government 4,595 million dollars (including 500 millions for stock ownership), and the public 252 millions.

The expansion and decline of the lending operations of the RFC which constitute loans to business are shown in the table on the following page.

This table excludes the great bulk of the assets shown by the RFC on its balance sheet. These are entries arising out of transfers of funds to other government agencies such as the allocation of funds to the Secretary of Agriculture, the Secretary of the Treasury, and the farm and home lending agencies. The RFC constitutes a circuitous route by which funds are transferred from the federal Treasury to other government relief and lending agencies.

RECONSTRUCTION FINANCE CORPORATION LOANS TO
BUSINESS, 1932-35[a]

(In millions of dollars)

Borrower	1932	1933	1934	1935
Banks and trust companies (including advances on the assets of closed banks)[b].	595	977	1,497	1,282
Building and loan associations.........	84	66	20	7
Insurance companies.................	62	65	55	36
Mortgage loan companies.............	77	178	161	138
Railroads.........................	272	337	377	396
Industrial and commercial business.....	—	—	7	41
Drainage, levee, and irrigation districts..	—	2	13	50
Marketing of agricultural commodities..	—	68	53	290
Miscellaneous......................	—	10	—	10

[a] Data, as of December 31, from annual reports of the Corporation.
[b] Including purchases of preferred stock.

The RFC is not being operated, as are the farm mortgage and urban home mortgage agencies discussed below, with a view to establishing a permanent field of activity of the federal government as a lending agency. At the end of 1935 its loans to railroads had already been liquidated to the extent of over 18 per cent, and those to banks to the extent of 57 per cent.[16] It has served in general the purpose it was intended to serve—easing the shock of liquidation—and will apparently be liqui-

[16] Including purchases of preferred stock and capital notes. If these are omitted, the percentage of repayments is above 79.

dated when its services as a rescue agency are no longer needed. The money which the RFC has advanced to non-governmental corporations has not been given away, and its policy has apparently been to make loans as nearly on a business basis as is consistent with its responsibility to extend aid to distressed institutions.

Probably the most important service which the RFC has rendered is the program of loans to banks during 1932 and the first two months of 1933. The creation of the Corporation and the inauguration of its program of lending to distressed banks had a very pronounced effect for nearly a year in checking the flood of bank failures, as may be seen from the accompanying table which shows the number of bank failures by months for 1931 and 1932, and January and February 1933.[17] The figures show very clearly how bank failures decreased immediately after the RFC began operations in February 1932.

Month	1931	1932	1933
January	198	342	242
February	77	121	154
March	86	46	
April	64	74	
May	91	82	
June	167	151	
July	93	132	
August	158	85	
September	305	67	
October	522	102	
November	175	93	
December	358	161	

In the winter of 1932-33, however, its efforts in this direction were not adequate. Likewise the Corporation's

[17] Data from *Annual Report of the Federal Reserve Board*, 1932, p. 154; *Federal Reserve Bulletin*, April 1934, p. 251.

loans to insurance companies and to railroads had a direct influence in stopping the wave of panic attacks on the banks and insurance companies.[18]

The loans made since the middle of 1933 have had a different setting. The primary objective has not been one of preventing the financial collapse of the borrowers, but of promoting general recovery by making expanded operations possible, and by increasing the flow of funds through the channels of trade. Very large sums have been loaned to closed banks,[19] and these have served to speed up the distribution of funds to depositors. Since the policy is to take collateral for these loans and to require repayments as the collateral is liquidated, the process has not increased the final return of depositors; in fact the payment of interest to the RFC by closed banks has reduced the amount that will be ultimately available for distribution. However, the release of funds to depositors at an earlier date than would otherwise have been possible has presumably facilitated the expansion of the total volume of spending which has been evident in the past three years.

Loans to industrial and commercial business (authorized by Sec. 5(d) of the RFC Act as amended June 19, 1934) have been intended to relieve local shortages of credit caused by bank failures and to enable industry (chiefly small-scale business) to obtain working capital on somewhat longer terms of payment than have been customary at the banks.[20] The volume of eligible applica-

---

[18] Compare above, pp. 331-32.

[19] Up to the end of 1935, 866 million dollars had been loaned to closed banks, building and loan associations, and mortgage loan companies, of which 621 millions had been repaid.

[20] The Federal Reserve Banks also have been authorized since the same date to make loans of this type, and at the end of 1935 had a total of 32 million dollars outstanding.

tions for direct loans has turned out to be much smaller than was expected at the time the program of industrial lending was initiated. The policy has been to refuse credit to applicants who can get what they need from banks on reasonable terms; and on the other hand it is to require that borrowers give adequate security. Loans which are adequately secured and still are not acceptable to the banks are not plentiful, and the program of direct lending has therefore moved slowly.

The lending activity of other agencies which deal directly with private business calls for little discussion. Loans to the shipping industry made by the Shipping Board (now the Shipping Bureau of the Department of Commerce) are a part of the long-established national program of encouraging the development of a domestic merchant marine; the volume of such loans has been contracting in recent years. The loss in connection with these loans has been very heavy and even the proportion of uncollectable interest has been high, in spite of extraordinary low rates.

2. The Federal Farm Loan program. The table on pages 340-41 shows in some detail the changes in the debtor and creditor positions of the federal agencies which make loans to farmers. The change after 1933 in volume of mortgages held by the Federal Farm Loan system reflects a definite change of policy which found expression in the Emergency Farm Mortgage Act and the Farm Credit Act, both passed in that year. These acts liberalized the lending power of the federal farm lending agencies in several ways, among which are the following:

First, they provided that no payments on the principal of mortgages held by the Federal Land Bank system were to be required during the five-year period beginning

July 11, 1933, provided borrowers were not in default with respect to any other obligations under their mortgages. The Land Banks were also authorized to grant debtors extensions of time to meet interest and tax obligations on a more liberal basis than previously. These provisions tend to hold up the total amount of the debt by obviating the normal amortization of loans by borrowers who are not in distress.

Second, the Federal Farm Loan Act, as amended, provides that the appraisals used as a basis for new loans may be made on the basis of the "normal agricultural value" of farm property. As the principal guide used in determining the normal value is the earning power of the land at the 1909-14 level of agricultural prices, the lending basis for many farmers has been increased. More important is the provision made for loans by the Land Bank Commissioner. These loans are made with funds supplied by the United States Treasury and are granted in cases where the character of the security or the amount of the loan needed by the farmer in order to retain possession of his property are such as to make Federal Land Bank loans impossible or inadequate. The loans may run as high as 75 per cent of the appraised value of the land or other property mortgaged, whereas Land Bank loans may not exceed 50 per cent of the value of the land plus 20 per cent of the value of the improvements. About one-third of the Land Bank Commissioner loans are secured by second mortgages. They are not made through local co-operative associations of borrowers, as are a large proportion of the loans made by the Land Banks. In 1934 the outstanding Land Bank Commissioner loans were taken over by the Farm Mortgage Corporation and since then they have been made by that agency.

The Corporation also has made large loans to the Land Banks on the security of farm mortgages. Such loans were authorized in order to enable the farm loan system to raise money on the strength of the credit of the government at times when the investment market would not absorb Land Bank bonds, Farm Mortgage Corporation loans being fully guaranteed by the federal government.

Another change made in 1933 was the provision that all of the Federal Land Banks should be jointly responsible for one another's bonds, issued in the future; a change which may have tended to lessen the sense of responsibility of the lending banks for the results obtained and thereby facilitated the expansion of the volume of lending.

Most of the long-term loans made by the Federal Farm Loan system during the last few years have been for the purpose of refinancing existing indebtedness.[21] In many cases the refinancing involved a reduction of indebtedness through compromise, and such reduction has been actively encouraged by the Farm Credit Administration. In 1933-35 it was reported that about 20 per cent of Land Bank Commissioner loans involved a scaling down of debts; the reduction in 1933 averaged 25 per cent of the original indebtedness.[22]

The reduction in the volume of Joint Stock Land Bank loans reflects the progress of liquidation of these agencies, which will soon disappear from the system. Most of the reduction of their loans has been effected either through direct purchase of mortgages by the Farm Mortgage Corporation, or by refunding through Land Bank and Land Bank Commissioner loans.

[21] In 1933 it was reported that 85 per cent of the proceeds of Land Bank Commissioner loans were of this character.

[22] Figures include scale-down of short-term as well as mortgage indebtedness.

The public agencies making short-term loans to farmers have also been completely reorganized during the period under review and have effected a marked increase in the volume of operations, though the totals naturally are much lower than those for mortgage loans. Details are shown in the table on pages 340-41. Production credit associations, supervised by the production credit corporations, have replaced the old regional agricultural credit corporations and a system of banks for cooperatives has been established. Emergency crop and seed loans and drought-relief loans, which have been made by the federal government in small volume since 1921, have been placed under the administration of the Farm Credit Administration and the amount of money available has been greatly increased.

The reduction in the volume of lending of the Intermediate Credit Banks since the end of 1934 has been due chiefly to the transfer of business to the banks for cooperatives. The capital used by the short-term lending agencies, except the Federal Intermediate Credit Banks, is furnished almost entirely by the federal government, though a small percentage of the stock of co-operatives and of the production credit associations has been sold to borrowers.

The Resettlement Administration loans are made independently of the Farm Credit Administration and are distinctly of relief character. They are secured chiefly by liens on farm equipment.

3. The Federal Home Loan program. As the table on page 350 shows,[23] the rise of the government agencies to a position of dominance in the financing of urban housing has been even more rapid than the similar change in the farm mortgage situation.

---

[23] Compare also table on pp. 340-41.

Here again what was primarily an emergency program designed to check the rush of liquidation almost immediately became a program of permanent financial activity. The HOLC is a depression stop-gap and has already begun to liquidate, but the Federal Home Loan Banks and the Federal Housing Administration embody a purpose to establish the federal government permanently in the business of home financing. The HOLC, which lent only on a showing of need, advanced 103

HOME MORTGAGE INDEBTEDNESS TO FEDERAL
AGENCIES, 1933-35[a]
(In millions of dollars)

Agency	1933	1934	1935
Home Owners' Loan Corporation	103	2,394[e]	2,897
Federal Home Loan Banks	85	87	103
Federal Savings and Loan Insurance Corporation	—	103[b]	370[b,c]
Federal savings and loan associations	[d]	81	186
Federal Housing Administration	—	30[b]	421[b]
Total	188	2,695	3,977

[a] Data, as of December 31, from annual reports of Federal Home Loan Bank Board and Federal Housing Administration.
[b] Amount insured.
[c] June 30, 1935.
[d] No data; amount very small.
[e] Includes accrued interest.

million dollars in loans in 1933; 2,091 millions in 1934; 743 millions in 1935; and 153 millions in 1936. The receipt of applications for new loans was stopped on June 27, 1935 and lending activity terminated on June 12, 1936, except that some purchase money loans are still granted to facilitate the sale of property acquired under foreclosure. The Home Loan Banks, on the other hand, were still expanding operations up to the end of 1935. However, the emergency activities have played, relatively speaking, a much larger part in the program of housing finance than in that of farm credit. At the end of 1933 the loans of the HOLC, the emergency agency, made up 55 per cent of the total volume of credit extended by the federal home lending agencies; in 1934, 85 per cent; and at the end of 1935, 73 per cent of the total.

In form the Federal Home Loan banking system is patterned on the Federal Reserve system. The banks lend only to members (building and loan associations), the loans being secured by pledge of first mortgage loans on urban homes, just as the Federal Reserve Banks make loans only to member banks on the security of paper obtained through loans to commercial borrowers. But the analogy with the Federal Reserve banking system is superficial. The Reserve Banks derive their working funds from the member banks themselves, partly by the sale of stock, but chiefly as demand deposits. The Reserve Banks make loans to members only on a temporary basis, and the effect of the depression has been to decrease the volume of credit which they extend in this manner. The bulk of their funds is invested in the securities of the federal government. The Reserve Banks are thus a source of credit for the government and not an outlet for governmental funds. The Federal Home Loan Banks, on the other hand, extend credit to their members on a permanent basis and derive only a small fraction of their working funds from their members. The bulk of their assets has been obtained by pledging the credit of the United States government to secure bond issues. The system is not a device to redistribute private credit, but a channel through which the government makes credit available to individuals.

At the end of 1935 the Federal Home Loan Banks and the HOLC together held one-seventh of the estimated total of urban home mortgages in the country. In addition, the FHA, which does not make any loans but merely guarantees them, accounted for 421 million dollars of loans. The total amount of federal credit in the housing field at the end of 1935 was 3,977 million dollars.[24]

To some extent the program of government lending at low rates and on easy terms to owners of farms and homes has been motivated by the belief that the depression was caused, or its severity increased, by the private debt situation. It has been partly motivated also by the desire to expand the volume of money in circulation. Primarily, however, the motive of the loan expansion appears to have been one of relief—this despite the fact that the beneficiaries are not as a rule in sufficient distress to qualify for public relief. Many of them are holders of steady jobs and have suffered no material reduction of income on account of the depression. Others are owners of income producing properties—farms and business enterprises—and while their incomes have in most cases been reduced they have rarely been wiped out.

Several factors underlie the debtor relief lending program. In the first place, individuals who contracted debts when their incomes were larger than they are now, if they fulfill their obligations, suffer a loss of consumable income that is disproportionate to the shrinkage in their gross incomes. Second, the debt of farmers and home owners is more serious than that of wage earners because it is more readily collectable. The debt of people whose borrowing power rests solely on their earning power does not create a problem of public policy because it promptly adjusts itself by becoming uncollectable. But the debts of farmers and home owners, as well

---

[24] This figure includes credit extended by the federal savings and loan associations, 188 million dollars, of which only about 130 million is government money.

as those of business corporations, do not adjust themselves in this way until there has been a transfer of ownership of property, and such transfers give rise to a strong demand for public intervention. Active dissatisfaction with one's own economic position moreover is determined not merely by absolute need but also by recent improvement or retrogression. Finally, owners of homes and farms are politically more powerful than are the mass of wage earners. Consequently the amount of public money and effort expended to relieve the position of debtors has been greater than that expended for the sake of individuals of comparable income positions who never owned enough property to get into debt.

VI. SUMMARY

Changes in the debt situation in the course of the depression may be summarized as follows:

The long-term debt of corporations and of individuals shows comparatively little change. Long-term indebtedness of railroads, public utilities, and other nonfinancial corporations increased between 1929 and 1933. Since the latter date, railroad long-term debt has decreased slightly and that of other classes of corporations has probably also declined, though definite information is available only for comparatively few industries. The long-term debt of insurance companies (policyholders' reserves) has increased steadily, while that of other financial corporations, chiefly real estate companies, decreased between 1929 and 1933 and has probably decreased further in recent years. Individual long-term debt, chiefly farm mortgages and home mortgages, has decreased more than has the debt of corporations. The debt of state and local governments has increased moderately and that of the federal government and its more important special agencies has expanded very rapidly.

With regard to short-term debt the picture is entirely different. The short-term debt of railroads decreased slightly until 1933 and increased by nearly one-third in 1934-35, largely because of the accumulation of unpaid matured funded debt and interest. Other public utilities showed a decrease of about two-thirds between 1929 and 1933, and non-financial corporations, other than utilities, showed a decrease of nearly one-third. Bank deposits, which constituted the most important form of short-term debt of financial institutions, were liquidated very rapidly between 1929 and 1933, and have since expanded with equal rapidity, though the level is still below that of 1929. Our knowledge of the short-term debt of individuals is very scanty, but indirect evidence seems to indicate a large liquidation of the indebtedness of individuals to banks. Other forms of short-term personal debt, aside from brokers' loans, seem to have changed but little. The short-term and demand debt of the United States government increased fivefold between 1929 and 1933, and has since shown a moderate decline. The short-term debts of state and local governments have been comparatively stable. Other financial agencies of the government have no significant volume of short-term debt.

Aside from the anticipated fiscal effects of the increase in government indebtedness, which have been dealt with in a preceding chapter, the changes in the national debt structure do not seem to be of tremendous significance for the recovery program. The debt which was incurred under prosperity conditions became under depression conditions an aggravating factor which made distress the more severe. If the country had had to look forward to an indefinite perpetuation of the volume of unemployment of men and resources which characterized the years 1931-32, further drastic reduction of the debt structure would have been inevitable. But just as a debt structure appropriate to a prosperity era seems far too heavy in a period of depression, so a debt structure appropriate to a period of depression seems light in a prosperity era. In other words, the process of debt creation is subject to the same alternation of expansion and contraction as are other forms of economic activity. Unfortunately, however, expansion of debt in prosperity eras is much easier than downward readjustment in periods of depression.

CHAPTER XIV

INTEREST RATES AND THE
AVAILABILITY OF CREDIT

In this chapter we shall describe certain changes which have taken place in the rate of interest and in the supply of funds for loans and investments during the post-war years. We shall also consider the extent to which, during the course of the depression, fluctuations in interest rates, combined with changes in the amount of debt and in the volume of business transacted, have changed the weight of the burden of interest charges on various types of corporate business. Before presenting any data we shall review briefly the general theory of the relationship of interest rates to prosperity and depression, in order that the relevance and meaning of the factual material may be more readily apparent.

It has long been observed that as a rule interest rates (at least those types of interest rates which are most readily observed and which fluctuate most widely) tend to be high in the later stages of prosperity and low in the later stages of depression. This fact is frequently interpreted as evidence that high rates tend to cause the prosperity era to come to an end, and that low rates tend to bring about recovery from depression. However, it is generally recognized that such a conclusion cannot safely be drawn merely from these historical sequences; at least a similar conclusion is not accepted with reference to wages, which also tend to be high in the later stages of prosperity and low in the later stages of depression. The facts are equally consistent with the interpretation that the line of causation is the other way; the prosperity era causing high interest rates and the depression low interest rates, through changes in the demand for money, just as the forces of prosperity and depression tend to bring about changes in wages and other prices with varying degrees of lag. A choice between the two theories must be based on the internal consistency and general plausibility of the doctrines, and not on a purely inductive study.

As we view it, there are three principal reasons for the general acceptance of the idea that a low interest rate is economically desirable. One has to do with the equality of distribution of income. On the whole, though with numerous individual exceptions, it may be said that interest is received by the wealthier members of the community to whom a given item of added income is less useful than it is to the laboring population. Low interest rates leave more of the social income for distribution to the other elements of the population, among whom the laboring element is the most important; consequently they make for a higher average standard of well-being.[1] The case for lowering interest rates is seldom, if ever, argued primarily on this basis, but it unquestionably colors men's thinking on the question and makes it easier for them to accept other arguments supporting the same conclusion.

A second reason has to do with the conditions of supply of the kind of service for which interest is generally assumed to be paid. This is the service of "waiting"; that is, postponing consumption in order that laborers and the owners of natural resources may be paid in

[1] In this respect the case is the same as the case for low profits, low rents, and low executive salaries.

advance for the values which are expected ultimately to emerge from the productive process. Now it seems clear that most individual saving is motivated chiefly by the desire to make provision for the future, and probably goes on at much the same rate regardless of the high or low level of interest that is expected.[2] Consequently, interest payments, though inevitable under competition, are in the main socially unnecessary in the sense that the service for which payment is made would be performed anyway if the payment was eliminated or greatly reduced. Moreover, a large volume of saving is done through the accumulation of corporate surpluses, and results from the superior convenience and certainty of getting funds in this way (for those concerns which have income to reinvest) rather than the desire to avoid interest charges.

In this analysis it is tacitly assumed that the only social service which is involved is that of saving, and that the act of saving leads automatically to the expenditure of funds of like amount in the creation of new productive resources.[3]

Both these arguments have to do with the want-satisfying power of income and not with the stimulus to business activity; they are equally applicable to any stage of the business cycle. Their application to the cycle problem is an example of the widespread tendency to assume that anything which is desirable for general social reasons must be also a means of alleviating cyclical disturbances.

The third reason has to do more directly with the phenomena of the cycle. Other things being equal, high

[2] For a general discussion of this question compare Gustav Cassel, *Theory of Social Economy* (McCabe's translation), Vol. I, pp. 230-38.

[3] Compare H. G. Moulton, *The Formation of Capital*, Chap. X; also below, pp. 359-60.

interest rates mean low profits. Interest is a payment made by the active elements in the productive organization to the relatively inactive; by the young to the old; by the enterprising and adventurous to the conservative; by the employers of labor and producers of goods, upon whose decisions depends the volume of investment and of productive activity, to those whose decisions have already been made. Specifically, since the value of capital goods depends directly on the rate at which anticipated income is capitalized, low interest rates[4] mean a high valuation of long-time durable goods and consequently a high incentive to capitalists to produce them. Since the fluctuations of productive activity are most pronounced in the case of production for the distant future, a low rate of capitalization, which gives high capital values and a maximum incentive to the production of capital instruments, tends definitely toward the creation or perpetuation of prosperity. Moreover, even in operations which do not look far to the future, such as the building up of inventories by traders, whatever must be paid as interest increases cost and thus reduces by that much the prospective profit.[5]

In addition to these familiar considerations, much emphasis has been laid in recent years on the existence of a discrepancy, now in one direction and now in the other, between the amount of money income that is saved and the amount that is actually expended in the production of capital goods. The desire to provide for the future is an inducement to save, but not necessarily to invest. Except for interest, savers would seek only

[4] That is, long-term rates. As is shown below, a low rate of capitalization may in fact coincide with a high level of short-term open market rates which are generally used to identify periods of high or low rates.

[5] This aspect of the question is emphasized especially in Hawtrey's analysis of the relationship between the money market and the pace of business activity.

safety in the case of their savings, and would often prefer to hoard rather than to lend. Thus interest serves not so much to induce saving as to induce those who save to forego the maximum of liquidity and safety, by exchanging liquid funds for equities in productive assets or securities based on them.[6]

When viewed from this angle the service for which interest is paid looms as much more important than in the older view which confines attention to the payment for "saving" and assumes that all savings are automatically converted into real capital. Moreover, the general level of interest rates loses significance and attention shifts to the structure of rates. For different classes of loan and investment transactions involve varying degrees of risk and of sacrifice of liquidity, and the same conditions which raise some rates depress others. When for any reason liquidity preference rises, long-term rates and rates on risky investments rise, but rates for short-term and highly safe uses of funds fall. Now the rates that are most commonly recorded and are generally quoted in discussions of the level of rates are those paid in the open market for very short and very safe loans. Such loans do not meet the needs of industry for funds for expansion and full utilization of existing plant, and an abundance of funds for such uses does not evidence a genuine abundance of capital. The very fact that owners of capital are unusually timid means that funds, though scarce and dear for genuine investment, are unusually abundant and cheap for financing the speculative turnover of existing goods and securities and for the small volume of genuine productive services for

[6] Compare J. M. Keynes, *General Theory of Employment and Money,* 1936, Chap. 13; also review of this book by Charles O. Hardy, *American Economic Review,* 1936, Vol. XXVI, pp. 490-93.

which no long-term commitment of resources is necessary.

Vice versa, in a period when confidence in the future is running high and money is abundant for stock investments, long-term bond issues, and the underwriting of promotions, short-term money may be scarce and dear precisely because possible lenders wish to take advantage of the anticipated profitability of enterprise by making long-term commitments. The problem is greatly complicated, however, by the fact that interest rates for short-term money are influenced by the abundance or scarcity of bank reserves, which in turn is influenced by the state of gold production, by changes in legal or customary requirements as to bank reserves, by central bank policy, and by the money market situation in other countries with which the community in question is linked by the gold standard or by exchange stabilization.

I. INTEREST RATES

Before carrying the discussion further, we present, in the table on pages 362-63, a record of the movement of a number of types of interest rates as measured by annual averages, for the years since 1919. The charts on pages 365 and 369 show the monthly fluctuations of some of these series.

Some caution is necessary in using statistical data as a basis for inferences concerning the interrelations between the money market and business activity. In the first place the rates which are published, while probably accurate in themselves, are not fully representative of the price that money commands; and in the second place there are wide fluctuations in the volume of funds that are available at the rates quoted, and in the rigidity of credit standards.

Most of the rates which are included in our table, and

DOMESTIC INTEREST

(Average

Type of Loan	1919	1920	1921	1922	1923	1924
Short-term:						
Call loans[a]..............	6.27	7.78	5.98	4.29	4.85	3.08
Commercial paper[b]........	5.42	7.37	6.53	4.43	4.98	3.91
Over-the-counter:[c]						
Southern and Western						
cities (27)............	6.00	6.75	6.99	6.14	5.94	5.71
Northern and Eastern						
cities (8).............	5.73	6.74	6.76	5.48	5.50	5.11
New York City.........	5.51	6.25	6.34	5.07	5.19	4.60
Earnings on national bank						
loans[d]................	...	...	...	...	...	...
U. S. Treasury bonds[e]......	...	...	4.83	3.47	3.93	2.77
Long-term:						
Railroad bonds[a]..........	5.29	5.79	5.57	4.85	4.98	4.78
Railroad bonds — second						
grade[f]..................	6.03	6.83	6.51	5.57	5.91	5.56
Public utility bonds[a].......	5.84	6.73	6.56	5.46	5.41	5.22
Industrial bonds[a].........	5.40	6.01	5.96	5.21	5.26	5.21
Municipal bonds[a].........	4.46	4.98	5.09	4.23	4.25	4.20
Real estate bonds[a]........	...	...	...	6.91	6.58	6.50
Earnings on national bank						
investments[d]...........	...	...	...	...	...	...
U. S. Treasury bonds[g].....	4.62	5.32	5.09	4.30	4.36	4.06
Common stocks (dividend						
yield)[h]................	...	...	...	...	...	...

[a] Annual averages as published in the *Survey of Current Business*. The
compiled by the Standard Trade and Securities Service. The yield of real
icle and represents the yield to the investor from the purchase of new issues,
compiled by the Federal Reserve Board. For 1931 and preceding years the
Business, 1932 Annual Supplement, pp. 76–77, 98–99. Later data are from
  [b] Standard Trade and Securities Service yearly averages of rates quoted
  [c] Data collected by the Federal Reserve Board; published in its annual
  [d] Computed for this study from data published in *Annual Reports of the*
  [e] For 1921–33, offering yield of 3–6 month bills and certificates; for 1934,
of Current Business, 1932 Annual Supplement, pp. 98–99; for 1933 computed
Reserve Bulletin.
  [f] Dow-Jones averages as published in the *Survey of Current Business*;
  [g] Market yield of all issues outstanding except those of less than eight
Federal Reserve Board, 1935, p. 185.
  [h] Yield of 90 common stocks compiled by the Standard Trade and Secur-
Supplement; later data from current issues of the *Survey*. Figure shown for

RATES, 1919-35
for year)

1925	1926	1927	1928	1929	1930	1931	1932	1933	1934	1935
4.20	4.50	4.06	6.04	7.61	2.94	1.74	2.05	1.15	1.00	0.56
4.03	4.24	4.01	4.84	5.78	3.56	2.64	2.84	1.87	1.14	0.91
5.58	5.61	5.60	5.70	6.14	5.72	5.39	5.62	5.56	5.17	4.69
4.98	5.06	4.88	5.34	6.04	5.07	4.61	5.05	4.83	4.29	3.87
4.47	4.67	4.53	5.15	5.88	4.69	4.22	4.49	4.02	3.33	2.70
...	...	5.65	5.69	6.23	5.57	5.17	5.45	5.05	4.73	4.60
3.03	3.25	3.11	3.97	4.38	2.23	1.15	0.78	0.26	0.24	0.15
4.67	4.51	4.31	4.34	4.61	4.39	4.61	5.99	5.64	4.65	4.93
5.22	4.93	4.69	4.71	5.04	4.71	5.53	11.66	8.72	5.90	7.01
5.06	4.90	4.78	4.68	4.86	4.65	4.60	5.36	5.18	4.61	4.31
5.06	4.91	4.83	4.88	5.06	4.95	5.51	7.46	6.93	5.54	4.61
4.09	4.08	3.98	4.05	4.27	4.07	4.07	4.99	4.71	3.94	3.16
6.29	6.18	6.03	5.89	6.05	5.90	5.59	5.54	...	...	...
...	...	4.53	4.56	4.59	4.52	4.03	4.16	3.70	3.37	3.00
3.86	3.68	3.34	3.33	3.60	3.28	3.31	3.66	3.31	3.10	2.70
...	4.94	4.76	4.00	3.47	4.51	6.15	7.42	4.26	3.72	4.33

yields of railroad, public utility, industrial, and municipal bonds are those
estate bonds is from data compiled by the *Commercial and Financial Chron-*
based on coupon rates and offering prices. Call loan figures are from data
averages are those computed for and published in the *Survey of Current*
current issues of the *Survey.*
weekly in the *Commercial and Financial Chronicle.*
reports and in the *Federal Reserve Bulletin.*
Comptroller of the Currency.
6-month bills, and for 1935, 9-month bills. Data for 1921–31, from *Survey*
from monthly data in the *Survey*; for 1934 and 1935 from data in *Federal*

converted from price to yield basis.
years' maturity. Data from *Annual Report of the Board of Governors of the*

ities Service. Data for 1927–31 from *Survey of Current Business,* 1932 Annual
1935 is average of first four months, series having been discontinued in May.

most of those published elsewhere, are considerably lower both in good times and in bad than the average rates paid throughout the country for the use of money, and also much more variable. They are open market rates; that is, the rates for large blocks of money lent under conditions which afford the lender not only first-class security, but a high degree of liquidity. Such rates are fixed by the free play of supply and demand with a minimum of influence either of convention or of agreement among lenders, but they are not the rates which are most important from the standpoint of those who wish to borrow for productive purposes. The bond rates are not the rates at which borrowers could secure new capital from investment bankers or other lenders. They are the yields at market prices of old bonds which had a broad market, most of them listed on the New York Stock Exchange.

Call and time rates at the stock exchange represent new lending but lending of a highly specialized character. These loans are outlets for temporary surpluses of lending institutions and carry no obligation to renew, nor are the borrowers under any obligation to carry deposits with the lenders or submit their affairs to the scrutiny and advice of the lending banks. Like the bond yields, they depict the costs of and the income from financial operations which in the short-run are substantially dissociated from the creation and maintenance of employment in productive activity.

"Commercial paper" does represent the financing of industrial and commercial operations, but such loans constitute a negligible proportion of the total of current financing. At the maximum, only a few thousand firms ever had access to this method of financing and these only for a small fraction of their capital needs. Moreover, the market was declining in importance before the

SHORT-TERM MONEY RATES, 1927-35[a]

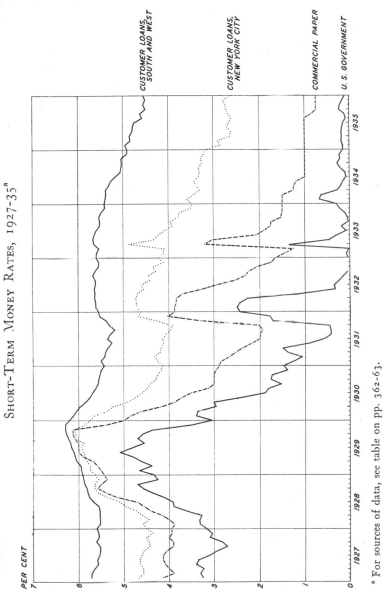

PER CENT

CUSTOMER LOANS,
SOUTH AND WEST

CUSTOMER LOANS,
NEW YORK CITY

COMMERCIAL PAPER

U. S. GOVERNMENT

[a] For sources of data, see table on pp. 362-63.

onset of the depression and has since suffered a further decline. The volume of such paper now outstanding is usually less than 20 million dollars.

The open market rates, in short, represent the return which can be obtained with a minimum of sacrifice of liquidity. The obligations which they represent are the next thing to being money. The very fact that they carry with them such a high degree of liquidity and such a low degree of risk unfits them for service as measures of the cost of money for investment in expansion of business. Any sort of productive activity requires investment, at least in working capital. Investment means that funds which are withdrawn from income or disgorged from hoards must be irrevocably committed by some one to the production of fixed or working capital goods. The individual investor may withdraw his money by selling his claim against industry to some other investor, but such transfers add nothing to the supply of real capital, the production of consumption goods, or the volume of employment. Marketability gives liquidity to the investment from the standpoint of the individual owner; it does not directly affect the supply of capital available to finance the productive process.

The "over-the-counter" rates are more satisfactory in that they represent the cost of advances of sufficiently permanent character, so that they can and do serve as the means of financing a wider range of industrial and commercial business. Apparently they represent primarily the cost of advances by large city banks to large borrowers. They conceal a wide divergence between borrowers and probably between banks, and fluctuate more than do the rates on the bulk of the smaller loans. Many banks in the East and Mid-West charged 6 per cent on small unsecured loans straight through the period of high rates in 1928-29 and the recent period of low rates. In the South and Southwest higher rates are common.

Moreover, there is a tremendous volume of borrowing both for business use and for other private purposes which involves much higher rates than those shown in the published series. Business finance companies, which buy accounts receivable and make chattel loans, do a large volume of business at rates around 15 and 18 per cent. Rates charged by household finance companies operating under the uniform small loan law are generally 2.5 per cent a month, rarely less than 2 per cent. Deferred payments on purchases of automobiles and household goods financed through finance companies have generally cost about 15 or 18 per cent, with much higher rates on many purchases of used cars. In 1935, however, money for purchases of new automobiles became available at about 12 per cent. Merchants who fail to take their cash discounts generally pay as much as 14 per cent per annum for the use of money. Moreover, a very high payment for the use of money is concealed in the prices paid for goods purchased on the instalment plan.

It is probable, however, that the published rates are more significant as an influence on the business situation than are the more stable rates paid by farmers, household consumers, and small business men. At least they tend to be the rates paid in connection with those types of business which are most subject to fluctuation in the course of the business cycle. Keeping these qualifications in mind we call attention to four things which are strikingly brought out by these exhibits.

First, in general the interest rates for all types of loans and investments where the risk is not considered to be serious, such as call loans, commercial paper, and government securities, have tended to lag behind changes in business activity and in prices. They were relatively high during the later stages of prosperity in 1919-20 and 1928-29. They remained high and in some cases rose further during the financial crises of 1921 and 1929 and during the earlier stages of the two depressions. They were relatively low during most of the depressed eras and remained so during the earlier stages of recovery.

Second, for types of loans and investments where risk rather than use of capital is the determining factor, rates do not show this lag, but have tended to be relatively low during prosperity and high during depression. This difference may be seen readily by comparing the yields of common stocks and low-grade bonds with those of the highest grade securities.[7]

Third, short-term rates have fluctuated much more violently than long-term rates. In periods of dear money, short-term funds have been dearer than long-term, and during periods of cheap money they have been cheaper than long-term. These three characteristics of the war and post-war eras are in harmony with what has been observed in pre-war business cycles.

Fourth, so far as concerns rates on types of lending that are considered safe, the tight money era of 1928-29 was much less severe than that of 1919-21. This is apparent from a comparison of rates on call money and commercial paper and on short-term government securities. On the other hand, on securities that carry a relatively high degree of risk, the yields went higher during the later depression than in the earlier one.

These facts suggest strongly that the significance of our data is not merely in the sequence of periods of rela-

---

[7] Compare chart on p. 369. Data are not available for similar comparison of safe and risky short-term loans. Here the difference shows itself primarily in the availability of funds rather than in rates paid.

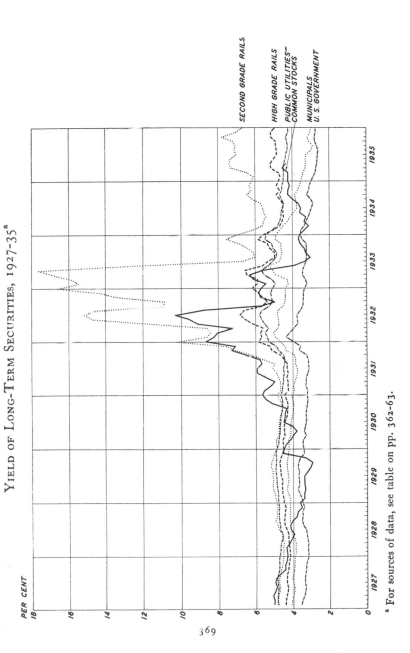

YIELD OF LONG-TERM SECURITIES, 1927-35[a]

PER CENT

SECOND GRADE RAILS

HIGH GRADE RAILS

PUBLIC UTILITIES—
COMMON STOCKS

MUNICIPALS
U. S. GOVERNMENT

[a] For sources of data, see table on pp. 362-63.

369

tively high and relatively low rates, but rather in changes in the rate structure. We shall analyze the data further, first in terms of the weight of the burden of interest on business enterprise; second, as evidence of deeper changes in the attitudes and perhaps the capacities of both borrowers and lenders—in other words, in terms of the availability of credit and the willingness to accept it; and third, in terms of the rate structure.

II. THE BURDEN OF INTEREST PAYMENTS

In the accompanying table we present estimates of the amount of interest paid by certain groups of corporations and individuals in 1929 and in later years.

INTEREST CHARGES ON CERTAIN TYPES OF DEBT, 1929-35
(In millions of dollars)

Borrower	1929	1930	1931	1932	1933	1934	1935
Aggregate:							
Railroads—long-term debt[a]	581	589	593	591	590	570	...
Railroads—short-term debt[a]	15	14	20	27	29	32	...
Public utilities—long-term debt[b]	491	511	533	549	555	551	543
Farm mortgages[c]	553	536	521	503	480	412	...
Non-farm real estate mortgages[b]	2035	2064	2020	1923	1759	1760	1777
Samples:[d]							
Public utility corporations (25)	226	234	247	239	249	252	241
Manufacturing corporations (17)	38	26	27	25	24	23	24
Trading corporations (16)	6	8	8	8	7	7	6

[a] Data from the *Statistics of Railways*, Statement 24. Does not include switching and terminal companies.

[b] From Leonard Kuvin, "Private Long-Term Debt in the United States," *National Industrial Conference Board Studies No. 230*, 1936, p. 42.

[c] Computed on the basis of debt figures as given above, p. 337, and interest rates as estimated in Kuvin (preceding reference), p. 50. The debt estimates used by Mr. Kuvin in computing interest totals (p. 42) are higher, for recent years, than those which we have used.

[d] Samples compiled for this study from annual reports. The samples include only corporations which reported some interest paid in 1935 and also reported sales and interest payments for the entire period covered, except that in the case of one or two corporations which did not report for some one year figures have been interpolated.

The total amount of interest paid is obviously less significant as a means of determining the interest burden than is the ratio of interest to total receipts or gross sales. In the table below, therefore, we present data for representative groups in the form of percentage ratios. Blanket figures for total interest reported by different groups of corporations and individuals for income tax purposes are not presented because the changes in the totals which took place between 1929 and later years were largely due, especially for individuals, to the shrinkage and expansion of the reporting groups incident to sharp changes in the national income.

INTEREST PAID BY CORPORATIONS AS PERCENTAGE OF TOTAL COMPILED RECEIPTS OR GROSS SALES, 1929-35

Borrower	1929	1930	1931	1932	1933	1934	1935
Aggregate:[a]							
Industrial corporations	1.9	2.2	2.8	3.5	3.1	...	...
All manufactures	1.0	1.1	1.4	1.7	1.3	...	...
Textiles	.9	1.0	.9	.9	.7	...	...
Chemicals	1.1	1.2	2.0	2.2	1.6	...	...
Metal manufacturing	.8	1.0	1.3	2.0	1.4	...	...
Transportation and public utilities	8.5	9.6	12.0	13.8	14.0	...	...
Trade	.64	.69	.69	.70	.61	...	...
Railroads[b]	8.4	10.0	12.8	17.2	17.3	16.0	15.3
Samples:[c]							
Public utility corporations (25)	8.0	8.4	10.0	11.0	12.1	11.6	10.6
Manufacturing corporations (17)	1.5	1.3	2.0	3.6	2.5	2.0	1.6
Trading corporations (16)	.46	.61	.70	.80	.71	.62	.51

[a] Except for railroads, data are from the *Statistics of Income*, and represent the ratio of interest paid to total compiled receipts.

[b] Ratio of interest paid to railway operating revenue plus non-operating income, for Class I roads and their non-operating subsidiaries. Computed from data in the *Statistics of Railways*; items for 1935 supplied by the Bureau of Statistics of the Interstate Commerce Commission in advance of publication.

[c] Ratio of interest paid to gross sales. See note *d* to preceding table.

The sample data shown in the two tables were compiled in order to ascertain the changes that took place in 1934 and 1935, years for which no aggregate data are available. The sample is very small, and is made up chiefly of corporations that are much larger than the average of those included in the aggregate data. Nevertheless, the agreement between the ratios shown for the sample and those in the aggregate data, for 1929-33, is close enough to justify use of the sample data as a basis for conclusions as to what happened in 1934 and 1935.

It will be noticed that the rise and fall of these ratios is not closely related to the fluctuation in interest rates shown in the table on pages 362-63. What it does reflect, except for the trading corporations, is the stability of interest charges in the face of shrinking and rising income. This is especially true of the railroads and public utilities, but it is true also in lesser degree of the manufacturing corporations.[8]

It will be noted that only in the case of the trading corporations was the level of 1935 as low as that of 1930. The better recent showing of this last group reflects the larger proportion of short-term bank credit which they use (the rates on this type of loans having fallen most) and also the fact that the revival has been more pronounced in the consumer goods than in the production goods industries. The business of the trading concerns consists chiefly of consumers goods, while the manufacturing corporations include both classes. The public utilities, of course, are dealing to a large extent directly with the consumer, but here the preponderance of bond interest and the relatively small proportion of borrowings that have been refunded keep the interest

[8] Compare Appendix G, Section VIII.

charge relatively high as compared with the trading corporations.[9]

The burden of interest presumably has some importance in determining the net profit of industry and consequently the willingness of industry to borrow in order to maintain or expand operations, but changes of the magnitude which we have indicated can hardly be of major importance in determining the pace of business activity. The bulk of interest payments of corporations and a very large part of those made by individuals are made under long-term contracts. Changes in the rates at which such contracts can be entered into may be of major significance in controlling long-term investments, but changes in the volume of current disbursements, such as occur in the course of a single cycle, are certainly not major elements of the trend of activity.[10]

III. THE AVAILABILITY OF FUNDS

It was noted above that fluctuations in interest rates, even those which are most unstable, do not measure adequately the changes in the conditions surrounding the supply of loanable funds. Interest rates are one visible index of the availability of capital, but do not measure the extent to which it changes. The fluctuation in the availability of capital is reflected also in the credit standards that are applied and in the quantity of capital that

[9] The rise in the proportion of interest to sales of trading corporations in our sample from 1929 to 1930 is somewhat puzzling. It was due almost entirely to an increase in interest paid, in spite of lower rates, as sales were about the same in the two years. Of 15 corporations reporting for both years, 11 showed increases in interest paid, 2 decreases, and 2 no change.

[10] Compare Carl Snyder, "Influence of the Interest Rate on the Business Cycle," *American Economic Review*, 1925, Vol. XV, pp. 684-99; Waldo F. Mitchell, "Interest Cost and the Business Cycle," the same, 1926, Vol. XVI, pp. 209-21; Carl Snyder, "Interest Rates and the Business Cycle," the same, 1926, Vol. XVI, pp. 451-52.

can be obtained for certain purposes irrespective of the interest rate offered.

High interest rates are due, of course, to scarcity of funds, and scarcity of funds means curtailment of new investment. Scarcity of funds, however, may be due to an absolute shortage (in terms of the demands of solvent borrowers) or it may be due to timidity of capitalists and a consequent unwillingness to part with funds except under conditions of maximum liquidity and safety. The two kinds of shortage must be sharply distinguished. A shortage of the former type can occur only in a period of great confidence when demand is running high, as it did in 1920 and 1921. A shortage of funds of the latter type occurs in a period of low confidence in the future, and coincides with low demand for loans, except from distressed borrowers.

The former type of shortage registers itself in high rates for nearly all kinds of loans. The latter type registers itself in what is ordinarily referred to as a period of low interest rates; that is, very low rates are paid for those uses of money which offer the minimum of risk, such as the open market loans ordinarily quoted, but very high yields for stocks and low-grade bonds. These are accompanied by an absolute drying up of new security issues, and by the application of stringent credit standards in the granting of short-term loans.

In other words, the conventional interest rate series omit the most important factor determining the availability of capital, namely, changes in lending standards which determine the ability of a given borrower to get money at the quoted rates, or at any rate. The bank rate may remain unchanged at 6 per cent and the finance company rate at 15 per cent, and still the effective rate may have risen greatly if credit standards have been tightened so that many borrowers who formerly enjoyed access to bank credit now have to resort to the finance company. Likewise the rates charged respectively for first mortgage and second mortgage loans may be unchanged with a substantial rise in the real cost of borrowing, if the amount which typically can be secured on the first mortgage has been reduced.

REAL ESTATE BOND FINANCING, 1927-32[a]

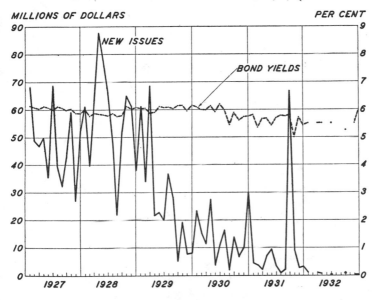

[a] New issues: volume of long-term corporate capital issues covering chiefly apartments and hotels, and office and commercial buildings. Bond yields: yield to maturity of new real estate bond issues. See note *a* to table on pp. 362-63.

An illustration of the possible disparity between rates and availability is furnished by the market for real estate bonds. As the accompanying chart shows, rates on new lending actually declined a trifle in 1932, but the volume of issues shrank almost to zero.

In 1919-21, as was noted above, interest rates were very high, both for long-term and for short-term obligations. These rates were the reflection of a genuine shortage of loanable funds. They did not result from any general distrust of the future and unwillingness of savers to lend or invest, nor from unwillingness on the part of industrial managers to accept capital—quite the contrary. Indeed, much larger sums could have been lent at high rates had not the reserves, both of commercial banks and of the Reserve Banks, been down to their legal minima so that further bank expansion was impossible.

With regard to long-term securities, it is not so easy to distinguish the two types of shortage. New issues, both of stocks and bonds (aside from government securities) almost disappeared after 1930[11] but statistics do not readily answer the question whether this was due to lack of buyers for new securities or to lack of willing borrowers of good credit, or to both factors. The best evidence on this question is furnished not by interest rates, but by comparison of the volume of issues for new capital purposes with the volume of refunding issues. In 1931, 1932, and most of 1933, both types of issues shrank to practically nothing. This shrinkage went on both in 1930-31 while rates were falling, and in 1932-33 while they were rising and high. But in 1934 and 1935, with steadily falling rates on high-grade long-term securities, refunding issues expanded rapidly, while new capital issues lagged.

We conclude that in 1931-33 the lack of new capital issues was due to a lack of confidence on both sides; there was no effective demand, and if there had been an effective demand there would still have been no effective supply of funds to take up new securities. If there had been a decent market for new long-term securities, refunding issues would not have stopped, even though no capital was sought for expansion and betterment. In 1934 confidence revived somewhat on the side

[11] See chart on p. 377.

of the suppliers of capital. Funds became available for new issues, but borrowing demand was practically limited to offerings of refunding issues; there was still no

NEW CORPORATE FINANCING, 1927-36[a]

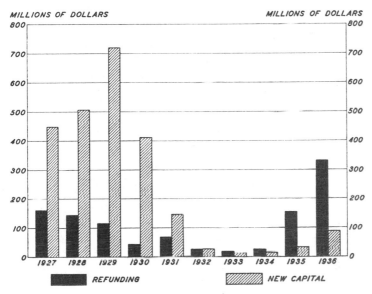

[a] Monthly averages for the calendar years indicated. Data collected by the *Commercial and Financial Chronicle*, as reprinted in *Standard Trade and Securities Service*. Items shown for 1936 are averages for the first eight months of the year.

willingness on the part of sound corporate borrowers to make large commitments.[12]

IV. LONG-TERM AND SHORT-TERM RATES

Whatever conclusion may be reached as to the importance of interest rates in determining the willingness of business men to borrow, it is safe to say that the long-

[12] Another reason for the slackness of borrowing demand was the fact that, for reasons discussed elsewhere, large corporations are usually well supplied with liquid funds. However, this consideration should have just as much tendency to hold down issues for refunding as those for new capital purposes.

term rates on new borrowing are more important than the short-term rates. Short-term borrowings can be made in view of an immediate and often a certain profitable use of money, and reduced or paid off whenever the business finds it has more money on hand than it can profitably use; whereas long-term borrowing commits the industry to a fixed charge against receipts that must be forecast in the face of uncertainty. Ordinarily individual business men are willing to pay more for short-term than for long-term accommodations. Lenders tend to require higher rates on short-term loans because of the greater expense of managing them, and because of the risk of having them paid off at inconvenient times. For concerns of good standing, however, the difference is not usually great. For stock market loans and the small volume of commercial lending that is made through the open market,[13] rates are usually lower than for any other type of loans, because these serve as secondary reserves for banks and "dumping" markets for their surplus funds.

One of the most striking facts about the money market situation in the United States just before and just after the oncoming of the depression was the extraordinary difference between long-term and short-term interest rates, first in one direction and then in the other. As the charts on pages 365 and 369 show, in 1922-27 the prevailing rates for both call money and commercial paper were always considerably below the quoted yields of high-grade corporation bonds, while over-the-counter rates were generally higher. But in 1928 short-term rates began to move up rapidly, while long-term rates remained comparatively stable at a level below that of 1922-26. Short-term open market rates were much

---

[13] Compare above, pp. 364-65.

above high-grade bond yields in the last half of 1928 and nearly all of 1929, and very much lower than the bond yields in 1930. There were three months in 1929 in which the call money rates averaged over 9 per cent; there were five months in which 90-day time loans on stock exchange collateral ranged up to 9 per cent; prime commercial paper was as high as 6 per cent in every month from March to November, and the best customers' loans ranged from 5.5 to 6 per cent throughout the year. Meantime, bond yields rose very moderately, most indexes failing to reach the levels of 1925, while common stock yields fell below those of United States bonds.

The high rate structure of short-term rates collapsed almost immediately after the stock market debacle. The average call rate was down to 4.31 per cent in January 1930, and to 2 per cent in October and November of that year, while commercial paper was down to 3 per cent by the middle of the year. Over-the-counter loans went below 5 per cent in March and ranged around 4 per cent for most of the year. Since 1930 there has been a pronounced downward trend, interrupted for a short time in 1931 and again in 1932-33 on account of banking difficulties. In 1934, and still more strikingly in 1935-36, open market rates were so low as to be almost nominal, and over-the-counter rates were also the lowest on record. Long-term rates remained comparatively steady in 1930 and ran up to extraordinarily high levels in 1931-33. Recently they have fallen, but they are still far above short-term rates.

Such a shift in the relative rates on short-term and long-term paper is a characteristic feature of alternations of prosperity and depression, though the spreads in this case have been unusually wide and have persisted unusually long. It is not remarkable that short-term rates go higher than long-term rates in times of dear money, and lower when money is cheap. For it is obvious that when money is scarce and rates on all forms of loans are high (in comparison with what is expected to prevail in the future) borrowers will prefer to finance as far as possible on a short-term basis and can afford to pay a premium to postpone long-time financing. Rates of 7 to 9 per cent, such as were frequently paid in 1929 for loans on the very best collateral, are not deemed ruinous if the borrower expects to be able to refinance at lower rates in a few months. Moreover, the very high rates which prevailed in 1928 and 1929 were in large part the result of the prevailing enthusiasm for stock market speculation. A speculative borrower operates for fairly short terms and can close out his position at any time. If he feels very sure the market is going his way, the interest rate makes very little difference.[14] But it would be financial suicide to contract to pay such rates for long periods to obtain capital for ordinary industrial and commercial operations.

Investment in new capital facilities can be postponed when more favorable money market conditions are anticipated, and will not be undertaken if it involves an excessive burden of fixed charges. Even such refunding operations as must be undertaken in a period of tight money frequently take the form of the issuance of notes of fairly short maturity, leaving the final refinancing for a more favorable period. The reported corporate bond issues, which had exceeded 450 million dollars in every year from 1924 to 1927, fell to 350 millions in 1928 and 258 millions in 1929.[15] The lender, on the other hand, when rates are above those which are ex-

[14] Compare R. N. Owens and Charles O. Hardy, *Interest Rates and Stock Speculation*, rev. ed., 1929, pp. 121-23.

[15] Another factor which certainly was extremely important in holding

pected to prevail in the future, prefers long-term non-callable obligations, and to get them will accept a comparatively small premium above what are regarded as normal rates; if he ties up his money for short periods and expects to have it come back on him when rates are lower, he must be compensated by a premium considerably above what he can get on long-term lending. From the standpoint either of lender or borrower, 10 per cent for one year and 4 per cent for the next 14 years is equivalent to 4.5 per cent for 15 years.

It would be a mistake, however, to assume that the very high rates charged for short-term money in 1928 and 1929 were due merely to the willingness and ability of speculators to pay high rates and the unwillingness of possible lenders themselves to forego prospective profits of speculation on their own account. The stock market rose in 1924-27 almost as rapidly as it did in 1928-29, yet money rates remained comparatively stable. Nor was the upward movement of interest rates due to gradual exhaustion of a reserve of bank lending capacity. The banks did not, in 1924-27, have a surplus

---

down the yield of bonds as compared with short-term interest rates during the period of high rates in 1928-29 was the availability of share capital. The average dividend yield of listed stocks (Standard Statistics Index of 90 stocks), which was just below 5 per cent in 1926 and 1927, dropped to 4 per cent in 1928 and 3.5 per cent in 1929. Businesses whose form of organization and financial standing were such that they could market stocks very generally took advantage of the speculative situation to provide for their future needs, and even to refund their existing debt through the issuance of new shares. While new bond issues were falling off, as was noted in the preceding paragraph, stock issues rose from less than 150 millions a year to 300 millions in 1928 and over 575 millions in 1929. This meant that institutions such as savings banks and life insurance companies, which could not buy stocks, had to compete for a limited volume of new bond issues. Some of their money was diverted indirectly to the purchase of stocks, through the medium of call and time loans "for account of others," but the bulk of it continued to go into bonds and mortgages. The volume of funds seeking investment from these sources is always very large and served to protect bond borrowers from the forces which were making for a run-away interest rate.

of unused lending capacity which had to be used up before the expansion of demand made itself effective. The new and decisive factor in the last year and a half of the boom was not in the speculative demand nor in the banking situation nor in the attitude of private and corporate lenders—it was the decision of the Federal Reserve system to restrict the available supply of credit. This decision was carried out through the sale of most of the government securities owned by the Reserve Banks and through successive increases of rediscount rates.[16]

In 1930 and the years which followed, the relationship between short-term and long-term rates was affected by conditions precisely the opposite of those which prevailed in 1928-29. After the stock market crash, and especially after the financial collapse which occurred in Europe in 1931, there was a loss of confidence in the future on the part both of investors and of potential borrowers, with the result that funds for long-time investment, and especially for investment involving any considerable degree of risk, became almost unobtainable, while at the same time the demand for such funds on the part of sound borrowers also disappeared. In the market for highly liquid and highly safe securities, especially short-term loans, the supply of funds expanded enormously in comparison with the demand, whereas in the long-time securities market both the supply and the demand for new capital almost disappeared, and open market short-term rates were low except for brief flurries. But long-term rates shot up to levels far higher than the peak of 1920-21.[17]

[16] For detailed discussion compare Charles O. Hardy, *Credit Policies of the Federal Reserve System*, Chaps. VII and VIII.

[17] Compare chart on p. 369.

The relative cheapness of short-term money as compared with long-term, which is a characteristic depression phenomenon, was accentuated by Federal Reserve action. Reversing its policy of 1928-29 when the conditions which gave rise to it were past, the system used its powers vigorously, though intermittently, to make liquid funds abundant and cheap. Holdings of government securities rose by 218 million dollars in the course of 1930, 89 millions in 1931, 1,038 millions in 1932, and 545 millions in 1933. Since the close of 1933 they have remained practically constant. Rediscount rates were lowered frequently during these years, and at the middle of 1931 ranged from 1.5 to 3 per cent. Increases were made at all banks in the fall of 1931 because of the outflow of gold after the British abandonment of the gold standard, and at the end of the year ten Reserve Banks were charging 3.5 per cent and the other two 4 per cent. Rates were lowered very slowly at most of the banks through the next four years, and at the end of 1935 stood at 2 per cent at ten banks and 1.5 at two banks. However, after 1931 the rediscount rates had very little significance because the member banks had large excess reserves, and therefore had no occasion to rediscount.[18]

V. RATES ON PUBLIC AND PRIVATE BORROWINGS

One striking effect of the depression has been the creation of a discrepancy between rates paid by the government and those paid by private industry and by individuals. This has been true not only of the United States but of other countries, wherever the credit of the

[18] Member bank borrowings, which were above one billion dollars all through 1928 and 1929, were below 200 millions on all call dates in 1933, below 100 millions through 1934, and less than 20 millions throughout 1935.

government was strong. In the United States, in spite of a greatly expanded volume of short-term borrowing, the rates paid by the government on short-term certificates have been almost at zero level for several years.

The preference of the money market for government over private securities is a phenomenon of exactly the same character as its preference for short-term over long-term loans. It reflects the prevalence of an enhanced degree of caution. The banks buy short-term government securities and expand their deposit accounts in the process. Then as the government expends the proceeds of the loans, capital which in more normal times would flow from the investment institutions directly into industrial expansion goes into expenditures for public works and relief.

VI. SUMMARY

The abundance of funds for investment in short-term liquid securities, and its scarcity for uses which involve loss of liquidity, point to a weakness in the financial structure of modern society; namely, the dissociation of the saving process from the productive utilization of funds. This difficulty is only accentuated, not created, by the depression. The unwillingness of many investors to part with their money except on the basis of a maximum assurance that they can get it back on demand, coupled with inability on the part of borrowers to make any productive use of purchasing power without immobilizing it, creates a perpetual problem. For, unless a connection is maintained between these savings and the growth of real capital, the saving process will exercise a perpetual downward pull on the money income of the community.

The dilemma has been partially solved for a private

enterprise economy through two devices: first, the marketability of stocks and bonds; and second, the institution of commercial banking. The marketability of stocks and bonds enables the individual in ordinary times to get his money out of an investment almost at will, though with some risk of capital loss, without exposing the borrower to the risk of having to pay off his borrowings on short notice. And the banks bridge the gap between potential lenders who demand liquidity and potential borrowers who must have funds on a quasi-permanent basis by assuming obligations to pay on demand, or short notice, and then accumulating claims against industry and government, which in fact if not in form are payable only gradually over a long period. The banks do this by accumulating both securities and working capital loans as an offset against their demand obligations.

When a wave of caution sweeps over a country, both devices fail. Security markets collapse because too many people try to liquidate long-term investments at once, and banks collapse because they are called to pay off demand obligations the proceeds of which have been invested in the fixed and working capital of industry and in the permanent obligations of governments. Orthodox banking theory regards the tying up of bank funds in slow loans and investments as unsound banking, and admittedly such practice involves them in an obligation to perform the impossible. Nevertheless it is essential to the performance of the banks' most important function—that of keeping the volume of money saving in line with the volume of investment.

In the current recovery the United States has assumed the financial responsibilities under which the banks and the stock markets broke down. It has borrowed funds short, and lent them long or invested them permanently or given them away, for the purpose of reversing the downward spiral of the flow of funds through incomes and the channels of trade. It has thus sought to bridge the gap between lenders' desire for liquidity and the community's need to expend saved funds in ways that are inconsistent with liquidity. The credit of the government has been utilized directly through the issuance of government securities, and indirectly through the quasi-guarantee of bank deposits and of the assets of building and loan associations and the salvage operations of such agencies as the Reconstruction Finance Corporation and the Home Owners' Loan Corporation. The effects of this on government finance have been discussed in Chapter XII, while the problems which it raises for the future will be discussed in Chapter XVIII.

During the past two years there has been a sizable volume of refunding of bond issues at lower rates. While such refunding does not bulk large in the debt totals, it does mean substantial savings to the firms concerned. However, the significance of this saving for the future productivity of industry must not be exaggerated. A decline of rates which is due to a rise in the levels of income and of saving is a sign of progress, and a condition of further progress. But a decline which is due merely to a lack of demand on the part of industry, with an unchanged or lowered volume of income and saving, means merely a redistribution of wealth as between stockholders and bondholders; it does not indicate either in the present or in the future any increase in the country's productive capacity or, probably, in the effective utilization of that capacity. Refunding at lower rates means that the corporations will have larger net incomes for reinvestment or for distribution as dividends; that the bondholders will have smaller incomes. There is no reason to suppose that the proportion saved out of bondholders' and stockholders' incomes is significantly different, and therefore no prospect that the future supply of funds available for expansion will be different because of this decline in bond rates. It is a temporary phenomenon due to the dearth of new offerings of securities for expansion of plant and equipment. Only to the extent that it may encourage future borrowing or sale of stocks on the basis of increased profit margin of these concerns is it significant of a present or prospective betterment of the economic structure as a whole. Moreover, it does not carry promise of substantial relief for concerns which suffer seriously under the burden of fixed charges, for in general the concerns which are able to refund at low rates in a period of low demand for investment funds are the ones that are already in a strong position.

From the studies which are summarized in this and the preceding chapter we conclude that the readjustments that have taken place in the volume of debt and the size of the interest burden are not of major importance in the process of recovery. The internal debt of the country was not a major factor undermining the prosperity of the twenties, though in many cases it caused serious difficulty after the decline of prices and of business activity got under way. The major element in the debt structure of corporate business consists of bonded debt, and neither the volume of such debt nor the interest charges which it involves have been reduced enough to change greatly the capacity of industry to function effectively. The reductions in the amount of short-term debt are larger, and the reduction of interest rates greater than in the case of long-term debt. But the reduction of indebtedness reflects chiefly liquidation incident to the contraction of business operations; the recovery process is re-creating this debt, and will continue to do so. This means simply that the savings of the inactive fraction of the community are being utilized more effectively. And the reduction in both long-term and short-term interest rates reflects the fact that the supply of funds offered in the markets has revived, under the combined influence of reviving confidence and of expanded governmental expenditure, more rapidly than have the borrowing demands of industry. There is no reason to anticipate an indefinite continuance of these rates as industry returns to a normal level of activity.

In the case of individual indebtedness the readjustments are probably more far-reaching than in the case of corporate business. The burden of interest on agriculture has been materially reduced, largely through the activity of government lending agencies; to a less extent through the processes of foreclosure and other types of forced sale, which have relieved the farmers of their debts by relieving them of the property by which the indebtedness was secured. As insurance companies and other lenders sell out the farms they have bought in, new debts will be incurred by the buyers; whether this debt will be unduly burdensome will depend on the correctness of the anticipations which determine the prices at which the land is sold. A similar situation exists in the home mortgage field, though here the relative importance of the operations of government as compared with debt reduction through foreclosures is probably greater than in the agricultural field. The future growth of home mortgage indebtedness and the interest burden associated with it depend largely on the policies which the government follows with regard to its permanent place in home financing.

More important from the standpoint of recovery is the availability of capital, and here the trend since 1933 is encouraging. The success of refunding issues, the fall in the yield of medium-grade bonds, and the rising level of stock prices indicate that there is no longer a dearth of funds for the financing of expansion. But the depression psychology still seems to control on the side of the borrower. The revival, so far as private industry is concerned, consists chiefly of a fuller use of existing plant and equipment; in other words, in the type of enterprise which involves the minimum sacrifice of liquidity. Certain industries have made a notable recovery, but they have been financing their needs out of their own accummulated balances rather than through the security market of the banks. The flow of new issues, aside from government securities, remains a trickle, and the government continues to fill the gap between the volume of private saving and the volume of private investing.

CHAPTER XV

TRENDS IN INTERNATIONAL TRADE AND FINANCIAL RELATIONS

We turn now from the domestic factors which have influenced the processes of depression and recovery in the United States to the country's international trade and financial relations. There are two principal ways in which these relations bear upon the economic life of the United States. First, foreign markets normally provide outlets for the surplus-producing branches of American agriculture, mining, and manufacturing industry; conversely, surplus production in foreign countries serves as a source of supply of those commodities which cannot be produced in the United States, or are produced in insufficient quantities, or can be produced only at a prohibitive cost to the consumer. Second, American citizens have large investments in other countries and foreigners have substantial investments here; the resulting flow of current receipts and payments constitutes an element in the formation and utilization of the national income.

The years which have elapsed since the depression began have produced many changes in the functioning of economic relations between the United States and the rest of the world, and the purpose of this chapter is to trace the salient features of the developments which have occurred. Accordingly, an analysis is first made of the magnitude, commodity composition, and geographic distribution of exports and imports of merchandise; the position of the United States in world trade; and the relation of exports to the country's production and of imports to its consumption. In the second division, a similar analysis is made of the country's international creditor-debtor position, private and inter-governmental, long term and short term. The data presented there relate to the capital value of investments and debts, as well as to the annual receipts and payments on all debts. Since, in addition to merchandise trade and the movements of funds resulting from new investments and from the transfer of interest and dividend payments, American citizens engage in a large variety of other international transactions which involve a flow of funds to and from the country, the total international movement of income and outgo is discussed in the third division.

No attempt is made to appraise the economic significance of the shifts which have taken place in all these phases of the country's international economic relations. Such interpretation as appears feasible at the present time will be deferred to a later chapter.[1]

I. FOREIGN TRADE DEVELOPMENTS

The foreign trade of the United States has, during the years that have elapsed since the depression began, followed in general the same lines of development as have characterized the international trade of the world as a whole. During the depression period there was a sharp decline in the value of both exports and imports and a less marked decrease in the physical volume of trade. During the recovery period, there has been a rise in both value and volume. As in other countries, foreign trade has continued to show a greater decline than domestic production. In addition to these general trends, in the case of the United States there have been a number of

[1] See Chapter XIX.

shifts in the structure of foreign trade. These relate to both the commodity composition of exports and imports and to their geographic distribution. While in some instances the shifts have been quite pronounced, it is impossible to judge to what extent they represent permanent trends since they have been conditioned by numerous and complex factors.

1. Total trade and balance. The chart on page 393 shows the value of the merchandise exports and imports of the United States yearly during the years 1926-35, with the average annual figures for the period 1921-25 added for purposes of comparison. The data relate to trade in all commodities with the exception of gold and silver. Figures for the movements of the precious metals will be given separately.

The value of exports increased steadily during the period under consideration until it reached its maximum of 5.2 billion dollars in 1929. It declined sharply during the next three years, reaching its lowest level of 1.6 billion dollars in 1932. There was a rise in the value of exports in 1934 and a less substantial improvement in 1935. Expressed as an index, with the figure for 1929 equalling 100, the value of exports declined to 30 in 1932 and recovered to 43 in 1935. The value of imports rose sharply in 1926 as compared with the average for the preceding five years, declined during the next two years, but regained the 1926 level of 4.4 billion dollars in 1929. Thereafter, it fell off rapidly, reaching its lowest point at 1.3 billion dollars in 1932. Its recovery was moderate in 1933 and 1934 and substantial in 1935. Expressed as an index, with 1929 as 100, the value of imports stood at 30 in 1932 and at 47 in 1935.

The relationship between the value of exports and of imports has varied from year to year, but the fluctuations since 1929 have been no more sharp than during the period immediately preceding that year. Since, however, the total value of trade declined severely and has regained only a small portion of the loss, the absolute amount of the trade balance has shrunk proportionately.

VALUE OF TOTAL UNITED STATES EXPORTS AND IMPORTS, 1921-35[a]
(In billions of dollars)

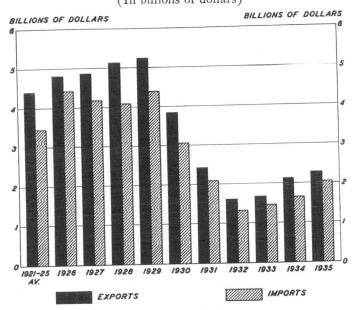

BILLIONS OF DOLLARS   BILLIONS OF DOLLARS

1921-25 AV. 1926 1927 1928 1929 1930 1931 1932 1933 1934 1935

EXPORTS   IMPORTS

[a] For data see Appendix H, Table 2.

Our foreign trade has continued to show an excess of exports over imports, but the export surplus decreased from 841 million dollars in 1929 to 236 millions in 1935.

In terms of physical volume, both exports and imports showed a steady increase prior to 1929, a continuing sharp decline thereafter, which reached its lowest point in

1932, and an increase since then. Expressed as indexes, with 1929 as 100, the volume of exports dropped to 52 in 1932 and stood at 59 in 1935, while the volume of imports fell off to 60 in 1932 and rose to 81 in 1935. It will be noted that the volume of imports did not decline as severely as did the volume of exports and recovered more rapidly from the low point. The year-to-year changes in the physical volume of exports and imports are indicated in the charts on pages 397-98.

2. *Commodity composition of exports and imports.* The chart on page 395 shows the exports and imports of the United States grouped by broad economic classes, in terms of percentages of the total value for each year. The figures are averaged for the years 1921-25 and are given annually thereafter. It will be seen that, so far as exports were concerned, there was a steady increase in the share represented by finished manufactures up to and including the year 1930; a decrease in the relative importance of this class of commodities during the following three years; and an increase since then. The exports of raw materials showed an exactly opposite movement. The share represented by semi-manufactures increased slightly, while that of foodstuffs, especially non-manufactured, declined almost continuously. On the import side, the share represented by raw materials declined during the period under consideration; shares represented by finished manufactures and semi-manufactures fluctuated somewhat but assumed no definite trends; while that of foodstuffs, especially manufactured, showed an almost continuous increase, which was especially marked from 1932 on. On the whole, finished products and raw materials have, throughout the period, clearly continued to hold a position of overwhelming importance in the export trade, while on the side of imports, trade has tended to be more evenly divided among

United States Exports and Imports, by Economic Classes, 1921-35[a]

(As percentages of the total value for each year)

I. EXPORTS

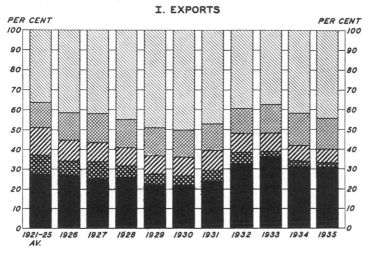

II. IMPORTS

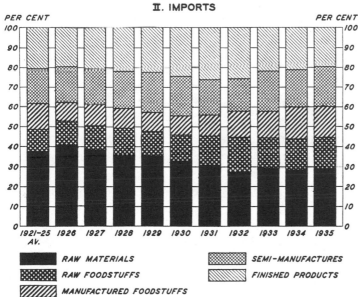

RAW MATERIALS   SEMI-MANUFACTURES

RAW FOODSTUFFS   FINISHED PRODUCTS

MANUFACTURED FOODSTUFFS

[a] For data see Appendix H, Table 3.

the five economic classes, with raw materials and food-stuffs as the largest single groups.

These shifts in the relative importance of the various classes of commodities reflect substantial year-to-year changes in both the physical volume of trade in each of the classes of goods and in the prices at which these goods were sold. The charts on pages 397-98 reveal these changes in quantity, unit value, and total value for the entire trade and for each of the five classes over the whole period here under review.

Turning first to the export side, we find that the quantity of raw materials shipped abroad was, in 1932, slightly greater than it had been in 1929, while the quantities in all other classes showed a large decline, which was especially pronounced in the case of finished goods. Over the next three years, the quantity of raw material exports showed a decline, while the volume of exports of foodstuffs fell substantially below the level of 1932. On the other hand, the exports of semi-manufactures and of finished products recovered in substantial measure. The price situation.showed a reverse tendency. By 1932 the unit value of the exports of raw materials and foodstuffs declined much more precipitately than the unit value of semi-manufactures and of finished products. By 1935 the former had recovered far more than the latter.

The price factor was thus primarily responsible for fluctuations in the relative importance of raw materials in the total export trade, while the quantity factor played a determining role as to the relative importance of semi-manufactures and finished products. In the case of foodstuffs, even a substantial rise in unit price following 1932 was not sufficient to overcome the severe decline in the volume of exports.

On the import side, the chart reveals for 1932 a marked decline in quantity for all five classes, the

INDEXES OF CHANGES IN QUANTITY, UNIT VALUE, AND
TOTAL VALUE OF UNITED STATES EXPORTS, BY
ECONOMIC CLASSES, 1926-35[a]

(1929 = 100)

I. QUANTITY

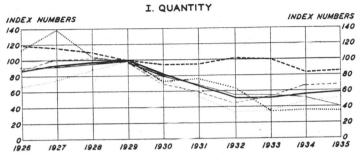

II. UNIT VALUE

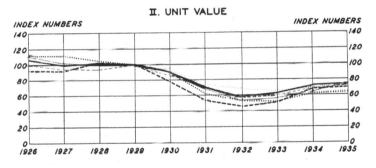

III. TOTAL VALUE

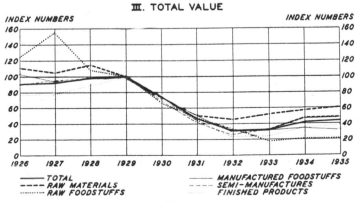

——— TOTAL   ——— MANUFACTURED FOODSTUFFS
– – – RAW MATERIALS   – – – SEMI-MANUFACTURES
········ RAW FOODSTUFFS   ········ FINISHED PRODUCTS

[a] For data see Appendix H, Table 5.

Indexes of Changes in Quantity, Unit Value, and Total Value of United States Imports, by Economic Classes, 1926-35[a]

(1929 = 100)

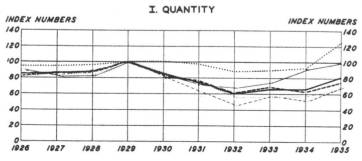

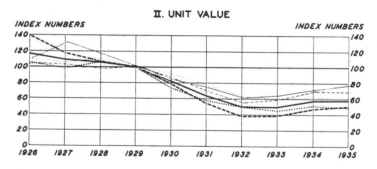

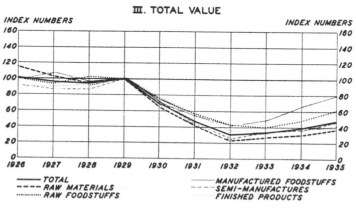

——— TOTAL
– – – RAW MATERIALS
············ RAW FOODSTUFFS

———MANUFACTURED FOODSTUFFS
– – –SEMI-MANUFACTURES
········· FINISHED PRODUCTS

[a] For data see Appendix H, Table 5.

shrinkage being especially pronounced in the case of semi-manufactures and finished products and least in the case of foodstuffs. Over the next three years there was an increase in the volume of imports of all five classes, the rise being especially noticeable in the case of foodstuffs. The price situation with regard to imports was substantially similar to that which was just noted in connection with exports, except that the rise in the prices of raw materials and foodstuffs was not nearly so striking.

Considered in terms of individual commodities, the export trade of the United States involves an immense variety of agricultural, mineral, and industrial products. The foreign sales of some of these commodities represent very large sums to the producers involved. The accom-

PRINCIPAL COMMODITIES IN UNITED STATES EXPORT
TRADE, 1926-35[a]
(In millions of dollars)

Commodity	1926–30 (Average)	1932	1933	1934	1935
Raw cotton	766	345	398	373	391
Machinery	490	132	133	218	265
Petroleum and products	524	208	200	228	249
Automobiles, including parts, etc...	406	76	91	190	227
Tobacco	145	66	83	125	134
Chemicals and related products....	135	70	77	93	103
Fruits and nuts	122	77	70	74	94
Iron and steel-mill products	171	29	46	89	88
Coal and coke	122	45	40	57	52
Copper, ores and manufactures	150	21	25	50	49
Packing-house products	194	57	66	67	43
Sawmill products	101	26	32	43	41
Cotton manufactures	124	46	39	43	39
Iron and steel advanced manufactures	78	20	20	28	31
Rubber and manufactures	67	16	18	22	22
Paper and manufactures	30	15	15	19	21
Leather	47	13	14	16	17
Furs and manufactures	31	13	15	21	17
Naval stores, gums and resins	30	12	15	14	16

[a] Values as reported in official statistics of exports and imports.

panying table indicates the principal commodities or
groups of related commodities exported from the United
States, ranked according to the value which they represented in 1935.

Agricultural products such as cotton, tobacco, fruits
and nuts, and packing-house products (mostly lard);
minerals and metals such as petroleum, copper, coal and
coke; semi-manufactures such as iron and steel-mill
products and saw-mill products; finished goods such as
machinery, automobiles, cotton goods, and rubber and
paper manufactures, have continued to be our principal
export commodities. A comparison of the figures given
on page 399 readily reveals the striking changes which
have occurred in the income derived from foreign sales
by the producers of the commodities concerned.

PRINCIPAL COMMODITIES IN UNITED STATES IMPORT
TRADE, 1926-35[a]

(In millions of dollars)

Commodity	1926–30 (Average)	1932	1933	1934	1935
Coffee	282	137	124	133	137
Cane sugar	207	97	108	118	133
Crude rubber	294	33	46	102	119
Raw silk	368	114	103	72	96
Paper and manufactures	151	94	77	87	93
Pulp and other paper-base stocks	114	54	65	71	82
Vegetable oils	82	29	35	35	79
Tin	89	16	51	45	70
Chemicals and related products	133	48	60	65	69
Fruits and nuts	85	44	37	46	55
Furs and manufactures	115	28	38	41	53
Hides and skins	118	22	46	35	46
Wines and spirits	b	b	15	49	41
Cotton manufactures	64	28	32	32	41
Petroleum and products	132	61	26	36	37
Oilseeds	66	16	27	23	34
Copper, ores and manufactures	108	24	25	28	33
Burlaps	72	17	24	28	33

[a] Values as reported in official statistics of exports and imports.
[b] Very small amounts.

The import trade of the United States also involves a very large variety of products. The principal commodities or groups of related commodities imported during recent years are indicated in the table on page 400, in which they are ranked according to the value they represented in 1935.

For both exports and imports, the fluctuations in total value were due to changes in both quantity and price. As was indicated in the discussion of trade by economic classes, variations in quantity have been more pronounced in the case of manufactured products and semi-manufactures, while variations in price have affected more the value of foodstuffs and crude materials.

3. Geographic distribution of trade. The chart on page 402 indicates the distribution of the export and import trade of the United States by continents. The figures represent for each year the percentage of the total value of exports taken, and the percentage of the total value of imports supplied, by each continent.

The diagrams reveal clearly the dominant position held by Europe as a market for our exports. During the decade 1926-35, Europe's share of our total exports varied between 44.5 and 50.7 per cent of the total. After 1929, it increased through 1933, fell off during the next year, and showed again an upward tendency in 1935. Next in importance as a market for United States exports are the countries of North America. Their share of the total, however, has shown a decline since 1929. Asia, the next most important continental market, has shown a marked increase in its share of American exports since 1929. The shares of South America and Oceania have declined, while Africa's share has shown a slight increase. The relative importance of the various continents as sources of American imports has shown a remarkable degree of stability during the decade.

DISTRIBUTION OF UNITED STATES EXPORTS AND IMPORTS BY CONTINENTS, 1921-35[a]

(As percentages of total value for each year)

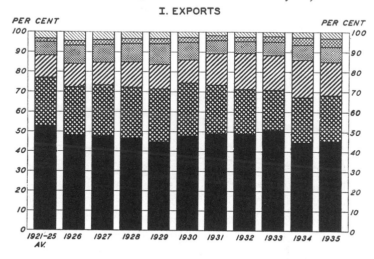

I. EXPORTS

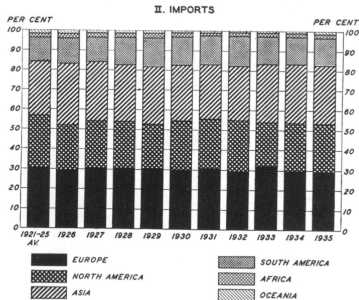

II. IMPORTS

EUROPE

NORTH AMERICA

ASIA

SOUTH AMERICA

AFRICA

OCEANIA

[a] For data see Appendix H, Table 4.

Of individual countries, the United Kingdom and Canada have consistently occupied first and second places as the largest single markets for American products. Of the next three largest markets, Germany changed from third place during the period 1926-30 to fifth place in 1935; France, from fifth to fourth place; while Japan advanced from the fourth to the third place. On the import side, Canada, Japan, the United Kingdom, British Malaya, Cuba, and Brazil have been the most important sources of American purchases abroad.

The value of exports and imports by continents and leading countries is given in Appendix H.[2] The figures not only show the relative importance of individual countries as markets for exports and sources of imports, but also reveal the multi-angular rather than directly bilateral character of the financial settlements involved in American foreign trade. As a rule, the United States has an excess of exports over imports in its trade with the industrial countries of Europe, and an excess of imports over exports in its trade with the raw material and food producing countries of Asia and South America. In this manner, funds representing export surpluses in trade with some countries have been available for payment of import surpluses in trade with other countries. Thus in 1935 American exports to Europe exceeded imports from that continent by 429 million dollars, while American imports from Asia exceeded exports to that continent by 227 million dollars, and imports from South America exceeded exports to that continent by 107 million dollars.

4. Position of United States in world trade. One of the most striking developments in the field of foreign trade has been a decline during recent years in the relative importance of the United States in the international

[2] See Table 6.

trade of the world. With the entire world trade measured in terms of gold, the share of the United States in total exports was 15.6 per cent in 1929; 12.2 per cent in 1932; and 11.0 per cent in 1933 and 1934. Similarly, the share of the United States in total imports changed as

SHARE OF UNITED STATES IN IMPORTS AND EXPORTS OF
SELECTED COUNTRIES, 1929 AND 1932-35[a]

Country	Imports from United States as Percentage of Total Imports of Country Indicated					Exports to United States as Percentage of Total Exports of Country Indicated				
	1929	1932	1933	1934	1935	1929	1932	1933	1934	1935
EUROPE:										
Belgium.....	9.5	8.7	8.1	7.3	7.8	6.8	4.8	5.1	4.4	6.1
France......	12.3	9.8	10.3	9.5	8.5	6.7	4.9	4.7	4.7	4.6
Germany....	13.3	12.7	11.5	8.4	5.8	7.4	5.0	5.0	3.8	4.0
Italy........	16.7	13.5	15.0	12.5	—	11.5	9.4	8.6	7.4	—
Switzerland..	9.0	6.7	5.8	5.4	5.5	10.0	7.2	7.0	5.8	6.1
United Kingdom......	16.1	11.9	11.2	11.2	11.6	6.2	4.2	5.2	4.4	5.4
NORTH AMERICA:										
Canada.....	68.8	58.3	54.2	57.2	56.8	45.1	33.9	32.8	34.1	36.5
Cuba.......	58.8	56.6	53.5	56.2	58.3	76.6	74.1	67.7	75.3	79.3
Mexico......	69.1	63.8	59.9	60.7	65.3	60.7	65.3	47.9	51.8	62.8
SOUTH AMERICA:										
Argentine....	26.4	13.5	12.7	14.8	14.4	9.8	3.4	7.7	5.1	11.6
Brazil.......	30.1	30.1	21.2	23.6	23.3	42.2	46.2	46.7	38.9	39.4
Chile........	32.2	23.1	22.4	28.8	27.1	36.8	28.1	17.6	19.0	23.0
ASIA:										
British India.	7.3	7.8	6.2	6.7	6.6	12.0	7.5	9.5	8.4	9.8
British Malaya....	3.7	1.9	1.6	1.8	1.9	42.2	22.5	33.5	33.2	36.7
China.......	18.0	25.4	21.9	26.2	18.9	13.6	12.2	18.5	17.6	23.7
Japan.......	29.5	35.6	32.4	33.7	32.7	42.5	31.6	26.8	18.4	21.4

[a] Data from *Foreign Trade of the United States*, 1934 and 1935.

follows: 12.2 per cent in 1929; 9.5 per cent in 1932; 8.9 per cent in 1933; and 8.2 per cent in 1934. This diminution in the relative importance of the United States in international trade is revealed even more strikingly by the accompanying table, which shows the percentages of total imports of a number of selected countries supplied by the United States during recent years and the percentages of total exports of the same countries taken by the United States.

The United States has continued, during the decade

under consideration, to occupy a position of great importance in international trade, usually ranking as the world's first or second largest exporter and importer. But its relative importance, both as a seller and as a buyer of merchandise, was in 1935 substantially smaller than it had been prior to the depression.

5. *Relation of exports to production.* Since the depression began the decline in exports has been consistently greater than the decrease in total production. There are several ways of indicating the relation of the export trade to the country's productive activity. The total value of exports may be compared with the estimated total value of product for the nation as a whole. On this basis exports constituted in 1929 about 6.4 per cent of total product. This percentage declined to 3.8 in 1933 and rose to about 4.3 in 1935. Again exports may be compared with the total value of movable goods. On this basis the percentage was 9.8 in 1929; 6.6 in 1933; and about 7.5 in 1935. These percentages are necessarily only rough estimates, but they indicate nevertheless a clear trend. The value of exports fell much more rapidly than the value of total production as the depression developed. Although, as the process of recovery has gone forward, the value of exports has risen somewhat more rapidly than the value of total production, it still shows a proportionately greater decline from the 1929 level. Expressed in the form of indexes, with the year 1929 as 100, the total value of movable goods stood in 1935 at approximately 58, while the total value of exports stood at 44.

A more significant method is to compare the exported quantity of each commodity with the total physical quantity of production of that commodity. The ratio of exports to production for a number of individual commodities is shown in the table on page 406. Where physical quantities are not reported, the comparison is made in terms of value. Unfortunately, production data for the year 1935 are not available in the case of all the commodities listed, and in such instances comparison is made on the basis of the latest available year. An examination of the figures reveals clearly the loss of production

UNITED STATES EXPORTS IN RELATION TO PRODUCTION, 1929 AND 1935[a]

Commodity	Unit of Measurement	Production		Exports		Exports as a Percentage of Production	
		1929	1935[b]	1929	1935[b]	1929	1935
Cotton	thousand bales	15,760	10,638	8,637	5,301	54.8	49.8
Leaf tobacco	million pounds	1,373	1,046	566	375	41.2	35.8
Phosphate rock	thousand dollars	13,153	*10,040	5,387	*5,009	41.0	*49.9
Lard	million pounds	1,763	662	866	115	49.1	17.4
Canned salmon	million pounds	236	*402	41	*49	12.2	*12.2
Canned sardines	million pounds	232	**98	124	**26	53.5	**26.1
Rice	million pounds	1,206	1,064	393	121	32.6	11.4
Wheat	million bushels	913	497	164	22	17.9	4.3
Barley	million bushels	330	118	60	4	18.3	3.5
Cottonseed oilcake	thousand tons	2,282	1,614	297	3	13.0	0.2
Linseed oilcake	thousand tons	752	**403	328	**203	43.6	**50.4
Fresh apples	million bushels	177	121	27	11	15.5	9.2
Fresh pears	million bushels	24	24	5	6	22.3	23.6
Dried fruits	million pounds	939	**999	432	**397	46.0	**39.7
Canned fruits	million dollars	137	**82	31	**17	22.8	**20.8
Patent leather	million square feet	81	**42	23	**27	28.2	**64.8
Gum rosin	thousand barrels	1,865	1,665	1,133	847	60.8	50.9
Gum turpentine	thousand gallons	28,000	25,000	14,175	9,691	50.6	38.8
Cornstarch and corn flour	million pounds	1,046	**985	235	**59	22.5	**6.0
Wooden doors	million'dollars	59	**12	4	**2	6.7	**16.4
Kerosene	million barrels	60	56	20	6	35.4	11.6
Lubricating oil	million barrels	34	28	11	8	31.4	30.1
Lubricating greases	million pounds	288	**204	117	**73	40.6	**35.9
Paraffin wax	million pounds	630	450	319	230	50.7	51.1
Carbons and electrodes	million dollars	17	**9	3	**2	18.1	**21.7
Crude sulphur	thousand tons	2,437	*1,614	855	*507	35.1	*31.4
Refined copper	thousand tons	1,370	*445	496	*296	36.2	*66.5
Radio apparatus	million dollars	412	**112	23	**16	5.6	**14.4
Mining machinery	million dollars	294	**89	54	**14	18.5	**15.2
Metal-working machinery	million dollars	228	**35	33	**8	14.7	**23.2
Sewing machines	million dollars	41	**12	12	**4	29.8	**35.0
Printing machinery	million dollars	69	**15	19	**6	27.6	**38.8
Office appliances	million dollars	178	**58	54	**16	30.2	**27.0
Agricultural implements	million dollars	561	**193	141	**57	25.1	**29.7
Automobiles	thousands	5,358	4,009	692	353	12.0	8.8
Aircraft, engines and parts	million dollars	70	**25	9	**9	13.0	**37.8
Borax	thousand tons	170	**242	80	*104	47.0	*42.8
Carbon black	million pounds	284	**313	92	*121	32.4	*38.6

[a] Data from *Summary of United States Trade with World, 1935*, pp. 28–30.
[b] Production data for 1935 are not available for all commodities. Figures marked with a single asterisk* refer to 1934 data: those marked with a double asterisk (**) refer to 1933 data.

suffered by a number of vitally important lines of economic activity as a result of curtailment of the volume of exports.

6. *Relation of imports to consumption.* Data on the relation of imports to consumption, comparable with those just presented in the case of the relation of exports to production, unfortunately are not available. An important feature of the relationship may, however, be indicated by calculating the ratio of imported raw materials to the total of such materials used in the United States. The value of raw materials used in American factories has been estimated at 15.1 billion dollars for the year 1929 and at 6.4 billions for the year 1933. Of these amounts, imports accounted for 3.1 billions in 1929 and 1.1 billions in 1933. In other words, imports supplied 21 per cent, in value, of the country's raw material requirement in 1929 and 17 per cent in 1933.

II. CHANGES IN CREDITOR-DEBTOR POSITION

The United States entered the period of the depression as the world's greatest lending nation and second largest international creditor. This pre-eminent position in world finance was achieved by the country in a remarkably brief period of time. At the outbreak of the World War, the United States was a net debtor, still owing some of the financially powerful countries of Europe comparatively enormous sums of money borrowed in the process of American economic expansion during the nineteenth century. As was noted in Chapter I, the war quickly converted the United States from a net debtor into a net creditor on an enormous scale.

The international financial position of the United States since 1929 has been characterized by the following important developments: (1) a decrease in the volume of American long-term investments abroad and increase in the volume of foreign investments in the United

States; (2) a much greater decrease of American short-term debts to foreigners than of American short-term claims against foreigners; and (3) almost universal suspension of payments on the war-debt account. In spite of these changes, the United States has retained a large net creditor position, and is still the world's second largest creditor nation. The substantial net creditor position of the country is clearly shown by the continuing, though reduced, excess of receipts over payments on current interest and dividend account.

1. Private long-term investments and debts. Data relating to international movements of capital and to the value of outstanding investments and debts must, of

MOVEMENT OF PRIVATE LONG-TERM INVESTMENT FUNDS
OUT OF AND INTO THE UNITED STATES, 1926-35[a]

(In millions of dollars)

Year	Total Outflow	Total Inflow	Net Movement[b]
1926	1,928	1,326	−602
1927	2,332	1,609	−723
1928	3,253	2,591	−662
1929	2,465	2,328	−137
1930	2,428	2,161	−267
1931	1,301	1,520	+219
1932	645	862	+217
1933	1,456	1,505	+ 49
1934	958	1,160	+202
1935	1,547	2,009	+462

[a] Data from U. S. Department of Commerce, *The Balance of International Payments of the United States,* 1935, pp. 82-83.
[b] Plus sign indicates net inflow; minus sign net outflow.

necessity, be estimated since no machinery exists either in the United States or anywhere else in the world for a precise evaluation of the amounts involved. The table on this page presents the best available estimates of the annual movements of long-term investment funds out of and into the United States during the period 1926-35. The figures are subject to varying margins of error, which will be discussed on pages 421 and 424.

It should be borne in mind that an outflow of funds from the United States may represent either new investment by American citizens or repurchase from foreigners of American securities or properties. Similarly, an inflow of funds into the United States may represent either new investment by foreigners or repurchase by them of existing obligations. Hence, a net outflow of funds may mean either an increase in the total American investments abroad or a decrease in the total foreign investments in the United States. Conversely, a net inflow of funds may mean either a decrease in the total American investments abroad or an increase in the total foreign investments in the United States.

The net movement of funds, therefore, represents changes in the *net* creditor-debtor position and should not be confused with the year-to-year changes in the total American investment abroad or foreign investment here. Moreover, such investments consist in part of bonds, which are usually taken at their par value in a computation of the total, and in part of equities or direct investments, the estimate of which is usually based upon a combination of book and market values. Changes in these latter factors tend to affect the capital value of total investment independently of the flow of investment funds.

The best available estimates of the capital value of American long-term investments abroad, as of the end of each year during the decade 1926-35, are given in the table on page 410. "Direct investments" represent equities, and "portfolio" consists of bonds.

The table on page 410 shows a continuous increase in the total of long-term investments abroad through the year 1930 and a persistent decline since that year, although the figure at the end of the period was still substantially higher than it had been at the beginning. The decrease in the total was the result primarily of a decline in the foreign bond holdings of American investors. This change reflects a substantial excess of repurchases

ESTIMATES OF UNITED STATES LONG-TERM INVESTMENTS
ABROAD, 1926-35
(In millions of dollars)

Year-End	Direct Investments	Portfolio	Total
1926............	6,451	5,279	11,730
1927............	6,806	5,887	12,695
1928............	7,233	6,806	14,039
1929............	7,694	7,070	14,764
1930............	7,966	7,273	15,239
1931............	8,096	6,604	14,700
1932............	8,122	6,035	14,157
1933............	7,767	6,032	13,799
1934............	7,818	5,293	13,111
1935............	7,835	4,795	12,630

by foreigners of bonds held in the United States over purchases by American investors of new foreign securities. Such repurchases were especially heavy during the last three years of the period under review, because of the sharp declines in the prices at which many foreign securities were offered for sale by American investors. The volume of repurchases has been estimated, on a par basis, at 815 million dollars in 1933; at 1.1 billion dollars in 1934; and at a similar amount in 1935.

Systematic estimates, similar to those just given for the year-end totals of American long-term investments abroad, unfortunately do not exist for the total of foreign long-term investments in the United States. A recent, extremely thorough study carried out by the Finance Division of the Bureau of Foreign and Domestic Commerce of the United States Department of Commerce indicates that at the end of 1935 foreign long-term investments in the United States aggregated 5,025 million dollars. This figure probably represents an increase over 1929 of something like 500 million dollars.

2. *Changes in short-term debts and claims.* During the years following 1929, violent fluctuations occurred in the volume of American short-term debt to foreigners. This type of indebtedness declined from over 3 billion dollars in 1929 to less than 500 millions in 1933, and then rose to 1,220 million dollars in 1935. Fluctua-

SHORT-TERM DEBTS AND CLAIMS OF THE UNITED STATES
1929-35*
(In millions of dollars)

Year	Due to Foreigners	Due from Foreigners	Balance
1929	3,077	1,566	−1,511
1930	2,737	1,802	−935
1931	1,465	1,239	−226
1932	870	1,053	+183
1933	487	1,082	+595
1934	614	1,217	+603
1935	1,220	853	−367

* Data from *The Balance of International Payments of the United States*, 1931, p. 62; the same, 1935, p. 50.

tions in the volume of American short-term claims against foreigners were also substantial, but much less pronounced; their amount increased in 1930 over 1929, declined during the following year, rose steadily during the next three years, and fell off sharply in 1935. As a result of these fluctuations, there were marked changes in the creditor-debtor position of the country on short-term account. In 1929 the United States was a large net debtor. By 1932 this country was a small net creditor and during the next two years increased its net creditor position. In 1935 it changed again into a short-term net debtor.

The accompanying table indicates year-to-year changes in the international short-term debts and claims of the United States during the period 1929-35.

The fluctuations were the result of both foreign and domestic developments. The sharp shifts which occurred in 1931-32 were largely a part of the general international financial panic described in Chapter II. The changes in the next two years were connected with the unsettled monetary conditions in the United States. The pronounced alteration of the short-term creditor-debtor position in 1935 was due in part to a persistent flight of capital from Europe and in part to a steady repatriation of American funds.

3. Net creditor position on private account. Bringing together the data relating to the American private investments abroad and the foreign investments in the United States on both long-term and short-term accounts, we can now indicate roughly the changes which have occurred since 1929 in the net creditor position of the United States on private account. Because of the absence of complete estimates of foreign long-term investment in the United States during the whole period, it is not possible to present a year-to-year picture. In the following table the estimated international assets and liabilities are given only for the years 1929 and 1935.

ESTIMATES OF PRIVATE INTERNATIONAL ASSETS AND LIABILITIES OF THE UNITED STATES, 1929 AND 1935
(In billions of dollars)

Item	1929	1935
ASSETS..........................	**16.4**	**13.5**
Long-term investments...........	14.8	12.6
Short-term claims...............	1.6	0.9
LIABILITIES......................	**7.6**	**6.2**
Long-term debts................	4.5	5.0
Short-term debts................	3.1	1.2
NET CREDITOR POSITION............	**8.8**	**7.3**

In spite of the fact that American long-term investments abroad decreased by 2.2 billion dollars and that American short-term claims against foreigners declined by 0.7 billions, the net creditor position of the country was in 1935 only 1.5 billion dollars less than it was in 1929. The increase in the foreign long-term investments in the United States was more than offset by the reduction in American short-term debts to foreigners. In 1935, as in 1929, the international assets of the United States on private account were more than double the country's liabilities to foreigners.[3]

4. The war debts. The obligations of all but three debtor governments were funded during the first postwar decade, and scheduled payments with respect to them were met in full up to the inauguration of the Hoover moratorium in June 1931. Upon the expiration of the one-year moratorium, several abortive attempts were made in 1932 and 1933 to negotiate new settlements. In the meantime, Finland alone of the eighteen war debtors resumed payments in full and has continued to meet the required instalments. Great Britain and several of the smaller debtors met in full the instalment which fell due in December 1932 and made small token payments in June and in December 1933, when even these payments were suspended. The other debtor governments have failed to resume payments, except that Greece began in 1936 to make partial payments on a portion of her debt.

The war indebtedness of the various governments concerned, as it stood on the books of the United States Treasury at the beginning of 1936, is indicated in the table on page 414. Since the obligations were incurred,

[3] See also discussion on p. 424.

the United States government has received payments with respect to them aggregating 2,748 million dollars.

WAR DEBTS OWED TO THE UNITED STATES AS OF THE
BEGINNING OF 1936[a]

(In millions of dollars)

Country	Principal Unpaid	Interest Postponed and Payable under Moratorium Agreements	Interest Accrued and Unpaid under Funding and Moratorium Agreements	Total Indebtedness
FUNDED DEBTS	11,229.1	184.2	646.2	12,059.4
Austria	23.8	—	0.1	23.9
Belgium	400.7	3.8	19.0	423.5
Czechoslovakia	165.2	—	0.2	165.4
Estonia	16.5	0.5	2.0	19.0
Finland	8.3	0.2	—	8.5
France	3,863.7	38.6	138.9	4,041.2
Great Britain	4,368.0	131.5	451.1	4,950.6
Greece	31.5	0.4	1.3	33.2
Hungary	1.9	[b]	0.2	2.2
Italy	2,004.9	2.5	6.7	2,014.1
Latvia	6.9	0.2	0.7	7.8
Lithuania	6.2	0.2	0.6	7.0
Poland	206.1	6.2	25.2	237.5
Rumania	63.9	—	0.1	64.0
Yugoslavia[c]	61.6	—	—	61.6
UNFUNDED DEBTS	204.9	—	173.6	378.5
Armenia	12.0	—	9.5	21.5
Nicaragua	0.3	—	0.2	0.5
Russia	192.6	—	163.9	356.5
GRAND TOTAL	11,433.9	184.2	819.7	12,437.8

[a] Official figures of the U. S. Treasury.
[b] Less than $100,000.
[c] This government refused to accept the provisions of the moratorium.

Of this amount 757 million dollars was credited as repayment of principal and the remaining 1,991 millions as interest. British payments accounted for 2,025 million dollars; French payments for 486 millions; and Italian payments for 101 millions.

5. *Annual international debt receipts and payments.*

Changes in the volume of American private investments abroad and of foreign investments in the United States and the reduction and finally virtual disappearance of war-debt payments naturally found reflection in the

ANNUAL RECEIPTS AND PAYMENTS OF UNITED STATES ON
ALL INTERNATIONAL DEBT ACCOUNTS, 1926-35[a]

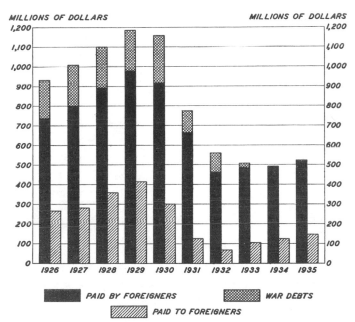

[a] For data see Appendix H, Table 7.

amounts annually received and paid by the United States in the form of interest and dividends. Such receipts and payments were also affected by general business conditions in so far as the latter determine the earnings of direct investments. In recent years outright defaults, transfer moratoria, and other measures resulting in diminution or cessation of debt payments which have been made operative in a number of foreign countries also served to curtail our international debt receipts. As a result of all these influences, annual receipts by the United States on the various debt accounts declined steadily between 1929 and 1934, but have since that year shown a slight upward tendency. Payments to foreigners also declined sharply between 1929 and 1932, but have increased since that year. These movements are graphically represented in the chart on page 415.

From the high point of 1,186 million dollars in 1929, our total international debt receipts declined to their low point of 494 millions in 1934, and rose slightly in 1935. Our total payments to foreigners were at their lowest in 1932, when they totalled only 68 million dollars, as compared with 414 millions in 1929. They rose then to 146 millions in 1935. The excess of receipts over payments decreased from 857 million dollars in 1930, when it was at its highest level, to 375 millions in 1935. While these data are estimated throughout they are sufficiently reliable to indicate the persistence of the net creditor position of the United States and the substantial magnitude of the continuing excess of receipts over payments.

III. CHANGES IN INTERNATIONAL BALANCE OF PAYMENTS

In the first two divisions of this chapter, we noted the changes which occurred during the decade 1926-35 with respect to the three most important factors involved in the transactions in which American citizens engage in their economic intercourse with the rest of the world. We set forth the value of the American export and import trade; the magnitude of the sums collected annually by American investors abroad (including the Treasury receipts on the war-debt account) and of the sums paid annually to foreign investors in the United States; and the amounts involved each year in the outward and inward movements of investment funds. In addition to these transactions, there are many others in which American citizens are engaged internationally.

Shipping and freight charges are collected and paid; expenditures of American tourists abroad and of foreign tourists in the United States require transfers of funds out of and into the country; immigrant and charitable remittances to and from the country, as well as expenses and remittances by the American government abroad and by foreign governments in the United States, require similar financial transactions. Finally, payments and receipts flow back and forth in connection with a large miscellany of other less extensive service transactions. The amounts involved in all these operations also fluctuated from year to year during the decade under consideration.

1. The balance of payments. Bringing together for a particular year all of the payments made by Americans to foreigners and all of the payments made by foreigners to Americans, we obtain a picture of the country's international balance of payments during that year. The table on page 419 presents a summary of the international balance of payments of the United States for each year from 1926 to 1935. The various types of trade, service, and financial transactions are grouped in a manner convenient to the purposes of this discussion.

The figures are in terms of net balances for each of the major groups of transactions. It should be borne in mind that such offsetting against each other of the amounts involved in export and import trade, or in tourist traffic from and to the country, or in outward and inward movements of debt payments, or in the similar movements of capital funds constitutes merely a statistical device. In reality, the dollars obtained by foreigners from the sale of goods or the rendering of services to Americans may or may not be used in direct payment of similar purchases made or similar services received from Americans. Through the operation of the foreign exchange process, the monetary proceeds of all transactions become, to all intents and purposes, a single pool.[4] Nevertheless, the statistical evaluation of net balances for major groups of transactions is extremely useful for the purpose of disclosing the general character of the country's economic relations with the rest of the world.

In the table on page 419, item 1 indicates the excess of exports over imports in the merchandise trade—that is, the amounts by which each year the number of dollars obtained by foreigners from sales of merchandise to Americans fell short of the amounts they needed in order to pay for their purchases of American goods. Item 2 shows the net balance on such service transactions as shipping, tourist traffic, all kinds of international remittances, and so forth.[5] The minus sign indicates that

[4] Foreigners receiving dollar bills of exchange in payment for the goods they sell and the services they render to Americans or as the proceeds of loans contracted by them in the United States dispose of these bills in the foreign exchange markets and thus obtain the equivalent in their own currencies or the means of meeting their own obligations in other countries. The dollar bills are bought in the foreign exchange markets by persons who desire to use them in paying for goods or services purchased from Americans or who wish to make investments in the United States. A dollar bill of exchange may thus pass through several hands and even through several countries, and its precise origin when employed in the settlement of any particular transaction with the United States is, in practice, entirely immaterial. Exactly the same process takes place with respect to bills of exchange expressed in foreign currencies when purchases from Americans are paid for with such bills.

[5] In addition to shipping and freight services, tourist expenditures, and immigrant, charity, and government remittances, this group of transactions included the following: for the years 1926-32, silver movements; unrecorded parcel post; motion picture royalties; bunker-fuel sales; sale of vessels; ship chandlering, etc.; estimate of smuggling, of goods brought

Summary of United States International Balance of Payments, 1926-35[a]

(In millions of dollars)

I. Non-Capital Accounts

Item	1926	1927	1928	1929	1930	1931	1932	1933	1934	1935
1. Merchandise trade as recorded (exclusive of gold and silver)	+378[b]	+681	+1,037	+841	+782	+334	+289	+225	+478	+236
2. Service transactions (exclusive of debt receipts and payments)	−884[b]	−899	−1,053	−1,166	−1,010	−823	−650	−414	−385	−403
3. Total of items 1 and 2	−506	−218	−16	−325	−228	−489	−361	−189	+93	−167
4. Interest and dividend receipts and payments (including war-debt receipts)	+662	+725	+741	+772	+857	+649	+492	+404	+368	+375
5. Net balance on all merchandise and service accounts (exclusive of item 6)	+156	+507	+725	+447	+629	+160	+131	+215	+461	+208
6. Gold, silver, and currency movements[c]	−112	+99	+232	−135	−258	+166	−91	+83	−1,329	−2,076
7. Net balance on all non-capital accounts	+44	+606	+957	+312	+371	+326	+40	+298	−868	−1,868

II. Capital Account

Item	1926	1927	1928	1929	1930	1931	1932	1933	1934	1935
8. Long-term capital movements	−602	−723	−662	−137	−267	+219	+217	+49	+202	+462
9. Short-term capital movements	+350	+900	−188	−80	−485	−709	+409	−385	+184	+1,075
10. Net balance on capital account	−252	+177	−850	−217	−752	−490	−192	−336	+386	+1,537

III. Residual Item

Item	1926	1927	1928	1929	1930	1931	1932	1933	1934	1935
11. Errors and omissions	+208	−783	−107	−95	+381	+164	+152	+38	+482	+331

[a] For detailed data see Appendix H, Table 7. Plus sign indicates net income; minus sign net outgo. [c] Silver included only in 1934 and 1935

419

the number of dollars made available by Americans to foreigners in connection with the rendering of all these services consistently exceeded the amounts required by foreigners for payment to Americans in connection with similar transactions. Combining the two balances, we find in item 3 that during each year of the decade except 1934 total payments to foreigners on all merchandise and service accounts (with the exception of the movements of gold, currency, interest and dividend payments throughout the period, and of silver in 1934-35) exceeded total receipts from foreigners with respect to similar transactions by amounts which varied from 16 to 506 million dollars.

But as was noted earlier in this discussion the United States is a net creditor on the investment account. Throughout the decade the country's net international debt receipts were sufficiently large, by the amounts shown in item 5, to offset the net payment requirements indicated in item 3. In item 6 are shown the net balances of gold, silver,[6] and currency movements (mostly gold) which shifted several times during the decade from a net inflow to a net outflow, and vice versa.

Item 7 shows the final result of all the offsettings of transaction against transaction and of net balances of groups of transactions against each other. It reveals, for the first eight years of the period, the net amounts by which foreign payments to the United States relating to trade, services, and the movements of the precious metals exceeded similar payments by Americans to foreigners.

---

in under exemption for travelers, and other commodity adjustments; insurance; import of Canadian power; newspapers and advertising; patents and copyrights; cablegrams, etc.; for the year 1933, the same as above with the addition of stock-transfer taxes, brokerage fees, etc.; for the years 1934-35, the same items as for 1933, with the exception of silver movements.

[6] For the years 1934-35 only.

For the last two years of the period, item 7 shows a reverse picture. It discloses the amounts by which the country's receipts from abroad on all these accounts fell short of its similar payment requirements to foreigners. The net excess of receipts over payments or of payments over receipts on all current trade and service accounts including gold is necessarily represented by lending or borrowing, since such operations are the only other means by which international payments can be made. It is clear, therefore, that during the years 1926-33 the United States was, on balance, making new loans to the world, while during the years 1934-35 the country was, on balance, borrowing from the world or rather reducing its net international creditor position.[7] Items 8, 9, and the summation in item 10 in the table represent an attempt to indicate the type of lending and borrowing which took place during the period.

If the financial results of all the transactions included in the balance of payments could be determined with exact precision, the figures for each year in items 7 and 10 would have been identical. Since, however, some of the data are merely estimated, there is bound to be a margin of error. Item 11 indicates the amounts by which, in each year, the official estimate of the net balance on all trade and service accounts failed to coincide with the similar estimate of the net balance on the capital account. While for some years the amounts of "errors and omissions" are substantial, the data as presented in the table on page 419 are believed to be sufficiently reliable to indicate the general character of the financial results of the country's economic relations with the world during the years 1926-35.

2. *Gold and capital movements.* The most striking

---

[7] See discussion on pp. 412-13.

features of the developments which occurred during the decade under consideration, as revealed by the table on page 419, were the change during the last two years of the period from net receipts to net payments on current non-capital accounts and the corresponding change from net outflow to net inflow on the capital account. Directly connected with these changes were the movements of the precious metals, especially gold.

Prior to 1934 net annual exports or imports of gold were moderate in size and played a relatively unimportant role in the determination of the net balance on all trade and service accounts. It is true that in some years, notably 1931 and 1932, there were heavy exports of the metal during some months and heavy imports during other months, but these movements tended to offset each other in substantial measure. The exports and imports of silver during these years were almost negligible. During the years 1934 and 1935 there was an enormous inflow of gold and a growing inflow of silver, accompanied by very small outward movements of the two metals. During these years, the net excess of gold and silver imports over exports played a dominant role in the determination of the net balance on all trade and service accounts and was solely responsible for converting that balance from an excess of receipts to an excess of payments. The annual exports and imports of gold and silver are shown graphically in the chart on page 423.

The increase in the importation of silver and to some extent in the importation of gold was caused directly by the changes which occurred in the monetary policy of the United States, which will be discussed in the chapter which follows. Such imports represented deliberate purchases of the precious metals by the United States Treasury. The greater portion of the gold imports, especially

UNITED STATES EXPORTS AND IMPORTS OF GOLD AND SILVER, 1926-35[a]
(In millions of dollars)

I. GOLD

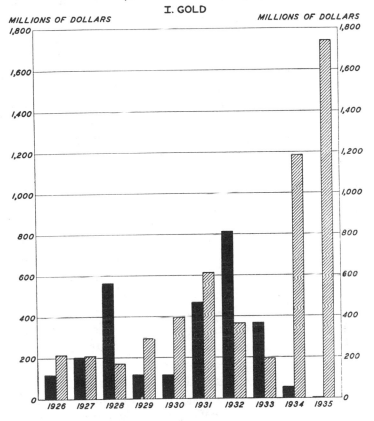

II. SILVER

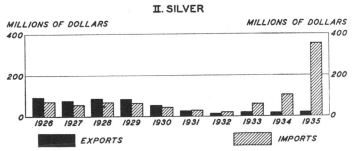

■ EXPORTS   ▨ IMPORTS

[a] For data see Appendix H, Table 1.

in 1935, was only indirectly connected with monetary policy and was brought about by other factors.

The years 1934-35 were characterized by a large net inflow of capital funds from abroad, especially of the short-term type. This influx represented, in part, the repatriation of American owned funds which had left the country when the monetary uncertainty of 1933 and the early part of 1934 induced a substantial flight of capital. The repatriation was the result of a growing clarification of monetary policy in the United States as well as of a deterioration of political and economic conditions abroad. These same circumstances were largely responsible for a steady inflowing stream of foreign owned funds seeking in the United States either greater safety or more favorable investment than could be obtained at home. The repurchase at bargain prices of American held foreign securities also contributed to the influx of foreign capital to the United States. This steady flow of funds from abroad represented a continuous demand for dollars which, under existing circumstances, could be satisfied only by gold shipments to the United States.

The withdrawal of American capital from abroad and the increase of foreign investment in the United States produced as their consequence a decrease in the net creditor position of the country. On the assumption that the whole amount of "errors and omissions" should be applied to the capital account, there occurred in 1934-35 a reduction in the net creditor position of the United States amounting to 2,736 million dollars. Since, however, the "errors and omissions" item should in all probability be distributed between the trade and service and the capital accounts, the change attributable solely to the movement of investment funds was probably somewhat smaller.[8]

[8] The reader will recall from the discussion on pp. 412-13 that the

The reduction in the net creditor position had as its direct counterpart an increase in the gold stocks of the United States, resulting from importation, of 2,956 million dollars and a similar increase in silver stocks of 422 million dollars. Two things happened in the process: first, some American investments abroad were liquidated and the proceeds came to the United States in the form of gold and silver imports; second, precious metals were shipped to the United States and exchanged by foreigners either for new deposits in American banks, American securities, or foreign securities owned by Americans.

---

capital value of total investment is also affected by changes in the book and market value of direct investments. In connection with that discussion, we estimated the reduction of the net creditor position between 1929 and 1935 at 1.5 billion dollars. Since during the years 1929-33 the United States was, on balance, an exporter of capital, the reduction in the net creditor position during the period 1929-35, as derived from the balance of payments figures given on p. 413, would appear to be approximately 1.7 billion dollars.

CHAPTER XVI

CHANGES IN MONETARY RELATIONS

Up to the beginning of 1933 the United States operated on the basis of a full gold standard. The dollar was defined as 25.8 grains of gold, nine-tenths fine, and the price of the metal was thus fixed by statute at $20.67 per ounce. All forms of United States currency were by law directly or indirectly exchangeable for gold at the rate set by the statutory price, and all gold was exchangeable for currency at the same rate. There was free coinage of gold, no limitation on private holding of or dealings in the metal, and complete freedom of gold imports and exports. Under this system, the exchange value of the dollar in terms of other gold currencies remained stable, within certain narrow and defined limits, while its exchange value in terms of non-gold currencies fluctuated in accordance with the degree to which these other currencies depreciated with respect to gold.

Although the abandonment of the gold standard by Great Britain and a number of other countries, which was described in Chapter II, served on several occasions to place a strain upon the maintenance of the gold standard system in the United States, a disruption of that system did not occur until the early part of 1933. Even then the abandonment of the gold standard took place not so much as a result of external strain as in pursuance of a domestic policy which was believed to require definite action in the monetary field.

426

I. ABANDONMENT AND PARTIAL RE-ESTABLISHMENT OF THE GOLD STANDARD

The gold standard was suspended in the United States in connection with the national banking holiday proclaimed by President Roosevelt on March 5, 1933. Upon the termination of the holiday all banks in the United States were forbidden, by executive order of March 10, to pay out or export gold except by permission of the Secretary of the Treasury. At the same time, all foreign exchange transactions were placed under control. Shortly after, the suspension of the gold standard was converted into its virtual abandonment. All gold held within the country was nationalized and was expropriated by the government at the statutory price. The gold clause, which had been widely used in connection with debt obligations, was abrogated. Over a period of several months a number of measures were taken for the establishment of a managed currency system, directed toward regulation of the purchasing power of the dollar in terms of commodities rather than the maintenance of stability in the foreign exchange value of the dollar. The most important of these measures and some of the principal reasons for their adoption were as follows.

On April 19 the embargo on gold exports was made absolute by executive order. At the same time an amendment to the Agricultural Adjustment bill was introduced in Congress which granted the President wide monetary powers, including authority to reduce from time to time the gold content of the dollar though by not more than 50 per cent. These provisions went into effect on May 12, when the bill was approved as enacted. The primary purpose of both of these measures was to bring about a depreciation of the dollar in terms of gold and therefore in terms of foreign currencies.

The Administration's preoccupation with the problem of commodity prices was mainly responsible for the policy of depreciation. President Roosevelt and some of his principal advisers had become converted to the theory that economic recovery in the United States was impossible without an antecedent rise of commodity prices; that, while many different measures might be required to bring about such a price rise, fundamentally it could not be achieved without a reduction in the gold content of the dollar; and that prosperity in the future should be sought largely through a stabilization of domestic commodity prices on a predetermined level. The depreciation of the dollar was considered desirable also from the viewpoint of the competitive position of American foreign trade as it was affected by the depreciation of foreign currencies. Accordingly, in conferring upon President Roosevelt the power to devalue the dollar, Congress stated explicitly that the amount of reduction in the gold content of the dollar should be such "as he [the President] finds necessary from his investigation to stabilize domestic prices or to protect the foreign commerce against the adverse effect of depreciated foreign currencies." This and the other monetary powers granted to the President at the same time were also intended to enable him "to secure by international agreement a stabilization at proper levels of the currencies of various governments."[1]

These three basic aims—continuing price manipulation, freedom to engage in competitive depreciation, and exchange stabilization at a "proper" level—were in large measure irreconcilable alternatives. The price level to be achieved and subsequently stabilized was to have reference primarily to domestic requirements, especially the

[1] Agricultural Adjustment Act, Title III, Sec. 43.

exigencies of the internal debt situation and the relation between agricultural and industrial prices. Since the theory under which the government was operating required for this purpose a reduction in the gold content of the dollar, the depreciation of the dollar in the foreign exchanges was regarded as necessary from the point of view of the price policy. Depreciation directed to this end could, however, be of use only incidentally in any effort to attain the objective of improving the competitive position of American export trade. Moreover, concentration of attention on the price problem meant the abandonment of all efforts to secure a stabilization of the dollar exchange rate—at least until the price-raising objective had been fully attained, and possibly permanently if the program of price control was to be fully carried out.

After a brief period of uncertainty, monetary management in terms of commodity prices was definitely made the central objective. This new policy was given its first clear exposition in President Roosevelt's message to the World Monetary and Economic Conference. On July 3 he said:

> The sound internal economic system of a nation is a greater factor in its well-being than the price of its currency in changing terms of the currencies of other nations. It is for this reason that . . . old fetishes of so-called international bankers are being replaced by efforts to plan national currencies with the objective of giving these currencies a continuing purchasing power which does not greatly vary in terms of the commodities and needs of modern civilization. Let me be frank in saying that the United States seeks the kind of dollar which a generation hence will have the same purchasing and debt-paying power as the dollar value we hope to attain in the near future.

Two days later the American delegation to the Conference was instructed to present the following even more explicit statement of policy:

The revaluation of the dollar in terms of American commodities is an end from which the government and the people of the United States cannot be diverted. We wish to make this perfectly clear: We are interested in American commodity prices. What is to be the value of the dollar in terms of foreign currencies is not and cannot be our immediate concern.

The next important monetary measure was taken at the end of October, when the so-called gold purchase plan was inaugurated. Under this scheme the government began a program of monetary management based upon an attempt to regulate commodity prices by altering the price of gold in terms of dollars. For several weeks thereafter the appropriate governmental agencies steadily advanced the price at which they were prepared to buy all gold brought to them, and at which they were, in fact, purchasing substantial quantities of the metal abroad.

The experiment in managed currency based on the gold purchase plan was abandoned within a few weeks of its inauguration. On January 30, 1934 Congress passed the Gold Reserve Act, which laid the foundation for the restoration of a monetary system based upon the principles of a gold standard. The act reaffirmed the provisions of Title III of the Agricultural Adjustment Act as they concerned the President's power to devalue the dollar, but prescribed that the new gold content of the dollar should be fixed within the limits of 50 and 60 per cent of the old content. By proclamation issued on January 31, 1934 the President formally devalued the dollar by fixing its gold content at $15\frac{5}{21}$ grains of gold, nine-tenths fine. The statutory price of gold thus became fixed once more, but at $35.00 rather than $20.67 per ounce. In this manner the dollar was officially devalued by 40.94 per cent, or by just less than the minimum percentage fixed in the act. The action, however, was provisional in character, since in his proclamation the President specifically reserved the right to change the gold content of the dollar within the prescribed limits.

The Gold Reserve Act did not restore the convertibility of currency into gold nor the right of individuals to hold or deal in the metal. All gold remained the property of the federal government. However, the Secretary of the Treasury announced on January 31, 1934 that as a matter of policy he was prepared to release gold for exportation to countries still on the gold standard, whenever the exchange rate of the dollar in terms of the currencies of such countries should reach the gold-export point.

As a result of the Gold Reserve Act, the presidential proclamation, and the announcement of the Secretary of the Treasury mentioned above, the dollar became again to all intents and purposes a gold currency. The combined effect of these three measures was to restore the operation of the essential features of the gold standard mechanism as it relates to the maintenance of exchange stability. They represented a tacit abandonment of all attempts to establish a system of monetary management in terms of commodity prices.

The devaluation increased the dollar value of the gold stocks that had been accumulated in the hands of the government and thus produced a profit of about 2.8 billion dollars, which became the property of the government. Out of this profit the sum of 2 billion dollars was segregated to constitute an Exchange Stabilization Fund designed to assist in maintaining the exchange stability of the dollar.

The provisions of the Gold Reserve Act relating to the powers of the President to change the gold content of the dollar and to the existence of the Exchange Stabilization Fund were made terminable upon the issuance of a presidential proclamation declaring the emergency at an end, but not later than within two years from the date of enactment. The President was, however, authorized to continue the operation of these provisions by proclamation for not more than one additional year. On January 10, 1936 the President extended the life of the provisions to the full term of three years, ending January 30, 1937.

In connection with the provisional restoration of the dollar to a gold basis, the system of foreign exchange control was practically abolished. On November 12, 1934 the Secretary of the Treasury, by formal announcement, granted a general license for all foreign exchange transactions, requiring only the reporting of such transactions.

An important step in the field of monetary relations was taken with the passage of the Silver Purchase Act, approved by the President on June 19, 1934. By the terms of this act it became mandatory for the Treasury to increase its stocks of silver until they equalled in value one-third of the monetary stocks of gold held by it, or until the market price of silver should reach $1.29. The act provided for the nationalization of all silver bullion held in the country, which placed the Treasury in possession of a substantial amount of the metal. The remainder of the required accumulation was to come from domestic production of newly mined silver and through importation of the metal from abroad. Since the domestic production is relatively insignificant,[2] the bulk of the purchases must be effected in other parts of the world.

[2] The record annual output in the history of the country was 75 million ounces in 1915; in 1932, the production amounted to 24 million ounces.

Foreign purchases of silver were continued at a substantial rate up to the middle of 1935. Since then they have been made at a somewhat reduced rate.

The latest measure in the field of monetary policy was taken at the end of September and the beginning of October 1936, in connection with the devaluation of their currencies by the "gold bloc" countries. On September 25 the government of the United States joined with the governments of Great Britain and France in announcing "its intention to continue to use appropriate available resources so as to avoid as far as possible any disturbance of the basis of international exchange" resulting from the readjustment of the French currency. The joint declaration was, in effect, an undertaking on the part of the three countries to maintain, in the absence of unforeseen developments, the exchange relationship of their respective currencies on approximately the basis which became established after the gold content of the French franc was reduced by about 29 per cent.

On October 12 the joint declaration was implemented by an announcement of the Secretary of the Treasury to the effect that he was prepared to sell gold at a fixed price of $35 per fine ounce (plus one-quarter per cent handling charge) to "the exchange equalization or stabilization funds of those countries whose funds likewise are offering to sell gold to the United States." It was stipulated that the sales of gold to the United States must be on such terms as "the Secretary may deem most advantageous to the public interest," and that the whole arrangement may be rescinded on twenty-four hours' notice.

The countries which satisfied the stipulation as to the terms on which they were prepared to sell gold to the United States were to be announced daily. At the beginning Great Britain and France were the only countries so announced. Later Belgium, the Netherlands, and Switzerland were added to the list. As among these six countries, therefore, a system of foreign exchange relationships based on gold shipments was thus provisionally re-established.

II. MOVEMENTS OF THE DOLLAR EXCHANGE RATE

Under the influence of the measures and developments just described, after March 1933 the foreign exchange value of the dollar underwent a number of important changes. The movements of the dollar exchange rate with respect to those foreign currencies which remained on the gold basis reflected, in general, the depreciation of the dollar in terms of gold. The movements with respect to non-gold currencies reflected not only the relation of the dollar to gold, but also the relation to gold of these other currencies. These fluctuations are graphically represented in the accompanying chart.

The curve representing the relationship between the dollar and the French franc is typical of the changes which have taken place in the dollar exchange rate on the gold currencies in general. As the dollar depreciated in relation to gold, the value of these currencies in dollars rose correspondingly. The amount of the rise fluctuated markedly during the last three quarters of 1933 and the first quarter of 1934. From the time of the formal devaluation of the dollar until September 1936, its exchange rate with respect to these currencies moved within a very narrow range around 169 per cent of the pre-depreciation parity. The Belgian currency was devalued at the beginning of 1935 by 28 per cent and has since remained stable at that level.

The other six currencies shown on the chart had all

Exchange Rates of Selected Currencies in Terms of United States Dollar[a]

(Monthly averages of noon buying rates for cable transfers in New York)

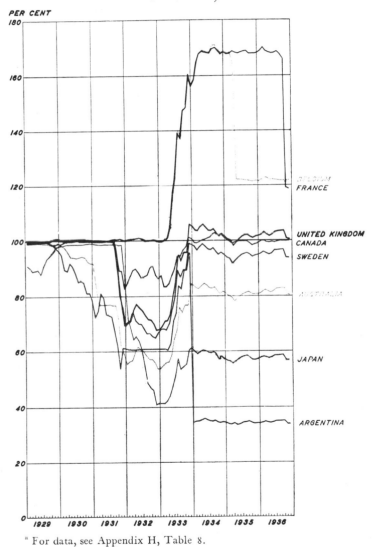

undergone depreciation with respect to gold prior to the abandonment of the gold standard by the United States. As a result, the value of these currency units in dollars declined, especially during the year 1932 and the first quarter of 1933. Since then their value in dollars has risen as the dollar depreciation tended to match and, in some cases, outstrip their own. The pound sterling and the Canadian dollar reached, during the year 1935, a level of almost the same degree of depreciation as the dollar and have remained, since the early part of that year, in a condition of stability with the dollar on the basis of approximately the same exchange rates as those which prevailed prior to the second half of 1931. The Swedish krona, the Australian pound, and the Japanese yen also attained a condition of stability with the dollar during the same period, though on the basis of varying degrees of relatively greater depreciation. The Argentine peso was sharply reduced in value in 1934.

The movements of these six depreciated currencies are typical of the behavior followed by the other non-gold monetary units. On the whole, from the early part of 1935 until October 1936, a condition of substantial stability has prevailed in the field of foreign exchange relations. The chart shows clearly, however, how far the gold values of the world's currencies have diverged from one another. This divergence, which was in part reduced as a result of the devaluation of the "gold bloc" currencies, has had important economic consequences, some of which continue to operate.

PART III
READJUSTMENTS REQUIRED
FOR RECOVERY

INTRODUCTION

In the two preceding divisions of this analysis we have reviewed in a broad way the sweep of world events since the end of the Great War, and traced in considerable detail the effects of the depression upon the economic system of the United States and the progress of recovery to the present time. The primary purpose of the series of chapters constituting the second part of the investigation has been to assemble the factual information essential for a broad gauge consideration of the recovery problem as it presents itself today.

In Part III an attempt is made to relate the study as a whole to the immediate economic situation with a view to suggesting modifications of governmental and business policy which might prove helpful in promoting further recovery. The first step is to review the government program in so far as it relates to recovery as distinguished from permanent reform. This analysis is followed by three chapters dealing respectively with the problem of fiscal and monetary stability, international economic relations, and certain phases of industrial and labor policy. In the final chapter an effort is made to give an integrated picture of the economic situation today and to summarize the major conclusions to which the analysis leads.

CHAPTER XVII

THE RECOVERY PROGRAM OF THE UNITED STATES GOVERNMENT

As a first step in discussing the readjustments required for a more complete recovery, it is essential to review the efforts that have been made by the federal government to arrest the depression and promote revival. In undertaking this task we shall not attempt to make any extended appraisal of each of the numerous measures that have been adopted, but will direct attention rather to their significance as interrelated parts of a general program of recovery. In other words, our primary purpose is not to consider whether each particular act might have been justified as an independent policy, under the conditions existing at the time of its passage, but whether the series of acts which constitute the government recovery program resulted in a consistent whole.

As was pointed out in Chapter V, the present depression marks the first time in industrial history that the power of government has everywhere been extensively invoked to stem the tide of depression and stimulate the process of recovery. In the United States governmental efforts to influence or control the course of the depression did not begin with the coming to power of the Democratic party. As a background for a consideration of the comprehensive program evolved in 1933, it will be of interest therefore to consider briefly the measures undertaken by the preceding Administration.

I. UNDER THE HOOVER ADMINISTRATION

In 1929 the view was held in the highest official circles that it was possible under government leadership to control, at least in substantial degree, the fluctuations of the so-called business cycle. It may be recalled in this connection that there was published in the spring of that year the Report of the Committee on Recent Economic Changes, of which Mr. Hoover had served as chairman. Both the staff of the National Bureau of Economic Research, under whose auspices the survey was conducted, and the members of the Committee had been greatly impressed with the increasing intelligence with which government officials and business men had been managing the complex problems presented by modern economic organization. In the recapitulating words of Dr. Wesley C. Mitchell, "All of the changes making for prosperity . . . can be summed up under a single head—applying fresh intelligence to the day's work."[1] The Committee itself summarized its thinking as follows: "There has been balance between the economic forces—not perfect balance, but a degree of balance which has enabled the intricate machine to produce and to serve our people. . . . Our situation is fortunate, our momentum is remarkable. Yet the organic balance of our economic structure can be maintained only by hard, persistent, intelligent effort. . . . Informed leadership is vital to the maintenance of equilibrium."[2]

In the light of the conclusions reached by the Committee on Recent Economic Changes, and in view of the efforts that had been made by Mr. Hoover as Secretary of Commerce to promote co-operation both among the members of the various industries and between these industries and the government, it was to be expected that a vigorous effort would be made by President Hoover's Administration to check the downward course of the

[1] *Recent Economic Changes in the United States*, Vol. II, p. 867.
[2] The same, Vol. I, pp. XXI, XXII.

depression which soon began. Such an effort was promptly undertaken and agreements were reached with many important business groups to continue as usual their production programs, particularly as they related to new capital construction—in the belief that the shock occasioned by the stock market crisis in 1929 would thus soon be absorbed. While the evidence indicates that this program served to retard the decline of industrial activity during the first half of 1930, it could not ultimately check the downward sweep of the depression.[3]

An effort was also made to arrest the depression by means of "financial controls." During the stock market boom rediscount rates were raised as high as 6 per cent. After the crisis they were gradually lowered until in the middle of 1931 they ranged, at the different banks, from 1.5 to 3.0 per cent. During the gold export crisis of the autumn of 1931 they were raised to a level of from 2.5 to 4.0 per cent; and they remained at about that level until after the banking crisis of 1933. At the same time the Federal Reserve Banks engaged extensively in open market operations with a view to easing the money market situation generally. In the two years 1930-31 they purchased about 300 million dollars of government securities and in 1932 over a billion. It was expected that the resulting increase in loanable funds in the hands of private institutions would, through the reduction of rates, stimulate recovery.

The third aspect of the Hoover program related to agriculture. A farm aid plan was conceived and passed before the coming of the depression and constituted a significant attempt to use the powers of government in

[3] Some students have contended that the result was to make the situation worse than it would otherwise have been. In the light of the analysis in Chaps. I and II, it is our conclusion that this program probably had little influence upon the severity of the ensuing decline.

aid of private economic enterprise. In the preamble to the Agricultural Marketing Act of June 15, 1929, it was declared,

to be the policy of Congress to promote the effective merchandising of agricultural commodities in interstate and foreign commerce, so that the industry of agriculture will be placed on a basis of economic equality with other industries . . . by aiding in preventing and controlling surpluses in any agricultural commodity, through orderly production and distribution, so as to maintain advantageous domestic markets and prevent such surpluses from causing undue and excessive fluctuations or depressions in prices for the commodity.

It will be observed that this declaration of policy gave a place both to "orderly production" and "orderly distribution." Indeed, special provisions of the act empowered the Federal Farm Board "to investigate conditions of over-production of agricultural commodities and advise as to the prevention of such over-production," and to make studies of land utilization and the "reduction of the acreage of unprofitable marginal lands in cultivation." Primary emphasis was, however, placed upon the marketing problem, and a revolving fund of 500 million dollars was provided to facilitate the stabilization of supplies in both domestic and foreign markets. Whatever degree of success the Board, with its revolving fund, might have had under conditions of continuing prosperity, it was wholly unable to check the catastrophic decline of agricultural prices which accompanied the world-wide depression of 1930-31.

Another important feature of the government program prior to 1933 was the setting up of government financial agencies to safeguard the financial structure. The Railroad Credit Corporation was organized in late 1931 with a view to increasing and pooling railroad revenues in the interests of distressed companies. The Reconstruction Finance Corporation was established in February 1932 for the purpose of making loans in support of distressed private enterprises, including railroads, banks, insurance companies,[4] and other financial institutions; and by the end of March 1933 loans aggregating 2,587 million dollars had been authorized. Finally, an act of June 1932 provided for the establishment of a Home Loan Bank system for the purpose of extending additional capital to building associations, savings banks, and similar institutions, and of making direct loans to home owners.

Reference must also be made to the effort to ease the international situation by means of a moratorium on war debts and co-operation with European countries with respect to other international financial and monetary problems;[5] and to the unavailing efforts of President Hoover, late in his term, to work out in co-operation with the President-elect a plan for alleviating the banking crisis before it might degenerate into panic.

These financial policies of the Hoover Administration have been not incorrectly defined as essentially defensive rather than offensive in character. That is to say, their primary purpose was to prevent further disintegration rather than directly to promote expansion. The assumption was, however, that once stable foundations were assured ordinary business processes would in due course lead to a new forward movement. In brief, this program was one of controlling or checking deflation rather than of stimulating reflation.

II. UNDER THE ROOSEVELT ADMINISTRATION

From the early frenzied weeks of the new Administration to the closing days of the recent political cam-

[4] For a fuller statement, see Chap. XII.
[5] See Chap. II, pp. 43-49.

paign the Roosevelt recovery program has been of compelling and universal interest. In the hysteria and hyperbole of public discussion it has been acclaimed as the sole cause of the vast improvement in business which has occurred, and denounced as a positive barrier to recovery. In the calmer atmosphere afforded by detachment alike from government and business and in the light of the analysis made in the foregoing chapters of this inquiry, it should be possible to clarify the primary economic issues involved in this collective effort to promote recovery—even though one may not aspire to give a definitive judgment with respect to its ultimate effects upon the functioning of the economic system. In any case, a general review of the program launched by the Administration in 1933 is an essential orientation for a new look forward at the present juncture.

In the effort to throw light upon the issue thus raised, it will be necessary first to outline briefly the major features of the general program that was evolved. When currently absorbed in discussions or controversies over particular phases of government policy one is prone to forget or overlook the larger aspects of the program as a whole. Even the Administration itself, when frantically endeavoring, under pressure, to accomplish results of far-reaching significance in the shortest possible period of time, is almost certain to overlook to some extent the importance of co-ordination or unification, particularly when the objectives include both immediate recovery and permanent reform. Accordingly, attention should here be focussed upon the various policies as related parts of a general program, with particular reference to recovery.

It is perhaps well to recall at the outset that the recovery program was by no means fully developed, or even conceived in its entirety, before March 1933, either in the mind of the President or any of his advisers, official or otherwise. Much of it, indeed, was developed after the inauguration; and significant parts were of course promoted by groups of individuals who had little interest in other phases of the program. It must also be noted that the central emphasis in the program as a whole shifted during the course of the four-year period. Though the fact is not commonly appreciated, the recovery program may be divided into two more or less definite stages.

1. The first phase. The major planks or steps in the early program of the Roosevelt Administration may be listed as follows: (1) liquidating the banking situation and reconstructing the commercial and investment credit system; (2) extending financial aid to and underwriting the credit of distressed economic institutions and groups; (3) establishing public credit on a sound basis through the balancing of the federal budget; (4) reducing the extraordinary barriers to international trade; (5) raising the general level of commodity prices through devaluation of the dollar; (6) restoring agricultural purchasing power by raising the prices of agricultural products through benefit payments and other devices provided by the Agricultural Adjustment Administration; and (7) stimulating employment and purchasing power by means of the National Recovery Administration and extensive appropriations for public works. Such enterprises as the civilian conservation camps, resettlement, unemployment relief, the development of the Tennessee Valley, and so forth were of minor significance, so far as the *recovery* program was concerned. The first three of the policies enumerated were essentially of a defensive nature, intended to re-establish financial stability and thus to restore business confidence. The other four were offensive or constructive in character, conceived as positive aids in promoting recovery.

There appears to be general agreement that the first of these policies was on the whole soundly conceived and effectively carried out. The policy of granting aid to distressed institutions and groups, begun by the preceding Administration but continued on a much broader scale under the Roosevelt Administration, also seemed an indispensable requirement of the situation.

The placing of the credit of the federal government upon a sound basis was regarded during the early months of the new Administration as of major importance. A special committee was organized prior to the inauguration and requested to draft proposals for substantial economies in government expenditures; the rate of pay of government employees was cut 15 per cent in the first Roosevelt budget; and taxes were increased. While the exigencies of the situation were such as to make a genuine balancing of the budget impossible at that juncture, sound finance remained for many months a goal to be attained if possible. It was with this objective in view that the Public Works Administration was at first tied in with the National Recovery Administration—the idea being that the amount of public expenditures might be adjusted in the light of the degree of recovery in private industry.

The reduction of the impediments to international trade and the expansion of international commerce represented a policy in line with traditional Democratic opinion; and it happened that the way had been prepared for the accomplishment of early results by the work already done by international experts in preparation for the World Economic Conference called for June.

The reduction in the weight of the gold dollar had two principal objectives: on the one hand, such action was deemed essential as a means of restoring our competitive position in international markets, which had suffered from the currency depreciation of other countries; and, on the other hand, it was deemed essential to raise the general level of domestic prices as a means of mitigating the burden of indebtedness. The policy was pressed upon the Administration by the so-called "Committee of the Nation," the membership of which included many prominent business men and bankers and some economists. In its first phase—and this was all many of the advocates of currency inflation were interested in—it involved merely cutting the dollar adrift from gold and allowing it to depreciate in the foreign exchanges—with stabilization to be effected at a more satisfactory level. Its second aspect involved the outright devaluation of the dollar and the assumption by the President of responsibility for managing the currency and controlling the level of prices.

The agricultural policy was the outgrowth of years of antecedent efforts to restore parity between agriculture and industry. The objectives of the Agricultural Adjustment Administration were not essentially different from those of the Farm Board, though the machinery provided was of a new order. The price-raising program for agriculture was basic in the whole recovery effort and had been more fully developed at the time of the inauguration than any of the other measures in the program.

The National Industrial Recovery Act, which also authorized the public works program, was the last of the initial policies of the New Deal program to be formulated. Public works appropriations on a vast scale had, to be sure, long been under consideration, and it is also true that no little attention had been given by various groups to problems pertaining to labor and industry. Nevertheless, the comprehensive industrial plan which was envisaged by the National Recovery Administration emerged somewhat later than other phases of the program. Moreover, the scope of the NRA expanded rapidly, both during the evolution of the law and after the passage of the act—which was couched in terminology intended to give a maximum of flexibility in its administration.

Its scope was extended in two directions. Instead of being confined to a selected group of major industries, its operations were quickly extended to cover nearly the entire range of business activity. Instead of merely setting minimum standards with respect to wages, hours, and so on, thereby establishing a foundation from which a new forward movement in industry might begin, it sought to generate expansion by means of reductions in hours and increases in wages. Moreover, instead of confining its activities to recovery measures, as the title suggested, its administrators sought to make it an instrumentality for permanent reforms.

2. *The second phase.* Several significant modifications of policy marked what we are designating as the second stage of the Roosevelt program. The first was the deferment of the goal of a balanced budget. It is difficult to say precisely when Administration policy shifted from the position that an unbalanced budget is an evil to be avoided as far as humanly possible, to the view that large deficits are to be regarded as a virtue in time of depression. But in the face of lagging recovery, especially in the autumn and winter of 1933-34, the opinion gradually crystallized that huge governmental expendi-

tures were the primary requisite for recovery.[6]

The policy of priming the industrial pump through the medium of vast governmental disbursements was henceforth vigorously pursued. The National Recovery Administration had fallen far short of its objective and the Public Works program was both slow in developing and comparatively small in magnitude. Hence, the Civil Works and Works Progress Administrations, in turn, became the principal instrumentalities for disbursing public funds. These agencies, to be sure, were considered essential to the provision of necessary public relief; but they were also definitely regarded as means of stimulating recovery. The theory was that only by greatly accelerating the volume and speed of government disbursements could processes of real recovery be generated.

The second important modification was in the field of monetary policy. In January 1934 the gold content of the dollar was fixed provisionally. While the President still possesses the power to make additional reductions in the weight of the dollar, no further modifications have in fact been made. Shortly after this return to a policy of stable currency the program designed to remove trade barriers and to reopen the channels of international trade was inaugurated and vigorously pushed. A willingness was also officially expressed to co-operate with foreign countries in re-establishing international monetary stability as soon as conditions might be propitious.

Some significant developments also occurred in the field of finance. The control over the issuance of securities was liberalized somewhat with a view to encouraging the resumption of capital goods construction. The burden

---

[6] This theory was endorsed by numerous economists, notably by John Maynard Keynes of Great Britain.

of interest was also alleviated, particularly by the reductions in the cost of credit to farmers and home owners through the aid of the Farm Credit Administration and the Home Owners' Loan Corporation. In the field of short-term credit no important actions were taken. There has been no increase in the security holdings of the Federal Reserve Banks since the end of 1933. Measures already adopted during the Hoover Administration, together with the very large inflow of gold from abroad and the abundance of loanable funds, rendered any further action intended to lower short-term interest rates quite unnecessary.[7]

It may be recalled, also, that since 1934 certain important modifications of policy were made necessary by decisions of the Supreme Court, notably with respect to the Industrial Recovery and Agricultural Adjustment programs. The former resulted in the outright abandonment of the effort to expand purchasing power through the medium of code agreements; the latter necessitated important changes in the methods of extending aid to agricultural producers and reduced its amount.

3. *Conflicting policies.* In the light of this summary account of the numerous phases of government policy, we may now consider the extent to which the program as a whole involved inconsistent elements. Again we shall consider separately the two stages of development.

It is readily apparent that certain phases of the early Roosevelt program were fundamentally incompatible: (1) the efforts to re-establish business confidence through the reconstruction of the credit system and the reduction of expenditures by the regular federal departments were in large measure nullified by the uncertainty arising out

[7] For a discussion of the factors involved in the money market situation, see Chap. XVIII, pp. 469-74.

of the program of dollar devaluation and currency management. (2) The authorization of billions of dollars for public works was seen as a menace to the program of fiscal stability. (3) The currency policy necessitated independent national action, and it thus disrupted the World Economic Conference and deferred the program intended to mitigate trade barriers and reopen the channels of international commerce. (4) The sharp increase in industrial prices fostered by the NRA program of increasing wages and shortening hours worked directly at cross purposes with the AAA policy of restoring price parity between agriculture and industry. It should also be noted that some of the permanent reform implications of the Administration's general program—however meritorious they may be—inevitably occasioned uneasiness and hence served to impede the recovery program.

The changes which occurred during the second stage (1934-36) served to eliminate some of the major conflicts within the program. The abandonment of currency management carried with it an abandonment of the policy of economic isolation, and paved the way for the reopening of negotiations intended to encourage international trade development. The dissolution of the National Recovery Administration eliminated the program of progressively raising industrial costs and prices, and thus removed a serious obstacle to the restoration of agricultural and industrial price parity.

The new policy of promoting recovery through vast governmental expenditures presented, however, a fresh complication. The rapidly increasing public indebtedness was viewed as a menace to the stability of public credit, and thus to the stability of the dollar. In other words, while the reduction of the value of the dollar as a matter of definite policy had apparently been abandoned, it was feared that currency stability might be undermined in another—and less controllable—way. The great question became whether the stimulus resulting from government expenditures might generate a sufficient expansion in business activity to make possible in good season a restoration of fiscal equilibrium. No one could definitely forecast the outcome.[8]

III. GOVERNMENT POLICIES AND RECOVERY

Because of the complex factors involved in the process of economic recovery, it is difficult to establish conclusively whether government policies as a whole have been a stimulating or retarding influence. The available evidence does, however, definitely enable one to limit the area of doubt and to indicate whether the policies pursued were of decisive importance, one way or the other. To throw light on the issue thus raised we may compare the time and extent of recovery in the United States with that in other countries and also indicate how closely the degree of actual recovery in the United States at various stages articulated with the recovery program that was being evolved.

In the first place, it is clear that the recovery in this country has been part of a world movement. It was shown in Chapter IV that the bottom of the depression in general was reached in the summer of 1932, and that the slow, if halting, process of recovery was under way in the second half of that year. Even in the United States the lowest level of industrial output was reached in July 1932. The index of industrial production rose from 48.7 in that month to about 56 in the late autumn, only to decline again to 49.6 at the time of the banking crisis

[8] For an analysis of the present status of the fiscal problem, see Chap. XVIII.

in March 1933. During this period industrial production in Great Britain rose from about 78 to 85; in Sweden from 67 to 81; in Germany from 51 to 57; and in Japan from 95 to 117. The monthly data indicate that the new American decline in the first quarter of 1933 exercised a restraining influence upon, but did not altogether check, the advance elsewhere.

In the light of these facts, it seems a fair presumption that as soon as the American banking crisis was cleared up a new advance in the United States would have begun, even had no further governmental action been taken. The question remains, however, whether other policies may not have accelerated the forward movement. In attempting to throw light on this issue, it will be necessary to divide the period of recovery into several segments.

The first period is the three-month interval from March to May 1933. The most significant developments in these months were the reopening of the banks, the setting up of the Agricultural Adjustment Administration, the emphasis upon a balanced budget, and the gradual downward drift of the dollar in the foreign exchanges. It should be borne in mind that a definite decision to devalue the currency had not yet been reached, and that the National Industrial Recovery Act was still only in the stages of preliminary discussion.

During this period the index of industrial production in the United States showed a marked rise, from 49.6 in March to 65.5 in May. Meanwhile, industrial output in Great Britain, Germany, Sweden, and Japan[9] showed little change. During these three months the

---

[9] For present purposes international comparisons will be confined to these four important countries. The data for twelve selected countries are shown graphically in the charts on pp. 78-79.

American recovery movement may be said to have caught up with, and even passed, that of other leading countries. It is impossible to assign responsibility for this strong upward surge to any single development; it would probably be safest to attribute it to a combination of factors, including the new spirit of hopefulness engendered by the President.

The next period to be considered separately is June and July 1933. It was in the former month that the policy of depreciating the currency was definitely adopted and that the National Industrial Recovery program was announced. Industrial production jumped sharply, from 65 in May to 84 in July. Meanwhile, in Germany, Great Britain, Japan, and Sweden there was little change in the level of output. One must conclude, therefore, that the policies of the United States government were a powerful stimulus at this particular juncture. The prospect of substantially higher costs and prices, arising from monetary and industrial code policies, led to a rapid expansion of output in anticipation of the changes to come.

In the following months there was a sharp reversal of trend, the index of industrial production declining from 84.0 in July to 60.5 in November—well below the level of May. This period was one of liquidation of excessive inventories accumulated in anticipation of the new level of costs. During these months, however, there was a strong advance in other countries. Measured from the low point of the depression to December 1933 the degree of recovery in the United States had been somewhat less than that in Great Britain, Germany, Sweden, and Japan.

The next period requiring scrutiny is the first eleven months of the year 1934. The index of industrial output in the United States fluctuated between about 60 and 72. It stood at 65.5 in January, reached a high of 72.3 in May, and then declined to an average of about 61.0 in September, October, and November. This was just about the level of the preceding autumn. Meanwhile, there was a further advance of over 10 per cent in the level of production in Great Britain, Germany, Sweden, and Japan.

A rather sharp recovery occurred in December 1934 and January 1935. For the first half of 1935 as a whole, however, the index of industrial production was only about four points above the level of the first half of 1934. It is of interest to note also that in June 1935 the level of industrial output was below that of June 1933 and materially below the peak reached in July of that year. Moreover, the degree of recovery by June 1935 had been less than that in any of the other countries with which we are here making comparisons.

Since the middle of 1935 there has been a fairly steady and strong forward movement. The index of industrial output advanced from 72.3 in June 1935 to 86.6 in June 1936 and to 91.6 in September of this year. This advance has been somewhat more pronounced that that in most other countries. At the present time, however, the degree of recovery in the United States is still considerably less than that in various other countries.[10]

The best-sustained recovery movement thus began shortly after the National Industrial Recovery Act was declared unconstitutional. It is evident that the grave fears entertained that the abandonment of the codes would lead to a new period of business disorganization were not well founded. It should be observed in this

[10] See charts, pp. 78-79.

connection, however, that the ensuing improvement in business did not result from downward wage readjustments—for the fact is that wage rates have tended to rise rather than fall.[11]

One would not be justified in attributing all of the improvement which has occurred since the middle of 1935 to the disappearance of the codes. Other factors have doubtless played a part, such as the relative increase in farm income, the increasing confidence resulting from the modification of government policy with respect to currency, and the continued forward movement in other countries. Moreover, recovery is ordinarily a cumulative process and in the absence of definitely retarding influences one would expect to find an expanding volume of production as the months pass.

When the degree of recovery is considered more broadly, in relation to the two phases of the Roosevelt recovery program, a conclusion of primary significance may be drawn. It will be recalled that in the first stage of the recovery program the internal inconsistencies were much greater than in the second stage. These conflicts of policy manifested themselves most strikingly during the first year or so; and it was during this period that the recovery movement was most halting, and most uneven in character. One may fairly conclude, therefore, that the conflicting and confusing character of the early Roosevelt program tended on the whole to retard the recovery program.

It is interesting to note in this connection that the two measures which gave the greatest initial impetus to industrial expansion, namely, dollar depreciation and the anticipation of the NRA program to raise costs and price, were the very measures which in the end threat-

[11] For the movement of wages and prices, see pp. 254-56.

ened to undermine the whole recovery program. Dollar depreciation not only engendered fear over the future stability of values, but it produced serious international complications which impeded the recovery of world trade.[12] The NRA not only became administratively impossible and a source of endless confusion and controversy, but it failed to increase the real income of the laboring classes as a whole,[13] and tended to checkmate the policy of increasing the real purchasing power of the agricultural population.

During the second phase of the government's recovery effort, the spending program came to occupy a place of primary importance. It is impossible to gauge accurately the bearing of this policy upon recovery, for one cannot segregate its effects from those of other factors in the situation. It may be pointed out that the spending program was vigorously pushed throughout the year 1934 and that it was not until after the middle of 1935 that a strong forward movement began. Was this simply a natural lag, or does it suggest rather that the benefits were for the time being nullified by the adverse effects of other phases of the government program? No one can answer this question conclusively.

It is evident, however, that the spending program operated as a sort of two-edged sword. On the one hand, it undoubtedly served as a direct stimulus to retail trade, and through retail trade to the processes of production. On the other hand, it produced uneasiness with reference to the future stability of the dollar, and thus militated against long-term credit operations. A considerable period of time elapsed before the fears re-

[12] For a discussion of this phase of the problem, see Chap. XIX.

[13] For detailed discussion, see *The National Recovery Administration,* published by the Brookings Institution, 1935.

sulting alike from the devaluation and budget unbalancing programs subsided; and it was not until 1935 that long-term credit operations—even refunding operations—were resumed on any considerable scale.

The effects of the spending program on business activity, however, tended to be cumulative in character. At the outset the influence was exerted chiefly in the markets for consumers' goods; but as time passed the expansion movement gradually extended to the field of capital construction.[14] It is possible that an earlier and more rapid expansion might have occurred had confidence not been impaired by fiscal policy; but one cannot tell from any available evidence.[15]

In considering the influence of the spending program on recovery, it will be helpful again to make comparisons with the experience of other countries. Both Great Britain and Sweden have attained a greater degree of recovery than has the United States, and neither has permitted any material increase in the public debt.[16] It is evidently possible, therefore, to have recovery, even from a world depression, without vast outlays of public funds.

However, it must also be noted that Germany and Japan have had an even greater degree of expansion than Great Britain, and that their budgets have been even more seriously unbalanced than has that of the United States. It is clearly evident, therefore, that an unbalanced budget is not an insurmountable barrier to

[14] For a discussion of the degree of expansion which has occurred in the several divisions of the durable goods industries, see Chap. VIII.

[15] For a discussion of the relation of the Agricultural Adjustment disbursement program to recovery, see Edwin G. Nourse, J. S. Davis, and J. D. Black, *Three Years of the Agricultural Adjustment Administration*.

[16] See data on p. 89.

recovery. But at the same time there is no doubt that if recovery is achieved without a piling up of government indebtedness there exists a much sounder basis for enduring prosperity. Unbalanced budgets and public debts leave an aftermath of complications which threaten both financial and economic stability.

In connection with these international comparisons it must be borne in mind that the comparisons are not between one country in which vigorous efforts were made by the government to promote recovery and other countries in which economic trends were allowed to run a normal course uninfluenced by government policy. As was shown in Chapter V, all countries endeavored in one way or another to use the powers of government in promoting business revival. We must therefore repeat here what was said at the close of that chapter, namely, that it is impossible to make a simple direct comparison of results in countries which invoked the powers of government with the outcome in countries following a policy of strict laissez faire—for there were none of the latter.

CHAPTER XVIII

GOVERNMENT CREDIT AND GENERAL FINANCIAL STABILITY

As has been pointed out in preceding chapters, a striking feature of the current depression period has been the rapid growth of public indebtedness in most of the nations of the world. This expansion of government debt has occurred not merely during the period of acute deflation and shrinking national income but has in many instances been even more pronounced during the years of recovery. The United States is conspicuous among nations which have employed the credit resources of the government in a deliberate effort to promote business revival as well as to relieve distress and suffering. In view of the basic importance and ramifying influence of public finance we shall begin our discussion of the adjustments necessary for further recovery with an analysis of the problem of public credit in the United States.

We have already traced the growth of public indebtedness in this country and indicated the changing character of federal revenues and expenditures.[1] We have not, however, attempted to analyze what is involved in re-establishing fiscal stability or to indicate the significance of sound public credit from the standpoint of the successful operation of the economic system as a whole. This is the task of the present chapter. We shall begin the discussion by endeavoring to clear up some of the mystery as to how the government has been able to procure the funds required to carry out its vast program

[1] See Chap. XII.

of expenditures; why the sources of government credit
have been so apparently illimitable; and why, as the
government debt has mounted, the rates of interest on
new flotations have fallen rather than risen.

I. THE SOURCES OF GOVERNMENT FUNDS

Governments in pressing need of money always appear able to procure it by one means or another. In
former times, when the currency consisted chiefly of
metallic coins, it was a common practice for the king's
treasurer to sweat or clip coins passing through his
hands, thereby acquiring a profit which was the equivalent of an increase in taxes. But since the resulting lack
of uniformity in coins disorganized the currency system
it was found to be a better device to recoin the entire
circulation, replacing existing coins by new units of
value containing a larger percentage of base metal. With
the development of paper money the process of dilut-
ing the currency became simpler, for it was necessary
merely to print government promissory notes and pass
them out in payment of current obligations. This method
was employed, for example, in financing the American
Revolution, the Confederate government during the
Civil War, and, to the extent of some 400 million dollars, the United States government during the same
struggle.

With the evolution of banking and credit currency,
more refined methods of procuring an increase of fiscal
receipts have been devised. Instead of issuing its own
promissory notes in the direct payment of obligations,
the Treasury commonly borrows what it requires from
the banks, with the latter assuming the role of issuing
agency. The process involves giving the banks interest
bearing obligations of the government payable at future
dates in exchange for non-interest bearing promises

on the part of the banks to pay the bearer on demand. These demand obligations may assume the form either of bank notes or checking accounts. Sometimes these government notes are sold as a straight business proposition to private banking institutions and sometimes they are sold to government controlled central banks. During the World War both of these alternatives were extensively employed. When government obligations are sold in the financial markets there is an outside check on the credit standing of the government—though even here considerations of patriotism or public necessity may make such a check more nominal than real. When the government exercises its control over a central bank in order to borrow from it, there is no external judgment; to put the matter another way, the government is merely issuing its notes through a subsidiary agency. It has the practical advantage, however, of keeping up appearances and of obscuring the true situation.

While it has been relatively easy for governments to procure virtually unlimited funds by resort to such devices, it has always proved impossible, ultimately, to avoid fluctuations in the value of the currency. A reduction in the weight of metallic currency immediately affects its value in the foreign exchange markets, where coins are exchanged by weight and fineness only; and the moment a nation's currency depreciates as compared with foreign currencies the number of units required in payment for commodities is altered. In other words, the prices of goods entering into international trade are affected. Similarly, as soon as the issuance of irredeemable government paper money assumes such proportions as to cast doubt upon the *ultimate* ability of the government to redeem such paper in standard metal, its value depreciates in the international exchange markets. Discussion of the ultimate consequences flowing from this process must be reserved for later pages.

During the course of the present depression several methods of creating currency have been available to the United States government. It has had the power: (1) to coin money and to adjust the value of existing coinage; (2) to issue non-interest bearing notes, within limits and for express purposes; and (3) to borrow in the general financial markets. Only the last has been extensively utilized.

The power to coin and to regulate the value of gold and silver has been employed chiefly with a view to price adjustment rather than as a fiscal expedient. However, the devaluation of the gold dollar in January 1934 to 59.06 per cent of its former value did yield a profit to the Treasury of 2.8 billion dollars. Of this amount two billions was set aside as a Stabilization Fund, of which to date only 200 millions has been withdrawn for stabilization operations. The balance of the gold profit was placed in the general fund of the Treasury and the greater part used to retire national bank notes.[2] Similarly, the operations under the Silver Purchase Act of 1934, and previous legislation, resulted in substantial seigniorage profits to the Treasury. About 700 million dollars worth of new silver coin and currency has been issued, most of which has entered the channels of circulation.

The so-called Thomas Amendment authorized the President to direct the Secretary of the Treasury to enter into agreements with the Federal Reserve Board[3]

---

[2] The President's devaluation power, which has been extended to Jan. 30, 1937, limits him to a range of operations between 50 and 60 per cent of the original gold value.

[3] By the Banking Act of 1935 the Federal Reserve Board was dissolved and reconstituted as the Board of Governors of the Federal Reserve system.

to purchase 3 billion dollars of government obligations in the open market, in addition to their present holdings; and if the Secretary should be unable to secure the assent of the Board, or if operations should be inadequate for the purposes in view, the President was further authorized to direct the Secretary to issue an aggregate amount of 3 billions of United States notes for the purpose of purchasing outstanding government securities or meeting maturities. These powers have, however, not been utilized, and the present legislation expires January 30, 1937. It remains true, however, that the resources of the Federal Reserve Banks—and also the Stabilization Fund, which can be invested in government bonds—may be drawn upon in support of public credit.

The government has relied primarily upon the sale of its securities in the financial markets. To some extent they have been purchased from the money savings of the people, but, as we shall see, the largest portion has been sold to commercial banking institutions. The interest bearing debt of the federal government increased between December 31, 1930, when the deficits began to accumulate, and June 30, 1936 by 16,270 millions of dollars.[4] The following table shows how these issues were absorbed:

	Millions of Dollars
Federal Reserve Banks[5]	1,701
Member banks of Reserve system[5]	7,596
Mutual savings banks[6]	1,698

[4] This figure does not include 945 million dollars of Adjusted Service bonds, the issuance of which did not involve receipt of funds by the Treasury.

[5] From *Federal Reserve Bulletin*.

[6] Increase based on figures for June 1930 and June 1936 as shown in *Reports of the Comptroller of the Currency*.

Life insurance companies[7] 2,419
Held in United States government trust funds or
   owned by United States government and government agencies[8] 612
                                          ─────
                                          14,026
Balance absorbed by individuals and other institutions[9] 2,244
                                          ─────
   Total 16,270

It is not possible to indicate with any precision what proportion of the total purchases was made from the money savings of individuals, what amount represented a shifting of assets, and what amount originated in bank credit expansion. However, it is evident from the fact that there was an increase of 9,297 millions of government securities in the holdings of Federal Reserve and member banks that the commercial banking institutions are the primary direct source from which government funds have been derived. The process involves the sale of government obligations to the banks in exchange for deposits against which the Treasury may draw in meeting its current obligations.

The banks have purchased both long- and short-term obligations. The following chart shows the member bank holdings of the three principal classes of government issues annually from December 31, 1930 to

[7] This is an estimate of the increase from Dec. 31, 1930 to June 30, 1936, based on actual figures for the period December 1930 to December 1935, as shown by the *Proceedings . . . of the Association of Life Insurance Presidents*, 1935, Table 1, p. 43.

[8] An estimate based upon figures for June 1930 and June 1935 obtained from the *Annual Report of the Secretary of the Treasury*, 1935 (compiled from Table 44-B, p. 425, and Table 45-B, p. 427). The figure is net, and includes an increase of 773 million dollars in holdings of Postal Savings banks, between December 1930 and June 1936.

[9] Includes the holdings of non-member banks, the precise volume of which is not known.

June 30, 1936, in relation to other loans and investments.

CHANGING CHARACTER OF BANK ASSETS, 1930-36[a]

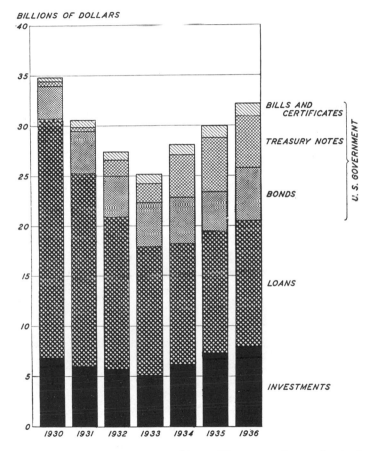

BILLIONS OF DOLLARS

BILLS AND CERTIFICATES

TREASURY NOTES

BONDS

U. S. GOVERNMENT

LOANS

INVESTMENTS

1930 1931 1932 1933 1934 1935 1936

[a] For data, see Appendix F, Table 12. Figures are for member banks of Federal Reserve system.

The diagram indicates a rapid increase in the percentage of bank assets that are in the form of government securities—from 12 per cent in 1930 to 37 per cent in 1936. Of particular interest is the expansion of bank holdings of intermediate term notes and short-term Treasury bills and certificates. The one- to five-year notes have been acceptable to the banks, for it was assumed that the comparatively short duration would be a protection against being enmeshed in government fiscal difficulties. The Treasury bills and certificates provided a temporary use for funds and yet enabled the banks to maintain a highly liquid position; the only fly in the ointment has been the negligible and sometimes negative yields that have come to prevail.[10]

It should be borne in mind in considering this problem that business demands for commercial loans during these years have been relatively small. In consequence the banks have welcomed these investments in government securities as a source of current income, however modest. Business demands for banking accommodations during the recovery period have been slack, in part because the volume of business has remained comparatively low, especially in dollar terms; in part because the government has done a large portion of the borrowing required for expansion; and in part because of the increased financial independence of business corporations. Prior to the depression, business corporations were accumulating larger working capital resources, which together with the reduction of costs incident to the deflation process from 1929 to 1933 enabled most of the larger corporations to enter the period of recovery with cash resources adequate to finance, on the lower cost basis, the modest requirements entailed by

---

[10] The question has often been raised as to why the banks should purchase bills at a price which would not pay the out-of-pocket costs. The answer is that it is assumed that they will always be given preference when these obligations are refunded and thus obtain new issues at more favorable rates.

partial recovery. These cash resources have since been augmented by the government's financial program. Not until business recovery is much more extensive and prices are materially higher will the demand for commercial loans approach those of former times.

It will be observed, however, that meanwhile the structure of banking is being profoundly altered. Bank assets and deposits expand not in relation to business requirements but in response to government exigencies and policies; and the security back of these assets is taxing power and taxation capacity rather than specific business assets and earnings. If the money procured by the government were all employed in the production of salable commodities the situation would not be different from what it is when loans are directly expanded for private enterprise. But, to the degree that government loans are used for relief purposes or are devoted to the creation of non-revenue producing public properties, such loans are of course not self-supporting. They are thus a charge against the taxpayer in general.

II. WHY INTEREST RATES ARE LOW

Attention was called in Chapter XII to the fact that the more the government debt has been increased the lower has become the rate at which the government has been able to borrow. Does this suggest steadily increasing confidence in the soundness and stability of government credit, or may it be otherwise explained? In order to understand this phenomenon we must consider the relation of the government's financial operations to the money market and also other factors relating to the supply of available funds.

We must first trace the flow of funds resulting from government borrowing operations. When banks purchase government securities they immediately set up a deposit account for the Treasury. From time to time, as needed, the Treasury transfers these funds to the Federal Reserve Banks and then in meeting its manifold disbursements draws checks against these balances. Individuals or corporations receiving these government checks normally deposit them to their accounts in their respective banks; and, in due course, private checks are drawn against such accounts with the recipients thereof redepositing them in their banks. Thus the initial expansion of bank deposits arising out of the government loans is not liquidated; it returns as deposits somewhere in the banking system conceived as a whole. With each succeeding government issue this process is repeated.

It has sometimes been assumed that such an expansion of bank deposits is peculiarly related to government borrowing. This is not the case, for it is also what happens in a period when bank loans are being extended to private borrowers who take deposit accounts and draw checks against them, which in turn are redeposited somewhere in the banking system. But, as was pointed out on a preceding page, there is a marked difference in the character of the assets which the bank obtains in the process—in the one case government obligations and in the other loans directly related to commercial operations.

1. The importance of bank reserves. The ultimate power of the banks to purchase government securities is determined by the situation with reference to bank reserves. The expansion of bank deposits in the process of financing the government means that, other things equal, the ratio of deposits to cash reserves will decline. If continued long enough the ratio of deposits to reserves will reach the minimum deemed compatible with the safety of the banking system.

During recent years, however, bank reserves have been enormously augmented as a result of the increasing gold supply of this country. This accumulation be-

MONETARY GOLD STOCKS OF THE UNITED STATES
BY YEARS, 1914-35[a]

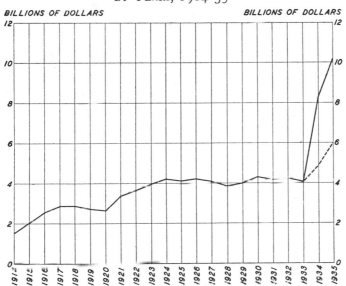

BILLIONS OF DOLLARS   BILLIONS OF DOLLARS

[a] Year-end figures in dollars of 1929 gold content through 1933; thereafter in dollars of present content. See *Annual Report of the Board of Governors of the Federal Reserve System*, 1935, p. 115.

gan in the World War period, continued intermittently in the period of the twenties, and has been greatly accelerated during the past three years. The growth is shown in the chart on this page.[11] The supply of bank reserves has also been materially increased by the "open market" purchases of bonds by the Federal Reserve Banks, especially in 1931-33.

[11] For a detailed discussion of this gold movement, see Charles O. Hardy, *Is There Enough Gold?*.

As a result of these various developments the reserves became so "excessive" that it seemed desirable in 1936 to raise the reserve requirements as a means of restraining the possibilities of commercial inflation. However, even after this action, the excess reserves remain far larger than they ever were prior to the year 1934.

In considering further possible increases in reserve requirements it is to be noted that something of a dilemma exists. On the one side, the appearance of strong speculative tendencies in the financial and commercial markets would seem to demand not only a tightening of margin requirements but also of interest rates; but on the other side an increase in interest rates would seriously affect the government's fiscal problem. It should also be noted that the reserve situation might be quickly altered by extensive shifts in the international investment situation and a consequent export of gold.[12]

2. *The dearth of private financing.* Another important factor in the long-term money market situation is the negligible volume of private security issues as compared with the amount of private funds available for investment. The flotation of private securities for the expansion of capital has been of insignificant proportions throughout the recovery period.[13] This fact is attributable in part to the slow rate of growth of new productive capital and in part to the fact that private business corporations have been able to finance the greater part of such expansion directly from their own funds. In any event, neither the railways, public utilities, industrial corporations, commercial and finan-

---

[12] See pp. 421-25.
[13] See chart and discussion on p. 377.

cial companies, nor state and local governments and agencies have issued any significant volume of new securities in recent years, which would absorb current money savings.

The purchase of federal government securities has thus provided a welcome alternative to the normal investment outlets. The large volume of available investment money, together with the superabundance of loanable bank funds, as compared with business requirements for capital purposes, explains the extraordinarily low interest rates and yields on high-grade bonds and stocks. It follows that not until new private financing is resumed on a large scale, through the issue of securities, will the supply of funds seeking investment in government bonds be appreciably reduced or will interest rates rise.

Moreover, not until private enterprises increase substantially their short-term borrowings from commercial banks will there be any appreciable rise in short-term rates of interest—though, as noted above, it is conceivable that a modification of reserve requirements might quickly alter the short-term market situation and appreciably affect long-term rates.

3. The limits of government credit. It should not be concluded from the preceding analysis that the practical limits of government credit are governed solely by the reserves of the banking system and the supply of private investment credit. While the situation which we have disclosed is the explanation of the ability of the government thus far to borrow all the funds required, and at progressively lower rates of interest, it does not follow that the government will indefinitely be able to procure all the funds required irrespective of the amount of the public debt. The process can be continued only so long as confidence in the government's ability to balance the budget remains. Should confidence be severely shaken, the ability of the government to borrow from the public at low rates of interest would cease—with serious effects upon the value of government obligations. The vital question at issue at the present juncture, then, is whether the credit of the United States government has been in any serious degree imperilled or to what extent the process of borrowing might be further continued without destroying confidence. Efforts have here and there been made to set some total debt figure which would measure the upper limit of safety under present methods of financing. Such estimates, running as high as 60 or 70 billion dollars, have little significance taken by themselves. The problem has to be considered in terms of the possibilities of bridging the gap between current expenditures and current revenues.

The danger point in public debt is that point at which it becomes clear that the budget cannot, as a practical matter, be brought into balance. In Chapter XII we reviewed the rise of the public debt and disclosed the amount of the current deficit, but we did not there discuss the issues involved in bringing about a balance between current expenditures and current revenues. To this problem we now direct attention.

III. THE BUDGET PROBLEM

In order to reveal what is involved in bringing the federal budget into stable equilibrium it is necessary as a first step to have before us in summary form the major classes of expenditure at the present time. The following table gives the estimates for 1937 as contained in the *President's Budget Statement* of September 1936. The figures are in millions of dollars.

Interest	825	Public works	834
Pensions (military)[14]	600	Aids to home owners	188
National defense	920	Miscellaneous	216
Civil departments and		Debt retirement	580
agencies	946	Social security	405
Relief (WPA and			
CCC included)	1,659	Total[15]	7,822
Agricultural aid	649		

In analyzing the budget problem from the point of view of expenditures, we shall not consider the possibility of increases or reductions in the estimates for the current fiscal year ending June 30, 1937.[16] For the purpose of this analysis we shall assume that current expectations will be realized, and then face the problem as it will present itself in the ensuing year.

1. Interest. In estimating the future interest charges we shall assume that the debt does not increase after the end of the present fiscal year and that the accumulated debt will be consolidated on a relatively permanent basis. The amount of the interest burden would then depend upon (1) the total of the debt, and (2) the rate of interest at which the debt may be permanently consolidated.

The amount of the interest bearing debt as of June 30, 1936 was 32,989 million dollars. The current budget calls for expenditures of 7,822 millions, plus 560 millions carry-over on account of the bonus, making total outlays of 8,382 millions. Revenues for the year are estimated at 5,666 millions (including 325 millions from social security taxation). In addition, it is

[14] Does not include 560 millions to be paid this year to government trust funds as compensation for cancellation of veterans' loans.

[15] Net repayments on loan and investment accounts have not been deducted from expenditures, which are given as gross figures.

[16] Subsequent official statements indicate probable increases.

estimated that recoveries from loans and investments will yield 620 millions, making total estimated receipts of 6,286 millions. The difference between gross expenditures and receipts would thus be 2,096 millions. However, expenditures for debt retirement (580 millions) should obviously be deducted before computing the actual deficit, which leaves 1,516 millions. Adding this deficiency of revenues for the current year to the June 30, 1936 debt gives a total interest bearing debt of 34,505 millions.

It will be recalled, however, that the government has a substantial amount of recoverable assets which must be regarded as an offset to public debt. On the basis of our analysis in Chapter XII, it would seem that something like 2 billion dollars would be a reasonable estimate of the aggregate recoveries that may be expected, over and above the 620 millions included in this year's estimates.[17] While it will be several years before these recoveries will be realized, we shall nevertheless for simplicity subtract the full amount from the debt as it would otherwise stand on June 30, 1937.

On this basis of computation the debt would be approximately 32,500 millions. To the extent that delay is experienced in effecting a complete balance between revenues and expenditures this total will of course be increased. Everything considered, a round figure of 33 billions may be taken as a minimum total on which to compute interest charges for the future.[18]

In computing the amount of the interest burden it

[17] See pp. 286-91.

[18] The stabilization fund of 2 billion dollars has not been subtracted from the debt because of the probability that it will have to be reserved for some years to come for stabilization purposes. Moreover, its utilization for debt retirement might involve a further substantial increase in bank reserves, a result which is not desired at the present time.

is necessary again to call attention to the abnormally low rates now prevailing. It must also be recalled that the present debt includes long-term bonds (18,628 millions); one- to five-year notes (11,861 millions); and Treasury bills and certificates (2,500 millions). The rate on the one- to five-year notes issued in the past year averages about 1.5 per cent and that on the short-term obligations a mere fraction of one per cent. The computed rate on the entire debt as of June 30, 1936 was 2.56 per cent. If the federal debt is to be consolidated and placed upon a permanent basis it is essential that a considerable proportion of the five-year notes and short-term bills and certificates be converted into longer term issues. While no definite principle can be laid down as to the proportion of the total debt that might remain more or less permanently in the form of these shorter term obligations, we shall assume that a consolidated debt should show not more than 5 billions in the former class and not more than one billion in the latter.

It is impossible to say at this time at what precise rate of interest the government debt might be consolidated and placed on a permanent basis. Taking advantage of the present unusually favorable investment market situation, the government recently floated a 17-year loan on a 2.5 per cent basis; but the average coupon rate on the outstanding long-term issues is still above 3 per cent.

We cannot, however, count on the continuance of as favorable a money market situation as has recently prevailed. If there is a resumption of demand for investment funds on the part of private enterprise, as will undoubtedly occur if we have continued economic expansion, the rates at which the government could borrow would of course be materially affected. Not only would the general money market rate stiffen, but there would be a tendency to shift from government bonds to other securities, thus reducing the price of outstanding government issues. Similarly, increasing demands for ordinary commercial bank loans, resulting from an increasing volume of business, greater speculative activity, or higher levels of cost and prices, would substantially increase the rate on government intermediate and short-term accommodations. A reduction in reserve ratios either because of an outflow of gold or a change of reserve requirements would also work in the same direction.

In the following computation we show what the interest charge would be on the aggregate indebtedness at varying rates of interest.

27 billions	(long-term) at 3 per cent	810	millions
5 "	(intermediate term) at 2 per cent .	100	"
1 "	(short-term) at ¼ per cent	2.5	"
	Total	912.5	"

27 billions	(long-term) at 3.5 per cent	945	millions
5 "	(intermediate term) at 2½ per cent	125	"
1 "	(short-term) at ½ per cent	5	"
	Total 1,075		"

27 billions	(long-term) at 4 per cent 1,080		millions
5 "	(intermediate term) at 3 per cent .	150	"
1 "	(short-term) at 1 per cent	10	"
	Total 1,240		"

It may also be noted that a flat rate of 3 1/4 per cent on the entire debt would mean an annual charge of 1,070 millions.

It is evident then that a refunded or consolidated

debt would probably involve annual interest charges—
even though all further increase in the debt be arrested
at the end of this year—of well over a billion dollars.
This is some 200 millions in excess of the estimate for
1937 and 300 millions above the actual outlays for
1936.

2. *Military pensions.* Apart from the special bonus
granted in 1936, military pensions have ranged around
600 million dollars in recent years. As noted above,
there is a carry-over item this year of 560 millions to be
paid to government trust funds as compensation for
cancellation of veterans' loans (not a recurring item).
The present level of outlay will doubtless be expanded
somewhat by increases in the amount of domiciliary care
and in rates of compensation for the disabled.[19] A more
important potential cause of increased payments lies in
the procuring of pensions for the widows of all veterans,
which is now an objective of the veterans' organizations.

Ultimately the magnitude of the pension bill will
depend upon whether "service pensions," which are
based upon age rather than disability, are secured. Estimates have been made which indicate that if service
pensions were granted on a basis comparable to those
of the past the outlays for veterans would rise to well
over a billion dollars in the next 15 or 20 years, and
possibly to as much as 2 billions. It is evident, therefore,
that future pension policy will have a very important
bearing on the budget situation. For the purpose of the
present analysis we shall assume that pensions will continue at approximately the existing level of 600 millions.

3. *National defense.* As the chart at page 301 indi-

---

[19] This has already been forecast by the head of the Veterans' Administration.

cates, expenditures for national defense ranged around
700 million dollars in the early thirties. The estimate
for 1937 is 920 millions, despite the substantial reduction in the cost of supplies and materials. This increase
is attributable to the assumed necessity of increasing
armaments in view of military programs elsewhere and
also to the desire to provide employment and promote
recovery. In other words, military outlays have been
incorporated as a feature of the Public Works program.
When this reason for large military outlays passes it
would seem that some reduction might be made in the
military budget even though the general situation with
respect to the possibilities of war remains unchanged.
However, in view of the high cost and rapid obsolescence
of modern armament, too much need not be expected.
Moreover, the present five-year program of providing
adequate defense does not suggest curtailment.

4. *Civil departments and agencies.* The possibility
of reducing expenditures in the civil departments and
agencies depends upon two factors—the gradual elimination or reduction of certain activities and a more economical administration of essential functions. It is undoubtedly possible to effect some reductions without
sacrificing efficiency or crippling necessary services; but
we are not prepared to suggest here the magnitude of
such economies.[20]

These four categories of expenditures constitute the
greater part of the regular or traditional outlays. Our
analysis has shown that one item—interest—seems certain to increase by something like 200 million dollars.
The other three are comparatively inflexible; but for
the sake of conservatism we shall assume that the econ-

---

[20] The Brookings Institution is at present engaged on a special investigation of this problem at the request of congressional committees.

omies which might be effected in these categories would be sufficient to offset the assured increase in interest.

5. *Social security.* The total listed under this heading in the 1937 budget is 405 million dollars; but this includes a special appropriation of 265 millions to an old-age reserve account, which transaction is not an actual expenditure but merely a method of setting up claims on the basis of which future benefits will be paid. For the fiscal year 1938, the expenditures under the Social Security Act are tentatively estimated at a little over 400 millions, exclusive of the provisions for old-age annuities.[21] While in the earlier years these expenditures may be more than offset by special revenues collected for the purpose of reserve accumulation, they must nevertheless be included in the gross expenditures of the government.

6. *Relief and emergency outlays.* It is apparent from the foregoing analysis that if the present level of 7,822 millions of gross expenditures is to be substantially reduced it must be accomplished chiefly in the classifications arising out of recent relief and emergency requirements. The extent to which these items can be reduced without serious consequences will depend in part upon the extent to which business improves and provides employment, in part upon the elimination of wasteful and extravagant outlays, and in part upon a more economical administration of essential relief. We have not made the investigations necessary to warrant a statement as to the extent to which reductions might be made in the

---

[21] The expenditures for annuities will be only a few millions annually in the next few years, but they rise to 143 millions in 1944, to 505 millions in 1950, and to a peak of about 3.5 billions in 1980. It is to be noted that about 1.5 billions of the amount required to cover these maximum expenditures will be derived from interest on reserve investments in government obligations.

various types of outlays. The magnitude and character of the problem involved may, however, be indicated by pointing out the extent of the reductions that would be required in order to reduce total expenditures to a level approximating that of estimated tax revenues.

In the following summary we indicate, on a purely arbitrary basis, the extent of the reductions which would be required in the relief and emergency classifications to bring total budget outlays down from around 7,800 million dollars to 6,000 millions.

	1937 Estimate	Assumed Reductions
	(In Millions)	
Relief (including WPA and CCC)	1,659	1,000
Agricultural aid	649	300
Public works	834	300
Aids to home owners	188	100
Miscellaneous	216	100
Total reductions		1,800

Estimated revenues for the budget year ending June 1937, exclusive of social security taxation, amount to 5,341 million dollars. With revenues continuing at this level and with reductions of expenditures as indicated above, we would still be over 600 million dollars short of balancing the budget and providing a sinking fund for purposes of gradual debt retirement.

In considering the practicability of bridging this gap by increasing taxes, it should be borne in mind that taxes will in any event substantially increase over present levels during the next few years in carrying out the requirements of the social security program. The present old-age annuity program calls for special collections estimated at 253 millions in the fiscal year 1937, 560 millions in 1938, and 714 millions in 1940, with the amount rising annually thereafter to as much as 1,877 millions in 1950.[22] Under the existing law it would be possible to use these revenues in meeting current government expenditures; but if they are thus diverted[23] the requirements for the security program will obviously not be currently fulfilled, and larger tax burdens will be in store for later years.

In the light of this scheduled increase in taxation for a specific purpose it is evident that in balancing the budget primary attention should be directed to the curtailment of expenditures. It will be recalled that 6 billions of federal taxes, plus 6 billions of state and local taxes, means 20 per cent of the existing national income.[24] If taxation at a level which might seriously impede economic activity and progress is to be avoided and if at the same time the contractual obligations arising out of the security program are to be met, it is obvious that in balancing the budget primary emphasis must be placed upon the drastic curtailment of the more flexible elements of expenditure.

The establishment of a sound fiscal situation thus still presents a problem which is of the first order of difficulty. To accomplish the goal will demand resolute resistance, on the part both of Congress and of the Administration, to pressures from many directions for increased appropriations; it will require the ruthless elimination of extravagant outlays for purposes which

---

[22] In addition to the 6 per cent payroll taxes for old-age benefits, there is also a tax on payrolls, increasing from one per cent in the calendar year 1936 to 3 per cent in 1938, levied for the purpose of unemployment insurance. However, the taxpayer may credit against this tax, up to 90 per cent of its amount, payments made to unemployment funds established under state law. The government is estimated to receive from this source in 1937 about 72 million dollars.

[23] See note on p. 284.

[24] See Chap. XII, p. 317.

cannot be justified on either economic or social grounds;
it will involve the overhauling of the whole system of
relief; and it will necessitate the introduction throughout the government organization of economies in the
administration of essential functions.

IV. FISCAL INFLATION?

The possibility of a serious breakdown of government finance still exists. We are still gambling, so to
speak, upon a sufficiently rapid growth in national income to permit a balancing of the budget before confidence in the credit of the government wanes. The continued ability of the Treasury—for reasons discussed
above—to obtain all the funds required at low rates of
interest has given rise to a false sense of security. We
are working on a very narrow margin; and adverse developments could quickly upset all present calculations.

There is always a tendency when predicted crises,
whether in business or public finance, are slow in reaching an acute stage, to assume that the dangers have
been grossly exaggerated, if indeed they are not altogether fanciful. Whether the present fiscal situation
will lead to a breakdown of government credit and a
disastrous period of inflation, no one can predict with
certainty. One may fairly conclude, however, that
though the task of establishing financial stability is not
insurmountable, it is one which cannot be taken lightly.
This discussion may therefore well be concluded by a
brief statement with reference to the process and effects
of fiscal inflation. What is involved in such inflation and
what are its practical consequences?

If confidence in the stability of government credit
is once severely shaken, and funds can no longer be
borrowed in the investment market, it will become nec-

essary for the Treasury to resort to other means of procuring the funds required. The Federal Reserve Banks might be required to advance the needed credits, or the Treasury might issue its own direct promissory notes in meeting its obligations.

Once either of these means of procuring funds was resorted to on a large scale, the value of the dollar would depreciate in the exchange markets. History is replete with illustrations of this natural phenomenon—*natural* because foreigners are unwilling to exchange goods at the same rate as before for currency of doubtful stability; and they cannot be compelled to do so. Exchange stabilization funds might for a short time prevent a depreciation of the dollar, but they could not ultimately check the downward movement.

Once out of hand the process of financial and economic disintegration is cumulative. The depreciation of the dollar leads to a "flight of capital" which exerts further direct and powerful pressure on the foreign exchange rate; it demoralizes international trading operations; it checks business investments involving longtime commitments; and it engenders wholesale speculation in real estate, in commodities, and in stock equities—the prices of which may be expected to rise. In order to prevent the dissipation, or evaporation, of liquid working capital, business corporations spend it in piling up inventories or in constructing additional plant and equipment without reference to market requirements. One half of a nation's business activity represents a desperate struggle to avoid or minimize losses —the other half an effort to capitalize on disaster and reap a speculative harvest.

An accompanying result of the mounting prices is the shrinkage in the value of incomes that are of a fixed character. The investments of individuals, business enterprises, and institutions, whether made directly in bonds and mortgages or through the intermediation of insurance companies, savings banks, or other investment agencies, progressively decline in purchasing power. Even those who shift from bonds to stocks and commodities cannot as a rule wholly escape the effects of the financial disintegration; they may win large paper profits for a time, but in the end they usually do not enjoy a *real* enhancement of wealth or income.

Nor can the wage-earning masses escape a degradation of living standards. Wages may be progressively raised as prices advance, but there is always a serious lag in the adjustment. Inevitably the distortion of productive activity that accompanies the inflation process means that the real standards of living of the masses will be adversely affected. National income—in terms of goods and services—is greatly reduced.

Assertions such as the foregoing are not the result of theoretical cogitations. They are based upon plain facts as recorded in historical incidents. A few statements summarizing the economic effects of actual inflationary movements will perhaps best serve to reveal their devastating character. The revolutionary war, as a matter of practical expediency, was largely financed by the issue of irredeemable paper money. By the end of the struggle the paper currency had become practically worthless, as is evident from the still surviving expression, "not worth a Continental." The effects are described by an historian of the time as follows:

The aged who had retired from the scene of active business, to enjoy the fruits of their industry, found their substance melting away to a mere pittance. . . . The widow who lived comfortably on the bequests of a deceased husband experienced a frustration of all his well-meant tenderness. . . . The blooming virgin who had grown up with an unquestionable title to a liberal patrimony was legally stripped of everything but her personal charms and virtues. The hapless orphan, instead of receiving from the hands of an executor a competency to set out in business, was obliged to give a final discharge on the payment of six pence in the pound. . . .[25]

The impossibility of controlling the value of the currency, as well as its demoralizing influence, is indicated in the following quotation:

Congress resolved [January 11, 1776] that "whoever should refuse to receive in payment Continental bills, etc., should be deemed and treated as an enemy of his country, and be precluded from all trade and intercourse with the inhabitants. . . ." This ruinous principle was continued in practice for five successive years, and appeared in all shapes and forms, i.e., in legal tender acts, in limitations of prices, in awful and threatening declarations, in penal laws with dreadful and ruinous punishments . . . and all executed with a relentless severity by the highest authorities then in being, viz., by Congress, by assemblies and conventions of the states, by committees of inspection, and even by military force; and though men of all descriptions stood trembling before this monster of force, without daring to lift a hand against it during all this period, yet its unrestrained energy ever proved ineffectual to its purposes . . . ; at best its utmost effect was like that of water sprinkled on a blacksmith's forge, which indeed deadens the flame for a moment, but never fails to increase the heat and force of the internal fire. . . .

It has polluted the equity of our laws; turned them into engines of oppression and wrong; corrupted the justice of our public administration; destroyed the fortunes of thousands who had most confidence in it, and has gone far to destroy the morality of our people."[26]

The ultimate consequences of paper money inflation in France in the period of the French Revolution have been summarized as follows:

[25] David Ramsay, *History of American Revolution* (1789), Vol. II, pp. 134-35.
[26] Pelatiah Webster, *Strictures on Tender Acts* (1780).

What the bigotry of Louis XIV and the shiftlessness of Louis XV could not do in nearly a century, was accomplished by this tampering with the currency in a few months. . . . The result was that capitalists declined to embark their means in business. Enterprise received a mortal blow. . . . The business of France dwindled into a mere living from hand to mouth. . . . With the masses of the people the purchase of every article of supply became a speculation. . . . Says the most brilliant apologist for French revolutionary statesmanship, "Commerce was dead; betting took its place."[27]

In the German inflation of 1920-23 the total volume of currency increased between August 1922 and the end of 1923 from the stupendous amount of 252 billion marks to the unimaginable total of 497 quintillian marks.

The stampede to spend (in place of the desire to save) only intensified the effects of inflation, for it simultaneously raised the prices of goods, and increased the velocity of circulation of money. Prices rose and the value of the mark declined, therefore, not only because of the violent increase in the quantity of money, but also because all the money in the country was kept in endless and rapid circulation. No one wanted to keep it; no one even considered saving it."[28]

The value of savings deposits and investments in bonds and mortgages, both public and private, was almost completely obliterated; and the German economy has not even now recovered from the economic and social consequences of the widespread financial ruin that was wrought.

The Confederate currency of the Civil War became utterly worthless. Even so modest an issue of irredeemable "greenbacks" by the United States government as 400 million dollars was accompanied by a depreciation

[27] Andrew D. White, *Paper Money Inflation in France.*
[28] Philip G. Wright, *Inflation and After* (published by the Duke Endowment, 1933).

of over 60 per cent at the maximum; and it was not until 14 years after the war was over that this currency became redeemable in gold and hence no longer a disturbing factor in the financial system.

In this analysis of the process of fiscal disorganization we have endeavored to give an extreme but nevertheless realistic picture of the ultimate consequences of an unrestricted "run-away" inflationary movement, arising out of fiscal and currency disorganization. To complete and to balance the story we must in conclusion note that sometimes governments have been able by heroic measures to halt a serious inflationary movement before it resulted in the disintegration of the entire economic system. For example, the French government in 1927 checked a disastrous fall in the franc by a financial program which involved sharp increases in taxes, already extremely onerous, and the stabilization of the franc at a level some 25 per cent lower than the hitherto prevailing rate. Even here the consequences both to taxpayers and owners of fixed income securities were serious; and there was left a legacy of economic distress and discontent which has remained to this day a potent source of social and political instability.

While it may thus prove possible in some cases to arrest the fateful process of fiscal inflation at some intermediate stage, such a result cannot be guaranteed. Once confidence in government credit is undermined, the forward pressures become well-nigh irresistible. To play along with an unbalanced budget is to play with fire. The only safe and sound financial procedure is to achieve fiscal stability *now*—while it is still possible.

CHAPTER XIX

INTERNATIONAL ECONOMIC POLICIES

The persistent lag of exports behind production is a major maladjustment in the American economic system. Our analysis has shown that while there has been a substantial recovery in the export trade since the bottom of the depression, the percentage of the national production that is exported remains substantially below that of 1929. The discrepancy between production and foreign trade is, moreover, a world phenomenon, resulting from the operation of certain powerful and persistent factors in international economic and financial relations.

The economic system of the United States is interlinked with that of the rest of the world through foreign trade, the investment of funds, and the operation of the monetary system. The changes in these relationships which have occurred during the course of the depression were revealed in earlier chapters. The task here is merely to indicate the bearing of these changes upon the recovery problem today.

I. THE IMPORTANCE OF FOREIGN TRADE

It has been frequently asserted in recent years that foreign trade is not of any great significance since its entire value represents but a small percentage of the value of the total national production. The reader will recall from the data given in Chapter XV that in 1929, when exports had reached their peak, their value accounted for only 6.4 per cent of the estimated total value of national product and 9.8 per cent of the total output of movable goods. In 1935, these percentages were, respectively, 4.3 and 7.5. It is argued, therefore, that even a complete cessation of export trade would make little difference in the scale of operation of the national economic machine, and that, therefore, a drastic diminution in the volume of exports could not materially affect the economic life of the country.

The fallacy inherent in this superficially plausible reasoning becomes immediately apparent if the relationship of the export trade to the operation of the national economic machine is examined in terms of specific industries. Many lines of activity are directly dependent upon the maintenance of a large export trade. In Chapter XV we showed the relation of exports to production in the cases of such commodities as cotton, tobacco, lard, canned fish, rice, wheat, oilcake, fresh and canned fruits, leather, rosin and turpentine, various petroleum products, sulphur, copper, automobiles, and a wide range of machinery, implements, and appliances. Many of these commodities were shipped abroad in 1929 in quantities representing from one-quarter to over one-half of total output. In more recent years, while both domestic consumption and exports declined, the latter still constituted a substantial, though in many instances reduced, share of total production. In addition to these outstanding articles of exportation, there are hundreds of others the exports of which, though less substantial in relation to total output, nevertheless constitute a sufficiently large share of the latter to affect the profitableness of operation in the industries concerned.

In the cases of some of these commodities, the decrease in exports has been much more responsible for the curtailment of total production than the decline in domestic consumption. To give a few striking examples, the reduction in the exports of cotton and tobacco between 1929 and 1935 accounted for nearly two-thirds of the decline in the total production of these commodities. The drop in the exports of rice, kerosene, and some other products was greater than the entire diminution of total output.

All these branches of production are geared to a scale of operations yielding an output far in excess of domestic consumption requirements. A decline in exports imposes upon them, therefore, the choice between two painful adjustments. If full production is continued in the face of shrinking foreign markets, stocks pile up, prices decline, and incomes are depressed. If production is curtailed, idle capacity increases, unemployment ensues, and incomes are again depressed.

Depression in the exporting industries, resulting from decreased exports, has far-reaching repercussions throughout the entire economic system. The decline in the income of those producers who depend for their prosperity upon adequate exports reduces their purchasing power for the products of all branches of production. If cotton planters, or tobacco growers, or hog raisers and processors, or the owners and employees of the various mining and machine manufacturing industries find their incomes diminished, their ability to purchase the products of those industries which work primarily for the domestic market becomes correspondingly smaller. Relative over-production and the resulting price declines, or, alternatively, curtailment of production and ensuing unemployment, quickly appear in these latter industries. The vicious spiral of business depression, though it may have its inception in the industries dependent upon exports, inexorably extends its effects to the whole mechanism of national production. Furthermore, trade involves a large number of facilitating services. Railway traffic, shipping, port activity, and banking and merchandising organizations are caught in the vicious spiral of depression when the volume of foreign trade declines.

Thus the country's economic machine does not operate in such a way that a small portion of it, representing 5 or 7 or 10 per cent of the total output, produces only goods and services connected with the export trade, while the remainder, working independently, produces wholly for the domestic market. If this were true, it might have been possible to slow down or even stop entirely the operation of the part of the machine which is concerned with exports and leave the remainder functioning as efficiently as before. But the fact is that the exporting industries and the facilitating services involved in the export trade operate for both the foreign and the domestic markets; and when they are depressed through loss of foreign markets the effects are felt throughout the whole national economic system.

The reduced volume of exports is responsible for a substantial share of continuing unemployment in the United States. The number of gainfully employed workers in the United States in 1929 was estimated at 47 millions. Since during that year the value of exports constituted 6.4 per cent of the estimated total national product, roughly 3 million persons were directly engaged in production for foreign markets. Allowing for necessary adjustments, the number of persons so engaged in 1935 was probably no more than 1.5 millions.

Imports are also essential to the economic well-being of the nation, both intrinsically and as a necessary counterpart of the export trade. They represent in part raw materials which are indispensable for many branches of American industry and foodstuffs and other products necessary for balanced national consumption. Some of these commodities cannot be produced at all within the country, because of accidents of natural endowment or climatic conditions. Others may be produced, but either in insufficient quantities or of inferior quality. In part, imports also consist of commodities which are produced both in the United States and in some foreign countries, but less efficiently here than abroad. To the extent to which such imports are permitted to enter the country, even on the basis of a reasonable degree of tariff protection for the domestic producers, they force upon the latter the need of improving their technical production methods, result in lower cost of such products to the consumers, and thus lead to greater consumption.

American purchases abroad represent the creation in the hands of foreigners of the means of payment for their purchases of American products. Trade is thus necessarily a two-way affair. American exports can take place only when foreign purchasers have the means with which to pay for them. And while such means of payment may be created in several different ways, in practice imports constitute the most important single element in this process.

The disappearance or a sudden and drastic reduction of foreign trade imposes upon a nation the need of far-reaching reorganization and readjustment, which are inexorably involved in any plans for economic isolation. In order to approach a condition of "autarchy," under some scheme of economic nationalism, it is necessary for a nation to curtail imports and by that very process to forego exports. The elimination of imports will mean that some indispensable commodities formerly obtained abroad will become unavailable, except in so far as substitutes may be developed to take their place—usually at a very high cost to the consumer. Labor and resources rendered idle by the curtailment or disappearance of exports may theoretically be employed in the production of such substitutes. But in any event the net result of such a process will be the curtailment of those branches of production in which the country has developed a relatively greater degree of efficiency and an expansion of those branches in which previous efforts had failed to secure a similar degree of efficiency. This will inevitably impair the effectiveness of the economic machine and thus reduce standards of living for the nation as a whole.

II. TRADE EXPANSION THROUGH TRADE AGREEMENTS

The volume of foreign trade depends upon two primary factors. In the first place, fluctuations in general business conditions within any country are certain to produce, under normal conditions, an expanding or contracting effect upon both production and international trade. In the second place, the volume of international trade is powerfully affected by the character and extent of governmental regulation of trade movements. The fact that during the period of deepening depression international trade declined relatively more than production and that during the years of the recovery trade has continued to lag behind production has been due primarily to the existence of extraordinary barriers to world commerce which have sprung up since 1929.

The United States has both contributed to the impairment of a proper functioning of the mechanism of international trade and fallen victim to similar action on the part of other countries. The enactment of the Hawley-Smoot Tariff at the outset of the depression was an important stimulus to the growth of exaggerated protectionism everywhere in the world—both as an example and as an occasion for retaliatory action. Many other factors combined to produce the protectionist race which developed with startling rapidity as the depression unfolded itself; and in this race the United States, formerly the greatest prototype of trade protectionism, was soon far outstripped by some other countries, which were using more drastic and more effective techniques.

In the acute stage of the depression, as was pointed out in Chapter II, most of the nations of the world in rapid succession abandoned the gold standard and resorted to a wide variety of trade restrictions of almost unprecedented severity. Increased customs duties; quotas and other forms of quantitative regulation; foreign exchange controls; competitive currency depreciation; clearing, compensation, and payment agreements and arrangements; subsidies of various kinds; attempts to balance trade bilaterally between pairs of countries; the application of discriminatory treatment of goods originating in different countries—all served to obstruct the movements of goods across national frontiers and to divert the currents of trade from their accustomed channels of natural advantage.

The destructive effects of these policies upon world trade in 1931 and 1932 led to an international movement for the re-establishment of the gold standard and the removal of other obstructions to international trade. The World Monetary and Economic Conference of June 1933 was, however, disrupted by the decision of the United States government to embark upon a policy of currency depreciation and monetary management. The result was to intensify and prolong the period of monetary instability and international trade restrictions. Whether under the conditions then existing the high hopes entertained for a rapid rehabilitation of the world economic structure would have been realized is a question which need not here be considered. In any case, the breakdown of the World Economic Conference delayed for some little time the inauguration of policies designed to promote the recovery of international trade. A far-reaching change in the commercial policy of the United States occurred with the adoption of the Trade Agreements Act of June 12, 1934. By means of this act, Congress authorized the President, for a period of three years, to enter into trade agreements with foreign governments and, in connection with such agreements, to modify customs duties, to impose new import restrictions, and to bind, against change, for the period of a particular agreement, the existing customs treatment accorded the commodities specified in the agreement. The President may not, however, increase or decrease any duty by more than 50 per cent, and he may not transfer any article from the dutiable to the free list or vice versa.

The Trade Agreements Act constitutes an explicit recognition of two basic ideas. The first is that an expansion of exports is indispensable to economic prosperity in the United States. In the preamble to the act, the expansion of foreign markets for the products of the United States is described as "a means of assisting in the present emergency in restoring the American standard of living, in overcoming domestic unemployment and the present economic depression, in increasing the purchasing power of the American public, and in establishing and maintaining a better relationship among various branches of American agriculture, industry, mining, and commerce."

The second principle is that an inextricable interconnection exists between exports and imports. The President is authorized to exercise the powers granted him "whenever he finds as a fact that any existing duties or other import restrictions of the United States or any foreign country are unduly burdening and restricting the foreign trade of the United States" and to enter into negotiations with foreign governments in order that "foreign markets will be made available to those branches of American production which require and are capable of developing such outlets by affording corresponding market opportunities for foreign products in the United States."

Prior to the adoption of the Trade Agreements Act, the United States was the only commercially important country which continued to fix its customs duties by unilateral action rather than through a process of negotiation with the countries which supply the imports affected by such duties. As a result, this country was not in a position to seek modifications of customs duties and other trade restrictions imposed by foreign countries upon American exports. The act represented a change from an "autonomous" to a "conventional" tariff system, thus bringing American commercial policy in line with the principles which had long ago become dominant in the contractual trade relations of the world.

Each trade agreement negotiated under the authority of the act consists of three parts. There is, first, the list of commodities imported into the United States on which duty concessions—in the form of reductions or bindings—are granted to the foreign country in question. Second, there is a similar list of commodities exported from the United States on which the other party to the agreement grants concessions to American trade— in the form of duty reductions or bindings, better quota treatment, and so forth. Finally, there is a set of general provisions which embody various undertakings on the part of the signatories with regard to administrative and other kinds of treatment accorded to each other's trade, as well as safeguards relating to future contingencies. The preparation and negotiation of a trade agreement is a task of great complexity. The final decisions are made on the basis of exhaustive factual studies prepared by a series of committees, consisting of representatives of the Departments of State, Treasury, Commerce, and Agriculture, and the Tariff Commission. The co-ordination of this inter-departmental organization and the primary responsibility for the actual negotiations devolve upon the Department of State. By means of written presentations and public hearings, full opportunity is provided for business groups and all other interested persons to present their views.

In entering upon negotiations with a particular country, the government of the United States transmits to the other government a list of American exports to that country with respect to which the existing duties, quotas, or other devices are considered to be particularly restrictive to trade and with respect to which, therefore, an improvement in the existing treatment is desired. The government of the other country transmits to the government of the United States a similar list of requests for duty concessions. Each agreement thus represents a direct attack upon those trade barriers in the two countries which are particularly obstructive to their mutual trade. This is one of the principal advantages of the method of bilateral negotiations for the adjustment of restrictions upon international trade, as well as one of the important reasons why the bilateral agreement method was chosen in preference to unilateral downward revision of the tariff.

Another important reason for the choice of the

method now being employed was that under the unilateral method there would have been no assurance that a general reduction of tariff duties by this country would have been followed by similar action on the part of other countries. Bilateral agreements, on the other hand, by their very nature result in a reduction of trade barriers by all the countries with which such agreements are concluded.

When a sufficient number of agreements have been negotiated, consideration will have been given to practically all the commodities listed in the American tariff schedules. Action, possibly no less comprehensive in scope than a general tariff revision, will have been taken, but on the basis of far more adequate information than is available to Congress when it undertakes this task, and with at least as great a degree of care in safeguarding the economic interests of the country. And in addition, each agreement will constitute a potent instrument for the reopening of foreign markets to American exports.

The choice of the bilateral method imposed the need of a far-reaching decision with regard to the so-called most-favored-nation principle. It seldom happens that a particular commodity is supplied to a country exclusively by another single country. Usually there are several supplying countries. Hence, in reducing a duty on a particular commodity in a bilateral trade agreement, a country has to decide the kind of treatment it will accord to the other supplying countries. The Trade Agreements Act provides that any duties reduced by virtue of an agreement with any country shall apply to imports of the commodities concerned from all countries, except that the President is empowered to deny the reduced duties to countries which discriminate against American commerce, or are guilty of acts or policies which in his opinion tend to defeat the purposes of the act.

This adoption of a policy based upon the unconditional most-favored-nation principle was dictated by eminently practical considerations. The underlying purpose of the trade agreements program is the creation of conditions under which international trade will be able to expand and under which American exporters will be able to obtain a fair share of the increased total. The first of these objectives requires a reduction of trade barriers. The second can be achieved only if American traders find themselves on a footing of equality with their foreign competitors; and the most-favored-nation principle is the sole practicable instrument for assuring such equality.

Under the operation of that principle, American exporters can have full assurance that their competitive position in any particular market will not be impaired by adverse discrimination, since the application of the principle means that whenever a concession is granted by that country to any country, the benefits of that concession will immediately and automatically be extended to American products. And in order to demand and obtain such equality of treatment for American trade it was obviously necessary for the United States to grant other countries similar equality. Hence the adoption of the unconditional most-favored-nation policy.

Up to the end of 1936, fifteen trade agreements had been negotiated under the authority of the act—one in 1934, eight in 1935, and six in 1936—and all but one were in full effect and operation. The fifteen countries with which these agreements have been negotiated are as follows:

Country	Signed	Effective
Cuba .... Aug. 24, 1934	Sept. 3, 1934
Brazil .... Feb. 2, 1935	Jan. 1, 1936
Belgium .... Feb. 27, 1935	May 1, 1935
Haiti .... Mar. 28, 1935	June 3, 1935
Sweden .... May 25, 1935	Aug. 5, 1935
Colombia .... Sept. 13, 1935	May 20, 1936
Canada .... Nov. 15, 1935	Jan. 1, 1936
Honduras .... Dec. 18, 1935	Mar. 2, 1936
The Netherlands, including Netherland India, Netherland Guiana, and Netherland West Indian Islands .... Dec. 20, 1935	Feb. 1, 1936
Switzerland .... Jan. 9, 1936	Feb. 15, 1936
Nicaragua .... Mar. 11, 1936	Oct. 1, 1936
Guatemala .... Apr. 24, 1936	June 15, 1936
France and its colonies, dependencies, and protectorates other than Morocco. May 6, 1936	June 15, 1936
Finland .... May 18, 1936	Nov. 2, 1936
Costa Rica .... Nov. 28, 1936	1

All of these agreements, with the exception of that with Cuba, are based on the most-favored-nation principle.[2] The concessions granted in them have so far been generalized to all countries except Germany and Australia, which are deemed to be discriminating against American trade. Each agreement provides for substantial duty reductions or other methods of mitigating the existing trade barriers.

The following figures indicate approximately the extent of tariff revision achieved in the United States as a result of the agreements: Exclusive of Cuba, the trade

---

[1] Thirty days from date of exchange of instruments of approval and ratification.

[2] The agreement with Cuba, because of the peculiar historic association between that country and the United States, is based on the principle of preferential treatment.

agreements which were in effect at the end of 1936 contained 386 duty reductions; 20 bindings of duties; and 81 bindings on the free list. The value of the commodities subject to duty reductions constituted about 20 per cent of the total value of dutiable imports into the United States; the bindings represented about 35 per cent of the total value of duty-free imports. The liberalization of trade restrictions by the other signatories to the agreements was fully as substantial.

The trade agreements thus represent a sizable break in the multitude of trade diverting and trade destroying restrictions which arose out of the disorganization produced by the depression. It is of course too early to appraise the effects upon the American economic system as a whole. But there can be no doubt that the substantial reductions in trade barriers which are being effected are reopening the channels of international trade. At the same time the reassertion by the United States of the unconditional most-favored-nation principle is laying the foundation for a return to a régime of equal treatment in international commercial relations on the basis of which international trade had, in the past, attained its greatest and most fruitful development.

III. TRADE POLICY AND DEBT RECEIPTS

So far we have considered foreign trade in its bearing upon the general economic situation in the United States. But foreign trade also has a vital significance in connection with the country's international financial relations and its creditor-debtor position. It is an important element in the process by means of which the United States, as a net creditor nation, receives payments on its foreign investments.

In that process, interest and dividend payments to

Americans must, generally speaking, be made in dollars, since that is the currency in which American private investors or the American Treasury as creditor on the war-debt account can utilize income. Foreign debtors, on the other hand, initially have in their possession their own currencies, which they must convert into dollars in order to meet their obligations in the United States. This transfer process can operate only if there is available abroad a volume of dollar exchange over and above the volume required to meet all other foreign payments to the United States.

There are four principal ways in which dollar exchange in excess of non-debt payment requirements can become available for debt payments. These are: (1) when Americans import more goods than they export; (2) when Americans buy more services from foreigners than they sell to foreigners; (3) when more gold is imported into the United States than is exported from the country; and (4) when new American loans to foreigners exceed the flow of foreign funds into the United States. It is obviously not necessary that all four of these conditions be fulfilled simultaneously; it is merely necessary that the net result of all these operations be such as to enable foreigners to obtain a sufficiently large number of dollars to meet both their debt and non-debt payments to Americans. The manner in which this net result is brought about may, however, be of the utmost importance.

As we saw in Chapter XV, during the decade 1926-35 the commodity trade of the United States showed an invariable excess of exports over imports, while service operations, exclusive of debt receipts and payments, showed an excess of payments over receipts. The net payments to foreigners on the service accounts were, in each year except 1934, greater than the import balance on the commodity account; but they fell short, in each year, of the amounts actually transmitted to the United States on account of current net interest and dividend payments.

The difference was not made up by means of gold shipments to the United States, except in 1934 and 1935. In 1926, 1927, 1929, 1930, and 1931, gold imports into the United States exceeded exports, but the net inward shipments of the metal were sufficient to meet only a part of the foreign requirements of dollar exchange for the purpose of debt payments. During the other three years of the period, gold exports from the United States exceeded imports. For the whole eight years, there was a total export surplus of gold amounting to nearly 300 million dollars. Only in 1934-35 were gold imports more than sufficient to enable foreigners to meet their payment requirements to the United States.

Except for the years 1934 and 1935, net exports of American capital constituted the source from which foreigners obtained the dollars with which to meet the deficiency in their total payments to the United States. Without this net outflow of American funds, one of three things would have happened: either debt payments to the United States would have broken down; or exports would have declined in relation to imports; or gold would have steadily flowed to the United States to the detriment of monetary and financial stability in other countries. During the years 1934 and 1935, it was net imports of gold and silver that rendered possible a continuation of substantial receipts on the debt account and the maintenance of a relatively large export surplus in the merchandise trade.

At the present time, with the war-debt instalments almost entirely in suspension and with payments on a substantial portion of the private debts in default, our net receipts on the various debt accounts are on a level of approximately 400 million dollars a year. While from an economic point of view the interests of the United States and of the world would be best served by a complete and formal elimination of the war debts, it is not improbable that, for political reasons, some readjustment of war-debt settlements will be made and payments on that account resumed on some reduced scale. This would add to the volume of the country's net debt receipts.

The volume of collections will also expand if conditions in the debtor countries and international monetary and financial relations improve sufficiently to permit the resumption of some of the payments which are now in default. Finally, the improvement of these conditions and relations is likely to cause an outflow from the United States of foreign funds which have entered the country in recent years. This would diminish the amount of debt payments made by Americans to foreigners and thus serve to increase still further the volume of net debt receipts by the United States.

It may be anticipated that the net payments to foreigners on service operations will increase and thus serve to offset in part the increased net receipts on the debt account. But it is not likely that in the future, as in the past, the outlays of our citizens for tourist expenditures, shipping charges, immigrant remittances, and other services will be sufficiently large to provide a vehicle for the transfer of debt receipts and at the same time permit the maintenance of a substantial export surplus in the merchandise trade. Nor is it to be anticipated that net imports of gold will solve our balance of payments problem as they did in 1934-35. It is more likely that sooner or later the abnormal flow of gold into the United States which is taking place during the present disturbed condition of the world will turn into an outflow.

In practice, there are only two ways in which we can, in the future, get payment on our foreign investments. The first is by expanding imports faster than exports in our merchandise trade. The second is by a resumption of lending. Looking at the matter realistically, the solution probably lies in developments along both of these lines.

As was shown in the preceding two sections of this chapter, an expansion of exports is indispensable to full recovery and continued economic prosperity in the United States. At the same time, a complete loss or even a substantial impairment of our huge private investment abroad—which would be inevitable if we were to refuse to make it possible for our debtors to secure the means of meeting their payments—would scarcely be conducive to either full recovery or prosperity in this country. Theoretically, we can safeguard our foreign investments by a forcible reduction of exports below the level of imports by means of a drastic system of trade control, but that would involve sacrificing trade advantages for debt collection. The constructive solution calls for an expansion of both exports and imports, with the latter increasing somewhat more rapidly.

It is doubtful, however, that any practicable policy can be devised which will bring about, within a short period of time, a relatively more rapid increase of imports than of exports. Such a development, if it is to help rather than hurt, can come about only gradually. Under these conditions, it may be desirable for the United States to bridge the gap through the resumption of foreign lending on private account. There are several factors which tend, in any event, to favor a resumption of foreign lending by American citizens. There is in this country an unquestionable abundance of loanable funds. It appears probable that relatively low interest rates will persist for some time to come. There is a legitimate and pressing need for new capital in many parts of the world. These various factors are likely to create a desire among American investors for new foreign lending as soon as economic and monetary conditions abroad provide an adequate basis for new loans.

To be sure, pre-depression experience in the field of international finance is a strong reminder of the need of far greater care in the choice of foreign investment than was exercised in the past, and it is probable that the lessons of the recent defaults are sufficiently vivid to render unlikely a repetition of the frenzied international finance of the twenties. Moreover, governmental action may be helpful in providing adequate machinery for better scrutiny of foreign flotations with a view to avoiding the unloading of worthless securities upon American investors. Such machinery, in fact, exists in the form of the Securities and Exchange Commission.

It is extremely doubtful that governmental action should go further than the activities of the Commission and assume the form of official control over foreign lending, as has been suggested on many occasions in recent years. So long as foreign lending proceeds with reasonable moderation, action on the part of the government designed to impede or deny to legitimate foreign borrowers access to the American capital market would harm rather than promote the best interests of this country and of the world as a whole. We must bear in mind, however, that loans cannot provide a permanent solution. While a certain amount of new lending may be helpful in order to make our foreign trade and our net creditor position positive factors in promoting full economic recovery, in the end difficulties can be avoided only if our commercial policy develops along the lines of creating conditions in which both exports and imports can develop as freely and as fully as possible. From this point of view, the commercial policy which is being put into effect under the Trade Agreements program is unquestionably an important step in the right direction.

IV. MONETARY RELATIONS

Both an expansion of foreign trade and a satisfactorily functioning system of international financial relations require stability of foreign exchange rates. These rates are the ratios at which the various national monetary units exchange for each other. They are important for two primary reasons. The first is that they render possible pecuniary calculations involved in international commercial and financial transactions in the absence of a single monetary unit for all countries. The second reason is that they constitute a vital element in determining the terms of commercial competition between producers and traders in various countries.

When a time obligation to pay is created within a country as a result of any kind of transaction, there is no question as to the number of monetary units which that obligation may represent at the time it matures.

A promise to pay one thousand dollars three months hence will represent one thousand dollars when it falls due, provided the entire transaction is confined to the United States. The worst that could happen would be a change in the purchasing power of each unit. This is not the case, however, when the creation and the discharging of a time obligation to pay involves a creditor and a debtor separated by a national frontier.

For example, when an American cotton planter sells a shipment of his product to a buyer in England, he receives in payment, typically, a bill of exchange, under the terms of which his debtor undertakes to pay him, within 90 days, a certain number of pounds sterling. By knowing the exchange ratio which exists between the pound and the dollar on the day on which the bill is drawn, the American seller knows how many dollars he is to receive. Obviously the number of dollars which the bill represents will be the same on the day of maturity as on the day on which the transaction took place only if the ratio between the pound and the dollar is the same. If the ratio changes in the interval before maturity, one or the other of the parties to the transaction sustains a loss. When such changes occur at frequent intervals and are of substantial magnitude, the risks of trade become so great as to lead to an inevitable contraction of the volume of trade. The same considerations apply to payments involved in financial transactions.

When a country depreciates its currency there is an immediate alteration in the rates at which its monetary unit exchanges for the monetary units of other countries. As a result, its exporters find it possible to lower their prices in terms of other currencies. For example, before the dollar was depreciated and its exchange rate in terms of the French franc was one to 25, an article sold in France for 25 francs brought the American seller one dollar. After the dollar was depreciated by 40 per cent, the exchange rate in terms of the franc became one to 15. Hence it became possible for the American exporter to sell his commodity in France for 15 francs and still get one dollar.

The advantage thus acquired by the country which depreciates its currency tends to be sooner or later destroyed by a number of factors. The depreciation causes a rise in the prices of imported and, to some extent, of exported commodities, and may set into operation other forces which tend to raise commodity prices in general. Thus the competitive advantages of the depreciation are gradually offset. Other countries may retaliate, either by lowering their prices, or by depreciating their currencies, or by establishing special barriers to imports from countries with depreciated currencies. The net result is a disorganization of trade and its inevitable contraction.

At this stage, it is no longer necessary to discuss the question whether or not instability of foreign exchanges resulting from currency depreciation has, in its domestic effects, advantages which outweigh its disastrous effects upon international trade and financial relations. In the light of the evolution of monetary policy in the United States, outlined in Chapter XVI, and of similar developments in other countries, it is clear that the world is moving toward a re-establishment of a system of stable foreign exchanges. There is today almost as universal a recognition of the vital need for exchange stability as there was prior to the time when, under the impact of the depression, the ideas of monetary management in terms of purely domestic factors gained widespread support and were actually put to the test of application in a number of countries.

There is a similar unanimity of opinion that the only practicable way to re-establish foreign exchange rates on a basis of stability is through the restoration of an international gold standard. Such a standard will once more become operative when each country again defines by law the fixed gold content of its monetary unit and permits gold to be obtained freely in exchange for currency for purposes of international payments and to be freely shipped abroad. When these conditions are fulfilled, the cost of shipping gold between any two countries will again become the determining factor in fixing the narrow limits beyond which the exchange ratio between the monetary units of the countries concerned cannot fluctuate.

The arrangements made in September and October 1936 in connection with the devaluation of the "gold bloc" currencies represented an important forward stride in the world's progress toward the restoration of a gold standard. That action has greatly mitigated the grave economic consequences which had resulted from the dispersion of the gold values of the principal national monetary units, the extent of which was indicated in Chapter XVI. In the words of one competent observer,

. . . certain rigidly antagonistic elements in the previous situation have been eliminated. What we can say today is that in the place of opposing systems difficult to reconcile, we now have a state of general flux—a sort of common, though still fluid, denominator for the main currencies of the world. The situation has become malleable.[3]

---

[3] F. H. Fentener van Vlissingen (president of the International Chamber of Commerce), "Currency Adjustment and Trade Barriers," *World Trade*, November 1936.

The final restoration of a fully functioning international gold standard still requires the solution of many technical problems as well as the determination of many important questions of policy. Action along these lines cannot be taken by any one country alone, but requires concerted measures by the principal countries. In this process the United States has an important role to play along the lines already laid down by the recent evolution of our monetary policy.

CHAPTER XX
WAGE AND PRICE POLICIES

Although government policies have come to exert an increasingly important influence over economic affairs, it remains true that the American economic system is operated by private business managers who direct labor and capital to the production of goods and services for sale in the markets. The absorption of the unemployed and the attainment of complete economic recovery, as well as the promotion of further economic progress, thus depend largely upon policies pursued in the realm of private enterprise. Accordingly, attention must now be focussed upon certain factors, tendencies, policies, and requirements in the broad field of industry and labor, which may have an important bearing upon economic developments in the years immediately ahead.

There is universal agreement with respect to the desired goal, namely, progressive improvement in the standards of living of the masses of the people. Wide differences of view exist, however, as to what is involved, economically, in accomplishing this objective. The first essential in clarifying the problem is to establish a groundwork of fact with reference to present standards of living and the production requirements involved in the attainment of higher standards. For this purpose it will be necessary to recapitulate some of the results reached in the analyses of earlier chapters.

I. LIVING STANDARDS AND PRODUCTION REQUIREMENTS

The plane of living in the United States may be roughly and summarily indicated as follows: The national income is estimated for the year 1936 at approximately 60 billion dollars—equivalent on a comparable price basis to about six-sevenths that of 1929. If it were divided equally among the entire population each person would receive about $470—the equivalent of about $1,800 per family. If all the unutilized labor power in 1936 had been employed in productive enterprise the national income would have been increased by not more than 20 per cent, giving a total of something like 72 billion dollars.[1]

If a national income of 72 billion dollars were distributed equally it would amount to about $2,200 per family. But since income is not divided equally the great majority of families would receive substantially less than this average—probably not more than $1,500, while many would receive far less than this amount.[2] It is evident without argument that a family income of $1,500 is sufficient to provide little more than minimum necessities. A level of income at least double this amount is essential for what is ordinarily regarded as a "reasonably satisfactory" standard of living; and even such a level cannot be accepted as the ultimate goal of society.

The goods and services required for the satisfaction of human wants flow from the productive process. Hence if we are to gauge what is involved in raising standards of living we must analyze the production side of the problem. The first fact to be clearly apprehended is that a great economic conflagration, such as that through which we have recently passed, inevitably carries with it

---

[1] This rough method of estimating undoubtedly exaggerates the possible increase in production—for it assumes that the average level of efficiency would not be reduced as the unemployed were absorbed. The figure is low as compared with 1929 potential capacity because of the reduction in hours.

[2] In 1929, for which year we have more detailed data than for 1936, average family incomes amounted to over $2,600, on the price level then existing; but the great majority of families received incomes of less than $1,800. (See *America's Capacity to Consume*, p. 52.)

a material reduction in the producing capacity of the economic machine. Existing plant and equipment deteriorate for want of adequate maintenance expenditures; and the growth of new plant and equipment is largely suspended. Meanwhile, however, population continues to grow at about the usual rate; hence, as measured on a per capita basis, producing power appears less adequate still.

While we have emerged from the depth of the depression, we are still far below the levels of production attained in 1929. Industrial output is still some 10 per cent below the plane of 1929—although we have had in the last seven years a 5 per cent increase in population. On a per capita basis we are operating at roughly 85 per cent of the pre-depression level.

Thus the minimum production task before us now is: (1) to make good the actual deterioration of plant and equipment sustained during the depression; (2) to increase productive capital in line with the growth in population; and (3) to expand the production of consumption goods in accordance with this growth of population. In our investigations we have endeavored to gauge the magnitude of the production requirements involved in the fulfillment of such a program. For the purpose in hand we tentatively set as a goal, to be achieved in five years, a per capita level of production (and consumption) equal to that of 1929. In other words, we assumed that it would probably take five years to re-establish per capita production on the pre-depression plane.

The production requirements for carrying out such a program may be briefly recapitulated as follows: In the durable goods industries it would be necessary to produce at the rate of approximately 33 billion dollars annually from 1937 to 1941. This is in comparison with an actual production of about 21 billion dollars in 1936 and an average production between 1925 and 1929 of about 25 billion dollars.[3] In other words, to make good accumulated deficiencies and provide for the needs of an expanding population, we should have to produce in the field of durable goods during the next five years at a rate 60 per cent higher than the present rate and one-third higher than the level attained in the boom period 1925-29.[4]

What would such a production program mean in terms of employment? Our analysis shows that it would require the full-time employment of from 8 to 9 million additional workers annually over the next five years. At the same time a considerable increase in the output of non-durable goods would be necessary to restore the 1929 per capita level of consumption. Hence the production requirements—on the basis of present working hours—appear more than sufficient to absorb the entire volume of existing unemployment.[5]

II. LIVING STANDARDS AND WORKING HOURS

The large volume of unemployment which has persisted even during the recovery period has not unnaturally suggested to many people that a remedy must be sought in the form of shorter working hours. This point

[3] The actual figure is about 30 billions; but since prices then averaged more than 15 per cent higher than the present level the dollar figure has been reduced accordingly.

[4] The figures are conservative, representing minimum requirements. For detailed analysis, see Chap. VIII.

[5] Our analysis of the volume of unemployed labor power—counting not only outright unemployment but part-time work as well, indicates the equivalent, on a full-time basis, of approximately 9.5 million men in 1936. The computation is based on the assumption of an average working week in industry of from 42 to 43 hours. For detailed analysis see Chaps. VI, VII, and IX.

of view has been strengthened by the fact that employment in manufacturing production has for some years been practically stationary. For example, during the period of expansion from 1923 to 1929 the number of workers employed showed virtually no change, although the output of manufacturing industries increased by about 25 per cent. This tendency has continued during the course of the depression. Such a development seems to suggest that an increasing volume of unemployment is an inevitable accompaniment of technological advancement and that the only solution is rapid decreases in working hours. This policy also finds support in the philosophy that we have reached the age of plenty and that we suffer from or are threatened with chronic overproduction.

As a background for considering the present situation it may be recalled that between 1900 and 1929 per capita production and income in the United States increased by about 38 per cent, while the length of the working day in industrial lines was reduced by about 13 per cent. The people thus received the benefits of increasing efficiency partly in the form of greater leisure, but more largely in the form of increased incomes. In 1929 the length of the working week in industrial activities, generally, averaged close to 49 hours. Since 1929 it has been reduced to an average of about 40 hours, or by roughly 20 per cent.

As an outgrowth of the unemployment situation there has recently been evolved a policy regarded by its exponents as of vital significance to labor. It is enunciated as a definite principle that working hours should be reduced at the present juncture sufficiently to absorb the existing unemployment,[6] and that henceforth they

[6] In a pamphlet published by the American Federation of Labor in support of the 30-hour week the following argument is made: "For

should be systematically reduced in proportion to increases in productive efficiency. What would be the economic results of such a policy upon living standards and what would be its bearing upon recovery?

If the principle of reducing ████ hours in proportion to increases in productive efficiency had been in operation between 1900 and 1929 it would have meant that *all* of the gains resulting from the increase in productive efficiency would have had to be realized in the form of greater leisure—none in the form of higher standards of living. If such a plan were to be put into operation now with a view to absorbing existing unemployment it would mean that the volume of national production would be frozen at its present low level—concretely, at about $470 per capita. If the principle of reducing working hours in the future in direct proportion to increasing efficiency were adopted and enforced there could henceforth be no increase in production per worker or in living standards.

The advocates of this principle are apparently quite unconscious of its implications from the standpoint of production. The confusion of mind arises from concentration of attention upon *money income* to the exclusion of everything else. What is seen is that if the working week is shortened sufficiently to absorb unemployment, but without any reduction in weekly wages per person, the total volume of money flowing to the laboring population would be increased. What is not seen is that the

---

every 100 units of product turned out by an average factory worker in 1919, 171 are turned out today in the same amount of time. In 1919 the average work week in our factories was 52¼ hours. With a 71 per cent increase in the worker's producing capacity, work which took about 52 hours in 1919 can now be done in 30 hours." (William Green, *The Thirty Hour Week*, p. 32.)

This policy is apparently incorporated in a bill recently prepared by Senator O'Mahoney for the regulation of industrial corporations.

expenditure of this increased money income in the markets would not bring forth any larger volume of goods and services—since the very process by which the increased volume of money income is made available prevents any increase in production. We would have on the one side an increasing flow of money into trade channels; but on the other side a flow of goods and services of unchanging magnitude. The certain outcome would be rising prices. By the very nature of the plan real income—in terms of goods and services—would have to remain stationary. Labor would merely obtain increased leisure.

It is also assumed that this plan assures, in any event, a more "equitable participation in the output of industry." Even the most "equitable" distribution of a fixed and limited national income of 60 billion dollars would not enable labor to obtain any significant increase in real wages. If the profits of 1936 were completely diverted to employees the increase accruing to each working-class family would be less than $150. It is, moreover, by no means certain that the plan would lead to an increase in wages at the expense of profits. The rise in prices might leave profits much the same as before.

The adoption of this plan as a means of absorbing present unemployment would, however, undoubtedly lead to a different distribution of real income among the laboring groups themselves. Those who would secure employment as a result of the scheme would of course receive an increase in money income and in real purchasing power. On the other hand, those who now have jobs would find their real purchasing power reduced as a result of rising prices. Putting the matter more directly, since a larger number of workers would have claims against an unchanging volume of production, the share going to labor *now employed* would inevitably be reduced. The salaried and fixed income groups, together with the 30 million people constituting the agricultural population, would likewise be adversely affected. Because of the sharp increases in costs that would be entailed, legislation requiring a universal shortening of the working week would be certain to halt the present recovery movement and precipitate a new period of reaction. The interests of labor quite as much as those of the employer demand that hours of labor be adjusted in the light of production and consumption requirements rather than for the purpose of absorbing unemployment.

It is sometimes alleged that the real objective of the short work week is not so much to reduce actual working hours as to place labor in a position to exact extra pay for *overtime*, computed on a shorter standard week. Hence, it is argued that the shorter work week would not necessarily mean a smaller volume of work performed, though it would mean larger money wages. It is obviously true that a 30-hour regular week plus ten hours of overtime would actually be the equivalent of 40 hours of work. But it does not follow that this would increase the standard of living of labor in general. This is because no increase in efficiency would result from the process. The increase in wage costs would promptly lead to an effort to recoup the added outlays through advancing prices. It may be recalled that this is precisely what occurred under the NRA program of forcing shorter hours with a view to increasing wage rates. Here and there, in highly profitable enterprises, the increased costs might be absorbed without proportionate increases in prices; but in the great majority of cases it would result either in advancing prices or crippled operations and the discharge of labor.

In many industries and companies, moreover, the result of such a program would be to make further expansion practically impossible. In the railroad industry, for example, where prices (rates) cannot readily be advanced, the increase in wage costs would destroy the margins of income and credit which are essential to the reconstruction of railway properties. It would thus prevent not only the desired improvement of railway operating efficiency but also the expansion of employment that would normally accompany the rehabilitation.

Summarizing the discussion thus far, we find that the reduction of working hours during the course of the last seven years has been nearly double that of the preceding generation. Meanwhile great production deficiencies have accumulated, particularly in the field of durable commodities. To make good these deficiencies and at the same time provide an increase in production in line with the growth of population would necessitate a vast increase in employment. Our analysis of the requirements for carrying through a production program that would at the end of five years place this country on a plane of production and consumption equal to that of pre-depression days indicates a probable need of longer rather than shorter hours than those now prevailing. For the economic system as a whole, reduction in working hours during the depression has undoubtedly not been matched by a corresponding increase in efficiency.

III. WAGES AND PRICES IN RELATION TO RE-EMPLOYMENT

In the light of the foregoing analysis it is evident that the basic need is to absorb the unemployed in the production of additional goods and services in the field of private industry. Apart from the great human issues involved, re-employment in productive work is essential to the restoration and improvement of living standards, and also to the reduction of the relief outlays which still imperil the stability of the federal budget. By what processes, or as the result of what policies, may we expect this re-employment to come about?

In beginning this discussion it must be emphasized that the absorption of the unemployed in private industry will not depend upon any single factor. The economic system, as we have repeatedly pointed out, is of great complexity and operates in response to varied stimuli. Just as numerous factors of maladjustment combined to produce the great depression, so various adjustments and harmonies are essential to the process of recovery. Some of these have been considered in immediately preceding chapters and a general summary of the factors involved will be presented in the chapter which follows. Accordingly, we shall here be giving consideration merely to one phase of the recovery process, namely, that pertaining to the expansion of the purchasing power of the masses. We make this the center of our interest not only because of the social importance of raising living standards but also because of the direct relationship of mass purchasing power to the stimulation of production.

It should be noted first that during a period of business recovery there are two ways in which the buying power of industrial workers may be increased. The first and most obvious is through the mere expansion of employment. Whenever additional workers are placed upon the payroll the volume of wage disbursements is of course increased. Similarly, when individuals who have been employed irregularly or on a part-time basis are given the opportunity to work more continuously and a greater number of hours per month, wage payments are enlarged. Such an increase in aggregate wages has of course been taking place during the course of the present recovery movement in conjunction with the expansion of employment that has occurred.

The second means of enlarging the purchasing power of the workers is through increasing wage rates relatively to prices, or decreasing prices relatively to wage rates. This process differs from the former in that it may operate both during a period of recovery and permanently. Indeed, once the slack in employment has been completely taken up the increase in the ratio of wage rates to prices is the only means by which standards of living may be further increased.[7] This conception is so important to an understanding of the requirements for sustained prosperity and progress that it must be given emphasis before we continue the analysis of its relation to the recovery movement.

In a pecuniary society—in which incomes are received in the form of money and disbursed for goods selling on a money price basis—*the process of raising the standard of living of wage earners necessarily involves increasing the spread between wage rates and prices.* That is, a wage earner can increase the volume of his purchases from year to year only if wage rates are increased *relatively* to the prices of the commodities which he buys. If he gets more dollars and prices remain unchanged, his purchasing power is expanded. If he gets the same number of dollars and prices decline, his purchasing power is expanded. If his wages increase twofold while prices increase only 50 per cent, his purchasing power is expanded. If prices decline 20 per cent and wages fall but 10 per cent, his purchasing power is expanded. It cannot be expanded, however, unless the spread between wages and prices is increased.

---

[7] Assuming of course no lengthening of the hours of work.

It is perhaps well to recall in this connection that over the years the benefits of technological progress have been disseminated among the masses of the people precisely in this way—through a changing relationship between wage rates and prices. At certain periods the result has been brought about chiefly through advances in money wages; at other times, chiefly through price reductions. During some periods both wage rates and prices have increased, but with the former moving up more rapidly; sometimes both wages and prices have fallen, with prices falling more rapidly than wages; and again wages and prices have moved in opposite directions, the former rising and the latter falling. But whatever the character of the shifts an increasing spread between wages and prices has been the means by which the great rise in living standards in modern times has been brought about.

A second principle—too often forgotten—must also be emphasized. It is that *an increasing spread between wage rates and prices depends fundamentally upon increasing the efficiency of production.* Only inconsequential increases in wages can, as we have seen, be achieved by trenching upon profits. The primary requirement for an improvement in the wage-price ratio is increased productive output through the acceleration of technical advances, improved management, increased labor efficiency, and so forth. Any practices or policies that tend to work in this direction are economically sound; and any that work in the opposite direction are economically unsound.

With these principles in mind we may return to the consideration of recent trends. Our studies of wage and price changes during the course of the recovery movement provide the basis for a significant observation. As the chart on page 255 indicates, the present recovery has been marked by an increasing spread between wage rates and wholesale prices in manufacturing industries. The same generalization, moreover, holds, until recently, with respect to the comparison between wage rates and the cost of living. During the early months of the recovery period, wage rates were sharply increased as a result of the code agreements. These advances were made with a view to increasing purchasing power and were not directly related to efficiency. Prices of manufactured goods advanced even more quickly than wage rates, though on the whole they did not rise to quite the same extent.[8] Since the end of 1933, wage rates have continued to increase at a moderate pace. The prices of manufactured goods have, however, remained practically stationary; indeed the trend was slightly downward until the last quarter of 1936. Meanwhile, the net profits of industry have shown a very substantial rise.

Two factors in the situation have made it possible to have higher wage rates relatively to prices and at the same time much larger profits. The first is the increase in productive efficiency that has been occurring in many lines of manufacturing industry, and a decline in other costs than wage rates.[9] The second is the reduction in unit costs which has accompanied increasing output; as the percentage of utilization of plant capacity rises the overhead charges are distributed over an expanding volume of business.

In the present recovery period, especially since the

[8] Workers employed in industries outside the codes, amounting to about one-third of the total wage-earning population, suffered a reduction in real wages as a result of the rise in prices. For a detailed discussion, see *The National Recovery Administration*, published by the Brookings Institution.

[9] See Chap. VII.

end of 1933, we have thus had a double force operating to increase purchasing power among the masses. The absorption of additional workers has automatically increased the flow of funds to the working population; and at the same time those regularly employed have had an expanding purchasing power resulting from the increasing spread between wage rates and prices. Had prices risen faster than wage rates, the decreased real purchasing power of those already employed would have tended to offset the gains resulting from the reabsorption of those who had been out of work. Moreover, had prices been rising, other groups of consumers, with stationary money incomes, would have had declining purchasing power.

The present recovery movement has been unique in this regard. Not only in the United States but in other countries as well the prices of manufactured goods have remained practically stable for three full years. The current recovery, though less intense in character, has meanwhile continued for a longer period without serious interruption than any other recovery movement of modern times.[10]

The theory has often been advanced that recovery requires an increase of prices relatively to wage rates—rather than the reverse. Underlying this line of reasoning is the assumption that the increase in prices is essential to the establishment of profit margins. The facts with respect to the present recovery movement conclusively refute the theory that the only means of re-establishing a profit margin is to increase prices faster than wage rates.

Profits which result from increasing efficiency and an expansion in the total volume of production are soundly

[10] See discussion in Chap. IV.

based, while those arising out of price advances are not. Profits derived from rising prices tend to be offset by the shrinking purchasing power of those whose incomes from wages, salaries, or investments are not expanding proportionally. Rising prices may indeed stimulate an increase in production and produce an industrial boom. But since the buoyant activity that results merely from rising prices is not accompanied by corresponding increases in the purchasing power of the masses, it is not self-sustaining.

The encouraging feature of the present recovery movement has been its failure—thus far—to generate a period of rapidly advancing prices. The purchasing power of the industrial working population has been expanding in proportion to the recovery of production. Similarly the stability of the prices of manufactured goods has contributed in a vital way to the rise in the real purchasing power of the farm population. It is not surprising, therefore, that we have witnessed no piling up of speculative inventories or other evidence of a growing disequilibrium between production and consumption.

IV. DANGERS AHEAD?

The generally favorable wage-price situation that has been outlined appears, however, to be in some danger of succumbing to pressures and temptations inherent in the immediate situation. In the last quarter of 1936 tendencies have developed which threaten a reversal of recent trends. Increasing taxes, rising prices of important raw materials, and pressures for further substantial increases in wages are exerting powerful influence in the direction of price advances. These are very real forces—perhaps irresistible. In any case, once an advance in prices is under way the process becomes cumulative—

since the selling prices of commodities in the intermediate stages of production appear as costs in succeeding stages.

The recent expansion of business activity has moreover been creating a situation in which it appears readily possible to advance prices without checking demand. Concurrently the doctrine seems to have been growing that the *happy* way forward from here is to step up prices all along the line—thereby making more money for division between share owners and workers in the form of dividend and wage bonuses.

The drift in the direction of higher prices of manufactured goods is the gravest danger which we face today. Whether forced by increasing costs, or embraced as a means of stimulating rapid expansion, it is the sure road to an inflationary boom with its customary spiral of rising prices, wages, costs, and again prices. An increase in the volume of production would for a time no doubt be stimulated, and in any event large speculative gains would be realized. But on the other hand there would be a great increase in industrial unrest, resulting from the rising cost of living. Not the least significant result would be the changing ratio of industrial to agricultural prices and consequent renewed efforts to use the machinery of government to protect the relative position of the farmer.

The primary necessity at this particular juncture is to resist the pressures toward higher prices, just as far as possible, with a view to preserving and improving the existing favorable ratio of wage rates to prices. To the extent that the spread can be increased we shall be laying foundations for further solid growth; to the extent that it is narrowed, we shall be undermining the basis of sustained recovery.

As output continues to expand and efficiency to increase, prices should be reduced. Even under present conditions it may be desirable in many instances to lower prices as a means of increasing demand and promoting a fuller utilization of productive capacity. The basic principle remains that price reductions, as a general policy, constitute the surest means of promoting continuous economic progress.

To guard against possible misunderstanding it is perhaps well to add here that we do not hold that an increasing ratio of wage rates to prices would insure permanent prosperity. We do not believe that there is any *single* cause of, or cure for, depressions. The complex economic machine may suffer dislocation in numerous ways; and it will be recalled that our analysis of the situation in 1929 disclosed several sources of maladjustment. We are merely contending here that a continuous expansion of purchasing power among the masses is a primary essential to sustained prosperity and economic growth.

V. VARIATIONS WITHIN THE PRICE STRUCTURE

In the foregoing analysis attention has been concentrated on the general level of prices in relation to wage rates. It must now be recalled that during the course of the last seven years both the price structure and the wage structure have undergone marked changes. During the depression there occurred a wide dispersion of prices with respect to broad groups of commodities, such as raw materials and finished products, foodstuffs and manufactured goods, and also as between the various classes of manufactured products. These variations are attributable to a variety of factors, including governmental regulation, monopolistic control, and the power of labor organizations. During the course of the recovery, these disparities have been greatly reduced, though not wholly eliminated. Indeed, in some very important lines, prices are now considerably higher relatively to the general level than was formerly the case. The question must now be asked whether this situation impedes the process of recovery.

On the basis of general reasoning the answer to the query seems to be in the affirmative. In the case of producer goods, high prices appear as costs in the successive stages of the productive process, and thus tend to limit the possibilities of price reductions in goods destined for the ultimate consumer. In the case of finished goods, consumer demands tend to be restricted by high prices, and hence production and employment are held in check. As a general proposition it would therefore appear that the persistence of high prices is a retarding influence in the process of further recovery and expansion.

A contrast needs to be made between conditions existing in the depth of depressions and during the course of a recovery movement. On the downswing of the cycle, further declines in prices may serve merely to prolong depression by inducing potential buyers to wait for still further price recessions. But when a forward movement is under way price reductions, made possible by increasing efficiency and the gains resulting from a fuller utilization of capacity, need produce no such unfortunate repercussions; on the contrary, they should induce an expansion of demand and consequent increase of profits as well as employment. It should be noted in this connection that the degree of recovery has in fact been most pronounced in certain industries in which a policy of maintaining low prices prevails.

A conspicuous example is of course the automobile

industry; and others which may be mentioned are farm machinery and fertilizer materials. Conditions vary so considerably in different lines that generalizations are hazardous; but there can be little doubt that the industries which since the end of 1933 have followed a policy of reducing prices have contributed most to the process of recovery and at the same time have enjoyed the most satisfactory profits. The automobile industry has been a leader throughout the recovery period; and the farm machinery industry registered a rapid forward movement following the substantial reductions of prices which were made effective mid-way in the recovery period. It is of interest to note, also, that reductions of railway passenger rates during the past three years have resulted in increased traffic and increased net earnings. The gains thus accruing to particular industries do not represent a mere shifting of demand from other products. Through offering more goods or services for a given amount of money, or the same amount of goods or services for less money, expansion in the total volume of production is stimulated.

In some instances the high prices now existing are attributable in no small degree to high wage rates. Such is the case, for example, in the building industry— though it should also be borne in mind that the relatively high prices of building materials and other costs are contributing factors. While admitting the economic importance of high wages it must at the same time be recognized that wage *rates* may under certain circumstances be so high as to reduce annual *wages*.

In the building industry, for example, wage *rates* are exceptionally high; but in consequence of restricted construction and the large number of idle days in the year, annual wages in the industry are far from satisfactory.

Under such conditions a reduction in wage *rates*, as well as other costs, might well serve to increase *aggregate wages* through promoting steadier employment; for, as our analysis of the present housing situation has revealed, there is an enormous need for new construction at this time. While other factors are in part responsible, high wage rates, high prices of building materials, high interest and other financial charges, have undoubtedly served to retard the recovery of the building industry. The result has been detrimental alike to living standards in general and to the earnings of all who are connected with the industry.

It must always be remembered that, fundamentally, wages as well as interest and profits depend upon production; and that the maximum returns will usually be realized under conditions which promote maximum output.

CHAPTER XXI

SUMMARY AND CONCLUSIONS

Although the present world recovery movement has been under way for approximately four years, the degree of economic improvement has been far from sufficient to absorb unemployment and to restore former standards of living. Moreover, elements of instability still exist which make the continued and orderly expansion of production a matter of uncertainty. Accordingly in this final chapter we shall attempt to draw together the threads of the investigation as a whole with a view to indicating the significant economic elements in the present situation and suggesting the policies which are most likely to be conducive to further constructive expansion.

The degree of recovery in the United States, in which we are here chiefly interested, has been appreciably less than that in many other countries. The fact is that, as measured by the recovery of industrial production, the United States falls definitely in an intermediate group —considerably above the former "gold bloc" nations, but considerably below numerous other countries. On a per capita basis industrial output is still approximately 15 per cent below the level of 1929; and the per capita national income, with allowance for price changes, is less than six-sevenths what it was seven years ago. A great increase in production is still necessary if we are merely to restore the standards of living formerly enjoyed by the American people.

Perhaps the best means of clarifying the recovery problem in the United States as it presents itself today is through a recapitulation of significant trends and developments of the past four years. Many of the changes that have occurred may be regarded as constituting favorable factors in the present situation, while others must be set down as unfavorable. In the following summary the order in which these factors are listed is not intended to indicate their relative importance.

I. FAVORABLE FACTORS IN THE PRESENT SITUATION

An abundance of loanable funds is available at low rates of interest. Owing to a combination of causes, the supply of both short-term banking accommodations and long-term investment money is now unprecedentedly large. Interest rates are extraordinarily low, and the prospect is that they will remain comparatively low for some time to come. While the abundance of funds at low rates may possibly stimulate speculative activity, it must nevertheless be set down as an important essential for business expansion.

The burden of private indebtedness has been materially reduced in the course of the last three years. The argument has often been made that recovery is impossible without a vast writing down of the bond and mortgage indebtedness that has been built up over a long period of years. Our investigation shows that the private debt situation does not now constitute a deterrent to further recovery. As a result of a substantially higher level of prices, refunding at lower rates of interest and the replacement of bonds by stock, financial reorganizations and scaling down of mortgages, the shifting of debt from private to governmental hands, and a reduction in interest rates by government lending agencies, the burden of private debt has been appreciably mitigated. While there are still some difficult situations, in general there is no pressing need of further adjustment at this time.

The trend with respect to wage and price relationships has been unusually satisfactory. Since the end of 1933 wage rates have gradually increased, while the prices of manufactured goods have remained at a practically stationary level. The purchasing power of the laboring population has thus been steadily expanded. Increasing efficiency of production and a fuller utilization of capacity have made it possible for wage rates to advance relatively to prices, and at the same time for profits to increase satisfactorily. It is to be noted on the other side, however, that in some important lines both wage rates and prices are so high as to impede the process of recovery and the expansion of employment.

The balance between agriculture and industry has been materially improved. This is attributable in part to normal recovery from the extreme depths reached during the depression; in part to the effects of dollar devaluation, which raised the prices of staple export commodities; in part to weather conditions; and in part to the government program of restricting agricultural production. There are still uncertain and complicating elements in this situation, but for the present at least the balance between the two great divisions of economic activity has been greatly improved.

Uncertainty with respect to monetary and banking policies has almost wholly disappeared. Legislation with respect to both commercial and investment banking has largely alleviated the fears of depositors and investors with reference to the security of savings. As a result of the business recovery that has occurred and the waning political importance of the groups which had been most insistent on accomplishing revival through money panaceas, there now appears to be little likelihood of further changes in currency policies. The Administration itself has for three years followed a policy of monetary stability and has taken a definite stand in favor of international stabilization, to be achieved as soon as conditions in general are propitious.

Developments in the field of commercial policy have been laying foundations for an expansion of foreign trade. As a result of the breakdown of the international monetary system between 1931 and 1933 and the growth of multifarious commercial restrictions, international trade was enormously curtailed; and its restoration has shown a serious lag throughout the recovery period. The trade agreements being consummated under the leadership of the United States government are eliminating uneconomic restrictions and barriers and are thus clearing the way for a renewed expansion of international trade.

The enormous accumulated deficiency of production is a powerful stimulus to further expansion. The back log of requirements in the field of durable goods is so great that we do not need to wait upon the development of any new industries to lead the way forward. The mere process of making good deferred maintenance and expanding production sufficiently to provide an increased population with the usual types of consumption goods would tax the nation's productive energies for some years. The opportunity for a great expansion along clearly defined, established lines has never been greater than it is today. Indeed, the impetus from this direction is largely responsible for the substantial increase of business activity during the course of the past year.

Finally, the confusion with respect to government policies has been greatly reduced. The conflicts and inconsistencies which were the inevitable accompaniments of a government recovery program, forced by insistent pressures and undertaken with the double objective of recovery and reform, have been largely, though not wholly, eliminated during the course of the past three years. Moreover, the atmosphere of doubt, uncertainty, and distrust arising from conflicting theories, opinions, and policies as between governmental and business leaders has in substantial degree been dissipated.

II. UNFAVORABLE FACTORS IN THE PRESENT SITUATION

On the darker side of the picture, interest centers not so much in the number of adverse factors as upon the vast potential significance of some of them. In fact, any one of several possible trends or developments might completely change the whole economic outlook.

The maintenance of fiscal stability remains a problem of major difficulty. Our analysis shows that an early balancing of the federal budget is economically possible, but that such a consummation will require resolute action in curtailing wasteful and unnecessary federal expenditures. There is undoubtedly a strong disposition now to place the federal credit upon a secure foundation; but economic, social, and political pressures for the continuance or expansion of government disbursements are powerful, and it remains an open question whether they can be successfully withstood. If fiscal stability is not achieved, the resulting financial and monetary disorganization and price inflation would in due course completely disrupt the process of constructive economic expansion now under way.

There is some danger of an inflationary movement generated by forces operating in the field of private en-

terprise. The existence of super-abundant bank reserves and investment funds, as has already been indicated, provides a basis for and something of a stimulus to speculative activities and credit and price inflation, both in the security and commodity markets. This situation has, however, existed for some little time without producing the results so frequently predicted. Thus, one must conclude that the money market situation is not necessarily of controlling importance with respect to commercial inflation. The most direct pressure in the direction of higher prices is that exerted by factors related to industrial costs and market conditions. Rapidly rising costs in a time of expanding and buoyant business activity lead to a rising spiral of prices, costs, and again prices. An abundance of credit which lenders are desirous of putting to work makes possible, facilitates, and encourages such a price inflation. At the present juncture the possibility of such an inflationary movement—having temporarily stimulating effects but promoting longer run instability—is very real.

Emerging labor policies endanger the recovery process. The most important among these policies is that pertaining to the reduction of working hours, on the mistaken theory that we can thus raise standards of living. The sharp rise in costs, unrelated to efficiency, would be certain to result either in rapid rises in industrial prices, with profoundly disturbing effects upon the operation of the economic system as a whole, or the immediate halting of business activity with a consequent increase in unemployment. The struggle now going on within the ranks of labor over conflicting theories of labor organization and the intensive efforts being made to strengthen the power of labor over industry constitute a serious menace to the continuance of business prosperity.

Ill-conceived industrial legislation would also serve to check the recovery movement. Current discussions and preliminary drafts of legislative measures indicate at one and the same time a laudable desire to safeguard public welfare through legislative provisions with respect to industrial practices, price policies, wages, hours of work, output, capital expansion, and so forth, and endless confusion and conflicts of opinion as to the regulatory policies that would bring about the desired results. Premature legislation along these lines would give rise to a new period of uncertainty and confusion.

Finally, mention must be made of highly unstable elements in the international situation. In many countries the expansion of business activity has not been built on sound foundations. In numerous instances it is largely attributable to military programs which, while they generate temporary business prosperity, do not directly raise standards of living or increase wealth producing capacity. They involve at the same time vast expenditures of public funds which simultaneously increase the burdens of taxation and threaten financial stability. The condition of public finance in the world at large constitutes a fundamental factor of instability everywhere. A new series of fiscal and currency breakdowns with adverse effects upon American trade and finance is quite within the bounds of possibility. The threat of new wars not only forecasts the possibility of renewed wealth destruction, but also constitutes a barrier to the re-establishment of constructive international economic policies. The present recovery movement is unique in this regard.

III. AN INTEGRATED PROGRAM

The foregoing recapitulation readily suggests the primary requisites and elements of an integrated program designed to promote further recovery. The underlying necessity, to which every policy must be related, is the reabsorption of the unemployed in productive activities. Only thus can improving standards of living be realized. Whatever merit production restriction programs may have possessed as a means of correcting in special cases serious maladjustments in the depths of depression and of stimulating the beginnings of recovery, they have no regular place in the continuous process of economic progress. An expansion in *real* incomes depends upon an increase of productive activity; it cannot be derived from an artificial expansion of *money* incomes, unaccompanied by increases in the output of goods and services.

In brief, the essential requirements for a consistent program of further recovery may be summarized as follows:

The re-establishment of a balanced federal budget as a foundation on which to build enduring progress.

The continuance of the present policy of maintaining a fixed price of gold and the establishment through international co-operation of a system of stable foreign exchanges.

The extension of the program of reciprocal trade agreements as the most practical means of reducing artificial barriers to commerce and reopening the channels of international trade.

The preservation of the generally favorable ratio of prices and wage rates, in the interest of progressively expanding the real purchasing power of workers and creating a demand for added production and employment—placing emphasis upon price reductions as a means of carrying the benefits of technological progress to all groups within the nation.

The maintenance, in general, of prevailing hours of labor, as the only means of meeting the production requirements involved in restoring during the next few years the standards of living of the laboring masses and promoting the economic advancement of the nation as a whole.

The elimination of industrial practices and policies—private and public—which tend to restrict output or to prevent the increase of productive efficiency.

Shifting the emphasis in agricultural policy from restricted output and rising prices to the abundant furnishing of the supplies of raw materials and foodstuffs required by gradually expanding markets.

The economic situation today is one of delicate adjustment and precarious balance. In a very real sense the world stands at the crossroads. We may move gradually forward along a broad front, achieving progressively higher levels of well-being; or we may suffer a reversal of current trends and enter upon a new period of recession, involving further deterioration of living standards and bringing a new era of disorganization, the consequences of which no one can foresee. Which way we go will largely depend upon private and public policies now in the making.

The lesson of the world depression is that all groups

are indissolubly linked in a common enterprise. No nation, no class, and almost no individual could escape the devastating effects of the collapse of the economic system which began in 1929. The economic advancement of laborers, clerical workers, professional groups, business men, and farmers all depends upon our pulling together, with the aid of government, toward the common objective of increased production and higher living standards.

APPENDIXES

APPENDIX A

STATISTICS RELATING TO WORLD TRENDS

The material in this appendix is supplementary to the first four chapters. Data presented in the first six tables are from new world indexes recently compiled and published by the League of Nations to replace old League indexes. Tables 1-4 give sub-series used in the computation of the League's new composite world index of primary production, and Table 5 gives 12 of the 81 individual items used in the calculation of the same index. Table 6 presents one of the League's new indexes of industrial production—manufacturing only.

The new composite world index of primary production and its component series are aggregative in type and weighted by world prices in 1930. They are described in detail in Appendix I of the League's *World Production and Prices, 1935-36*. The new world indexes of industrial production are calculated as weighted arithmetic averages of the 23 national indexes (described briefly under Table 8 below), some necessary adjustments having been made to make the sub-series comparable. The weights used are based on value added by manufacture during 1925-29 as shown by the industrial censuses or other relevant information for the countries included. For a fuller description, see pages 21-22 and Appendix II of the League's *World Production and Prices, 1935-36*.

1. INDEXES OF PRODUCTION OF CRUDE FOODSTUFFS, BY CONTINENTS, 1925-35[a]
(1925-29 = 100)

Continental Group	1925	1926	1927	1928	1929	1930	1931	1932	1933	1934	1935[b]
Europe—											
incl. USSR........	96	95	100	104	106	108	104	104	106	107	109
excl. USSR.......	97	92	99	105	107	106	109	112	114	115	115
USSR..............	92	102	102	101	102	111	90	81	86	86	92
North America......	95	99	101	104	100	102	103	100	101	105	90
Latin America.......	97	98	101	105	99	102	101	100	106	105	101
Africa..............	98	94	100	102	108	106	106	116	111	118	122
Asia, excl. USSR[c]....	98	98	100	102	102	104	105	105	108	101	101
Oceania............	95	99	98	105	103	115	118	130	130	131	133
World total—											
incl. USSR........	96	97	100	104	103	106	104	104	106	106	104
excl. USSR[d]......	97	96	100	104	103	105	106	107	109	109	106

[a] League of Nations, *World Production and Prices, 1935-36*, p. 15.
[b] Provisional.
[c] Excluding China with the exception of Manchuria.
[d] Furnished by the League of Nations.

2. INDEXES OF PRODUCTION OF RAW MATERIALS, BY CONTINENTS, 1925–35[a]
(1925–29 = 100)

Continental Group	1925	1926	1927	1928	1929	1930	1931	1932	1933	1934	1935[b]
Europe—											
incl. USSR........	88	85	104	106	116	107	98	89	96	109	119
excl. USSR.......	90	85	105	105	115	102	90	80	87	97	103
USSR..............	75	87	100	113	126	144	157	155	166	197	232
North America......	93	101	96	101	109	94	82	63	72	74	83
Latin America.......	91	92	94	108	116	107	93	79	87	107	110
Africa.............	95	95	93	105	112	111	96	90	112	113	122
Asia, excl. USSR....	92	94	100	105	109	111	98	100	111	117	120
Oceania............	94	101	101	103	102	97	98	104	103	106	103
World total—											
incl. USSR........	91	94	99	104	112	102	91	79	88	95	103
excl. USSR[c]	92	94	99	103	111	100	88	76	84	91	97

[a] League of Nations, *World Production and Prices, 1935–36*, p. 18. [b] Provisional.
[c] Furnished by the League of Nations.

3. INDEXES OF PRODUCTION OF AGRICULTURAL RAW MATERIALS, BY CONTINENTS, 1925–35[a]
(1925–29 = 100)

Continental Group	1925	1926	1927	1928	1929	1930	1931	1932	1933	1934	1935[b]
Europe—											
incl. USSR........	93	91	102	101	114	101	108	96	99	101	112
excl. USSR.......	95	92	106	93	115	87	91	84	89	92	98
USSR..............	92	89	97	110	113	119	128	112	111	112	128
North America......	104	115	87	96	98	94	113	88	88	68	76
Latin America.......	97	101	101	100	101	103	104	93	112	130	123
Africa.............	97	96	90	104	112	109	96	98	116	109	117
Asia, excl. USSR....	96	95	101	106	103	107	90	94	103	101	98
Oceania............	91	101	98	106	103	101	109	114	109	110	104
World total—											
incl. USSR........	98	101	96	102	104	102	102	94	100	95	98
excl. USSR[c].....	98	102	96	101	103	100	100	93	99	94	95

[a] League of Nations, *World Production and Prices, 1935–36*, p. 17 [b] Provisional.
[c] Furnished by the League of Nations.

4. INDEXES OF PRODUCTION OF NON-AGRICULTURAL RAW MATERIALS, BY CONTINENTS, 1925–35[a]
(1925–29 = 100)

Continental Group	1925	1926	1927	1928	1929	1930	1931	1932	1933	1934	1935[b]
Europe—											
incl. USSR........	88	84	105	107	117	108	96	88	96	110	120
excl. USSR.......	90	84	105	106	115	104	89	80	87	97	104
USSR..............	61	84	102	115	137	166	183	193	215	271	323
North America......	91	99	97	102	111	95	76	59	69	75	84
Latin America.......	87	87	90	113	123	108	88	71	75	95	104
Africa.............	90	93	98	106	113	116	98	87	100	124	133
Asia, excl. USSR....	86	92	98	105	118	117	110	108	122	143	154
Oceania............	99	99	106	98	98	89	74	81	89	97	109[c]
World total—											
incl. USSR........	89	92	100	104	114	102	87	75	84	95	104
excl. USSR[d].....	90	92	100	104	113	100	84	71	80	90	98

[a] League of Nations, *World Production and Prices, 1935–36*, p. 17. [b] Provisional.
[c] In the chart on p. 61 this entry is given as 103, which was the preliminary figure furnished by the League prior to the publication of *World Production and Prices, 1935–36*.
[d] Furnished by the League of Nations.

5. INDEXES OF WORLD PRODUCTION OF SELECTED RAW MATERIALS, 1925–35[a]
(1925–29 average = 100)

Products	1925	1926	1927	1928	1929	1930	1931	1932	1933	1934	1935[b]
Cotton.............	105	106	90	100	99	98	103	90	99	89	97
Raw silk...........	87	93	99	108	113	110	107	97	100	103	92
Wool..............	92	98	100	104	106	102	102	102	99	99	99
Crude rubber.......	80	95	93	100	131	125	121	107	129	154	132
Mechanical wood pulp	88	96	98	104	114	112	103	96	103	118	...
Coal..............	95	95	103	100	107	98	87	77	81	88	91
Petroleum.........	86	88	101	106	119	113	109	104	114	120	130
Sulphur...........	84	98	105	101	112	114	97	71	89	91	91
Pig iron[b].........	95	92	107	99	107	92	65	44	50	68	80
Copper............	89	91	94	106	120	100	87	57	65	80	...
Potash............	94	83	96	109	118	110	76	65	80	101	...
Natural phosphates..	89	97	103	103	107	125	89	76	88	101	109

[a] League of Nations, *World Production and Prices, 1935–36*, pp. 125–26.
[b] Partly based on estimates; subject to revision.

6. INDEXES OF MANUFACTURING ACTIVITY, BY CONTINENTS, 1925–35[a]
(1925–29 average = 100)

Continental Group	1925	1926	1927	1928	1929	1930	1931	1932	1933	1934	1935[b]
Europe, excl. USSR..	90	89	103	107	111	102	90	78	85	94	100
North America......	95	98	96	102	108	87	73	58	69	72	83
World, incl. USSR...	91	93	99	105	111	98	88	77	86	94	106

[a] League of Nations, *World Production and Prices, 1935–36*, p. 23.
[b] Provisional.

7. INDEXES OF VOLUME OF WORLD TRADE, BY GROUPS
OF COMMODITIES, 1930–35[a]
(1929 = 100)

Year	Total	Foodstuffs[b]	Raw Materials[b]	Manufactured Articles[b]
1930..................	93	...	...	...
1931..................	86	...	...	...
1932..................	75	91	82	58
1933..................	76	85	88	60
1934..................	79	84	90	66
1935..................	82	86	94	69

[a] League of Nations, *Review of World Trade*, 1935, p. 15.
Not given separately prior to 1932.

8. National Indexes of Industrial Production

Indexes of industrial production are compiled by methods which vary considerably from country to country. The choice of the industries covered and their grouping and weighting are determined not only by the economic structure of each country, but also by the availability or lack of regular data on production in the various industries. The diversity of manufactured products and the absence of comprehensive production statistics render impossible in almost all countries an exact measurement of the fluctuations in the physical output of industry.

Annual Indexes of Industrial Production in Selected Countries
1930–35[a]
(1929 = 100)

Country	1930	1931	1932	1933	1934	1935
Germany	85.9	67.6	53.3	60.7	79.8	94.0[b]
United States	80.7	68.1	53.8	63.9	66.4	75.6
Poland	82.0	69.5	53.9	55.6	63.0	66.4
Canada	84.8	71.0	58.1	60.3	73.5	81.3
Czechoslovakia	89.2	80.7	63.5	60.2	66.5	69.9
Netherlands	91.4	79.0	62.3	69.1	69.8	66.3
Austria	84.9	74.3	64.3	65.4	72.2	79.6
Italy	91.9	77.6	66.9	73.7	80.9	...
France	100.4	88.9	68.8	76.7	71.0	67.4
Belgium	88.8	81.1	69.1	71.4	72.3[c]	80.6
Hungary	93.8	87.4	76.9	83.9	97.5	110.9
Chile	100.9	77.9	87.0	95.8	105.1	120.1
Estonia	98.7	90.8	78.3	81.9	96.4	106.4
Norway	101.0	78.3	92.7	93.8	97.7	105.1
Sweden	96.4	84.5	79.1	81.8	100.0	[d]
Finland	90.8	80.0	83.3	95.8	116.7	125.0
United Kingdom	92.3	83.8	83.5	88.2	98.8	105.7
Spain	98.6	93.2	88.4	84.4	85.5	86.9
Rumania	96.9	102.1	88.5	102.6	123.9	...
Denmark	108.0	100.0	91.0	105.0	117.0	121.0
Japan	94.8	91.6	97.8	113.2	128.7	141.8
Greece	103.4	107.0	100.9	109.8	125.2	140.7
USSR	130.5	160.9	182.9	198.1	238.2	288.2

[a] League of Nations, *Monthly Bulletin of Statistics*, August 1936, p. 347.
[b] Since March 1935 including the Saar.
[c] February to July—labor dispute in the wool industry.
[d] Suspended pending recast of the index.

The indexes vary widely in scope. Some cover almost the entire range of national industry; others are limited to important industries or branches of industry which are considered to be representative. Some are based mainly on returns of actual quantities produced; others on values produced, corrected by a price index to show quantity changes. Some make extensive use of indirect gauges of activity such as hours worked, imports of raw materials, orders filed, etc. These indirect measurements may be influenced by changes in working efficiency, the seasonal character of orders and shipments, the importance of stocks, the trend of prices, etc. Some are adjusted for seasonal variations and others are not. The majority of the indexes shown should thus be regarded as merely furnishing a rough measure of changes in industrial activity.

We present below the essential facts with reference to the character of the production indexes for the countries included in the discussion in the latter part of Chapter III. As given in the accompanying table these indexes have been recomputed by the League of Nations from their original bases to a 1929 base, a form which was essential for the purposes of our discussion. In nearly all cases the descriptions given below are those furnished by the agencies responsible for the indexes, and in all cases the original base period is given.

Austria

Compiler: Öesterreichisches Institut für Konjunkturforschung, Vienna.
Base period: 1923-31.
Scope: Based on ten series relating to consumption of electric current and to production of coal, lignite, iron ore, pig iron, steel, cotton yarns, wood pulp, paper, and alcohol. Shows accurately the movements of production in only the most important industries, but is believed to reflect rather closely the trend of total industrial production.
Method: A simple arithmetic average of the ten component series, each of which is adjusted for seasonal fluctuations.
Source: League of Nations, *Statistical Yearbook, 1935-36*, p. 183.

Belgium

Compiler: Institut des Sciences économiques, Louvain.
Base period: 1923-25.
Scope: Based on ten series, the majority of which are computed from direct production data which relate in most cases to a part only of the industries concerned. The annual index, which was used in constructing the index shown on page 550, is fairly comprehensive although it omits such important industries as construction and chemicals. The monthly index is much less comprehensive than the annual, completely omitting five of the series and giving only one component of a sixth. The differences between the annual and the monthly indexes are within reasonable limits, however.

Method: A weighted average of the component series. The weights, based mainly on capital invested and its yield and the number of workers employed, are: coal and related industries 20; iron and steel 27; textiles 24; glass 7; paper 2; foodstuffs 9; quarries, cement, etc. 5; non-ferrous metals 4; tobacco 1; matches 1.

For the most part the series are based on production for a standard month of 25 days, but seasonal variations are not eliminated.

Source: Bulletin de l'Institut des Sciences économiques (Louvain), August 1931, pp. 367-412; November 1931, pp. 3-26; League of Nations, *Statistical Yearbook, 1935-36,* p. 185.

Canada

Compiler: Dominion Bureau of Statistics.

Base year: 1926.

Scope: Includes 32 series relating to manufacturing, 9 series relating to mineral production, one construction series, and one electric power series, and is sufficiently comprehensive to indicate accurately the trend of industrial production.

Method: Aggregative type of index, quantitative data being multiplied by average prices during 1926. Series for which only value data are compiled are converted to a volume basis by means of appropriate indexes of prices and costs. The industrial group is given a weighting of 67.5 in the general index, distributed as follows: foodstuffs 23.5; tobacco 2.7; pneumatic tire casings 2.9; crude rubber imports 1.4; boots and shoes 2.7; textiles 2.0; wood and paper 15.7; iron and steel 12.4; coke 0.9; petroleum imports 3.3. The remaining weights are: mineral production 11.1; construction 15.8; electric power 5.6.

Adjusted for seasonal variations.

Source: Supplements to the following issues of the *Monthly Review of Business Statistics* issued by the Dominion Bureau of Statistics: November 1932, pp. 1-3; May 1934, pp. 1-2; June 1935, pp. I-II.

Chile

Compiler: Dirección General de Estadística, Santiago.

Base period: 1927-29.

Scope: Covers 24 industries including among others clothing, woolen yarn, footwear, paper, paperboards, malt, liquor, sugar, tobacco, and gas and electric power. These industries are divided into two groups: (1) manufacturing and (2) light and power. Almost the entire production of the industries included is represented, but since important industries are omitted the index covers only a relatively small portion of total industrial production.

Method: Aggregative type of index, quantitative data being multiplied by average wholesale prices during the base period.

Seasonal fluctuations and inequalities in the length of months are eliminated.

Source: Dirección General de Estadística (Santiago), *Estadística*

Chilena, March 1931, pp. 75-77; August-September 1931, pp. 222-23; October 1931, pp. 254-55; December 1935, p. 487.

Czechoslovakia

Compiler: Dr. Karel Maiwald.

Base year: 1929.

Scope: Covers 14 series which include 44 main industries. In the cases of mining and metallurgy direct monthly production data are available. The other component series are based on indirect measures of the physical volume of production, such as consumption of raw materials and auxiliary supplies; employment statistics; and export (or export and railway transport) statistics for industries exporting more than 80 per cent of their total production.

Method: An arithmetic average of the component series, weighted on the basis of estimates of the relative importance of each industry in terms of the number of workers employed, the horse-power of machinery installed, and estimates of the value of manufacturing production and of value added by manufacture. The weights are as follows: mining 11; metallurgy 23; glass 3; porcelain 2; stone and clay other than porcelain 5; chemicals 5; wood 8; paper 3; printing 2; textiles 21; leather 2; clothing 8; foodstuffs 5; electricity 2.

The group series are similarly constructed from the individual series upon which they are based.

The index is not adjusted for seasonal fluctuations, but incidental influences in the constituent series are smoothed.

Source: Obzor Narodohospodarsky, No. 6, 1934.

Denmark

Compiler· Statistiske Departement, Copenhagen.

Base year: Annual index, 1927. Monthly index, 1931.

Scope: Both annual and monthly indexes cover eight representative series. For the most part the annual index (used in constructing the index shown on page 550) is based on volume of production data but in several cases value figures, corrected by price data to show quantity changes, are used. The monthly index is based in part on volume of production, and in part on consumption of raw materials, hours worked, and wages.

Method: Aggregative type of index. The weights are based on value added by manufacture in 1926, as follows: foodstuffs 37.3; textiles 6.7; clothing 2.0; leather 3.3; wood 3.5; quarries, tiles, and glass 10.2; metals 27.8; chemicals 9.2. A method is provided for linking the monthly figures with the annual index.

The monthly index is corrected for inequalities in the length of months. Some series, such as those relating to the textile, confectionery, and building industries, are adjusted for seasonal variations.

Source: Statistiske Departement (Copenhagen), "Produktionsstatistik, 1928," *Statistiske Meddelelser,* Apr. 3, 1929 and *Statistiske Efterretninger,* No. 22, June 25, 1934, pp. 121-22.

Estonia

Compiler: Estonian Institute of Economic Research, Tallinn.

Base period: 1927-31.

Scope: Includes twelve series which cover large-scale industries and handicrafts. These series in turn cover 28 individual series, 15 of which are based upon direct volume of production data and 13 (including the important textile, engineering, leather, and clothing industries) upon the number of man-hours worked. Practically all large-scale production (concerns employing 20 or more workers) is represented, but medium and small-size establishments, which employ about two-thirds of all persons engaged in industry, are not included. Hence the index reflects closely changes in the volume of large-scale production only and merely indicates the trend of total industrial production.

Method: Both the group indexes and the general index are arithmetic averages of the component series, weighted by net value of production during 1928-31, as follows: mines and quarries 5.4; mineral working 4.8; engineering 13.6; chemicals 3.6; leather 2.4; textiles 22.6; woodworking 7.9; paper 13.1; polygraphics 4.1; foodstuffs and beverages 16.6; clothing and drygoods 1.9; electric power 4.0.

No adjustments are made for seasonal fluctuations and inequalities in the length of months.

Source: Konjunktuur (monthly review of the Estonian Institute of Economic Research, Tallinn), No. 15 (2), 1936, pp. 137-38, 165.

Finland

Compiler: Nordiska Föreningsbanken (Pohjoismaiden Yhdyspankki).

Base year: 1926.

Scope: Based on ten series which include from 60 to 65 per cent of total industrial production (about 90 per cent of total output for exports and 40 per cent of total output for home consumption). Monthly and quarterly indexes are computed: the monthly index was used in constructing the general index shown on page 550. For the export industries volume of production data are used; for the home industries, value figures adjusted by wholesale price indexes to show changes in quantity.

Method: An arithmetic average of the component series, weighted by the value of production in 1926. The weights are as follows: sawn wood 28.8, cellulose, 9.0, newsprint paper 4.5, mechanical pulpwood 1.35, plywood 1.35, or a total of 45.0 for export industries; metal work and machinery 13.2, stone and earthen ware 4.4, textiles 11.6, leather and footwear 4.9, foodstuffs and beverages 20.9, or a total of 55.0 for home market industries.

Monthly and quarterly indexes are adjusted for seasonal variation.

Source: Unitas, quarterly review of Nordiska Föreningsbanken.

France, including Alsace and Lorraine

Compiler: Statistique Générale de la France, Paris.

Base year: 1913.

Scope: Includes 18 series which directly or indirectly represent approximately one-half of total industrial production. Fourteen of these appear in the general monthly index as parts of four group series—engineering, metallurgy, textiles, and mining. The metallurgy and mining series, as well as the cotton and the wool series, are based on direct production data. All others are based on indirect measurements of production.

Method: Arithmetic average of component series, weighted by the approximate proportion of all industrial workers employed by the industry in the base year. The weights are as follows: mining (5 series) 4.0; textiles (3 series) 12.0; metallurgy (3 series) 3.0; engineering (3 series) 17.0; building 8.5; paper 1.0; leather 4.0; rubber 0.5. The component indexes are also arithmetic averages weighted in the same way.

The series for metallurgy, cotton, and wool-weaving are adjusted for inequalities in months; those for rubber, building, leather paper, motor vehicles, silk and wool, for seasonal variations. The mining series is adjusted for both.

Source: Bulletin de la Statistique Générale de la France, October 1924, pp. 71-109; April 1926, pp. 297-328.

Germany

Compiler: Institut für Konjunkturforschung, Berlin.
Base year: 1928.
Scope: Both the annual and the quarterly index include 69 series which represent approximately two-thirds of net industrial production. Three of these (foodstuffs, tobacco, and beverages) are excluded from the monthly index because of their violent seasonal fluctuations, but the margin between this index and the others is extremely small. Series relating to steel, metal goods, lumber, electricity, and optical goods are omitted for lack of data, but these goods are taken account of in the weighting of their respective group indexes. Since March 1935 production in the Saar Territory has been included, but it has not been added to production data for the base year. In the index the 69 series are divided into four main groups according to sensitiveness in registering cyclical changes. The index is outstanding for its comprehensiveness and elaborate method of construction and is a reliable indicator of the course of industrial production.

Method: A weighted arithmetic average. The weighting of the individual series is based on the number of workers employed and the total horse-power installed in each industry, corrected by the net value of output. These weights have been revised on the basis of the provisional results of the 1933 census of industrial establishments. The weighting of the four main groups is based on the net total output of all industries falling within each group during 1927-29. That is, each group is given the weight which it would command if it actually included all industrial branches pertaining to it. The weights are: investment goods (27 series) 40; sundry producers' goods (15 series) 20; consumers' goods with elastic demand (14 series) 25; consumers' goods with inelastic demand (13 series) 15.

Inequalities in the length of months are eliminated. The annual and the quarterly index are published both with and without seasonal fluctuations, but the monthly index is not adjusted for them.

Source: Institut fur Konjunkturforschung (Berlin), *Vierteljahrshefte zur Konjunkturforschung,* 1930, No. 4, Pt. A, pp. 37-41; 1933, No. 4, Pt. A, pp. 263-64; and *Wochenbericht des Instituts für Konjunkturforschung,* June 19, 1935, pp. 97-100.

Greece

Compiler: Conseil Supérieur Économique, Athens.
Base year: 1928.
Scope: Described by the compiler as being based on actual production of 57 manufactured goods and as covering nearly all industrial production. Since 1933 a monthly index has also been compiled.
Method: Arithmetic average of component series, which are weighted by value of production in base year. The weights for the more important groups are: textiles 26.3; foodstuffs 23.3; tobacco 3.4; chemicals 12.8; leather 15.3; metallurgy 1.2; engineering 1.4; building 6.3; paper 1.5; clothing 1.6; electricity 6.9.
The monthly index is adjusted for seasonal variations.
Source: Banque de Grèce, *Bulletin Mensuel,* Supplement of December 1934, pp. 1-10; March 1936, pp. 137-38.

Hungary

Compiler: Ungarisches Institut für Wirtschaftsforschung, Budapest.
Base year: 1927.
Scope: The general index covers 19 series based on quantities and reflects fairly closely the trend of the country's total industrial production.
Method: An arithmetic average, weighted by value of production of component industries in the following 19 series: workmen employed in manufacturing; consumption of coal and coke by industry; consumption of motor power; production of raw steel; consumption of raw steel; imports of the six most important raw metals; consumption of cast iron; consumption of bricks; consumption of cement; consumption of lime; production of table glass; consumption of iron girders; production of cotton goods; production of woolen goods; production of silk goods; production of artificial silk (rayon) goods; production of jute goods; production of paper; production of beer.
Seasonal variations are eliminated.
Source: League of Nations, *Monthly Bulletin of Statistics,* December 1933, pp. 481-82.

Italy

Compiler: Ministero della Corporazioni, Rome.
Base year: 1928.
Scope: Comprises 32 individual series, combined into 6 groups, and reflects fairly well the trend of industrial production. The series relating to metals, paper, gas, electricity, and textiles (spinning and weaving of flax, hemp, and jute, and silk-weaving excepted) represent quantities

produced, while all the others represent indirect measures such as activity of machines, workers employed, building permits, etc.

Method: This monthly index is a weighted geometric average of the group indexes, which in turn are weighted geometric averages of their individual series. The weights for the individual series are based on the number of persons employed according to the census of 1927; for the group series additional weights are used, based upon estimates of the value added by manufacture. The group weights are as follows: textiles 37; metallurgy 3.1; engineering 32.9; paper 3; construction 19; electricity and gas 5.

The index is not corrected for seasonal fluctuations but inequalities in the length of months are removed.

Source: Numeri Indici Mensili della Produzione industriale in Italia, July 1935, pp. 209-10; *Economia,* October 1934, pp. 361-64; and Instituto Centrale di Statistica (Rome), *Compendio Statistico Italiano,* Vol. XIII, Chap. XXI. For a description of an annual index, see League of Nations, *Statistical Yearbook, 1935-36,* p. 189.

Japan

Compiler: Ministry of Commerce and Industry, Tokyo.

Base period: 1931-33.

Scope: Includes 31 series, of which 25 represent manufacturing and 6 mining or extractive industries. With the exception of electricity, which is based on consumption of electric power, the series are all based on actual producton data. In some cases the whole industry is covered by the series, and in most cases all of the principal companies are included. Since 1930 the index has been comprehensive in scope and a good indicator of the total volume of industrial production. For the years 1927-29, however, it has been linked to a less representative index and indicates changes in production for only a few important industries.

Method: Arithmetic weighted average of the component series. For mining the weights are derived from the total value of output, and for manufacturing from the net value added by manufacture during the base period. In some cases this net value has been estimated according to capital invested, profits, and other indirect indications. The weights are: mining (12.3) broken down into coal 8.4, petroleum 0.5, copper 2.3, gold 0.7, silver 0.2, sulphur 0.2; and manufacturing (87.7) broken down into pig iron 2.3, steel 5.0, machinery 15.2, cotton yarns 6.8, woolen yarns 1.1, raw silk 9.1, spun silk yarns 0.7, cotton tissues 8.0, silk tissues 6.4, woolen tissues 2.9, rayon tissues 1.8, rayon yarns 1.8, sulphate of ammonia 1.4, nitro-lime 0.5, superphosphate of lime 0.7, bleaching powder 0.2, soda ash 0.5, caustic soda 0.2, cement 2.9, glass (plate and sheet) 0.7, paper 4.1, wheat flour 0.7, refined sugar 2.9, electricity 8.9, gas 2.9.

No adjustment is made for inequalities of length of month or seasonal variations.

Source: League of Nations, *Monthly Bulletin of Statistics,* August 1935, pp. 338-39.

Netherlands

Compiler: Centraal Bureau voor de Statistiek, The Hague.
Base period: 1922-25.
Scope: Covers eight series representing imports of raw materials in excess of those exported or used in the manufacture of exports. It reflects only roughly the trend of industrial activity of the country.
Method: Arithmetic average of the component series, which are weighted by estimated value added by manufacture. The weights are: pig iron, iron, and structural steel output of blast furnaces 41.6; wood 4.2; raw cotton and cotton yarns 20.6; raw wool and woolen yarns 8.3; tallow, oil seeds, and whale oil 12.5; cocoa beans 4.2; hides and skins 4.2; wood for paper manufacture, wood pulp 4.2.
Source: Centraal Bureau voor de Statistiek (The Hague), "Nederlandsche Conjunctuurlignen le kwartaal, 1928," supplement to the quarterly *Economische en Sociale Kroniek; De Nederlandsche Conjunctuur,* September 1931, p. 14. See also League of Nations, *Statistical Yearbook, 1935-36,* p. 191, and H. W. Methorst and J. Tinbergen, "Les Recherches Relatives a la Conjuncture au Bureau Central de Statistique des Pays-Bas," *Revue de l'Institut International de Statistique* (The Hague), April 1934, pp. 37-55. For description of a new and more comprehensive index, see Centraal Bureau voor de Statistiek, *Maandschrift,* Apr. 30, 1934, pp. 479-505.

Norway

Compiler: Statistiske Centralbyrå, Oslo.
Base year: 1927.
Scope: Includes 13 series representing main groups of industries. They are based on quantitative production returns, except in the cases of iron and metal and of printing, for which the number of hours worked (corrected for increase in productivity) is employed. The annual index gives a fairly complete picture of the fluctuations of total industrial production, while the monthly index reflects only the trend of production in key industries.
Method: A weighted geometric average of the individual series, which are of the aggregative type, quantity being multiplied by prices in 1927. The weights, which represent value added by manufacture in 1927, are as follows: mining and smelting 3.7; earth and quarries 4.2; iron and metals 14.7; chemicals 7.4; oils and fats 3.0; gas 1.0; wood 5.1; paper 15.2; leather and rubber 1.6; textiles 5.7; clothing 4.9; foodstuffs 29.0; printing 4.5.
There is also a monthly index with the base period January-June 1933. It is an arithmetic average of its component series. These series are constructed from production returns and, in a few instances, from the number of hours worked, the consumption of raw materials, etc. They are weighted in accordance with value added by manufacture in 1932 and cover the most important industries only.
Source: Statistiske Meddelelser (Oslo), Nos. 1 and 2, 1934.

Poland

Compiler: Institute of Research on General Business Movements and Price Formation, Warsaw.

Base year: 1928.

Scope: Includes 17 series of which 4 relate to mining, 2 to metallurgy, and 11 to manufactures. The mining and metallurgy data are direct production figures but the basic data for the finishing industries cover hours worked in establishments which employ at least 20 workers.

Method: An arithmetic average of the component series, each of which is weighted by the proportion of all workers which it employed in the base year (in the case of the finishing industries, the proportion of working hours). The weights are: mining 18.0; metallurgy 8.2; manufactures 73.8.

Adjustment is made for inequalities in the length of months and for normal seasonal fluctuations.

Source: Central Statistical Office (Warsaw), *Konjunktura Gospodarcza w Polsce, 1924-27; Konjuntura Gospodarcza, 1929,* No. 4; *Travaux de l'Institut des Rescherches sur le Mouvement général des Affaires et sur la Formation des Prix,* Vol. II, No. 2, 1933.

Rumania

Compiler: Institutul Românesc de Conjunctură, Bucharest.

Base year: 1927.

Scope: Includes 18 series which are divided into four main groups: manufacturing industries, extractive industries, monopoly industries, electricity. The index portrays with a fair degree of reliability the trend and changes in the volume of total industrial production.

Method: Arithmetic average of the 18 series, which are weighted by average value of production during 1927-31. The weights are: manufacturing industries (73.2)—food 20.3, chemicals 14.3, textiles 11.0, metals 10.9, wood 5.8, hides, skins, and leather 4.7, paper and printing 3.3, building materials 1.9, plate glass and ceramics 0.8, electro-technical products 0.2; extractive industries (13.7)—petroleum 9.0, coal 3.3, natural gas 0.6, various metals 0.5, quarries 0.3; monopoly industries (8.2) —tobacco 7.3, salt 0.9; electricity 4.9.

There is no adjustment for inequalities in the length of months or seasonal variations.

Source: Institutul Românesc de Conjunctură (Bucharest), *Buletin Trimestrial,* No. 34, 1933.

Spain

Compiler: Banco de España.

Base year: 1928.

Scope: Represents 15 branches of industry, namely, pig iron, steel, copper, silver metal, lead, zinc, superphosphates, cement, coal, electricity, gasoline, lubricating oils, cotton, wool, and tobacco.

Method: Constructed by the aggregative method, quantities being multiplied by prices. The component series are said to be weighted in accordance with the value of production, but weights are not available.

Source: League of Nations, *Monthly Bulletin of Statistics,* July 1935, p. 290.

Sweden

Compiler: Sveriges Industriförbund, Stockholm.

Base period: 1925-30.

Scope: Includes 14 series which represent industrial establishments which employ 35.6 per cent of all industrial workers in the industries included in the index. It shows accurately the course of production in the key industries and roughly indicates changes in the total volume of production. It is less inclusive than the annual Kommerkollegium index, to which it has been linked.

Method: An arithmetic average of the component series, which are weighted by the relative number of workers employed in 1930, corrected, where necessary, by relative values of production. The weights are: mining 2.6; iron and steel 7.7; metallurgy 2.6; engineering 20.5; wood pulp 6.4; sawn wood 9.0; earth 5.1; stones 2.6; chemicals 2.6; paper 5.1; textiles 14.1; leather 5.1; household goods 11.6; foodstuffs and beverages 5.1.
Adjusted for seasonal variations.

Source: K. G. Nilson, "Den Industrielle Productionens Volym i Sverige Aren, 1913-23," *Kommersiella Meddelanden,* Feb. 28, 1925; *Industriförbundets Meddelanden,* No. 2, 1933; *Sweden Yearbook,* 1936, p. 40.

Union of Soviet Socialist Republics

Compiler: Central Board of National Economic Accounting of the Gosplan, Moscow.

Base year: 1928.

Scope: Includes 27 series covering large-scale industries only. Such industries include all enterprises which are equipped with motive power and employ 16 or more workers, and all industries without motive power which employ 30 or more workers. They represent from 85 to 89 per cent of total industrial production. The index reflects the trend rather than actual volume of production.

Method: Aggregative type of index, the aggregate value of production being calculated at October 1926-September 1927 prices. The weights assigned to the component series are: electricity 1.1; coal 2.2; crude petroleum extraction 1.8; petroleum refining 2.3; iron ore 0.2; basic chemical production 0.5; dye-stuffs 0.3; rubber 1.1; chemical treatment of wood 0.2; glass and porcelain 0.8; metallurgy (ferrous metals) 1.3; engineering 12.6; coke ovens 0.5; woodwork 3.0; paper 1.0; printing 0.9; cotton 16.2; linen 1.2; wool 3.2; silk 0.4; fats and soap 1.7; foodstuffs 21.8; timber felling (not yet published); building materials 1.5; cement 0.4; matches 0.1.

Sources: Central Board of National Economic Accounting of the

Gosplan (Moscow), *The USSR in Figures, 1934,* pp. 32-35; *The USSR in Figures, 1935,* pp. 110-11; *Planovoie Khoziaistvo,* January-December 1934; Central Direction of Statistics of Public Economy of the State Plan, *Plan,* No. 21, 1935; League of Nations, *Statistical Yearbook, 1935-36,* pp. 180-81.

United Kingdom

Compiler: Board of Trade, London.

Base year: 1930.

Scope: Comprises two main industrial series, mining and manufacturing, with the latter subdivided into nine series. The grouping follows that of the 1930 census of production as closely as possible. Data relating to the production of paper, pianos, and cement and to the consumption of rubber, although not set up as separate series, are taken account of in the weighting of the appropriate groups. About 90 per cent of the production of the component groups (30 per cent in the case of building), and over 70 per cent of total mining and manufacturing activity are directly or indirectly represented in the index. It is therefore a reliable indicator of the trend of production and also of month-to-month changes in the volume of production. The index is characterized by its comprehensiveness and elaborate methods of construction. Of the branches of industry not covered the most important are clothing (other than boots and shoes) and public utility services (other than gas and electricity).

Method: Weighted arithmetic average of component group indexes, which in turn are weighted averages of the single branches of industry within each group. The weights, which are based on value added in production or manufacture in 1930, are as follows: mining (13.7); manufactures (86.3)—iron and steel and their products 9.0, non-ferrous metals 1.2, engineering and shipbuilding 23.3, textiles 12.6, chemical and allied trades 3.5, leather and boots and shoes 3.4, food and drink and tobacco 16.3, gas and electricity 7.2, building materials and building 4.2. (In addition to the manufactures listed above, paper, pianos, and rubber are included in the index.)

There is no adjustment for seasonal variations or inequalities in the length of months.

Source: Board of Trade Journal, July 26, 1928, pp. 104, 107; Feb. 21, 1929, pp. 253-54; Mar. 28, 1935, pp. 515-17; May 21, 1936, pp. 723-24. League of Nations, *Statistical Yearbook, 1935-36,* p. 192.

United States of America

Compiler: Federal Reserve Board, Washington, D.C.

Base period: 1923-25.

Scope: Made up of two component indexes, manufactures and minerals, which comprise 54 individual industrial series. Changes in about 35 of the industries covered are measured by direct production data, and in the others by indirect data. The index represents directly and indirectly nearly 80 per cent of total production and is therefore one of the most comprehensive of its kind. It is distinguished by elaborate methods of construction. The base period is fairly recent, but the component series have been computed and combined in such a way as to allow, so far as possible, for changes in the relative importance of industries during recent years.

Method: The index is of the aggregative type, physical quantity figures being multiplied by price data. The weight for each manufacturing industry is a composite of the unit value added by manufacture in a given industry and a factor representing the importance of that industry and of certain related industries not directly represented in the index. For mining, average prices in the base period are used for weighting. The weights assigned to the main groups of industries are: iron and steel 20.64; textiles 18.38; food products 9.05; paper and printing 10.00; lumber and allied products 8.29; transportation and equipment 5.96; leather and its manufactures 3.62; stone and glass 2.30; metals other than iron and steel 1.62; chemicals and allied products 3.18; rubber products 1.59; tobacco 1.02; total manufacturing 85.85; minerals 14.15.

Inequalities in the length of months are eliminated and adjustments for seasonal fluctuations are made.

Source: Federal Reserve Bulletin, February 1927, pp. 100-03; March 1927, pp. 170-75; March 1932, pp. 194-96; September 1933, pp. 584-87.

9. Trend of Unemployment in Selected Countries

Unemployment data are still so fragmentary and incomplete in character as to make it impossible to present a comparable and accurate picture of employment conditions in the different countries. The International Labor Office, however, has for some years published figures on unemployment for a selected group of countries. In some of these countries the data are presented in terms of the actual number of unemployed, in others as a percentage of the eligible workers unemployed, and in still others in terms of the number of applications for work. The percentage of eligible workers unemployed naturally reflects increases or decreases in the growth of the population. In the following table we give the data as published by the International Labor Office:

Unemployment in Selected Countries, 1925-35

Year	United States (Unemployed, in thousands)	Great Britain and Northern Ireland (Percentage of workers unemployed)	France (Number of applications for work)	Belgium (Percentage of workers unemployed)	Germany and Saar Territory (Number of unemployed)	Japan (Persons wholly unemployed, 1929=100)
1925....	...	11.5	11,167	6.0	647,848	...
1926....	...	12.6	11,705	4.2	2,016,753	...
1927....	...	9.7	47,289	5.7	1,256,871	...
1928....	2,034	10.8	15,275	4.4	1,356,871	...
1929....	1,813	10.4	10,052	4.3	1,898,547	100
1930....	4,921	16.0	13,859	11.5	3,034,866	133
1931....	8,634	21.3	75,215	27.8	4,540,667	153
1932....	12,803	22.1	308,096	39.7	5,616,932	170
1933....	13,176	19.9	307,844	34.2	4,843,177	140
1934....	11,382	16.8	376,320	36.2	2,752,850	125
1935....	11,446	15.5	465,796	30.7	2,117,008	118

Year	Italy (Number of unemployed)	Sweden (Percentage of workers unemployed)	Canada (Percentage of workers unemployed)	Australia (Percentage of workers unemployed)	Czecho-slovakia (Number of applicants for work)	Denmark (Percentage of workers unemployed)
1925....	119,486	11.0	7.0	8.9	49,369	14.7
1926....	125,839	12.2	5.1	7.1	67,851	20.7
1927....	375,538	12.0	.49	7.0	52,869	22.5
1928....	362,879	10.6	4.5	10.8	38,636	18.5
1929....	316,941	10.7	5.7	11.1	41,630	14.5
1930....	448,845	12.2	11.1	19.3	105,442	13.7
1931....	763,175	17.2	16.8	27.4	291,332	17.9
1932....	1,039,910	22.8	22.0	29.0	554,059	31.7
1933....	1,052,839	23.7	22.3	25.1	738,267	28.8
1934....	995,723	18.9	18.2	20.5	676,994	22.1
1935....	791,281	16.2	15.4	16.5	686,269	19.8

Year	Estonia (Number of unemployed)	Finland (Number of unemployed)	Latvia (Number of applications for work)	Netherlands (Percentage of workers unemployed)	New Zealand (Number of unemployed)	Norway (Number of unemployed)
1925....	2,399	29531	2,721	9.5	386	14,928
1926....	2,178	1,956	2,794	8.7	1,158	23,467
1927....	2,957	1,868	3,131	9.0	1,930	23,889
1928....	2,629	1,735	4,700	6.8	2,143	21,759
1929....	3,181	3,906	5,617	7.1	2,895	18,089
1930....	3,089	7,993	4,851	9.7	5,003	19,353
1931....	3,542	11,522	8,709	18.1	41,430	27,479
1932....	7,121	17,581	14,587	29.5	51,549	32,705
1933....	8,207	17,139	8,156	31.0	46,971	35,591
1934....	2,970	10,011	4,972	32.1	39,235	35,121
1935....	1,779	7,163	4,825	36.3	38,469	35,261

10. MONTHLY INDEXES OF INDUSTRIAL PRODUCTION FOR SELECTED COUNTRIES, JANUARY 1931–JUNE 1936
(1929=100)

Year and Month	Canada	United States	Chile	Japan	Germany	Belgium	France	Poland	Sweden[b]	Czecho-slovakia	Hungary	United Kingdom
1931:												
Jan.	75.6	70.6	80.3	87.7	65.5	80.9	95.0	74	74.5	77		
Feb.	78.0	72.3	81.2	86.5	65.5	77.9	95.0	73	80.9	75		84.8
Mar.	79.5	73.1	88.0	85.1	69.3	80.9	94.3	72	83.6	76	68.6	
Apr.	73.2	73.9	96.6	88.1	73.7	80.1	93.6	71	88.2	80		
May	73.2	73.1	84.6	91.8	73.1	74.3	92.1	72	81.8	81		82.1
June	66.1	69.7	84.6	89.9	74.3	77.2	90.0	72	80.9	78	68.6	
July	70.9	68.9	82.1	94.4	73.1	78.7	87.9	72	86.4	78		
Aug.	68.5	65.5	64.1	92.6	69.1	78.7	86.4	70	86.4	81		79.5
Sept.	71.7	63.9	65.8	93.0	67.5	77.2	85.5	69	85.5	82	68.6	
Oct.	66.9	61.3	66.7	92.8	63.3	77.9	83.6	66	85.2	82		
Nov.	67.0	61.3	69.2	91.6	62.0	75.7	81.4	63	88.2	79		86.6
Dec.	63.0	62.2	67.5	91.3	57.8	69.1	79.3	58	91.8	73	62.7	
1932:												
Jan.	63.0	60.5	65.0	85.9	51.9	71.3	75.0	52	88.2	65		
Feb.	63.8	58.0	72.6	89.5	52.4	67.6	71.4	52	86.4	60		84.8
Mar.	60.6	56.3	85.5	96.7	53.0	66.9	70.0	53	90.9	58	82.4	
Apr.	53.5	52.9	85.5	93.6	53.3	66.9	67.9	55	79.1	56		
May	59.1	50.4	85.5	95.7	54.8	65.4	67.1	55	82.7	56		83.9
June	60.6	49.6	84.6	93.3	53.3	62.5	66.4	54	72.7	55	66.7	
July	58.3	48.7	88.0	95.6	51.0	48.5	65.7	55	67.3	54		
Aug.	58.3	50.4	90.6	95.2	50.3	50.7	66.4	55	73.6	55		77.7
Sept.	56.7	55.5	89.7	97.9	53.3	64.7	67.1	53	77.3	57	68.6	
Oct.	55.1	56.3	99.1	101.4	56.6	66.6	67.9	56	75.5	58		
Nov.	56.7	54.6	103.4	106.4	57.6	70.6	69.3	57	77.3	56		84.8
Dec.	53.5	55.5	92.3	111.8	55.2	69.9	70.0	49	79.1	54	75.5	
1933:												
Jan.	48.8	54.6	96.6	105.2	52.2	69.1	71.4	47	79.1	59		
Feb.	48.0	52.9	100.9	103.2	53.7	66.9	73.6	51	80.9	57		84.8
Mar.	49.6	49.6	98.3	116.6	57.1	69.1	75.0	46	80.0	56	73.5	
Apr.	51.2	55.5	94.9	113.5	57.9	67.6	76.4	53	76.4	58		
May	57.5	65.5	95.7	117.2	58.9	72.1	77.9	55	79.1	60		86.6
June	63.0	76.5	94.9	107.6	60.3	68.4	79.3	58	77.3	60	78.4	
July	65.4	84.0	88.0	113.9	60.5	66.2	80.0	58	79.1	58		

Aug.	70.9	76.5	99.1	115.8	62.3	64.0	79.3	57	82.7	61	83.3
Sept.	70.9	70.6	94.9	114.2	64.7	65.4	78.6	59	81.8	61	89.2
Oct.	68.5	63.9	95.7	121.1	67.1	66.2	77.1	59	84.5	65	
Nov.	66.1	60.5	95.7	122.4	68.3	71.3	76.4	61	90.9	65	
Dec.	66.9	63.0	90.6	124.5	68.1	69.9	75.7	61	91.8	62	
1934:											
Jan.	66.9	65.5	92.3	118.6	70.3	71.3	75.7	59	93.6	59	89.2
Feb.	66.1	68.1	98.3	116.2	74.3	66.9	75.0	61	94.5	61	
Mar.	72.4	70.6	100.0	125.3	79.7	58.4	74.3	62	97.3	66	
Apr.	71.7	71.4	101.7	126.0	78.6	57.6	73.6	65	100.0	70	95.1
May	78.7	72.3	100.9	126.2	80.4	66.2	72.1	64	100.9	71	
June	74.8	69.7	100.0	128.0	80.0	65.4	70.7	62	101.8	69	
July	75.6	63.9	102.6	130.0	81.6	65.4	70.0	61	97.3	67	90.2
Aug.	78.7	61.3	106.8	124.4	80.7	65.2	69.3	62	101.8	68	
Sept.	77.2	59.7	106.8	136.9	84.1	66.2	67.9	63	101.8	69	
Oct.	75.6	61.3	116.2	137.5	83.9	68.4	67.1	64	100.9	67	103.9
Nov.	76.4	62.2	118.8	145.4	83.3	69.9	67.1	67	103.6	66	
Dec.	71.7	71.4	112.8		83.5	58.4	66.5	65	103.6	65	
1935:											
Jan.	76.8	76.5	109.4	131.6	84.2	66.9	66.7	64	105.5	65	106.1
Feb.	79.4	74.8	117.9	130.9	85.1	65.6	66.7	65	106.4	65	
Mar.	73.2	74.0	115.9	142.7	91.1	66.9	66.7	65	109.1	65	
Apr.	76.7	72.3	118.5	143.0	93.8	71.8	66.7	67	107.3	66	103.2
May	81.9	71.4	119.6	143.1	95.5	72.8	66.7	67	109.1	68	
June	78.3	72.3	123.8	137.2	92.8	70.0	66.7	65		68	
July	81.6	72.3	117.3	141.7	94.7	69.6	66.7	68		67	114.0
Aug.	86.6	74.0	117.4	139.9	95.5	70.8	66.7	66		68	
Sept.	80.5	74.8	121.5	141.0	102.4	70.8	67.4	67		73	
Oct.	85.9	79.8	129.9	148.8	101.1	73.3	68.1	68		75	120.5
Nov.	89.1	82.4	129.2	147.8	100.1	77.8	68.1	67		79	
Dec.	85.4	87.4	120.8	152.8	96.5	81.7	68.8	69		80	
1936:											
Jan.	84.0	82.4	107.8	135.3	95.7	78.8	69.5	68		75	127.0
Feb.	82.3	79.0	124.6	139.8	96.2	80.3	71.0	69		74	
Mar.	81.7	78.2	125.1	150.5	99.6	80.6	72.4	68		75	
Apr.	85.7	84.0	126.8	148.0	103.4	80.6	73.4	72		78	
May	86.8	84.9	122.2	149.3	105.2	79.1	73.1	71		77	
June	87.6	86.6	121.3	...			70.3	72			

a League of Nations, *Statistical Yearbook* for the years since 1931; and *Monthly Bulletin of Statistics*, August 1936.
b Suspended pending recast of index.

11. Monthly Indexes of Wholesale Prices at
(Monthly average

Period	Argen-tine	Aus-tralia	Bel-gium	Canada	Czecho-slovakia	France	Ger-many
1929:							
Mar.	102.1	99.4	101.6	100.7	104.2	104.7	102.2
June	99.0	99.4	100.0	97.3	99.8	100.8	98.5
Sept.	100.0	103.0	99.2	102.0	96.9	96.9	100.7
Dec.	97.9	97.6	96.8	100.7	93.3	95.3	97.8
1930:							
Mar.	99.1	91.4	91.0	96.0	90.7	89.0	92.1
June	96.2	91.9	88.1	91.7	89.7	86.1	90.7
Sept.	94.2	85.0	83.7	85.9	84.9	88.7	89.5
Dec.	90.3	77.6	79.8	81.3	82.5	86.3	85.9
1931:							
Mar.	90.3	80.8	77.6	77.9	82.8	85.9	83.0
June	89.8	79.0	75.4	75.1	83.9	82.6	81.9
Sept.	90.1	77.2	70.2	72.9	78.3	75.4	79.2
Dec.	97.0	79.0	67.3	73.6	76.6	70.5	75.6
1932:							
Mar.	95.5	79.8	64.4	72.2	75.4	70.8	72.7
June	93.4	77.1	60.4	69.5	73.4	67.8	70.1
Sept.	91.7	79.9	62.6	68.9	74.6	65.9	69.3
Dec.	88.7	75.8	61.3	66.9	72.4	65.9	67.3
1933:							
Mar.	87.9	73.9	59.2	67.3	70.9	62.2	66.4
June	88.5	79.8	59.6	70.6	73.6	64.3	67.7
Sept.	87.6	82.1	58.3	72.1	72.1	63.3	69.2
Dec.	96.7	79.7	56.9	72.2	70.9	64.9	70.1
1934:							
Mar.	100.2	80.9	56.2	75.3	72.6	62.8	69.9
June	102.0	81.1	55.5	75.4	76.5	60.4	70.8
Sept.	104.4	82.8	55.2	75.3	75.3	58.2	73.2
Dec.	102.3	80.9	55.0	74.5	76.0	54.9	73.6
1935:							
Mar.	100.7	79.9	54.5	75.3	76.3	53.4	73.4
June	99.7	81.3	65.2	74.8	79.1	52.6	73.8
Sept.	100.2	82.9	65.8	75.6	77.0	53.0	74.6
Dec.	102.4	81.0	68.0	75.9	77.9	56.5	75.4
1936:							
Mar.	101.9	82.4	67.9	75.7	77.0	60.0	75.5
June	101.2	84.5	67.0	75.6	76.6	60.3	75.8

ª League of Nations, *Statistical Yearbook* for the years since 1932; and

QUARTERLY INTERVALS, MARCH 1929-JUNE 1936*
for 1929 = 100)

India	Japan	Nether-lands Indies	Nor-way	Poland	Sweden	Union of S. Africa	United King-dom	United States
101.4	103.0	101.4	101.3	103.1	102.9	100.9	102.2	100.7
97.9	101.2	100.7	98.0	99.0	99.3	99.1	99.3	99.3
101.4	98.8	100.0	100.7	97.9	100.0	97.4	99.3	100.7
95.0	93.4	97.3	98.7	95.8	95.7	92.2	97.1	97.8
88.7	89.1	93.9	94.0	91.1	89.3	92.5	91.3	94.6
82.3	82.4	90.5	91.9	88.6	87.9	89.7	88.4	91.1
78.7	78.0	87.2	91.3	87.0	85.0	85.9	84.9	88.6
70.9	73.2	85.1	87.2	83.1	83.6	85.7	80.5	83.5
70.9	72.0	75.0	83.2	79.7	80.7	88.0	78.1	79.8
66.0	68.6	70.3	80.5	79.4	78.6	85.4	75.8	75.7
64.5	68.0	66.9	78.5	74.9	76.4	84.6	73.7	74.7
69.5	68.7	64.2	81.9	72.9	79.3	85.0	78.1	72.0
66.7	72.1	61.5	81.9	70.5	77.9	81.4	76.8	69.3
61.0	66.6	56.8	80.5	70.2	77.1	76.8	72.8	67.1
64.5	76.2	55.4	82.6	65.5	78.6	74.9	75.2	68.5
62.4	84.0	52.7	82.6	62.0	77.1	75.3	74.3	65.7
58.2	80.7	48.7	81.2	62.1	75.0	77.6	72.4	63.2
63.1	81.7	48.7	81.2	62.4	75.7	82.1	75.5	68.2
62.4	83.0	46.6	82.6	60.3	77.9	86.0	76.9	74.3
63.1	79.8	45.3	81.9	59.8	78.6	91.4	76.7	74.3
62.4	80.5	45.9	81.9	59.5	80.0	89.7	77.2	77.3
63.8	79.4	45.3	82.6	57.9	81.4	84.4	77.0	78.3
63.1	81.5	45.3	84.6	57.1	81.4	85.0	77.4	81.4
62.4	82.4	45.3	83.9	55.5	82.1	82.3	76.9	80.7
61.7	83.5	43.9	84.6	54.1	82.1	80.0	76.1	83.2
64.5	82.0	43.9	84.6	54.6	82.9	81.9	77.4	83.7
63.1	85.9	43.9	85.9	56.3	82.1	82.8	78.5	84.7
66.0	87.3	43.9	87.9	54.7	84.3	85.8	80.0	84.9
64.5	86.8	43.2	88.6	54.1	84.3	86.0	80.3	83.5
63.8	88.1	...	88.6	56.0	84.3	83.1	81.1	83.1

Monthly Bulletin of Statistics, August 1936.

12. National Indexes of Production of Investment and
Consumption Goods, 1930–35[a]
(Average for 1929 = 100)

Country	1930	1931	1932	1933	1934	1935
Belgium:						
Producer inv. goods....	88.8	79.4	66.2	68.1	77.3	80.5
Building only.........	87.3	93.4	93.2	92.6	77.0	99.5
Current cons. goods....	84.2	75.4	68.1	66.0	57.6	74.1
Canada:						
Producer inv. goods....	68.5	39.5	25.7	31.6	50.3	65.4
Automobiles only......	58.2	30.1	23.5	26.0	43.2	70.0
Building only.........	79.0	55.6	26.3	17.3	21.8	29.7
Current cons. goods....	95.5	94.6	87.6	93.4	101.8	102.3
Czechoslovakia:						
Producer inv. goods....	85.2	70.6	42.5	43.0	49.0	58.3
Building only.........	65.5	75.0	87.6	62.4	50.3	35.5
Current cons. goods....	92.0	87.1	74.6	70.1	79.8	79.7
Finland:						
Producer inv. goods....	82.4	69.1	67.4	78.5	100.8	106.1
Building only.........	59.8	113.4	36.0	44.8	102.0	120.8
Current cons. goods....	98.5	89.9	96.8	110.8	126.5	139.8
France:						
Producer inv. goods....	99.8	84.9	59.4	68.4	62.0	60.7
Automobiles only......	97.4	83.0	65.1	71.1	69.0	61.3
Building only.........	111.4	111.6	81.3	74.0	66.7	55.7
Current cons. goods....	95.7	87.6	71.6	85.8	79.9	76.3
Germany:						
Producer inv. goods....	78.8	51.5	33.7	41.7	68.6	95.3
Automobiles only......	72.4	51.3	31.4	65.5	104.9	149.4
Building only.........	88.0	55.7	37.6	46.2	76.0	100.1
Current cons. goods....	94.3	88.0	77.7	82.5	92.0	92.6
Italy:						
Producer inv. goods....	95.8	86.8	72.4	76.6	74.3	...
Automobiles only......	81.8	64.5	69.9	76.0	78.0	...
Building only.........	87.3	52.8	45.1	53.1	88.6	...
Current cons. goods....	91.7	83.1	72.2	80.9	80.6	...
Netherlands:						
Producer inv. goods....	86.6	62.9	45.9	55.2	55.8	47.2
Building only.........	110.6	103.3	71.5	117.1	100.1	80.0
Current cons. goods....	96.3	98.5	83.0	85.9	86.1	89.6
Norway:						
Producer inv. goods....	106.3	75.0	88.3	93.2	98.1	105.3
Building only.........	105.4	108.6	154.8	105.6	145.0	165.8
Current cons. goods....	96.0	81.9	97.4	94.8	97.4	105.1
Poland:						
Producer inv. goods....	81.1	60.5	43.2	49.6	58.9	65.6
Building only.........	67.3	39.2	21.5	18.1	23.9	26.8
Current cons. goods....	85.6	76.8	65.5	65.1	72.5	76.1
Sweden:						
Producer inv. goods....	98.4	89.8	80.2	84.4	112.9	...
Building only.........	107.4	85.9	76.8	47.9	102.5	126.7
Current cons. goods....	100.8	100.1	98.6	105.3	118.1	...
United Kingdom:						
Producer inv. goods....	91.7	73.3	69.6	77.7	93.1	103.1
Automobiles only......	94.6	87.8	103.0	123.3	145.8	178.5
Building only.........	105.7	91.5	105.9	140.8	157.2	177.2
Current cons. goods....	92.0	91.3	94.7	98.9	107.9	114.2
United States:						
Producer inv. goods....	74.3	48.9	28.0	42.4	45.6	61.8
Automobiles only......	63.0	44.4	25.9	35.6	51.1	71.1
Building only.........	59.3	49.1	19.0	18.8	16.6	35.0
Current cons. goods....	86.8	85.2	75.9	84.2	83.4	87.6

[a] League of Nations, *World Production and Prices, 1935–36*, pp. 52–53. Of the countries listed by the League, we have included only those which show at least three classes of commodities. These are sub-indexes of the League's national indexes, briefly described under Table 8 of this appendix.

APPENDIX B

RECOVERY LEGISLATION IN FOURTEEN
SELECTED COUNTRIES

We present in this appendix a thumb-nail picture of the scope and varied character of government legislation during the course of the depression in fourteen representative countries.[1]

1. England. Measures taken by the British government for the purpose of alleviating the depression and promoting recovery were of varied character. Money, credit, and fiscal policies were emphasized as of far-reaching general importance; but at the same time efforts were also made to protect and foster domestic industry, to stimulate agriculture and foreign trade, and to provide employment and promote recovery by means of subsidies, especially of the housing industry.

Money and Credit

Loans of 130 million pounds secured in Paris and New York to check exchange crisis (August 1931).

Gold standard abandoned (September 1931).

Exchange Equalization Fund created to control sterling rates (March 1932).

Equalization Fund increased 2 million pounds (May 1933); Fund used to prevent fall in sterling (July 1933).

Decision reached by governments of British Empire to bring about mutually stable exchange rates (July 1933).

Fifteen million pounds lent to Canada (July 1933).

[1] Because of the enormous mass of legislation and other measures adopted, the task of selection has presented great difficulties. No doubt special students in the various countries will find much to criticize or regret; and actual errors may well have crept in. Nevertheless, it is believed such a survey affords a useful illustration of the range and character of governmental measures designed to alleviate the depression and promote recovery.

The Budget

Commission formed to cut state expenses (February 1931).

Expenditures reduced: unemployment relief, 10 per cent; salaries of civil servants, 10 per cent; road building, 8 million pounds; army and navy, 5 million pounds (September 1931).

Income, beer, tobacco, petrol, and entertainment taxes increased (September 1931).

Five per cent war loan of 2.1 billion pounds converted to 3.5 per cent basis (June 1932).

Short-term indebtedness consolidated by means of conversion loan (March 1933).

Various taxes decreased (1934-35).

Labor and Unemployment

Contribution of 90,227,852 pounds to housing program made by government (1929-36); 11,925,426 pounds to March 1933 by local governments.

New Unemployment Law established (June 1934).

Transitional payment abolished and Unemployment Assistance Board created (June 1934).

Unemployment insurance increased from 26 to 52 weeks, and compulsory age reduced from 16 to 14 years (June 1934).

Two commissions appointed to improve social and economic conditions in depressed areas; fund, partly governmental, created to further the work (November 1934).

Agriculture

Through Agricultural Marketing Act a majority of producers permitted to regulate marketing; decisions binding on minority (1932).

Wheat Quota Law passed guaranteeing producers minimum price (April 1932).

Marketing schemes adopted for hops, milk, pigs and bacon, and potatoes (1932-33).

Marketing boards for various products established under Agricultural Marketing Act; empowered to regulate supplies of imports and domestic products; provided with funds (July 1933); given increased financial powers (December 1933).

Importation of eggs limited by Ministry of Agriculture (March 1933).

Minimum price for two years guaranteed milk producers by government (April 1934).

Beet-sugar subsidy extended (July 1935).

Industry

Cheap loan made to and money invested in shipping company to help build the S.S. *Queen Mary* (July 1934).

Bill passed making it possible to cease operating 10 million looms, or 25 per cent of capacity (July 1934).

Two million pounds subsidy granted for ships in operation; 10 million pounds appropriated for modernizing and building ships—conditional upon destruction of two old tons for every modernized or new ton (December 1934).

Company created to finance railway construction through bond issue of 27 million pounds, with capital and interest guaranteed by the government (December 1934).

Foreign Trade

The "Abnormal Importations Customs Act" enacted (November 1931).

Levying of duties up to 100 per cent authorized where imports exceeded the normal level (November 1931).

Duties on a wide variety of products increased (March 1931-March 1932).

Ottawa Agreement Act with Dominion of Canada adopted (November 1932).

Agreement reached with Polish coal mine owners relating to exports and prices (December 1934).

Trade agreements to expand exports consummated with 16 countries (1933-35).

Iron and steel duties increased (April 1935).

Agreement reached by British Iron and Steel Federation and International Iron and Steel Cartel on import quotas to England (April 1935).

2. *France.* The measures passed by the government of France cover a wide range of economic activity, especially in the later years. Particularly noteworthy are the continuous efforts to prevent fiscal disorganization; the attempts to reduce costs and stabilize industry; and the

various measures designed to relieve agricultural distress.

Money and Credit

Gold standard maintained without depreciation until September 1936.

Loan of 4,570 million francs to colonies (February 1931).

Clearing system established for regulating French claims and debts with countries having exchange control (February 1932).

Discount rates adjusted by Bank of France to meet changing conditions (1931-35).

The Budget

State loan of 85 billion francs (one-third of total debt) converted at lower interest (September 1932).

Military budget reduced 1.5 billion francs (1932-33).

Income tax increased (1932-33).

Algeria given loan of 3.3 billion francs to enable it to repay loan of 1.4 billions to French government (1932-33).

Ten billion franc loan voted to cover deficit of three preceding years (January 1933); issued in course of year.

New 10 billion franc deficit loan authorized (December 1933).

Government administration reorganized by 14 decrees; number, salaries, pensions of civil employees reduced (April 1934).

Luxury tax abolished and income tax decreased; general turnover tax established (June 1934).

Supplementary work and over-time for civil servants prohibited (1935).

By decree disbursements of states, municipalities, etc. reduced 10 per cent, involving cuts in salaries, pensions, and interest (July 1935).

Taxes increased on high incomes, armament profits, and security transfers (July 1935).

Labor and Unemployment

Government voted 100 million francs for purposes of relief (February 1931).

Government granted 3.5 billion francs for employment of French workers only, on public works—electrification, water supply, schools, museums, libraries, hospitals (November 1931).

State's share of municipal unemployment dole increased (January 1932).

Plan adopted for increasing public works, involving 1,000 million franc contribution from government and 2,725 million franc government guaranteed loan by railways for improvement purposes (June 1934).

Supplementary work and over-time among civil servants eliminated; encouragement given to spreading of work in private industry (1935).

By decree rents reduced 10 per cent, with owners compensated by 10 per cent reduction in mortgage interest (1935).

By decree municipalities required to use funds secured through economies effected (see above) for public works, especially waterworks, hospitals, granaries (July 1935).

Public works program accelerated; six-year program to be carried out in four (August 1935).

Agriculture

Importation of various commodities restricted in aid of French agriculture (1932-33).

Minimum price established on wheat (August 1, 1933).

Minimum wheat price abolished and measures taken to get rid of surplus (December 1934).

Production controls established on wheat and wine (December 1934).

Transport rates reduced on wine and cider (December 1934).

Law involving reduction in vineyards passed to relieve the viticultural crisis (July 1935).

Agreement to finance wheat crop reached by Bank and government (October 1935).

Department of Agricultural Co-operatives favored (1935).

Power of local authorities to fix maximum meat prices extended (1935).

Industry

Formation of cartels made compulsory in any industry in which the majority desired it (February 1932).

Railways and shipping companies reorganized with state control increased; 14-year subvention of 50 to 150 million francs guaranteed to shipping (July 1933).

Price decreases on gas and electricity, fertilizers, and coal decreed by government (July 1935).

Foreign Trade

Quota system to ration imports initiated (September 1931).

Licensing imports to offset exchange controls authorized (December 1931).

Special import tax levied on all goods (March 1932).

One hundred additional commodities subjected to import quotas (January 1934).

Law passed increasing import duties on finished and semi-finished goods (March 1934).

General change in commercial policy made, involving modification of quota system and negotiation for export advantages (July 1934).

3. Belgium. Governmental policy here involves two distinct stages—a comparatively passive one until 1934 and then an active program of far-reaching ramifications involving devaluation of the currency, banking and credit reorganization, and a program of public works.

Money and Credit

Gold standard maintained until 1935.

Control over all foreign exchange operations established by government (March 1935).

Currency devalued 28 per cent; then reattached to gold on new fixed parity (April 1935).

Steps taken by government to prevent collapse of credit system: reduction of discount rate; mortgage moratorium; reduction of cost of credit to industry; establishment of National Industrial Bank to take over long-term bank credits; reorganization of commercial banking and investment banking systems; and provision for "controlled management" of companies threatened with insolvency (1934).

Loan of 1.5 billion francs at 4 per cent obtained from Holland bankers (December 1934).

New commercial banking law passed (July 1935).

By decree mortgage office regulating mortgage loans created (January 1936).

Office created to centralize all interventions of the state in credit institutions (April 1936).

The Budget

Systematic efforts made to prevent budget disorganization by: administrative economies, salary reductions, and increase of direct and indirect taxes (1932-35).

Moderate tax reductions made (May 1935).

State bonds to the amount of 25 billion francs converted at one-third reduction in interest rates (May 1935).

Salaries of public employees increased 5 per cent (September 1935).

Labor and Unemployment

By decree special commissions empowered to determine wage rates for allocating unemployment benefit and to provide "means" test (July 1932).

Local unemployment funds replaced by national agencies for employment and payment of dole (October 1934).

By decree tenants of certain small dwellings empowered to claim reduction of rent to pre-war level (November 1934).

Decision to stimulate public works made by government and subsidies authorized if persons entitled to unemployment pay were employed (December 1934).

Office created to fight depression and unemployment through stimulation of public works (April 1935).

Three and a half billion francs appropriated for public works program, 1936-38 (August 1935).

Agriculture

Valorization scheme to raise price of wheat established (September 1932).

Import of foreign flours and soft wheat prohibited (September 1932).

Law passed providing for temporary reduction of farm rents (August 1933).

Foreign Trade

Government authorized to establish quota system (June 1931).

License system extended to many imports (1931-34).
Trade agreements reached with 17 countries (1932-36).

4. Germany. The relation of the state to economic activity in Germany has traditionally been closer than in Anglo-Saxon countries. This fact, together with extraordinary economic difficulties and political transformations, has resulted in a more varied and extensive program of recovery than is to be found in most countries. The range of government influence over and participation in economic activity was greatly increased after the advent of the present government.

Money and Credit

Gold standard maintained, nominally, throughout depression.

Foreign exchange regulations introduced under control of Reichsbank (July 1931).

Payment of short-term foreign bank credits postponed by standstill agreement (September 1931).

Acceptance and Guarantee Bank founded with capital supplied by government and eleven large banks, for prevention of bank runs (July 1931).

Banking Board of Control and a Commission of Banking created (September 1931).

Distressed banks rehabilitated, and banking system placed under strict governmental control (February 1932).

Acceptance and Guarantee Bank allowed to give credit to financial institutions (March 1932).

Industrie Finanzierung Institut created to put liquid funds at disposal of banking institutions. (September 1933).

Amortization Institut created to relieve banks of frozen debts (September 1933).

Transfer moratorium declared (July 1933).

Reichsbank allowed to use bonds as collateral to follow more forceful policy in influencing money market (October 1933).

Supervisory Committee created for all banking and credit institutions except Reichsbank and Golddiskont Bank (December 1934).

Price Commissioner appointed to control commodity prices (December 1934).

The Budget

Systematic effort made to control budget by reducing salaries, pensions, and other outlays and by increasing both direct and indirect taxation (1930-31).

Poll and intoxicants' tax increased by communal governments (October 1931).

Assistance in meeting floating debt of states and communes agreed to by Reich (October 1931).

Eight billion reichsmark 6 per cent government bonds converted to 4.5 per cent (January 1935).

Loans and Treasury bonds to the amount of two milliard marks converted from 6 to 4.5 per cent (February 1935).

Consolidation of debt started and new Reich loan issued for first time since 1929 (March 1935).

General Measures to Promote Recovery

To help export markets comprehensive program instituted for reduction in production costs, involving reductions of: wages by not more than 15 per cent; salaries of civil workers; interest rates on outstanding issues by about 25 per cent; cartel prices 10 per cent and more; railway tariffs, public utility rates, etc.; rents on pre-war buildings by 10 per cent. Efforts made to reduce retail prices. (December 1931.)

To encourage employers to renew fixed capital tax immunity on new machinery granted (June 1933).

To encourage industrial expansion, postponements of turnover, income, and land taxes amounting to 40 per cent granted to everyone in exchange for tax vouchers payable 1934-39; even larger postponements granted railways (September 1933).

Subsidies granted to individuals to rehabilitate houses (1933).

Employers given premium of 100 reichsmarks quarterly for each new worker employed (September 1933).

Extensive government public works program begun; financed by Public Works Company, created 1930 (1932).

Outlays for military program greatly increased (1934-36).

Labor and Unemployment

Unemployment Board created to direct voluntary service on land and transport improvement, forests, etc. (June 1931).

All persons under 25 permitted to enroll in voluntary service (June 1932).

Voluntary contributing fund created to foster national employment (June 1933).

Marriage loan created to raise marriage and birth rates and give vacated jobs to men (June 1933).

Workers' right to choose place and kind of work restricted (May 1934).

Prohibition of "outside" workers, in districts with heavy unemployment, permitted (May 1934).

Number of persons for obligatory work service raised by 100,000 (July 1934).

Persons under 25 required to be replaced by older workers (August 1934).

Farm workers prohibited from migrating (February 1935).

Employment in military service increased (1934-35).

Agriculture

Subsidies given to agriculturalists during crisis (1930-31).

Interest on distressed mortgages reduced by emergency decree (December 1931).

Cut in mortgage rates decreed (September 1932).

Burden on agriculture greatly relieved by decrease in Reichsbank discount rate (September 1932).

Severe quota policy introduced regulating import of agricultural products (1932).

"Reich Nourishment Order" established to increase production of food products which Germany lacked: minimum prices for bread grain fixed; Minister empowered to regulate production, sale, prices, and profits (September 1933).

Producers prohibited from offering for sale butter, cheese, and eggs unless first offered to Reich center market; prices fixed by "Reich Nourishment Order" (December 1933).

Moratorium declared on farm foreclosures (1933).

Export of corn, wheat, flour, and oatmeal banned by government (June 1934).

Minister of Agriculture given right to apportion sales of wheat and rye producers, thus regulating mill activity and commercial transactions (July 1934).

Wheat and rye prices raised (July 1934).

Agricultural price increases prohibited by Minister of Agriculture; maximum for meat, potatoes, cheese fixed; and increase in price of beef and pork to March 1935 level ordered (August 1935).

Central bureau for trade in cereals created (October 1935).

Foreign Trade

Import price of textile raw materials, metals, hides and skins controlled (March 1934).

Control extended to finished goods and additional raw materials (July 1934).

Twenty-five "Ueberwachungstellen" authorized to act as foreign exchange control offices to ensure that imports corresponded to foreign currency available at any time (September 1934).

Fund created for favoring exportation of German industrial products (June 1935).

Various bilateral trade agreements consummated (1934-35).

Economic dictatorship with undefined powers of control established (1934-36).

5. Sweden. The measures passed by the Swedish government were less numerous and less varied in character than those of most European countries. This may perhaps be attributed to the fact that the depression itself was somewhat less acute and recovery began relatively early. Government policies were concerned chiefly with financial measures and the provision of relief for labor and agriculture, especially the latter.

Money and Credit

Gold standard abandoned. Intent to maintain internal buying power of the krona announced by Minister of Finance (September 1931).

Foreign reserves accumulated and credit restrictions gradually eased (October 1931 and following).

Intent to increase wholesale prices moderately, within the limits of an unchanged cost of living, announced by government (March 1932).

During Kreuger crisis 200 million krona loan to Skandinaviska Bank made by government (May 1932).

Savings banks induced by Riksbank to lower rates (June 1933).

Krona stabilized at 1,940 kronor to the pound sterling; much foreign exchange purchased by Riksbank (July 1933).

New commercial banking law passed with rigid restrictions against speculative loans (1935).

Statute set up to provide long and intermediate term credits for companies unable to float bond issues; 5 million kronor provided by government and 3 millions by banks (1935).

The Budget

Budget balanced by taking 165 million kronor from reserves of alcoholic drink account (1932-33).

Funds borrowed by government to be used for non-self liquidating public works in aid of recovery (1933-35).

Death duties increased (1933-35).

Surtax levied on large properties and incomes (1934-35).

Public works provided for out of current revenues (1935-36).

Income tax reduced (1936-37).

Labor and Unemployment

Under law of 1915, public works authorized to provide employment (1930-33).

Some money relief provided both by national and local governments (1930-33).

Wage rate for relief workers made equal to that of regular common labor (1933).

Principal public work projects postponed by strikes (1933); intensified activity in following year.

Unemployment insurance law passed (May 1934).

Old-age pensions increased (June 1935).

Agriculture

Millers required to increase percentage of Swedish wheat and rye used in milling flour (June 1930).

Subsidy established for beet-sugar producers (1930 and 1931).

Grain corporation established and given monopoly on grain imports; agreement made to purchase all grain at fixed prices (April 1931).

Monopoly control established over sugar industry; designed to equalize the retail price of sugar and guarantee a minimum price for sugar beets (February 1932).

Fees levied on milk production to support the butter market (June 1932, July 1933).

State Milk Board given import monopoly on milk and dairy products (February 1933).

Tariff duties increased on potatoes (November 1932), oil cake, and fodder (June 1933, May 1934, April 1935); proceeds of duties on oil cake and fodder divided 90 per cent for milk regulation fund, 10 per cent for assisting egg production.

State monopoly established for the manufacture of potato flour (June 1933); price of potato flour fixed (September 1934).

Minimum wholesale price for butter fixed (July 1933).

By royal proclamation, duties levied on import of grain and fodder, and licenses required for import (December 1933).

Slaughtering Board given funds to subsidize pig exports (January-September 1934).

Subsidy granted to provide for refrigeration of domestic pork (October 1934).

Foreign Trade

Agreement made between Riksbank and Swedish Bankers' Association for informal control of exchange to limit imports (November 1931).

Credit restrictions on imports lifted (August 1932).

Commercial agreements made with nine countries (1933).

Trade agreement reached with United States (May 1935).

(*See also trade restrictions under* Agriculture.)

6. *Norway.* The measures passed by the Norwegian government relate to all of the major classifications, but primary emphasis has been placed upon money and credit and fiscal policies.

Money and Credit

Gold standard abandoned, following example of England (September 1931).

Decree issued postponing provisions of bankruptcy law as they related to the important private banking institutions (December 1931).

Agreement made by Bank of Norway to support credit of important private banks (March 1932).

Law established creating guaranty fund for savings banks (June 1932).

Series of reductions in discount rates made by Central Bank (1931-32).

The Budget

Cigarette, tobacco, and alcohol taxes increased (1931-32).

Turnover tax of 2 per cent established; customs duties and income taxes increased (1932-33).

Wages of civil workers reduced; customs duties and rates on government railways increased (1933-34).

Numerous public loan conversions carried out (1934).

Small appropriations made for crisis relief (1933-34).

Seventy-three million kroner earmarked for crisis relief (January 1935).

Additional turnover tax of 1 per cent levied (July 1935).

Tax of 25 per cent levied on interest paid to bank depositors (January 1936).

Labor and Unemployment

Under government arbitration, hours and wages reduced in collective contracts (September 1931).

Recommendation that adjustments in hours of work be handled separately by each industry made by government committee (November 1933).

Agreements reached to prolong existing collective contracts to 1940 (last half of 1935).

Agriculture

Government loan fund established to aid farmers and fishermen (June 1932).

Food imports limited; tax on margarine levied (1933-34).

Additional loan funds provided for agriculture; department established to aid in converting farm mortgages (1934).

Funds provided to subsidize reductions in price of butter to important public agencies (August 1935).

Industry

Agreement made by whale fishers to limit oil production (June 1932).

Building of tankers restricted by government regulations (January 1935).

Law passed giving King right to limit whale companies' implements and production (June 1935).

Area and duration of fishing period fixed by royal decree (June 1935).

Foreign Trade

Voluntary agreements made by Norwegian banking institutions to ration exports of foreign currencies (September 1931).

Customs duties increased (first half of 1932).

State guaranty of export credits extended to new commodities and additional countries (November 1933).

Import of certain goods provisionally prohibited by government and others licensed (June 1934).

Agreement reached with foreign whale fishing companies with reference to control of oil production (autumn 1934).

Agreement reached with Sweden and Finland to divide exports of paper pulp (April 1935).

7. *Finland.* A decline in building activity brought on depression in Finland in the third quarter of 1928. Hence as early as 1929 relief measures became necessary. During the depression as a whole the legislation has related primarily to the budget and agricultural relief.

Money and Credit

Insurance companies permitted to carry depreciated bonds at cost price (February 1931).

Gold exchange standard abolished and currency restrictions of 1922 reintroduced (October 1931).

Discount rate increased to 9 per cent by Central Bank (October 1931).

After severe depreciation, mark stabilized at 18 per cent above sterling par (1931-32).

Discount rate progressively reduced by Central Bank (1933).

The Budget

Eight million marks authorized for unemployment and 8 millions for relief (1929).

Fifteen million marks appropriated for unemployment and 5 millions for roads and bridge building (1930).

Outlays for relief work and particularly for large-scale road construction increased (1932).

Tax imposed on beer (May 1931).

Alcohol company created for production and trade in light drinks (December 1931).

Tax rates on beer increased (December 1931).

Customs duties increased on large group of consumption goods (1932).

Salaries and wages of government employees reduced by 5-10 per cent (December 1932).

Many public loan conversions carried out and short-term debt repaid (1934-35).

Agriculture

Bonds of Agricultural Mortgage Society up to 400 million marks guaranteed by state; and, similarly, the foreign loans of Industrial Mortgage Bank (May 1929).

Two million marks set aside for purchase and improvement of agricultural properties (May 1929).

Export credits to 75 per cent of value of exports guaranteed by state (May 1929).

Customs duties increased on most agricultural products (December 1929).

Twenty million marks earmarked for purchase and improvement of agricultural properties (January 1930).

Loans of a joint stock company guaranteed by government to reduce interest rates to peasants (January 1931).

Bonds of a joint stock company guaranteed and a share of its capital contributed by the government (October 1931).

Laws passed to bring about further reductions in mortgage interest rates (March 1932).

Subsidy granted to small holders for expanding beet acreage (October 1932).

Export bounty established on butter and cheese (December 1932).

Export bounties on butter, eggs, cheese, and pork increased; imports of pork, butter, etc., prohibited (1934).

Foreign Trade

Quota policies established (1931-32).

Coal treaty concluded with England (November 1933).

Trade treaty negotiated with Germany (April 1934).

Imports of coal and coke restricted to expand markets for forest products (1934).

(*See also* Customs duties *under* Agriculture.)

8. Denmark. The government of Denmark resorted to extreme measures in the control of production and trade, the regulation of prices, and the alleviation of the burden of farm indebtedness.

Money and Credit

Export of gold prohibited (September 1931).

Gold standard abandoned; Bank required to act in agreement with Minister of Commerce and give profits arising from nonredemption in gold to the state (September 1931).

Discount rate reduced by National Bank—a link in policy to reduce general level of interest (November 1932).

New currency law passed (December 1932).

Currency Expert Committee created to help control the carrying out of currency regulations (December 1932).

Crisis Fund created to improve liquidity conditions, encourage normal lending, and lower interest rates (January 1933).

Maximum interest rate set at 3.5 per cent on 3-month deposits and 3 per cent on those of shorter notice (January 1933).

Co-operative Credit societies permitted to convert mortgage loans at lower rates of interest (January 1933).

Exportation of certain types of securities prohibited (December 1934).

National Bank changed from self-supporting joint stock company into the National Bank of Denmark (April 1936).

The Budget

An extra quarter's income tax imposed (June 1932).
Certain customs duties increased provisionally (June 1932).
A 30 million krone 5 per cent loan converted to 4.5 per cent (November 1932).

Labor and Unemployment

Wages in excess of 1.10 kroner subjected to reductions (April 1931).

Eleven million kroner decreed for extraordinary unemployment relief (October 1931).

Additional holidays given (1932).

Wages of slaughter-house workers reduced 3 per cent (May 1932).

Provisional state advance to municipalities to help unemployment provided by law (June 1932); continued in 1933.

Relief to members of Unemployment Insurance Fund extended; 80 per cent of expenses incurred covered by the state (June 1932).

Thirty million kroner to be used for loans for new buildings and 10 millions for land improvement rendered available by government (January 1933).

Distribution of beef to unemployed ordered by law; advances to aid municipalities made by state and continued through 1934-35 (January 1933).

Compulsory arbitration law passed (April 1933).

Law passed ordering strikers to resume work at once and giving organizations five days to settle disputes (May 1935).

Six million kroner appropriated to distribute pork to needy (April 1936).

Agriculture

Through "Accord Law" 20 million kroner placed at disposal of farm owners to help them in securing reductions of mortgage debt to a level with tax value of land plus inventory and herds (1931).

By decree 30 million kroner given agriculturalists to help them pay rent and taxes (October 1931).

Temporary postponement of payment of mortgage debts granted (1932-33).

Three-year moratorium given under Moratorium Law for debts exceeding value limit prescribed in Accord Law (January 1933).

Minister of Agriculture given control over production, refining, importing, or exporting of sugar and potatoes; prices fixed by law (January 1933).

Pig production regulated (April 1933).

Tax levied on cattle slaughtered for consumption in order to obtain funds with which to purchase and destroy inferior cattle (January 1933).

Eleven million kroner provided for purpose of splitting up big farms (January 1933).

Taxes on agricultural real estate reduced 20 million kroner (January 1933).

New taxes levied on import of corn, flour, grain, and other foodstuffs to bring up home market prices; proceeds to be distributed among agricultural properties (August 1935).

One hundred million kroner placed by state in fund for loans to owners of agricultural properties (April 1936).

Foreign Trade

Quota system agreed upon for 1932 (November 1931).

All imports put under control; office created to issue licenses (January 1932).

Agreement made with England to limit export of pigs (January 1932).

Imports of butter, milk, and margarine prohibited (November 1933).

More commodities put on quota list (December 1933).

Currency Board created to help work out proposals for quotas for each country (December 1934).

9. Poland. A very extensive recovery program was inaugurated, with special emphasis placed upon the control of industry and the reduction of costs. Extensive public loans were also made with a view to providing work relief for the unemployed.

Money and Credit

Deflationary policy pursued by central bank in order to prevent exchange depreciation (1931).

Specie payments suspended by several of the important private banks (1931).

Straight gold standard substituted for foreign exchange standard (August 1932).

Validity of gold clause with respect to debts abroad declared subject to law of country where contracted (July 1934).

Control of gold transfer and foreign currency transfer established (April 1936).

The Budget

Government expenditures systematically reduced by salary cuts, dismissals, and curtailment of social services (1931-33).

Circulation of subsidiary coins increased, the government profiting from the seigniorage (August 1932).

Program for conversion of short-term debts elaborated by autonomous administrations (1933).

Bonds to the amount of 100 million zlotys issued for financing public works (January 1934).

Discount rates lowered by Bank of Poland (June 1934).

Agreement made by joint stock banks to reduce interest rates (June 1934).

Customs duties increased on many goods (October 1934).

Bonds to the amount of 150 million zlotys issued for roads, water supplies, agricultural reform, port improvement, and electrification (April 10, 1935).

Bond issue of 70 million zlotys authorized to finance railway program (April 22, 1935).

Taxes of from 7 to 25 per cent levied on salaries of civil servants (November 1935).

Rent and tax on dwellings of one or two rooms reduced 21 per cent (November 1935).

Debts of the autonomous administration and agriculture reduced (November 1935).

Credit of 20 million zlotys furnished by Bank of Poland for construction of roads, providing four months' employment for 40,000 workers (1935).

Agriculture

Moratorium established to reduce debts of rural properties, with enforcement power vested in arbitration commissions (August 1932).

Acceptance banks created for purpose of converting agricultural debts (1933).

Moratorium extended for three years (September 1935).

Credit for establishment of silos and granaries created by government (1936).

Industry

Financially distressed industries relieved by a compulsory general bankruptcy law (1933).

Individual industries "stabilized" by forcing establishment of syndicates or cartels—petroleum, dye, cement, woolen spinning, iron and steel (1932-35).

Taxes on consumption reduced (1934).

Automobile industry placed under commission control (July 1935).

"Inflexible prices" reduced by negotiation or decree; reductions made in tariffs on petroleum, mineral oils, coal, transportation, electricity, postal services (1934-35).

Minister of Commerce empowered to dissolve cartels which raised prices; 44 dissolved (November 1935).

Price commissioner appointed to study measures for enforcing price reductions (December 1935).

Foreign Trade

New customs tariff imposed, increasing duties on imports (August 1932).

Imports from countries banning Polish goods prohibited by decree (August 1934)

Imports licensed under quota (October 1934).

Import restrictions extended (July 1935).

Import of certain luxuries prohibited (October 1935).

Various bilateral trade and compensation agreements concluded (1934-35).

10. Italy. In view of the centralized control of the Italian government over economic affairs in general, it is not surprising to find during the depression many new laws and decrees relating to all phases of economic life. Of particular interest are those directed toward the control of industrial activity, prices, and wages. In the following brief summary, measures taken in connection with the Abyssinian war are not included.

Money and Credit

Gold standard maintained without devaluation until October 1936.

Restrictive policy in granting of credits relaxed and discount rate reduced (April 1930).

Exchange regulations introduced for payment of imports (May 1932).

Life of Liquidation Institute of 1926 extended to 1940 (May 1932).

By decree maximum rate of interest for loans and mortgages fixed at 5 per cent (September 1932).

Two decrees to curb flight of capital made (May 1934).

By decree interest on all mortgage loans of real estate credit establishments reduced to 4 per cent (September 1934).

Strict control established over foreign exchange (December 1934).

The Budget

Wages and salaries of civil servants reduced by decree 8 and 12 per cent respectively (November 1930).

Most customs duties increased 15 per cent (September 1931).

Wages and salaries of civil workers cut 6 to 20 per cent (April 1934).

Wages and salaries of government employees again reduced (July 1934).

Dividends, interest, coupons, bonuses, etc., taxed 10 per cent (August 1935).

Labor and Unemployment

Provision of 800 million lire for road building made by government and Autonome Institute (August 1931).

Loan of 1,200 million lire for state railway electrification made by Credit Consortium (June-July 1933).

Work week reduced to 40 hours, and over-time prohibited (September 1933).

Agreement made between government and farmers assuring for one year a definite number of days of work to a fixed number of workers (October 1933).

Large landed proprietors invited, under penalty of expropriation, to divide land into medium-size holdings upon which necessary buildings might be constructed (December 1934).

Use of machinery during next harvest banned by Inter-Syndical Committee of Bologna (January 1935).

Industry

Seven corporations formed by government to give directive aid to major industries, but not empowered to deal with concrete problems (1930).

State consumption organizations competing with private retailers created (November 1930).

Stock exchange placed under control of Finance Minister (August 1932).

Issue of industrial loans without government authorization prohibited by decree (December 1932).

Institute for Industrial Reorganization formed for gradual elimination of unsound industry and rebuilding of private industries with government financial aid (January 1933).

Corporations established for control of iron and steel, silk, and cotton industries (May 1933).

Twenty-two additional corporations for control of major industries established by government (May 1934).

Number of pages in daily papers limited by government decree (June 1935).

Wage and Price Control

Minister of Corporations authorized to fix prices of certain commodities (November 1930).

Wages of industrial workers reduced 8 per cent and rents lowered 10 per cent by decree (November 1930).

Retail prices of foodstuffs reduced 10 per cent for civil servants and state pensioners (April 1934).

Wages of industrial workers cut 10 per cent (July 1934).

"Indemnities of directors" of industrial companies reduced 40 per cent (July 1934).

Commission formed for the purpose of controlling export prices (November 1934).

Variable dividends distributed by commercial and industrial companies limited by decree (August 1935).

Foreign Trade

Duties increased on phosphates, nitrates, and building materials (January 1932).

Importation of copper alloys prohibited without special authorization (November 1934).

License system extended to many products (1934-35).

Exporters and importers required to obtain permit to use barter system (March 1935).

Bilateral trade agreements instituted (1934-35).

Monopoly created for foreign purchases of coal, copper, lead, and nickel (July 1935).

11. Austria. Because of the extraordinarily acute financial difficulties resulting from the panic of 1931, Austrian relief measures center largely upon money and credit, fiscal and foreign exchange problems. Much of the reconstruction was carried out in co-operation with the League of Nations.

Money, Credit, and Exchange

Law passed to reorganize Kreditanstalt in co-operation with National Bank and Rothschilds (May 14, 1931).

Liabilities of Kreditanstalt guaranteed by government under certain conditions (May 31, 1931).

Foreign exchange regulations approved (January 1932).

Transfers of maturities due abroad suspended (June 1932).

Entire portfolio of Kreditanstalt bills taken over by government from National Bank (November 1932).

To provide basis for external loan, statement made by League Protocol that Austria planned to return as soon as possible to stable money and exchange (December 1932).

Agreement reached with foreign creditors for reconstruction of Kreditanstalt, under joint ownership of foreign creditors and government (January 1933).

Trust Company established to assist banks in reconstructing capital (March 1933).

Agreement reached with foreign creditors of Anstalt to postpone debt payments for two years; other "standstill" agreements renewed (May 1933).

International loan procured (August 1933).

Gold standard definitely abandoned (1933).

Domestic lottery loan floated (November 1933).

Gold value of schilling reduced and foreign exchange regulations abolished by government (April 1934).

Agreement made by League Control Committee to extend guaranty on 1923 loan from 1943 to 1959 (September 1934).

Domestic lottery loan floated (May 1935).

Other Important Measures

"Extraordinary" measures in aid of agriculture authorized by federal law (July 16, 1930).

Imports of 73 articles forbidden (April 1932).

12. New Zealand. New Zealand's recovery policies have related largely to money and credit and public finance, with relief to agriculture also assuming an important place.

Money and Credit

Currency depreciated in relation to gold (April 1930).

Gold standard suspended (September 1931).

Exchange accruing from exports pooled; set aside for government use in meeting external debts, with balance only available for imports (September 1931; terminated June 1932).

Currency depreciated compared with sterling, giving protection to local industry (January 1933).

A Reserve Bank established; domestic interest rates shortly reduced (August 1933).

Announcement made that on January 1, 1936 government would take control of money and credit (December 1935).

The Budget

Salaries and wages of public employees reduced (April 1931).

National Expenditures Adjustment Commission appointed to effect government economies (early 1932).

Wages of public employees again reduced (early 1932).

Sales tax levied on wide range of products (early 1933).

Taxes increased further and additional economies in expenditures effected (early 1933).

Internal public debt "voluntarily" converted; taxed if not converted (early 1933).

Labor and Unemployment

To aid the unemployed, tax levied on wages, salaries, and other incomes (1931).

Foregoing tax increased (1932).

With budget balanced, this tax reduced (1934).

Public works program of 5 million pounds proposed by Governor General (September 1935).

Forty-hour week established for government employees and workers on public enterprises.

Agriculture

Mortgagors' Relief Act passed to relieve debtors (1931).

Commission established to promote conciliation between mortgagors and mortgagees (1931).

Expenditures Act passed to effect reductions in mortgage interest rates, rents, and other fixed charges (1932).

Executive Commission of Agriculture established (1934).

Decision made by dairy industry to organize on Denmark co-operative plan (1935).

Proposal made by government to guarantee export price of important agricultural products (1936).

Foreign Trade

Tariff Commission established; moderate but widespread reductions in tariffs on British goods made (1933).

Importation of tax-free mutton into Great Britain arranged for (1933).

13. Australia. The measures passed by the Australian government have been of wide and varied character. Efforts have, however, in the main been directed toward balancing the budget, reducing costs of production, affording relief to the unemployed, and protecting domestic industry through bounties and tariffs. The several states within the Commonwealth have also passed a great deal of legislation pertaining to public works, unemployment relief, control of industry, agriculture, and so forth. These are not included in the present summary.

Money and Credit

Gold standard suspended (December 1929).

Commonwealth Bank given control of gold and gold shipments (1930).

Loans for financing deficits placed under control of Loan Council (1931).

Reserves against note issue by Bank reduced from 25 to 15 per cent in order to use gold reserve to meet short-term debts in London (June 1931).

Amendment provided that reserves could be held in "English" sterling or gold (May 1932).

Public works required to be financed out of public loans and not by Treasury bills (1932).

The Budget

Sales tax of 2.5 per cent authorized (1930).

Increased postal rates authorized (1930).

Heavy additional taxation provided (1930).

Conversion loan issued for 9.5 million pounds (1930).

Premiers' Plan adopted (June 1931):

(1) Reduction of 20 per cent in salaries, wages, and pensions of civil workers;

(2) Conversion of internal debts on basis of 22.5 per cent reduction of interest;

(3) Increased taxation, both Commonwealth and state;

(4) Reduced bank and savings bank interest rates on deposits and loans;

(5) Relief in respect of private mortgages.

Various New South Wales revenues appropriated to the service of the Commonwealth by the Financial Agreement Enforcement Act (1932).

Financial Agreements Act made Commonwealth responsible for interest payments on state debts, and affirmed complete liability for principal of state debts; Commonwealth empowered to sue states for money owed (1932).

Numerous public loans converted (1932-33).

Gradual reductions of taxes and advances of wages of civil workers made possible by improved budget (1933-35).

Unemployment

Basic wage rate reduced 10 per cent (1930).

Relief funds for states provided by special levies on wages of employed (1930-32).

States given one million pound government grant for relief purposes (1930).

Three million pounds provided for relief, 1.2 millions by states and 1.8 millions by government (April 1932).

Money for public works provided to states by Loan Council and Central Bank (1933).

Foreign Trade

Bounty on galvanized iron sheets and wine increased, and bounty on flax imposed (1930).

Trade agreement concluded with Canada (July 1931).

Numerous duties increased (1931-32).

Customs Tariff enacted to provide for allowances for exchange from fixed duties in "protective" items of the tariff (December 1933).

Regulation of internal and external trade in various commodities provided for in numerous acts (December 1933).

Many duties reduced (December 1934).

Bilateral trade agreements concluded with Belgium and Sweden (1935).

14. Japan. Among the measures passed by the Japanese government special emphasis has been placed upon the expansion of credit, industry, and foreign trade. Military outlays have played an important part in stimulating industrial activity and providing employment.

Money and Credit

Gold embargo imposed (December 1931).

Law passed to prevent flight of capital, giving Finance Minister power to control transactions in foreign currencies (1932).

Law passed raising limits for issue of convertible bank notes from 120 to 1,000 million yen (1932).

Law for the prevention of speculative exchange transactions (May 1933).

Law passed governing purchase of gold by the Bank of Japan to encourage production of gold in Japanese territory and to increase the gold holdings of the Bank (April 1934).

The Budget

Reductions in rate of sugar consumption, textile consumption, and business profits taxes (1931).

Considerable sums voted for emergency relief, for public works and other undertakings designed to provide unemployment, and for aid to local authorities in financing primary schools (September 1932).

Decision reached to rely upon bond issues instead of increased taxation for needed federal revenues. Treasury obligations sold direct to Bank of Japan (1932).

Military expenditures greatly increased (1931-36).

Agriculture and Industry

Substantial appropriations made for relief of agriculture and fisheries (1931).

Funds provided for the stabilization of the prices of rice and silk (1931).

Law passed for the control of staple industries (1931).

Industrial guild law amendments passed to extend the scope and increase the capital funds of industrial guilds (1932).

Numerous laws passed for control of various industries such as rice, silk textiles, iron and steel, petroleum, etc. (1933-34).

Foreign Trade

Reduction or abolition of protective duties on articles which no longer need protection enforced (May 1930).

Rebate allowed on railway freight on goods destined for export (April 1930).

Government authorized to lend funds at low interest to small traders and manufacturers in order to promote export trade (April 1930).

Import duty on artificial silk reduced (April 1931).

"Specific" duties raised by 35 per cent (June 1932).

Duties raised on numerous commodities (June 1932).

Several new duties imposed; some duties raised (1933-34).

License required for manufacture of aquatic products for export (May 1934).

Government allowed to alter import duties or restrict or prohibit imports if necessary (May 1934).

Trade agreements reached with various nations (1930-34).

APPENDIX C

DATA RELATING TO EMPLOYMENT, PRODUCTION, AND WAGES

The following tables and notes are to supplement Chapters VI, VII, IX, and X. For the most part the tables are self-explanatory. In a few cases, however, methodology is briefly explained in accompanying text. It should be evident from the nature of the material that the figures are by no means final. They are for the most part rough approximations and should not be used apart from the qualifications incorporated in footnotes and text. The material of this appendix is presented under five headings: the labor force; current estimates of employment and unemployment; equivalent full-time employment and unemployment; production and productivity; and wages.

I. THE LABOR FORCE

This section contains Tables 1 to 7, inclusive. Special comment is necessary only with respect to Table 5, which shows estimates of the new workers who have become employable for the first time since 1929. The estimates in this table are composed of two parts: first, the estimated annual replacements required to maintain the complex of gainful workers as it was at the time of the last decennial census in April 1930; and second, the additions to the labor force on account of population growth.

The annual replacements are based on the number in the highest frequency age as shown by the Census of Occupations of 1930. It has been assumed that as the workers in this age group are moved on annually to successive age groups until their ranks are depleted by death, disease, and retirement, the full number in this age of highest frequency has to be replaced each year from the lower ages and hence from new recruits. This method of computing replacements does not take account of the workers entering gainful occupations at later ages than the age of highest frequency, nor does it account for the losses below the age of highest frequency. The error due to the first

(Please turn to p. 607.)

1. Age and Sex Distribution of Gainful Workers in the United States, 1930

I. By Industry[a]

(In thousands)

Industry and Occupation	Males and Females				Males				Females			
	Total	Under 18 Years	18 to 65 Years	65 Years and Over	Total	Under 18 Years	18 to 65 Years	65 Years and Over	Total	Under 18 Years	18 to 65 Years	65 Years and Over
ALL INDUSTRIES	48,830	2,146	44,479	2,205	38,078	1,425	34,714	1,939	10,752	721	9,765	266
AGRICULTURE[b]	10,484	976	8,677	831	9,570	776	8,018	776	914	200	659	55
Unpaid family workers on farms	1,660	750	893	17	1,185	575	600	10	475	175	293	7
ALL INDUSTRIES, EXCLUSIVE OF AGRICULTURE	38,346	1,170	35,802	1,374	28,508	649	26,696	1,155	9,838	521	9,106	211
Forestry and fishing	269	7	250	12	267	7	248	12	2	—	2	—
Extraction of minerals	1,156	20	1,107	29	1,149	20	1,100	29	7	—	7	—
Manufacturing and mechanical industries, exclusive of building	11,767	468	10,956	343	9,390	251	8,832	307	2,377	217	2,124	36
Building	2,575	26	2,414	135	2,550	25	2,390	135	25	1	24	—
Transportation and communication	4,438	78	4,240	120	3,998	56	3,824	118	440	22	416	2
Trade	7,530	259	7,001	270	5,815	176	5,386	253	1,715	83	1,615	17
Public service[c]	1,050	7	989	54	928	6	870	52	122	1	119	2
Professional service	2,966	22	2,822	122	1,335	9	1,228	98	1,631	13	1,594	24
Recreation and amusement	443	19	410	14	313	15	287	11	130	4	123	3
Domestic and personal service	4,814	208	4,408	198	1,661	43	1,545	73	3,153	165	2,863	125
Not specified industries and services	1,338	56	1,205	77	1,102	41	986	75	236	15	219	2

II. By Occupation[d]
(In thousands)

	48,830	2,146	44,479	2,205	38,078	1,425	34,714	1,939	10,752	721	9,765	266
ALL OCCUPATIONS	48,830	2,146	44,479	2,205	38,078	1,425	34,714	1,939	10,752	721	9,765	266
SELF-EMPLOYED	9,641	2	8,737	902	8,956	2	8,123	831	685	—	614	71
Farmers	6,012	—	5,339	673	5,749	—	5,121	628	263	—	218	45
Professional	514	—	476	38	453	—	418	35	61	—	58	3
Others	3,115	2	2,922	191	2,754	2	2,584	168	361	—	338	23
SALARIED EMPLOYEES	12,185	318	11,540	327	7,397	167	6,965	265	4,788	151	4,575	62
Professional	2,432	8	2,367	57	1,045	3	1,003	39	1,387	5	1,364	18
Executive	806	—	762	44	766	—	723	43	40	—	39	1
Foremen and lower managerial	1,141	—	1,076	65	851	—	814	37	290	—	262	28
Other salaried	7,806	310	7,335	161	4,735	164	4,425	146	3,071	146	2,910	15
WAGE EARNERS	25,344	1,076	23,309	959	20,540	681	19,025	833	4,804	395	4,283	126
Skilled	5,432	12	5,185	235	5,393	11	5,148	234	39	1	37	1
Semi-skilled	7,523	406	6,911	206	5,397	209	5,028	160	2,126	197	1,883	46
Unskilled, total	12,389	658	11,213	518	9,750	461	8,850	439	2,639	197	2,363	79
Farm	*2,733*	*225*	*2,374*	*134*	*2,562*	*201*	*2,232*	*129*	*171*	*24*	*142*	*5*
Non-farm	*9,656*	*394*	*8,886*	*376*	*7,188*	*224*	*6,662*	*302*	*2,468*	*170*	*2,224*	*74*
UNPAID FAMILY WORKERS ON FARMS	1,660	750	893	17	1,185	575	600	10	475	175	293	7

a "Gainful Workers by Industry and Occupation," *Fifteenth Census of the United States: 1930*, pp. 6-9.
b Includes unpaid family workers on farms.
c The Census classification "Public Service," includes only a portion of the individuals employed by governments; for instance, school teachers are included under "Professional Service."
d Compiled from "General Report on Occupations," *Fifteenth Census of the United States: 1930, Population*, Vol. V.

2. Occupational and Industrial Distribution of Gainful Workers in the United States, 1930[a]

I. Male Workers

(In thousands)

Occupation	All Industries	Agriculture	All Industries Exclusive of Agriculture											
			Total	Forestry and Fishing	Extraction of Minerals	Manufacturing and Mechanical Industries — Building	Manufacturing and Mechanical Industries — All Other	Transportation and Communication	Trade	Public Service[b]	Professional Service	Recreation and Amusement	Domestic and Personal Service	Not Specified Industries and Service
ALL OCCUPATIONS	38,078	9,570	28,508	267	1,149	2,550	9,390	3,998	5,815	928	1,335	313	1,661	1,102
SELF-EMPLOYED	8,956	5,749	3,207	6	15	154	204	98	2,016	—	453	48	211	2
Non-professional	8,503	5,749	2,754	6	15	154	204	98	2,016	—	—	48	211	2
Professional	453	—	453	—	—	—	—	—	—	—	453	—	—	—
SALARIED EMPLOYEES	7,397	74	7,323	18	84	85	1,643	1,145	2,862	408	681	170	95	132
Professional	1,045	—	1,045	1	10	21	166	51	14	43	584	144	—	11
Executive	766	—	766	1	15	19	283	96	224	119	—	2	—	7
Foremen and lower managerial	851	66	785	12	34	21	289	293	33	39	22	10	28	4
Other salaried	4,735	8	4,727	4	25	24	905	705	2,591	207	75	14	67	110
WAGE EARNERS	20,540	2,562	17,978	243	1,050	2,311	7,543	2,755	937	520	201	95	1,355	968
Skilled	5,393	—	5,393	5	100	1,817	2,463	716	81	112	15	8	21	55
Semi-skilled	5,397	—	5,397	7	22	67	3,437	798	214	219	12	4	417	200
Unskilled, total	9,750	2,562	7,188	231	928	427	1,643	1,241	642	189	174	83	917	713
Farm	2,562	2,562	—	—	—	—	—	—	—	—	—	—	—	—
Non-farm	7,188	—	7,188	231	928	427	1,643	1,241	642	189	174	83	917	713
UNPAID FAMILY WORKERS ON FARMS	1,185	1,185	—	—	—	—	—	—	—	—	—	—	—	—

II. Female Workers
(In thousands)

	10,752	914	9,838	2	7	25	2,377	440	1,715	122	1,631	130	3,153	236
ALL OCCUPATIONS	10,752	914	9,838	2	7	25	2,377	440	1,715	122	1,631	130	3,153	236
SELF-EMPLOYED	685	263	422	—	—	—	46	1	127	—	61	1	186	—
Non-professional	624	263	361	—	—	—	46	1	127	—	—	1	186	—
Professional	61	—	61	—	—	—	—	—	—	—	61	—	—	—
SALARIED EMPLOYEES	4,788	5	4,783	1	7	23	579	427	1,532	116	1,506	119	280	193
Professional	1,387	—	1,387	—	—	—	13	—	2	4	1,267	100	—	1
Executive	40	—	40	—	—	—	10	3	15	11	—	—	—	1
Foremen and lower managerial	290	1	289	1	7	23	28	4	6	5	22	2	221	1
Other salaried	3,071	4	3,067	1	7	23	528	420	1,509	96	217	17	59	190
WAGE EARNERS	4,804	171	4,633	1	—	2	1,752	12	56	6	64	10	2,687	43
Skilled	39	—	39	—	—	2	37	—	—	—	—	—	—	—
Semi-skilled	2,126	—	2,126	—	—	—	1,656	3	10	1	1	1	424	30
Unskilled, total	2,639	171	2,468	1	—	—	59	9	46	5	63	9	2,263	13
Farm	*171*	*171*	—	—	—	—	—	—	—	—	—	—	—	—
Non-farm	*2,468*	—	*2,468*	*1*	—	—	*59*	*9*	*46*	*5*	*63*	*9*	*2,263*	*13*
UNPAID FAMILY WORKERS ON FARMS	475	475	—	—	—	—	—	—	—	—	—	—	—	—

a Compiled from "Gainful Workers by Industry and Occupation," *Fifteenth Census of the United States: 1930.*

b The Census classification "Public Service" includes only a portion of the individuals employed by governments; for instance, school teachers are included under "Professional Service."

3. Population and Gainful Workers in the United States, 1929–36
(In millions)

| Year | Population | | Gainful Workers[c] | | Increase in Number of Gainful Workers Since Jan. 1, 1930 | | |
	Total[a]	15–64 Years Inclusive[b]	Total	Exclusive of Unpaid Family Workers on Farms in April 1930	Total	Males[d]	Females[d]
1929—July 1....	121.8	79.3	48.4	46.7			
1930—Jan. 1....	122.5	79.8	48.7	47.0			
July 1....	123.1	80.3	49.0	47.3	0.3	0.23	0.07
1931—July 1....	124.1	81.3	49.6	47.9	0.9	0.7	0.2
1932—July 1....	125.0	82.4	50.2	48.5	1.5	1.2	0.3
1933—July 1....	125.8	83.4	50.8	49.1	2.1	1.6	0.5
1934—July 1....	126.6	84.5	51.4	49.7	2.7	2.1	0.6
1935—July 1....	127.5	85.5	52.1	50.4	3.4	2.6	0.8
1936—July 1...	128.4	86.6	52.7	51.0	4.0	3.1	0.9

[a] Estimates for July 1, 1930 to July 1, 1935 are from a release of the Bureau of the Census, *Estimated Population of the United States as of July 1, 1935*, Feb. 12, 1936. Estimates for other dates have been extrapolated from census figures. (In using the 1930 census data Thompson and Whelpton, in the study cited in note *b* have increased the 1930 census figures by an allowance of 4 per cent for under-estimation by the census of children under five years of age. This allowance has not been incorporated in the series presented here.)

[b] Based on Warren Thompson and P. K. Whelpton, *Estimates of Future Population by States* (National Resources Board, December 1934), p. 3.

[c] The gainful workers exclusive of unpaid family workers on farms have been estimated from the population 15–64 years of age by means of the ratio existing between these groups at the census date, April 1930.

It is impossible to estimate the number of unpaid family workers on farms as distinct from paid workers. The number fluctuates according to season and also according to business conditions outside of agriculture. In projecting the estimates of the total gainful workers beyond 1930 it was thought much more accurate to leave out the unpaid family workers. However, in order to make the estimates for subsequent years more or less comparable with the aggregate reported by the census for 1930, the number of unpaid family workers as of April of that year (1.7 millions) was added as a constant to the estimates for the subsequent years. The actual number of unpaid family workers on farms during the several years was, of course, not constant. It appears from the Census of Agriculture that in 1935, for instance, the number of unpaid family workers was considerably above that reported for 1930. But the difference was drawn largely from the aggregate charged to non-agricultural occupations.

[d] The increases have been distributed between the sexes on the basis of the ratio existing between male and female gainful workers at the time of the census in 1930.

4. Population, by Age Groups, April 1930 and 1935

| Age in Years | Total Population[a] (In millions) | | Change between 1930 and 1935 | |
	1930	1935	In millions	As a Percentage
0– 4.............	11.91[b]	10.83	−1.08	−9.6
5–14.............	24.64	24.21	−0.43	−1.7
15–39.............	50.62	52.45	+1.83	+3.6
40–64.............	29.42	32.82	+3.40	+11.5
65 and over........	6.64	7.49	+0.85	+12.8
All ages........	123.23[b]	127.80	+4.57	+3.7

[a] Warren Thompson and P. K. Whelpton, *Estimates of Future Population by States* (National Resources Board, December 1934), United States Summary Table, p. 3.

[b] This is the census figure plus an "allowance of 4 per cent for under-enumeration by the census of children under five years of age."

5. CUMULATED NUMBER OF PERSONS WHO UNDER NORMAL CONDITIONS WOULD HAVE SOUGHT EMPLOYMENT FOR THE FIRST TIME BETWEEN JAN. 1, 1930 AND JULY 1, 1930–36[a]

(In thousands)

Industry and Sex	1930	1931	1932	1933	1934	1935	1936
All Industries and Services:							
MALES	755	2,275	3,825	5,275	6,825	8,375	9,925
Replacements to maintain 1930 number and composition	525	1,575	2,625	3,675	4,725	5,775	6,825
Additions on account of population growth[b]	230	700	1,200	1,600	2,100	2,600	3,100
FEMALES	335	995	1,625	2,355	2,985	3,715	4,345
Replacements to maintain 1930 number and composition	265	795	1,325	1,855	2,385	2,915	3,445
Additions on account of population growth[b]	70	200	300	500	600	800	900
MALES AND FEMALES	1,090	3,270	5,450	7,630	9,810	12,090	14,270
Replacements to maintain 1930 number and composition	790	2,370	3,950	5,530	7,110	8,690	10,270
Additions on account of population growth[b]	300	900	1,500	2,100	2,700	3,400	4,000
Industries and Services, Exclusive of Agriculture:							
MALES	630	1,900	3,200	4,400	5,700	7,000	8,300
Replacements to maintain 1930 number and composition	400	1,200	2,000	2,800	3,600	4,400	5,200
Additions on account of population growth[b]	230	700	1,200	1,600	2,100	2,600	3,100
FEMALES	320	950	1,550	2,250	2,850	3,550	4,150
Replacements to maintain 1930 number and composition	250	750	1,250	1,750	2,250	2,750	3,250
Additions on account of population growth[b]	70	200	300	500	600	800	900
MALES AND FEMALES	950	2,850	4,750	6,650	8,550	10,550	12,450
Replacements to maintain 1930 number and composition	650	1,950	3,250	4,550	5,850	7,150	8,450
Additions on account of population growth[b]	300	900	1,500	2,100	2,700	3,400	4,000
Agriculture:							
MALES	125	375	625	875	1,125	1,375	1,625
Replacements to maintain 1930 number and composition	125	375	625	875	1,125	1,375	1,625
Additions on account of population growth	—	—	—	—	—	—	—
FEMALES	15	45	75	105	135	165	195
Replacements to maintain 1930 number and composition	15	45	75	105	135	165	195
Additions on account of population growth	—	—	—	—	—	—	—
MALES AND FEMALES	140	420	700	980	1,260	1,540	1,820
Replacements to maintain 1930 number and composition	140	420	700	980	1,260	1,540	1,820
Additions on account of population growth	—	—	—	—	—	—	—

[a] These estimates of replacements and additions are net figures; they do not include entrants who have since dropped out. For method, see pp. 599,607–08.
[b] See Table 3, p. 604.

6. Unemployment among Male Gainful Workers in the United States by Age Groups, April 1930

Age in Years	Number of Male Gainful Workers (In thousands)				Number of Unemployed Males[a] (In thousands)		Ratio of Unemployed to Urban Employees	
	Total[b]	Agriculture[c]	Entrepreneurs Exclusive of Farmers[d]	Urban Employees[e]	Class A	Classes A and B	Class A	Classes A and B
10–14.......	273	224	—	49	1	2	2.0	4.1
15–19.......	2,752	1,080	26	1,646	192	242	11.7	14.7
20–24.......	4,800	1,157	180	3,463	332	424	9.6	12.2
25–29.......	4,714	902	341	3,471	244	323	7.0	9.3
30–34.......	4,454	826	431	3,197	204	274	6.4	8.6
35–39.......	4,572	896	466	3,210	211	284	6.6	8.8
40–44.......	4,036	849	459	2,728	198	264	7.2	9.7
45–49.......	3,569	845	407	2,317	188	248	8.1	10.7
50–54.......	2,996	802	354	1,840	163	211	8.9	11.5
55–59.......	2,257	662	266	1,329	129	165	9.7	12.4
60–64.......	1,685	539	193	953	97	123	10.2	12.9
65–69.......	1,073	386	115	572	62	78	10.8	13.6
70 and over..	866	389	91	386	37	47	9.6	12.2
Unknown....	31	5	—	26	1	1	—	—
Total.....	38,078	9,562	3,329	25,187	2,059	2,686	8.2	10.7

[a] *Fifteenth Census of the United States: 1930, Unemployment*, Vol. 1, p. 13. Class A includes "persons out of a job, able to work, and looking for a job"; Class B includes "persons having jobs but on lay-off without pay, excluding those sick or voluntarily idle."
[b] *Abstract of the Fifteenth Census of the United States*, p. 472.
[c] The same, p. 336. The difference between the total for this distribution and the 9,570,000 shown in Table 2 on p. 602 is due to "other salaried workers" 'in agriculture who are not included in this distribution.
[d] Compiled from "General Report on Occupations," *Fifteenth Census of the United States: 1930, Population*, Vol. V.
[e] Total gainful workers minus gainful workers in agriculture.

7. Percentage of Employable Workers Unemployed in Massachusetts and Detroit, by Age Groups, 1934 and 1935

Age in Years	Massachusetts[a] (Jan. 2, 1934)				Detroit, Michigan[b] (Jan. 14, 1935) Males
	Entire State		Boston Only		
	Males	Females	Males	Females	
15................	62.4	59.7	67.4	76.2	—
16................	66.1	60.9	73.1	77.5	—
17................	61.5	51.3	71.3	68.2	—
18................	56.3	45.7	64.7	57.4	—
19................	50.2	40.0	57.4	50.7	—
20................	43.5	32.4	49.6	41.0	—
21–24............	33.7	21.2	39.9	25.6	—
25–29............	25.0	13.9	30.9	16.5	11.5
30–34............	21.0	13.7	26.8	16.1	10.4
35–39............	20.7	15.9	26.0	19.4	11.3
40–44............	20.9	16.7	26.6	20.1	13.4
45–49............	22.8	19.0	28.7	23.3	16.9
50–54............	24.1	19.9	29.2	23.2	21.6
55–59............	26.3	21.9	31.0	25.6	28.6
60–64............	28.4	20.7	32.6	24.4	34.0
65–69............	31.2	21.0	35.5	25.8	
70 and over........	26.3	14.3	34.6	17.1	36.1

[a] Massachusetts Department of Labor and Industries "Report of the Census of Unemployment in Massachusetts as of Jan. 2, 1934," *Labor Bulletin No. 171*, pp. 14 and 91.
[b] William Haber and Paul L. Stanchfield, *Unemployment Relief and Economic Security—A Survey of Michigan's Relief and Unemployment Problem* (Lansing, Mich., 1936), p. 155.

consideration is not significant for the current years, since there have been practically no accretions to the labor force through immigration, and it is only in the professions that individuals enter active life at an age which is higher than our class of reference. The ages of highest frequency used in the computation and the frequencies thereof are:

All occupations:
Males . . . . Approximately 22 years   1.05 millions
Females . . . . Approximately 19 years   0.53 millions

All occupations, exclusive of agriculture:
Males . . . . Approximately 28-29 years 0.80 millions
Females . . . . Approximately 21 years   0.50 millions

Thus it is estimated that the annual replacements required in order to maintain the full quota of gainful workers as it was in April 1930 amounted to approximately 1.58 million individuals for all occupations and 1.3 millions for all occupations outside of agriculture.

In our computations the number of individuals required to maintain the 1930 aggregate of gainful workers in agriculture is estimated by accepting the difference between all occupations and non-agricultural occupations. When the estimates are carried out directly, the replacements for agriculture appear to be somewhat higher. This difference is more marked for females than males; for females the total accretion between January 1930 and July 1936 when computed directly amounts to 221,000 whereas the number obtained by subtraction is only 195,000; for males the two estimates are 1,716,000 and 1,625,000 respectively. These discrepancies are accounted for by the fact that in agriculture the age of highest frequency is lower than in other occupations and that the turnover, particularly of females, is much higher than elsewhere. In this connection it should be pointed out that among the gainfully employed in agriculture a considerable number are unpaid workers on home farms, not all of whom remain for any length of time in agriculture. Some enter other occupations and a majority of the females marry. Hence among the agricultural replacements there is a considerable portion of individuals who normally remain in this occupation only a short time.

The additions to the labor force because of growth in population were estimated by multiplying the mid-year estimates of the population 15-64 years of age by the ratio of gainful workers to the population of these ages. These additions were subdivided into males and females on the basis of the sex distribution of gainful workers in April 1930. It was assumed that the entire addition due to population growth accrued to the nonagricultural labor force since agriculture is a contracting rather than an expanding industry.[1] This assumption is not invalidated by the fact that in reality during the depression there has been an increase in the number of workers on farms. As explained on page 146, this city-to-farm movement is considered only temporary.

It should be observed that in all of these calculations we have assumed the proportions existing in 1930 to have been unchanged. This assumption is, of course, not strictly tenable; during the past six years there has been, in fact, a considerable change in the age and sex composition of the persons whom the Census would classify as gainful workers.[2] The changes, however, do not invalidate the general significance of our estimates.

II. CURRENT ESTIMATES OF EMPLOYMENT AND UNEMPLOYMENT

Table 8 presents the estimates of employment and unemployment compiled by the American Federation of Labor, the President's Committee on Economic Security, and the National Industrial Conference Board.[3] As stated on page 131, the methods used by the three agencies differ only in detail. The procedure in each case was substantially as follows: (1) to establish the employment situation as it existed in April 1930 when the first federal Census of Unemployment was taken; (2) to project estimates of employment in the several branches of industry on the basis of indexes of the United States Bureau of Labor Statistics, the Interstate Commerce Commission, and miscel-

[1] For more detailed explanation, see pp. 146-47 and Table 10, p. 621.

[2] Owing to increased longevity, the age composition of the entire population is undergoing changes. During the depression fewer of the older workers have been able to "retire," and there has also been a tendency for persons who under ordinary conditions would be in "nongainful" activities to seek remunerative work.

[3] The present discussion and all subsequent references to the unemployment estimates of the National Industrial Conference Board pertain to the series made available prior to the Board's revision of Nov. 13, 1936.

laneous employment surveys; (3) to project estimates of total gainful workers reported in the Census of Occupations in 1930 in accordance with a population factor; and (4) to subtract the number employed from the total number of gainful workers—the residual representing the number of gainful workers unemployed.

The major differences among the several estimates arise from two sources. In the first place there is some difference of opinion as to the accuracy of the unemployment census for 1930. The National Industrial Conference Board has accepted this census as being substantially correct, while the American Federation of Labor and the President's Committee on Economic Security have made some upward adjustments for the understatement of unemployment in April 1930. This difference in the estimate for the base month is carried through the subsequent years. The second source of difference hinges on the fact, already mentioned, that a marked change has been taking place in the age composition of the population of the United States. On account of a decrease in the birth rate and an increase in longevity, the proportion of adults in the population has been increasing. The estimates of the total number of gainful workers will therefore depend upon whether the number is varied in accordance with the total population or with the population of specified ages. In fact, the principal difference between the estimates of the American Federation of Labor and those of the President's Committee on Economic Security is explained by the fact that the former has used the adult population (that is, persons 15 years of age and over), while the latter has used the total population as the basis for estimating total gainful workers. Since the unemployment figure is a residual derived by deducting the number employed from the total number of gainful workers, the results vary according to the method selected for estimating the gainful workers.

From what has just been said it can be seen that the totals of the unemployed include not only those who have lost their jobs since 1929 and those unemployed in 1929, but also the increment in the number of workers seeking employment. It should also be clear that the terms "employed" and "unemployed" are used rather broadly. There is no attempt to define degree of employment or unemployment. The employed category includes persons self-employed and "unpaid family workers on farms" as well as hired employees, and the unemployed (in some of the estimates, at least) include those who are temporarily idle from choice or through disability[4] as well as those who are able to work and are seeking work. In 1930, according to census data, roughly 1.3 per cent[5] of the gainful workers were not employable in the strict sense. Furthermore, as previously indicated, the unemployed contain a fair percentage of aged persons and of minors.

Another qualification of the unemployment figures is that the total number of employed in the later years of the depression includes a large number of individuals who have left the cities to enter agriculture as an escape from the depression. These individuals, though technically employed, are in many respects part of the non-agricultural labor force and to that extent they may still be considered as unemployed. This question is treated in the discussion on pages 146-47.

[4] In the estimates prepared by both the National Industrial Conference Board and the American Federation of Labor, adjustments have been made to exclude those of the unemployed who were not seeking work.

The National Industrial Conference Board series purports to trace unemployment among those who are able to work and looking for work; it excludes those who are employed and also those who are unemployed but not in a position to be employed. Thus its annual estimates of total gainful workers include a constant of 619,000 persons who are not distributed among either the employed or unemployed. The 619,000 represent those included in Classes C through F of the Census of Unemployment for 1930 whom the Board considers outside the problem of employment and unemployment because they were not at work for reasons of personal disability or were not seeking work. (In the revised estimates of the Board, published in November 1936, the "unemployables" were apparently thrown into the unemployed group.)

The American Federation of Labor series of unemployed includes some who are unemployed but who presumably are not looking for work at the time. In establishing its base the Federation deducted from the number of gainful workers reported by the Census of Occupations for April 1930 all those classified by the Census of Unemployment as "persons out of a job and unable to work" (Class C) and half of those classified as "persons out of a job and not looking for work" (Class E). This represented a total deduction of approximately 217,000.

The unemployment figures of the President's Committee on Economic Security include all the gainful workers who are not working, whether or not they are able or willing to work at the time.

[5] Exclusive of farmers and unpaid family workers on farms the percentage is 1.5.

A recent survey conducted by the *New York Sun,* which compares average employment in 1929 and in 1935 for a sample of identical establishments, casts some doubt on the accuracy of the employment estimates discussed in the foregoing paragraphs. According to the replies obtained by the *New York Sun* the number employed in major industrial groups in 1935, expressed as percentages of 1929, were as follows: mechanical and manufacturing industries (exclusive of construction), 93.6; trade, 108.0; extraction of minerals, 72.8; transportation and communication, 70.3. The corresponding percentages underlying the estimates of the President's Committee on Economic Security, which, as said before, are in the aggregate essentially the same as those of the American Federation of Labor and the National Industrial Conference Board, are 78.9, 87.9, 65.5, and 67.2 respectively.

When the two sets of percentages are applied to the same estimates of employment for 1929,[6] we find that according to the *New York Sun* survey employment in the major industrial groups mentioned above decreased from 21,840,000[7] to 20,550,000, while according to the estimates of the President's Committee the decline was to 17,380,000. The *Sun* survey therefore indicates that in the industries covered the number unemployed was about 3 millions less than is shown by the other estimates.

If the ratio of employment in 1935 to that in 1929 for the *New York Sun* sample were extended to all industries,[8] including those not covered by the survey, the discrepancy in the employment estimates would be raised to 5 millions. Thus instead

[6] Estimates of the President's Committee on Economic Security are here used.

[7] The *Sun* claims that its sample is applicable to a total of 27,968,000 persons in 1929. Two and one-half millions, however, are in construction and the *Sun* itself feels that its sample for construction "must be accepted with reservations." (It shows that employment in building construction in 1935 was 60.5 per cent of 1929, which is improbable in view of existing data relative to volume of construction.) It is safer to disregard the *Sun's* construction figures. Another cause of the *Sun's* overstatement of the number of persons to which its sample is applicable is that whereas the reports from the different establishments refer to numbers employed, the calculation of the raised aggregate refers to *employables.* There was considerable difference between the two concepts even in 1929.

[8] Exclusive of unpaid family workers on farms.

(In millions)

Year and Month	Number of Gainful Workers			Number of Employed			Number of Unemployed		
	American Federation of Labor[a]	President's Committee on Economic Security[b]	National Industrial Conference Board[c]	American Federation of Labor[a,d]	President's Committee on Economic Security[b,d]	National Industrial Conference Board[c]	American Federation of Labor[a]	President's Committee on Economic Security[b]	National Industrial Conference Board[c]
1929:									
Jan.......	47.7	48.4	...	44.7	45.8	...	3.0	2.6	...
Feb......	47.8	48.4	...	44.7	45.5	...	3.1	2.9	...
Mar......	47.9	48.5	...	45.3	45.6	...	2.6	2.9	...
Apr......	47.9	48.5	...	45.9	46.3	...	2.0	2.2	...
May.....	48.0	48.5	...	46.2	46.7	...	1.8	1.8	...
June.....	48.0	48.5	...	46.6	47.0	...	1.4	1.5	...
July......	48.1	48.5	...	46.9	47.5	...	1.2	1.0	...
Aug......	48.1	48.6	...	47.1	48.0	...	1.0	0.6	...
Sept......	48.2	48.6	...	47.6	47.7	...	0.6	0.9	...
Oct......	48.3	48.7	...	47.4	48.2	...	0.9	0.5	...
Nov......	48.3	48.7	...	46.4	46.8	...	1.9	1.9	...
Dec. :	48.4	48.7	...	45.8	45.9	...	2.6	2.8	...
Average ..	48.1	48.6	...	46.2	46.8	...	1.9	1.8	...
1930:									
Jan.......	48.4	48.7	...	44.5	44.7	...	3.9	4.0	...
Feb......	48.5	48.8	...	44.2	44.4	...	4.3	4.4	...
Mar......	48.5	48.8	...	44.2	44.2	...	4.3	4.6	...
Apr......	48.6	48.8	...	44.6	44.4	...	4.0	4.4	3.2
May.....	48.7	48.9	...	44.9	44.6	...	3.8	4.3	3.2
June.....	48.7	48.9	...	44.8	44.7	...	3.9	4.2	3.7
July......	48.8	48.9	...	44.3	44.7	...	4.5	4.2	4.4
Aug......	48.8	48.9	...	43.9	44.1	...	4.9	4.8	4.8
Sept......	48.9	48.9	...	43.9	43.9	...	5.0	5.0	4.6
Oct......	48.9	49.0	...	43.4	43.5	...	5.5	5.5	4.8
Nov......	49.0	49.0	...	42.7	42.5	...	6.3	6.5	5.5
Dec......	49.1	49.1	...	42.2	42.1	...	6.9	7.0	5.8
Average ..	48.8	48.9	49.0[e]	44.0	44.0	43.9	4.8	4.9	4.5[e]
1931:									
Jan.......	49.1	49.1	...	40.9	41.0	...	8.2	8.1	6.8
Feb......	49.2	49.1	...	40.9	40.8	...	8.3	8.3	7.0
Mar......	49.2	49.2	...	41.1	40.9	...	8.1	8.3	7.0
Apr......	49.3	49.2	...	41.5	41.1	...	7.8	8.1	6.8
May.....	49.3	49.2	...	41.5	41.2	...	7.8	8.0	7.0
June.....	49.4	49.2	...	41.5	41.2	...	7.9	8.0	7.3
July......	49.5	49.2	...	41.1	41.3	...	8.4	7.9	7.9
Aug......	49.5	49.2	...	40.7	40.8	...	8.8	8.4	8.2
Sept......	49.6	49.3	...	40.7	40.6	...	8.9	8.7	8.3
Oct......	49.6	49.3	...	40.1	40.2	...	9.5	9.1	8.6
Nov......	49.7	49.3	...	39.3	39.4	...	10.4	9.9	9.1
Dec......	49.7	49.4	...	38.8	38.8	...	10.9	10.6	9.3
Average ..	49.4	49.2	49.3[e]	40.7	40.6	40.9	8.7	8.6	7.8
1932:									
Jan.......	49.8	49.4	...	37.9	37.9	...	11.9	11.5	10.2
Feb......	49.8	49.4	...	37.6	37.6	...	12.2	11.8	10.3
Mar......	49.9	49.5	...	37.5	37.3	...	12.4	12.2	10.5
Apr......	49.9	49.5	...	37.4	37.1	...	12.5	12.4	11.0
May.....	50.0	49.5	...	37.0	36.7	...	13.0	12.8	11.3
June.....	50.0	49.5	...	36.6	36.4	...	13.4	13.1	11.8
July......	50.1	49.5	...	36.3	36.1	...	13.8	13.4	12.4
Aug......	50.1	49.6	...	36.2	36.0	...	13.9	13.6	12.5
Sept......	50.2	49.6	...	36.7	36.5	...	13.5	13.1	12.1
Oct......	50.2	49.6	...	36.8	36.8	...	13.4	12.8	11.9
Nov......	50.3	49.7	...	36.4	36.5	...	13.9	13.2	12.2
Dec......	50.3	49.7	...	36.1	36.1	...	14.2	13.6	12.3
Average ..	50.1	49.6	49.7[e]	36.9	36.8	37.5	13.2	12.8	11.5

[a] *American Federationist*, January 1936, Vol. XLIII, No. 1, pp. 64–72, and September 1936, p. 98 press release of American Federation of Labor, July 3, 1936.

[b] Robert R. Nathan, "Estimates of Unemployment in the United States, 1929–35," *International Labor Review*, January 1936, Vol. XXXIII, No. 1, pp. 49–73. The series have been continued by means of the indexes described by Mr. Nathan.

[c] National Industrial Conference Board, Inc., *Memorandum, Unemployment Estimates*, Apr. 29, 193 (mimeographed). The series begins with April 1930. (The figures have since been revised. See *Conference Board Bulletin*, Nov. 13, 1936.)

[d] It should be noted that the figures in these series, for 1934 and 1935 at least, understate the actual employment within the definitions used on account of an under-estimate of the number of gainful workers in agriculture. Each series presumes that a "gainful worker" on the farm is an employed person. The under-estimates are disclosed by the Census of Agriculture for 1935, the results of which were not available.

(In millions)

Year and Month	Number of Gainful Workers			Number of Employed			Number of Unemployed		
	American Federation of Labor[a]	President's Committee on Economic Security[b]	National Industrial Conference Board[c]	American Federation of Labor[a,d]	President's Committee on Economic Security[b,d]	National Industrial Conference Board[c]	American Federation of Labor[a]	President's Committee on Economic Security[b]	National Industrial Conference Board[c]
1933:									
Jan......	50.4	49.7	...	35.2	35.2	...	15.2	14.5	13.0
Feb.....	50.4	49.8	...	35.1	35.2	...	15.3	14.6	13.0
Mar.....	50.5	49.8	...	34.8	34.7	...	15.7	15.1	13.5
Apr.....	50.5	49.8	...	35.4	35.1	...	15.1	14.7	13.2
May.....	50.6	49.8	...	36.0	35.5	...	14.6	14.3	12.9
June.....	50.6	49.8	...	36.8	36.3	...	13.8	13.5	12.2
July.....	50.7	49.9	...	37.2	37.1	...	13.5	12.8	11.8
Aug.....	50.8	49.9	...	38.1	37.8	...	12.7	12.1	11.0
Sept.....	50.8	49.9	...	38.9	38.5	...	11.9	11.4	10.2
Oct......	50.9	50.0	...	39.0	38.8	...	11.9	11.2	10.1
Nov.....	50.9	50.0	...	38.5	38.3	...	12.4	11.7	10.6
Dec.....	51.0	50.0	...	38.2	38.0	...	12.8	12.0	10.5
Average ..	50.7	49.9	50.0[e]	37.0	36.7	37.5	13.7	13.2	11.9
1934:									
Jan......	51.0	50.1	...	37.6	37.5	...	13.4	12.6	10.8
Feb.....	51.1	50.1	...	38.1	38.0	...	13.0	12.1	10.1
Mar.....	51.1	50.1	...	38.7	38.5	...	12.4	11.6	9.7
Apr.....	51.2	50.2	...	39.2	39.0	...	12.0	11.2	9.6
May.....	51.2	50.2	...	39.5	39.3	...	11.7	10.9	9.4
June.....	51.3	50.2	...	39.6	39.5	...	11.7	10.7	9.5
July.....	51.3	50.3	...	39.1	39.3	...	12.2	11.0	10.1
Aug.....	51.4	50.3	...	39.0	38.9	...	12.4	11.4	10.3
Sept.....	51.4	50.3	...	39.0	38.4	...	12.4	11.9	10.4
Oct......	51.5	50.3	...	39.3	38.7	...	12.2	11.6	10.1
Nov.....	51.5	50.3	...	38.9	38.3	...	12.6	12.0	10.3
Dec.....	51.6	50.4	...	39.2	38.3	...	12.4	12.1	10.0
Average ..	51.3	50.2	50.3[e]	38.9	38.6	39.7	12.4	11.6	10.0
1935:									
Jan......	51.6	50.4	...	38.5	37.8	...	13.1	12.6	10.4
Feb.....	51.7	50.5	...	38.9	38.1	...	12.8	12.4	10.2
Mar.....	51.7	50.5	...	39.1	38.3	...	12.6	12.2	10.0
Apr.....	51.8	50.5	...	39.4	38.7	...	12.4	11.8	9.9
May.....	51.8	50.5	...	39.4	38.9	...	12.4	11.6	9.9
June.....	51.9	50.5	...	39.5	39.1	...	12.4	11.4	10.0
July.....	51.9	50.6	...	39.4	39.2	...	12.5	11.4	10.2
Aug.....	52.0	50.6	...	39.8	39.5	...	12.2	11.1	9.9
Sept.....	52.0	50.6	...	40.2	39.7	...	11.8	10.9	9.5
Oct......	52.0	50.6	...	40.6	40.0	...	11.4	10.6	9.3
Nov.....	52.1	50.6	...	40.6	39.9	...	11.5	10.7	9.3
Dec.....	52.1	50.6	...	40.7	40.0	...	11.4	10.6	9.1
Average ..	51.9	50.5	50.7[e]	39.6	39.1	40.3	12.3	11.4	9.8
1936:									
Jan......	52.2	50.7	...	39.6	39.0	...	12.6	11.7	9.8
Feb.....	52.2	50.7	...	39.7	39.3	...	12.5	11.4	9.8
Mar.....	52.3	50.7	...	40.1	39.6	...	12.2	11.1	9.6
Apr.....	52.3	50.8	g	40.8	40.5	g	11.5	10.3	g
May.....	52.4	50.8	...	41.1	40.7	...	11.3	10.1	...
June.....	52.4	50.8	...	41.3	40.9	...	11.1	9.9	...
July.....	...	50.8	...	...	41.2	...	11.2	9.6	...
Aug.....	...	50.9	...	...	41.5	...	10.8	9.4	...
Sept.....	...	50.9	...	...	41.9	...	...	9.0	...
Oct......	...	...	...	...	...	...	...	...	...
Nov.....	...	...	...	...	...	...	...	...	...
Dec.....	...	...	...	...	...	...	...	...	...
Average ..	...	...	...	...	...	...	...	...	...

at the time the estimates were prepared. From the Census it appears that at the beginning of 1935 there were about 2 million more "workers" on farms than are included in these estimates. See pp. 138-39.

The National Industrial Conference Board made no attempt to estimate changes in agricultural employment but assumed the number working on farms remained constant. (A different assumption has apparently been made in the estimates of Nov. 13, 1936. See note c.)

[e] Includes 619,000 persons falling in Classes C to F of the Census of Unemployment for 1930. These individuals, who were not working at the time of the Census because of personal disability or were not seeking work, have not been distributed among the employed or unemployed since the National Industrial Conference Board has considered them outside the problem of employment and unemployment. (Apparently this is no longer true in the revised estimates of November 1936. See note 3, p. 608.)

[f] Average for nine months.

[g] Series has not been continued beyond March 1936.

of a total unemployment in 1935 of 12.5 millions, the *Sun* survey would point to a total of only 7.5 millions.

However, the ratios published by the *New York Sun* cannot be accepted as conclusive. Such judgment as may be formed from the inadequate classification of the published summary indicates that some types of establishments are disproportionately represented and that an entirely different result might be obtained if the weighting of the different groups were made according to their actual importance with respect to employment in 1929. For instance, according to the Census in 1929, chain stores had about 20 per cent of all the full-time employees in retail trade. Yet in the *Sun* sample chain stores account for at least 64 per cent of the employees in retail outlets.[9] Chain stores have suffered less during the depression than other retail establishments: between 1929 and 1933 the number of full-time employees in all retail outlets decreased about 30 per cent, but in chain stores it decreased only 13 per cent. The significance of the discrepancy in weighting is indicated by the fact that the *Sun* sample shows employment in chain stores as 19.0 per cent higher in 1935 than in 1929 while in department stores it was 2.6 per cent lower.

Until the data collected by the *New York Sun* are analyzed in greater detail with a view to assigning proper weights to the several component parts, it is impossible to judge whether the survey actually invalidates the estimates made by other agencies on the basis of the information collected by the United States Bureau of Labor Statistics.

One defect of the Bureau of Labor Statistics indexes of employment cannot, however, be overlooked. Because of the method of collecting the data these indexes cannot incorporate currently employment by new enterprises, and hence in a period of rising activity they do not fully register the increase in employment. This defect is recognized by the Bureau of Labor Statistics as well as by those using the indexes in estimating total employment. However, there is no basis for determining the magnitude of the error involved. This bias is opposite to that existing in the *New York Sun* survey. The *Sun* sample is based on firms existing at the time of the survey and does not reflect the reduction in employment of firms which have gone out of business during the de-

[9] In the *Sun* classification wholesale trade is not classified separately. But out of a total of 711,000 employees in retail and wholesale establishments, 454,000 employees were reported by chain stores for 1929.

pression, while it includes new firms which have entered business during the upturn.

III. EQUIVALENT FULL-TIME EMPLOYMENT

Tables 9 to 16 inclusive, presented in this section, deal with the estimates of employment and unemployment on a full-time equivalent basis. The need for distinguishing full-time equivalent employment from the ordinary measures referring to mere counts of workers without regard to actual time worked is indicated on page 142.

Employees in all industries. In estimating the equivalent full-time number of wage earners and salaried workers use was made of existing data on aggregate wages and salaries and average full-time earnings. The work of the Department of Commerce in connection with its estimates of national income was relied upon in practically all the estimates. However, the categories used in the Department of Commerce estimates have not been followed in each case. Manufacturing, for instance, consists of a somewhat different industrial component in our figures than in the Department's figures.

The number of equivalent full-time employees was obtained by dividing total wages and salaries by annual estimates of average full-time earnings of employees. Separate averages have been computed for the several industries. In five of them, namely, manufacturing, construction, mining, steam railways, and agriculture, it was possible to compute separate averages for wage earners and salaried workers, but for the other industries, which were chiefly service industries, such a segregation could not be made because the distinction between wage earners and salaried workers in these industries is ordinarily not clearly drawn. The averages for the different groups were weighted in accordance with the approximate number in the respective groups. On the whole, our results correspond very closely with those published by the Department of Commerce since in most instances the same figures were used and refinements with respect to the concept of full time have been possible in the cases of only a few industries. In manufacturing, for instance, the Department of Commerce accepts the average number on payrolls as the equivalent full-time employees in the case of wage earners as well as salaried workers. In our estimates for manufacturing, however, the average full-time earnings of wage earners have been computed on the basis of average hourly earnings and a standard number of hours per year. In other words, in the Department of Commerce figures the number of hours representing full-time employment changes from year to year, while in our estimates an attempt has been made to keep the number of hours stationary, at the level established in 1929. Thus in our estimates for manufacturing, full-time work was considered to be about 2,400 hours in 1932 as well as in 1929 although the average wage earner on the payrolls was employed on a considerably lower hour basis in the later year.

The self-employed in agriculture. The estimates of the full-time equivalent of the self-employed in agriculture are shown in Table 10 on page 621. These figures represent only rough estimates based primarily on a conceptual classification of the farm operators in 1929 and on the assumption that, because there has been no increase in demand for or production of farm products, no farmers added since 1929 are engaged in commercial farming. Thus the number of full-time self-employed commercial farmers is kept constant at 4.9 millions. When the noncommercial farmers are included, the total is estimated to have increased from 5.4 millions in 1929 to 5.9 millions in 1935.

The steps involved in estimating the full-time equivalent number of farmers in 1929 are as follows:

Total number of farms as reported by the Census of Agriculture[10] 6,289,000
Number operated by managers[10] 56,000
Number operated by owners or tenants 6,233,000
Equivalent full-time workers represented by the days
    worked by farmers for pay off their own farms[11] . 628,000
Estimated equivalent full-time workers represented
    by *self-employment* of farmers at other occupations[12] 221,000

Total man-years at other occupations 849,000
Corrected estimate of number of farmers 5,384,000

---

[10] *Fifteenth Census of the United States: 1930, Agriculture,* Vol. IV, p. 146.

[11] The volume of days of other occupations of farm operators (*Agriculture,* Vol. IV, pp. 430-31) divided by 300. The outside occupations of farm managers have been excluded.

[12] The difference between the enumeration of the Census of Agriculture and that of the Census of Occupations. This would seem to be conservative in view of the number of farmers who operate country stores, gasoline stations, etc. There are no figures of the actual number of such operators.

Subtracting from the above result 498,000 farmers reported as self-sufficing, we find that the full-time equivalent of "commercial" farmers may be set at approximately 4,886,000.

The situation revealed by the foregoing analysis is fully confirmed by the available data on the value of products sold from the farm. Dr. O. E. Baker has estimated on the basis of the Census of Agriculture that, in 1929, 15.3 per cent of the farmers (comprising nearly one million of the units reported) accounted for less than one per cent of the total value of farm products sold. The sale from one-half of the farms—representing some 3 millions of the so-called farmers—constituted less than 12 per cent of the total.

The increase of 523,700 farms between 1930 and 1935 was accompanied by an increase in the number of days given by farm operators to non-agricultural occupations. In 1929 farm operators worked 189 million days for pay away from their farms, but in 1934, despite the decrease in employment possibilities, the volume of such work rose to 202 million days.[13] The explanation lies, of course, in the fact that a large proportion of the new operators were "part-time" farmers with non-agricultural employment connections.

It is impossible to determine the exact relationship of these new farmers to the farm industry, but for our immediate purposes it will be convenient to consider the entire increment as "self-sufficing" farmers, although, as has been suggested, many would more correctly fall into the class of *part-time* farmers.[14] This places the number of "self-sufficing" or "subsistence" farmers at the beginning of 1935 at something more than one million,[15] in addition to the estimate of 4,886,000 commercial farmers.

In agriculture it is difficult to treat the self-employed apart from the supplementary farm labor consisting of unpaid family workers and hired laborers. In many respects the three groups are interchangeable. For example, it is reasonable to believe

[13] *U. S. Census of Agriculture: 1935, Part-Time Farmers* (rotoprint release), p. 2.

[14] Incidentally, in our calculations the category of part-time farmer is eliminated, the time devoted by farmers to non-agricultural pursuits being reduced to an equivalent full-time basis and then subtracted from the total number of farm operators.

[15] See Table 10, p. 621.

that the women reported as farm operators for the most part devote their time to household duties while the actual operations on their farms are carried on by other members of the family (reported as unpaid family workers) or by hired help. Likewise, during the depression there has been an increase in the number of operators and unpaid family workers with an attendant decrease in the number of wage earners in agriculture.

It is not possible to make a precise evaluation of the volume of work and the productive contribution of unpaid family workers on farms. The only data available concern their number as of a specified date. Because the volume of work varies greatly with the season, the number as of a given date is a poor index of the average for the year. The reduction of the unpaid family workers to a full-time basis must therefore be made in a rather arbitrary manner in the light of qualitative considerations connected with the age and sex distribution of these workers as reported by the Census. We have already seen that about 475,000 of the 1.7 million unpaid family workers reported in the 1930 Census were females. It is believed that these may be definitely excluded from the count of *producers* in the narrow sense of the word since it may be assumed that their work consisted chiefly of household functions in their own homes which are not ordinarily included in the computation of production and income. Their assistance on the farm proper was merely incidental and could not have been of much consequence. The 575,000 boys under 18 years of age and the 10,000 men over 65 who were included in this group undoubtedly contributed a very considerable amount of work to the farm business. Yet in view of the uneven distribution of farm work throughout the year and in view of the long periods of idleness—in some parts of the country at least—on the part of adults as well as children, it would perhaps not be too inaccurate to offset the idle time of the full-time workers by the part-time work of the minors and the aged. This leaves 600,000 males between the ages of 18 and 64 who may rightly be considered as full-time workers. However, as has already been pointed out, there were 263,000 female operators whom we considered as merely nominal farmers. On the assumption that adult males reported as unpaid family workers conducted the actual operation on these farms, 263,000 of the 600,000 may be shifted to the self-employed group in order to offset the inclusion of female operators. The net addition to the equivalent full-time labor force on account of the unpaid family workers is therefore reduced to 337,000.

The number of full-time wage earners in agriculture has been calculated for the different years on the basis of the estimated annual wages in agriculture and the average full-time compensation of agricultural laborers.[16] The number of full-time wage earners by this calculation was 2.0 millions in 1929 and 1.5 millions in 1935.[17]

Co-ordinate with the reasoning followed in the case of the self-employed in agriculture, it is assumed that there has been no change during the depression in the number of supplementary workers, that is, wage earners and unpaid family workers, on commercial farms. This assumption, like the other, is ultra-conservative since the decrease in demand for and the production of agricultural products has not necessitated keeping so large a personnel in the industry as in 1929.[18] On the basis of this assumption it is possible to reason that the decrease in full-time wage earners during the depression has been made up by an equivalent number of unpaid family workers. Furthermore, it may be assumed that the unpaid workers over and above the quota required to replace the wage earners are not engaged in additional production. Such chores as they perform merely represent relief from the work for the regular workers. Thus it is estimated in the table on page 621 that the full-time equivalent workers represented by the unpaid family workers increased from 337,000 in 1929 to 873,000 in 1935.

[16] This method is used by the Department of Commerce in connection with the income estimates.

[17] The 1935 Census of Agriculture gives the total number of hired help on farms as 1,646,000 as of Jan. 1, 1935. *U. S. Census of Agriculture: 1935, Farm Labor* (rotoprint release), p. 2.

[18] The index of physical volume of output in agriculture computed by the National Bureau of Economic Research and converted to a 1929 base is as follows: 1929, 100.0; 1930, 100.0; 1931, 105.9; 1932, 98.9; 1933, 96.0; 1934, 91.0. National Bureau of Economic Research, "Income Originating in Nine Basic Industries, 1919-34," *Bulletin 59*, p. 24.

9. Equivalent Full-Time Employment of "Employees" in All Industries, 1929-35[a]

Year	Department of Commerce Estimates (Changing hour content per wage earner)[b]		Adjusted Estimates (1929 hours per wage earner kept constant)[c]	
	In Thousands of Employees	*As a Percentage of 1929*	In Thousands of Employees	*As a Percentage of 1929*
1929....	34,485	*100.0*	34,341	*100.0*
1930....	32,373	*93.9*	31,649	*92.2*
1931....	28,943	*83.9*	27,724	*80.7*
1932....	25,308	*73.4*	23,914	*69.6*
1933....	25,358	*73.5*	23,683	*69.0*
1934....	27,325	*79.2*	25,173	*73.3*
1935....	28,094	*81.5*	26,175	*76.2*

[a] Exclusive of work relief.

[b] Robert R. Nathan, "Expansion in the National Income Continued in 1935," *Survey of Current Business*, July 1936. These estimates take no account of the violent changes in average hours of work which have taken place during the depression. They present the average number on payrolls for each year irrespective of length of working day. In a few industries adjustments have been made for part-time employees.

[c] Based on figures from U. S. Department of Commerce, *National Income in the United States, 1929-35*, 1936. Except for wage earners in the principal non-service industries—manufacturing, mining, construction, and transportation—the Department of Commerce data, as given, have been incorporated in the present estimates. For the wage earners mentioned, however, the average hours of work in 1929 (provided they did not exceed 2,400 hours) have been retained as full-time in all the subsequent years. The equivalent numbers have been obtained by dividing the aggregate payrolls for the wage earners in question by the current average annual earnings for a working year of the 1929 number of hours. The maximum hours considered normal in 1929 was 2,400; that is, 48 hours per week for 50 weeks. In railroad transportation the average worked in 1929 was more than 2,400 hours. Hence the adjustment made in the number of wage earners in that industry in 1929 gave a higher number than reported by the Interstate Commerce Commission.

10. Equivalent Full-Time Employment in Agriculture, 1929–35
(In terms of thousands of workers)

Year[a]	Grand Total	Self-Employed			Unpaid Family Workers[d]	Wage Earners[d,f]
		Total	Commercial Farmers[b]	Non-commercial Farmers[c]		
1929.....	7,727	5,366	4,886	480	337[e]	2,024
1930.....	7,757	5,396	4,886	510	468	1,893
1931.....	7,817	5,456	4,886	570	592	1,769
1932.....	8,167	5,806	4,886	920	839	1,522
1933.....	8,247	5,886	4,886	1,000	806	1,555
1934.....	8,267	5,906	4,886	1,020	889	1,472
1935.....	8,272	5,911	4,886	1,025	873	1,488

[a] Average for the year or as of July 1.

[b] Owners and tenants exclusive of self-sufficing farmers, and corrected for time given to other occupations. It is assumed that since there was no increase in demand for agricultural products and no increase in production, there was no increase in the volume of time given to commercial farming. See pp. 616–19.

[c] Includes self-sufficing and, subsequent to 1930, some part-time farmers who gave time to other employment. The increase between 1930 and 1935 has been distributed in accordance with the Department of Agriculture estimates of growth in farm population.

[d] It is assumed that no additional labor was required in agriculture during the depression. Hence the combined total of unpaid family workers and wage earners is kept stationary, the decrease in wage earners being compensated by additions to the unpaid family workers. The actual number of unpaid family workers increased much more during the depression than is here indicated, but not the work.

[e] This is the number of males in the ages 18–64 reported in the Census of Occupations with a deduction to allow for female farm operators. See p. 618.

[f] Estimated by the Department of Commerce on the basis of total farm wages and average full-time annual pay of farm labor without board.

11. Equivalent Full-Time Employment of "Commercially Self-Employed" in All Industries, 1929–35
(In terms of thousands of workers)

Year	Total	Agriculture[a]	Other Industries[b]
1929	8,813	4,886	3,927
1930	8,795	4,886	3,909
1931	8,777	4,886	3,891
1932	8,717	4,886	3,831
1933	8,767	4,886	3,881
1934	8,864	4,886	3,978
1935	8,897	4,886	4,011

[a] See Table 10, p. 621.
[b] U. S. Department of Commerce, *National Income in the United States, 1929–35*, 1936.

12. Equivalent Full-Time Employment of "All Workers" in All Industries, 1929–35[a]
(In terms of thousands of workers)

Year	Total		Self-Employed		Others	
	Including Self-Sufficing Farmers	Commercial Activities Only	Commercial[b]	Non-Commercial[c]	Employees[d]	Unpaid Family Workers on Farms[e]
1929	43,971	43,491	8,813	480	34,341	337
1930	41,422	40,912	8,795	510	31,649	468
1931	37,663	37,093	8,777	570	27,724	592
1932	34,390	33,470	8,717	920	23,914	839
1933	34,256	33,256	8,767	1,000	23,683	806
1934	35,946	34,926	8,864	1,020	25,173	889
1935	35,970	35,945	8,897	1,025	26,175	873

[a] Exclusive of work relief.
[b] See Table 11 above.
[c] Agriculture only. See Table 10, p. 621.
[d] See Table 9, p. 620.
[e] See Table 10, p. 621.

[h] These alternative estimates are based on the fact that the employment indexes of the Bureau of Labor Statistics, which enter into the original calculations, are subject to a downward bias. In the absence of the final data of the 1935 Census enumerations this bias cannot be fully evaluated. Preliminary checks, however, indicate that in 1935 the error in our figures resulting from the bias was perhaps as high as 400,000 workers on a full-time basis (500,000 corrected for reduction in hours between 1929 and 1935). Since the Bureau of Labor Statistics indexes have already been corrected in accordance with the Census of 1933, the error in our estimate for 1934 may be placed as roughly one-half of that in 1935, or about 200,000. By 1936 the bias may have raised the error to 500,000.

[i] Preliminary. See note *g* above.

13. Volume of Unemployment on Equivalent Full-Time Basis, 1929–36
Exclusive of Non-Commercial Activities[a]
(In terms of millions of workers)

Year	Gainful Workers[b]		Full-Time Equivalent Employment in Commercial Activities[e]	Approximations of Unemployment[f]
	Gross Estimates[c]	Adjusted for Overstatement in Agriculture[d]		
1929....	48.4	46.6	43.5	3.1
1930....	49.0	47.2	40.9	6.3
1931....	49.6	47.8	37.1	10.7
1932....	50.2	48.4	33.5	14.9
1933....	50.8	49.0	33.2	15.8
1934....	51.4	49.6	34.9–35.1[h]	14.7–14.5[h]
1935....	52.1	50.3	35.9–36.3[h]	14.4–14.0[h]
1936....	52.7	50.9	37.9[g]–38.4[h]	13.0[i]–12.5[h]

[a] Excludes subsistence farming and work relief. If individuals in these activities were counted as employed, the estimates of unemployment in the last four years would be greatly reduced. (In September 1936 about 3.4 million people were on work relief.)

For wage earners in manufacturing, transportation, mining, and construction the full-time equivalent in the several years is based on a constant number of hours of work per year—the number which approximately obtained in 1929. If the computations for these industries were made on a progressively reduced working year, the estimates of full-time equivalent employment in the years following 1929 would be higher.

[b] As of middle of year.

[c] See Table 3, p. 604.

[d] Gross estimates less 1.8 million workers in agriculture as follows: self-sufficing farmers, 498,000; female farm operators, 263,000; female unpaid family workers on farms, 475,000; and male unpaid family workers under 18 and over 65 years of age, 585,000. It is assumed that these workers included in the 1930 Census of Occupations and carried in the annual gross estimates are not available for employment in the commercial sense. (See pp. 617–18.)

[e] See Table 12, p. 622. Since correction for part-time and short hours could be made only for a portion of the personnel, these figures fail to indicate the full extent of the decline in employment. The error is progressively reduced as we move up from the low point of the depression. On the other hand, actual recovery has been more rapid than here indicated, since the expansion in average hours which has taken place for salaried workers, entrepreneurs, and some wage earners is not here accounted for.

[f] Difference between preceding two columns.

[g] Preliminary estimate based on current estimates of employment (American Federation of Labor and President's Committee on Economic Security) for first six months of 1935 and 1936 and corrected for increase in average hours of work per week for wage earners in the industries for which such corrections have been made for other years. Employment in all industries in the first eight months of 1936 appears to have been about 4 per cent higher than in the same period of 1935, and on the basis of the Bureau of Labor Statistics figures it is estimated that the average hours per week worked by employed wage earners in the first eight months of 1936 was approximately 6 per cent higher than in 1935.

(See opposite page for continuation of footnotes.)

14. Estimated Number of Equivalent Full-Time Workers in
Manufacturing Industries, 1919–35[a]

(In thousands)

Year	Equivalent Full-Time Wage Earners[b]	Salaried Workers[c]	Entrepreneurs and Firm Members[d]	All Workers
1919	9,348	1,438	180	10,966
1920	9,104	1,451	176	10,731
1921	6,398	1,146	173	7,717
1922	7,814	1,262	160	9,236
1923	8,958	1,355	148	10,461
1924	8,024	1,256	140	9,420
1925	8,430	1,341	133	9,904
1926	8,598	1,365	133	10,096
1927	8,300	1,450	133	9,883
1928	8,305	1,450	133	9,888
1929	8,692	1,567	133	10,392
1930	7,067	1,560	117	8,744
1931	5,618	1,386	103	7,107
1932	4,390	1,179	67	5,636
1933	4,732	1,113	73	5,918
1934	5,115	1,201	85	6,401
1935	5,604	1,240	94	6,938

[a] Industries covered by the Census of Manufactures.

[b] Total annual payrolls divided by estimated average full-time earnings on a 2,400-hour per year basis. See Table 22, p. 632.

[c] Includes employees in central administrative offices. Data for the census years 1919 through 1929 are from the Census of Manufactures with minor adjustments to make the series comparable throughout the period; data for the intercensal years in this period have been interpolated by means of the Bureau of Labor Statistics index of employment in manufacturing. Beginning with 1930 the data are based on annual estimates of salaried employees shown in U. S. Department of Commerce, *National Income in the United States, 1929–35*, 1936.

[d] Data for the census years 1919 through 1929 are from the Census of Manufactures, and those for the intercensal years in this period have been estimated from census data by means of arithmetic straight-line interpolation. Beginning with 1930 the data are based on the annual estimates of the Department of Commerce.

15. Estimates of Wage Earners in Manufacturing Industries, on Three Bases, 1919–36[a]

Year	Equivalent Full-Time[b]		Average Number on Payrolls[c]		Wage Earners Attached[d]	
	In Thousands	As Percentage of 1929	In Thousands	As Percentage of 1929	In Thousands	As Percentage of 1929
1919.......	9,348	107.5	9,000	101.8	9,709	104.1
1920.......	9,104	104.7	9,081	102.7	9,670	103.7
1921.......	6,398	73.6	6,947	78.6	9,631	103.3
1922.......	7,814	89.9	7,649	86.5	9,592	102.8
1923.......	8,958	103.1	8,778	99.3	9,554	102.4
1924.......	8,024	92.3	8,137	92.0	9,516	102.0
1925.......	8,430	97.0	8,394	95.0	9,478	101.6
1926.......	8,598	98.9	8,545	96.7	9,440	101.2
1927.......	8,300	95.5	8,358	94.6	9,402	100.8
1928.......	8,305	95.5	8,358	94.6	9,364	100.4
1929.......	8,692	100.0	8,839	100.0	9,327	100.0
1930.......	7,067	81.3	7,716	87.3	9,289	99.6
1931.......	5,618	64.6	6,523	73.8	9,252	99.2
1932.......	4,390	50.5	5,401	61.1	9,215	98.8
1933.......	4,732	54.4	6,071	68.7	9,178	98.4
1934[e]......	5,115	58.8	6,934	78.4	9,141	98.0
1935[e]......	5,604	64.5	7,230	81.8	9,105	97.6
1936[e]......	6,320[f]	72.7[f]	7,630[f]	86.3[f]	9,068	97.2

[a] Industries covered by the Census of Manufactures.
[b] Total annual payrolls divided by estimated average full-time earnings on a 2,400-hour per year basis. See Table 22, p. 632.
[c] Data for census years are from the Census of Manufactures with minor adjustments to make the series comparable throughout the entire period; data for intercensal years have been interpolated by means of the Bureau of Labor Statistics index of employment in manufacturing.
[d] For 1919 and 1929 the number on the payrolls in the month of highest employment as reported in the Census of Manufactures, was assumed to represent the number of effectives "attached" to manufacturing. Estimates of effectives for other years were computed from logarithmic straight line based on 1919 and 1929. These estimates have been raised by 1.5 per cent to allow for the "non-effectives" reported in the Census of Unemployment for 1930 under Classes C through F, that is, persons not working on account of disability or temporary voluntary idleness. (The estimate of 1.5 per cent represents the ratio of the total for Classes C through F to all gainful workers except farmers and unpaid family workers on farms.)

The estimates are rather rough, and since they are based on the acceptance of the highest employment months in 1919 and 1929 as determinants they are arbitrary. They are subject to question because the highest employment in the two years just mentioned came in different months, December and September respectively. Some refinement in the data might be introduced by correcting the figures in accordance with the seasonal index for the two months in question: the ratio of the number of wage earners in the highest months to the average for the year was 1.06 in 1919 and 1.04 in 1929. If it were assumed that the allowance for slack as between the highest month and the average for the year should be 6 per cent in 1929 as it was in 1919, the estimate of the number attached in 1929 would be about 9,535,000 instead of 9,327,000. This would give a somewhat different slope, but the difference would not be material.

[e] Subject to revision; Census of Manufactures data for 1935 not yet available.
[f] This is a rough estimate based on data for first eight months of year.

16. The Unemployment Situation in 1936[a]

Item	Millions of Workers
Unemployment in 1929...........................	3.1[b]
Decrease in employment, 1929–36....................	5.1[c]
Increase in labor force, 1929–36.....................	4.3[d]
Gross unemployment in 1936......................	12.5[e]
Voluntary and disability unemployment...............	0.7[f]
"Normal" idleness occasioned by securing initial employment and changing jobs.................................	1.0[g]
Allowance for reduction in working hours of industrial wage earners..	1.3[h]
Total allowances and corrections for 1936.............	3.0[i]
Net unemployment requiring absorption on a full-time basis..	9.5[j]

[a] These figures, which are in terms of "full-time equivalents," differ from the unadjusted estimates of the American Federation of Labor and other agencies (see p. 1₅5). As in the unadjusted estimates, however, the increase in the number of subsistance farmers (some 500,000), the rise in the number of "unpaid family workers" on farms (between one and 2 millions), and the number on federal work relief (about 3.4 millions) are not counted among the employed and hence are included in the estimates of unemployment.

[b] See Table 13, p. 623.

[c] This is based on a preliminary estimate for 1936 which includes a 4 per cent increase over 1935 in the number employed and a 6 per cent increase in average working hours for industrial wage earners. (See note *g*, Table 13, p. 62₅.) The general reliability and meaning of this figure may be indicated by the following rough computation. The probable national income in 1936 is generally given as approximately 60 billion dollars, which is the same as about 70 billions in 1929 dollars, or about 14 per cent below the income of 1929. The full-time equivalent of 1929 employment in "regular" activities approximated 43.5 million workers. Fourteen per cent of this number constitutes 6 million persons.

[d] See Table 3, p. 604. Based on growth of population only; does not allow for possible change during the depression in the proportion of adults seeking employment.

[e] See Table 13, p. 623. The estimate there given is 13.0–12.5 millions.

[f] On the basis of the 1930 Census voluntary and disability unemployment are estimated as about 1.3 to 1.5 per cent of the gainful workers, or approximately 700,000. This is perhaps low. U. S. Public Health Service studies for industrial workers indicate that time lost through illness alone averages between 2 and 3 per cent.

[g] This is a rough estimate based on conditions in 1929.

[h] This is a rough estimate in accord with the assumption that the decreased hours for industrial workers brought about by the influence of the NRA will for the most part persist within the next few years. The figure implies a reduction of hours of about 14 per cent from the 1929 average.

This allowance is several times as great as the "normal" reduction indicated by the predepression trend and almost as great as that shown by the actual hours now obtaining for industrial workers on payrolls. (From the data compiled by the National Industrial Conference Board it appears that the 1936 average of actual hours of work for industrial workers is about 82 per cent of that in 1929.) Exactly what the hours of actual work will be in the near future cannot, of course, be forecast. The average has increased considerably since the bottom of the depression, and it is not unlikely that with further recovery it will expand even more. The allowance made for purposes of the present calculation imputes a weekly average for manufacturing of about 41 to 42 hours as compared with about 48 to 49 hours per week in 1929. (To attain these averages of actual hours of work the "standard" or nominal hours per week must be from two to three hours higher.) In recent months the actual average for manufacturing has been between 39 and 40 hours. The correction for hours is made only for the selected industries for which, in our original computation of full-time equivalents, the 1929 hours have been taken as a constant for each of the subsequent years. See note *j* below.

i This is the total of the foregoing three items and perhaps approximates the true situation more closely than the individual estimates composing it. At best, however, the analysis—particularly that concerning working hours —must rest largely on conjecture.

j This rough figure is subject to the qualifications indicated in the foregoing footnotes. It assumes that the shift of gainful workers to agriculture is only temporary, as is also the provision of employment through work relief. From some points of view the standard of full-time employment exacted by this estimate may perhaps be considered too high. It requires somewhat more complete employment (if no offset is made for the imputed reduction in working hours) than was experienced in 1929. The estimate would be reduced by something more than one million if the attainment of the 1929 employment situation were taken as the aim. In part this difference is due to under-employment in seasonal industries. The extent to which this is offset by our allowance for reduction in hours and changing jobs cannot be indicated.

IV. PRODUCTION AND PRODUCTIVITY

17. Indexes of Physical Volume of Output in Eight Industries, 1919–34[a]

(1929=100)

Year	Composite Index for Eight Industries[b]	Agriculture	Mining	Electric Light and Power and Gas	Manufacturing[c]	Construction	Steam Railroad Transportation	Street Railways	Telephone
1919	71.1	86.1	63.2	43.5	67.1	59.3	91.8	103.8	50.9
1920	75.0	90.1	70.9	47.2	71.1	53.9	100.8	108.2	54.0
1921	63.1	82.1	58.8	44.8	55.7	63.2	76.5	101.4	57.9
1922	74.6	91.0	62.0	50.7	69.8	81.2	81.8	106.7	64.1
1923	83.6	94.0	84.8	59.6	79.2	84.9	97.0	109.0	69.2
1924	81.4	96.0	81.0	62.7	75.2	86.8	91.4	106.6	73.0
1925	87.2	96.0	82.9	69.1	83.2	94.6	96.1	105.5	77.6
1926	91.5	101.0	89.8	78.1	87.2	95.7	101.6	106.0	82.9
1927	91.6	98.0	91.8	84.9	87.2	100.1	97.8	103.7	87.1
1928	96.9	103.0	91.8	91.3	93.9	107.8	97.5	101.0	92.6
1929	100.0	100.0	100.0	100.0	100.0	100.0	100.0	100.0	100.0
1930	88.2	100.0	88.6	98.2	84.5	83.3	85.7	89.2	98.3
1931	78.4	105.9	75.3	94.6	72.5	62.9	69.3	80.8	94.3
1932	62.6	98.9	62.0	84.7	55.7	32.0	52.6	68.8	84.5
1933	65.7	96.0	67.1	85.5	62.4	27.7	55.1	64.6	78.6
1934	68.7	91.0	72.7	91.2	67.1	30.9	59.7	68.1	81.1

[a] Simon Kuznets, "Income Originating in Nine Basic Industries," *National Bureau of Economic Research Bulletin 59*, p. 24.
[b] The composite index has been computed by weighting the indexes for the eight industries by the income produced in these industries in 1929, which is shown on pp. 22–23 of *Bulletin 59*.
[c] This is a later revision of the National Bureau index than that reproduced in column 2 of Table 18 following.

18. Trends of Production, Productivity, and Number of Producers in the United States, 1909–35

(1929 = 100)

Year	Physical Volume of Production		Productivity			Number of Producers	
	All Industries and Services[a]	Manufacturing Only[b]	All Industries and Services		Manufacturing Only (Per full-time worker)[e]	All Industries and Services[f]	Manufacturing Only[g]
			Per Capita[c]	Per Gainful Worker[d]			
1909.......	60.5	44.0	81.4	71.5	...	73.2	...
1910.......	61.4	46.2	81.0	74.1	...	75.1	...
1911.......	63.4	45.1	82.3	75.8	...	76.4	...
1912.......	66.0	51.3	84.4	78.1	...	77.5	...
1913.......	68.7	53.9	86.0	79.8	...	79.2	...
1914.......	66.8	51.8	82.2	76.6	...	80.8	...
1915.......	71.1	61.6	86.0	81.5	...	81.2	...
1916.......	76.3	74.1	91.1	86.4	...	82.6	...
1917.......	69.9	74.6	82.2	78.0	...	84.2	...
1918.......	67.4	74.6	78.4	73.7	...	86.4	...
1919.......	69.9	65.8	81.0	77.0	63.6	86.2	102.7
1920.......	64.4	69.9	73.6	71.7	68.8	85.9	102.4
1921.......	66.9	55.4	74.9	73.3	75.0	87.6	102.2
1922.......	77.5	69.4	85.6	83.7	78.5	89.2	101.9
1923.......	85.4	77.7	92.7	91.1	78.6	90.9	101.6
1924.......	87.3	73.6	93.0	91.8	83.0	92.7	101.3
1925.......	91.9	81.9	96.6	95.4	87.3	94.3	101.1
1926.......	94.3	87.0	97.6	96.8	89.7	95.8	100.8
1927.......	95.6	87.0	97.6	97.2	91.7	97.3	100.5
1928.......	97.3	93.8	98.4	98.1	98.6	98.7	100.3
1929.......	100.0	100.0	100.0	100.0	100.0	100.0	100.0
1930.......	89.4	85.5	88.4	88.8	100.5	101.3	99.7
1931.......	79.2	73.0	77.7	78.0	106.0	102.6	99.5
1932.......	66.8	56.0	65.1	65.4	102.8	103.9	99.2
1933.......	71.6	62.7	69.4	69.6	109.7	105.2	98.9
1934[h].......	74.6	66.8	71.8	71.9	108.9	106.5	98.7
1935[h].......	77.4	77.7	74.0	74.1	117.4	107.9	98.4
Annual percentage rate of growth	2.53[i,j]	3.99[i,k]	1.03[i,l]	1.58[i,m]	3.49[n]	1.48[o]	−0.25[n]

[a] Based on total income from current production deflated by a composite price index representing value of goods and services produced. (See *America's Capacity to Consume*, p. 149.)

[b] Compiled by National Bureau of Economic Research. Revised figures (as of February 1936) for 1914–34 furnished by Charles A. Bliss of the Bureau; these were linked to index for earlier years appearing in Frederick C. Mills, *Economic Tendencies*, p. 567. A subsequent revision of this index for 1919–34 was published in *National Bureau of Economic Research Bulletin 59*, and is used in Tables 17 and 20. (See also footnote *e* below.) No attempt has been made to incorporate the revision published in *Bulletin 59* in this column because of the uncertainty as to whether it would correspond with the figures back of 1919.

[c] Same as column 1 on per capita basis.

[d] Same as column 1 on basis of the total number of gainful workers (exclusive of unpaid family workers on farms) corrected for trend since 1909 in the standard hours of work per week.

[e] Index of physical volume of production divided by index of full-time equivalent workers. See Table 20, p. 631. A later revision of the National Bureau index of physical volume of production was used in this computation than is shown in column 2.

[f] Based on estimated number of gainful workers in all industries, exclusive of unpaid family workers on farms.

[g] Based on estimate of the number "attached," including wage earners, salaried workers, entrepreneurs, and firm members.

[h] Preliminary; subject to revision.

[i] Estimated on basis of 1909–15 and 1923–29. Other years have been omitted because of disturbances in production and prices caused by the war and the depression.

[j,k,l,m] A logarithmic straight line fitted to all the points 1909–29 has a slope of: *j* — 1.0246 instead of 1.0253 as shown here; *k* — 1.0369 instead of 1.0399; *l* — 1.0095 instead of 1.0103; *m* — 1.0151 instead of 1.0158.

[n] From logarithmic straight line fitted to data for 1919–34 inclusive. Because of its preliminary nature, the 1935 estimate was not included in the computation of the trend.

[o] This is an average for 1909–34 (estimated along logarithmic straight line) and is somewhat higher than the trend indicated by the most recent years. At present the rate of growth in the number of gainful workers is approximately 1.1 per cent per annum.

629

19. DEVIATIONS OF INDEXES OF PRODUCTION AND PRODUCTIVITY FROM TRENDS, 1929–35ᵃ

Index	1929	1930	1931	1932	1933	1934	1935	1936
PHYSICAL VOLUME OF PRODUCTION, ALL INDUSTRIES AND SERVICES:								
As computed	100.0	89.4	79.2	66.8	71.6	74.6	77.4	119.1
Fitted trend	100.0	102.5	105.1	107.8	110.5	113.3	116.2	...
Percentage deviation from trend	—	*-12.8*	*-24.7*	*-38.0*	*-35.2*	*-34.2*	*-33.4*	...
PHYSICAL VOLUME OF PRODUCTION, MANUFACTURING ONLY:								
As computed	100.0	85.5	73.0	56.0	62.7	66.8	78.4	128.6
Fitted trend	97.8	101.7	105.8	110.0	114.4	118.9	123.7	...
Percentage deviation from trend	*+2.2*	*-15.9*	*-31.0*	*-49.1*	*-45.2*	*-43.8*	*-36.6*	...
PRODUCTION, ALL INDUSTRIES AND SERVICES (PER CAPITA):								
As computed	100.0	88.4	77.7	65.1	69.4	71.8	74.0	107.4
Fitted trend	100.0	101.0	102.1	103.1	104.2	105.3	106.3	...
Percentage deviation from trend	—	*-12.5*	*-23.9*	*-36.9*	*-33.4*	*-31.8*	*-30.4*	...
PRODUCTION, ALL INDUSTRIES AND SERVICES (PER GAINFUL WORKER):								
As computed	100.0	88.8	78.0	65.4	69.6	71.9	74.1	111.8
Fitted trend	100.2	101.8	103.4	105.0	106.7	108.4	110.1	...
Percentage deviation from trend	*-0.2*	*-12.8*	*-24.6*	*-37.7*	*-34.8*	*-33.7*	*-32.7*	...
PRODUCTIVITY, MANUFACTURING ONLY (PER FULL-TIME WORKER):								
As computed	100.0	100.5	106.0	102.8	109.7	108.9	117.4	123.4
Fitted trend	97.0	100.4	103.9	107.5	111.3	115.2	119.2	...
Percentage deviation from trend	*+3.1*	*+0.1*	*+2.0*	*-4.4*	*-1.5*	*-5.5*	*-1.6*	...

ᵃ See Table 18, p. 629.

20. PRODUCTIVITY IN MANUFACTURING INDUSTRIES, 1919–35
(1929 = 100)

Year	Index of Physical Volume of Production[a]	Index of Equivalent Full-Time Workers		Index of Productivity			
		Wage Earners Only[b]	All Workers[c]	Wage Earners Only		All Workers	
				As Computed[d]	Fitted Trend[e]	As Computed[d]	Fitted Trend[e]
1919.......	67.1	107.5	105.5	62.4	67.4	63.6	71.0
1920.......	71.1	104.7	103.3	67.9	70.1	68.8	73.5
1921.......	55.7	73.6	74.3	75.7	72.9	75.0	76.1
1922.......	69.8	89.9	88.9	77.6	75.8	78.5	78.8
1923.......	79.2	103.1	100.7	76.8	78.9	78.6	81.5
1924.......	75.2	92.3	90.6	81.5	82.1	83.0	84.3
1925.......	83.2	97.0	95.3	85.8	85.4	87.3	87.2
1926.......	87.2	98.9	97.2	88.2	88.8	89.7	90.2
1927.......	87.2	95.5	95.1	91.3	92.4	91.7	93.3
1928.......	93.9	95.5	95.2	98.3	96.1	98.6	96.6
1929.......	100.0	100.0	100.0	100.0	100.0	100.0	100.0
1930.......	84.5	81.3	84.1	103.9	104.0	100.5	103.5
1931.......	72.5	64.6	68.4	112.2	108.2	106.0	107.1
1932.......	55.7	50.5	54.2	110.3	112.6	102.8	110.8
1933.......	62.4	54.4	56.9	114.7	117.1	109.7	114.7
1934.......	67.1	58.8	61.6	114.1	121.8	108.9	118.7
1935[f].......	78.4	64.5	66.8	121.5	126.8	117.4	122.8

[a] Simon Kuznets, "Income Originating in Nine Basic Industries," *National Bureau of Economic Research Bulletin 59*, p. 24.
[b] Index of man-hours obtained by dividing total annual wages by average hourly earnings in manufacturing.
[c] Includes salaried workers, entrepreneurs, and firm members, as well as wage earners. See Table 14, p. 624.
[d] Index of physical volume of production divided by indexes of full-time equivalent workers.
[e] Least-squares line (fitted to logarithms of data for 1919–34 inclusive) moved up so that 1929 would equal 100.
[f] Preliminary; subject to revision.

21. MAN-HOUR PRODUCTIVITY IN MANUFACTURING INDUSTRIES, 1919–35[a]

Year	Index of Productivity		
	As Computed	Fitted Trend	*Percentage Deviation from Trend*
1919.................	62.4	66.7	*−6.5*
1920.................	67.9	69.4	*−2.2*
1921.................	75.7	72.2	*+4.8*
1922.................	77.6	75.1	*+3.3*
1923.................	76.8	78.2	*−1.8*
1924.................	81.5	81.3	*+0.2*
1925.................	85.8	84.6	*+1.5*
1926.................	88.2	88.0	*+0.2*
1927.................	91.3	91.6	*−0.4*
1928.................	98.3	95.0	*+3.5*
1929.................	100.0	99.1	*+0.9*
1930.................	103.9	103.1	*+0.7*
1931.................	112.2	107.3	*+4.5*
1932.................	110.3	111.6	*−1.2*
1933.................	114.7	116.1	*−1.2*
1934.................	114.1	120.8	*−5.5*
1935.................	121.5	125.7	*−3.4*

[a] Wage earners only. See Table 20 above.

V. WAGES

22. Earnings of Wage Earners in Manufacturing Industries, 1919–36[a]

Year	Annual Payrolls (In millions of dollars)[b]	Average Hourly Earnings (In cents)[c]	Average Yearly Earnings					
			Per Equivalent Full-Time Wage Earner		Per Wage Earner on Payroll		Per Wage Earner Attached	
			In Dollars[d]	As Percentage of 1929	In Dollars[e]	As Percentage of 1929	In Dollars[f]	As Percentage of 1929
1919......	10,414	46.4	1,114	83.3	1,157	88.0	1,073	86.1
1920......	12,518	57.3	1,375	102.8	1,378	104.8	1,294	103.9
1921......	8,202	53.4	1,282	95.9	1,181	89.8	852	68.3
1922......	8,752	46.6	1,120	83.8	1,144	87.0	912	73.2
1923......	11,009	51.2	1,229	91.9	1,254	95.4	1,152	92.5
1924......	10,238	53.2	1,276	95.4	1,258	95.7	1,076	86.3
1925......	10,740	53.1	1,274	95.3	1,279	97.3	1,133	90.9
1926......	11,083	53.7	1,289	96.4	1,297	98.6	1,174	94.2
1927......	10,856	54.5	1,308	97.8	1,299	98.8	1,155	92.6
1928......	10,921	54.8	1,315	98.4	1,307	99.4	1,166	93.6
1929......	11,621	55.7	1,337	100.0	1,315	100.0	1,246	100.0
1930......	9,448	55.7	1,337	100.0	1,224	93.1	1,017	81.6
1931......	7,186	53.3	1,279	95.7	1,102	83.8	777	62.4
1932......	4,908	46.6	1,118	83.6	909	69.1	533	42.8
1933.....	5,271	46.4	1,114	83.3	868	66.0	574	46.1
1934[g]....	6,726	54.8	1,315	98.4	970	73.8	736	59.1
1935[g]....	7,638	56.8[h]	1,363	101.9[h]	1,056	80.3	839	67.3
1936[g]....	8,680[h]	57.2[h]	1,373[h]	102.6[h]	1,138[h]	86.8[h]	957[h]	76.8[h]

[a] Industries covered by the Census of Manufactures.

[b] Data for census years are from the Census of Manufactures with minor adjustments to make the series comparable throughout the entire period; data for intercensal years have been interpolated by means of the Bureau of Labor Statistics index of payrolls in manufacturing.

[c] Beginning in 1932 the annual averages are weighted averages (number on payrolls used as weights) of the monthly figures published by the Bureau of Labor Statistics; prior to 1932 the basic data are the National Industrial Conference Board averages which have been adjusted to correspond with those of the Bureau of Labor Statistics.

[d] On basis of 2,400 hours per year.

[e] Annual payrolls divided by the average of the number of wage earners at the middle of each month as reported in the Census of Manufactures.

[f] Annual payrolls divided by the estimated number of workers attached to manufacturing industries. See Table 15, p. 625.

[g] Subject to revision; Census of Manufactures data for 1935 are not yet available.

[h] This is a rough estimate based on data for the first eight months of year.

23. Average "Real" Earnings of Wage Earners in Manufacturing Industries, 1919–36[a]

Year	Index of Cost of Living[b] (1929 =100)	Average Yearly Earnings (In terms of 1929 purchasing power)					
		Per Equivalent Full-Time Worker		Per Wage Earner on Payroll		Per Wage Earner Attached	
		In Dollars[c]	As Percentage of 1929	In Dollars[c]	As Percentage of 1929	In Dollars[c]	As Percentage of 1929
1919.........	106.6	1,045	78.2	1,085	82.5	1,006	80.8
1920.........	121.9	1,128	84.4	1,130	85.9	1,062	85.2
1921.........	106.4	1,205	90.1	1,110	84.4	801	64.2
1922.........	98.8	1,133	84.7	1,158	88.1	923	74.1
1923.........	100.0	1,229	91.9	1,254	95.4	1,152	92.5
1924.........	100.3	1,272	95.1	1,254	95.4	1,073	86.1
1925.........	102.2	1,247	93.3	1,251	95.1	1,109	88.9
1926.........	102.9	1,253	93.7	1,260	95.8	1,141	91.5
1927.........	101.4	1,290	96.5	1,281	97.4	1,139	91.4
1928.........	100.0	1,315	98.4	1,307	99.4	1,166	93.6
1929.........	100.0	1,337	100.0	1,315	100.0	1,246	100.0
1930.........	97.4	1,372	102.6	1,256	95.5	1,044	83.8
1931.........	88.7	1,442	107.8	1,242	94.4	876	70.2
1932.........	80.5	1,389	103.9	1,129	85.9	662	53.1
1933.........	76.8	1,451	108.5	1,130	85.9	747	60.0
1934[d].......	80.0	1,644	123.0	1,212	92.2	920	73.8
1935	80.8	1,687	126.2	1,307	99.4	1,038	83.3
1936	81.8[e]	1,678[e]	125.5[e]	1,391[e]	105.8[e]	1,170[e]	93.9[e]

[a] Industries covered by the Census of Manufactures.
[b] Based on index of the Bureau of Labor Statistics. See Harold G. Moulton, *Income and Economic Progress*, pp. 183–85.
[c] Average earnings shown in Table 22 divided by index of cost of living.
[d] Subject to revision; Census of Manufactures data for 1935 not yet available.
[e] This is a rough estimate based on data for first eight months of year.

24. Wages and Salaries Compared with National Income, 1929–35
(Dollar items are in millions)

Year	Income Paid Out[a]	Income Produced[a]	Difference between Income Produced and Paid Out	Wages and Salaries		
				Amount[a]	As Percentage of Income Paid Out	As Percentage of Income Produced
1929.....	$78,362	$81,034	$2,402	$50,550	64.3	62.4
1930.....	72,932	67,917	−5,015	46,208	63.4	68.0
1931.....	61,704	53,584	−8,120	38,675	62.7	72.2
1932.....	48,362	39,545	−8,817	29,821	61.7	75.4
1933.....	44,321	41,123	−3,198	27,828	62.8	67.7
1934.....	48,785	47,008	−1,776	31,240	64.1	66.4
1935.....	52,274	51,646	− 628	33,739	64.5	65.3

[a] Robert R. Nathan, "Expansion in the National Income Continued in 1935," *Survey of Current Business*, July 1936. Work-relief payments are excluded.

25. Wages and Profits in Manufacturing Industries, 1922–33

Year	Total Wages, All Manufacturing Industries[a]		Estimated Profits before Taxes, All Manufacturing Corporations[b]	
	In Millions of Dollars	As Percentage of 1929	In Millions of Dollars	As Percentage of 1929
1922........	8,752	75.3	2,832	58.3
1923........	11,009	94.7	3,784	77.8
1924........	10,238	88.1	2,978	61.3
1925........	10,740	92.4	3,973	81.7
1926........	11,083	95.4	4,041	83.1
1927........	10,856	93.4	3,405	70.0
1928........	10,921	94.0	4,280	88.0
1929........	11,621	100.0	4,861	100.0
1930........	9,448	81.3	1,530	31.5
1931........	7,186	61.8	−501	−10.3
1932........	4,908	42.2	−1,388	−28.5
1933........	5,271	45.3	384	7.9

[a] See Table 22, p. 632.
[b] "Compiled net profits," as reported in *Statistics of Income*, corrected for inter-corporate dividends.

piled by the Bureau of Agricultural Economics, U. S. Department of Agriculture. The figures here given are different from the composites published by the Department of Agriculture in that the prices of food, feed, and seed have been excluded. In combining the remaining indexes, weights roughly representing farm consumption have been used as follows: clothing, 5; operating expenses, 2; furniture and furnishings, 1; building materials for house, 1: farm machinery, 4; fertilizer, 1; building materials for other than house, 2; equipment and supplies, 2. To use weights purporting to represent general rather than farm consumption would be misleading. The composite is only suggestive of the movement of retail prices in general.
[e] Data not available.

26. Quarterly Indexes of Average Hourly Earnings in Manufacturing and of Wholesale and Retail Prices of Finished Manufactured Products, 1920–36

(1929 = 100)

Year and Month[a]	Average Hourly Earnings[b]	Wholesale Prices of Finished Products[c]	Retail Prices of Finished Products[d]	Year and Month[a]	Average Hourly Earnings[b]	Wholesale Prices of Finished Products[c]	Retail Prices of Finished Products[d]
1920—March.....	e	161.1	e	1929—March....	99.6	100.3	100.5
June......	e	165.8	e	June......	100.1	100.5	100.2
Sept.......	102.9	161.0	e	Sept......	100.5	100.5	100.0
Dec......	103.0	133.8	e	Dec......	100.3	98.1	100.1
Annual average ..	103.0	158.5	133.4	Annual average ..	100.0	100.0	100.0
1921—March.....	96.2	116.5	e	1930—March....	100.3	96.2	99.0
June......	90.8	106.5	e	June......	100.0	93.5	97.3
Sept.......	85.9	103.6	e	Sept......	100.1	91.4	95.5
Dec......	83.2	100.7	e	Dec......	98.2	87.6	94.0
Annual average ..	89.1	109.3	104.2	Annual average ..	100.0	93.1	96.5
1922—March.....	e	99.0	e	1931—March....	97.8	84.2	90.9
June......	e	103.1	e	June......	96.2	80.4	87.7
Sept.......	82.7	103.6	e	Sept......	95.4	80.3	85.4
Dec......	85.4	105.4	e	Dec......	91.3	77.5	83.4
Annual average ..	84.0	102.1	98.7	Annual average .	95.9	81.5	86.9
1923—March.....	86.2	108.3	99.9	1932—March....	86.9	75.6	80.0
June......	92.2	105.5	101.1	June......	84.4	74.0	77.4
Sept.......	93.8	104.0	99.9	Sept......	79.3	74.5	75.4
Dec......	95.2	101.8	99.5	Dec......	77.7	72.4	74.3
Annual average ..	91.8	105.0	100.0	Annual average ..	83.6	74.4	76.8
1924—March.....	95.2	102.9	101.1	1933—March....	78.1	69.5	71.3
June......	95.4	100.0	100.6	June......	75.0	73.0	71.4
Sept.......	95.4	101.0	100.3	Sept......	92.2	79.1	79.6
Dec......	95.5	104.7	100.3	Dec......	94.4	79.1	81.2
Annual average ..	95.4	101.9	100.6	Annual average ..	83.3	74.6	75.9
1925—March.....	95.0	106.7	102.2	1934—March....	95.3	81.7	83.1
June......	95.6	106.3	102.1	June....	98.5	82.7	83.4
Sept.......	94.9	106.1	101.7	Sept......	100.3	84.7	83.0
Dec......	95.2	107.4	102.1	Dec......	100.5	84.1	83.0
Annual average ..	95.2	106.5	102.0	Annual average ..	98.3	82.8	83.0
1926—March.....	95.2	106.2	102.1	1935—March....	102.0	86.4	82.3
June......	96.4	106.7	102.4	June......	103.2	86.9	82.3
Sept.......	96.7	105.6	101.7	Sept......	101.0	87.9	82.4
Dec......	97.2	104.0	101.3	Dec......	102.6	87.9	82.4
Annual average ..	96.4	105.8	102.0	Annual average ..	101.9	87.0	82.5
1927—March.....	97.2	100.6	101.0	1936—March....	102.6	86.0	81.9
June......	97.9	99.7	100.6	June......	103.2	85.4	81.8
Sept.......	98.1	100.2	100.9	Sept......	102.2	87.1	82.2
Dec......	98.0	100.8	100.6	Dec......	...	...	...
Annual average ..	97.8	100.5	100.7	Annual average ..	...	...	...
1928—March.....	97.4	99.9	101.2				
June......	98.1	101.2	100.5				
Sept.......	98.4	104.0	101.1				
Dec......	98.9	100.7	101.1				
Annual average ..	98.2	101.5	101.0				

[a] The series for average hourly earnings is not strictly comparable with the other two series prior to 1929 since the indexes are based on quarterly averages rather than on an average for the month indicated. However, beginning in 1929 this series also represents earnings in the months specified.
[b] Indexes for 1920–31, inclusive, are based on average hourly earnings of wage earners in manufacturing industries as computed by the National Industrial Conference Board; beginning in 1932 they are based on averages computed by the Bureau of Labor Statistics.
[c] Index of the Bureau of Labor Statistics.
[d] Prices of manufactured goods, exclusive of food, bought by farmers, based on indexes com-

(See opposite page for continuation of footnotes)

27. Annual Indexes of Wages, Prices, and Productivity in Manufacturing Industries, 1919–36
(1929 = 100)

Year	Average Hourly Earnings[a] In Current Money	Average Hourly Earnings[a] In Terms of Physical Product[d]	Wholesale Prices[b] All Manufacturing[e]	Wholesale Prices[b] Finished Products	Productivity[c]
1919........	83.3	60.3	140.6	138.2	62.4
1920........	102.8	64.9	176.1	158.5	67.9
1921........	95.9	87.7	114.5	109.3	75.7
1922........	83.8	82.0	111.8	102.1	77.6
1923........	91.9	87.5	113.9	105.0	76.8
1924........	95.4	93.6	108.8	101.9	81.5
1925........	95.3	89.4	112.0	106.5	85.8
1926........	96.4	91.1	109.2	105.8	88.2
1927........	97.8	97.3	102.6	100.5	91.3
1928........	98.4	96.9	101.4	101.5	98.3
1929........	100.0	100.0	100.0	100.0	100.0
1930........	100.0	107.4	93.0	93.1	103.9
1931........	95.7	117.4	81.9	81.5	112.2
1932........	83.6	112.4	76.6	74.4	110.3
1933........	83.3	111.7	77.7	74.6	114.7
1934........	98.4	118.8	85.6	82.8	114.1
1935........	101.9	117.2	85.0	87.0	121.5
1936........	102.6[f]	118.8[f]	86.3[f]	86.4[f]	

[a] See Table 22, p. 632.
[b] Indexes of the Bureau of Labor Statistics.
[c] Based on wage earners only. See Table 20, p. 631.
[d] Adjusted by means of wholesale price index of finished products. This index comes nearest to representing the product added by manufacturing. The result is, of course, rough since the price index reflects also cost of raw materials, transportation, etc.
[e] All commodities other than farm products and foods.
[f] This is a rough estimate based on data for the first eight months of the year.

28. Index of Average Hourly Earnings in Manufacturing Industries in Terms of Physical Product, 1919–35[a]

Year	As Computed	Fitted Trend	Percentage Deviation from Trend
1919..............	60.3	71.3	−15.4
1920..............	64.9	73.8	−12.1
1921..............	87.7	76.5	+14.6
1922..............	82.0	79.3	+ 3.4
1923..............	87.5	82.1	+ 6.6
1924..............	93.6	85.1	+10.0
1925..............	89.4	88.2	+ 1.4
1926..............	91.1	91.3	− 0.2
1927..............	97.3	94.6	+ 2.8
1928..............	96.9	98.0	− 1.1
1929..............	100.0	101.6	− 1.6
1930..............	107.4	105.2	+ 2.1
1931..............	117.4	109.0	+ 7.7
1932..............	112.4	113.0	− 0.5
1933..............	111.7	117.0	− 4.5
1934..............	118.8	121.2	− 2.0
1935..............	117.2	125.6	− 6.7

[a] See Table 27 above. Average hourly earnings in manufacturing industries are adjusted by index of wholesale prices of finished products. See note d, Table 27.

29. Indexes of Hourly Wages in Selected Industries, 1930–36[a]
(1929=100)

Industry	1930	1931	1932	1933	1934	1935	1936[b]
Manufacturing[c]	100.0	95.7	83.6	83.3	98.4	101.9	102.8
Mining[d]	97.0	92.9	85.4	84.5	103.7	108.9	111.5
Steam railways[e]	101.7	103.8	95.2	95.2	96.4	104.3	106.6
Production and distribution of electricity[f]	103.2	103.8	102.7	103.5	114.4	117.8	117.2
Building construction[g]	103.9	104.7	93.3	88.8	89.1	91.6	90.4
Road building: common labor[h]	100.0	92.3	82.0	89.7	105.1	105.1	101.3
Average exclusive of farm wages[i]	99.8	96.9	83.7	83.1	95.3	99.5	99.9
Farm wages[j]	90.8	71.4	54.1	49.9	55.4	60.0	64.3
Average, including farm wages[k]	98.4	92.0	77.9	76.6	88.0	92.8	93.8

a The series are for the most part average earnings. Exceptions are the figures for building construction (for 1929–33), road building, and agriculture, for which only rates are available. The movement of actual earnings is, of course, somewhat different from the movement of rates, but it is impossible to evaluate the difference. The discrepancy is perhaps less serious in road building and farm wages than in building construction.

b Rough estimates based on data for first part of year.   c See Table 22, p. 632.

d Based on Bureau of Labor Statistics (see *Trend of Employment*) average hourly earnings for anthracite and bituminous coal mining, metalliferous mining, quarrying and non-metallic mining, and crude petroleum producing.

e Based on average hourly earnings compiled by the National Industrial Conference Board (see *Wages, Hours, and Employment in the United States, 1914–36*) from data collected by the Interstate Commerce Commission from Class I railroads.

f See source cited in note e above. Based on average hourly earnings.

g Based on National Industrial Conference Board hourly rates for 1929–34 and on Bureau of Labor Statistics hourly earnings from 1934 to date.

h Based on rates compiled by the Bureau of Public Roads, U. S. Department of Agriculture (see *Survey of Current Business*).

i Weighted average of above, including indexes of hourly earnings for laundries and cleaning and dyeing. Weights based on estimated number of man-hours worked each year.

j Based on rates compiled by the Bureau of Agricultural Economics, (see *Survey of Current Business*).

k Weighted average. Estimated full-time equivalent number of wage earners employed used as weights.

APPENDIX D

DATA RELATING TO DURABLE GOODS

The data in this appendix supplement Chapter VIII.

I. VALUE OF DURABLE GOODS PRODUCTION

On page 181 of the text there is presented a chart showing the relative importance of the various types of durable production goods. The basic figures are given herewith.

1. RELATIVE IMPORTANCE OF DURABLE GOODS PRODUCTION, 1919–33[a]
(In millions of 1929 dollars)

Year	All Com- modities	Durable	Non- Durable	Con- sumers' Durable	Pro- ducers' Durable	Public and Semi- Public
1919	46,287	19,736	26,551	7,909	10,305	1,522
1920	43,911	18,713	25,198	6,499	10,656	1,558
1921	45,040	17,157	27,883	7,156	8,036	1,965
1922	51,412	22,059	29,353	9,666	9,801	2,592
1923	56,524	25,654	30,870	11,928	11,553	2,173
1924	58,267	26,464	31,803	12,766	11,136	2,562
1925	62,156	29,491	32,665	14,363	12,060	3,068
1926	64,194	30,857	33,337	14,789	12,931	3,137
1927	65,032	30,174	34,858	13,991	12,657	3,526
1928	65,476	30,775	34,701	13,933	13,106	3,736
1929	68,705	31,906	36,799	13,430	14,771	3,705
1930	62,144	26,859	35,285	10,227	12,625	4,007
1931	54,172	21,102	33,070	8,271	9,045	3,786
1932	46,043	14,545	31,498	5,719	5,817	3,009
1933	44,133	12,940	31,193	5,516	5,359	2,065

[a] All the data underlying these series, except in so far as they relate to construction expenditures, have been taken from the *National Bureau of Economic Research Bulletin 52*. Our own estimates for construction have been used throughout. Their derivation involved the compilation of estimates for about a dozen separate types of construction and their conversion into 1929 dollars by as many different deflators. These operations were too numerous and varied to justify a detailed description here.

II. RESIDENTIAL CONSTRUCTION

The figures underlying the chart on page 185 are given in Table 2 below.

2. TRENDS IN THE HOUSING INDUSTRY, 1919-36
(Non-farm only)

Year	Thousands of Family Units Standing on Dec. 31	Thousands of Family Units Occupied Dec. 31	Potential Occupancy	Percentage Vacant	Thousands of Units Erected During Year[a]
1919.......	18,110	17,480		3.5	
1920.......	18,290	17,990		1.6	213
1921.......	18,700	18,330		2.0	446
1922.......	19,340	19,020		1.7	705
1923.......	20,130	19,810		1.6	846
1924.......	20,950	20,390		2.7	872
1925.......	21,810	20,970		3.9	951
1926.......	22,570	21,620		4.2	845
1927.......	23,260	22,130		4.9	781
1928.......	23,900	22,590		5.5	736
1929.......	24,300	23,090		5.0	472
1930.......	24,510	23,180	23,510	5.4	260
1931.......	24,670	23,040	23,930	6.4	200
1932.......	24,710	22,740	24,350	8.0	80
1933.......	24,760	22,860	24,770	7.7	70
1934.......	24,780	23,350	25,190	5.8	60
1935.......	24,900	23,750	25,610	4.6	150
1936.......	25,150	24,400	26,030	3.0	300

[a] Data which became available after this table went to press indicate that the estimates for 1925, 1926, and 1936 should be reduced by 30,000-50,000, while those for 1920 and 1929 should be increased by a similar amount.

Number of family units standing. The first step in deriving this series was to estimate the volume of vacant units at the end of 1919, when it begins. After careful consideration, this was put at about 3.5 per cent of all non-farm dwellings then available. This made it possible to compute the total number of dwellings from the Census figures for occupied dwellings. Having thus obtained a base figure for 1919, subsequent figures were derived by adding each year the estimated number of units constructed and subtracting the estimated number demolished.

Number of dwelling units occupied. To obtain actual, as contrasted with potential occupancy, estimates for the number of non-farm families normally occupying separate quarters were adjusted to allow for deviations of the marriage rate from its trend line,[1] and for estimated depression "doubling up." There is, admittedly, no satisfactory measure for the latter. The various real property inventories and surveys made in recent years as white-collar relief projects fail to distinguish clearly between doubling up attributable to the depression and the very considerable amount of doubling that is normal in prosperity. The estimates reflected in the chart are little more than guesses which appear to the author to harmonize best with the various bits of indirect evidence available.

Number of family units constructed. For 257 cities covered since 1921 by the building permit data of the Bureau of Labor Statistics, the number of family units erected was taken as the number for which permits were issued, minus an allowance of 2 per cent for non-execution of permits. (Data for 1920 and 1936 are estimated.) For the non-farm area outside of the 257 cities, an estimate for the decade 1920-30 was first obtained by assuming that the number of new units erected bore the same relation to the increase in the number of families that prevailed in a group of smaller cities included in the 257 (82 cities with a population of 25,000-50,000). This estimated total for the decade as a whole was then distributed among the ten years in accordance with the distribution of the decade's construction shown by these 82 cities. For years since 1929, construction in the non-farm area outside the 257 cities has been estimated by other methods, too varied to detail here.

As to the volume of demolitions since 1919, only the most fragmentary evidence is available. Without undertaking to review it here, suffice it to say that the total for the decade 1920-30 was taken as 700,000 family units. This was distributed by years in accordance with the distribution of the decade total of commercial and public construction. Experience has shown that the great bulk of residential demolitions result from the

---

[1] The dissolution of families by death proceeds with little disturbance from business depressions, whereas the formation of new families by marriage is responsive in considerable measure to them. Hence the one-sided adjustment.

conversion of the site to commercial or public purposes; hence the use of these types of construction to gauge their trend. For years since 1929 demolitions have been estimated at 40,000-50,000 a year.

Percentage of vacancies. This was computed by comparing the figures for the number of family units standing with those for actual occupancy.

Potential occupancy. This is the occupancy which would theoretically exist (1) if the marriage rate were normal; (2) if there were no depression doubling up; and (3) if the number of farm families had remained at the 1920-30 level instead of being greatly increased by an exodus of urban population resulting from depression influences.

III. COMPUTATION OF POTENTIAL HOUSING REQUIREMENTS

On page 187 of the text residential construction requirements for the five-year period 1937-41 were estimated at the following number of units:

For accumulated deficiency, 1929-36 2,000,000
For increase in number of urban families, 1937-41 2,000,000
For replacements of demolished housing, 1937-41 500,000

These estimates were derived by the following method:

In the first place, in making these computations we assumed that the volume of vacancies at the beginning of 1930 might be regarded as normal. This does not seem over-liberal in view of the fact that the total number of units standing will be considerably higher in 1941, and that the percentage of vacant units will be correspondingly reduced. It must be noted also that, in view of the protracted duration of many of these vacancies during the depression and the effect of prolonged vacancies on maintenance, it is probable that many of these structures will become more or less permanently untenantable.

In computing accumulated deficiency in 1936 we estimated the demolitions at between 40,000 and 50,000 units a year (as compared with 70,000 in the pre-depression period). The construction of new units since 1929 amounted to about 1,100,000—giving a net increase of from 800,000 to 850,000.

In estimating the requirements resulting from the growth

of population during the period (1929-36), we assumed that the reduction in the marriage rate was but a temporary factor, that the doubling up in houses would be discontinued with a return of prosperity, and also that the shift of urban families to farms is not a permanent factor. In other words, we simply computed the increase in housing requirements as determined by the normal increase in non-farm population and families. As a practical matter the undoubling of families, the increase in the marriage rate, and the return of farm families to the cities would be spread over a period of years. It seemed simpler, however, to take account of these factors in the figures for 1936 rather than to include them in the estimates of requirements over the next five years.

The growth in the number of families from 1937 to 1941 has been computed on the basis of the forecasts of population by Thompson and Whelpton. The increase in the number of families would be expected to run from 400,000 to 450,000 annually; and we assume that practically all of these would reside in urban centers. This would give an increase in the number of urban families of at least 2 million between 1937 and 1941. We estimate the demolitions to run at a somewhat higher rate than in the pre-depression period, because of the increased average age of dwellings and the decreased rate of demolitions during the depression period.

IV. PASSENGER AUTOMOBILES

The data underlying the chart on page 189 of the text are given in Table 3 on the following page. The following statements indicate sources of data and methods employed.

Gasoline consumption. Estimates of gasoline consumption by passenger cars were prepared by H. A. Breakey of the Federal Bureau of Mines.

Cars in use. The figures for registrations of passenger automobiles compiled by the federal Bureau of Public Roads do not give the number of cars in use at any given time, since they cumulate all registrations occurring within a twelve-month period. For various reasons into which we need not enter here, no very satisfactory method of estimating the number of cars in use is possible without additional information not now available.

A rough approximation may be made for January 1 by subtracting from the total registrations for the succeeding year those of new cars sold and registered during that year. By averag-

3. Production, Consumption, and Supply of
Automobiles, 1925–1935

Year	Gasoline Consumption by Passenger Automobiles (In thousands of barrels)	Average Cars in Use during the Year (In thousands)	New Car Sales at Retail (In thousands)	Increase in Cars in Use Jan. 1– Jan. 1 (In thousands)	Apparent Scrappage during the Year (In thousands)
1925.......	155	15,106	3,198	1,479	1,719
1926.......	181	16,666	3,457	1,641	1,816
1927.......	206	17,800	2,792	625	2,167
1928.......	227	18,596	3,321	969	2,352
1929.......	257	19,721	4,073	1,281	2,791
1930.......	270	20,398	2,745	62	2,683
1931.......	277	20,123	1,986	−601	2,587
1932.......	257	19,500	1,137	−646	1,783
1933.......	259	19,439	1,541	523	1,018
1934.......	280	19,774	1,941	148	1,793
1935.......	295	...	2,808	...	...
1936.......	...	...	3,500[a]	...	...

[a] Estimated from data for eight months.

ing the estimates thus derived for the beginning and end of each year a figure may be derived for the average number of cars in use during the year. Estimates so derived are subject to considerable error, but are nevertheless a better indication of the number of cars in use than the gross registration figures as published. They are used here simply for want of anything better. The data have been adjusted to include passenger cars not subject to registration and to exclude buses.

New car sales at retail. New car registrations as compiled by the R. L. Polk Company, adjusted for estimated undertabulation.

Increase in cars in use. The estimate for cars in use on each January 1, derived as described above, was subtracted from the estimate for the succeeding January 1 to give the increase (or decrease) during the year.

Apparent scrapping. New car sales minus the increase during the year in cars in use. There is probably some overstatement of scrapping on the down-swing, and a corresponding understatement on the recovery, owing to the fact that a considerable but unknown number of cars were withdrawn from registration as conditions worsened and subsequently re-registered when they improved.

V. STEAM RAILROADS

The data underlying the chart on page 199 are given in Tables 4-6, which indicate the railroad plant and equipment situation during 1921-36.

4. ROAD AND EQUIPMENT BUILT, 1921-35[a]
(1929 = 100)

Year	Loco-motives[b]	Freight Cars	Passenger Cars	Miles of Road Constructed
1921	116	49	102	49
1922	135	81	54	47
1923	370	214	120	66
1924	187	138	172	95
1925	101	129	188	89
1926	167	108	174	131
1927	103	77	142	122
1928	60	49	108	141
1929	100	100	100	100
1930	105	91	101	69
1931	20	16	16	75
1932	11	4	3	48
1933	6	3	1	18
1934	10	31	21	5
1935	20	8	16	7

[a] Data compiled by the *Railway Age*, except for road built, for which the source is the Interstate Commerce Commission.

[b] Original figures include production for Canadian market before 1929. These have been adjusted by subtracting average of Canadian orders for the preceding year and the current year.

5. Amount of Equipment Owned and Maximum Percentage
Operated, 1921–36

	Amount of Equipment Owned, Dec. 31[a] (1929 = 100)			Maximum Percentage of Equipment Active[b]		
Year	Loco-motives	Freight Cars	Passenger Cars	Freight Cars	Freight Loco-motives	Passenger Loco-motives
1921.....	113	102	106	. . .	. . .	. . .
1922.....	112	101	106	. . .	. . .	. . .
1923.....	113	102	106	91	. . .	. . .
1924.....	113	104	107	87	81	85
1925.....	111	104	106	88	83	85
1926.....	109	103	106	90	85	85
1927.....	107	102	104	88	82	86
1928.....	103	101	102	90	84	83
1929.....	100	100	100	89	85	82
1930.....	98	100	100	78	80	83
1931.....	96	97	97	67	68	77
1932.....	93	94	94	62	62	71
1933.....	88	89	89	66	65	69
1934.....	84	85	84	68	64	70
1935.....	81	80	79	74	68	74
1936.....	79	77	75	81	74	79

[a] Data through 1935 compiled by the Interstate Commerce Commission. They cover all roads in the United States. The figure for 1936 is estimated on the basis of data for the first eight months of the year compiled by the Association of American Railroads.

[b] Active equipment is computed by subtracting from the total number of units reported "on line" those reported as unserviceable ("bad order" freight cars, and locomotives "awaiting classified repairs") plus those reported as "surplus" (in the case of locomotives those "stored, serviceable"). Since the various items have been reported with differing frequency, ranging from weekly to monthly, it is likely that the maximum utilization of equipment during each year was slightly higher than it happened to be on the reporting dates showing the highest ratios of use.

6. Maintenance of Road and Equipment, 1921–36

Year	Man-hours of Equipment Maintenance per 1,000 Car-miles Run[a]	Man-hours of Road Maintenance per 1,000 Car-miles Run	Percentage of Locomotives Awaiting Classified Repairs[b]	Percentage of Freight Cars in Bad Order[b]
1921	...	...	...	13.9
1922	49	36	...	13.3
1923	52	35	...	8.0
1924	46	33	9.4	8.2
1925	43	32	9.0	7.9
1926	40	32	8.5	6.7
1927	38	32	7.8	6.1
1928	35	30	7.7	6.4
1929	34	31	7.4	6.1
1930	32	28	8.4	6.4
1931	30	24	11.3	8.0
1932	29	22	16.1	11.2
1933	27	20	21.4	14.3
1934	28	21	22.5	15.2
1935	28	21	22.6	15.2
1936	...	...	21.0	14.6

[a] Both series are computed from data published by the Interstate Commerce Commission.

[b] Annual averages computed from data of the Association of American Railroads. Figures for 1936 are for the first eight months of the year. In the case of locomotives only units needing major or "classified" repairs are included.

VI. PUBLIC UTILITIES

The data underlying the chart on page 207 are given in Table 7 below.

7. Public Utility Construction and Maintenance
Expenditures, 1919–36
(In millions of dollars)

Year	Electric Power[a]	Telephones[b]	Transit[c]	Gas[d]
1919............	300	205	...	...
1920............	380	290	...	...
1921............	400	320	...	...
1922............	540	365	...	...
1923............	895	435	...	...
1924............	1,000	505	419	...
1925............	950	516	436	...
1926............	875	550	373	...
1927............	903	554	352	...
1928............	867	628	343	..
1929............	964	818	357	290
1930............	1,036	824	339	280
1931............	696	600	311	210
1932............	375	422	207	130
1933............	219	345	179	90
1934............	237	365	226	105
1935............	285	380	271	110
1936............	425[e]	447[e]	280[e]	...

[a] For construction expenditures during 1921–35 we have used the estimates of the Edison Electrical Institute, as given in *Statistical Bulletin No. 3*, June 1936, p. 8. For 1919 and 1920 the Institute supplied estimates by letter. We have estimated 1936 on the basis of the gain over 1935 shown by the *Electrical World* forecast, in the issue of Jan. 4, 1936. Maintenance expenditures for the years 1923–32 are taken from data compiled by the Federal Employment Stabilization Board and published in Gayer's *Public Works in Prosperity and Depression*, p. 60. For other years we have made approximations.

[b] Estimates for the industry were supplied by the American Telephone and Telegraph Company.

[c] Data taken from various issues of the *Transit Journal*. For the years 1924 to 1926 inclusive we have estimated expenditures for maintenance labor.

[d] Estimates are based on data in *Bulletin 21* of the American Gas Association. We have supplied estimates for maintenance expenditures in the natural gas industry.

[e] Preliminary estimate.

VII. INDUSTRIAL ENTERPRISES

The data underlying the chart on page 219 are given in Table 8 below.

8. CAPITAL AND MAINTENANCE EXPENDITURES IN INDUSTRIAL LINES, 1919–36
(In millions of dollars)

Year	Total	Construction[a]	Machinery and Equipment[b]
1919	7,597	1,184	6,413
1920	8,233	1,311	6,922
1921	4,867	629	4,238
1922	5,254	1,012	4,242
1923	6,404	977	5,427
1924	6,210	968	5,242
1925	6,807	1,338	5,469
1926	7,355	1,545	5,810
1927	7,147	1,443	5,704
1928	7,622	1,542	6,080
1929	8,480	1,660	6,820
1930	6,439	983	5,456
1931	4,184	485	3,699
1932	2,578	192	2,386
1933	2,563	263	2,300
1934	...	312	...
1935	...	322	...
1936	...	505[c]	...

[a] Estimates through 1935 by Mr. Lowell Chawner of the Construction Division of the Bureau of Foreign and Domestic Commerce. The estimate for 1936 is based on data for the first eight months of the year.

[b] From the estimates for the output of producers' machinery and equipment of all kinds, prepared by the National Bureau of Economic Research and published in *Bulletin 52*, we have subtracted estimates for agricultural machinery, railroad rolling stock, and equipment for public utilities. The result approximates machinery and equipment used by industrial enterprises. All of the figures used are preliminary, and will be altered by revisions now under way.

[c] Estimated from first eight months.

VIII. PUBLIC CONSTRUCTION AND MAINTENANCE

The data underlying the chart on page 227 are given in Table 9 below.

9. EXPENDITURES FOR PUBLIC CONSTRUCTION AND MAINTENANCE, 1923-34
(In millions of dollars)

Year	Total	Roads and Streets[a]	All Other[b]
1923	2,240	1,110	1,130
1924	2,625	1,320	1,305
1925	2,915	1,435	1,480
1926	2,875	1,455	1,420
1927	3,225	1,640	1,585
1928	3,415	1,810	1,605
1929	3,435	1,820	1,615
1930	3,570	2,100	1,470
1931	3,020	1,765	1,255
1932	2,020	1,325	695
1933	1,750	1,070	680
1934	2,165	1,215	950

[a] For rural roads, the estimates for 1923-32 inclusive are from the Bureau of Public Roads. For 1933 and 1934, the Bureau's estimates for state highways were supplemented by our own estimates for local rural roads. Estimates for city roads and streets were prepared by us on the basis of data in *Financial Statistics of Cities.*

[b] For the period 1923-32 the estimates are by Arthur Gayer (*Public Works in Prosperity and Depression*, p. 248). For 1933 and 1934 these estimates were extrapolated on the basis of data compiled by the F. W. Dodge Corporation.

10. Durable Goods Requirements, 1937–41, Compared
with Production in 1936 [a]
(In billions of 1936 dollars)

Class of Goods	Deficiency at End of 1936	Regular Requirements, 1937–41	Total Requirements, 1937–41	Production in 1936
Residences (non-farm)....	9.0[b]	11.3[b]	20.3	1.3
Passenger automobiles....	2.2[c]	12.8[c]	15.0	2.6
Other consumers' durable goods................	1.0[d]	29.0	30.0	4.5
Steam railroads..........	2.3[e]	10.0	12.3	1.5
Public utilities..........	[f]	11.0[g]	11.0	1.3
Industrial enterprises.....	11.0[h]	40.0	51.0	6.0
Agriculture..............	1.5	5.0	6.5	0.8
Public and semi-public construction..............	...	17.5	17.5	3.0
Total..............	27.0	136.6	163.6	21.0

[a] Estimates compiled from statements in the text of Chap. VIII and this appendix. No claim of precision is made for any of the figures. The aggregates, however, are believed to be correct enough to give a fair picture of the production situation in durable goods. "Requirements" are those necessary to restore roughly the pre-depression standards of living.

[b] Computed at $4,500 per unit of housing.

[c] Computed at $750 per unit.

[d] Based on deficiency in residences. Equipment for one million new households at $1,000 each would give this amount.

[e] Computed at $2,200 per freight car, $30,000 per passenger car, and $100,000 per locomotive.

[f] Included in following column.

[g] Including 1936 deficiency.

[h] Includes allowance of one billion dollars for commercial and industrial buildings.

APPENDIX E
DATA RELATING TO PRICES

1. Index Numbers of Wholesale Prices of Raw
of the Cost of Living and of

(1929

Year and Month	Raw Mate- rials[a]	Semi- Finished Goods[a]	Finished Goods[a]	Cost of Living[b]	Prices Received by Farmers[c]	Prices Paid by Farmers for Home Mainte- nance[d]	Prices Paid by Farmers for Goods Used in Produc- tion[d]
1929:							
Jan......	101.3	100.7	100.2	99.9	100.7		
Feb......	100.6	100.7	99.8	99.9	99.3		
Mar.....	101.5	102.3	100.3	99.3	100.0	100.6	101.4
Apr......	99.5	101.0	100.5	99.1	98.6		
May....	97.7	99.0	100.1	98.9	97.3		
June....	99.1	98.4	100.5	99.2	97.3	100.0	100.0
July.....	101.6	99.5	101.2	100.0	100.7		
Aug.....	101.7	99.6	100.7	100.7	104.1		
Sept.....	101.4	100.6	100.5	100.8	102.7	100.6	100.0
Oct......	99.6	100.9	99.7	101.0	102.1		
Nov.....	97.2	99.1	98.3	100.9	99.3		
Dec.....	97.4	98.0	98.1	100.1	100.7	99.4	99.3
1930:							
Jan......	96.4	96.1	97.5	99.3	99.3		
Feb......	93.3	95.2	96.8	98.5	95.9		
Mar.....	91.6	93.8	96.2	97.8	92.5	98.1	96.6
Apr......	92.1	91.7	96.0	97.9	93.2		
May....	90.1	88.5	95.3	97.2	91.8		
June....	87.1	87.0	93.5	96.5	89.7	96.2	96.6
July.....	83.2	85.0	91.6	95.2	82.2		
Aug.....	83.9	83.8	91.2	94.7	80.8		
Sept.....	84.2	82.7	91.4	95.4	82.2	92.4	96.6
Oct......	81.9	81.8	90.4	94.8	77.4		
Nov.....	78.8	81.0	89.0	93.9	75.3		
Dec.....	76.1	80.0	87.6	92.6	71.2	88.6	91.8
1931:							
Jan......	74.6	78.5	86.2	91.1	69.2		
Feb......	72.4	77.7	85.0	89.6	65.1		
Mar.....	71.3	77.6	84.2	89.1	66.4	84.8	87.8
Apr......	70.1	76.1	82.9	88.2	66.4		
May....	68.2	74.3	81.4	86.9	63.0		
June....	66.4	73.8	80.4	85.9	58.9	81.6	85.0
July.....	65.9	73.8	80.5	85.9	58.9		
Aug.....	65.7	72.7	80.8	85.9	56.2		
Sept.....	64.3	71.0	80.3	85.6	54.8	78.5	79.6
Oct......	63.1	69.4	79.5	84.9	52.7		
Nov.....	63.6	69.1	79.2	83.9	54.1		
Dec.....	61.7	67.8	77.6	83.1	51.4	74.7	78.9
1932:							
Jan......	59.8	67.2	76.3	81.4	48.6		
Feb......	58.4	65.9	75.6	80.1	46.6		
Mar.....	57.5	64.7	75.7	79.6	47.3	71.5	76.2
Apr......	56.9	63.5	75.2	78.8	45.9		
May....	55.3	61.9	74.4	77.9	43.2		
June....	54.6	61.3	74.1	77.2	39.7	68.4	74.1
July.....	56.1	59.1	74.6	77.0	43.2		
Aug.....	57.1	61.7	74.8	76.8	44.5		
Sept.....	57.6	64.6	74.5	76.6	45.2	67.1	71.4
Oct......	56.0	64.6	73.7	76.1	43.8		
Nov.....	55.6	62.7	73.3	75.6	42.5		
Dec.....	53.4	61.4	72.4	75.1	43.2	65.2	70.7

MATERIALS, SEMI-FINISHED AND FINISHED GOODS, AND PRICES RECEIVED AND PAID BY FARMERS, 1929-JUNE 1936 =100)

Year and Month	Raw Materials[a]	Semi-Finished Goods[a]	Finished Goods[a]	Cost of Living[b]	Prices Received by Farmers[c]	Prices Paid by Farmers for Home Maintenance[d]	Prices Paid by Farmers for Goods Used in Production[d]
1933:							
Jan	51.5	60.6	70.6	73.7	41.1		
Feb	49.6	60.0	69.5	72.1	37.7		
Mar	50.7	60.6	69.5	71.8	37.7	62.7	68.7
Apr	51.3	61.0	69.5	71.5	39.7		
May	55.1	65.3	71.1	72.1	46.6		
June	57.6	69.5	73.0	72.8	48.6	64.6	70.7
July	63.4	73.6	76.4	75.2	56.8		
Aug	62.2	76.4	77.7	76.9	54.1		
Sept	63.3	77.6	79.2	77.9	54.8	74.1	77.6
Oct	63.4	77.5	79.8	78.0	53.4		
Nov	64.0	76.0	79.6	77.8	54.8		
Dec	63.5	77.0	79.2	77.3	53.4	74.1	77.6
1934:							
Jan	65.7	76.6	80.4	77.5	52.7		
Feb	67.7	79.7	81.5	78.3	56.8		
Mar	67.6	79.1	81.7	78.5	57.5	76.6	81.0
Apr	66.8	78.7	81.6	78.4	56.2		
May	66.8	78.5	82.3	78.6	56.2		
June	69.0	77.6	82.8	78.8	58.9	77.2	82.3
July	70.1	77.4	82.8	79.1	59.6		
Aug	73.4	77.3	83.8	79.6	65.8		
Sept	75.8	76.5	84.8	81.0	70.5	77.8	87.8
Oct	73.9	76.1	83.8	80.9	69.9		
Nov	74.1	75.7	83.9	80.8	69.2		
Dec	75.0	75.6	84.1	80.8	69.2	77.2	89.1
1935:							
Jan	78.5	75.8	85.5	81.6	73.3		
Feb	79.4	76.4	86.2	82.4	76.0		
Mar	78.6	76.5	86.4	82.4	74.0	78.5	89.1
Apr	79.5	77.0	87.1	83.2	76.0		
May	79.6	78.3	87.2	82.9	74.0		
June	78.4	78.7	87.0	82.7	71.2	78.5	88.4
July	77.7	77.5	86.8	82.6	69.9		
Aug	79.1	78.0	87.8	83.0	72.6		
Sept	79.3	79.2	87.9	83.5	73.3	78.5	83.0
Oct	79.1	81.3	87.5	83.9	74.7		
Nov	79.2	81.2	87.5	84.3	74.0		
Dec	79.7	80.1	87.9	84.8	75.3	78.5	81.0
1936:							
Jan	80.1	79.7	87.2	84.8	74.7		
Feb	81.1	79.4	87.0	84.4	74.7		
Mar	79.4	79.2	86.0	84.1	71.2	77.2	79.6
Apr	79.0	79.3	86.3	84.3	71.9		
May	77.7	78.9	85.2	84.6	70.5		
June	79.6	78.7	85.4	86.0	73.3	76.6	81.6

[a] Assembled from monthly issues of *Wholesale Prices*, Bureau of Labor Statistics, and converted from a 1926 to a 1929 base.
[b] Assembled from various bulletins of the National Industrial Conference Board.
[c] U. S. Department of Agriculture, *Index of Prices Received by Farmers 1910 to 1934* and *Crops and Markets* for December 1935 and October 1936. The index has been converted from a 1910-14 to a 1929 base.
[d] U. S. Department of Agriculture, *Index Numbers of Prices Paid by Farmers 1910-1934*, and *Crops and Markets* for December 1935 and October 1936. The index has been converted from a 1910-14 to a 1929 base.

2. Indexes of Wholesale Prices of Major

(1929

Year and Month	All Commodities	Farm Products	Foods	Hides and Leather	Textiles	Fuel and Lighting	Metals and Metal Products	Building Material	Chemicals and Drugs	House Furnishing Goods	Miscellaneous
1929:											
Jan......	100.6	101.0	99.0	103.9	102.3	101.4	99.6	100.1	101.5	99.6	100.1
Feb.....	100.1	100.5	98.2	99.8	102.1	99.9	100.1	100.5	101.6	99.5	100.1
Mar.....	100.8	102.2	98.4	99.2	102.2	98.9	101.8	101.4	101.2	99.5	99.8
Apr.....	100.2	100.0	98.1	98.8	101.3	98.7	101.8	100.9	100.5	99.7	99.2
May....	99.4	97.4	98.1	97.8	100.3	99.4	100.7	100.1	99.9	99.7	99.3
June....	99.9	98.5	99.2	98.9	99.7	101.8	100.7	99.8	99.2	100.3	99.8
July....	101.3	102.6	103.0	100.0	99.1	100.4	100.5	99.7	99.1	100.0	100.2
Aug.....	101.0	102.5	103.6	100.4	99.3	99.0	100.0	99.8	99.4	100.0	100.2
Sept.....	100.8	101.6	103.4	101.4	99.3	99.6	99.8	100.4	99.5	100.0	100.6
Oct......	99.8	99.1	101.5	101.1	99.0	100.1	99.3	100.5	99.8	100.4	100.7
Nov.....	98.1	96.4	99.0	99.3	98.0	100.2	98.2	99.0	99.6	100.3	99.8
Dec.....	97.9	97.1	98.8	98.4	97.1	100.1	98.0	99.0	99.3	100.4	99.5
1930:											
Jan......	97.1	96.3	97.4	96.3	96.5	98.4	96.7	98.9	98.7	99.5	98.4
Feb.....	95.9	93.4	95.9	95.2	95.6	97.5	96.4	98.5	98.0	99.3	98.3
Mar.....	94.6	90.3	94.4	94.6	93.8	95.7	96.1	98.4	97.0	99.2	97.9
Apr.....	94.4	91.3	95.0	94.1	92.9	95.8	94.8	98.0	96.8	99.2	98.0
May....	93.2	88.7	92.3	94.0	92.3	96.7	93.0	96.9	95.8	99.2	97.3
June....	91.1	84.7	90.9	93.9	90.3	95.1	91.4	94.2	94.9	99.1	94.9
July....	88.6	79.2	86.9	92.4	88.2	94.0	90.3	92.8	93.7	98.7	92.7
Aug.....	88.5	80.9	87.7	90.7	86.3	93.9	89.2	91.9	93.3	98.5	92.1
Sept.....	88.6	81.3	89.6	90.9	84.3	95.2	88.6	91.3	92.6	97.9	91.0
Oct......	87.1	78.6	88.9	88.5	82.6	93.5	87.5	90.5	92.0	97.7	90.4
Nov.....	85.3	75.6	86.3	86.3	82.1	90.7	87.4	89.6	91.3	97.0	89.7
Dec.....	83.5	71.7	82.5	83.8	81.5	89.2	87.5	88.9	90.9	94.2	89.0
1931:											
Jan......	82.1	69.7	80.8	81.3	78.9	88.3	86.5	87.8	89.7	93.6	87.4
Feb.....	80.6	66.8	78.1	79.7	78.4	87.3	86.1	86.5	88.4	93.4	86.6
Mar.....	79.7	67.3	77.7	80.3	77.4	82.3	86.0	86.5	88.0	93.3	87.2
Apr.....	78.5	66.8	76.4	80.2	75.4	78.8	85.3	85.4	86.3	93.2	86.6
May....	76.8	64.0	73.9	80.3	74.6	78.7	84.6	83.9	85.5	92.0	85.4
June....	75.7	62.3	73.4	80.7	73.7	75.8	84.0	83.1	84.3	91.6	84.4
July....	75.6	61.9	74.1	81.9	73.6	75.8	83.9	81.9	83.8	90.9	84.4
Aug.....	75.7	60.5	74.7	81.3	72.5	80.1	83.5	81.3	81.6	90.0	82.7
Sept.....	74.7	57.7	73.8	77.9	71.3	81.2	83.5	80.7	81.0	87.7	82.6
Oct......	73.8	56.1	73.4	75.6	69.7	81.7	82.4	79.9	80.3	85.9	80.6
Nov.....	73.7	56.0	71.1	74.8	68.8	83.6	82.2	79.9	80.8	85.8	83.2
Dec.....	72.0	53.1	69.2	73.1	67.3	82.3	81.8	79.4	80.8	83.2	80.9
1932:											
Jan......	70.6	50.3	64.8	72.7	65.9	81.8	81.4	78.4	80.4	82.4	79.4
Feb.....	69.6	48.2	62.6	71.8	65.8	82.3	80.5	76.9	80.1	82.2	78.3
Mar.....	69.3	47.9	62.4	70.9	64.2	81.8	80.4	76.7	79.9	81.8	78.3
Apr.....	68.7	46.9	61.1	68.7	62.1	84.6	79.9	76.0	79.0	80.9	78.3
May....	67.6	44.4	59.4	66.5	60.1	85.2	79.7	74.9	78.1	79.3	78.0
June....	67.1	43.6	58.9	64.9	58.3	86.3	79.5	74.2	77.6	79.2	77.7
July....	67.7	45.7	61.0	62.9	57.0	87.1	78.8	73.1	77.5	78.5	77.8
Aug.....	68.4	46.8	61.9	63.9	58.3	86.9	79.7	73.0	77.8	78.0	78.2
Sept.....	68.5	46.8	61.9	66.2	61.5	85.3	79.7	73.9	77.4	78.1	78.3
Oct......	67.6	44.7	60.6	66.7	60.8	85.7	79.9	74.1	77.2	78.1	77.6
Nov.....	67.1	44.5	60.7	65.4	59.6	86.0	79.2	74.1	76.9	78.1	77.1
Dec.....	65.7	42.0	58.4	63.8	58.6	83.5	79.0	74.2	76.8	78.0	76.8

GROUPS OF COMMODITIES, 1929-JUNE 1936[a]
=100)

Year and Month	All Commodities	Farm Products	Foods	Hides and Leather	Textiles	Fuel and Lighting	Metals and Metal Products	Building Material	Chemicals and Drugs	House Furnishing Goods	Miscellaneous
1933:											
Jan......	64.0	40.6	55.9	63.2	57.4	79.5	77.8	73.5	76.0	77.3	74.1
Feb.....	62.7	39.0	53.8	62.3	56.6	76.6	77.0	73.2	75.7	76.7	71.7
Mar.....	63.2	40.8	54.7	62.4	56.7	75.8	76.8	73.7	75.6	76.6	71.3
Apr.....	63.4	42.4	56.2	63.6	57.3	74.1	76.5	73.6	75.8	75.8	70.0
May....	65.8	47.9	59.5	70.5	61.8	72.8	77.3	74.8	77.7	76.0	71.3
June....	68.2	50.7	61.3	75.5	68.0	74.1	78.9	78.3	78.2	77.8	73.6
July....	72.3	57.3	65.6	79.1	75.2	78.7	80.2	83.3	77.7	79.3	77.5
Aug.....	72.9	54.9	64.9	84.1	82.5	78.9	80.8	85.2	77.6	82.3	79.2
Sept.....	74.3	54.3	65.0	84.6	85.1	84.8	81.7	86.7	77.2	84.1	78.8
Oct......	74.7	53.1	64.3	81.6	85.3	88.7	82.6	87.9	77.2	86.1	79.1
Nov.....	74.6	54.0	64.4	80.8	85.0	88.6	82.3	89.0	77.9	85.9	79.3
Dec.....	74.3	52.9	62.6	81.8	84.5	88.5	83.1	89.7	78.2	85.9	79.5
1934:											
Jan......	75.8	56.0	64.4	82.0	84.6	88.1	85.1	90.5	79.0	85.7	81.7
Feb.....	77.2	58.4	66.8	82.1	85.1	87.2	86.6	90.8	80.1	85.9	82.9
Mar.....	77.3	58.4	67.4	81.3	84.6	86.0	86.7	90.6	80.4	86.3	83.9
Apr.....	76.9	56.8	66.3	81.5	83.3	86.4	87.5	90.9	80.1	86.5	84.1
May....	77.3	56.8	67.2	80.6	81.4	87.3	88.7	91.5	80.0	87.0	84.5
June....	78.3	60.3	69.9	79.8	80.4	87.7	87.3	92.0	80.3	87.0	85.0
July....	78.5	61.5	70.7	79.1	79.1	89.0	86.4	91.2	80.0	86.5	84.6
Aug.....	80.2	66.5	74.0	76.8	78.3	89.9	86.3	89.9	80.4	86.7	85.0
Sept.....	81.4	70.0	76.2	77.1	78.7	89.9	86.2	89.7	81.2	86.7	85.0
Oct......	80.3	67.3	74.9	76.8	77.8	89.9	85.9	89.3	81.8	86.6	84.4
Nov.....	80.3	67.5	75.2	77.2	77.1	89.6	85.8	89.1	81.6	86.2	85.5
Dec.....	80.7	68.6	75.4	78.0	77.4	88.8	85.5	89.2	82.6	86.1	86.0
1935:											
Jan......	82.7	74.0	80.0	79.0	77.8	87.8	85.4	89.0	84.2	86.1	85.6
Feb.....	83.4	75.4	82.8	78.8	77.5	87.3	85.4	89.1	85.4	85.6	84.9
Mar....	83.3	74.6	82.0	78.3	76.8	88.0	85.3	89.0	86.5	85.6	83.8
Apr.....	84.1	76.6	84.6	79.1	76.5	87.7	85.5	88.7	86.0	85.6	83.2
May....	84.2	76.8	84.2	80.9	76.8	88.1	86.2	88.9	86.2	85.5	83.2
June....	83.7	74.6	82.9	81.5	77.5	89.4	86.5	89.4	85.7	85.4	82.8
July....	83.3	73.5	82.2	81.9	77.6	90.0	86.0	89.3	83.5	85.3	82.0
Aug.....	84.5	75.6	85.0	82.1	78.4	89.3	86.2	89.5	83.4	85.4	81.5
Sept.....	84.7	75.7	86.2	83.3	79.4	88.0	86.2	90.0	85.1	85.4	81.2
Oct......	84.5	74.5	85.1	85.8	80.6	88.4	86.1	90.3	86.1	85.5	81.7
Nov.....	84.6	73.9	85.2	87.1	81.2	89.8	86.5	89.9	86.2	85.9	81.6
Dec.....	84.9	74.6	85.8	87.4	81.0	89.9	86.4	89.6	85.6	85.9	81.7
1936:											
Jan......	84.6	74.5	83.6	89.0	79.3	90.5	86.3	89.8	85.5	86.3	82.1
Feb.....	84.6	75.8	83.3	88.1	78.5	91.7	86.3	89.6	85.0	86.4	82.4
Mar.....	83.5	72.9	80.2	87.0	78.3	91.8	86.2	89.4	84.2	86.3	82.7
Apr.....	83.6	73.3	80.3	86.7	77.7	92.0	86.2	89.8	83.3	86.4	83.1
May....	82.5	71.7	78.1	86.2	77.2	91.6	85.9	89.9	82.5	86.4	83.8
June....	83.1	74.5	80.0	86.0	77.0	91.7	85.8	89.9	82.8	86.3	84.4

[a] Assembled from monthly issues of *Wholesale Prices*, Bureau of Labor Statistics, and converted from a 1926 to a 1929 base.

3. INDEXES OF WHOLESALE PRICES OF SELECTED

(1929

Year and Month	Lumber	Fertilizer Materials	Petrol Products	Boots and Shoes	Furniture	Iron and Steel	Non-Ferrous Metal	Cotton Goods	Woolens and Worsted	Paper and Pulp
1929:										
Jan.......	99.3	102.7	100.8	100.4	99.4	99.6	95.4	101.6	103.5	100.0
Feb.......	101.3	102.8	96.6	100.3	99.3	99.8	99.4	101.0	103.4	100.0
Mar......	102.8	102.8	96.1	100.3	99.3	100.1	110.6	101.8	103.2	100.0
Apr.......	101.5	102.7	99.7	100.3	99.3	100.7	106.7	100.6	102.7	100.0
May.....	100.4	102.2	101.7	99.9	99.3	100.7	99.4	99.7	101.0	100.4
June.....	100.2	100.5	107.4	99.8	100.5	100.6	99.4	99.0	100.0	100.3
July.....	99.5	98.5	102.8	99.8	100.5	100.4	99.6	99.4	99.3	100.0
Aug......	99.7	98.3	98.6	99.8	100.5	100.2	99.4	99.4	98.3	100.0
Sept.....	101.2	97.6	98.5	99.8	100.5	100.1	99.2	99.6	98.2	100.0
Oct.......	101.9	97.8	99.3.	99.8	100.5	99.6	98.6	99.7	98.2	99.8
Nov.....	97.9	97.6	99.4	99.8	100.4	99.1	97.1	98.6	97.7	99.8
Dec.....	98.0	97.2	98.0	99.8	100.4	98.8	96.3	97.4	96.5	99.2
1930:										
Jan.......	98.4	97.5	94.4	97.6	99.8	96.9	95.5	95.9	96.1	99.1
Feb.......	97.5	97.2	92.1	97.6	99.8	96.3	95.2	93.9	95.4	98.8
Mar......	97.2	95.8	89.3	97.6	99.6	96.3	93.9	91.4	92.9	98.7
Apr.......	97.3	95.7	92.0	97.6	99.6	95.7	86.6	90.7	91.4	97.9
May.....	95.5	93.9	93.3	97.5	99.6	94.9	77.6	90.1	90.6	97.4
June.....	91.3	92.6	89.2	96.9	99.6	93.8	75.2	88.3	90.3	97.2
July.....	89.1	91.5	85.6	96.8	98.8	93.2	71.1	84.9	89.7	96.1
Aug......	87.1	90.4	85.4	94.6	98.8	92.7	70.2	82.1	88.1	96.1
Sept.....	86.5	90.2	87.0	94.5	98.4	92.3	69.0	79.6	86.0	95.7
Oct.......	85.1	90.8	83.3	94.3	98.3	91.8	65.7	77.9	84.9	95.7
Nov.....	85.5	89.1	74.8	94.3	98.1	91.5	66.5	78.4	84.6	95.2
Dec.....	83.4	88.4	71.7	91.9	97.4	91.3	67.6	76.5	83.7	94.5
1931:										
Jan.......	81.4	88.4	70.7	89.4	96.9	90.1	65.5	74.4	83.5	94.0
Feb.......	78.9	88.1	70.5	89.3	96.8	90.2	64.5	74.0	83.2	93.5
Mar......	79.6	87.7	58.6	89.2	96.7	90.0	65.3	73.3	81.3	92.9
Apr.......	78.3	87.5	52.5	89.2	96.7	88.6	63.6	72.3	78.1	92.4
May.....	74.0	87.4	50.4	89.2	95.2	88.3	59.7	70.0	77.6	91.7
June.....	73.0	86.6	43.1	89.0	94.5	88.0	57.7	68.4	77.0	90.8
July.....	71.6	85.5	42.5	88.0	93.8	87.1	57.9	67.6	76.3	90.7
Aug......	71.3	80.8	52.6	88.0	93.3	86.8	56.6	64.8	76.3	90.7
Sept.....	71.3	80.6	54.6	88.0	89.1	86.7	55.6	62.2	74.4	90.8
Oct.......	69.5	76.2	55.0	87.6	86.7	86.1	51.7	60.4	73.2	90.6
Nov.....	70.3	76.1	59.6	87.0	86.6	85.9	51.6	58.8	72.7	90.9
Dec.....	70.1	76.1	55.5	83.9	84.8	85.4	50.7	57.1	72.4	90.9
1932:										
Jan.......	69.9	75.9	54.4	83.5	83.7	84.2	52.2	56.5	71.7	87.7
Feb.......	67.1	75.8	54.1	83.3	83.7	83.6	49.7	57.1	71.5	86.3
Mar......	65.6	74.5	55.8	83.3	83.3	84.0	47.6	56.9	71.0	86.4
Apr.......	64.0	76.1	63.8	83.2	81.5	84.4	46.5	55.8	67.6	86.4
May.....	63.4	75.4	66.2	83.2	78.0	84.3	46.5	53.5	66.0	86.1
June.....	61.4	73.8	67.6	82.3	77.9	84.1	44.8	51.6	62.3	85.7
July.....	60.7	72.5	69.7	79.4	76.8	81.3	44.3	50.6	57.7	85.7
Aug......	59.2	72.1	68.6	79.4	76.4	82.9	45.7	53.2	60.5	85.8
Sept.....	60.0	69.1	65.5	79.4	76.5	84.0	48.6	58.6	64.2	84.9
Oct.......	60.3	68.8	66.5	79.6	76.6	84.7	47.8	56.9	64.0	82.6
Nov.....	60.3	68.9	67.6	79.2	76.5	83.7	46.3	54.3	62.6	82.6
Dec......	60.2	68.5	63.1	78.8	76.5	83.0	45.5	52.3	61.4	82.1

SUB-GROUPS OF COMMODITIES, 1929-JUNE 1936ᵃ
=100)

Year and Month	Lumber	Fertilizer Materials	Petrol Products	Boots and Shoes	Furniture	Iron and Steel	Non-Ferrous Metal	Cotton Goods	Woolens and Worsted	Paper and Pulp
1933:										
Jan......	59.6	67.6	54.3	78.4	76.1	82.7	43.7	50.7	60.5	81.0
Feb......	60.1	66.8	48.1	78.4	75.7	81.5	43.5	49.7	60.2	81.1
Mar......	61.6	67.2	46.4	78.3	75.6	80.5	45.1	50.6	60.2	81.2
Apr......	61.7	68.3	45.6	78.3	75.3	79.8	46.4	51.3	60.3	79.4
May.....	63.5	72.5	43.8	78.6	75.4	79.2	53.3	58.6	69.6	79.5
June.....	71.9	73.8	48.2	80.4	77.3	80.3	59.6	67.9	77.9	82.7
July.....	80.9	74.5	57.9	83.1	78.5	81.9	63.7	81.2	81.9	87.9
Aug......	84.6	74.9	57.4	90.4	80.8	82.8	64.3	94.6	89.4	91.1
Sept......	87.4	72.3	69.6	93.0	82.5	84.6	64.6	92.4	93.7	92.5
Oct......	89.8	73.4	73.9	93.0	84.0	86.8	63.1	89.9	95.7	92.7
Nov......	92.2	73.6	72.4	93.1	83.6	85.9	64.1	87.0	95.6	92.8
Dec......	93.8	73.9	72.4	92.8	83.5	88.1	62.8	86.5	95.5	92.8
1934:										
Jan......	93.2	74.3	71.7	92.7	82.9	88.1	62.3	87.6	95.5	93.4
Feb......	93.1	75.1	70.5	92.6	83.4	90.9	62.0	89.7	95.5	93.0
Mar......	92.1	75.5	68.3	92.7	84.0	90.9	62.5	90.2	95.1	93.0
Apr......	93.0	74.6	69.3	92.7	84.1	92.0	64.1	89.3	92.9	94.0
May.....	91.6	72.1	71.1	92.7	84.3	95.0	64.2	87.3	91.7	94.2
June.....	92.0	73.7	71.0	92.6	83.2	93.4	64.6	87.0	91.5	93.9
July.....	90.9	73.4	71.9	92.2	82.6	91.4	64.8	86.1	91.4	92.7
Aug......	87.2	70.4	72.4	92.1	83.1	91.3	64.9	89.4	89.4	92.7
Sept......	87.7	72.1	71.9	92.1	82.9	91.2	64.5	88.9	88.3	92.7
Oct......	87.4	71.3	70.7	91.9	83.2	90.8	64.2	87.7	84.8	92.7
Nov......	86.6	70.1	70.8	91.5	82.5	90.6	63.8	85.4	83.9	92.4
Dec......	86.6	70.9	69.8	91.4	82.3	90.2	63.6	85.3	83.8	91.7
1935:										
Jan......	85.2	72.2	68.4	91.3	82.3	90.3	63.7	85.1	83.6	91.7
Feb......	85.8	71.9	68.3	91.4	81.3	90.7	63.3	84.3	83.4	91.0
Mar......	85.2	72.0	69.8	91.4	81.4	90.6	63.2	83.4	82.8	90.7
Apr......	85.2	71.7	71.5	91.4	81.2	90.6	64.3	82.8	82.8	90.4
May.....	85.1	71.6	73.2	91.4	81.2	91.3	65.2	83.7	83.2	90.0
June.....	87.0	71.3	74.6	91.5	81.2	91.8	65.1	83.5	85.6	89.7
July.....	87.1	71.3	74.2	92.0	80.8	91.7	62.3	83.0	86.5	89.7
Aug......	87.4	72.5	73.5	92.5	81.1	91.8	63.1	83.5	86.5	89.7
Sept......	87.5	73.0	71.0	92.5	80.9	91.5	64.7	84.2	87.1	89.7
Oct......	87.4	73.0	70.3	92.9	80.9	91.6	66.8	85.5	89.6	89.7
Nov......	87.2	73.3	73.6	93.7	81.2	91.7	67.2	86.8	91.4	89.3
Dec......	86.9	70.0	74.1	94.2	81.2	91.6	66.5	87.0	91.7	89.1
1936:										
Jan......	87.6	69.9	76.3	94.5	82.0	91.8	65.7	81.4	92.2	89.8
Feb......	87.7	70.0	78.1	94.5	82.0	91.6	65.7	79.0	93.8	89.9
Mar......	88.1	70.4	78.5	94.4	82.0	90.9	65.9	78.0	94.9	90.3
Apr......	88.7	70.1	81.2	94.3	82.1	90.9	66.4	77.1	93.1	90.6
May.....	88.5	70.2	81.6	94.3	82.0	90.9	66.6	76.4	93.1	90.6
June.....	87.5	69.5	80.9	93.8	81.6	90.9	66.0	76.3	93.5	90.7

ᵃ Assembled from monthly issues of *Wholesale Prices*, Bureau of Labor Statistics, and converted from a 1926 to a 1929 base.

APPENDIX F

PUBLIC FINANCE SUPPLEMENT

The following pages contain supporting data and explanatory material bearing on Chapters XII and XVIII.

I. LOW AND HIGH POINTS OF FEDERAL INDEBTEDNESS, 1917-36

The fluctuations in the federal debt showing the lowest and highest points in the post-war period are revealed in Table 1.

1. FLUCTUATIONS IN UNITED STATES PUBLIC DEBT, 1917-36[a]
(In millions of dollars)

Item	Mar. 31, 1917 (Last pre-war)	Aug. 31, 1919 (Post-war high)	Dec. 31, 1930 (Post-war low)	June 30, 1936 (Present)
Gross debt.......	1,282	26,597	16,026	33,779
Net balance, general fund...	74	1,118	307	2,682
Net debt....	1,208	25,479	15,719	31,097

[a] *Preliminary Statement of the Public Debt*, June 30, 1936.

II. THE DECREASE IN THE FEDERAL DEBT, 1920-30

The reduction of the debt of the national government was accomplished chiefly by three means: (1) the regularly prescribed sinking fund; (2) the application of all excess ordinary revenues; and (3) special receipts, particularly on account of the war debts. The following table shows by sources the amount of funds made available for debt retirement during the fiscal years 1920-30 inclusive.[1]

Sinking fund	$3,187,486,300
Foreign government obligations	1,488,720,450
Other special receipts	230,425,944
Surplus of receipts	3,476,729,405
Decrease of general fund balance	913,382,020
	$9,296,726,119

[1] Assembled from *Annual Report of the Secretary of the Treasury*, 1930, p. 27.

III. SPECIAL-PURPOSE INTEREST BEARING DEBTS

As has been indicated in the text, a considerable volume of public indebtedness involves other than purely fiscal considerations. The following table lists all of these special forms of debts and the accounts outstanding as of June 30, 1930 and June 30, 1936:

2. SPECIAL-PURPOSE INTEREST BEARING PUBLIC DEBT, 1930 AND 1936[a]

Form of Debt	1930	1936
BONDS:		
2.5 per cent Postal Savings bonds....	$ 19,224,720	$ 120,881,020
United States Savings bonds.......	—	316,124,814
3 per cent Adjusted Service bonds..	—	944,516,650
2 per cent Consols and Panama Canal bonds.................	674,625,630	—
NOTES:		
4 per cent Retirement Funds series.	134,971,000	280,433,000
2 per cent Postal Savings System series......................	—	100,000,000
2 per cent Fed. Deposit Ins. Corp. series......................	—	100,000,000
4 per cent Adjusted Service Certif. Fund series.................	629,200,000	—
CERTIFICATES:		
2.5 per cent Unemployment Trust Fund series.................	—	18,909,000
4 per cent Adjusted Service Certificate Fund series..............	—	126,800,000
Total.......................	$1,458,021,350	$2,007,664,484

[a] 1930 data from *Annual Report of the Secretary of the Treasury,* 1930 p.551; 1936 data from *Preliminary Statement of the Public Debt,* June 30, 1936

Postal Savings bonds were designed for the small investor as an added facility to the deposit accommodation of the Postal Savings System and they have occupied a minor place in the public debt since 1910. Under pressure of recent emergency financing, the postal issues have been supplanted by the United States Savings bonds and they will gradually disappear from the debt within the next twenty years. United States Savings bonds are also a form of "small savings" debt, but, unlike the earlier postal issues, they are sold at a discount in lieu of interest, the principal amount being payable in not less than ten or more than twenty years. They are also redeemable before maturity at the option of the owner.

The issue of Adjusted Service bonds is a by-product of the method selected by the government in paying off a well-known special obligation, the Adjusted Service certificates. These certificates were actually obligations of the United States established in 1924 and with maturity twenty years from that date, but the maturity value was not immediately included as a part of the public debt. If this simplified method had been used, the Treasury would have only had to convert the certificates into some other form of debt as they were redeemed in cash. A more complicated device based on actuarial principles was selected to accomplish the same purpose. The issue of Adjusted Service Certificate Fund notes of 629 million dollars, which appears only in the 1930 tabulation, represents this means taken *progressively* to recognize the obligation which at maturity would have been about 3,500 million dollars.

A decision to pay the bonus in full immediately after June 15, 1936 precluded the continuation of this procedure and the Adjusted Service bonds consequently recognize the current nature of the obligation. Some of these bonds will be held to maturity as investments, but a large percentage of the holders have availed themselves of the privilege of immediate encashment.[2] The Treasury had to provide sufficient funds to meet this expenditure by borrowing in anticipation of later replenishing its depleted cash balance. Consequently, the effect of the bonus transaction will be an increase in some form of interest bearing debt, roughly comparable to the amount of Adjusted Service bonds redeemed, over and above whatever amount of the issue will remain outstanding to maturity in 1945, and with an additional amount of special obligations to compensate government trust funds for cancelled veterans' loans.[3]

Various trust funds administered by the Treasury are limited in their investments to United States securities. As the circumstances determine, special issues, such as the Retirement Funds

[2] Of these bonds $1,668,752,150 were issued on or shortly after June 15, 1936. By June 30, $724,235,500 had been redeemed for cash (*Daily Treasury Statement*, June 30, 1936). On Aug. 31, 1936 only 545 millions remained outstanding (*Preliminary Statement of the Public Debt*, Aug. 31, 1936).

[3] Legislation in 1931 authorized holders of Adjusted Service certificates to borrow up to 50 per cent of their maturity value. As a consequence, the

notes, are designed to fulfill their investment requirements. Treasury notes issued directly to the Postal Savings System and the Federal Deposit Insurance Corporation also represent a part of the government security investments of these agencies, the bulk of their investments being in regular public issues.

The Unemployment Trust Fund series of certificates represents the utilization of the more direct of two methods open for investment in government securities of this reserve established under the recent Social Security Act. An enormous reserve for old-age annuities may also be accumulated as a feature of the security program and it may be similarly invested in special obligations or public issues which comply with certain yield conditions. In any projection of the future of the debt, or of the fiscal situation as a whole, consideration of these reserves and the methods used for their investment is of paramount importance. On the basis of tentative actuarial schedules it is believed that the Old-Age Reserve Account will accumulate to about 48 billion dollars by 1980. The Unemployment Trust Fund will be a revolving fund reaching proportions of from one to 2 billions. These funds are to be formed from surplus receipts of special premium taxes levied by the federal government. The method of investment, whether in special issues or by purchase of publicly held debt, is of fundamental importance.

We have mentioned in the text that a large proportion of the pre-war bonds were used to secure national bank note circulation.[4] These securities, which are shown as the 2 per cent

---

special Adjusted Service Certificate Fund notes had to be redeemed by the Treasury, which borrowed publicly to provide the cash. The principal amount of these loans from the Adjusted Service Certificate Fund therefore operates as a deduction from the amount of *new* bonus financing for immediate payment in full. Similar loans were also made from the Government Life Insurance Fund, which presumably will be compensated by replacement with special government obligations inasmuch as 560 million dollars are being set aside for this purpose in the estimated expenditures for 1937 (*President's Budget Statement*, Sept. 1, 1936).

[4] As an emergency measure, this category of special-purpose debts was enlarged by a provision of the Federal Home Loan Bank Act of July 22, 1932 which attached the circulation privilege to all bonds of the United States bearing interest at a rate not in excess of $3\frac{3}{8}$ per cent, for a three-year period. These additional bonds amounted to about 3 billions, but

Consols and Panama Canal bonds in the 1930 tabulation, were called for redemption in 1935 and have disappeared from the debt.[5] Carrying out the intention of the original Federal Reserve Act, the currency system has also been simplified by the elimination of national bank notes as a medium of circulation.[6]

IV. THE OPERATION OF THE SINKING FUND

As indicated in the text on page 294, the operation of the statutory sinking fund requirement has been continued during the depression notwithstanding the existence of enormous deficits. The cumulative sinking fund was established in the fiscal year 1921. To this fund is made an annual appropriation, or *initial credit,* of 2.5 per cent of a fixed base amount of debt, and a *secondary credit* representing the amount of interest which would otherwise have been paid on the debt retired during the fund's operation.

In the fiscal years 1931-35, inclusive, a total of 2,248 millions of debt was retired by statutory provision, the greater part resulting from the operation of the sinking fund. The way in which this serves to reduce interest charges may be indicated by reference to the operation for the fiscal year 1935.

In that year initial and secondary credits were 296 millions and 198 millions respectively, to which may be added an unexpended balance from the previous year of 79 millions. All of the 593 millions of debt thus retired consisted of bonds of the First and Fourth Liberty Loans, bearing interest at from 3½ to 4¼ per cent. These bonds had been called for redemp-

---

their usefulness was restricted by the existing limitation of the national bank note issue to the amount of the banks' paid-in capital, which was about 1.5 billions. The banks actually availed themselves of only a modest proportion of this margin above their old circulation on 2 per cent bonds.

[5] The bonds were not retired by refunding, or use of the Treasury working balance, but by the release of gold certificates from the fund resulting from the devaluation of the gold dollar.

[6] As the banks have deposited money with the Treasury for retirement of their notes, following the redemption of the 2 per cent bonds, these notes have temporarily become obligations of the United States until collected and cancelled. This has caused a momentary rise in the non-interest bearing debt.

tion and consequently no funds were lost on payments of premiums. The funds used by the sinking fund came from other Treasury borrowings, but at substantially reduced rates, probably at rates less than those secured in the regular refunding operations of these war loans.

Appropriations will continue to be made to the sinking fund; but the savings of interest in the near future do not appear so great since there are no impending bond maturities and outstanding issues which would have to be purchased at substantial premiums. In the fiscal year 1936, only 403 millions of debt were actually retired, although the appropriation to the fund must have exceeded 500 millions.

3. Federal Expenditures, Classified According to
Function, 1915, 1919, and 1925[a]
(In millions of dollars)

Type of Function	1915	1919	1925
GENERAL:			
Legislative, executive, and judicial........	14	15	22
General administration.................	38	97	94
Total............................	52	112	116
MILITARY:			
National defense......................	260	11,239	570
Military pensions.....................	176	324	627
Miscellaneous.........................		164	42[b]
Total............................	436	11,727	1,155
CIVIL:			
Indian affairs.........................	13	12	13
Public domain........................	11	11	26
Commerce and industry................	3	7	15
Agriculture..........................	15	16	28
Marine transportation.................	17	1,898	72
Land transportation...................	4	355	13
Public health and education............	10	18	27
Public works.........................	99	72	200
All other............................	58	137	135
Total............................	221	2,526	529
NON-FUNCTIONAL (EXCLUSIVE OF DEBT RETIREMENT):[c]			
Loans to foreign governments...........	—	3,478	—
Other investments.....................	—	401[d]	—
Public debt interest...................	23	616	882
Trust funds, refunds, losses, etc..........	29	92	364[e]
Total (warrant basis).................	761	18,952	3,046
Adj. to cash......................	−1	−429	+ 18
Total.........................	760	18,523	3,064

[a] Figures assembled from *The Budget*, 1926 and 1927.

[b] Credit.

[c] The term non-functional distinguishes certain expenditures which have either deferred or recoverable characteristics and are therefore not readily allocable to the cost of purely current functional services. Debt service in the form of interest is non-functional only in the sense that it represents the deferred cost of previous functional activities which were covered by borrowing. Debt retirement is excluded from the figures as being associated with Treasury surpluses rather than budgeted costs.

[d] Includes capital stock war emergency corporations (305 millions) and purchases of Federal Farm Loan bonds (96 millions).

[e] Includes refunds of customs and internal revenue (170 millions) and payment to Adjusted Service Certificate Fund (99 millions). *The Budget*, 1927, Statement No. 1.

4. Aggregate Federal Debt, 1915–36[a]
(In millions of dollars)

Year Ending June 30	Interest Bearing	Matured	Non-Interest Bearing[b]	Total Gross Debt
1915	970	2	220	1,191
1916	972	1	252	1,225
1917	2,713	14	249	2,976
1918	11,986	20	238	12,244
1919	25,234	11	236	25,482
1920	24,061	7	230	24,298
1921	23,737	11	228	23,976
1922	22,711	25	228	22,964
1923	22,008	98	244	22,350
1924	20,982	30	239	21,251
1925	20,211	30	275	20,516
1926	19,384	13	246	19,643
1927	18,251	15	245	18,510
1928	17,318	45	241	17,604
1929	16,639	51	242	16,931
1930	15,922	32	232	16,185
1931	16,520	52	230	16,801
1932	19,161	60	266	19,487
1933	22,158	66	315	22,539
1934	26,480	54	518	27,053
1935	27,645	231	825	28,701
1936	32,989	169	620	33,779

[a] *Annual Report of the Secretary of the Treasury*, 1935, Table 19, p. 378; 1936 figures from *Preliminary Statement of the Public Debt*, June 30, 1936.
[b] Includes old demand notes; United States notes (less gold reserve); postal currency and fractional currency (less amount estimated to have been destroyed); and deposits held by the Treasury for the retirement of the Federal Reserve Bank notes and national bank notes. Does not include gold, silver, or currency certificates, or Treasury notes of 1890 for redemption of which an exact equivalent of the respective kinds of money or bullion was held in the Treasury.

5. Interest Bearing Federal Debt, 1930–36[a]
(In millions of dollars)

Year Ending June 30	Long-Term Bonds	Intermediate Term Notes	Short-Term Certificates	Short-Term Bills	Total
1930	12,111	2,390	1,264	156	15,922
1931	13,531	621	1,924	445	16,520
1932	14,250	1,465	2,831	616	19,161
1933	14,223	4,780	2,200	954	22,158
1934	16,510	6,932	1,635	1,404	26,480
1935	14,936	10,501	156	2,053	27,645
1936	18,628	11,861	146	2,354	32,989

[a] Issues of *Statement of the Public Debt* and of the *Federal Reserve Bulletin*.

6. Maturities of the Interest Bearing Federal Debt Outstanding in 1932 and 1936
(In millions of dollars)

Maturity (Calendar year)	Debt Outstanding, June 30, 1932[a]				Maturity (Calendar year)	Debt Outstanding, June 30, 1936[g]			
	Short Term Issues	1 to 5 Year Notes	Long-Term Bonds	Cumulative Total		Short-Term Issues	Intermediate Term Notes	Long-Term Bonds	Cumulative Total
1932[b]	1,889	600	600[c]	3,089					
1933	1,452			4,541					
1934		244		4,785					
1935		417		5,202					
1936			49	5,251	1936[h]	1,753	890		2,643
					1937	601	1,749		4,993
1938			6,294	11,545	1938		1,946		6,939
					1939		2,761		9,700
					1940		2,854		12,554
					1941		1,181	834	14,569
1943			898	12,443	1943			898	15,467
					1945			1,401	16,868
					1946			1,519	18,387
1947			2,416	14,859	1947			1,697	20,084
					1948			1,036	21,120
1949			821	15,680	1949			819	21,939
					1951			1,223	23,162
1952			759	16,439	1952			1,250	24,412
1954			1,037	17,476	1954			2,663	27,075
1955			800	18,276	1955			756	27,831
1956			489	18,765	1956			489	28,320
					1960			2,611	30,931
1961			50	18,815	1961			50	30,989
Special issues	105[d]	204[e]	36[f]	19,161	Special issues	146[i]	480[j]	1,382[k]	32,989
Total	3,446	1,465	14,250		Total	2,500	11,861	18,628	

[a] From *Annual Report of the Secretary of the Treasury*, 1932, Table 22, p. 409.
[b] Maturities from June 30 to end of year 1932.
[c] Consols, maturity after July 1, 1932.
[d] Adjusted Service Certificate Fund.
[e] Retirement Fund notes.
[f] Postal Savings bonds (3d to 49th series).
[g] From *Preliminary Statement of the Public Debt*, June 30, 1936.
[h] Maturities from June 30 to end of year 1936.
[i] Adjusted Service Certificate Fund and Unemployment Trust Fund.
[j] Retirement funds and special issues to Postal Savings System and FDIC.
[k] Postal Savings, United States Savings, and Adjusted Service bonds.

7. Interest Charges and Rate of Interest on the Federal Debt,
1915–36[a]

(Dollar items are in millions)

Year Ending June 30	Interest Bearing Debt	Computed Annual Interest Charge	Actual Interest Charge	Computed Interest Rate
1915............	$ 970	$ 23	$ 23	2.371
1916............	972	23	23	2.376
1917............	2,713	84	25	3.120
1918............	11,986	469	190	3.910
1919............	25,234	1,054	619	4.178
1920............	24,061	1,017	1,020	4.225
1921............	23,737	1,030	999	4.339
1922............	22,711	963	991	4.240
1923............	22,008	927	1,056[b]	4.214
1924............	20,982	877	941	4.180
1925............	20,211	830	882	4.105
1926............	19,384	793	832	4.093
1927............	18,251	723	787	3.960
1928............	17,318	671	732	3.877
1929............	16,639	657	678	3.946
1930............	15,922	606	659	3.807
1931............	16,520	589	612	3.566
1932............	19,161	672	599	3.505
1933............	22,157	742	689	3.350
1934............	26,480	842	757	3.181
1935............	27,583[c]	749	821	2.715
1936............	32,989	845	749	2.562

[a] Computed interest and interest rates for 1915–35 are from *Annual Report of the Secretary of the Treasury*, 1935, Table 32, p. 401; for 1936 they are preliminary Treasury figures. Actual interest data are from the same, Table 4, p. 322, and from *Daily Treasury Statement*, June 30, 1936.

[b] War Savings securities retirements to the amount of 97.5 million dollars were charged to *interest* in this year.

[c] Exclusive of United States Savings bonds.

THE RECOVERY PROBLEM

8. Receipts and Expenditures of the Federal Government, 1915–36-
(In millions of dollars)

Year Ending June 30	Receipts	Expenditures
1915.................	698	761
1916.................	783	734
1917.................	1,124	1,978
1918.................	3,665	12,697
1919.................	5,152	18,514
1920.................	6,695	6,403
1921.................	5,625	5,116
1922.................	4,109	3,373
1923.................	4,007	3,295
1924.................	4,012	3,049
1925.................	3,780	3,063
1926.................	3,963	3,098
1927.................	4,129	2,974
1928.................	4,042	3,103
1929.................	4,033	3,299
1930.................	4,178	3,440
1931.................	3,317	3,780
1932.................	2,121	4,862
1933.................	2,238	4,845
1934.................	3,278[b]	6,884[c]
1935.................	4,030[d]	6,539[e]
1936.................	4,374	8,781

[a] Data for 1915–35 are from *Annual Report of the Secretary of the Treasury,* 1935, Table 4, p. 322 (general, special, emergency, and trust accounts combined); for 1936 they are preliminary Treasury figures. Postal revenues and expenditures, with the exception of surpluses or deficits, are excluded, as are debt retirements chargeable against ordinary receipts.

[b] Exclusive of a 2,811 million dollar increment from devaluation of gold dollar.

[c] Exclusive of 2 billion dollars chargeable against increment on gold stabilization fund).

[d] Exclusive of a 1,738 thousand dollar increment from devaluation and 140 millions silver seigniorage.

[e] Exclusive of 113 million dollars chargeable against increment on gold.

[c] Excludes non-military expenditures.

[d] Includes payments to Adjusted Service Certificate Fund, and bonus in 1936.

[e] Includes sinking fund and other retirements from ordinary receipts.

[f] Includes AAA expenditures and other items shown in the table on p. 305.

[g] Excludes 125 million dollars in capital stock of Federal Land Banks (shown under civil expenditures).

[h] Legislative and executive only.

9. General Budget Summary, 1930–36[a]

(In millions of dollars)

General and Special Accounts	1930	1931	1932	1933	1934	1935	1936
RECEIPTS:—							
Revenues—							
Internal revenue.	3,039	2,430	1,561	1,604	2,641	3,278	3,513
Customs........	587	379	328	251	313	343	387
Miscellaneous....	282	293	95	184	153	169	216
Total revenue..	3,908	3,102	1,984	2,039	3,107	3,790	4,116
Realization on assets[b]	140	88	22	41	9	10	—
Total receipts..	4,048	3,190	2,006	2,080	3,116	3,800	4,116
EXPENDITURES:							
Legislative, executive, and judiciary	39	41	45	38	32	36	22[h]
Civil departments and agencies, etc..	1,005	1,276	1,535	1,076	574	499	720
National defense[c]...	699	699	708	668	480	534	765
Veterans' pensions and benefits[d].....	754	933	985	863	556	606	2,350
Debt charges—							
Interest........	659	612	599	689	757	821	749
Retirements[e].....	554	440	413	462	360	573	403
Recovery and relief[f].				768[g]	1,277	4,283	4,262	3,827
Refunds and miscellaneous........	132	91	101	70	63	45	44
Total expenditures	3,862	4,092	5,154	5,143	7,105	7,376	8,880
Less debt retirement..........	554	440	413	462	360	573	403
Total..........	3,308	3,652	4,741	4,681	6,745	6,803	8,477
DEFICIT.............	+740	462	2,735	2,601	3,629	3,002	4,361

[a] Prepared from issues of The Budget, the Daily Treasury Statement, Annual Report of the Secretary of the Treasury, and other official statements.

[b] Separation for 1936 is not available. Does not include RFC or other special Recovery and Relief account net repayments which in Treasury practice are deducted from current expenditures (for amount and character of repayments see table, p. 305). Whether repayments are included in receipts or deducted from expenditures does not affect the amount of the deficit, but the method now followed reduces the totals of both receipts and expenditures. A more adequate portrayal of loan and investment liquidation would show these repayments as receipts. If, however, the proceeds of liquidation are again turned into other loans or investments (and thus it is not a final realization) the present method has points of merit. There is, of course, greater flexibility and variation in the management of federal government investments, which are not specifically balance sheet assets, than would be possible in private practice.

(See opposite page for notes c through h.)

10. Federal Receipts, Classified by Sources, 1930–36[a]
(In millions of dollars)

General and Special Accounts	1930	1931	1932	1933	1934	1935	1936
Internal revenue:							
Income tax........	2,411	1,860	1,057	746	818	1,099	1,427
Miscellaneous internal revenue—							
Estates.........	65	48	47	30	104	140	219
Gifts...........	—	—	—	5	9	72	160
Capital stock and excess profits...	—	—	—	—	83	98	109
Alcoholic beverages..........	12	11	9	43	259	411	506
Tobacco........	450	444	401	403	425	459	501
Stamp taxes.....	78	47	32	57	67	43	69
Manufacturers' excises........	—	—	—	235	381	342	383
Sundry.........	23	20	15	85	156	109	88
Adjustment to daily Treas. stmt.	—	—	—	—	−14	−17	−26
Total misc. internal revenue.....	628	570	504	858	1,470	1,657	2,009
Processing taxes[b].	—	—	—	—	353	522	77
Total internal revenue..........	3,039	2,430	1,561	1,604	2,641	3,278	3,513
Customs..........	587	379	328	251	313	343	387
Miscellaneous revenues[b]...........	282	293	95	184	153	169	216
Total revenues...	3,908	3,102	1,984	2,039	3,107	3,790	4,116
Realization on assets	140	88	22	41	9	10	—
Total receipts....	4,048	3,190	2,006	2,080	3,116	3,800	4,116

[a] Prepared from issues of *The Budget*, the *Annual Report of the Secretary of the Treasury*, and other official statements.
[b] Includes interest, fines, fees, sales of services, etc.

11. Outstanding Public Debts, 1915–35[a]
(In millions of dollars)

Year Ending June 30	United States Government[b]	States, Counties, Cities, etc.[c]	Total
1915.............	970	4,644	5,614
1916.............	972	5,049	6,021
1917.............	2,713	5,371	8,084
1918.............	11,986	5,622	17,608
1919.............	25,234	5,951	31,185
1920.............	24,061	6,645	30,706
1921.............	23,737	7,268	31,005
1922.............	22,711	8,415	31,126
1923.............	22,008	9,015	31,023
1924.............	20,982	9,921	30,903
1925.............	20,211	10,975	31,186
1926.............	19,384	11,672	31,056
1927.............	18,251	12,610	30,861
1928.............	17,318	13,452	30,770
1929.............	16,639	14,358	30,997
1930.............	15,922	15,888	31,810
1931.............	16,520	17,458	33,978
1932.............	19,161	17,829	36,990
1933.............	22,158	17,098	39,256
1934.............	26,480	16,924	43,404
1935.............	27,645	17,234	44,879

[a] Prepared from *Annual Report of the Secretary of the Treasury*, 1935, Tables 43 and 44, pp. 424–25. Figures represent the estimated amount of securities, outstanding interest on which is wholly or partially exempt from federal income tax. The data are therefore very inclusive as virtually all governmental debts are so exempt either wholly or in part.

[b] Actual interest bearing debt as of June 30.

[c] Net of amounts held in sinking funds. For the years 1934 and 1935 debts of drainage, levee, and irrigation districts compromised through the RFC are not included. Loans of the RFC to such districts outstanding on June 30, 1935 were $27,596,000.

12. Classified United States Government Securities and Other Loans and Investments of All Member Banks of the Federal Reserve System[a]

(In millions of dollars)

Securities and Investments	1930	1931	1932	1933	1934	1935	1936
UNITED STATES GOVERNMENT SECURITIES.....	4,125	5,319	6,540	7,254	9,906	10,501	11,721
Certificates and bills.	369	679	795	927	1,030	1,192	1,266
Treasury notes......	485	441	1,649	1,916	4,217	5,403	5,161
Bonds.............	3,271	4,199	4,096	4,411	4,659	3,905	5,295
OTHER LOANS AND INVESTMENTS.........	30,735	25,257	20,930	17,965	18,245	19,484	20,537
Loans.............	23,870	19,261	15,204	12,883	12,028	12,175	12,541
Investments[b].......	6,864	5,996	5,726	5,132	6,216	7,309	7,995
TOTAL.............	34,860	30,575	27,469	25,220	28,150	29,985	32,592

[a] Member bank *Call Report* for December of the years 1930–35 and June 1936.

[b] Including investments fully guaranteed by the United States government as reported on the following dates: Dec. 31, 1934, 989 millions; Dec. 31, 1935, 1,768 millions; June 30, 1936, 1,950 millions.

APPENDIX G

SUPPLEMENTARY MATERIAL RELATING
TO PRIVATE DEBTS AND INTEREST
PAYMENTS

The data for the different types of institutions whose assets and liabilities are listed in Chapter XIII differ widely with regard to the availability and accuracy of information concerning them. In some cases it has been necessary to make estimates on a somewhat arbitrary basis.[1] Sections I-VII of this appendix present the sources and methods of computation used.

In Section VIII we give the supplementary data called for in Chapter XIV under the discussion of the burden of interest payments.

I. NON-FINANCIAL CORPORATION DEBTS

Railroads. Statistics of Railways, published annually by the Interstate Commerce Commission (Statements 1-A, 42, 43, 55-A, 55-B, 55-E, 55-F). Switching and terminal companies and their subsidiaries are not included because they are classified with other utilities in *Statistics of Income.* Long-term debt data are for Classes I, II, and III railways, their non-operating subsidiaries, and all proprietary companies. Short-term debt includes all current liabilities and tax liability of Class I roads and their non-operating subsidiaries, and the unpaid matured funded debt of proprietary companies. Data are not available for Classes II and III.

Other public utilities. Figures for 1929 have been obtained by subtracting railroad data from totals for transportation and other utilities shown in *Statistics of Income.* Data for 1933

---

[1] In using data from balance sheets published in *Statistics of Income* no adjustment has been made for corporations which failed to submit balance sheets. The resulting understatement probably averages about 2 per cent.

are taken from a breakdown of income tax data for that year, furnished by the Bureau of Internal Revenue.

Corporations other than railroads and public utilities. Statistics of Income.

II. HOLDERS OF RAILWAY SECURITIES

Railroads other than issuing corporation. Statistics of Railways, Statement No. 22. Data include bonds of affiliated and non-affiliated companies held for investment; miscellaneous securities of other railway companies; bonds held in sinking, insurance, and other funds (minus bonds of respondent companies); and bonds controlled through non-reporting subsidiaries.

National banks. Figures for 1929 and 1933 are from annual reports of the Comptroller of the Currency. Items shown are averages of adjacent June 30 figures. For 1934-35, year-end figures from *Call Report No. 4* of the Federal Deposit Insurance Corporation.

All insured banks. Federal Deposit Insurance Corporation, *Call Report No. 4.*

United States Treasury. Loans authorized by the Transportation Act of 1920, as reported in issues of *Statement of the Public Debt of the United States.*

Life insurance companies. Estimated from reported holdings of companies having about 92 per cent of total assets of United States life insurance companies. Data are from *Spectator Yearbook,* except those for 1935, which are from the *Annual Report of the Life Insurance Presidents.*

Railroad Credit Corporation: Annual reports of the Corporation published in the *Commercial and Financial Chronicle.*

Reconstruction Finance Corporation and Public Works Administration. Daily Treasury Statement, Jan. 31, 1936 (statement of assets and liabilities of governmental corporations and credit agencies of the United States).

"Other." This is a balancing item obtained by subtracting the total of all items from the total long-term railway debt. The figures are not precise because a small proportion of the securities reported by the agencies listed may be classified as short term, and also because some securities of switching and terminal companies are probably included in the reported hold-

ings of financial institutions. These are not included in our total of long-term railroad debt.

III. FUNDED DEBT OF SPECIFIED TYPES OF PUBLIC UTILITIES

Manufactured gas companies. American Gas Association, *Annual Statistics of Manufactured Gas Industry.* The data cover companies distributing manufactured gas in the years shown; hence they do not check with data shown in *Statistical Bulletin No. 17,* which are for identical companies distributing manufactured gas throughout a six-year period.

Switching and terminal companies. Total long-term debt as reported in *Statistics of Railways.*

Electric light and power companies and electric railway companies. Census of Electrical Industries.

Telephone, telegraph, and interstate pipeline companies, and express companies. Telephone and telegraph data for 1934 are from the *Annual Report of the Federal Communications Commission.* Other items are from *Statistics of Railways.* (Data for 1935 were furnished in advance of publication by the Bureau of Statistics of the Interstate Commerce Commission.)

Holding companies. Estimated for this study from data in *Moody's Investment Manual.*

IV. CONDITION OF FINANCIAL INSTITUTIONS

National banks. Annual reports of the Federal Reserve Board and the Comptroller of the Currency; also, for 1934 and 1935, Federal Deposit Insurance Corporation, *Call Report No. 4.* Long-term assets consist of mortgage loans, United States government securities (except Treasury bills and certificates), and other bonds. Short-term and demand assests consist of bank balances, cash and cash items, loans and discounts other than mortgage loans, customers' liability on account of acceptances, acceptances of other banks sold with endorsement, securities borrowed, and short-term government securities. Long-term liabilities consist of preferred stock and mortgages outstanding. Figure for 1935 is preferred stock as of November 1 (*Federal Reserve Bulletin,* January 1936). Short-term and demand liabilities consist of deposits, bills payable, rediscounts, acceptances (including those of other banks for account of reporting banks), securities borrowed, accrued interest, and "other" liabilities. Mortgage loans, which are not shown separately for December 31 except for 1934 and 1935, have been estimated for 1929 on the basis of the percentage of loans secured by mortgages on June 30, 1929 and June 30, 1930, and for 1933 on the basis of the percentage of June 30, 1934. Likewise the proportions of short-term United States securities and of bonds among the total investments have been estimated for 1929 and 1933 on the basis of ratios computed from adjacent June 30 data.

State banks. Data for 1929 and 1933 are drawn from annual reports of the Comptroller of the Currency; for 1934-35 from annual reports of the Federal Deposit Insurance Corporation, with an allowance for uninsured banks, based on the reported volume of deposits of such banks. Long-term obligations include preferred stock and capital notes and debentures, also a small amount of bonded debt and mortgages reported by the Federal Deposit Insurance Corporation. For 1933 the long-term debt is computed on the basis of the Reconstruction Finance Corporation's investment in preferred stock and capital notes and loans secured by preferred stock, plus bonded debt and mortgages reported by the Commissioner of Internal Revenue. The long-term debt for 1935 has been estimated as follows: preferred stock and capital notes outstanding November 1 (*Federal Reserve Bulletin,* January 1936) plus Reconstruction Finance Corporation's investment in non-member banks, plus bonded debt and mortgages shown in the call report of the Federal Deposit Insurance Corporation cited above.

Mutual savings banks. Deposits, loans, and investments are as reported in annual reports of the Federal Reserve Board; loans have been prorated between long- and short-term on the basis of data for adjacent June 30 dates shown in the reports of the Comptroller of the Currency.

Federal Reserve Banks. Annual reports of the Federal Reserve Board.

Postal savings. Annual reports of the Postmaster General reprinted in annual reports of the Comptroller of the Currency. Data for 1935 were furnished by the Post Office Department.

Building and loan associations. Long-term assets consist of mortgages owned, as reported by the Building and Loan League (data reprinted in annual reports of the Comptroller of the Currency), plus an allowance for United States bonds owned. The latter is an estimate based on the ratio of bonds owned to total assets reported in 1929 by states which held about 22 per cent of the total assets of building and loan associations. As the bonds make up less than 2 per cent of the total assets, the error due to this item is very small. For 1935 the data are preliminary figures for mortgages furnished by the Secretary of the United States Building and Loan League. Short-term assets for 1934 are based on data obtained from the Federal Home Loan Bank Board. Short-term assets for other years have been estimated on the basis of the ratio of short-term to total assets for 1934.

Life insurance companies. Data from *Spectator Yearbook,* except for 1935. For 1935 computed from the tabulation in the report of the Association of Life Insurance Presidents. Details not shown there have been estimated by stepping up the 1934 data by 7 per cent, except long-term assets, which have been stepped up by 4 per cent. These ratios were arrived at by comparison of the items which are reported for both years.

Veterans' Administration. Annual reports of the Veterans' Administration. Figure for 1935 was furnished in advance of publication by the Veterans' Administration.

Joint Stock Land Banks. Annual reports of the Federal Farm Loan Board and the Farm Credit Administration.

Federal Deposit Insurance Corporation. Annual reports of the Corporation.

Railroad Credit Corporation: Annual reports published in the *Commercial and Financial Chronicle.*

All other financial institutions. The figures for 1933 are from a breakdown of income tax data made available through the courtesy of the Statistical Division of the Bureau of Internal Revenue. Figures shown for short-term and demand assets consist of cash plus notes and accounts receivable. A similar breakdown is not available for 1929, though certain items not shown in *Statistics of Income* for 1930, 1931, and 1932 are shown in Senate Document No. 124, 73 Congress, 2 session *(National Income, 1929-32).* Data for 1929 have been estimated as follows: long-term debt is 97.8 per cent of total long-term debt for the entire financial group of corporations as reported in *Statistics of Income,* this being the percentage for 1930 as shown in Senate Document No. 124, page 236. Short-term and demand liabilities are similarly computed from total notes and accounts payable of financial corporations as reported in *Statistics of Income* for 1929, the ratio applied (96.2 per cent) being drawn from the 1935 data because not available for any earlier date.

Long-term creditor assets are taken at the same figure for 1929 as 1933 on the basis of the change in total investments of financial corporations, as shown in *Statistics of Income,* compared with the changes in investments of banks, life insurance companies, and Joint Stock Land Banks, as shown in the various sources of information cited above. As the change in invest-ments of these institutions seems substantially to account for the entire change in the group, no better basis of estimate suggested itself than to carry back the 1933 figure unchanged.[2] Short-term and demand assets have been estimated for 1929, for lack of a better basis, on the assumption that they bore the same relation to short-term and demand liabilities in 1929 as in 1933. It is impossible to make an estimate on the basis of the proportion of short and demand assets of "other financial" to total financial, because of the change in the character of bank lending and investment operations which took place between 1929 and 1933, and upset the previous ratios of assets within the group.

V. FORMS OF INDIVIDUAL DEBTS

Home mortgages. Rough estimate based on various studies for nearby dates. Compare text, pp. 338-39.

Farm mortgages. Estimates of the Bureau of Agricultural Economics, with a deduction for bonded debt and mortgages of agricultural corporations, as reported in *Statistics of Income.*

Bank loans. Total reported loans of banks other than those secured by real estate and inter-bank loans (from annual reports

[2] There is a considerable margin of error in this figure, as there is in all figures obtained by subtracting data obtained from other sources from the Bureau of Internal Revenue figures for larger groups. For example, for 1933 the amount of tax-exempt securities reported for banks in the banking reports, plus the amount shown for life insurance companies in the *Spectator Yearbook,* is greater than the amount shown for the entire financial group in *Statistics of Income.*

of the Comptroller of the Currency), minus estimated notes payable of corporations to banks. The latter item has been estimated from notes and accounts payable as reported in *Statistics of Income,* on the assumption that the ratio of notes payable to accounts payable was the same in later years as in 1927, the last year for which the items were reported separately, with an allowance of one-eighth for notes payable to others than banks. The figure is too high, as no allowance has been made for loans to governmental units and to philanthropic and educational institutions which do not report to the Bureau of Internal Revenue.

Brokers' borrowings from non-bankers. Loans for account of "others" as reported by New York City member banks, plus borrowings from private banks, brokers, foreign agencies, et cetera, as reported by members of the New York Stock Exchange, plus customers' credit balances estimated at three-eighths brokers' borrowings as reported by New York Stock Exchange. Ratio based on 1935-36 data; published in *Federal Reserve Bulletin,* September 1936, pages 693, 725.

Brokers' loans to customers. These were assumed to be 50 per cent greater than the total borrowings of brokers as reported by the New York Stock Exchange. Ratio based on 1935-36 data, cited in preceding paragraph.

Debts to retailers. From break-up of income tax reports of trading corporations for 1933 furnished us by the Bureau of Internal Revenue, we estimated total receivables from retail trade 2,112 million dollars; from wholesale trade, 1,833 millions. One-half of "wholesale and retail" and one-half of "all other" were put in each category; all "commission" was counted as wholesale. Gross sales of corporations were apportioned in the same way and the ratio of receivables to gross sales for retail trade was computed as 16.6 per cent. This percentage was applied to *total* retail sales for 1933 reported in the *Census of American Business.* For 1929 we stepped down the ratio in the proportion of 14.9 to 17.4, the receivables-sales ratio for all trade being 14.9 per cent in 1929 and 17.4 per cent in 1933, giving 14.2 as the estimated ratio of receivables to retail trade for 1929. This ratio was applied to 49,115 million dollars, the figure for total retail trade shown in the *Census of Retail Distribution* for 1929.

Non-corporate debts to wholesalers. To get year-end debt to wholesalers for 1933 we multiplied the gross wholesale sales, 32,152 million dollars, by 0.175, the ratio of incorporated wholesalers' receivables to sales, computed in the same manner as the retail ratio discussed above. The result was multiplied by 0.022 to get sales to home consumers, 0.81 to get sales to retailers and industries, and 0.168 to get sales to other wholesalers (percentages from the *Census of Wholesale Distribution,* Volume 1, page 63). To eliminate corporation debt we multiplied by 0.492 for retail and industrial business and 0.674 for wholesalers. The ratio used for wholesalers was based on the ratio of corporation sales, as reported in *Statistics of Income,* to all wholesale sales, as reported to the Census Bureau; that used for retailers and industrials likewise was based on the ratio of retail corporation sales to all retail sales (assuming for lack of better standard that the proportion of unincorporated industrial companies' purchases to all industrials' purchases from wholesalers was the same as the ratio of unincorporated retailers' sales to all retailers' sales). The same method was used for 1929, using the distribution between home consumers, retailers, industrials, and wholesalers, as of 1933 for lack of 1929 data.

Debts to small loan companies. The estimate for 1929 is taken from Louis N. Robinson and Rolf Nugent, *Regulation of the Small Loan Business,* 1935, page 169. The figure for 1933 is from Franklin W. Ryan, "Short-term Loans in the United States during 1932 and 1933," *Journal of Business,* Volume VII, 1934, page 267.

Debts to life insurance companies. Policy and premium loans, from the *Spectator Yearbook.*

Debts to government life insurance. Policy and premium loans, from reports of the Veterans' Bureau.

Miscellaneous items. The figure for 1933 is taken from the article by Ryan cited above under "Debts to small loan companies." The figure for 1929 is based on an article by the same author, "Family Finance in the United States," *Journal of Business,* Volume III, 1930, page 404. In the latter reference, estimates are given only for the annual volume of business; the figure for the amount outstanding is computed on the assumption that the ratio of loans outstanding at the end of the year to annual volume of business was the same as in 1933.

No attempt has been made to estimate the debt of individuals to other individuals outside the categories indicated in the table. Debt to building and loan associations is omitted on the theory that this represents merely the shareholders' use of their own money; possibly debt to life insurance companies should be omitted for the same reason.

VI. HOLDERS OF OUTSTANDING FARM MORTGAGES

Banks. Data for Federal Reserve member banks are from annual reports of the Federal Reserve Board. We cannot present similarly detailed tables for all banks, but incomplete data indicate a reduction similar to that which occurred in the case of national banks. Federal Deposit Insurance Corporation reports show 499 millions held by all insured banks at the end of 1934, and 488 millions at the end of 1935. The Comptroller of the Currency's totals indicate a large increase in holdings of state banks from 1933 to 1934, but this is due entirely to the fact that the totals for 1934 represent all states, while those for 1933 represent only about half the states. All states which report for both years show decreases, except New Mexico.

Life insurance companies. Estimated on the basis of reports of companies holding 91.9 to 92.1 per cent of total assets of life insurance companies of the United States. Data are from the *Spectator Yearbook.*

Joint Stock Land Banks and Federal Farm Loan system. Annual reports of the Federal Farm Loan Board and the Farm Credit Administration.

Farm mortgages outstanding. Data for 1929 and 1933 are as estimated by the Bureau of Agricultural Economics. The figure for 1934 is from a release issued by the Farm Credit Administration dated March 5, 1936. The 1935 figure is a preliminary estimate also furnished by the Farm Credit Administration.

VII. FINANCIAL CONDITION OF GOVERNMENTAL AND QUASI-GOVERNMENTAL AGENCIES

United States Government. All data are from issues of *Statement of the Public Debt of the United States* and *Daily Treasury Statement.* Long-term debt includes all interest bearing debt except certificates of indebtedness and Treasury bills. Short-term debt consists of Treasury certificates and bills; matured debt on which interest has ceased, and obligations which bear no interest, such as United States notes (less gold reserve), and national bank notes and Federal Reserve Bank notes assumed by the United States; silver dollar liabilities; Treasury checks outstanding; and deposit liabilities, except those of the Post Office Department. Long-term assets include all securities listed in the public debt statement except foreign obligations and capital stock of governmental corporations, excluding amount due the United States from Central Branch of the Union Pacific Railroad, which is excluded by the Treasury from the total of securities owned. Short-term assets include all asset items in the general fund except gold.

Federal trust funds. Amounts shown are averages of amounts shown for adjacent June 30 dates. They include investments of the District of Columbia Teachers' Retirement Fund, Civil Service Retirement Fund, Canal Zone Retirement Fund, Adjusted Service Certificate Fund, United States Government Life Insurance Fund, and the Alien Property Trust Fund. Some other very small trust funds are omitted.

United States territories and possessions. Items shown are averages of adjacent June 30 figures shown in estimates of tax-exempt securities outstanding, in annual reports of the Secretary of the Treasury.

State and local governments. Long-term debt data are from Treasury estimates of tax-exempt securities outstanding. They include amounts held by United States government or by governmental lending agencies. Short-term debt consists of short-term funded debt as estimated by the Treasury, without allowance for warrants or other current indebtedness.

Long-term assets. The figure is a very rough estimate based on data for trust funds of states and cities for 1931-32 in the *Decennial Census of the Financial Statistics of States and Cities.* As we have no basis for an estimate of the direction in which this item has been changing, we have used the same figure throughout. Short-term assets consist of deposits of public funds in all banks, as shown in reports of the Comptroller of the Currency (average of figures for June 30 before and after date indicated).

Reconstruction Finance Corporation. Quarterly reports of the Corporation.

Farm lending agencies, except Resettlement Administration. There are numerous minor discrepancies between the figures given for these agencies in different official sources, and in some cases we have not been able to reconcile them. Data shown are from the *Annual Report of the Federal Farm Loan Board* for 1929 and the *Annual Report of the Farm Credit Administration* for 1933, 1934, and 1935 except emergency crop and drought loans for 1929 and 1933, Regional Agricultural Credit Corporation loans for 1933, and Agricultural Marketing Act Revolving Fund for 1929 and 1933, which are from the *Statistical Abstract of the United States,* 1935, page 253. Obligations matured and unpaid by borrowers have been counted as short-term assets, no account being taken of reserves for bad debts. United States government obligations are counted as long-term assets. Securities sold under repurchase agreements counted as assets and the liability to repurchase counted as short-term debt. Cash balances with the United States Treasury are not included as assets. Bonds of the Federal Land Banks owned by the Federal Farm Mortgage Corporation are included among the liabilities of the Banks and the assets of the Corporation. The duplication on account of this item amounts to 579 million dollars in 1934, and 755 million dollars in 1935.

Resettlement Administration. Statement of the Public Debt of the United States, December 31, 1935.

Home lending agencies. Annual reports of the Federal Home Loan Bank Board and the Federal Housing Administration.

Public Works Administration and Shipping Board. Statement of the Public Debt of the United States.

VIII. EXAMPLES OF THE BURDEN OF INTEREST PAYMENTS

COMPILED RECEIPTS OR GROSS SALES OF SELECTED CORPORATIONS,
COMPARED WITH INTEREST PAYMENTS, 1929–35[a]

(In millions of dollars)

Year	Utility Corporations (25)		Manufacturing Corporations (17)		Trading Corporations (16)	
	Revenue	Interest	Revenue	Interest	Revenue	Interest
1929......	2,829	226	2,624	38	1,252	6
1930......	2,772	234	2,054	26	1,251	8
1931......	2,482	247	1,323	27	1,192	8
1932......	2,180	239	706	25	1,018	8
1933......	2,062	249	952	24	1,022	7
1934......	2,162	252	1,140	23	1,148	7
1935......	2,283	241	1,431	24	1,239	6

[a] Data are from annual reports published in the *Commercial and Financial Chronicle* and in *Moody's* and *Poor's Manuals*. For discussion of sampling, see p. 370.

APPENDIX H

DATA ON INTERNATIONAL TRADE AND FINANCE

1. UNITED STATES EXPORTS AND IMPORTS OF GOLD AND SILVER, 1926–35[a]

(In millions of dollars)

Year	Gold		Silver	
	Exports	Imports	Exports	Imports
1926	115.7	213.5	92.26	69.60
1927	201.5	207.5	75.63	55.07
1928	560.8	168.9	87.38	68.12
1929	116.6	291.6	83.41	63.94
1930	116.0	396.1	54.16	42.76
1931	466.8	612.1	26.49	28.66
1932	809.5	363.3	13.85	19.65
1933	366.7	193.2	19.04	60.22
1934	52.8	1,186.7	16.55	102.73
1935	2.0	1,741.0	18.80	354.53

[a] Bureau of Foreign and Domestic Commerce, *Monthly Summary of Foreign Commerce of the United States*, December 1935, p. 3, and June 1936, p. 3.

2. Total Value of United States Exports and Imports, 1921–35[a]
(Dollar items are in millions)

Year	Total Exports	Total Imports	Excess of Exports over Imports	Imports as a Percentage of Exports
1921–25 (av.) ...	$4,397	$3,450	$ 947	78.5
1926	4,809	4,431	378	92.1
1927	4,866	4,185	681	86.0
1928	5,128	4,091	1,037	79.8
1929	5,241	4,400	841	83.9
1930	3,843	3,061	782	79.6
1931	2,424	2,091	334	86.2
1932	1,611	1,322	289	82.1
1933	1,675	1,450	225	86.5
1934	2,133	1,655	478	77.6
1935	2,283	2,047	236	89.7

[a] As reported in the official statistics of exports and imports.

3. United States Exports and Imports, by Economic Classes, 1921–35[a]
(As percentages of the total value for each year)

Year	Exports					Imports				
	Crude Materials	Crude Foodstuffs	Manufactured Foodstuffs	Semi-Manufactures	Finished Manufactures	Crude Materials	Crude Foodstuffs	Manufactured Foodstuffs	Semi-Manufactures	Finished Manufactures
1921–25 (av.)..	27.5	9.7	13.9	12.5	36.3	37.4	11.1	13.0	17.7	20.9
1926	26.8	7.1	10.7	13.9	41.5	40.5	12.2	9.4	18.1	19.8
1927	25.1	8.8	9.7	14.7	41.6	38.3	12.1	10.8	17.9	21.0
1928	25.7	5.9	9.3	14.2	44.9	35.8	13.4	9.9	18.6	22.2
1929	22.2	5.2	9.4	14.1	49.1	35.4	12.2	9.6	20.2	22.6
1930	21.9	4.7	9.6	13.6	50.2	32.7	13.1	9.6	19.9	24.7
1931	23.8	5.3	10.4	13.4	47.1	30.7	14.6	10.6	17.8	26.3
1932	32.6	5.7	9.7	12.4	39.6	27.1	17.6	13.2	16.4	25.8
1933	35.9	2.9	9.4	14.4	37.4	29.3	15.0	13.4	20.3	22.1
1934	31.1	2.8	8.0	16.3	41.8	28.2	15.5	16.1	18.8	21.4
1935	30.5	2.6	7.0	15.6	44.3	28.6	15.8	15.6	20.1	19.9

[a] Data from *Statistical Abstract of the United States*, 1935.

4. DISTRIBUTION OF UNITED STATES EXPORTS AND IMPORTS,
BY CONTINENTS, 1921-35[a]
(As percentages of total value for each year)

I. Exports

Year	Europe	North America	Asia	South America	Africa	Oceania
1921–25 (av.)...	52.7	24.4	11.3	6.8	1.6	3.2
1926..........	48.0	24.4	11.7	9.2	2.1	4.4
1927..........	47.6	25.7	11.5	9.0	2.2	4.0
1928..........	46.3	25.8	12.8	9.4	2.3	3.5
1929..........	44.7	26.6	12.3	10.3	2.5	3.6
1930..........	47.8	26.6	11.7	8.8	2.4	2.8
1931..........	48.9	24.4	15.9	6.6	2.5	1.7
1932..........	48.7	22.7	18.1	6.0	2.2	2.3
1933..........	50.7	20.3	17.4	6.8	2.6	2.1
1934..........	44.5	22.7	18.8	7.6	3.6	2.7
1935..........	45.1	23.2	16.6	7.6	4.2	3.2

II. Imports

Year	Europe	North America	Asia	South America	Africa	Oceania
1921–25 (av.)...	30.4	26.4	27.3	12.2	2.1	1.6
1926..........	29.0	22.9	31.6	12.8	2.2	1.5
1927..........	30.5	23.6	30.0	12.4	2.2	1.3
1928..........	30.5	23.5	28.6	13.9	2.2	1.3
1929..........	30.3	22.3	29.1	14.5	2.5	1.3
1930..........	29.7	24.8	28.0	14.2	2.2	1.1
1931..........	30.6	24.8	27.4	14.7	1.6	0.9
1932..........	29.4	27.1	27.4	15.2	1.8	0.6
1933..........	31.9	22.0	29.4	14.0	1.9	0.9
1934..........	29.6	24.1	29.6	13.8	2.0	0.9
1935..........	29.3	24.1	29.5	13.7	2.0	1.3

[a] Data from *Foreign Trade of the United States*, for 1935 and preceding years.

4. INDEXES OF CHANGES IN QUANTITY, UNIT

IMPORTS, BY ECO-

(1929

I. Exports

Year	Total			Raw Materials		
	Quantity Index	Unit Value Index	Value Index	Quantity Index	Unit Value Index	Value Index
1921–25 (av.).	73.5	113.8	84.3	87.6	119.7	104.7
1926	87.1	105.7	91.3	118.6	92.1	110.5
1927	93.9	98.9	92.2	115.0	90.8	104.7
1928	97.0	101.1	98.3	109.7	102.6	114.0
1929	100.0	100.0	100.0	100.0	100.0	100.0
1930	82.6	89.7	73.9	93.8	77.6	73.3
1931	67.4	69.0	46.1	94.7	52.6	50.0
1932	52.3	58.6	30.4	101.8	44.7	45.3
1933	52.3	62.1	32.2	100.0	51.3	52.3
1934	56.1	72.4	40.9	83.2	68.4	57.0
1935	59.1	74.7	43.5	85.8	69.7	60.5

	Raw Foodstuffs			Manufactured Foodstuffs		
1921–25 (av.).	143.6	109.0	154.8	120.7	103.1	123.8
1926	111.7	111.2	123.8	93.1	111.5	103.6
1927	139.4	111.2	154.8	93.1	103.1	95.2
1928	104.3	104.5	108.3	96.6	100.0	96.4
1929	100.0	100.0	100.0	100.0	100.0	100.0
1930	73.4	89.9	65.5	81.6	91.7	75.0
1931	75.5	61.8	46.4	71.3	70.8	51.2
1932	62.8	52.8	33.3	57.5	54.2	31.0
1933	34.0	51.7	17.9	56.3	57.3	32.1
1934	36.2	60.7	21.4	54.0	64.6	34.5
1935	35.1	62.9	21.4	42.5	75.0	32.1

	Semi-Manufactures			Finished Products		
1921–25 (av.).	73.9	100.0	73.9	52.3	120.2	61.9
1926	89.1	101.0	89.9	68.4	113.5	77.4
1927	101.7	95.0	95.8	76.4	102.2	78.1
1928	104.2	94.0	98.3	88.5	101.1	89.0
1929	100.0	100.0	100.0	100.0	100.0	100.0
1930	81.5	87.0	70.6	78.7	95.5	74.8
1931	61.3	71.0	43.7	57.5	76.4	43.9
1932	46.2	58.0	26.9	35.1	69.7	24.5
1933	53.8	60.0	32.8	36.8	66.3	24.5
1934	68.1	69.0	47.1	48.3	71.9	34.8
1935	69.7	68.0	47.9	53.4	73.0	39.4

[a] Basic data from *Summary of United States Trade with World, 1935*, p. 14.

VALUE, AND TOTAL VALUE OF EXPORTS AND
NOMIC CLASSES[a]
=100)

II. Imports

Year	Total			Raw Materials		
	Quantity Index	Unit Value Index	Value Index	Quantity Index	Unit Value Index	Value Index
1921–25 (av.)..	71.8	108.0	78.8	72.2	112.5	83.0
1926.........	85.5	117.2	100.9	82.0	140.0	115.1
1927.........	86.3	109.2	95.6	87.2	117.5	102.8
1928.........	87.8	105.7	93.8	87.2	107.5	94.3
1929.........	100.0	100.0	100.0	100.0	100.0	100.0
1930.........	84.7	81.6	69.9	81.2	78.8	64.2
1931.........	74.8	63.2	47.8	76.7	53.8	41.5
1932.........	60.3	49.4	30.1	60.9	37.5	22.6
1933.........	65.6	49.4	32.7	68.4	38.8	26.4
1934.........	65.6	57.5	38.1	62.4	46.2	29.2
1935.........	80.9	57.5	46.9	75.2	50.0	36.8

	Raw Foodstuffs			Manufactured Foodstuffs		
1921–25 (av.)..	87.5	80.5	70.6	71.5	149.2	105.8
1926.........	95.5	105.3	100.0	89.1	109.5	97.7
1927.........	95.5	98.2	93.7	81.0	130.2	105.8
1928.........	96.4	106.2	102.4	81.8	115.9	95.3
1929.........	100.0	100.0	100.0	100.0	100.0	100.0
1930.........	100.9	73.5	74.6	83.2	82.5	68.6
1931.........	97.3	57.5	56.3	70.8	73.0	52.3
1932.........	88.4	48.7	42.9	67.2	60.3	40.7
1933.........	89.3	44.2	39.7	74.5	63.5	47.7
1934.........	92.9	50.4	47.6	91.2	71.4	65.1
1935.........	125.0	47.8	60.3	100.0	77.8	79.1

	Semi-Manufactures			Finished Products		
1921–25 (av.)..	68.5	100.0	68.8	66.0	109.9	72.1
1926.........	88.1	103.1	90.4	80.9	108.8	88.4
1927.........	82.7	102.0	84.8	85.1	104.4	88.4
1928.........	89.0	96.9	85.6	83.7	109.9	90.7
1929.........	100.0	100.0	100.0	100.0	100.0	100.0
1930.........	80.3	85.7	68.8	85.8	89.0	76.0
1931.........	62.2	68.4	41.6	73.0	75.8	55.0
1932.........	44.9	54.1	24.8	56.0	61.5	34.1
1933.........	57.5	58.2	32.8	56.0	58.2	32.6
1934.........	51.2	68.4	35.2	58.2	61.5	35.7
1935.........	68.5	68.4	46.4	68.8	60.4	41.1

6. Value of United States Exports and Imports, by Continents and Leading Countries, 1926-35ᵃ

(In millions of dollars)

Continent and Country	Exports (including re-exports)						General Imports					
	1926-30 Average	1931	1932	1933	1934	1935	1926-30 Average	1931	1932	1933	1934	1935
Total	4,777.3	2,424.3	1,611.0	1,675.0	2,132.8	2,281.8	4,033.5	2,090.6	1,322.8	1,449.6	1,655.1	2,047.3
Europeᵇ	2,237.7	1,187.1	784.5	850.0	949.9	1,028.2	1,211.5	640.7	389.6	463.0	489.6	599.0
North America:												
Northern North America	829.6	403.7	245.7	214.8	308.0	329.5	479.7	277.1	181.4	190.7	238.5	292.9
Southern North America	403.2	187.1	119.2	126.0	178.0	201.7	460.5	239.9	157.1	127.1	160.7	201.6
South America	447.9	158.7	96.6	114.0	161.7	174.3	545.8	307.2	200.9	202.3	229.0	281.5
Asiaᵇ	571.9	386.1	292.3	292.0	401.2	377.9	1,191.7	573.7	361.8	425.1	489.4	604.4
Oceania	177.2	41.6	36.8	35.1	57.1	73.8	53.1	19.1	7.7	13.2	14.6	26.5
Africa	109.6	60.0	36.0	42.9	76.8	96.2	91.2	32.9	24.2	28.3	33.3	41.4
EUROPE												
Belgium	105.6	59.4	40.3	43.3	50.0	58.2	70.1	34.2	21.9	23.2	26.2	39.8
Czechoslovakia	5.4	3.8	1.9	1.6	2.7	3.2	34.5	23.2	13.0	14.7	17.6	21.4
Denmark	49.6	29.7	12.0	11.6	14.5	12.5	4.3	1.9	1.3	1.8	1.9	3.3
Finland	14.9	4.9	2.8	3.5	6.0	6.1	9.9	10.0	8.2	8.9	9.0	12.2
France	244.6	121.8	111.6	121.7	115.8	116.9	152.8	79.2	44.7	49.7	61.0	58.3
Germany	400.4	166.1	133.7	140.0	108.7	91.7	210.6	127.0	73.6	78.2	68.8	77.7
Greece	13.7	7.6	7.8	2.8	4.7	6.6	18.1	11.0	7.6	6.0	8.3	10.0
Irish Free State	13.9	6.4	4.5	4.1	7.2	7.3	2.8	2.3	0.4	0.5	0.7	0.6
Italy	141.1	54.8	49.1	61.2	64.6	72.5	101.9	62.7	42.4	38.6	35.7	38.7
Netherlands	131.9	65.6	45.3	48.7	51.0	48.5	81.5	35.0	22.4	31.0	28.4	40.7
Norway	22.7	12.2	6.9	7.1	11.2	13.6	21.7	16.9	10.4	13.2	6.9	16.5
Poland and Danzig	10.9	4.6	7.1	15.1	18.9	24.5	4.1	2.0	1.3	2.7	5.6	9.8
Portugal	12.5	5.7	4.6	5.8	8.0	10.8	5.5	3.5	2.8	3.4	4.1	3.6
Spain	73.6	34.0	26.7	30.8	38.0	41.3	34.4	16.6	11.4	13.7	18.9	19.9
Sweden	49.3	32.2	17.5	18.6	33.1	38.2	47.3	34.3	24.5	31.0	33.9	41.2
Switzerland	10.9	9.7	7.3	7.5	8.4	7.6	42.1	23.1	12.5	14.6	15.2	16.3
United Kingdom	837.2	456.0	288.3	311.7	382.7	433.4	325.9	135.5	74.6	111.2	115.4	155.3
USSR	77.7	103.7	12.6	9.0	15.0	24.7	17.6	13.2	9.7	12.1	12.3	17.8
NORTH AMERICA												
Canada	819.5	396.4	241.4	210.7	302.4	323.2	469.2	266.3	174.1	185.4	231.7	286.2
Newfoundland Labrador	10.1	7.2	4.2	3.9	5.3	6.1	10.0	10.4	7.1	4.8	5.2	6.3
Mexico	122.0	52.4	31.9	37.5	55.1	65.6	125.9	47.6	37.4	30.7	36.5	42.3
Central America	78.5	46.7	30.5	31.5	37.8	38.6	43.6	31.0	24.5	22.6	23.9	29.2
Honduras	9.6	6.0	5.0	5.0	6.0	5.6	11.1	11.9	9.0	7.0	7.8	6.3
Panama	35.4	23.6	15.6	15.9	18.3	20.8	5.5	4.6	3.5	3.4	5.6	5.1
Haiti	10.1	4.9	4.0	3.6	3.4	3.3	1.4	0.8	0.6	0.8	4.2	1.2
Cuba	133.2	47.0	28.8	25.1	45.3	60.2	207.9	90.1	58.3	58.5	78.9	104.6
Dominican Republic	14.7	6.0	4.6	5.5	5.8	4.5	8.9	5.1	3.4	3.3	3.8	5.0

Continent and Country	Exports (including re-exports)						General Imports					
	1926–30 Average	1931	1932	1933	1934	1935	1926–30 Average	1931	1932	1933	1934	1935
Jamaica	8.5	5.6	2.8	2.6	3.8	4.0	8.4	6.3	3.2	1.2	1.8	2.1
Netherland West Indies	14.6	9.6	6.5	10.3	13.4	14.4	50.3	50.8	24.2	6.5	8.9	12.5
Other West Indies and Bermuda	31.5	19.9	14.2	13.5	16.8	14.5	15.4	9.1	6.1	4.2	6.9	5.8
SOUTH AMERICA												
Argentine	165.2	52.7	31.1	36.0	42.7	49.3	94.8	36.0	15.8	33.8	29.5	65.4
Brazil	89.4	28.5	28.6	29.1	40.4	43.6	199.5	110.2	82.1	82.6	91.5	99.7
Chile	45.9	21.5	3.6	5.3	12.0	14.0	75.1	40.0	12.3	11.5	22.9	24.1
Colombia	46.1	16.1	10.7	14.6	21.9	21.6	94.7	75.5	60.8	47.6	47.1	50.4
Ecuador	5.5	2.9	1.8	1.9	2.3	2.8	5.7	3.6	2.4	1.9	3.1	3.3
Peru	23.9	7.9	4.0	5.0	9.9	12.2	22.8	9.0	3.7	5.5	6.2	7.5
Uruguay	24.8	9.5	3.2	3.6	6.1	6.2	14.4	3.3	2.1	3.8	4.7	6.9
Venezuela	38.1	15.6	10.2	13.1	19.3	18.6	35.8	26.8	20.3	13.5	22.1	21.4
ASIA												
Turkey	3.1	1.7	1.5	1.3	2.7	4.5	11.5	8.1	5.4	8.2	7.2	7.8
Other countries of Western Asia	7.5	4.8	5.5	7.4	12.1	13.9	19.4	11.1	6.3	8.3	8.4	10.7
British India	53.5	46.7	25.0	19.9	27.4	31.5	136.9	58.5	33.8	43.8	55.1	64.4
British Malaya	12.6	4.7	2.5	2.4	4.2	4.5	249.8	83.1	34.8	60.0	105.5	129.2
Ceylon	2.6	1.3	0.7	0.8	1.3	1.3	36.1	10.9	5.9	7.0	11.6	11.4
China	109.0	97.9	56.2	51.9	68.7	38.2	140.5	66.8	26.2	37.8	43.9	64.2
Hong Kong	18.0	14.4	9.7	8.6	9.0	9.1	12.1	5.8	4.3	3.9	5.3	9.0
Kwantung	7.5	2.2	1.2	2.7	3.9	4.2	3.4	1.2	0.9	1.3	1.6	5.3
Japan	246.0	155.7	134.9	143.4	210.5	203.3	379.6	206.3	134.0	128.4	119.3	152.9
Netherland India	33.9	15.3	7.8	6.9	10.1	10.9	87.5	34.2	29.8	33.1	42.4	50.4
Philippine Islands	73.7	48.9	45.0	41.8	47.1	52.6	114.1	87.1	80.9	93.0	87.8	96.8
OCEANIA												
Australia	139.1	27.2	26.8	26.3	43.2	57.1	33.1	12.5	4.6	7.7	8.5	14.7
New Zealand	35.8	13.5	9.3	8.2	13.0	15.6	16.6	4.4	2.2	4.8	5.6	10.4
AFRICA												
Algeria and Tunisia	8.3	4.5	2.7	2.2	2.6	2.5	4.2	1.8	1.2	1.3	1.8	3.0
British South Africa	53.1	28.6	16.0	22.4	46.3	53.6	10.9	4.5	2.4	4.1	3.2	4.0
British West Africa	11.8	5.1	3.8	3.4	3.8	5.4	23.2	12.5	8.9	9.3	9.2	13.9
Egypt	11.1	5.3	2.7	3.1	6.9	10.5	30.1	4.0	8.9	6.1	9.0	8.9
Portuguese Africa	6.9	5.3	2.7	3.1	5.4	5.9	4.4	2.5	1.4	2.1	2.7	1.8

a Data from *Summary of United States Trade with World, 1935*, pp. 26–27.
b Russia in Asia is included in Europe.

7. The Balance of International Payments of the United States, 1926–35[a]

(In millions of dollars)

Item	1926	1927	1928	1929	1930	1931	1932	1933	1934	1935
COMMODITY AND SERVICE ITEMS										
Merchandise trade (as reported):										
Exports (credit)	4,809	4,865	5,128	5,241	3,843	2,424	1,612	1,675	2,133	2,283
Imports (debit)	4,431	4,184	4,091	4,400	3,061	2,090	1,323	1,450	1,655	2,047
Balance	+378	+681	+1,037	+841	+782	+334	+289	+225	+478	+236
Shipping and freight services:										
By Americans to foreigners (credit)	127	140	147	206	155	117	73	49	61	63
By foreigners to Americans (debit)	188	206	227	272	251	189	118	65	96	99
Balance	−61	−66	−80	−66	−96	−72	−45	−16	−35	−36
Tourist expenditures:										
By foreigners in U.S. (credit)	142	153	163	183	160	112	71	71	86	117
By Americans abroad (debit)	640	681	715	821	762	568	446	292	331	409
Balance	−498	−528	−552	−638	−602	−456	−375	−221	−245	−292
Immigrant remittances, charity, etc.:										
By foreigners to U.S. (credit)	35	35	25	24	33	10	6	3	5	5
By Americans to foreigners (debit)	299	290	301	289	248	212	169	135	136	120
Balance	−264	−255	−276	−265	−215	−202	−163	−132	−131	−115
Interest and dividends:										
Paid by foreigners to U.S. investors (credit)	735	800	893	979	916	662	461	487	493	521
Paid to foreigners investing in U.S. (debit)	268	281	359	414	300	126	68	103	126	146
Balance	+467	+519	+534	+565	+616	+536	+393	+384	+367	+375
War-debt receipts	+195	+206	+207	+207	+241	+113	+99	+20	+1	—

Item	1926	1927	1928	1929	1930	1931	1932	1933	1934	1935
Government transactions:										
Expenses and remittances by foreign governments in U.S. (credit)	46	57	53	60	46	34	31	32	31	28
Expenses and remittances by U.S. government abroad (debit)	89	86	110	152	127	134	101	85	68	83
Balance	−43	−29	−57	−92	−81	−100	−70	−53	−37	−55
Miscellaneous commodity and service items (net)	−18	−21	−88	−105	−16	+7	+3	+8	+63	+95
Balance on commodity and service account	+156	+507	+725	+447	+629	+160	+131	+215	+461	+208
GOLD AND CURRENCY MOVEMENTS										
Net gold movements	−72	+154	+272	−120	−278	+176	−11	+173	−1,217	−1,739
Net silver movements									−86	−336
Net currency movements	−40	−55	−40	−15	+20	−10	−80	−90	−26	−1
Balance, gold, silver, and currency movements	−112	+99	+232	−135	−258	+166	−91	+83	−1,329	−2,076
CAPITAL MOVEMENTS										
Private long-term capital movement:										
Credit	1,326	1,609	2,591	2,328	2,161	1,520	862	1,505	1,160	2,009
Debit	1,928	2,332	3,253	2,464	2,428	1,301	645	1,456	958	1,547
Balance	−602	−723	−662	−137	−267	+219	+217	+49	+202	+462
Government capital account										
Net short-term capital movement	+350	+900	−188	−80	−485	−709	−409	−385	+184	+1,075
Balance on capital account	−252	+177	−850	−217	−752	−490	−192	−336	+386	+1,537
Residual item	+208	−782	−107	−95	+381	+164	+152	+38	+482	+331

a Data from *The Balance of International Payments of the United States in 1935*, pp. 82–83.

Year and Month	United Kingdom	Belgium	France	Japan	Canada	Argentine	Australia	Sweden
1929:								
Jan........	99.7	100.0	99.7	91.3	99.8	99.3	99.0	99.8
Feb........	99.7	99.9	99.7	90.7	99.6	99.3	99.0	99.7
Mar.......	99.7	99.9	99.7	89.3	99.4	99.0	99.0	99.7
Apr.......	99.7	99.9	99.7	89.5	99.2	99.0	99.0	99.7
May.......	99.7	99.9	99.7	89.6	99.3	99.0	99.0	99.7
June.......	99.6	99.9	99.7	88.0	99.2	98.8	98.9	99.9
July.......	99.7	99.9	100.0	91.4	99.5	98.8	98.9	100.0
Aug........	99.6	100.0	99.7	93.7	99.4	98.9	98.6	100.0
Sept.......	99.6	100.0	99.7	94.8	99.2	98.8	98.4	99.9
Oct........	100.1	100.4	100.3	95.8	98.8	98.5	98.7	100.2
Nov.......	100.2	100.6	100.5	97.8	98.4	97.3	98.7	100.3
Dec........	100.3	100.7	100.5	98.2	99.1	96.4	98.7	100.6
1930:								
Jan........	100.0	100.3	100.3	98.5	98.9	94.7	98.1	100.2
Feb.......	99.9	100.2	100.0	98.6	99.2	89.7	97.4	100.1
Mar.......	99.9	100.3	99.7	99.0	99.8	88.8	95.9	100.2
Apr.......	99.9	100.4	100.0	99.0	100.0	91.9	94.0	100.3
May.......	99.9	100.4	100.0	99.1	99.8	90.4	94.0	100.1
June.......	99.8	100.4	100.0	99.1	100.0	87.6	93.9	100.2
July.......	100.0	100.6	100.3	99.0	100.1	85.0	94.1	100.3
Aug........	100.1	100.6	100.3	99.1	100.1	85.5	94.2	100.3
Sept.......	99.9	100.4	100.3	99.1	100.1	84.8	94.0	100.3
Oct........	99.8	100.3	100.0	99.5	100.1	80.9	92.4	100.2
Nov.......	99.8	100.3	100.3	99.5	100.1	81.0	91.8	100.1
Dec........	99.8	100.4	100.3	99.5	99.9	78.3	91.8	100.1
1931:								
Jan........	99.8	100.3	100.0	99.2	99.8	72.2	83.1	99.9
Feb.......	99.8	100.3	100.0	99.1	100.0	74.6	76.6	99.9
Mar.......	99.8	100.2	99.7	99.0	100.0	80.9	76.6	99.9
Apr......	99.9	100.0	99.7	99.0	100.0	79.2	76.7	99.9
May.......	99.9	100.1	99.7	99.1	99.9	73.3	76.7	100.0
June.......	100.0	100.1	100.0	99.0	99.7	72.8	76.8	100.0
July.......	99.8	100.4	100.0	99.0	99.7	72.4	76.6	99.9
Aug........	99.8	100.3	100.0	99.0	99.7	66.9	76.6	99.8
Sept.......	93.1	100.1	100.3	99.0	96.2	61.9	71.5	97.3
Oct........	79.9	100.6	100.5	98.8	89.1	53.9	61.4	86.2
Nov.......	76.4	100.1	100.0	98.9	89.0	61.0	58.7	77.4
Dec........	69.3	100.0	100.0	87.2	82.7	60.7	55.2	69.8
1932:								
Jan........	70.5	100.1	100.3	72.2	85.1	60.4	56.3	71.6
Feb........	71.0	100.3	100.5	68.8	87.3	60.3	56.7	72.0
Mar.......	74.8	100.3	100.3	64.5	89.4	60.4	59.7	74.1
Apr.......	77.1	100.7	100.5	65.8	89.9	60.3	61.5	71.2
May.......	75.5	100.9	100.8	64.1	88.4	60.4	60.3	69.9
June.......	74.9	100.3	100.5	60.8	86.7	60.7	59.8	69.8
July......	72.9	99.8	100.0	55.1	87.1	60.7	58.2	68.0
Aug........	71.4	99.8	100.0	49.1	87.6	60.7	57.0	66.6
Sept.......	71.3	99.7	100.0	47.4	90.3	60.7	57.0	66.5
Oct........	69.8	99.9	100.3	46.3	91.2	60.7	55.7	65.4
Nov.......	67.3	99.8	100.0	41.4	87.3	60.7	53.7	65.0
Dec........	67.4	99.6	99.5	41.6	86.6	60.7	53.8	66.8

noon buying rates for cable transfers in New York.)

Year and Month	United King-dom	Belgium	France	Japan	Canada	Argen-tine	Aus-tralia	Sweden
1933:								
Jan........	69.1	99.7	99.5	41.6	87.5	60.7	54.9	68.3
Feb........	70.3	100.4	100.0	41.7	83.5	60.7	55.9	68.2
Mar........	70.5	100.6	100.5	42.6	83.5	60.4	56.0	67.9
Apr........	73.5	104.5	104.6	44.3	84.7	62.7	58.5	70.2
May.......	80.8	117.1	117.1	48.1	87.6	70.4	64.3	75.5
June.......	85.0	122.7	122.4	51.7	89.9	73.7	67.6	79.4
July.......	95.5	139.9	139.3	57.7	94.5	83.7	75.9	89.5
Aug........	92.5	137.8	137.0	54.0	94.3	82.3	73.6	86.7
Sept.......	95.9	148.9	147.2	54.7	96.5	89.2	76.3	89.7
Oct........	95.9	149.1	148.5	55.7	97.6	89.3	76.3	89.8
Nov........	105.8	160.6	159.9	60.9	101.2	95.4	84.2	99.1
Dec........	105.1	156.3	156.1	61.7	100.6	34.5	83.7	98.5
1934:								
Jan........	103.8	158.6	158.4	60.4	99.5	34.7	82.7	97.2
Feb........	103.4	164.7	164.8	59.7	99.2	34.8	82.4	96.9
Mar.......	104.7	167.6	167.9	60.2	99.8	35.2	83.4	98.0
Apr.......	105.9	168.6	168.9	60.8	100.2	35.6	84.4	99.1
May......	104.9	168.4	168.6	60.6	100.2	35.3	83.7	98.2
June......	103.7	168.1	168.4	60.0	100.8	34.9	82.7	97.1
July......	103.6	168.1	168.1	59.9	101.2	34.8	82.5	97.0
Aug..	104.1	170.6	169.9	60.2	102.4	35.0	82.9	97.5
Sept......	102.6	170.7	170.2	59.7	102.9	34.5	81.5	96.1
Oct.......	101.5	168.8	168.9	57.5	102.1	34.2	80.4	95.1
Nov.......	102.5	167.8	168.1	58.3	102.5	34.5	81.3	96.0
Dec.....	101.6	168.3	168.4	57.8	101.3	34.2	80.6	95.2
1935:								
Jan........	100.5	167.8	167.9	57.1	100.2	33.8	79.7	94.1
Feb.......	100.1	167.8	168.1	57.0	99.9	33.6	79.4	93.8
Mar.......	98.1	163.7	168.9	56.1	99.1	34.0	77.8	91.9
Apr.......	99.4	121.9	168.4	56.9	99.5	33.4	78.8	93.0
May......	100.4	121.9	168.1	57.6	99.9	33.7	79.6	94.0
June......	101.4	121.9	168.6	58.2	99.9	34.1	80.4	94.9
July......	101.9	121.7	168.9	58.5	99.8	34.2	80.8	95.4
Aug.......	102.1	121.5	169.1	58.8	99.8	34.3	81.1	95.6
Sept......	101.3	121.3	168.1	58.1	99.3	34.1	80.4	94.9
Oct........	100.8	121.2	168.1	57.5	98.6	33.9	80.1	94.4
Nov.......	101.2	121.5	168.1	57.5	98.9	34.0	80.3	94.7
Dec........	101.3	121.3	168.4	57.7	99.0	34.0	80.4	94.8
1936:								
Jan........	102.0	121.9	169.1	58.2	99.9	34.3	81.1	95.5
Feb........	102.8	122.6	170.4	58.4	100.1	34.5	81.8	96.2
Mar.......	102.1	122.2	169.1	58.1	99.8	34.3	81.4	95.6
Apr.......	101.6	121.7	168.4	57.9	99.5	34.2	80.9	95.1
May......	102.1	121.9	168.1	58.3	99.8	34.3	81.4	95.6
June.......	103.1	121.7	168.1	59.0	99.7	34.6	82.2	96.6
July......	103.2	121.6	168.9	58.8	99.9	34.7	82.2	96.6
Aug........	103.3	121.3	168.1	59.0	100.0	34.7	82.3	96.7
Sept......	103.5	121.5	166.1	59.0	100.0	34.8	82.4	96.9
Oct........	100.7	121.2	119.1	57.4	100.0	33.9	80.2	94.2
Nov.......	100.4	121.7	118.6	57.3	100.1	33.8	80.0	94.0

[a] Basic data from issues of the *Federal Reserve Bulletin.*

9. FOREIGN EXCHANGE HOLDINGS AND GOLD STOCKS[a]

(In millions of dollars;

Country	Foreign Exchange Holdings								
	1930	1931				1932			
	December	March	June	September	December	March	June	September	December
Albania	3.9	4.1	3.9	3.5	2.9	3.5	3.5	3.5	3.6
Austria	100.7	91.5	62.5	28.4	17.9	8.5	6.0	5.6	7.6
Belgium	134.9	127.0	121.6	—	—	—	—	—	—
Bulgaria	5.8	4.2	3.7	2.1	1.9	1.5	1.5	1.2	0.9
Czechoslovakia	72.5	65.2	56.9	34.9	31.5	23.2	31.1	32.6	30.5
Danzig	8.9	7.1	6.6	5.0	5.0	6.0	3.1	5.0	2.7
Denmark	26.8	20.8	15.4	9.8	4.6	2.5	3.5	14.7	5.9
Estonia	6.4	6.2	6.2	5.4	4.2	3.9	2.3	1.9	1.3
Finland	23.5	23.9	21.6	16.2	10.2	18.1	12.7	11.0	18.7
France	1,025.5	1,029.6	1,025.9	889.5	807.1	486.8	237.7	184.8	175.6
Germany	182.1	44.8	71.4	33.0	41.1	33.8	30.9	31.6	27.2
Great Britain.	—	—	—	—	—	—	—	—	—
Greece	32.4	29.3	25.5	24.1	13.7	2.9	4.2	4.8	12.8
Hungary	11.8	4.4	1.7	1.2	4.1	2.1	1.9	1.9	2.4
Italy	227.7	215.7	206.5	154.6	114.2	80.7	72.9	73.7	68.7
Latvia	6.9	6.0	4.2	4.2	2.5	2.7	2.3	2.3	2.3
Lithuania	8.7	7.1	6.8	5.4	3.3	2.5	1.9	1.5	1.6
Netherlands.	99.2	87.6	91.8	88.0	32.8	34.0	27.6	28.7	28.5
Norway	10.8	9.8	5.8	3.3	3.3	3.3	1.2	5.0	8.3
Poland	46.3	42.8	39.2	28.0	23.9	21.6	17.8	15.4	15.4
Portugal	9.3	9.3	7.3	20.8	21.0	20.6	18.3	18.5	—
Rumania	10.4	7.9	13.7	9.5	1.9	1.9	1.0	3.3	3.3
Spain	—	23.2	20.5	49.2	54.2	53.8	56.3	55.8	55.0
Sweden	104.6	80.8	78.9	8.7	13.1	30.1	35.7	47.7	57.3
Switzerland.	67.7	63.1	81.0	67.3	20.1	20.6	11.2	11.8	16.8
Yugoslavia	23.2	16.8	16.4	9.6	7.5	4.8	5.4	6.2	3.7
Total, Europe	2,250.0	2,028.2	1,995.0	1,501.7	1,242.0	869.4	590.0	568.5	550.1
United States	36.7	1.7	12.0	57.5	42.1	37.4	34.3	33.6	32.5
Japan	—	—	—	—	—	—	—	—	—
Total	2,286.7	2,029.9	2,007.0	1,559.2	1,284.1	906.8	624.3	602.1	582.6

[a] As reported by the central banks of the countries indicated.
[b] Less than $50,000.

OF PRINCIPAL CENTRAL BANKS, 1930-32

conversion at par of exchange)

Monetary Gold Stocks

1930 December	1931 March	June	September	December	1932 March	June	September	December
0.4	0.4	0.4	0.6	1.0	1.0	1.2	1.2	1.1
30.1	30.1	30.1	26.6	26.6	25.3	21.0	21.0	21.0
190.8	200.1	199.5	346.5	354.4	349.6	356.8	359.1	360.9
10.4	10.6	10.8	11.0	11.0	11.0	11.0	11.0	11.0
45.7	45.7	45.5	45.1	48.8	48.6	48.6	49.0	50.6
b	b	b	3.1	4.2	4.2	7.5	4.2	4.1
46.1	46.1	46.1	44.0	38.6	38.8	35.9	35.7	35.6
1.7	1.7	1.7	1.7	1.7	1.9	3.1	3.1	4.0
7.5	7.5	7.5	7.5	7.7	7.7	7.7	7.7	7.7
2,098.5	2,198.4	2,210.6	2,325.0	2,682.9	3,010.2	3,216.4	3,239.2	3,257.0
527.7	553.4	338.4	309.9	234.4	209.3	198.2	189.7	192.0
718.3	698.9	792.6	656.0	587.5	587.9	662.6	678.4	586.9
6.6	6.6	6.4	6.4	11.2	9.3	0.8	7.1	18.0
28.4	22.0	19.5	18.3	17.8	17.6	17.0	17.0	17.0
278.8	279.6	282.5	286.5	296.0	296.2	298.3	304.7	307.3
1.7	1.7	1.7	1.7	3.3	3.5	4.1	4.1	6.9
3.9	3.9	3.9	3.9	5.0	5.0	5.0	4.8	4.9
171.3	179.2	199.9	282.3	356.6	353.5	394.0	415.8	415.2
39.2	39.2	39.2	39.0	41.5	41.7	40.1	38.2	38.6
63.1	62.9	63.7	63.7	67.3	64.3	54.4	54.8	56.3
9.3	9.3	9.3	7.7	8.9	12.5	12.7	12.5	23.8
55.6	52.3	52.9	53.4	57.9	56.5	56.3	56.7	57.0
433.7	466.9	468.1	439.3	433.6	434.1	435.1	435.5	435.9
64.4	64.3	63.9	53.3	55.2	55.2	55.2	55.2	55.2
137.6	124.1	162.1	327.8	452.8	470.6	502.8	508.8	476.8
19.1	19.1	27.2	29.1	31.1	31.1	31.1	31.1	31.0
4,989.9	5,124.0	5,083.5	5,389.4	5,837.0	6,146.6	6,476.9	6,545.6	6,475.8
4,592.7	4,696.9	4,955.9	4,740.9	4,459.8	4,390.0	3,919.0	4,086.8	4,513.0
411.8	415.4	424.3	407.7	234.0	214.2	213.8	213.8	261.7
9,994.4	10,236.3	10,463.7	10,538.0	10,530.8	10,750.8	10,609.7	10,846.2	11,250.5

INDEX